Teacher Guidebook Level D

A Reason For Spelling® Teacher's Guidebook - Level D
2nd Edition

EAN#: 978-1-58938-267-1
ISBN#: 1-58938-267-6
TL#: SPTGD2020JPS
Published by Concerned Communications, LLC
P.O. Box 1000, Siloam Springs, AR 72761

Authors: Rebecca Burton, Eva Hill, Leah Knowlton, Kay Sutherland
Illustrations: James McCullough & Mark Decker

For more information about *A Reason For Spelling*,® *A Reason For Handwriting*,® *A Reason For Science*® and *A Reason For Guided Reading*® go to: ***www.AReasonFor.com***

Contents:

Acknowledgments:

Field Test Participants:

Virginia Allen, East Rockaway, New York • Mrs. Christine Baker, Belleville, Pennsylvania • Judy M. Banks, Carmichael, California • Darya Birch, San Clemente, California • Mari Anne Burns, Baton Rouge, Louisiana • Karen Dafflitto, St. Louis, Missouri • Kristen J. Dorsett, Prescott, Arizona • Ms. Laura Guerrera, East Rockaway, New York • Mrs. Anne Gutierrez, San Antonio, Texas • Jeanette O. Kappel, Winstead, Minnesota • Sharon K. Kobilka, San Antonio, Texas • Connie Kozitza, Winsted, Minnesota • Vivian I. Sawyer, Carmichael, California • Harold W. Souther, San Antonio, Texas • Cleo F. Staples, Auburn, California • Suezy Tucker, Auburn, California • Martha Woodbury, Los Angeles, California

Placement Tests

In order to evaluate readiness and accurately meet individual student need, a simple placement test is recommended at the beginning of each school year.

Step 1: *Administer the test*

Number your paper from one to twenty. I will say the word once, use the word in a sentence, then say the word again. Write a word beside each number on your paper.

(Allow ample time and carefully monitor progress.)

Step 2: *Evaluate the corrected tests using the following criteria:*

If the student correctly spells 17 to 20 words:
- Assign the student to Level D program
- Encourage the student to work independently
- Select and assign several Other Word Forms to spell and test

If the student correctly spells 8 to 16 words:
- Assign the student to Level D program
- Allow opportunities to work independently
- Offer Other Word Forms activities

If the student correctly spells 0 to 7 words:
- Administer Level C placement test
- Based on results, you may choose to:
  a) Assign student to Level C Worktext, or
  b) Assign student to Level D Worktext
- Be sure student completes all activities

Placement Test Level D

1.	**practice**	I have to **practice** the piano.
2.	**meant**	I **meant** to finish my project.
3.	**station**	I painted at the art **station.**
4.	**hollow**	The log is **hollow.**
5.	**rescue**	We will **rescue** the kitten.
6.	**dream**	She had a funny **dream.**
7.	**pretend**	I **pretend** to be a gorilla.
8.	**wreath**	He put a **wreath** on the door.
9.	**cough**	His **cough** is getting better.
10.	**decide**	I can't **decide** what to buy.
11.	**bounce**	I shouldn't **bounce** on the bed.
12.	**fault**	It is my **fault** the books fell.
13.	**garbage**	The **garbage** truck came today.
14.	**curious**	She is **curious** about the package.
15.	**choice**	We made a **choice** to obey.
16.	**rather**	I'd **rather** play tag than swing.
17.	**castle**	I made a large cardboard **castle.**
18.	**fountain**	The **fountain** is lit up at night.
19.	**cereal**	That is my favorite **cereal.**
20.	**herself**	She made cookies by **herself.**

Placement Test Level C

1.	**began**	We **began** to eat.
2.	**hello**	The children said **hello** to us.
3.	**north**	We traveled **north.**
4.	**place**	This **place** is pretty.
5.	**broke**	The window **broke** in the storm.
6.	**sudden**	The **sudden** noise scared us.
7.	**belong**	This does not **belong** to me.
8.	**rush**	He was in a **rush** to get home.
9.	**sight**	That was a funny **sight.**
10.	**cage**	My bird is in a **cage.**
11.	**seventh**	I was the **seventh** in line.
12.	**track**	She ran around the **track.**
13.	**paper**	My **paper** is torn.
14.	**busy**	Dad's new job keeps him **busy.**
15.	**smile**	She has a cheerful **smile.**
16.	**open**	He left the door **open.**
17.	**song**	That new **song** is fun to sing.
18.	**mouth**	My braces make my **mouth** sore.
19.	**apart**	I can't tell the twins **apart.**
20.	**able**	I will be **able** to go with them.

How to Use This Guidebook

Introduction

Level **D**

Day One

Literature Connection - Each week begins with a Scripture verse, followed by a theme story that develops the principles found in that verse. Topic and description are provided to inform the teacher of story content. Some teachers may choose to use this theme story for the Monday morning devotional.

Discussion Time *(optional)* - Discussion questions follow each story, giving the teacher the opportunity to evaluate student understanding, and to encourage students to apply the values found in the Scripture to their own lives.

1 Literature Connection
Topic: Honesty
Theme Text: Luke 16:10

A Matter of Math

Matthew finds out that being dishonest only makes him cheat himself.

Lesson 10 | Day 1

... beside Mrs. Burton's desk. He noticed there were still some M&M's in the jar beside her stapler. "I haven't learned division in math class—but I've learned a lot about being honest," he said to no one in particular. "Responsibility, too."

2 Discussion Time
Check understanding of the story and development of personal values.

- What subject in school is the hardest for you?
- Why did Matthew not like the new chapter in math?
- What did Matthew do at the grading table that wasn't honest?
- How did he do on the chapter test over division?
- Why did Mrs. Burton think he'd cheated on his homework?
- Why do you think Mrs. Burton gave the special milk money job to Tommy?

93

94

Day One (cont.)

Preview - The test—study—test sequence begins with this pre-test which primarily uses sentences related to the story. Research has shown that immediate correction by the student—under teacher supervision—is one of the best ways to learn to spell.

Customize Your List *(notepaper graphic)* - An opportunity is provided to test additional words of the teacher's choice.

Say *(bubble graphic)* - Instructions to the students that are to be read aloud by the teacher are marked with the "say" symbol for easy identification.

Progress Chart *(chart graphic)* - Students may record their Preview scores for later comparison against their Posttest scores. (Reproducible master provided in Appendix B.)

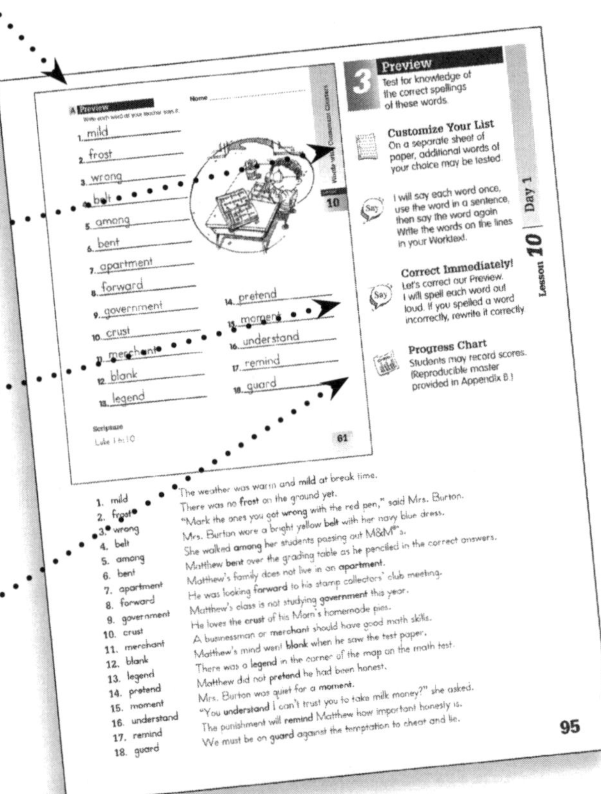

A Preview

1. mild
2. frost
3. wrong
4. belt
5. among
6. bent
7. apartment
8. forward
9. government
10. crust
11. merchant
12. blank
13. legend
14. pretend
15. moment
16. understand
17. remind
18. guard

Scripture
Luke 16:10

61

3 Preview
Test for knowledge of the correct spellings of these words.

Customize Your List
On a separate sheet of paper, additional words of your choice may be tested.

I will say each word once, use the word in a sentence, then say the word again. Write the words on the lines in your Worktext.

Correct Immediately!
Let's correct our Preview. I will spell each word out loud. If you spelled a word incorrectly, rewrite it correctly.

Progress Chart
Students may record scores. (Reproducible master provided in Appendix B.)

Lesson 10 | Day 1

1. mild — The weather was warm and **mild** at break time.
2. frost — There was no **frost** on the ground yet.
3. wrong — "Mark the ones you got **wrong** with the red pen," said Mrs. Burton.
4. belt — Mrs. Burton wore a bright yellow **belt** with her navy blue dress.
5. among — She walked **among** her students passing out M&M®s.
6. bent — Matthew **bent** over the grading table as he pencilled in the correct answers.
7. apartment — Matthew's family does not live in an **apartment**.
8. forward — He was looking **forward** to his stamp collectors' club meeting.
9. government — Matthew's class is not studying **government** this year.
10. crust — He loves the **crust** of his Mom's homemade pies.
11. merchant — A businessman or **merchant** should have good math skills.
12. blank — Matthew's mind went **blank** when he saw the test paper.
13. legend — There was a **legend** in the corner of the map on the math test.
14. pretend — Matthew did not **pretend** he had been honest.
15. moment — Mrs. Burton was quiet for a **moment**.
16. understand — "You **understand** I can't trust you to take milk money?" she asked.
17. remind — The punishment will **remind** Matthew how important honesty is.
18. guard — We must be on **guard** against the temptation to cheat and lie.

95

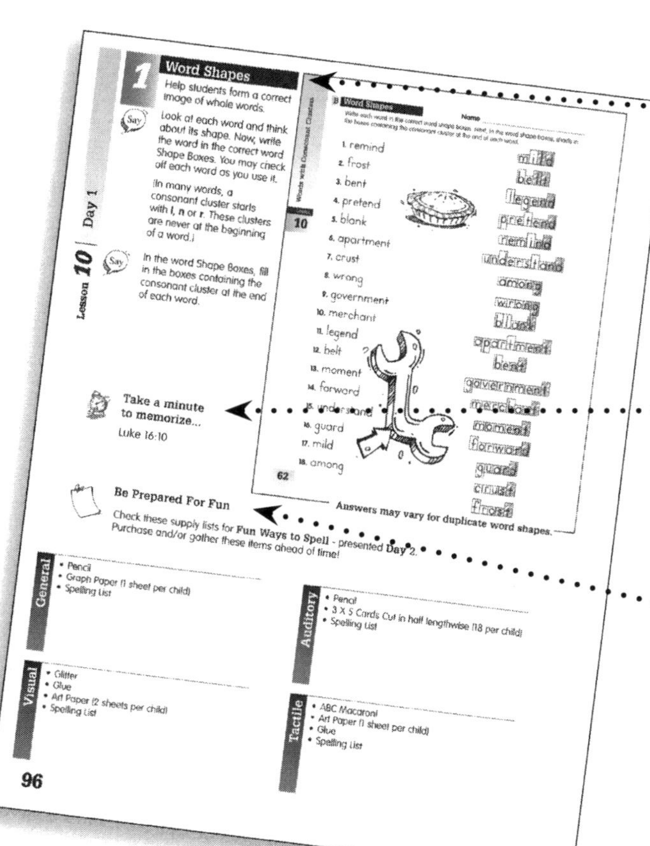

Day One (cont.)

Word Shapes - The use of "Shape Boxes" is a research-based method that helps students form a correct visual image of each spelling word. An additional exercise is provided to enhance student identification of spelling patterns and thus strengthen phonemic awareness.

Take a Minute *(clock graphic)* - Reminders are provided for committing to memory the Scripture verses upon which the stories are based.

Be Prepared for Fun *(list graphic)* - For teacher convenience, a weekly supply list is provided for "Fun Ways to Spell" on Day 1. Supplies for the "General" activity are readily available in most classrooms. Other categories may require minimal extra planning.

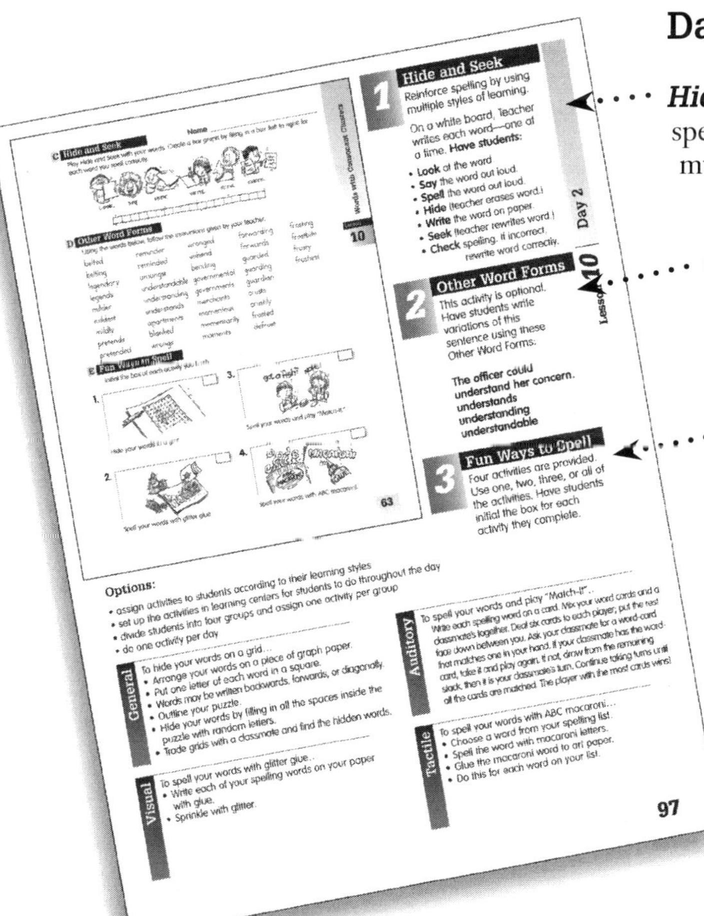

Day Two

Hide & Seek - This research-proven method of spelling instruction is highly effective for dealing with multiple intelligences and varying learning styles.

Other Word Forms *(optional)* - A variety of activities allow students to become familiar with other forms of the week's spelling words.

Fun Ways to Spell - Four options are offered each week. In addition to a "General" activity, "Auditory," "Tactile," and "Visual" options are provided for students with different learning styles. Suggestions are also given for adapting these activities to various classroom settings.

Level **D** | Introduction

Day Three

Language Arts Activity - Research studies show that meaningful, practical use of spelling words helps students become more familiar with the words they are studying. The weekly "Working with Words" activity is designed to offer practice in this area.

Take a Minute - Reminders to commit Scripture verses to memory are provided periodically.

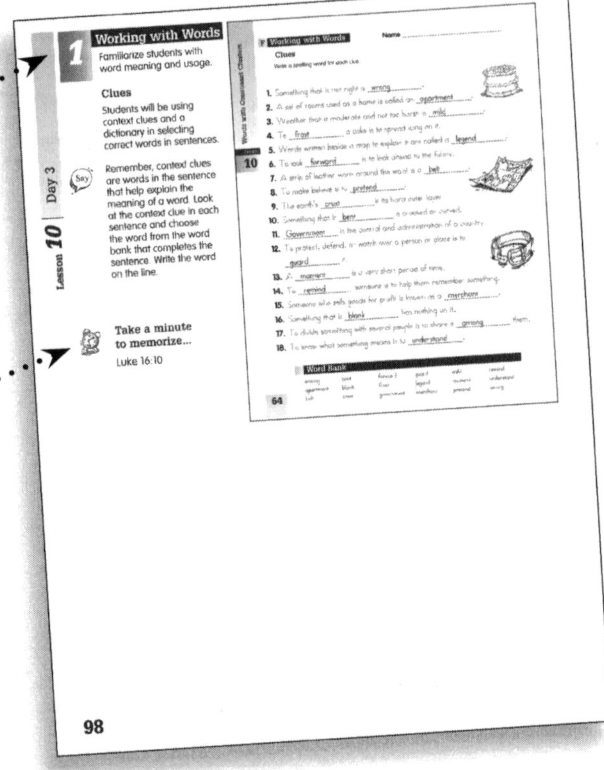

Lesson 10 | Day 3

1 Working with Words
Familiarize students with word meaning and usage.

Clues
Students will be using context clues and a dictionary in selecting correct words in sentences.

Say: Remember, context clues are words in the sentence that help explain the meaning of a word. Look at the context clue in each sentence and choose the word from the word bank that completes the sentence. Write the word on the line.

Take a minute to memorize...
Luke 16:10

98

Day Four

Dictation - Students write dictated words to complete sentences. This strengthens their word usage and context skills. Previously taught spelling words are also included in this activity, providing maintenance of spelling skills.

Proofreading - Proofreading allows students to become familiar with the format of standardized tests as they mark misspelled words. Proofreading is also a critical skill that can be incorporated in students' own writing.

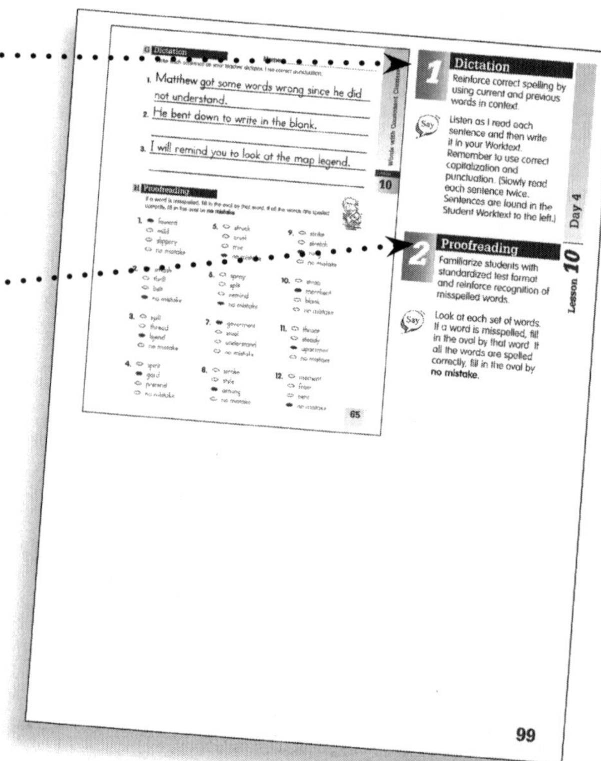

1. Matthew got some words wrong since he did not understand.
2. He bent down to write in the blank.
3. I will remind you to look at the map legend.

Lesson 10 | Day 4

1 Dictation
Reinforce correct spelling by using current and previous words in context.

Say: Listen as I read each sentence and then write it in your Worktext. Remember to use correct capitalization and punctuation. (Slowly read each sentence twice. Sentences are found in the Student Worktext to the left.)

2 Proofreading
Familiarize students with standardized test format and reinforce recognition of misspelled words.

Say: Look at each set of words. If a word is misspelled, fill in the oval by that word. If all the words are spelled correctly, fill in the oval by **no mistake**.

99

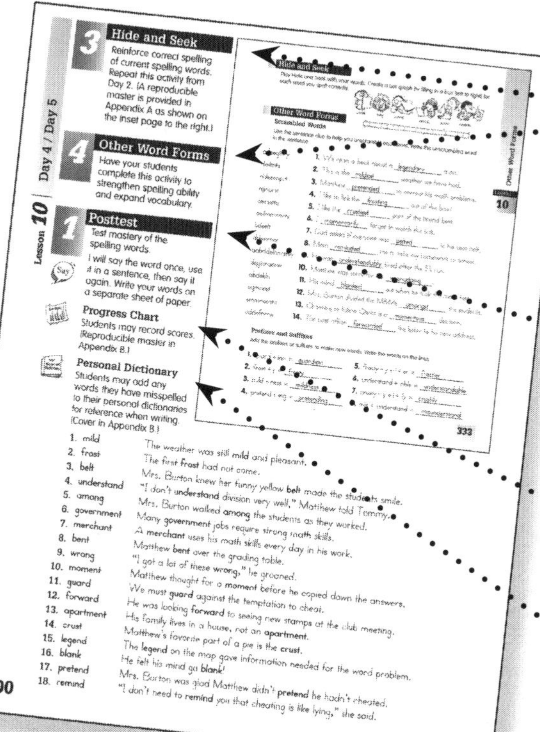

Lesson 10 | Day 4 / Day 5

3 Hide and Seek
Reinforce correct spelling of current spelling words. Repeat this activity from Day 2. (A reproducible master is provided in Appendix A as shown on the inset page to the right.)

4 Other Word Forms
Have your students complete this activity to strengthen spelling ability and expand vocabulary.

1 Posttest
Test mastery of the spelling words.

I will say the word once, use it in a sentence, then say it again. Write your words on a separate sheet of paper.

Progress Chart
Students may record scores. (Reproducible master in Appendix B.)

Personal Dictionary
Students may add any words they have misspelled to their personal dictionaries for reference when writing. (Cover in Appendix B.)

1. mild — The weather was still **mild** and pleasant.
2. frost — The first **frost** had not come.
3. belt — Mrs. Burton knew her funny yellow **belt** made the students smile.
4. understand — "I don't **understand** division very well," Matthew told Tommy.
5. among — Mrs. Burton walked **among** the students as they worked.
6. government — Many **government** jobs require strong math skills.
7. merchant — A **merchant** uses his math skills every day in his work.
8. bent — Matthew **bent** over the grading table.
9. wrong — "I got a lot of these **wrong**," he groaned.
10. moment — Matthew thought for a **moment** before he copied down the answers.
11. guard — We must **guard** against the temptation to cheat.
12. forward — He was looking **forward** to seeing new stamps at the club meeting.
13. apartment — His family lives in a house, not an **apartment**.
14. crust — Matthew's favorite part of a pie is the **crust**.
15. legend — The **legend** on the map gave information needed for the word problem.
16. blank — He felt his mind go **blank**!
17. pretend — Mrs. Burton was glad Matthew didn't **pretend** he hadn't cheated.
18. remind — "I don't need to **remind** you that cheating is like lying," she said.

100

Day Five

***Hide & Seek/Other Word Forms** (optional)* - These activities provide additional opportunity for students to practice other forms of their spelling words. (Note: These pages are not in the Student Worktext. A Reproducible master for each week is provided in Appendix A.)

Posttest - The test—study—test sequence of learning is completed with the posttest. Again, most sentences relate to the theme story. Visit the ***A Reason For*** website to download free, printable Posttest pages.

***Progress Chart** (chart graphic)* - Students may now record their posttest scores to evaluate their weekly progress.

***Personal Dictionary** (dictionary graphic)* - Students may add any words they have misspelled to their personal dictionaries. Each student may refer to his/her custom dictionary while journaling or during other writing activities. (Reproducible cover in Appendix B.)

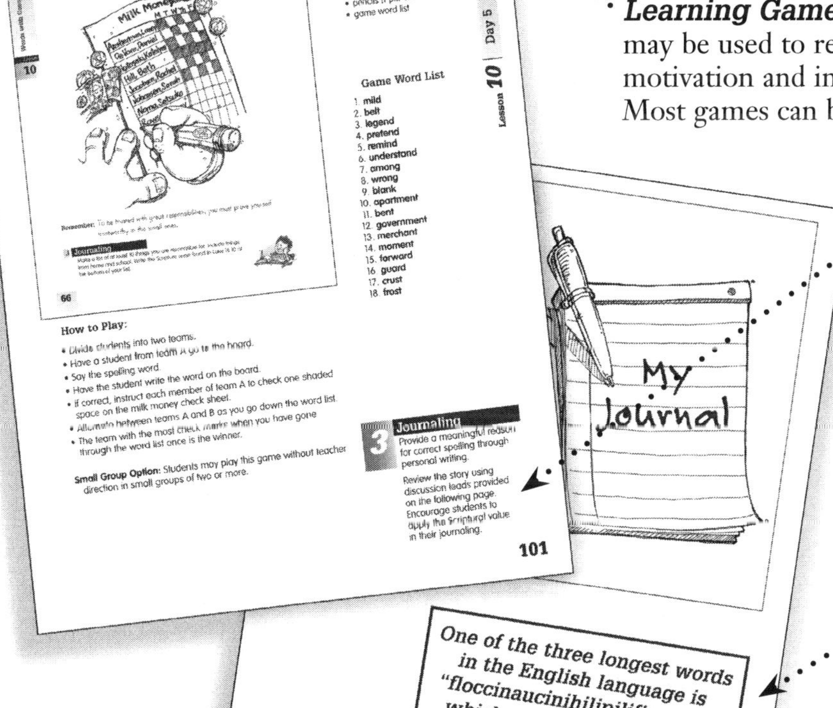

2 Game
Reinforce spelling skills and provide motivation and interest.

Materials
- game page (from Student Worktext)
- pencils (1 per child)
- game word list

Lesson 10 | Day 5

Game Word List
1. mild
2. belt
3. legend
4. pretend
5. remind
6. understand
7. among
8. wrong
9. blank
10. apartment
11. bent
12. government
13. merchant
14. moment
15. forward
16. guard
17. crust
18. frost

How to Play:
- Divide students into two teams.
- Have a student from team A go to the board.
- Say the spelling word.
- Have the student write the word on the board.
- If correct, instruct each member of team A to check one shaded space on the milk money check sheet.
- Alternate between teams A and B as you go down the word list.
- The team with the most check marks when you have gone through the word list once is the winner.

Small Group Option: Students may play this game without teacher direction in small groups of two or more.

3 Journaling
Provide a meaningful reason for correct spelling through personal writing.

Review the story using discussion leads provided on the following page. Encourage students to apply the Scriptural value in their journaling.

101

One of the three longest words in the English language is "floccinaucinihilipilification," which means "the action of estimating as worthless." There are 29 letters in the word.

Word Wow!

102

Day Five (cont.)

***Learning Game** (optional)* - The weekly "board game" may be used to reinforce spelling skills and produce motivation and interest in good spelling.
Most games can be played multiple times.

Journal Entry - The underlying goal of spelling instruction is to create better writers! This weekly journaling activity allows students to apply their spelling skills in a meaningful way, while encouraging them to make the featured value their own. Guided discussion questions are provided to assist in reviewing the value taught by the story.

Word Wow! - Interesting insights into words and their meanings are provided to capture student interest.

Research Basis

A Reason For Spelling® emphasizes a balance between spelling skills, application, and student enjoyment. In short, it is designed to be both meaningful and fun! Each level promotes successful classroom practices while incorporating the following research findings:

Research Findings:		***Application:***
Daily Practice. A daily period of teacher-directed spelling activities based on meaningful content greatly enhances student proficiency in spelling.		Daily lessons in ***A Reason For Spelling***® provide systematic development of spelling skills with a focus on Scripture verses and values.
Spelling Lists. The most productive spelling lists feature developmentally-appropriate words of highest frequency in writing.		Through daily lessons, challenge words, and other word forms, ***A Reason For Spelling***® focuses on the high frequency words children and adults use in daily writing.
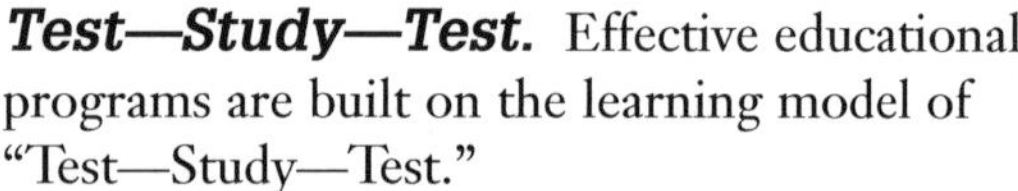 ***Test—Study—Test.*** Effective educational programs are built on the learning model of "Test—Study—Test."		***A Reason For Spelling***® follows a weekly pretest/posttest format, and also includes a cumulative review for each unit.
Accurate Feedback. Pretest and proofreading results are crucial in helping students identify words that require their special attention.		Regular pretests and proofreading activities in ***A Reason For Spelling***® help students identify words requiring their special attention.
Visual Imaging. Learning to spell a word involves forming a correct visual image of the whole word, rather than visualizing syllables or parts.		Every lesson in ***A Reason For Spelling***® features word-shape grids to help students form a correct visual image of each spelling word.
Study Procedures. The most effective word-study procedures involve visual, auditory, and tactile modalities.		***A Reason For Spelling***® uses the "look, say, hide, write, seek, check" method as a primary teaching tool.
Learning Games. Well-designed games motivate student interest and lead to spelling independence.		***A Reason For Spelling***® includes a wide variety of spelling games at each instructional level.
Self-Correction. Student focus, accomplished through such activities as self-correction of pretests, is an essential strategy for spelling mastery at every grade and ability level.		Teacher directed self-correction of pretests and reviews is encouraged throughout ***A Reason For Spelling***®.
Regular Application. Frequent opportunities to use spelling words in everyday writing contribute significantly to the maintenance of spelling ability.		***A Reason For Spelling***® provides opportunities for journaling in each lesson to promote the use of assigned spelling words in personal writing.

Cohen, Leo A. 1969. *Evaluating Structural Analysis Methods Used in Spelling Books*. Doctoral Thesis, Boston University.

Davis, Zephaniah T. 1987. Upper Grades Spelling Instruction: What Difference Does It Make? *English Journal*, March: 100-101.

Dolch, E.W. 1936. A Basic Sight Vocabulary. *The Elementary School Journal*, Vol. 36: 456-460.

Downing, John, Robert M. Coughlin and Gene Rich. 1986. Children's Invented Spellings in the Classroom. *The Elementary School Journal*, Vol. 86, No. 3, January: 295-303.

Fiderer, Adele. 1995. *Practical Assessments for Literature-Based Reading Classrooms.* New York: Scholastic Professional Books.

Fitzsimmons, Robert J., and Bradley M. Loomer. 1980. *Spelling: The Research Basis.* Iowa City: The University of Iowa.

Gardner, Howard. 1993. *Multiple Intelligences: The Theory in Practice.* New York: Basic-Books.

Gentry, J. Richard. 1997. *My Kid Can't Spell.* Portsmouth, NH: Heinemann Educational Books.

Gentry, J. Richard and Jean Wallace Gillet. 1993. *Teaching Kids to Spell.* Portsmouth, NH:Heinemann Educational Books.

Gentry, J. Richard. 1985. You Can Analyze Developmental Spelling-And Here's How To Do It! *Early Years K-8*, May:1-4.

Goswami, Usha. 1991. Learning about Spelling Sequences: The Role of Onsets and Rimes in Analogies in Reading. *Child Development*, 62, 1110-1123.

Graves, Donald H. 1977. Research Update: Spelling Texts and Structural Analysis Methods. *Language Arts 54* January: 86-90.

Harp, Bill. 1988. When the Principal Asks, "Why Are Your Kids Giving Each Other Spelling Tests?" *Reading Teacher*, Vol. 41, No. 7, March: 702-704.

Hoffman, Stevie and Nancy Knipping. 1988. Spelling Revisited: The Child's Way. *Childhood Education*, June: 284-287.

Horn, Ernest. 1926. *A Basic Writing Vocabulary: 10,000 Frequently Used Words in Writing.* Monograph First Series, No. 4. Iowa City: The University of Iowa.

Horn, Thomas. 1946. *The Effect of the Corrected Test on Learning to Spell.* Master's Thesis, The University of Iowa.

Horsky, Gregory Alexander. 1974. *A Study of the Perception of Letters and Basic Sight Vocabulary Words of Fourth and Fifth Grade Children.* Doctoral Thesis, The University of Iowa.

Lacey, Cheryl. 1994. *Moving On In Spelling.* Jefferson City, Missouri: Scholastic.

Lutz, Elaine. 1986. ERIC/RCS Report: Invented Spelling and Spelling Development. *Language Arts*, Vol. 63, No. 7, November: 742-744.

Marino, Jacqueline L. 1978. *Children's Use of Phonetic, Graphemic, and Morphophonemic Cues in a Spelling Task.* Doctoral Thesis, State University of New York at Albany.

Morris, Darrell, Laurie Nelson and Jan Perney. 1986. Exploring the Concept of 'Spelling Instructional Level' Through the Analysis of Error-Types. *The Elementary School Journal*, Vol. 87, No. 2, 195-197.

Nicholson, Tom and Sumner Schachter. 1979. Spelling Skill and Teaching Practice-Putting Them Back Together Again. *Language Arts*, Vol. 56, No. 7, October: 804-809.

Rothman, Barbara. 1997. *Practical Phonics Strategies to Build Beginning Reading and Writing Skills.* Medina, Washington: Institute for Educational Development.

Scott, Jill E. 1994. Spelling for Readers and Writers. *The Reading Teacher*, Vol. 48, No. 2, October: 188-190.

Simmons, Janice L. 1978. *The Relationship Between an Instructional Level in Spelling and the Instructional Level in Reading Among Elementary School Children.* Doctoral Thesis, University of Northern Colorado.

Templeton, Shane. 1986. Synthesis of Research on the Learning and Teaching of Spelling. *Educational Leadership*, March: 73-78.

Tireman, L.S. 1927. *The Value of Marking Hard Spots in Spelling.* Doctoral Thesis, University of Iowa.

Toch, Thomas. 1992. Nu Waz for Kidz tu Lern Rdn, Rtn. *U.S. News & World Report*, September 14: 75-76.

Wagstaff, Janiel M. *Phonics That Work! New Strategies for the Reading/Writing Classroom.* Jefferson City, Missouri: Scholastic.

Watson, Alan J. 1988. Developmental Spelling: A Word Categorizing Instructional Experiment. *Journal of Educational Research*, Vol. 82, No. 2, November/December: 82-88.

Webster's New American Dictionary. 1995. New York: Merriam-Webster Inc.

Wilde, Sandra. 1990. A Proposal for a New Spelling Curriculum. *The Elementary School Journal*, Vol. 90, No. 3, January: 275-289.

English as a Second Language (ESL)

Effective teachers are always sensitive to the special spelling challenges faced by ESL students. While it is not practical to provide specific guidelines for every situation where the teacher may encounter students with limited English proficiency, the following general guidelines for two of the most prominent cultural groups (Asian & Hispanic) may prove helpful.

alphabet Many Asian languages have a significantly different kind of alphabet and students may need considerable practice recognizing English letters and sounds.

vowels Some Asian languages do not have certain English vowel sounds. Speakers often substitute other sounds. Spanish vowels have a single sound: *a* as in *ball*, *e* as in *eight*, *i* as in *ski*, *o* as in *over*, *u* as in *rule*. The Spanish *a* is spelled *e*, *e* is spelled *i* or *y*, and *i* is often spelled *ai* or *ay*.

ô The variety of *ô* spellings may cause some problems for Spanish-speaking students.

ü, u̇ The *u̇* sound does not occur in Spanish, and may cause problems.

ou This sound is spelled *au* in Spanish.

r This sound does not exist in Spanish. Many Asian languages do not have words ending with *r*.

b, d, h, j Spanish and Asian speakers often confuse the sounds of *b* / *d* and *h* / *j*.

ge, gi, j In Spanish, *ge*, *gi*, and *j* most closely resemble the English *h*.

l, f Many Asian languages do not have these sounds.

k, q The letter *k* does not exist in Spanish, but the sound *k* is spelled with either *c* or *qu*. The letter *q* always occurs with *ue* or *ui*.

p, g In most Asian languages, the consonants *p* and *g* do not exist.

v In Spanish, the letter *v* is pronounced *b*.

w There are no Spanish-originated words with the letter *w*.

y In Spanish, *y* is spelled *ll*.

x, z In Spanish, *x* is never used in the final position. There is no letter or sound for *z*.

ch, sh The Spanish language does not have the sound *sh*. Spellers often substitute *ch*. Many Asian languages do not contain *sh* or *ch*.

wh, th The initial *wh* and *th* sounds do not exist in most Spanish and some Asian languages. The Spanish *d*, however, is sometimes pronounced almost like the *th*.

kn This sound may be difficult for native speakers of Spanish or Asian languages.

s clusters Spanish clusters that begin with s are always preceded by the vowels *a* or *e*. The most common clusters that will cause problems are *sc*, *sk*, *sl*, *sm*, *sn*, *sp*, *sq*, *st*, and *sw*. Many of these do not occur in Asian languages.

pl, fl, tr, fr, dr These sounds are used in Spanish, but may not be present in some Asian languages.

ng, nk, nt, nd Many Asian languages don't have *ng*, *nk*, *nt*, or *nd*. Spanish doesn't include the ng ending.

silent letters The only silent letter in Spanish is *h*. Silent consonants such as those in *mb*, *lk*, and *gh* do not occur in Spanish or Asian languages.

double consonants The only double consonants in Spanish are *cc*, *ll*, and *rr*.

ed In Spanish, the suffix *ed* is pronounced aid. This can be very confusing, especially when the *ed* has the soft *t* sound as in *dropped*.

plurals Spanish rules for adding plurals are: For words ending in a vowel, add *s*. For words ending in a consonant, add *es*. This may cause confusion both in pronunciation and spelling of English words.

contractions Only two contractions are used in Spanish: *a el* becomes *al*, and *de el* becomes *del*. Apostrophes do not exist.

syllables Many Asian languages consist entirely of one and two syllable words. Thus, many longer English words are often confusing.

Spelling Generalizations

In the English language, spelling cannot be taught primarily by rules or generalizations. It's a complex language that has evolved from many other languages and therefore contains many irregularities. There are exceptions to almost all spelling rules.

Research, however, indicates that some generalizations are of value in teaching children to spell. These generalizations have few exceptions and apply to a large number of words. Familiarity with these spelling rules can be helpful to many learners. In addition, generalizations that deal with adding suffixes to words can be quite valuable in expanding a student's ability to spell other word forms.

The following generalizations may prove to be helpful:

- The letter *q* is always followed by *u*.
- Every syllable contains a vowel. *Y* can also serve as a vowel.
- Words that end in silent *e*:
  ... drop the *e* when adding a suffix beginning with a vowel. (live, living)
  ... keep the *e* when adding a suffix beginning with a consonant. (time, timely)
- Words that end in *y*:
  ... are not changed when adding suffixes if the *y* is preceded by a vowel. (say, saying)
  ... change the *y* to *i* when adding suffixes if the *y* is preceded by a consonant, unless the suffix begins with *i*. (try, tried, trying)
- When *ei* or *ie* are used in a word, the *i* usually comes before the *e* except when they make the */ā/* sound, or follow after a *c*. (believe, eight, ceiling)
- Words ending in one consonant preceded by a single vowel usually double the final consonant when adding a suffix beginning with a vowel. (begin, beginning)
- Words ending with the sounds made by *x*, *s*, *sh*, and *ch* add the suffix *es* to form plurals or change tense. (mix, mixes)
- Proper nouns and most proper adjectives begin with capital letters.

Multiple Intelligences

In recognition of the multiple intelligences theory, ***A Reason For Spelling***® provides activities to meet the varied needs of your students. (See "Fun Ways to Spell," and "Hide & Seek.")

Scripture Translation

Each weekly lesson in ***A Reason For Spelling***® begins with a Scripture verse. This is followed by a contemporary theme story designed to bring out key values found in the verse.

Teachers are strongly encouraged to introduce each lesson by reading the "Theme Text" aloud (or have a student read the verse aloud). This helps set the stage for the principles and values students will be focusing on that week.

Scripture verses used in ***A Reason For Spelling***® are similar in most translations, allowing teachers to use the Scripture translation their school prefers, without affecting academic content.

Personal Spelling Dictionary

A great way to encourage students' spelling awareness is to help them develop and maintain their own Personal Spelling Dictionary at their desk to refer to when writing. This can be either a spiral-bound or loose-leaf notebook with a few pages designated for each letter of the alphabet. Throughout the school year, encourage students to constantly add words to their Personal Spelling Dictionary, not only from spelling class, but from other classes as well. These should include words a student finds difficult to spell, as well as words of particular interest. (Reproducible cover in Appendix B.)

Word Walls

Another excellent method of promoting spelling awareness is to create a word wall. This wall (often a large bulletin board) contains commonly used words and words of special interest. The word wall becomes a permanent reference list that students may refer to as they read and write.

Words may be arranged in a variety of ways. Some examples include traditional alphabetical order; groups (such as math words, weather words, color words); or by the targeted vowel. For example:

A	E	I	O	U
April	cheese	listen	worry	judge
capture	leather	price	bought	curious
carpet	perfect	tonight		pollute

Some words could even have picture or context clues added. Sample words from word families being studied, or interesting words students want to know how to spell are added throughout the year. Students should be reminded not to simply copy the words from the wall, but to look at the word needed, then write it from memory — or write the word they are having difficulty with, then check it against the word wall.

Games can be played using the word wall as well.

- Rhyming Words: Ask students to find a word that "rhymes with **phone**."
- Sentence Sense: Write the letter w on the board, then say "Look for a word that begins with a **w** and fits this sentence: I w_ _ _ _ _ _ Jesus."
- Dictate & Write: Dictate a sentence for students to write using words found only on the wall.
- Read My Mind:

I am thinking of one of the words on the wall. It has ______ letters. It begins with _____. The vowel is ______. It fits in this sentence: ________________.

Flip Folders

The Flip Folder is a great way for students to use the research-based, time-tested "Look—Hide—Write—Seek—Check" method to learn spelling words. They may do this activity on their own or with a partner.

On the front of a standard file folder, make two cuts to create three flaps (see diagram below). On a separate piece of paper, have students make three columns, then write the words they need to study in the first column. Now have students slide the paper into the folder so that the words are under the first flap.

- Open Flap 1 and ***Look*** at the first word.
- Now ***Hide*** the word by closing the flap.
- Open Flap 2 and ***Write*** the word in the middle column.
- Open Flaps 1 & 2 and ***Seek*** the word to ***Check*** your spelling. If the word is misspelled. . .
- Open Flap 3 and ***Write*** the word correctly in the third column.

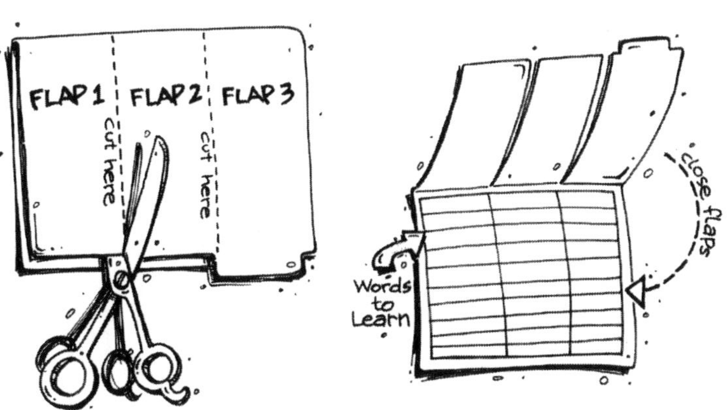

Inventive Spelling/Journaling

The goal of ***A Reason For Spelling***® is to create proficient and self-reliant spellers and writers. By combining inventive spelling (through journaling) with formal spelling instruction, an excellent environment is created for students to develop into expert spellers. (Reproducible Journal cover in Appendix B.)

As children learn to spell, they go through several stages. The move from one stage to another is gradual, even though students may spell from more than one stage at one time. Just as a toddler who is talking in complete sentences doesn't suddenly regress to babbling, so students tend to remain relatively stable within and between stages. Recognized stages of spelling development include:

Precognitive Stage: Children use symbols from the alphabet for writing words, but letters are random and do not correspond to sound. (eagle = dfbrt; eighty = acbp)

Semiphonetic Stage: Children understand and consistently represent sounds with letters. Spellings are often abbreviated representing only the initial and/or final sounds. (eagle = e; eighty = a)

Phonetic Stage: Students in this stage spell words like they sound. The speller perceives and represents every sound in a word, though spellings may be unconventional. (eagle = egl; eighty = aty)

Transitional Stage: Students think about how words appear visually. Spelling patterns are apparent. Spellings exhibit customs of English spelling such as vowels in every syllable, correct e-marker and vowel digraph patterns, inflectional endings, and frequent English letter sequences. (eagle = egul; eighty = eightee)

Conventional Stage: This stage develops over years of word study and writing. Correct spelling has different instructional levels. Correct spelling for a group of words that can be spelled by the average third grader would be "third grade level correct" spelling. (eagle = eagle; eighty = eighty)

An effective way to help students transition through the stages is to edit their first drafts, then talk with them about corrections. Discuss why changes are necessary. Encourage students to rewrite journal entries so others can read them easily. Display student work whenever possible. Teach students that inventive spelling makes it easier for the writer, but that revision to standard spelling is a courtesy to the reader.

Word Lists

Word lists in ***A Reason For Spelling***® are based on frequency of use in student and adult writing, frequency of use in reading materials, spelling difficulty, and grade level familiarity.

Studies used in the development of these lists include: *Dolch Basic Sight Vocabulary* (a list of 220 high frequency words); *The American Heritage Word Frequency Book* (a study of word frequency in print materials for grades three to nine); *Starter Words* (the 190 most frequently used words in children's writing, school materials, and adult print materials); and *A Basic Vocabulary of Elementary School Children.*

The following standard references were extensively cross-checked with other respected studies: Gates; Horn; Greene & Loomer; Harris & Jacobson. It is significant to note that very few differences were found among these sources.

The lesson number follows each word.

Level-C

able-27
address-8
afraid-16
ago-20
airport-23
alarm-25
allow-22
alone-20
amount-22
angel-13
angry-17
answer-1
anyhow-22
apart-25
April-27
argue-25
army-25
artist-25
asleep-14
August-21
aunt-9
autumn-21
awake-16
bark-25
began-1
behind-9
belong-9
berry-1
bicycle-19
body-1
boot-31
boss-14
bother-3
bottle-27
bought-21
bread-5
bright-11
broke-5
brook-29
brought-21
bump-9
burn-28
bushes-29
busy-17
butter-8
buzz-2
cactus-2
cage-13
candle-27
careful-15
carry-17
cattle-27
caught-11
cause-21
center-26
certain-14
chair-3
chalk-11
change-3
charge-25
cheek-3
cheese-3
cherry-3
chest-1
chill-1
choose-31
circus-14
classroom-8
clay-4
close-4
cloth-4
clothes-11
clown-22
collar-2
cookie-29
copy-15
corner-23
course-23
cover-15
crash-10
crayon-5
creek-17
crop-2
cross-5
crowd-22
date-16
daughter-21
deaf-2
December-26
deep-17
die-19
dirt-28
dollar-26
doubt-22
drank-9
drew-31
driver-26
drown-22
eagle-27
early-28
earn-28
earth-10
edge-13
eight-16
February-17
felt-2
field-17
fight-19
flag-4
flame-4
flash-4
flew-31
float-20
floor-23
follow-20
football-29
forget-26
fork-15
fort-23
fought-21
fourth-23
fresh-10
Friday-19
front-9
fruit-31
gas-14
gift-1
giraffe-13
glass-4
glove-4
goes-20
gold-20
good-bye-29
grab-5
grandfather-9
grandmother-9
gray-5
ground-22
group-31
half-11
hall-21
hammer-26
handle-27
happen-8
hatch-10
heavy-17
held-1
hello-2
herd-28
honey-17
hood-29
hook-29
horn-23
hour-22
huge-13
hurry-28
husband-9
ink-9
January-13
jar-13
jealous-13
jolly-13
judge-13
jug-13
juice-13
July-13
June-13
kept-15
key-15
kick-10
knee-11
knot-11
ladder-8
lady-16
lamb-2
later-26
lay-16
learn-28
leave-17
less-14
lesson-8
lie-19
life-19
lift-1
list-1
loose-31
loud-22
made-16
mail-16
March-25
mark-25
market-25
marry-17
match-10
meal-17
mean-17
merry-8
metal-27
middle-27
million-8
mirror-26
Monday-1
moon-31
mouse-22
mouth-22
nearby-19
neck-10
needle-27
neighbor-11
neighborhood-29
north-3
notebook-29
November-26
October-15
open-20
order-23
owe-20
pants-2
paper-16
park-25
pass-14
paw-21
person-28
pick-1
place-4
plain-4
plane-16
plant-4
please-4
plow-22
plus-4
pool-31
porch-10
pour-23
power-22
prayer-5
price-5
prize-5
proud-5
pulley-29
puppy-1
push-29
queen-15
quick-15
quiet-15
quilt-15
quite-15
race-14
rack-15
rage-13
rake-15
ranch-10
raw-21
really-8
remember-26
report-23
return-28
ripe-19
river-26
rode-20
rope-20
rubber-8
ruler-31
rush-10
sack-10
saddle-27
sail-16
salt-21
sandwich-10
sang-9
Saturday-28
save-14
score-23
scrap-7
scratch-7
scream-7
screen-7
scrub-7

search-28
sell-14
September-28
serve-28
seventh-14
sew-20
shade-16
shampoo-31
shark-25
sharp-25
shock-3
shook-29
shout-22
shown-20
shy-19
sidewalk-11
sight-11
sign-19
silver-26
since-14
skate-5
skin-5
skip-5
sleeve-4
slice-4
smart-25
smell-8
smile-19
smooth-31
soap-14
song-21
sore-23
sorry-14
spell-5
spend-5
splash-10
spoke-20
sport-23
spread-7
spring-7
sprinkle-27
squirrel-27
stamp-9
start-25
stiff-2
storm-23
straight-7
strange-7
straw-7
stream-7
street-7
string-7
strong-7
sudden-8
sugar-26
suit-31
summer-26
Sunday-2
sunny-8
supper-8
sweet-14
switch-10
table-16
taught-21
teacher-10
team-17
telephone-20
test-1
thankful-3
thirteen-3
thirty-28
though-11
threw-7
thumb-11
Thursday-3
tight-19
tiny-19
toast-20
track-15
travel-27
truth-31
Tuesday-31
turtle-27
twelve-2
twenty-17
unhappy-8
upon-21
visit-1
wagon-2
wait-16
wall-21
Wednesday-11
weigh-16
west-2
whale-3
wheat-3
whether-3
whip-3
whole-11
wild-19
wind-9
window-2
wing-9
wipe-19
wolf-29
woman-29
wonder-26
wool-29
wore-23
worse-28
wrap-11
young-9

Level-D

accept-2
across-14
against-3
agree-4
ahead-3
alike-5
all right-16
almost-16
aloud-15
alphabet-13
already-16
although-11
among-10
annoy-21
anyway-29
anywhere-26
apartment-10
appear-27
applause-16
appointment-21
April Fools' Day-31
Arbor Day-31
arrest-2
arrow-2
attic-2
author-16
avenue-7
avoid-21
awful-16
backyard-29
bandage-2
barber-17
bare-26
barnyard-17
bathroom-29
bathtub-29
battle-23
beard-27
beast-14
beautiful-7
became-4
bedroom-29
bedspread-29
behave-4
believe-4
belt-10
bent-10
birth-19
blade-8
blank-10
blanket-8
blood-1
bloom-7
bluff-13
bomb-11
bounce-15
branch-1
brand-1
breakfast-3
bridge-8
broom-7
built-3
bulldozer-20
bulletin-20
burst-19
butcher-20
button-25
cabbage-2
cane-4
cape-4
capture-22
cardboard-17
carnival-17
carpet-17
cart-17
castle-23
cave-4
cellar-14
cereal-27
champion-25
chance-14
cheer-27
chef-13
chicken-25
chief-4
choice-21
chose-5
Christmas-31
citizen-14
clear-8
climb-11
clue-7
coach-5
collect-2
Columbus Day-31
comb-11
comfort-3
common-25
compare-26
cord-16
cotton-25
cough-13
couldn't-28
county-15
couple-3
cousin-3
crack-8
craft-13
cream-8
crooked-20
crow-5
crust-10
cure-20
curious-20
curl-19
curtain-25
curve-19
dairy-26
damage-2
danger-22
dare-26
dead-3
decide-14
deer-27
delight-11
depend-2
dessert-19
destroy-21
dew-7
didn't-28
disappear-27
disappoint-21
dive-5
dock-1
dollhouse-15
donor-22
dragon-25
dream-8
drift-13
drum-8
due-7
dumb-11
during-20
dust-1
Easter-31
either-22
elephant-13
else-14
employ-21
enjoyment-21
enough-13
enter-22
everybody-29
evil-23
except-2
exciting-14
fail-4
fair-26
false-16
famous-14
fare-26
farmer-17
farther-17
fault-16
favor-22
fear-27
feather-22
fence-14
festival-23
fierce-27
final-23
finger-22
fireplace-29
firm-19
fist-1
flock-1
flour-8
flow-8
flute-7
fog-16
folks-11
footprint-20
forest-16
forward-10
fountain-25
freight-4
frost-10
frown-15
fry-8
fully-20
furious-20
furniture-19
further-19
garbage-17
garden-17
gear-27
general-23
gentle-23
germ-19
glance-14
glare-26
glue-7
goodness-20
government-10
gown-15
graph-13
grave-8
groan-8
Groundhog Day-31
growl-15
guard-10
hadn't-28
hair-26
Halloween-31
handful-20
Hanukkah-31
hardly-17
hare-26
harm-17
harsh-17
haul-16
hawk-16
he'd-28
he'll-28
here's-28
herself-29
hollow-5
homemade-29
homework-29
honor-22
hospital-23
however-15
human-7
humor-22
hung-1
I'd-28
Independence Day-31
instead-3
iron-5
it'll-28
jelly-4
joint-21
jungle-23
kitchen-25
knife-11
knob-11
label-23
Labor Day-31
laid-4
laugh-13
lazy-4
lead-3
lean-4
least-4
leather-3

legend-10
lemon-25
level-23
limb-11
lion-25
listen-25
loaf-13
lonely-5
loyal-21
marbles-17
Martin Luther King Day-31
May Day-31
meant-3
measure-3
Memorial Day-31
merchant-10
mild-10
model-23
moist-21
moment-10
motor-22
movement-7
movie-7
mustard-2
nature-22
near-27
neither-22
New Year's Day-31
newspaper-29
nothing-2
notice-5
noun-15
nurse-19
oak-5
object-2
offer-16
office-13
oily-21
orphan-13
ought-11
outdoors-15
oven-25
overalls-29
overlook-20
owl-15
owner-22
package-2
Passover-31
past-1
pasture-22
pause-16
peace-14
pear-26
pebble-1
perfect-19
period-27
photograph-13
picture-22
pile-5
pine-5
plank-8
plastic-2
playground-29
pleasant-3
plural-20
point-21
police-14
pollute-7
possible-23
pound-15
powder-15
practice-2
Presidents' Day-31
press-14
pretend-10
public-2
puddle-23
pumpkin-2
pure-20
purpose-19
quarrel-16
railroad-29
rather-22
rear-27
reason-25
recess-14
reign-11
rejoice-21
remind-10
repair-26
reply-5
reptile-1
rescue-7
ribbon-25
ridge-1
robin-25
roof-7
rose-5
rough-13
royalty-21
ruin-25
sauce-16
scarce-26
scare-26
scarf-17
scene-14
science-14
scout-15
secret-4
self-1
several-23
share-26
she'll-28
she's-28
shove-1
simple-23
sincerely-27
sink-1
sir-19
siren-25
skirt-19
slippery-9
smash-9
smoke-8
snap-8
somewhere-29
son-14
soybean-21
spark-17
speak-8
spear-27
spill-9
spirit-9
split-9
spray-9
stare-26
starve-17
station-4
steady-9
steer-27
stew-8
stool-9
stout-15
stove-5
strap-9
stretch-9
strike-9
stroke-9
struck-9
stuff-13
style-9
sunshine-29
supply-5
sure-20
sweat-3
swept-1
swift-13
tear-27
Thanksgiving-31
there's-28
they'd-28
thorough-11
thoughtful-11
thread-9
thrill-9
throat-9
tied-5
tiger-5
topsoil-21
total-23
touch-1
tough-13
tourist-20
toward-16
tower-15
tray-4
trouble-3
trout-15
true-9
trust-1
tune-7
turkey-19
uncle-23
underground-15
understand-10
unknown-11
upstairs-26
usual-7
Valentine's Day-31
visitor-22
voyage-21
we've-28
wealth-3
wear-26
weary-27
weird-27
weren't-28
what's-28
where's-28
who's-28
whom--7
whose-11
within-29
wooden-20
worry-19
worst-19
worth-19
wouldn't--28
wreath-11
wren-11
wrong-10
yarn-17
yesterday-3

Level-E

accent-1
account-29
accuse-11
acid-1
adapt-1
admire-9
admit-3
adopt-14
adult-5
adverb-26
aerobics-16
Africa-19
afternoon-23
aimless-27
aisle-17
Alabama-13
Alaska-21
album-5
alcohol-4
alibi-9
Amazon-22
anchor-26
angle-25
announcer-29
Antarctica-15
appeal-8
area-16
argument-15
Arizona-16
Arkansas-15
arrive-9
artery-15
artichoke-15
Asia-7
aspect-1
aspire-17
assist-3
astronaut-4
athlete-1
atlas-1
atomic-14
attend-2
audience-4
Australia-4
autograph-19
automatic-4
automobile-4
average-20
aware-16
awkward-4
backup-21
badge-20
banana-1
banjo-10
banner-1
banquet-21
bargain-15
barracks-16
barren-16
barrier-16
basketball-23
batch-1
biceps-17
blaze-22
blizzard-22
boldly-10
border-28
borrow-14
bottom-14
boundary-29
brief-8
broadcast-23
brother-in-law-23
browse-29
bruise-22
buffalo-10
bundle-25
burden-26
burial-25
byte-9
California-1
camera-1
Canada-1
candlestick-23
canoe-11
caramel-16
cardiac-15
cargo-10
cartilage-15
carton-15
cavern-1
cavity-1
central-25
chaos-21
chapter-26
chart-15
charter-26
chase-7
chorus-21
circuit-5
cirrus-27
citizen-22
citrus-27
clause-4
clerk-26
clever-26
cliffs-3
climate-17
closeness-27
closet-22
clout-29
coffee-4
college-14
colonies-14
Colorado-13
combat-13
combine-17
comment-14
commerce-14
compare-16
compartment-15
compile-17
compost-14
compound-29
concentrate-14
confuse-11
congress-27
Connecticut-31
construct-5
contact-14
contain-7
continent-14
control-10
conversation-14
cornea-28
cornerstone-28
corridor-28
counterfeit-29
courage-26
coward-29
coyote-17
crater-7
crawl-4
credit-2
creep-8
crew-11
crime-17
cringe-20
crisis-17
crocodile-14
crouch-29
crumb-5
crumple-25
crystal-25
cue-11

Curriculum Objectives

Literature Connection
To increase comprehension and vocabulary development through a value-based story.

Discussion Time
To check understanding of the story and encourage personal value development.

Preview
To test for knowledge of correct spellings of current spelling words.

Word Shapes
To help students form a correct visual image of whole words and to help students recognize common spelling patterns.

Hide & Seek
To reinforce correct spelling of current spelling words.

Other Word Forms
To strengthen spelling ability and expand vocabulary.

Fun Ways to Spell
To reinforce correct spelling of current words with activities that appeal to varying learning styles.

Dictation
To reinforce using current and previous spelling words in context.

Proofreading
To reinforce recognition of misspelled words, and to familiarize students with standardized test format.

Language Arts Activity
To familiarize students with word meaning and usage.

Posttest
To test mastery of current spelling words.

Learning Game
To reinforce correct spelling of test words.

Journaling
To provide a meaningful reason for correct spelling through personal writing.

Unit Tests
To test mastery of correct spelling of the words from each unit.

Action Game
To provide a fun way to review spelling words from the previous unit.

Certificate
To provide opportunity for parents or guardians to encourage and assess their child's progress.

Parent Letter
To provide the parent or guardian with the spelling word lists for the next unit.

Common Spelling Patterns

The following list of sounds and spelling patterns will help you easily identify words with similar patterns.

Sounds	Sample Words
a	**a**sk, h**a**t
ā	**a**pron, l**a**te, m**ai**l, pl**ay**
ä	f**a**ther, p**ar**t, he**ar**t
âr	aw**are**, f**air**, b**ear**, th**ere**
b	**b**erry, a**b**le, scru**b**
ch	**ch**eese, bun**ch**, la**tch**, na**tu**re
d	**d**og, la**dd**er
e	b**e**d, h**ea**vy, s**ai**d
ē	sh**e**, h**ea**t, fr**ee**, n**ie**ce, k**ey**
f	**f**ish, loa**f**, o**ff**, enou**gh**, pro**ph**et
g	**g**ive, for**g**ot, shru**g**
h	**h**as, any**h**ow, **wh**ole
wh	**wh**ine, **wh**ich
i	d**i**g, g**y**m
ī	f**i**nd, p**ie**, m**i**ce, tr**y**
îr	cl**ear**, d**eer**, p**ier**ce, c**er**eal, h**ere**
j	**j**ust, en**j**oy, **g**erm, hu**ge**, bu**dge**
k	**k**eep, hoo**k**, sti**ck**, s**ch**ool, **c**an
l	**l**eft, Ju**l**y, hau**l**, fu**ll**y, te**ll**
m	**m**eal, cal**m**, cli**mb**, co**mm**on, hy**mn**
n	**n**ice, fu**n**, tu**nn**el, **kn**ow
ng	alo**ng**, bri**nging**, tha**n**k
o	n**o**t, p**o**nd, w**a**tch

Sounds	Sample Words
ō	**o**ld, b**oa**t, h**oe**, gl**o**be, bl**ow**
ô	t**a**lk, c**au**se, dr**aw**, s**o**ft, th**ough**t
ôr	st**or**y, m**ore**, w**ar**d, f**our**
oi	p**oi**nt, b**oy**
ou	ab**ou**t, pl**ow**
p	**p**lan, re**p**ly, sna**p**, su**pp**ly
r	**r**an, me**rr**y, mo**r**e, **wr**ite
s	**s**ay, gue**ss**, **sc**ent, pri**c**e, **c**ity
sh	**sh**ip, ca**sh**, mi**ss**ion, ma**ch**ine, spe**ci**al, vaca**ti**on
t	**t**en, pu**t**, bu**tt**er, creas**ed**
th	**th**in, e**th**nic, wi**th**
t̲h̲	**th**em, wor**th**y, smoo**th**
u	c**u**p, d**o**ne, wh**a**t, y**ou**ng
ū	h**u**man, y**ou**, n**ew**, t**u**ne
ü	cl**ue**, d**o**, s**oo**n, fr**ui**t
u̇	t**oo**k, sh**ou**ld, p**u**sh
ûr	**ear**n, st**er**n, f**ir**st, w**or**k, Th**ur**sday
v	**v**isit, a**v**oid, arri**v**e
w	**w**ash, drive**w**ay
y	**y**oung, famil**i**ar
z	la**z**y, ja**zz**, pri**z**e, rai**s**e, rein**s**, e**x**ample
zh	mea**s**ure, ero**s**ion
ə	**a**bove, wat**e**r, anim**a**l, gall**o**n, thankf**u**l

Daily Lesson Plans

Letter

Provide the parent or guardian with the spelling word lists for the next unit.

Give your parents or guardian this letter that lists your spelling words for the next unit. Put it where you will remember to practice the words together.

Dear Parent,

We are about to begin our first spelling unit containing five weekly lessons. A set of eighteen words will be studied each week. All the words will be reviewed in the sixth week. Values based on the Scriptures listed below will be taught in each lesson.

Lesson 1	Lesson 2	Lesson 3	Lesson 4	Lesson 5
brand	attic	against	cane	alike
branch	bandage	ahead	cape	dive
past	cabbage	breakfast	cave	pile
reptile	damage	dead	became	pine
pebble	package	yesterday	behave	iron
self	plastic	instead	fail	tiger
swept	practice	lead	laid	tied
fist	accept	leather	lazy	reply
ridge	arrest	meant	station	supply
sink	arrow	measure	tray	coach
dock	collect	pleasant	freight	oak
flock	depend	sweat	lean	chose
shove	except	wealth	least	lonely
dust	object	built	agree	rose
touch	mustard	comfort	secret	stove
hung	nothing	couple	jelly	notice
blood	public	cousin	believe	crow
trust	pumpkin	trouble	chief	hollow
Mark 12:30, 31	John 15:26	John 1:4, 5	John 8:12	John 14:6

Have each student remove above letter from his or her Worktext prior to beginning Lesson 1.

1 **Literature Connection**
Topic: Helping Others
Theme Text: Mark 12:30, 31

Concept to Contemplate

Broken trash bags help Tommy teach Thorny about helping others.

"Hey, Thorny, those are neat looking roller blades. Where'd you get 'em?" Tommy Rawson thumped one of the flashy red in-line skates the boy next to him was putting on.

"Mr. Simmons purchased them for me this summer when I arrived at their house." The boy rubbed a smudge off the shiny red surface of his left skate.

Tommy finished fastening his own well-worn roller blades and leaned back, propping his elbows on the front porch step behind him. He waited, watching his new friend and neighbor, Hubert Thornton Remington III. Thorny, as Tommy called him, did everything with concentration and precision. He was taller than any of the other boys in Tommy's class, with fine, sand-colored hair that was always flopping into his face.

"Do you like living with the Simmons?" Tommy propped one foot across his other knee and ran his hand along the bottom of his roller blade, making the little wheels spin.

Thorny checked the fastenings on each of his skates before answering. "Well, as I've been in residence only a month, it is hard to predict how matters will progress. At this point, however, I can say that I find the family to be a refreshing change from some of the previous foster homes I've experienced in the last two years."

"Does that mean you like living with the Simmons or not?" Tommy jumped up. "How come you talk like that sometimes?"

"Like what?" Thorny stood and began gliding down the front walk.

"Oh, never mind." Tommy muttered. "I guess that's what happens to you when your dad was a scientist and your mom was a. . . a. . ." He hurried to catch up with Thorny. "What did you say your mom did?"

"She was an English professor." Thorny glanced at Tommy and added. "You know, a teacher who teaches about the English language."

"Yeah, I know what an English professor is." Tommy swerved around a hole in the pavement. "How come you didn't go live with an aunt or uncle or something when your parents died in that plane crash?"

"Because I don't have any relatives." Thorny held up his index finger. "I was an only child, as were both my parents. I never knew any of my grandparents. They all died when I was very little. My parents were older than most when they had me."

Tommy shook his head. "I guess I'm luckier than I thought. I've got a bunch of family, cousins and stuff. And my parents, my grandma, and my older sister." He shrugged. "Lisa's all right, even though she's a pest sometimes."

The boys whizzed back and forth past fields and pastures and an occasional house on the quiet road at the edge of town. "Race you!" Thorny's challenge snapped Tommy out of his feelings of pity for the other boy.

"You're on!" Tommy pointed down the road. "Let's race to the Clarks' mailbox. On your mark, get set, GO!"

"Oomph!" Tommy flopped onto the grass in the shade of a large oak across the road from the mailbox. "You won and I'm beat!"

Thorny rested one hand on the oversized black mailbox. "Because of the difference in height between us, my legs are longer, which provides the necessary span to increase. . ."

"Okay, okay!" Tommy picked up an acorn and tossed it at Thorny. "What're you standing out there in the sun for?" He chuckled. "Come over here in the shade to 'analyze' why you won the race."

"Actually, I'm not certain the race is over." Thorny lowered himself to the cooler pavement near Tommy.

"What're you talking about now?" Tommy fanned himself with a large oak leaf. "That's the Clarks' house and the Clarks' mailbox." He motioned across the road with the wilting leaf.

"So you say." Thorny's eyes sparked with laughter. "However, the mailbox in question does read 'lark' rather than 'Clark.'"

"Well, just 'cause the 'C' is missing doesn't mean I'm going to race 'til we find a mailbox that really says 'Clark!'" Tommy propped himself on one elbow and looked across the road at the well kept brick house. The yard was neatly mowed and there were a few flowers in front. "Oh, boy, look at that!" Tommy stood up and started across the road. "What a mess!"

Past the mailbox and the driveway, the front lawn near the road was littered with trash. "Looks like some dog tore apart these trash bags," Tommy called as he picked up a piece of black plastic with several gaping holes in it.

"May I ask what you are doing?" Thorny stood up and slowly skated towards the mess.

"Sure." Tommy bent to pick up an empty milk carton and a smashed cereal box. He poked them into the corner of the trash bag that wasn't ruined and reached for some papers that were starting to blow away.

"So?" Thorny stopped at the edge of the road.

"Huh?" Tommy grunted as he picked up some other stuff.

"So, what are you doing?" Thorny yelled.

Tommy looked up in surprise. "Picking up this trash. Come on, we're gonna need a couple of new trash bags."

"Now, wait just a minute." Thorny stopped

Story (continued)

Tommy as he started back down the road. "What do you mean 'we' need new trash bags? It's hot, you said you were beat, and that isn't even your trash!"

"No, but it needs to be picked up and I'm not that tired. Come on." Tommy took off for his house and Thorny followed more slowly.

Hubert Thornton Remington III was unusually quiet while they changed into their shoes and walked back to the Clarks' yard with large empty trash bags. With two of them working it didn't take too long to stuff all the scattered trash back into bags. Tommy whistled as they walked down the road toward his home again. "It doesn't make sense, you know." Thorny kicked a pebble down the road in front of him.

"What doesn't make sense?" Tommy grinned. "What are you analyzing this time?"

"Now that school has begun, there is little time for activities of your own choosing," Thorny began.

"You mean stuff like playing baseball or roller blading?" Tommy interrupted.

"Of course." Thorny nodded. "So, why would you choose to spend your time picking up trash for someone? Especially someone who doesn't even know what you did for them?"

Tommy picked up a long straight stick by the side of the road and trailed it along after him on the pavement. "Well, you know, it's like our handwriting verse says. It just. . . "

"Excuse me." Thorny caught Tommy's stick and stopped him. "What do you mean 'handwriting verse?'"

"Oh, yeah." Tommy flipped the stick out of Thorny's hand and walked on. "I forgot you've only been at our school a couple of days. All those words we've been practicing writing are part of a Scripture verse. We write a new one each week and learn about what it means. This week it's that Scripture that talks about loving others as much as you love yourself. You know."

"Actually," Thorny cleared his throat. "I don't."

"You mean your mom and dad didn't teach that one to you when you were a little guy?" Tommy flipped the end of his stick at some tall grass by the road.

"I don't think my parents believed in God." Thorny bent to pick up a pebble and toss it at a fence post. "At least they never said much about God to me. The Simmons are the first foster family I've been with that talk about such things. They're even spending the extra money to send me to Knowlton Elementary School so I can receive instruction in spiritual matters!" He tossed another pebble. "So what does this Scripture have to do with the Clarks' trash?"

"Well," Tommy scratched his head. "I guess it's just that when you really love God, you just sorta naturally love others, too. I mean, I think He puts His love for others in your heart. That Scripture's in Mark and it says we've got to love others as much as ourselves. You know, we've got to treat them like we'd like to be treated. See?"

"You always treat everyone like that?" Thorny stopped and stared at Tommy.

"Well, no." Tommy sighed. "I want to, and God wants me to, but sometimes I mess up." Tommy twirled his stick in the air. "At least I know He forgives me when I mess up. And I feel really good when I get it right!"

Both boys stepped off the road as a large truck approached. "Cole County Sanitation." Thorny read the large black letters on the door of the truck cab as the big white trash truck rumbled past them. He turned around to watch the truck wheeze to a stop in front of the Clarks' house for a moment before driving on down the road.

A few minutes later, Thorny headed the other direction down the road toward the Simmons' home. "Bye, Thorny! See you tomorrow!" Tommy called after him from the Rawsons' front porch. Thorny slung the red roller blades over one shoulder and waved with his free hand.

"'You must love others as much as yourself.'" Hubert Thornton Remington III repeated to himself as he walked down the road. "Now, there's a truly fascinating concept to analyze!"

2 Discussion Time

Check understanding of the story and development of personal values.

- Why do you think Tommy called his new friend "Thorny?"
- Why was Thorny living with the Simmons family?
- Who won the roller blade race?
- What problem did the boys discover at the Clarks' house?
- What did Tommy do about the scattered trash?
- How did Thorny feel about picking up the trash?
- Do you think Tommy was a good example for Thorny?
- In what ways can you show you love others as much as yourself?

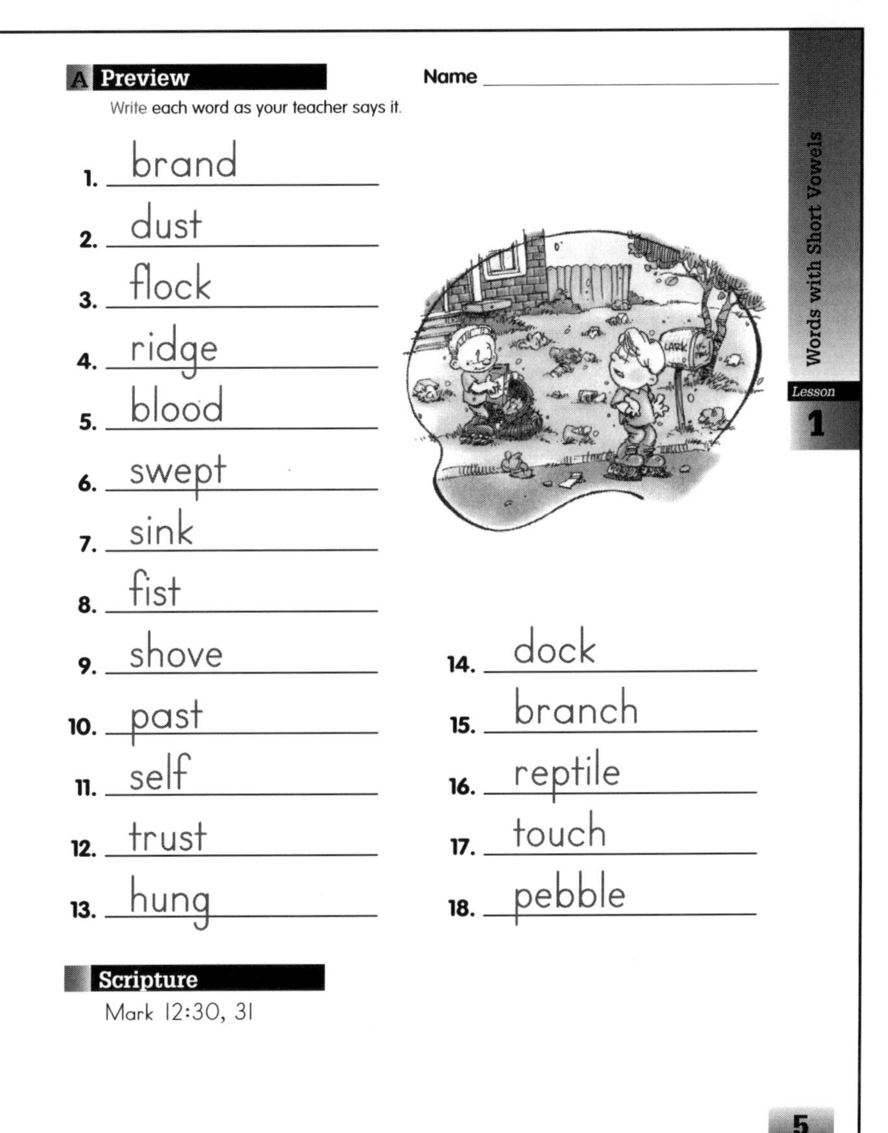

A Preview Name ______

Write each word as your teacher says it.

1. brand
2. dust
3. flock
4. ridge
5. blood
6. swept
7. sink
8. fist
9. shove
10. past
11. self
12. trust
13. hung
14. dock
15. branch
16. reptile
17. touch
18. pebble

Scripture

Mark 12:30, 31

Words with Short Vowels

Lesson 1

5

3 Preview

Test for knowledge of the correct spellings of these words.

Customize Your List

On a separate sheet of paper, additional words of your choice may be tested.

I will say each word once, use the word in a sentence, then say the word again. Write the words on the lines in your Worktext.

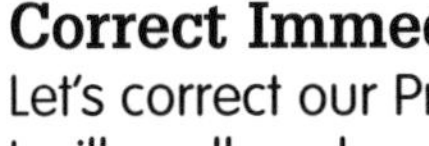

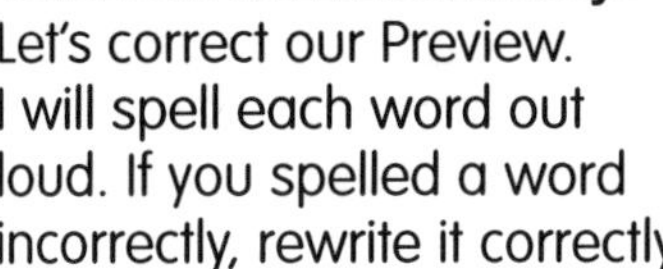

Correct Immediately!

Let's correct our Preview. I will spell each word out loud. If you spelled a word incorrectly, rewrite it correctly.

Progress Chart

Students may record scores. (Reproducible master provided in Appendix B.)

1. brand — Thorny is **brand** new to the neighborhood.
2. dust — Thorny liked to **dust** off his roller blades regularly.
3. flock — A **flock** of goldfinches scattered as the boys whizzed by on their skates.
4. ridge — The boys could see a mountain **ridge** off to their right.
5. blood — Tommy could feel the **blood** rushing to his heart as they raced.
6. swept — Thorny **swept** ahead of Tommy to win the race.
7. sink — Tommy can **sink** down on the grass to rest.
8. fist — Tommy packed the trash back into the torn bag with his **fist**.
9. shove — He tried to **shove** the trash down past the hole in the side of the bag.
10. past — Soon the white trash truck rumbled **past** them.
11. self — It is not always easy to put others before **self**.
12. trust — When you **trust** in Jesus, He gives you a desire to love others.
13. hung — Tommy **hung** his roller blades on a hook in the garage.
14. dock — Thorny and Tommy looked for a **dock** in the nearby pond.
15. branch — A large **branch** had fallen into the water.
16. reptile — They saw a **reptile** curled around the end of it.
17. touch — The boys did not **touch** the venomous snake.
18. pebble — Tommy skipped a flat **pebble** across the pond's surface.

Day 1

Lesson 1

4 Word Shapes

Help students form a correct image of whole words.

Look at each word and think about its shape. Now, write the word in the correct Word Shape Boxes. You may check off each word as you use it.

(Short vowels are usually found in syllables in which a vowel is immediately preceded and followed by a consonant, consonant cluster, or digraph.)

In the Word Shape Boxes, fill in the boxes containing the letter or letters that spell the short vowel sound in each word.

Take a minute to memorize...

Mark 12:30, 31

Words with Short Vowels — Lesson 1

B Word Shapes Name ____________________

Write each word in the correct Word Shape Boxes. Next, in the Word Shape Boxes, shade in the boxes containing the letter or letters that spell the short vowel sound in each word.

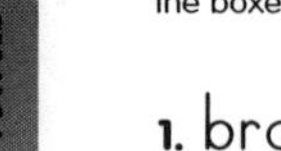

1. brand
2. branch
3. past
4. reptile
5. pebble
6. self
7. swept
8. fist
9. ridge
10. sink
11. dock
12. flock
13. shove
14. dust
15. touch
16. hung
17. blood
18. trust

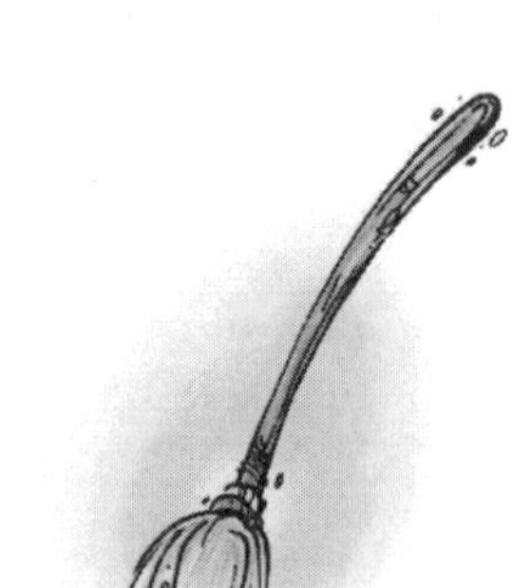

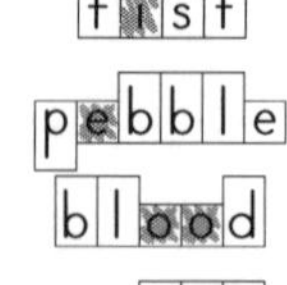

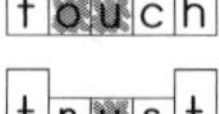

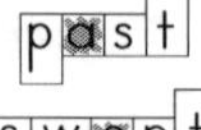

6

Answers may vary for duplicate word shapes.

Be Prepared For Fun

Check these supply lists for **Fun Ways to Spell** - presented **Day 2**. Purchase and/or gather these items ahead of time!

General
- Pencil
- Graph Paper (1 sheet per child)
- Spelling List

Auditory
- Voice Recorder
- Spelling List

Visual
- Water Color Paint Box (1 per child)
- Paint Brush (1 per child)
- Art Paper (3 or 4 sheets per child)
- Spelling List

Tactile
- Soccer Ball, Basketball, Tennis Ball, or 4-Square Ball
- Spelling List

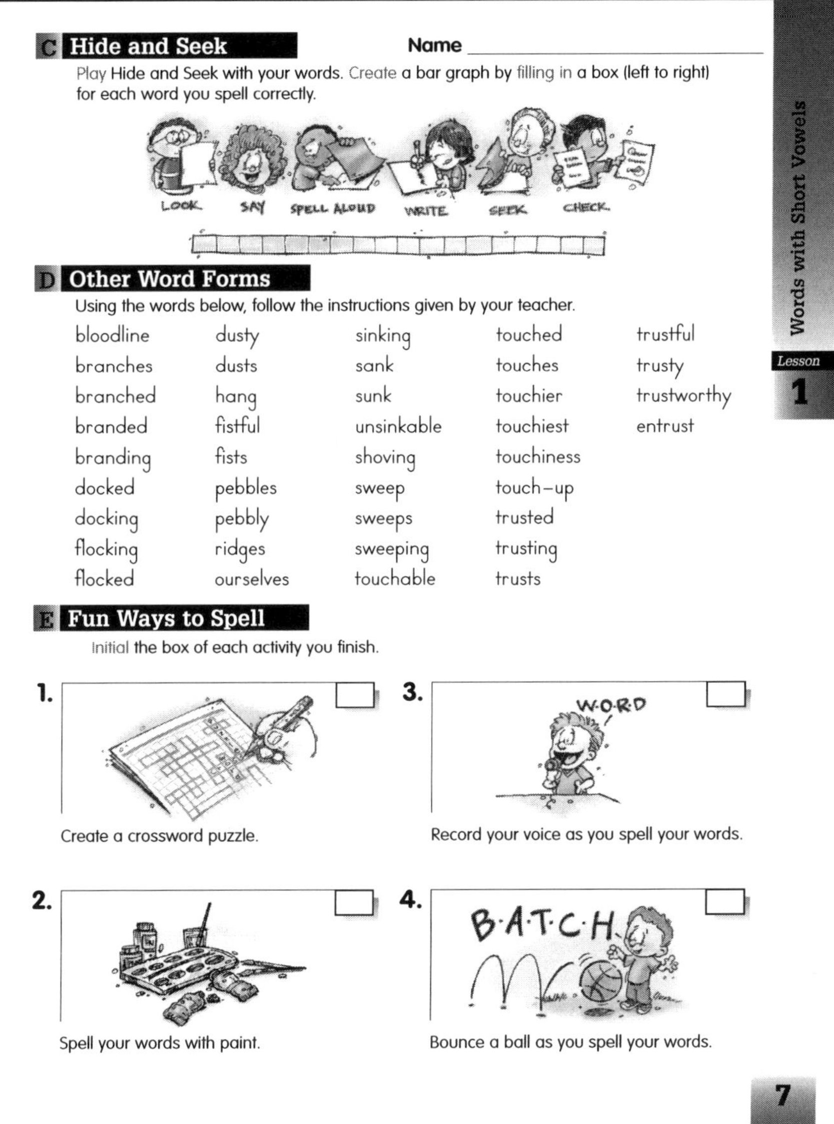

C Hide and Seek **Name** ______________________

Play Hide and Seek with your words. Create a bar graph by filling in a box (left to right) for each word you spell correctly.

D Other Word Forms

Using the words below, follow the instructions given by your teacher.

bloodline	dusty	sinking	touched	trustful
branches	dusts	sank	touches	trusty
branched	hang	sunk	touchier	trustworthy
branded	fistful	unsinkable	touchiest	entrust
branding	fists	shoving	touchiness	
docked	pebbles	sweep	touch-up	
docking	pebbly	sweeps	trusted	
flocking	ridges	sweeping	trusting	
flocked	ourselves	touchable	trusts	

E Fun Ways to Spell

Initial the box of each activity you finish.

1. Create a crossword puzzle.

3. Record your voice as you spell your words.

2. Spell your words with paint.

4. Bounce a ball as you spell your words.

Words with Short Vowels

Lesson 1

7

1 Hide and Seek

Reinforce spelling by using multiple styles of learning.

On a white board, Teacher writes each word — one at a time. **Have students:**

- **Look** at the word.
- **Say** the word out loud.
- **Spell** the word out loud.
- **Hide** (teacher erases word.)
- **Write** the word on paper.
- **Seek** (teacher rewrites word.)
- **Check** spelling. If incorrect, rewrite word correctly.

2 Other Word Forms

This activity is optional. Have students write original sentences using these Other Word Forms:

sweeping
bloodline
flocking
ourselves

3 Fun Ways to Spell

Four activities are provided. Use one, two, three, or all of the activities. Have students initial the box for each activity they complete.

Options:

- assign activities to students according to their learning styles
- set up the activities in learning centers for students to do throughout the day
- divide students into four groups and assign one activity per group
- do one activity per day

General

To create a crossword puzzle…
- Use a pencil to arrange your words on graph paper.
- Overlap words where letters are shared.
- Don't create any new words.
- Outline each word with a marker and number them.
- Write a clue for each word.
- Erase your words.
- Trade with a classmate and work each other's puzzles.

Auditory

To spell your words using a voice recorder…
- Record yourself as you say and spell each word on your spelling list.
- Listen to your recording and check your spelling.

Visual

To spell your words with paint…
- Paint each spelling word on your paper.
- Trade papers with a classmate and check each other's spelling.

Tactile

To bounce a ball as you spell your words…
- Look at the first word on your list.
- Bounce the ball as you say each letter of the word aloud.
- Do this with each word on your list.

Working with Words

Familiarize students with word meaning and usage.

Alphabetical Order

Write the words **break**, **bridge**, **bread**, and **breeze** on the board. Explain to the students that when words begin with the same letter, they need to look at the second letter to put the words in alphabetical order. If the first two letters are the same, look at the third letter, fourth letter, and so on. Guide the students in putting these four words in alphabetical order.

Look at each set of words. Write them in alphabetical order on the lines.

Dictionary Skills

Explain that some entry words in a dictionary have more than one meaning, or definition.

Read the definitions for each word. Write the word that matches both meanings.

Take a minute to memorize...

Mark 12:30, 31

Words with Short Vowels — Lesson 1

F Working with Words Name ____________________

Alphabetical Order

Dictionary words are listed in **alphabetical order**. Words beginning with **a** come first, then words beginning with **b**, and so on. It is simple to find a word in the dictionary if you know about **alphabetical order**. Remember, when words begin with the same letter, look at the second letter. If the first two letters are the same, look at the third letter.
Write the words in each group in alphabetical order.

1. brand fist branch flock
   branch, brand, fist, flock
2. dust blood past dock
   blood, dock, dust, past
3. swept trust self touch sink
   self, sink, swept, touch, trust

Dictionary Skills

Some dictionary entries have more than one meaning or definition. Read the definitions. Write the word that matches both meanings.

1. A part of a tree.
   A road that splits from a larger road. branch
2. Placed on a hook.
   Unable to make a decision. hung
3. A particular make of a product.
   Burn a mark on an animal's skin. brand

Word Bank

brand	reptile	swept	sink	past	hung
branch	pebble	fist	dock	dust	blood
past	self	ridge	flock	touch	trust

8

G Dictation

Name ____________________

Write each sentence as your teacher dictates. Use correct punctuation.

1. Thorny swept past his friends in the race.

2. The sun began to sink behind the ridge.

3. Thorny threw a pebble in the dust.

Words with Short Vowels

Lesson 1

H Proofreading

If a word is misspelled, fill in the oval by that word. If all the words are spelled correctly, fill in the oval by **no mistake**.

1. ○ brand ○ bump ○ past ● no mistake

2. ● reptiel ○ life ○ happen ○ no mistake

3. ○ berry ● dok ○ swept ○ no mistake

4. ○ cookie ○ branch ○ brook ● no mistake

5. ○ test ○ flock ○ plant ● no mistake

6. ○ wagon ● dunn ○ dust ○ no mistake

7. ○ hung ● blud ○ puppy ○ no mistake

8. ○ sorry ○ table ○ trust ● no mistake

9. ○ ridge ○ grab ● pebbel ○ no mistake

10. ○ sink ○ deep ○ mean ● no mistake

11. ○ rake ○ self ● tutch ○ no mistake

12. ○ fist ○ poor ○ loud ● no mistake

9

1 Dictation

Reinforce correct spelling by using current and previous words in context.

Listen as I read each sentence and then write it in your Worktext. Remember to use correct capitalization and punctuation. (Slowly read each sentence twice. Sentences are found in the Student Worktext to the left.)

2 Proofreading

Familiarize students with standardized test format and reinforce recognition of misspelled words.

Look at each set of words. If a word is misspelled, fill in the oval by that word. If all the words are spelled correctly, fill in the oval by **no mistake**.

3 Hide and Seek

Reinforce correct spelling of current spelling words. Repeat this activity from Day 2. (A reproducible master is provided in Appendix A as shown on the inset page to the right.)

4 Other Word Forms

Have your students complete this activity to strengthen spelling ability and expand vocabulary.

1 Posttest

Visit the **A Reason For** website to download free, printable Posttest pages.

I will say the word once, use it in a sentence, then say it again. Write your words on a separate sheet of paper.

Progress Chart

Students may record scores. (Appendix B)

Personal Dictionary

Students may add any words they have misspelled to their personal dictionaries. (Appendix B)

Hide and Seek

Play Hide and Seek with your words. Create a bar graph by filling in a box (left to right) for each word you spell correctly.

Other Word Forms

Sentence Clues

Use the sentence clue to help you unscramble each word. Write the unscrambled word in the sentence.

abdelmoorst	1. Exercise will improve the circulation of your bloodstream.
giiknns	2. He dove to keep the keys from sinking in the pond.
horrstttuwy	3. If you are trustworthy, people will respect you.
cfklos	4. Large flocks of ducks flew over, heading south.
-choptuu	5. Mom gave the scratched furniture a careful touch-up.
abdnr	6. Now there are scratches on my brand new car.
eepsw	7. Please sweep up the dirt you tracked into the house.
cdehotu	8. She carefully touched the soft chinchilla.
bbeelps	9. She stood and tossed pebbles into the creek.
degirs	10. The ridges on my boots kept me from sliding.
abcehnrs	11. The large branches are perfect for building a tree house.
ffilstu	12. The little boy grabbed a fistful of candy.
dehosv	13. Tommy shoved another bite of pizza into his mouth.
cdkos	14. We hurried to the docks to see which boat had won.
dginstu	15. When I finish dusting, I will vacuum the carpet.
eeilprst	16. We found two snakes for our collection of reptiles.

Prefixes and Suffixes

Add the prefixes and suffixes to make new words. Write the words on the lines.

1. touch + y = touchy
2. self – f + v + es = selves
3. en + trust = entrust
4. touchy – y + i + ness = touchiness
5. reptile – e + ian = reptilian
6. your + self = yourself

325

---

1. brand	The **brand** name of Tommy's skates was worn off.
2. flock	The **flock** of birds was startled by Thorny and Tommy.
3. branch	Thorny expertly jumped over a **branch** in the road.
4. blood	Their hearts worked hard to pump **blood** to all their muscles.
5. pebble	A **pebble** skipped along the pavement ahead of the boys.
6. ridge	The mountain **ridge** was beautiful in the distance.
7. fist	Tommy used his **fist** to punch trash down into the torn bag.
8. sink	The boys were careful not to **sink** into the mud in the ditch.
9. dust	A discarded vacuum cleaner bag was full of **dust**.
10. swept	Thorny and Tommy **swept** the yard clean of trash.
11. shove	The boys saw the garbage collector **shove** the bags into the truck.
12. past	In his **past**, Thorny had not been taught about God's love.
13. trust	Tommy wants Thorny to **trust** in Jesus.
14. self	To put others before **self**, we need God's help.
15. hung	Thorny had **hung** his roller blades in Tommy's garage.
16. dock	The boys did not find a **dock** at the pond.
17. reptile	They did see a **reptile** at the pond.
18. touch	They were careful not to **touch** the water moccasin.

I Game Name ______________________________

Help Tommy and Thorny pick up trash by moving one space for each word you or your team spells correctly from this week's word list.

Remember: Loving God means caring as much for others as you care about yourself!

J Journaling

In your journal, write about a time you showed your love for others by your actions, or a time when someone else showed their love for others by helping you.

Words with Short Vowels — Lesson 1

10

How to Play:

- Divide students into two teams.
- Have each student place his/her game piece on Start.
- Have a student from team A go to the board.
- Say the spelling word.
- Have the student write the word on the board.
- If correct, instruct each member of team A to move his/her game piece forward one space.
- Alternate between teams A and B as you go down the word list.
- The team to reach Thorny first is the winner.

Small Group Option: Students may play this game without teacher direction in small groups of two or more.

2 Game

Reinforce spelling skills and provide motivation and interest.

Materials

- game page (from Student Worktext)
- game pieces (1 per child)
- game word list

Game Word List

1. **brand**
2. **branch**
3. **past**
4. **reptile**
5. **pebble**
6. **self**
7. **swept**
8. **fist**
9. **ridge**
10. **sink**
11. **dock**
12. **flock**
13. **shove**
14. **dust**
15. **touch**
16. **hung**
17. **blood**
18. **trust**

3 Journaling

Provide a meaningful reason for correct spelling through personal writing.

Review the story using discussion leads provided on the following page. Encourage students to apply the Scriptural value in their journaling.

Journaling (continued)

- Have you ever heard someone speak with a different accent or use words that you're not familiar with?
- Why do you think Thorny used such big words when he spoke? (Because he was very intelligent. His parents had been well educated people.)
- Even though Thorny was intelligent, he didn't know much about God or the Scriptures. Why? (His parents hadn't believed in God and the foster homes he'd been in hadn't taught him about God either, until the Simmons.)
- How did Tommy's actions help Thorny learn more about God? (By picking up the Clarks' scattered trash, even though they'd never know about it, he showed what loving others as much as you love yourself means.)
- Have you ever had an opportunity like Tommy and Thorny did to help someone else?
- Thorny learned that showing love to others, especially when they don't know who helped them, can be a lot of fun. Maybe you'd like to work with a friend to secretly help out those around you. Ask God to help you see times when you can show His love by helping others and then be ready to help!

English is the language spoken in more nations than any other.

Who's Your Source?

Beth discovers the problem-solving power of regular Scripture reading.

"Mom, telephone's for you! It's Mrs. Schilling," Beth shouted from the top of the stairs.

"I'll get it down here. Thanks, Beth." Janette Hill wiped her hands on the blue kitchen towel and picked up the phone. "Hi, Elizabeth. No, we didn't... it's not true." Mrs. Hill shifted the phone on her shoulder as she opened a jar of peanut butter.

"Elisa Larkin said that? How rude! I know the Jacobson twins are noisy, but Helen took them out before the speaker started. Elisa might be more sympathetic if Laney weren't her only child....I agree. She's unbelievable! Well, I've got to go, Elizabeth. I don't want the kids to be late for school. I'll talk to you later. Bye." Mrs. Hill hung up the phone and hurriedly mixed pancake batter.

When Beth came into the kitchen a few minutes later she asked, "What did Matthew's mom want?"

"She called to find out if the school dress code allows shorts." Mrs. Hill put some baby carrots in Luke's lunch. "Elisa Larkin told her she'd heard the board voted to let kids wear shorts the first month of school while it's so hot."

"Well, did they?"

"Beth, I don't know how that rumor got started, but why would the board change the rule now? A dress code is already printed in the school handbook. It doesn't make any sense to change it a week after school starts. Maybe next year."

Beth grinned, "Just hoping, I guess. It's hot."

Forty-five minutes later Luke and Beth ran to catch up with the Schilling children as they walked up the sidewalk toward Knowlton Elementary. "Hi, Matthew. Look at this cave book I found at the library last night. Isn't it fun learning about stagtights and stuff?"

"Stalactites." Matthew corrected. "And yes, I like learning about the rock formations in caves. Mrs. Burton teaches us neat stuff."

"Yeah and she doesn't give us much homework." Beth smiled at Matthew, "Great shirt! Is it new?"

Matthew nodded. "It would be greater if I could wear the new shorts I got to go with it. Mom said the school board hasn't changed the rule yet. She called your mom to ask her since she's on the board."

"Yeah, I heard them talking." Beth looked down at her leather sandals. "What's wrong with Mrs. Larkin anyway? My mom said she's 'unbelievable.'"

"My mom says she's not very 'tolerant.' I think it's because she's from New York."

"Laney acts like she's better than us." Beth took off her backpack as she opened the big glass door. "She talks a lot to Rachel, but the rest of us are not quite good enough for her."

When the bell rang a few minutes later, Mrs. Burton walked to the front of the classroom. "This morning for our worship time we're going to go outside under the pine tree. Laney, I like the way your row is sitting quietly. You all may go first." Mrs. Burton smiled. "Thorny, now your row may go."

When everyone was seated in the shade of the tall pine, Mrs. Burton opened her Bible. "John 15:26 says, 'I will send you the Comforter—the Holy Spirit, the source of all truth. He will come to you from the Father and will tell you all about Me.' Raise your hand if you think Jesus sends the Holy Spirit to everyone in the world—even if they don't ask." Her eyes scanned the class seated around her. No hands were raised. "Will Jesus send the Comforter to anyone?" A few heads nodded.

"I'm going to tell you a story," Mrs. B. continued. "When I was in seventh grade our family moved to a new town where I knew only one girl. My old school had been a small country school with two grades in each classroom. I knew everyone, and only one teacher had taught me in both fifth and sixth grades. My new school was huge. We changed teachers for every class and had lockers in the hall. I had a hard time. The one girl I'd known from before was not very kind to me. One of her friends knocked my books out of my arms and scattered my papers all over the hall.

"Another time I was walking out the door at the end of school and someone pulled my slip down around my ankles and ripped my favorite dress. I didn't get invited over to other kids' homes. Some days no one would even talk to me. I don't know what I would have done without my mom. She realized what a struggle I was having and suggested I start reading a story from my Bible every night before I went to sleep. She got me a translation that was easy for me to understand and even let me stay up a little later every night to read it. She said I could always pray and Jesus would send the Comforter—the Holy Spirit.

"I don't know what bothers you or what difficulties you're facing, but no matter what problems you're working through, Jesus wants to send help. If the only thing you learn in my class is what a special friend Jesus is, I will feel I've been successful! That's the most important bit of information I have to teach you. Ask the Holy Spirit to come into your life. Jesus says the Comforter will come to you and help you understand God better.

"Before my seventh grade year was over I had made some special friends. Some of us

Story (continued)

went to school together all the way through college. I still keep in touch with them. I can't say I never felt uncomfortable again, but I did come to understand that if I wanted to have friends, I had to be friendly. I had to listen to people and find out what interests they had and what was important in their lives. My quiet study times helped me learn that. The same Comforter who helped me can teach you, too."

Everybody had a lot to think about as they filed back into the classroom.

Early the next morning Mrs. Hill headed downstairs to pack lunches and start breakfast. The kids wouldn't be up for another 15 minutes. She noticed the light on in Beth's room and poked her head in the door. "Whatcha doing, Bethy?"

Beth looked up. "I'm reading the story in the Bible about when Martha got mad at Mary because she wasn't doing her share of the work. It's in Luke 10. I've never read it in the Bible before."

Mom gave her daughter a thumbs up and hurried down to the kitchen.

The next morning she was surprised to see Beth reading her Bible again. "What are you reading this morning, Beth?"

"The one right before Mary and Martha." Beth put her finger on the page to keep her spot. "It's the story about the good Samaritan. It's hard to believe the priest and Levite could just walk by the guy who was all beat up. The good Samaritan was such a nice person. He paid the bill at the inn and everything. Didn't Jews hate Samaritans?"

Mom nodded. "Lots of times we judge people because we don't understand them."

"Yeah, Mrs. Burton was telling us about what a hard time she had in seventh grade."

"Really?" Mrs. Hill gazed out the window.

"That's why I'm reading my Bible. She told us how kids knocked books out of her arms and someone even pulled her slip down in the middle of the hall—right in front of everyone. Her dress got ripped too. I can't believe people would be so mean to her. She's such a nice person. Her quiet time helped her learn how to be a good friend."

Mom looked thoughtful. "Well, she was quiet—and a lot of us thought she was a snob. All her clothes were beautiful. She made straight A's. I'd known her before. We'd gone to fourth grade together in another state. I don't know why I pulled her slip down. Girls were doing it to each other, and she was the closest one to me. I never knew I tore her dress. She just ran on out the door."

Beth's eyes were huge. "You did that to her, Mom?"

Mrs. Hill looked down at the carpet. "I'm not proud of it. We went to school together all the way through twelfth grade and eventually became great friends. We've talked about it. I told her I was sorry."

"I think I need to try harder with Laney." Beth looked down at the Bible in her lap. "She's probably not really a snob. She's just new and New York is a lot different from our little town."

Mrs. Hill smiled at her daughter. "Me, too."

"Be nice to Laney?"

"No, Laney's mom, Elisa. She's probably lonely and doesn't know anyone except her new husband, Coach Larkin. I said some rather nasty things about her on the phone Monday morning. You'd think I'd learn." Mom looked at her watch. "I've got to hurry or you'll not have a lunch today. Hey, why don't we ask the Larkins over for dinner Thursday night?"

"That's a good idea," Beth answered. She looked down at her Bible and read the verses at the bottom of the page softly to herself. "Once when Jesus had been out praying, one of his disciples came to him as he finished and said, 'Lord, teach us a prayer... And this is the prayer he taught them: Father, may your name be honored for its holiness...'"

Sunlight was streaked across Beth's bed. She closed her eyes and bowed her head. "Father," she prayed, "be with the Larkins...and help me to make Laney feel welcome at Knowlton Elementary. Send Your Holy Spirit to help me know You better. I want to honor you. Amen."

2 Discussion Time

Check understanding of the story and development of personal values.

- Why did Mrs. Burton have a hard time when she was in seventh grade?
- What did Mrs. Burton's mom suggest she do about the problem?
- Did the quiet time help Mrs. Burton? How?
- How did Beth feel about Laney?
- How did Mrs. Hill feel about Elisa Larkin?
- What Bible story did Beth read that helped her realize she wasn't being fair with Laney?
- Can everyone have a quiet time with Jesus?

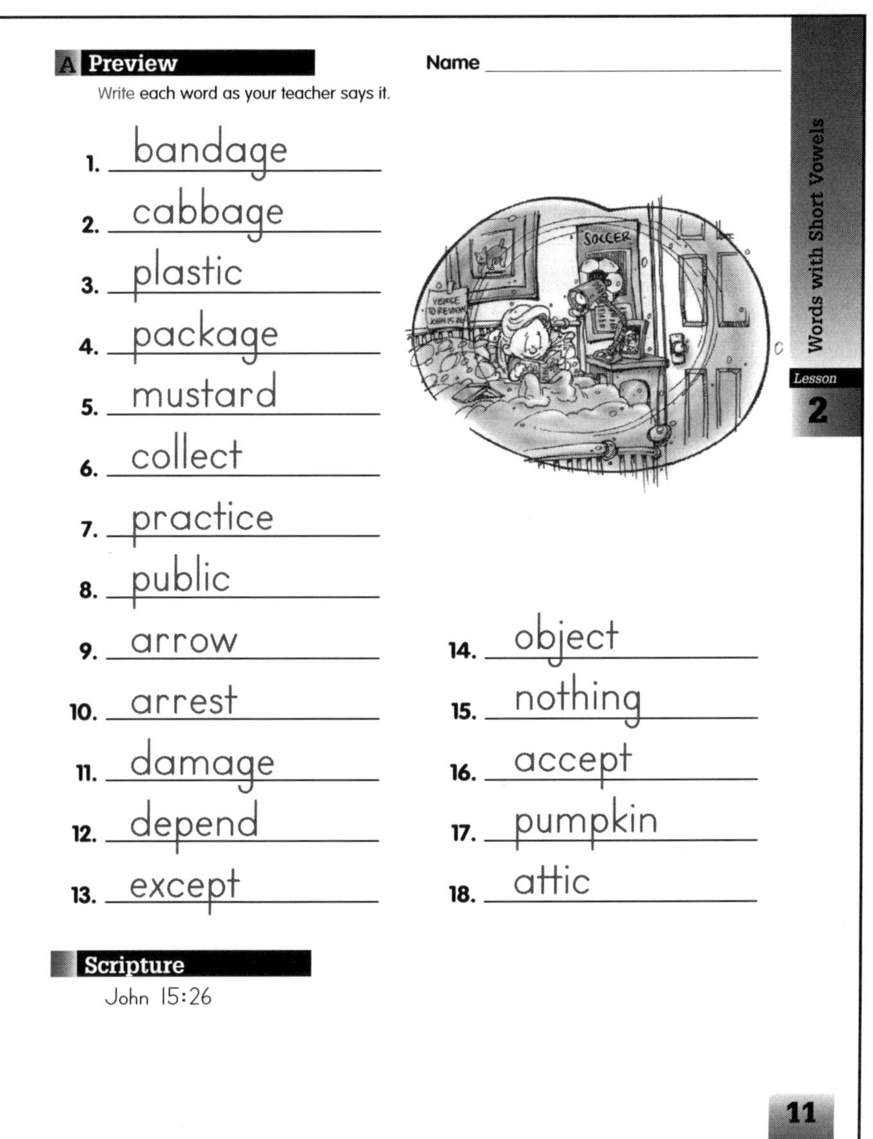

A Preview
Name
Write each word as your teacher says it.
1. bandage
2. cabbage
3. plastic
4. package
5. mustard
6. collect
7. practice
8. public
9. arrow
10. arrest
11. damage
12. depend
13. except
14. object
15. nothing
16. accept
17. pumpkin
18. attic
Words with Short Vowels
Lesson 2
Scripture
John 15:26
11

3 Preview

Test for knowledge of the correct spellings of these words.

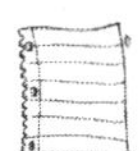

Customize Your List
On a separate sheet of paper, additional words of your choice may be tested.

I will say each word once, use the word in a sentence, then say the word again. Write the words on the lines in your Worktext.

Correct Immediately!
Let's correct our Preview. I will spell each word out loud. If you spelled a word incorrectly, rewrite it correctly.

Progress Chart
Students may record scores. (Reproducible master provided in Appendix B.)

1.	bandage	Mrs. Burton has a **bandage** in the classroom first aid kit.
2.	cabbage	Mrs. Hill put carrots, not **cabbage**, in Luke's lunch.
3.	plastic	She put them in a small **plastic** bag.
4.	package	Beth and Luke each got a **package** of cheese crackers.
5.	mustard	She spread **mustard** on the bread for their sandwiches.
6.	collect	Beth and Luke must **collect** their things to take to school.
7.	practice	It is a good **practice** to spend time alone with Jesus every day.
8.	public	It is not best to try to have your quiet time in a **public** place.
9.	arrow	Like an **arrow**, the Comforter will point us in the right direction.
10.	arrest	The Holy Spirit can help us to **arrest** our bad attitudes toward others.
11.	damage	We can **damage** someone's feelings if we do not treat them with kindness.
12.	depend	We can **depend** on the Holy Spirit to show us the truth.
13.	except	No one **except** God can see into our hearts and know our true feelings.
14.	object	Mrs. Hill did not **object** to Beth's being up early.
15.	nothing	Beth was learning that **nothing** could replace her time spent alone with God.
16.	accept	Mrs. Hill hopes the Larkins will **accept** her invitation to dinner.
17.	pumpkin	She can make a **pumpkin** pie for dessert.
18.	attic	Beth looked for her mom's yearbook in their **attic**.

Lesson 2 | Day 1

4 Word Shapes

Help students form a correct image of whole words.

Look at each word and think about its shape. Now, write the word in the correct Word Shape Boxes. You may check off each word as you use it.

(Short vowels are usually found in syllables in which a vowel is immediately preceded and followed by a consonant, consonant cluster, or digraph.)

In the Word Shape Boxes, fill in the boxes containing the letter that spells the short vowel sound in each word.

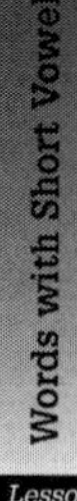

Words with Short Vowels — Lesson 2

B Word Shapes Name ____________________

Write each word in the correct Word Shape Boxes.

Word	Word Shape Boxes
1. attic	pumpkin
2. bandage	attic
3. cabbage	bandage
4. damage	practice
5. package	depend
6. plastic	damage
7. practice	collect
8. accept	package
9. arrest	mustard
10. arrow	accept
11. collect	arrest
12. depend	plastic
13. except	except
14. object	cabbage
15. mustard	object
16. nothing	arrow
17. public	nothing
18. pumpkin	public

OWIE!!

12

Answers may vary for duplicate word shapes.

Take a minute to memorize...

John 15:26

Be Prepared For Fun

Check these supply lists for **Fun Ways to Spell** - presented **Day 2**. Purchase and/or gather these items ahead of time!

General
- Pencil
- Notebook Paper
- Spelling List

Auditory
- Spelling List

Visual
- Pencil
- Paper
- Spelling List

Tactile
- Thick Pile Carpet Samples
- Spelling List

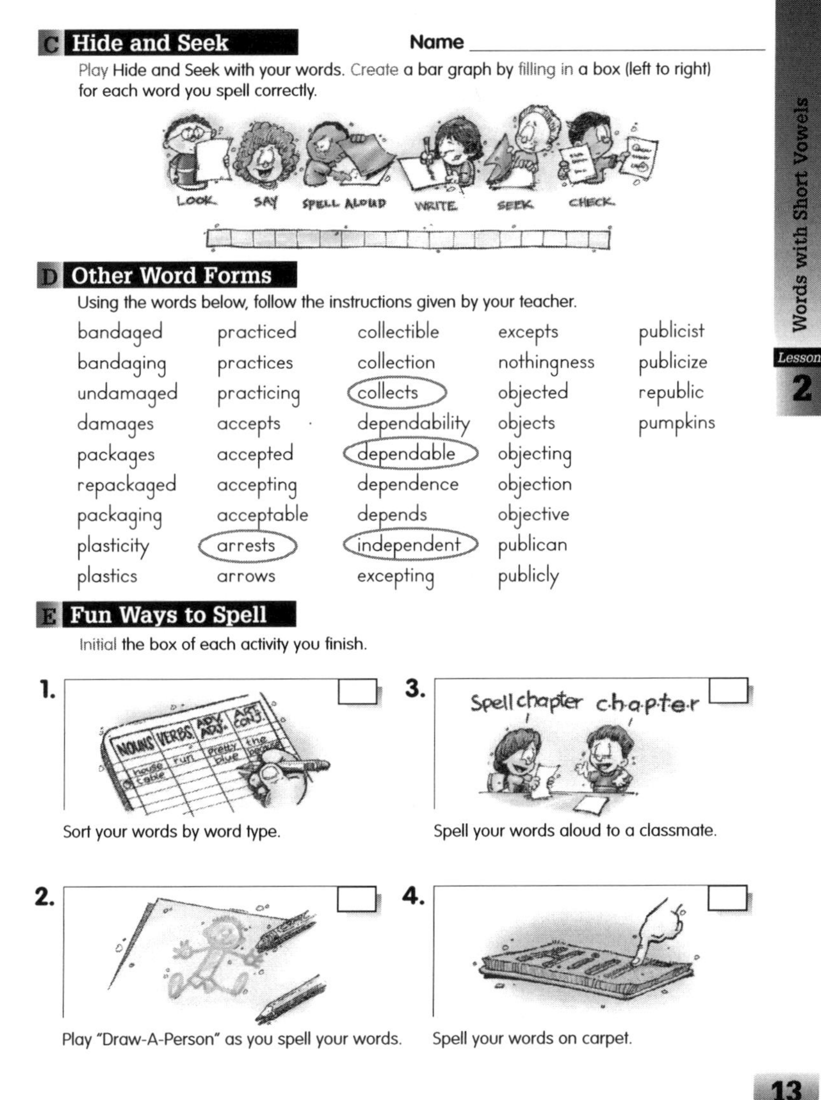

C Hide and Seek Name ____________

Play Hide and Seek with your words. Create a bar graph by filling in a box (left to right) for each word you spell correctly.

D Other Word Forms

Using the words below, follow the instructions given by your teacher.

bandaged	practiced	collectible	excepts	publicist
bandaging	practices	collection	nothingness	publicize
undamaged	practicing	collects	objected	republic
damages	accepts	dependability	objects	pumpkins
packages	accepted	dependable	objecting	
repackaged	accepting	dependence	objection	
packaging	acceptable	depends	objective	
plasticity	arrests	independent	publican	
plastics	arrows	excepting	publicly	

E Fun Ways to Spell

Initial the box of each activity you finish.

1. Sort your words by word type.

3. Spell your words aloud to a classmate.

2. Play "Draw-A-Person" as you spell your words.

4. Spell your words on carpet.

Words with Short Vowels

Lesson 2

13

1 Hide and Seek

Reinforce spelling by using multiple styles of learning.

On a white board, Teacher writes each word — one at a time. **Have students:**

- **Look** at the word.
- **Say** the word out loud.
- **Spell** the word out loud.
- **Hide** (teacher erases word.)
- **Write** the word on paper.
- **Seek** (teacher rewrites word.)
- **Check** spelling. If incorrect, rewrite word correctly.

2 Other Word Forms

This activity is optional. Have students find and circle the Other Word Forms that are synonyms of the following:

trustworthy
accumulates
apprehends
free

3 Fun Ways to Spell

Four activities are provided. Use one, two, three, or all of the activities. Have students initial the box for each activity they complete.

Options:

- assign activities to students according to their learning styles
- set up the activities in learning centers for students to do throughout the day
- divide students into four groups and assign one activity per group
- do one activity per day

General

To sort your words by word type...
- Make four columns on your paper.
- Label the columns: Nouns, Verbs, Adjectives/Adverbs, and Articles/Conjunctions.
- Write each of your spelling words in the appropriate column.

Auditory

To spell your words aloud to a classmate...
- Ask a classmate to read a word from your spelling list.
- Spell the word aloud to a classmate.
- Ask a classmate to check your spelling.
- Read a word to your classmate and continue taking turns.
- The person to spell the most words right wins!

Visual

To play "Draw-A-Person" when you spell your words...
- Ask a classmate to read a word from your spelling list to you.
- Write the word on your paper. Check your spelling.
- If you misspell the word, draw one part of a person on your paper.
- Read a word to a classmate and continue taking turns.
- The last one to finish drawing a person wins!

Tactile

To spell your words on carpet...
- Use finger tip to write a spelling word on carpet.
- Check your spelling.
- Smooth the word out with your hand and write another word.

Lesson 2 | Day 3

Working with Words

Familiarize students with word meaning and usage.

Sentence Skills

Explain that there are four kinds of sentences: **imperative**, **declarative**, **exclamatory**, and **interrogative**.

Rewrite the sentences in your Worktext, correcting the misspelled word. Then, circle the word that tells which kind of sentence it is.

Take a minute to memorize...

John 15:26

Words with Short Vowels — Lesson 2

F Working with Words Name ____________

Sentence Skills

An **imperative sentence** is a command and ends with a period or an exclamation point.
Get me a bandage for my knee. Give me that!
A **declarative sentence** tells something and ends with a period.
My knee has a bandage on it.
An **exclamatory sentence** shows strong feelings and ends with an exclamation point.
My knee really hurts!
An **interrogative sentence** asks something and ends with a question mark.
Do you think my knee needs stitches?

Write the sentences below, correcting the misspelled word. Circle the word that tells what kind of sentence it is.

1. Mrs. Hill is making punkin pies for dinner.
Mrs. Hill is making pumpkin pies for dinner.
imperative (declarative) exclamatory interrogative

2. Help me carry this packege.
Help me carry this package.
(imperative) declarative exclamatory interrogative

3. This cabbege salad is delicious!
This cabbage salad is delicious!
imperative declarative (exclamatory) interrogative

4. Will the Larkins axept the dinner invitation?
Will the Larkins accept the dinner invitation?
imperative declarative exclamatory (interrogative)

5. Beth is learning to deepend on the Holy Spirit.
Beth is learning to depend on the Holy Spirit.
imperative (declarative) exclamatory interrogative

Word Bank

accept	attic	collect	except	object	practice
arrest	bandage	damage	mustard	package	public
arrow	cabbage	depend	nothing	plastic	pumpkin

14

G Dictation

Name ______________________

Write each sentence as your teacher dictates. Use correct punctuation.

1. We took a walk to collect autumn leaves.
2. What is in the attic in those plastic boxes?
3. Learn to accept others and depend on the Lord.

Words with Short Vowels

Lesson 2

H Proofreading

If a word is misspelled, fill in the oval by that word. If all the words are spelled correctly, fill in the oval by **no mistake**.

1. ○ brand ○ branch ● attick ○ no mistake
2. ○ object ● bandeg ○ past ○ no mistake
3. ● cabige ○ reptile ○ mustard ○ no mistake
4. ○ public ○ pumpkin ○ damage ● no mistake
5. ○ pebble ○ self ● pakige ○ no mistake
6. ○ fist ○ ridge ● pracktis ○ no mistake
7. ○ swept ○ except ○ plastic ● no mistake
8. ○ sink ● acksept ○ dock ○ no mistake
9. ○ nothing ○ dust ○ arrest ● no mistake
10. ○ blood ○ trust ○ collect ● no mistake
11. ● arowe ○ touch ○ hung ○ no mistake
12. ○ flock ○ done ○ depend ● no mistake

15

Dictation

Reinforce correct spelling by using current and previous words in context.

Listen as I read each sentence and then write it in your Worktext. Remember to use correct capitalization and punctuation. (Slowly read each sentence twice. Sentences are found in the Student Worktext to the left.)

Proofreading

Familiarize students with standardized test format and reinforce recognition of misspelled words.

Look at each set of words. If a word is misspelled, fill in the oval by that word. If all the words are spelled correctly, fill in the oval by **no mistake**.

Day 4 / Day 5

3 Hide and Seek

Reinforce correct spelling of current spelling words. Repeat this activity from Day 2. (A reproducible master is provided in Appendix A as shown on the inset page to the right.)

4 Other Word Forms

Have your students complete this activity to strengthen spelling ability and expand vocabulary.

1 Posttest

Visit the **A Reason For** website to download free, printable Posttest pages.

I will say the word once, use it in a sentence, then say it again. Write your words on a separate sheet of paper.

Progress Chart

Students may record scores. (Appendix B)

Personal Dictionary

Students may add any words they have misspelled to their personal dictionaries. (Appendix B)

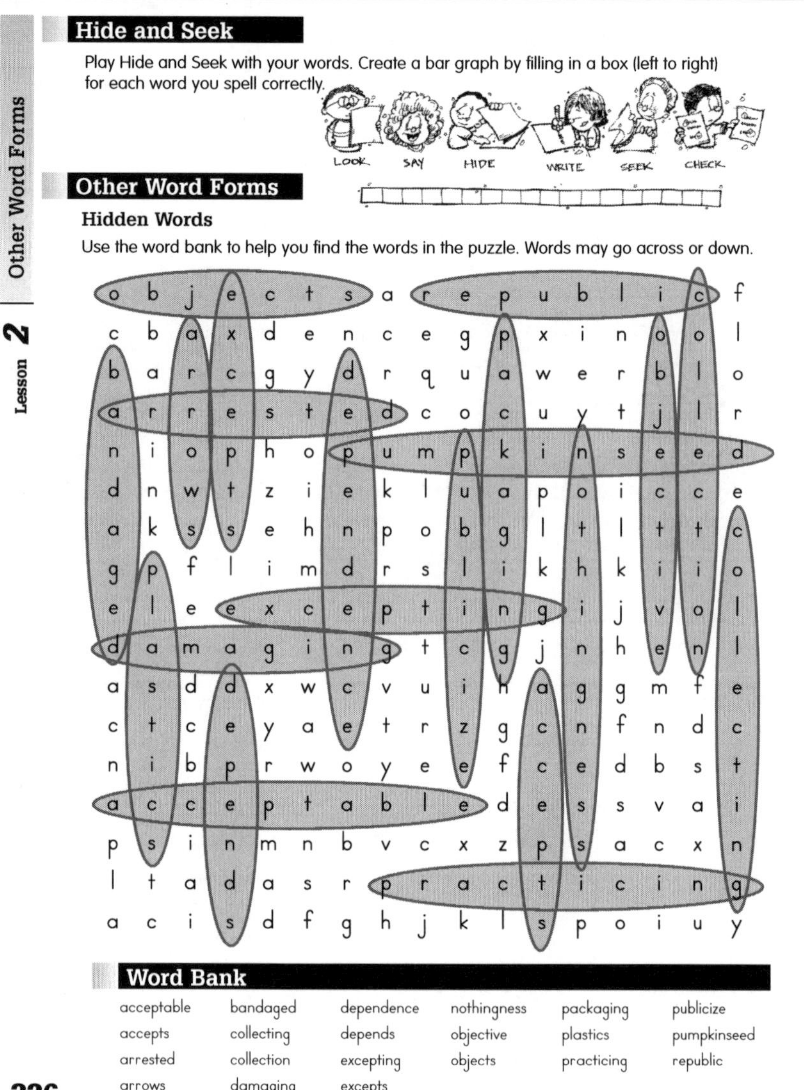

Lesson 2 Other Word Forms

Hide and Seek

Play Hide and Seek with your words. Create a bar graph by filling in a box (left to right) for each word you spell correctly.

Other Word Forms

Hidden Words

Use the word bank to help you find the words in the puzzle. Words may go across or down.

o b j e c t s a r e p u b l i c f
c b a x d e n c e g p x i n o o l
b a r c g y d r q u a w e r b l o
a r r e s t e d c o c u y t j l r
n i o p h o p u m p k i n s e e d
d n w t z i e k l u a p o i c c e
a k s s e h n p o b g l t l t t c
g p f l i m d r s l i k h k i i o
e l e e x c e p t i n g i j v o l
d a m a g i n g t c g j n h e n l
a s d d x w c v u i h a g g m f e
c t c e y a e t r z g c n f n d c
n i b p r w o y e e f c e d b s t
a c c e p t a b l e d e s s v a i
p s i n m n b v c x z p s a c x n
l t a d a s r p r a c t i c i n g
a c i s d f g h j k l s p o i u y

Word Bank

acceptable	bandaged	dependence	nothingness	packaging	publicize
accepts	collecting	depends	objective	plastics	pumpkinseed
arrested	collection	excepting	objects	practicing	republic
arrows	damaging	excepts			

326

1. **object** Beth needs to bring an **object** for the class drawing project.
2. **cabbage** Beth and Luke like broccoli better than **cabbage**.
3. **mustard** "Did you put **mustard** on my sandwich?" Beth asked.
4. **plastic** Beth put away the **plastic** bags for her mom.
5. **pumpkin** Mrs. Hill made delicious **pumpkin** cookies for their lunches.
6. **package** Beth took a **package** of them to Mrs. Burton.
7. **collect** Mrs. Burton will **collect** her things to take outside under the pine tree.
8. **arrow** The green **arrow** pointed to the exit leading to the playground.
9. **nothing** Mrs. Burton's students said **nothing** as she told them the story.
10. **except** No one **except** God knows every thought and feeling we have.
11. **depend** We can always **depend** on the Holy Spirit to show us the truth.
12. **public** Quiet time with God is a private, not **public**, activity.
13. **practice** Mrs. Burton encouraged them to **practice** having a daily quiet time.
14. **accept** "We must learn to **accept** direction from the Holy Spirit," she said.
15. **arrest** He can **arrest** our fears and bad attitudes, and show us the truth.
16. **damage** God can heal the **damage** others do to our feelings, too.
17. **bandage** His love is like a wonderful **bandage** on our hearts.
18. **attic** Mrs. Hill got her school yearbook down from the **attic**.

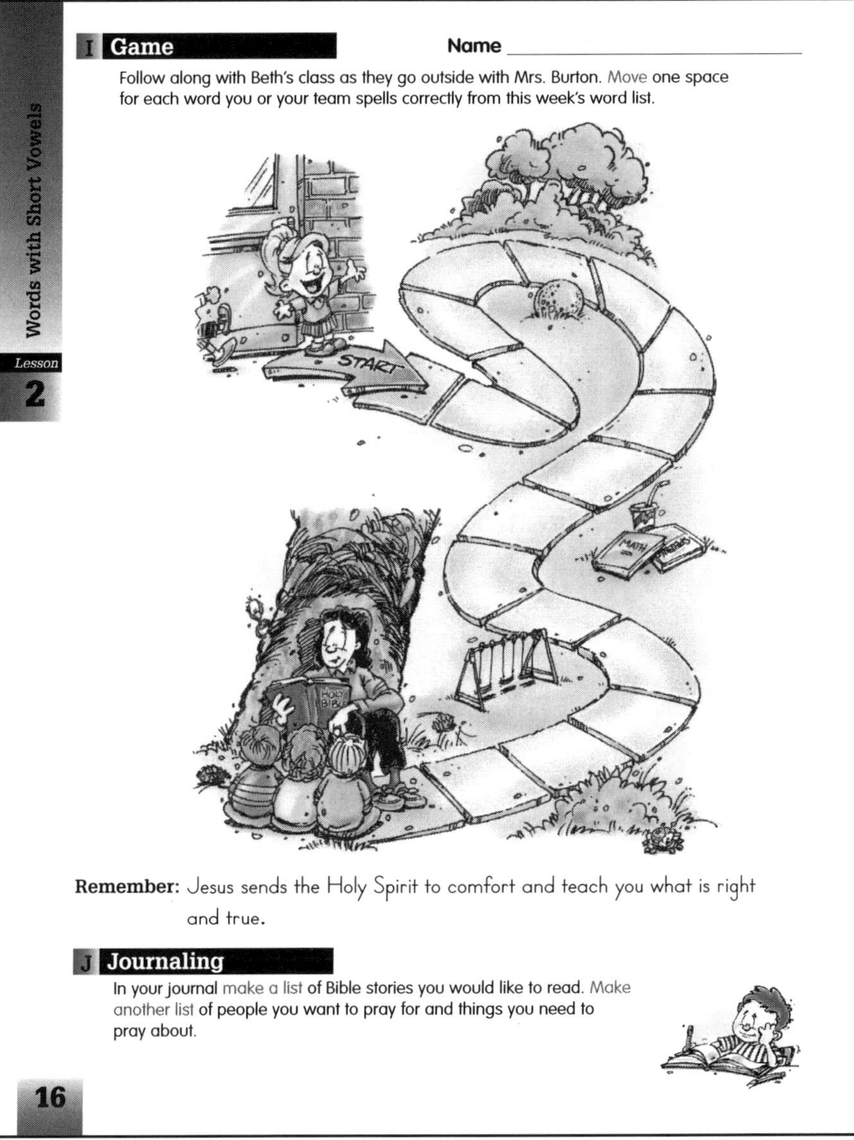

Words with Short Vowels

Lesson 2

I Game Name ______________________

Follow along with Beth's class as they go outside with Mrs. Burton. Move one space for each word you or your team spells correctly from this week's word list.

Remember: Jesus sends the Holy Spirit to comfort and teach you what is right and true.

J Journaling

In your journal make a list of Bible stories you would like to read. Make another list of people you want to pray for and things you need to pray about.

16

How to Play:

- Divide students into two teams.
- Have a student from team A go to the board.
- Say the spelling word.
- Have the student write the word on the board.
- If correct, instruct each member of team A to color one space, beginning at Start.
- Alternate between teams A and B as you go down the word list.
- The team to reach Mrs. Burton first is the winner.

Small Group Option: Students may play this game without teacher direction in small groups of two or more.

2 Game

Reinforce spelling skills and provide motivation and interest.

Materials

- game page (from Student Worktext)
- crayons or colored pencils (1 per child)
- game word list

Game Word List

1. **attic**
2. **bandage**
3. **cabbage**
4. **damage**
5. **package**
6. **plastic**
7. **practice**
8. **accept**
9. **arrest**
10. **arrow**
11. **collect**
12. **depend**
13. **except**
14. **object**
15. **mustard**
16. **nothing**
17. **public**
18. **pumpkin**

3 Journaling

Provide a meaningful reason for correct spelling through personal writing.

Review the story using discussion leads provided on the following page. Encourage students to apply the Scriptural value in their journaling.

Journaling (continued)

- Tell about a time you felt out of place or uncomfortable.
- Why did Mrs. Burton feel so out of place in seventh grade? (She was new in town. The only girl she knew was mean to her. She was used to a smaller school with fewer students and teachers.)
- What did Mrs. Burton's mother suggest she start doing? (Read a Bible story every evening and spend time in prayer.)
- What did Mrs. Burton say was the most important bit of information she had to teach her class? (What a special friend Jesus is.)
- Think about starting your own quiet time every day.

The English word with the most consonants in a row is "catchphrase."

Word Wow!

1 **Literature Connection**
Topic: Divorce
Theme Text: John 1:4, 5

Connected to the Current

When Tony's life is clouded by Papa's poor choices, God's love still shines through.

"Where's Papa?" Tony Vanetti watched the gray clouds boil in the darkening sky. "He said he was going to come and get me at six."

Maria Vanetti sat down beside her son on the porch swing and pushed it into motion with her bare toes. "Tony, Papa could be here any minute. He may have gotten caught in traffic or had a late meeting at work."

"He promised to come over and help me with my electricity project last week and never did. My teacher says it has to be finished by..." A bright streak of lightning lit up the black clouds, followed immediately by a deafening roar. "Wednesday!" Tony yelled.

"Nature is providing you with your own personal electrical display. Wasn't that spectacular?" Mama wrapped an arm around Tony and squeezed.

"I guess I could tie a key to the string of my kite and fly it up into those clouds like Benjamin Franklin did. He proved lightning has an electrical charge." Tony stood up and walked to the door of the duplex. "That could be my project, and I wouldn't need Papa."

"You will do no such thing, Antonio Marcus Vanetti. Benjamin Franklin was lucky doing that experiment. He could have been electrocuted if the string had been wetter or his kite had flown into the heart of the storm."

"You mean like—died?" Tony watched another streak of lighting zigzag across the horizon.

Mama waited until the deep rumble subsided. "Yes, like died. Benjamin Franklin knocked himself unconscious a couple of times while he was experimenting with electricity. No one had found a use for it yet. It was just a fascinating thing to feel and experiment with in Ben Franklin's day. It wasn't until Thomas Edison came along and invented the electric light bulb that electricity became a 'necessity' for every American household."

"Well, Papa needs to get over here and help me build my parallel circuit and my series circuit. He said he has everything we need." Tony frowned and looked down at the toes of his shoes.

"I hope your Papa comes, Tony-O," Mama said softly. "But if he doesn't, I'll help you."

"Thanks, Mama." Tony smiled halfheartedly and went inside just as another dramatic display of lightning lit up the sky. He plopped down on his bed in the darkened room and tossed his soccer ball pillow idly into the air. A flash of lightning lit up his dark room long enough for him to read the numbers on his clock. *Papa's always late. I bet he won't even come! He makes me so mad. He doesn't even care about his own son!* Tony thought. *Well, maybe his other son, Cutter. Papa always has time for Cutter. His wife Marilee is going to have another baby, too. I'll never get to see Papa then.*

He reached over and turned on the lamp beside his bed and noticed his Bible. It had kids on the cover playing soccer. Grandma Miller had gotten it for him at Christmas. He picked it up slowly and thumbed through the pages. He remembered what Grandma had said: "Read it, Tony. It will teach you about the most important things in life."

Mrs. Burton said Jesus will always be our friend, thought Tony. *She said He would send the Comforter. The verse we studied last week was from John. I think John is in the New Testament. This week's verse came from John, too.* Tony found the book of John and looked at all the pictures before reading the introduction and the devotional on the first page.

Tony jumped when Mama came in a little later and flipped on the overhead light. "Phone for you, Tony-O."

Tony put a marker in his Bible and headed for the phone. "Hello. Yes. Are you okay? Is it back on yet? Why do you have to stay?... But it's due on Wednesday... Mama will help me. No...Go to Cutter's program." Tony hung up the phone and headed back to his bedroom.

"He isn't coming, is he?" Mama sat down beside Tony on the edge of his bed.

"No. Cutter has some program tomorrow night, so he can't come tomorrow." Tony nudged his soccer ball with the toe of his shoe, "Cutter, Cutter, Cutter."

"What about tonight?" Mama gently rubbed her hand up and down Tony's back. "Your Papa was going to come tonight."

Tony rested his elbows on his knees and ran his fingers slowly through his dark hair. "The building Papa works in was hit by lightning. It blew something and they don't have any electricity. It messed up their phones, too. Papa had to use his cell phone to call me. He has to stay there while the phone people come to work on the phones and the electric company tries to figure out why they don't have any power."

"I see."

"Mama, I don't get it." Tears started to puddle in the corners of Tony's eyes. "Why does Papa keep his promise to go to Cutter's program—and not keep his promise to help me with my electricity experiments?"

Mama handed Tony a tissue before she answered. "Tony-O, your papa doesn't always make the best choices. He knows Marilee and Cutter will be very upset if he doesn't come to that program. Papa has to live with them... and he doesn't like to see them angry and agitated...so he usually chooses the path of least resistance."

"You mean like electrical current?"

"Good analogy. He usually chooses the easiest path, just like electrical current does. He doesn't have to see the disappointment on your face. One quick phone call takes care of us. I'm sorry you're hurting, Tony. I can assure you your papa loves you very much. In many ways he's not showing maturity. A mature person makes the right choice even if it's hard. A grown-up should know not to procrastinate and put things off 'till the last minute. But now he will hurt one of his sons no matter what he does."

It was a difficult conversation, and Mama paused to word her thoughts carefully. "Your papa is not trying to hurt you. He just needs to get his priorities straight. I'm trying to learn not to expect Papa to do things for you, so I won't get mad when he disappoints us again. And then when he does do something special for you, I can be happily surprised.

"He needs to make Jesus his special friend. I think that is the only thing that will help him. The choices he's making are like the clouds in this thunderstorm. They're making his life dark and unpredictable." Mama gave her boy another squeeze. "Let's see what supplies we have and then go to the store and get what we need for your experiments."

Tony wiped his eyes and followed Mama into the utility room.

A couple hours later Tony was lying on his back looking at the ceiling. The house was dark. Mama came in and sat down on the edge of his bed. A flash of lightning lit up the room, but only a distant rumble followed. Mama tucked the sheet up under Tony's chin and brushed the hair off his forehead. She reached over and flipped the switch on the lamp. Nothing happened.

"The electricity is off." Tony murmured.

"So it is." Mama smiled in the darkness.

"Mama."

"Yes, Tony."

"I was reading my Bible while I waited for Papa." Tony rolled over and looked out the window beside his bed.

"That's a good choice, Son."

"I was looking for the verse we're learning this week in spelling. It says, 'Eternal life is in Him, and this life gives light to all mankind. His life is the light that shines through the darkness—and the darkness can never extinguish it.' I found it in John."

"That's a good verse to remember, Tony-O. I'm glad you've memorized it. You know, God is the source of light in our lives—like electrical current is to the lights in the parallel circuit we worked on tonight. We can unscrew any of the three bulbs, and the other two will still shine because they are connected to the electric current. But the bulb that is unscrewed breaks contact with the circuit, and it no longer shines."

"And the other two bulbs of a parallel circuit still shine because their electrical current isn't broken," Tony added.

"The light of God's life shines through our darkest times, Tony." Mama slowly rubbed Tony's back. "Just like the verse you learned. The darkness can't put out the light. Only we can when we disconnect ourselves from the power source. Keep reading your Bible and praying. It will teach you how to live forever."

It was quiet for a few minutes as Tony relaxed and Mama was alone with her own thoughts. "I'm glad God is not like the series circuit we made," she smiled to herself.

"Tony," she whispered. When she got no response, Mama gazed at her precious son sleeping peacefully in the darkness. *I'm so glad he knows Jesus,* she thought. Then smiling, she tiptoed out of Tony's room.

2 Discussion Time

Check understanding of the story and development of personal values.

- What project did Tony need to finish by Wednesday?
- Who was going to help him with it?
- Why did Papa not come to help Tony make electrical circuits?
- What did Tony read while he waited for Papa?
- How did Tony feel when Papa didn't come?
- What would you say if one of your parents didn't do what he or she promised?
- How is God like the parallel circuit Tony and Mama built?
- What can you do when things go wrong and life seems dark?
- Is God always willing to light up your life?

A **Preview** Name ______

Write each word as your teacher says it.

1. against
2. pleasant
3. leather
4. yesterday
5. breakfast
6. meant
7. dead
8. ahead
9. sweat
10. instead
11. lead
12. measure
13. wealth
14. built
15. comfort
16. couple
17. cousin
18. trouble

Scripture

John 1:4, 5

Words with Short Vowels

Lesson 3

17

3 Preview

Test for knowledge of the correct spellings of these words.

Customize Your List

On a separate sheet of paper, additional words of your choice may be tested.

Say

I will say each word once, use the word in a sentence, then say the word again. Write the words on the lines in your Worktext.

Correct Immediately!

Say

Let's correct our Preview. I will spell each word out loud. If you spelled a word incorrectly, rewrite it correctly.

Progress Chart

Students may record scores. (Reproducible master provided in Appendix B.)

Lesson 3 | Day 1

1.	against	Tony's mama leaned **against** the back of the porch swing.
2.	pleasant	A **pleasant** smell came from a cake baking in the kitchen.
3.	leather	Tony stared down at the toes of his **leather** tennis shoes.
4.	yesterday	"I wish he had come **yesterday**!" mumbled Tony.
5.	breakfast	Tony had been planning for his dad's visit since **breakfast**.
6.	meant	Tony's dad **meant** to come that night, but he didn't make it.
7.	dead	The phones at his office were **dead** and the power was off, too.
8.	ahead	Tony's dad did not plan far enough **ahead** to see Tony.
9.	sweat	The warm air from the storm made Tony's forehead **sweat**.
10.	instead	Tony lay on his bed **instead** of sitting on the porch.
11.	lead	In his disappointment, Tony dragged his feet as if they were **lead**.
12.	measure	A multimeter is used to **measure** electrical current.
13.	wealth	Sharing your time is as important as sharing your **wealth**.
14.	built	Tony **built** the circuit with his mom.
15.	comfort	God's Word will give us **comfort** and direction.
16.	couple	Tony's papa was more than a **couple** of minutes late.
17.	cousin	Cutter is Tony's half brother, not his **cousin**.
18.	trouble	When **trouble** comes, we can count on Jesus to help us.

Lesson 3 | Day 1

4 Word Shapes

Help students form a correct image of whole words.

Look at each word and think about its shape. Now, write the word in the correct Word Shape Boxes. You may check off each word as you use it.

(Short vowels are usually found in syllables in which a vowel is immediately preceded and followed by a consonant, consonant cluster, or digraph.)

Say

In the Word Shape Boxes, fill in the boxes containing the letter or letters that spell the short vowel sound in each word.

B Word Shapes Name ____________

Write each word in the correct Word Shape Boxes.

Word	Word Shape Boxes
1. against	yesterday
2. ahead	breakfast
3. breakfast	dead
4. dead	wealth
5. yesterday	ahead
6. instead	meant
7. lead	against
8. leather	instead
9. meant	couple
10. measure	leather
11. pleasant	pleasant
12. sweat	sweat
13. wealth	measure
14. built	built
15. comfort	comfort
16. couple	cousin
17. cousin	lead
18. trouble	trouble

18

Answers may vary for duplicate word shapes.

Take a minute to memorize...

John 1:4, 5

Be Prepared For Fun

Check these supply lists for **Fun Ways to Spell** - presented **Day 2**.
Purchase and/or gather these items ahead of time!

General
- Pencil
- Notebook Paper
- Spelling List

Auditory
- Spelling List

Visual
- Pencil
- Scissors
- 3 X 5 cards (18 per child)
- Spelling List

Tactile
- Toothpicks
- Art Paper (3 sheets per child)
- Glue
- Spelling List

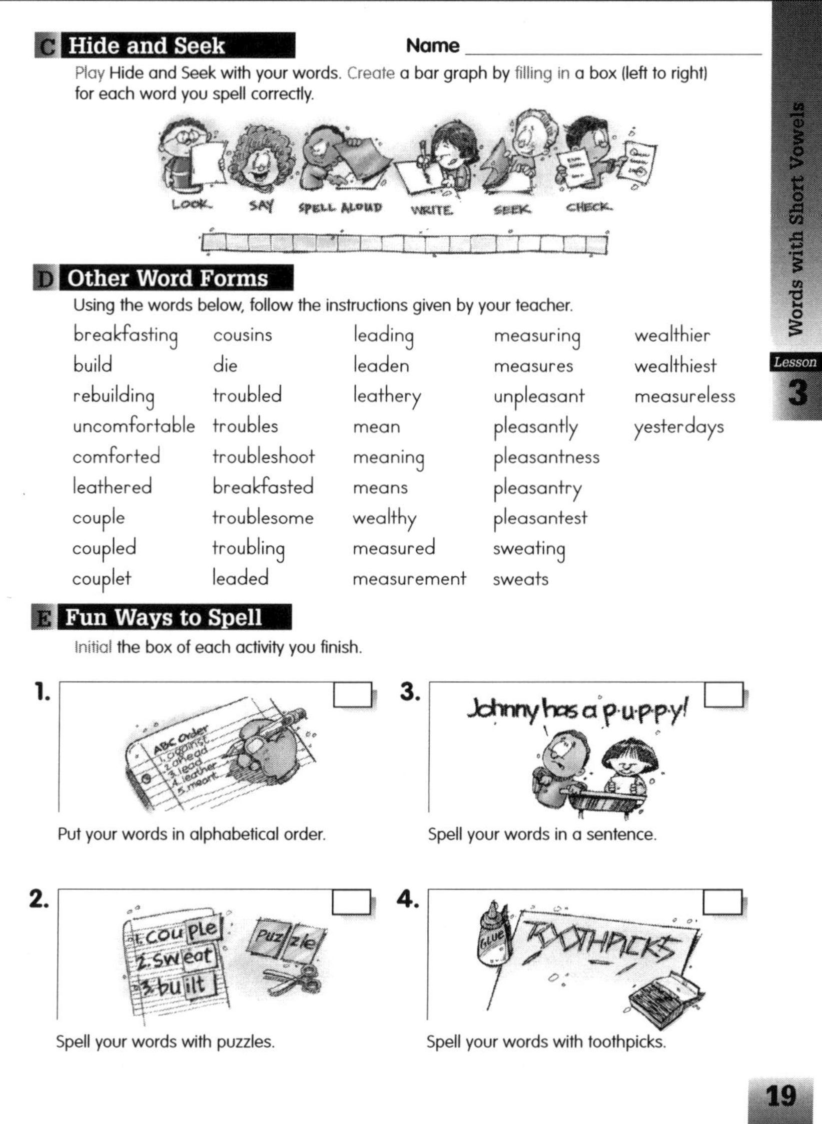

C Hide and Seek

Name ______________________

Play Hide and Seek with your words. Create a bar graph by filling in a box (left to right) for each word you spell correctly.

D Other Word Forms

Using the words below, follow the instructions given by your teacher.

breakfasting	cousins	leading	measuring	wealthier
build	die	leaden	measures	wealthiest
rebuilding	troubled	leathery	unpleasant	measureless
uncomfortable	troubles	mean	pleasantly	yesterdays
comforted	troubleshoot	meaning	pleasantness	
leathered	breakfasted	means	pleasantry	
couple	troublesome	wealthy	pleasantest	
coupled	troubling	measured	sweating	
couplet	leaded	measurement	sweats	

E Fun Ways to Spell

Initial the box of each activity you finish.

1.
Put your words in alphabetical order.

2.
Spell your words with puzzles.

3.
Spell your words in a sentence.

4.
Spell your words with toothpicks.

Words with Short Vowels · Lesson 3

19

Lesson 3 | Day 2

1 Hide and Seek

Reinforce spelling by using multiple styles of learning.

On a white board, Teacher writes each word — one at a time. **Have students:**

- **Look** at the word.
- **Say** the word out loud.
- **Spell** the word out loud.
- **Hide** (teacher erases word.)
- **Write** the word on paper.
- **Seek** (teacher rewrites word.)
- **Check** spelling. If incorrect, rewrite word correctly.

2 Other Word Forms

This activity is optional. Have students write these Other Word Forms in alphabetical order:

measureless
breakfasted
wealthy
leathered

3 Fun Ways to Spell

Four activities are provided. Use one, two, three, or all of the activities. Have students initial the box for each activity they complete.

Options:

- assign activities to students according to their learning styles
- set up the activities in learning centers for students to do throughout the day
- divide students into four groups and assign one activity per group
- do one activity per day

General

To put your words in alphabetical order...
- Write all the words in alphabetical order.
- Remember to look at the second, third, or fourth letters of the words when the first letters are the same.

Auditory

To spell your words in a sentence...
- Have a classmate read a spelling word to you.
- Say a sentence with that spelling word to your classmate.
- Ask your classmate to spell the word.
- Check your classmate's spelling.
- Read a word to your classmate, continue taking turns until you have each spelled all the words.

Visual

To spell your words with puzzles...
- Write each word on a card.
- Ask a classmate to cut each word apart between two letters.
- Arrange half of each word on your desk.
- Write the missing part of the word on a piece of paper.
- Do it again with the other half of your cards.
- Check your spelling.

Tactile

To spell your words with toothpicks...
- Choose a word from your spelling list.
- Arrange toothpicks to represent each letter of the word.
- Glue them to a piece of art paper.

Working with Words

Familiarize students with word meaning and usage.

Clues

Explain that context clues are words in the sentence that help explain the meaning of a word.

Look at the context clue in each sentence and choose the word from the word bank that completes the sentence. Write the word on the line.

Take a minute to memorize...

John 1:4, 5

F Working with Words Name ____________________

Clues

Write a spelling word for each clue.

1. Something that happened the day before, happened yesterday.
2. If you are not for something, you are against it.
3. Someone who is likable and friendly is pleasant to be with.
4. A difficult, dangerous, or upsetting situation is trouble.
5. If you are toward the front, you are ahead of others.
6. Another way to say a few days ago, is to say a couple of days ago.
7. If you stop suddenly and completely, you are stopped dead in your tracks.
8. When you finish making something from wood, it has been built.
9. The thin, black stick inside a pencil is called lead.
10. Animal skin that has been treated with chemicals is leather.
11. The meal that you eat in the morning is called breakfast.
12. Your aunt or uncle's child is called your cousin.
13. To substitute something means to use it or do it instead.
14. To comfort someone is to give them strength or hope.
15. To have an abundant supply of possessions and money is to have wealth.
16. The part of a musical staff between two bars is called a measure.
17. Drops of salty moisture on your skin are called sweat.
18. To have meant to do something is to have thought about it.

Word Bank

against	built	cousin	lead	measure	trouble
ahead	comfort	dead	leather	pleasant	wealth
breakfast	couple	instead	meant	sweat	yesterday

20

G Dictation

Name ______________________

Write each sentence as your teacher dictates. Use correct punctuation.

1. Dad did a couple of other things instead.
2. He had to measure when he built this.
3. Trust God for comfort in all your trouble.

Words with Short Vowels

Lesson 3

H Proofreading

If a word is misspelled, fill in the oval by that word. If all the words are spelled correctly, fill in the oval by **no mistake**.

1. ○ arrest ○ arrow ○ lead ● no mistake
2. ○ attic ○ comfort ● agenst ○ no mistake
3. ● ahed ○ bandage ○ cabbage ○ no mistake
4. ○ pumpkin ○ accept ● brekfast ○ no mistake
5. ● ded ○ damage ○ package ○ no mistake
6. ○ plastic ● cuple ○ yesterday ○ no mistake
7. ○ instead ○ practice ● bilt ○ no mistake
8. ○ collect ○ trouble ○ leather ● no mistake
9. ○ depend ○ except ○ meant ● no mistake
10. ○ wealth ● plesent ○ nothing ○ no mistake
11. ○ object ○ mustard ○ measure ● no mistake
12. ● cuzin ○ public ○ sweat ○ no mistake

21

Dictation

Reinforce correct spelling by using current and previous words in context.

Listen as I read each sentence and then write it in your Worktext. Remember to use correct capitalization and punctuation. (Slowly read each sentence twice. Sentences are found in the Student Worktext to the left.)

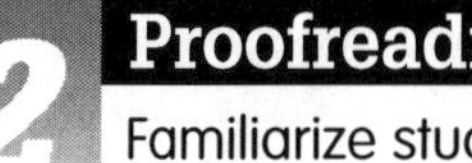

Proofreading

Familiarize students with standardized test format and reinforce recognition of misspelled words.

Look at each set of words. If a word is misspelled, fill in the oval by that word. If all the words are spelled correctly, fill in the oval by **no mistake**.

3 Hide and Seek

Reinforce correct spelling of current spelling words. Repeat this activity from Day 2. (A reproducible master is provided in Appendix A as shown on the inset page to the right.)

4 Other Word Forms

Have your students complete this activity to strengthen spelling ability and expand vocabulary.

Hide and Seek

Play Hide and Seek with your words. Create a bar graph by filling in a box (left to right) for each word you spell correctly.

Other Word Forms

Sentence Fun

Circle the word that completes each sentence.

1. A repairman came to (troubleshoot, troublesome) the computer.
2. Daniel (coupled, couplet) his model engine to the coal car.
3. I hope we get rain so the tomato plants don't (deader, die).
4. If you are hungry, grab a (couple, coupler) of pieces of fruit.
5. Mama (comforter, comforted) Tony during the electrical storm.
6. My three (cousin, cousins) are coming over for dinner.
7. Our neighbor waved and smiled (pleasantry, pleasantly).
8. We will be (breakfasting, breakfasts) on the terrace this morning.
9. What are you (build, building) with your blocks?
10. Our puppy likes to chew on (leathers, leathery) objects.
11. The boys' team was (leading, leaden) until the end of the game.
12. The next unit in math is about (measures, measuring).
13. These new shoes are not very (comfortable, comforted).
14. We were (sweats, sweating) by the time we finished running.
15. What is the (meaning, means) of this word?
16. This old, rusty bicycle is very (troublesome, troubles).

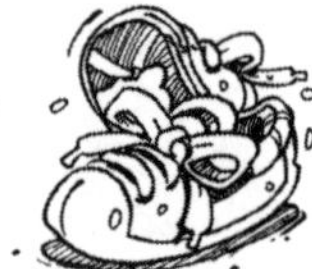

Prefixes and Suffixes

Add the prefixes or suffixes to make new words. Write the words on the lines.

1. trouble – e + ing = troubling
2. measure + ment = measurement
3. wealthy – y + iest = wealthiest
4. couple – e + ing = coupling
5. wealth + y = wealthy
6. dis + comfort = discomfort

327

Other Word Forms — Lesson 3

1 Posttest

Visit the **A Reason For** website to download free, printable Posttest pages.

I will say the word once, use it in a sentence, then say it again. Write your words on a separate sheet of paper.

Progress Chart

Students may record scores. (Appendix B)

Personal Dictionary

Students may add any words they have misspelled to their personal dictionaries. (Appendix B)

1. ahead — Tony planned **ahead** for his dad's visit.
2. breakfast — Tony's mama made a **breakfast** of omelets and hashbrowns.
3. yesterday — Mrs. Burton reminded the students about their project **yesterday**.
4. pleasant — The weather was **pleasant** right before the storm began.
5. against — Tony leaned his head **against** the back of the porch swing.
6. sweat — He wiped the **sweat** from his forehead.
7. leather — Tony's **leather** soccer cleats lay on the floor of his room.
8. lead — Tony's mom will **lead** the way to the phone.
9. meant — Papa said he had **meant** to come, but wouldn't be able to now.
10. instead — Tony's dad had to stay at his office **instead** of coming to see Tony.
11. dead — He used his cell phone to call Tony since the office phones were **dead**.
12. cousin — Cutter is not Tony's **cousin**; he is his half brother.
13. wealth — All the **wealth** in the world cannot take the place of God's love.
14. measure — We can **measure** electrical current, but never God's love!
15. couple — Tony needed a **couple** of supplies from the hardware store.
16. built — He and his mama **built** a parallel circuit that evening.
17. comfort — God's Word and the Holy Spirit gave **comfort** to Tony.
18. trouble — Jesus knows and cares about each **trouble** we face.

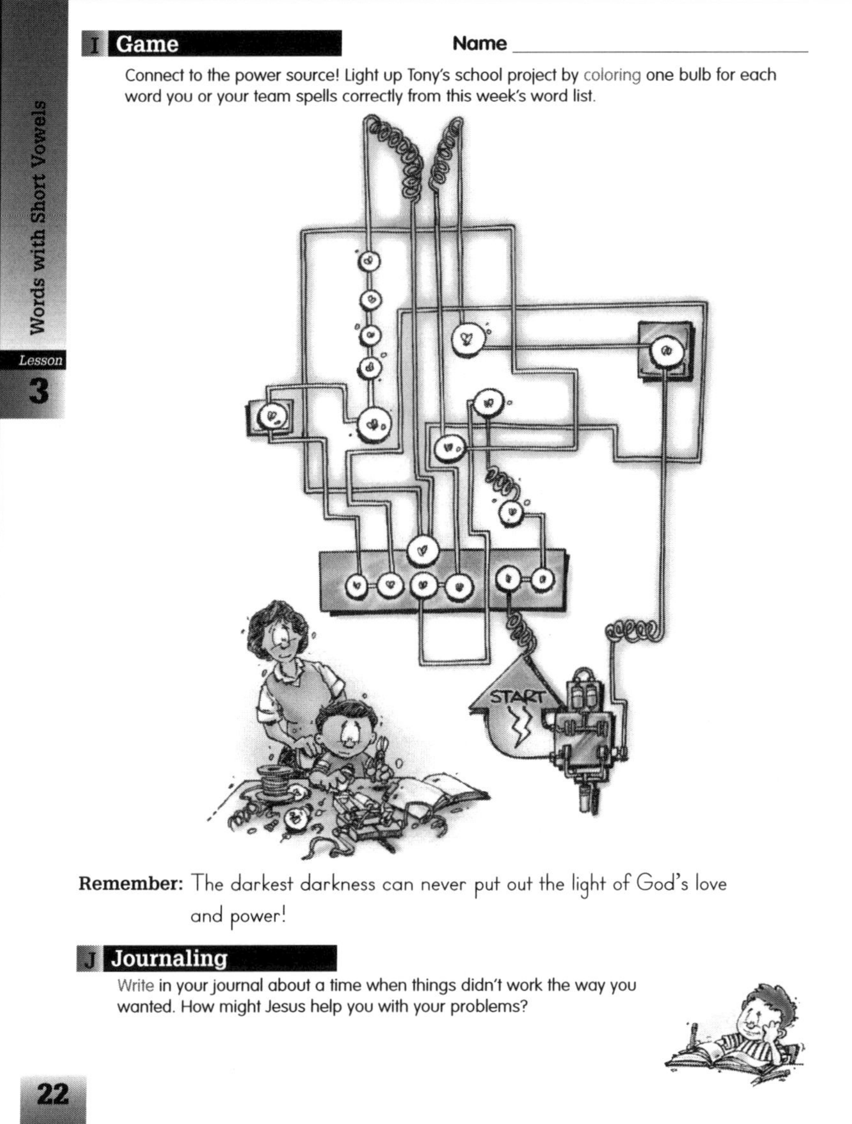
Words with Short Vowels

Lesson 3

I **Game** Name ____________________

Connect to the power source! Light up Tony's school project by coloring one bulb for each word you or your team spells correctly from this week's word list.

Remember: The darkest darkness can never put out the light of God's love and power!

J **Journaling**

Write in your journal about a time when things didn't work the way you wanted. How might Jesus help you with your problems?

22

How to Play:

- Divide students into two teams.
- Have a student from team A go to the board.
- Say the spelling word.
- Have the student write the word on the board.
- If correct, instruct each member of team A to color one light bulb, beginning at Start.
- Alternate between teams A and B as you go down the word list.
- The team to complete the circuit first is the winner.

Small Group Option: Students may play this game without teacher direction in small groups of two or more.

2 Game

Reinforce spelling skills and provide motivation and interest.

Materials

- game page (from Student Worktext)
- yellow crayons or colored pencils (1 per child)
- game word list

Game Word List

1. **against**
2. **ahead**
3. **breakfast**
4. **dead**
5. **yesterday**
6. **instead**
7. **lead**
8. **leather**
9. **meant**
10. **measure**
11. **pleasant**
12. **sweat**
13. **wealth**
14. **built**
15. **comfort**
16. **couple**
17. **cousin**
18. **trouble**

3 Journaling

Provide a meaningful reason for correct spelling through personal writing.

Review the story using discussion leads provided on the following page. Encourage students to apply the Scriptural value in their journaling.

Journaling (continued)

- Why was Tony angry at his papa? (Papa wasn't coming to help Tony with his project, but he was going to his son Cutter's program the next night.)
- Was it unusual for Papa not to do what he promised? Why? (No. Papa was often late or couldn't do what he promised because things came up he hadn't planned on.)
- What did Tony do while he was waiting for Papa? (He read his Bible.)
- What did Mama do to help Tony? (She put her arm around him and rubbed his back. She helped him on his project. She assured Tony that Papa loved him.)
- Mama told Tony that Jesus is the source of light in our lives. Who is always waiting to help you in your darkest times? (Jesus.)

"Was it a rat I saw?" is a palindrome.

1 **Literature Connection**
Topic: Dependence on God
Theme Text: John 8:12

Batty in the Dark

Lost in a dark cave, Christopher and Thorny pray for God's guidance.

"Bye!" Rosa waved as the white van backed slowly out of its parking place. "Have a good time!"

"Yeah! Don't drive the bats batty!" Daniel yelled. "And watch out for cave monsters!"

"We won't have to worry about any monsters in the cave today," Katelynn called back from an open van window, "...'cause you're not going with us!"

Mrs. Burton, the kids' teacher, walked over to the van and spoke with her husband for a minute before he drove off with eight excited students.

"Have you ever been in a cave?" Setsuko bounced on the seat beside Katelynn.

"Well, our family went to a cave once when we were on vacation." Katelynn bent down to pull up one of her socks. "It was a big cave where a guide leads the group and tells you stuff. They turned out the lights so we could see how total darkness feels. That kinda scared me, but I was little."

"Total darkness." Christopher repeated to himself. He flipped his flashlight on. "Hmmm. Is it getting dim?"

"What're you doing, Christopher?" Tony leaned across Thorny to thump Christopher's knee. "You better save your batteries for the cave." He sat back and held up his own big flashlight. "My mama gave me brand new batteries this morning. And a new bulb so I'll be able to see everything. I want to see some stag nights and stack tights."

"I presume you're referring to stalagmites and stalactites?" Thorny continued without waiting for Tony's answer, "It is highly unlikely that we will see any prime examples of these delicate formations in a cave such as the one we are visiting today. It is my understanding that many of these calcium carbonate deposits have been removed or damaged by thoughtless amateurs..."

"Whoa!" Tony thumped Thorny this time. "Hold it! What're you talking about?" He shook his head. "Don't try to explain. Isn't it great that Mr. Burton is taking us caving?"

"Spelunking." Thorny corrected.

"Whatever. I'm just glad I got to be in the first group. It's gonna be fun!"

"Can you guys believe Laney? She doesn't want to go." He shook his head in amazement.

"She can't stand getting dirty!" Tony mimicked.

Christopher kicked at his backpack of clean clothes. "It's not like we'll be dirty all the way home."

Tony laughed. "Who cares if we're covered with dirt in the cave? It'll be too dark to see!"

"Yeah, too dark to see." Christopher repeated weakly. "Total darkness." He patted his flashlight.

"We appear to have arrived." Thorny pointed to a sign that welcomed them to Willowwood State Park.

A ranger, dressed in dark green pants and khaki shirt, climbed into the front seat with Mr. Burton. Mr. Burton didn't have to raise his voice to get the kids' attention. "This is Mr. Davis. He'll be guiding us through the cave. Now, while we drive over to the entrance, Mr. Davis will tell you about Whispering Winds Cave."

Mr. Davis told them how the cave had been formed by an underground river. He said the cave contained several chambers and passageways. Native American tribes had used the room nearest the entrance for shelter; later robbers had hidden there. He explained that Whispering Winds Cave was home to bats, and told them what to do when they saw one.

The van arrived at the trail leading to the cave while he was still outlining safety rules. "So, remember, I'll lead and Mr. Burton will bring up the rear. Always keep track of the person behind you. And keep your head down. Many of these passageways are narrow and low. Watch where you're going so you don't bump your head, and pay attention to where you're going to step next. Any questions?"

Katelynn spoke up. "What happens if we get lost in there?"

Mr. Davis smiled reassuringly. "We've never lost anyone in this cave." His expression turned serious. "If you do find yourself separated from the group, just sit tight exactly where you are. We'll come to you. Everyone got that? Let's go have fun!"

The first passageway was tight, and even the children had to crawl. Christopher wasn't sure he liked spelunking, after all. He kept Tony's feet in sight and checked behind him often for Thorny's bobbing light.

But the first big room they entered was worth it. Mr. Davis gathered everyone in the center and flashed his powerful beam toward the ceiling. The dome of rock was 30 feet above them and had icicle-like stalactites pointing down. Thorny was fascinated and kept asking Mr. Davis questions. Finally Mr. Burton suggested they see what else the cave had to offer.

Christopher was getting used to the darkness. As they headed out, he kept sight of Tony. Especially when they reached a really twisty, turning section of passages. With the light bouncing off the rock walls and boulders, it was hard to tell which way to go. Then Christopher looked up and couldn't see Tony. Light from Tony's flashlight was shining over the large boulder wedged in the main passageway in front of him. But which way should he go to get to the other side of that boulder?

Story (continued)

Christopher's gaze bounced back and forth. *There's a passage on the right that looks like it goes through to the other side. But it's low and narrow. I'd have to crawl. This passage on the left is big enough to walk through, but it kinda looks like it heads away from the boulder. What am I going to do?*

Tony's light was fading. He had to act quickly. *Since Tony got through there so fast, he must have taken the left passage.*

Christopher glanced behind him to make sure Thorny's light was coming. Then he turned left.

He couldn't tell if he'd taken the right way. He kept hearing voices and seeing flashes of light that he thought were still ahead of him. He went quite a way before he was sure he'd taken the wrong turn. There were no more streaks of light bouncing off the rocks and no voices. He stopped and looked around. From where he was standing, passageways split off in four directions.

I don't even know which passage I came through to get here! If I go just a little ways down each direction, I should be able to tell. Christopher's heart thumped loudly. *But how will I know how to get back here if it's the wrong passage? I'll lay my flashlight on the ground, pointing toward the passage I go into so I can see a little way. If it's the wrong one, I'll just go back to my flashlight!*

Carefully placing his flashlight on the cave floor, Christopher started down the first passage. He was feeling pretty good about his plan when there was a crash behind him and his light went out!

"Help! Is anyone there?"

"Yes." Thorny's voice carried through the darkness. "But I don't know exactly where 'there' is."

Christopher felt a rush of relief. "Thorny, turn your light on so I can see how to get back to you."

"I would like to assist you." Thorny sounded strained. "However, I am unable to do so at this time. My flashlight is presently at some unknown location. When I tripped and fell, it flew from my hand. I do have your flashlight here. Unfortunately, it appears to have suffered damages when I landed on it."

Silence—for several long minutes. "Christopher?" Thorny cleared his throat. "I was not aware of it before this precise moment, but," his voice rose to a panicked squeak, "I believe I am suffering from claustrophobia!"

"It's okay, Thorny." Christopher tried to calm his own panic. "We'll be all right if we just stay put. Mr. Burton will find us."

"But, Christopher!" Thorny's voice sounded squeezed out of him. "I hate to admit it, but I feel as if the walls are tightening around us each second! Don't you feel it?"

"No, but I don't exactly like the dark," Christopher admitted.

"You're afraid of the dark?" Christopher could hear scraping sounds as Thorny jumped up and moved restlessly around. "What are we going to do?"

"We're going to stay exactly where we are, like Mr. Davis said." Christopher tried to keep his voice from shaking. "And we'll pray, of course." Christopher closed his eyes tightly to keep out the darkness around him and bowed his head. "Dear God, we're lost, but You know where we are. Help us not to be afraid and help it not to be too long till someone finds us."

"Christopher, Thorny?" Mr. Burton's voice bounced around the rocks. A light flashed through the darkness.

"We're here!" Thorny shouted. "Right here, Mr. Burton!"

Christopher stumbled toward the light. When he got back to Thorny, Mr. Burton had arrived. Christopher grinned straight into the powerful spelunking light attached to Mr. Burton's helmet. "God sure answered that prayer fast!"

Mr. Burton squeezed each boy's shoulder. "Well, let's thank Him before we join the others." He bowed his head and Christopher watched the light dance around on the cave floor while Mr. Burton prayed.

"Loving Father in Heaven, thank you for guiding me to these boys quickly. Thank you for caring for them and protecting them. Help them to see that You are the Light of the world. Help them to always remember that we can trust You to show us the way we should go every day."

On the way home, Christopher was almost asleep when Thorny asked, "Christopher, I was wondering…what made you think of praying?"

"Well, God's always there to help whenever we ask Him to." Christopher yawned. "And we needed help."

He flicked the switch on his flashlight and nothing happened. "I'm glad we can follow God's light and not worry about it going out like this flashlight, because I really don't like stumbling around in the dark!"

2 Discussion Time

Check understanding of the story and development of personal values.

- Where was Mr. Burton taking the students from his wife's class?
- Why do you think he didn't take all the students at one time?
- How did Christopher feel about being in the dark?
- What rules did Mr. Davis give the kids before they went into the cave?
- How did Christopher get lost?
- What happened to Christopher's and Thorny's flashlights?
- What did Christopher do when he and Thorny got lost?
- Who found the boys?
- Who is the Light of the world? Why?

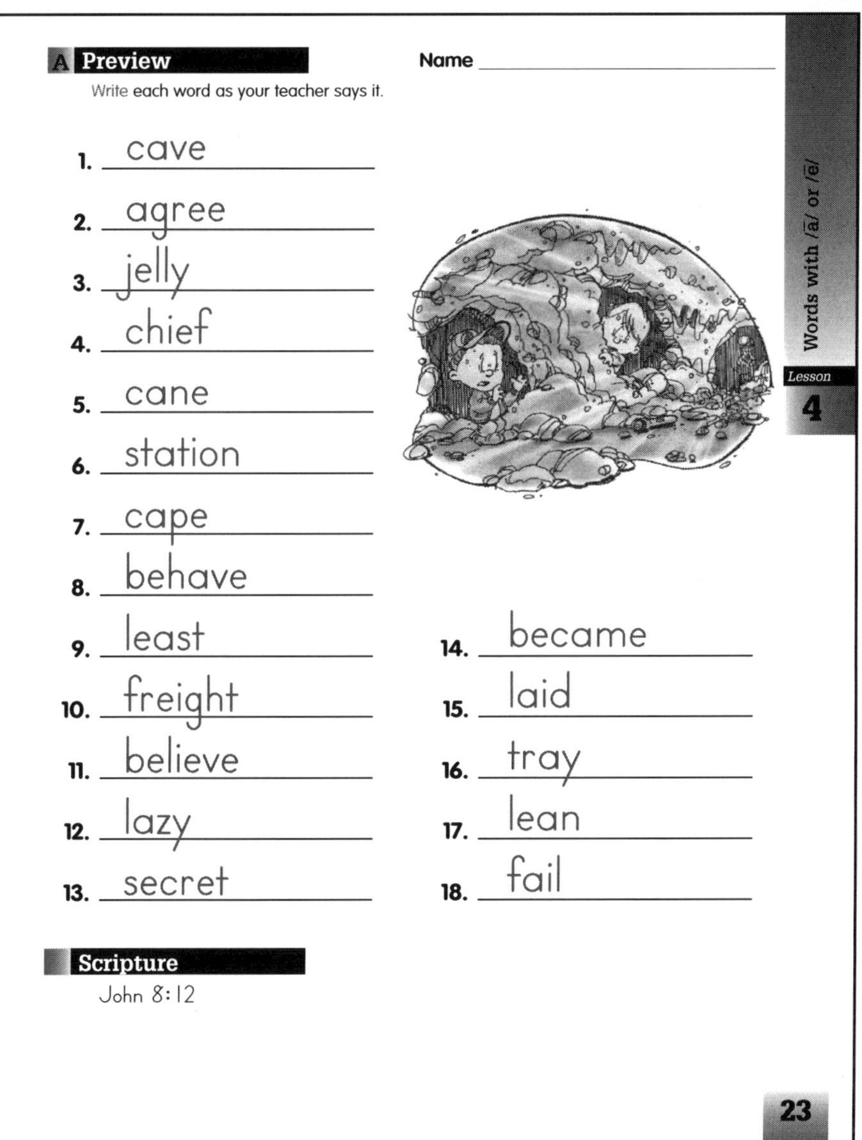

A Preview Name ______________

Write each word as your teacher says it.

1. cave
2. agree
3. jelly
4. chief
5. cane
6. station
7. cape
8. behave
9. least
10. freight
11. believe
12. lazy
13. secret
14. became
15. laid
16. tray
17. lean
18. fail

Words with /ā/ or /ē/

Lesson 4

Scripture

John 8:12

23

3 Preview

Test for knowledge of the correct spellings of these words.

Customize Your List

On a separate sheet of paper, additional words of your choice may be tested.

I will say each word once, use the word in a sentence, then say the word again. Write the words on the lines in your Worktext.

Correct Immediately!

Let's correct our Preview. I will spell each word out loud. If you spelled a word incorrectly, rewrite it correctly.

Progress Chart

Students may record scores. (Reproducible master provided in Appendix B.)

1.	cave	Mrs. Burton planned a field trip for her class to tour a **cave**.
2.	agree	Mrs. Burton's students were sure to **agree** that the cave was exciting!
3.	jelly	Tony brought along a peanut butter and **jelly** sandwich in his backpack.
4.	chief	The **chief** park ranger at Willowwood State Park was Mr. Davis.
5.	cane	There were some old chairs with **cane** seats outside the mouth of the cave.
6.	station	There was a first aid **station** located in the middle of the park.
7.	cape	Mr. Davis often wore a bright yellow rain **cape** to stay dry in the cave.
8.	behave	He told them how he expected them to **behave** in the cave.
9.	least	At **least** two native tribes had recorded their history on the cave walls.
10.	freight	A **freight** train could never fit through the tunnels of that cave.
11.	believe	"If you look carefully, I **believe** you'll see some bats," said Mr. Davis.
12.	lazy	You can't be **lazy** and be a good explorer; spelunking takes energy!
13.	secret	Christopher had a **secret** fear of the dark.
14.	became	In a few minutes, Christopher **became** certain he had taken a wrong turn.
15.	laid	Christopher **laid** his flashlight down on the floor of the cave.
16.	tray	A square piece of rock jutted out from the cave wall like a **tray**.
17.	lean	"We can **lean** on Jesus whenever we're afraid," Christopher told Thorny.
18.	fail	God will not **fail** us; His light will always shine to lead us.

Word Shapes

Help students form a correct image of whole words.

Look at each word and think about its shape. Now, write the word in the correct Word Shape Boxes. You may check off each word as you use it.

(In many words, the sound of **/ā/** is spelled with **a** at the end of a syllable, or with **a-consonant-e**, **ai**, **ay** and occasionally **ei**. In many words, the sound of **/ē/** is spelled with **e** at the end of a syllable, or with **ea**, **ee**, and **ie**. The spelling **y** can be used at the end of a word.)

In the Word Shape Boxes, fill in the boxes containing the letter or letters that spell the sound of **/ā/** or **/ē/** in each word.

Take a minute to memorize...

John 8:12

Day 1 | Lesson 4

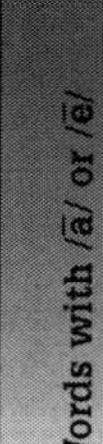

Lesson 4

B Word Shapes Name ____________________

Write each word in the correct Word Shape Boxes. Next, in the Word Shape Boxes, shade in the boxes containing the letter or letters that spell the sound of **/ā/** or **/ē/** in each word.

1. cane
2. cape
3. cave
4. became
5. behave
6. fail
7. laid
8. lazy
9. station
10. tray
11. freight
12. lean
13. least
14. agree
15. secret
16. jelly
17. believe
18. chief

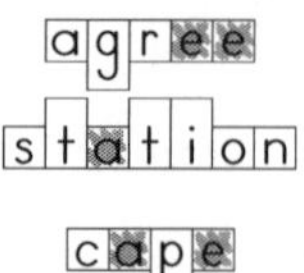

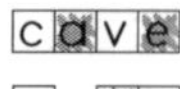

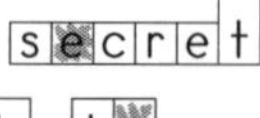
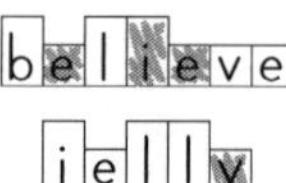
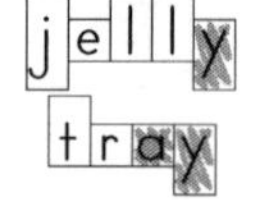
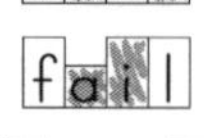

24

Answers may vary for duplicate word shapes.

Be Prepared For Fun

Check these supply lists for **Fun Ways to Spell** - presented **Day 2**.
Purchase and/or gather these items ahead of time!

General

- Pencil
- Graph Paper (1 sheet per child)
- Spelling List

Auditory

- Pencil
- 3 X 5 Cards Cut in half lengthwise (18 per child)
- Spelling List

Visual

- Glitter
- Glue
- Art Paper (2 sheets per child)
- Spelling List

Tactile

- ABC Macaroni
- Art Paper (1 sheet per child)
- Glue
- Spelling List

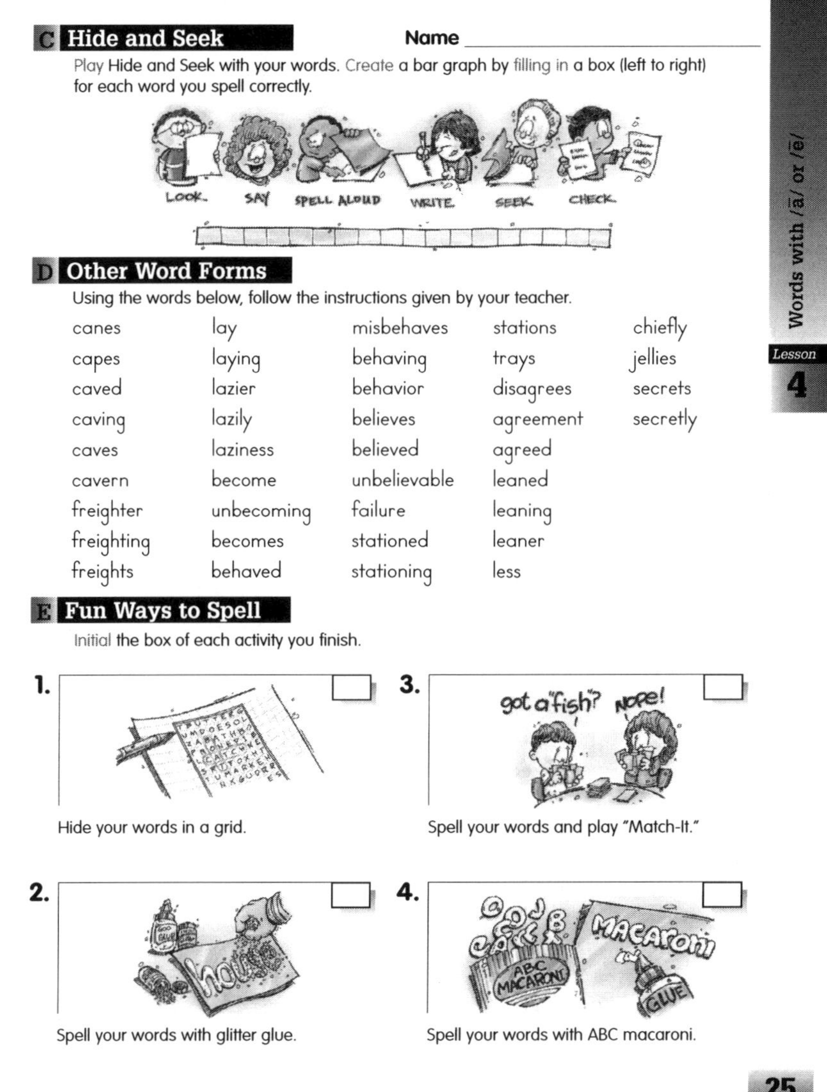

C Hide and Seek Name ______________

Play Hide and Seek with your words. Create a bar graph by filling in a box (left to right) for each word you spell correctly.

D Other Word Forms

Using the words below, follow the instructions given by your teacher.

canes	lay	misbehaves	stations	chiefly
capes	laying	behaving	trays	jellies
caved	lazier	behavior	disagrees	secrets
caving	lazily	believes	agreement	secretly
caves	laziness	believed	agreed	
cavern	become	unbelievable	leaned	
freighter	unbecoming	failure	leaning	
freighting	becomes	stationed	leaner	
freights	behaved	stationing	less	

E Fun Ways to Spell

Initial the box of each activity you finish.

1. Hide your words in a grid.

2. Spell your words with glitter glue.

3. Spell your words and play "Match-It."

4. Spell your words with ABC macaroni.

Words with /ā/ or /ē/

Lesson 4

25

1 Hide and Seek

Reinforce spelling by using multiple styles of learning.

On a white board, Teacher writes each word — one at a time. **Have students:**

- **Look** at the word.
- **Say** the word out loud.
- **Spell** the word out loud.
- **Hide** (teacher erases word.)
- **Write** the word on paper.
- **Seek** (teacher rewrites word.)
- **Check** spelling. If incorrect, rewrite word correctly.

2 Other Word Forms

This activity is optional. Have students write variations of this sentence using these Other Word Forms:

The soldier remained at his station.

stationed stationing stations

3 Fun Ways to Spell

Four activities are provided. Use one, two, three, or all of the activities. Have students initial the box for each activity they complete.

Options:

- assign activities to students according to their learning styles
- set up the activities in learning centers for students to do throughout the day
- divide students into four groups and assign one activity per group
- do one activity per day

General

To hide your words on a grid...

- Arrange your words on a piece of graph paper.
- Put one letter of each word in a square.
- Words may be written backwards, forwards, or diagonally.
- Outline your puzzle.
- Hide your words by filling in all the spaces inside the puzzle with random letters.
- Trade grids with a classmate and find the hidden words.

Auditory

To spell your words and play "Match-It"...

Write each spelling word on a card. Mix your word cards and a classmate's together. Deal six cards per player; put the rest face down between you. Ask classmate for a word-card that matches one in your hand. If the classmate has the word-card, take it and play again. If not, draw from the remaining stack, then it is your classmate's turn. Continue taking turns until all the cards are matched. Player with most cards wins!

Visual

To spell your words with glitter glue...

- Write each of your spelling words on your paper with glue.
- Sprinkle with glitter.

Tactile

To spell your words with ABC macaroni...

- Choose a word from your spelling list.
- Spell the word with macaroni letters.
- Glue the macaroni word to art paper.
- Do this for each word on your list.

Lesson 4 | Day 3

1 Working with Words

Familiarize students with word meaning and usage.

Secret Words

The boxed letters in the acrostic are a phrase from the Scripture verse for this week. Use the clues to write the words in the puzzle, then write the boxed letters on the lines to find the secret phrase.

Take a minute to memorize...

John 8:12

Words with /ā/ or /ē/ — Lesson 4

F Working with Words Name ______________________

Secret Words

Use the clues to write the words in the puzzle. Then use the boxed letters to fill in the lines below to find the secret words from this week's Scripture.

1. to be certain of
2. large, underground hole
3. changed
4. the smallest
5. a commander
6. a sleeveless coat
7. to be slothful
8. cargo
9. consent
10. be nice
11. serving platter
12. depot
13. unsuccessful
14. fruit preserves
15. mystery
16. thin
17. set down

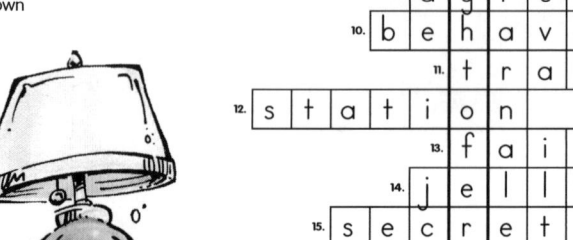

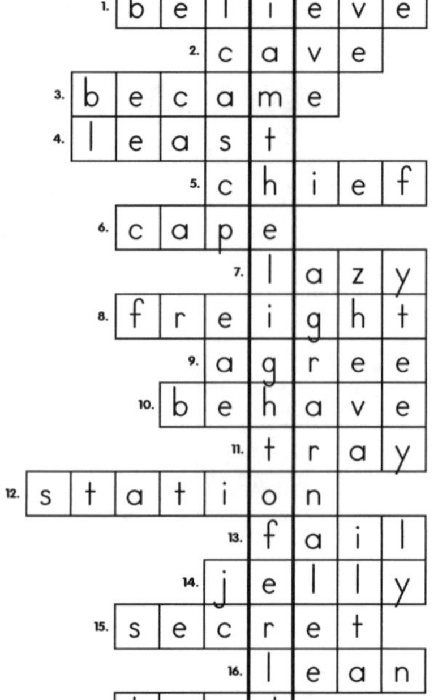

What is the secret phrase?

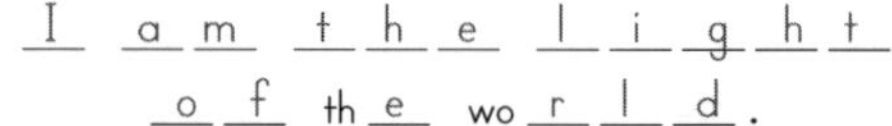

Word Bank

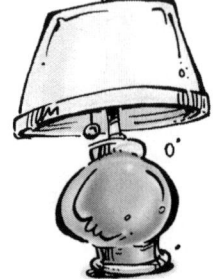

agree	believe	cave	freight	lazy	secret
became	cane	chief	jelly	lean	station
behave	cape	fail	laid	least	tray

26

G Dictation

Name ____________________

Write each sentence as your teacher dictates. Use correct punctuation.

1. Please behave when you are in the cave.
2. I believe at least one chief lived here.
3. He did not know what became of his light.

Words with /ā/ or /ē/

Lesson 4

H Proofreading

If a word is misspelled, fill in the oval by that word. If all the words are spelled correctly, fill in the oval by **no mistake**.

1. ○ against ○ cape ○ ahead ● no mistake
2. ○ breakfast ○ cave ○ dead ● no mistake
3. ○ cane ● jellie ○ behave ○ no mistake
4. ○ became ○ trouble ○ yesterday ● no mistake
5. ○ instead ○ lead ● fale ○ no mistake
6. ○ leather ○ secret ● lade ○ no mistake
7. ○ meant ○ lazy ○ believe ● no mistake
8. ● stashun ○ measure ○ pleasant ○ no mistake
9. ○ sweat ○ wealth ○ tray ● no mistake
10. ● agrea ○ freight ○ built ○ no mistake
11. ○ cousin ● cheif ○ lean ○ no mistake
12. ○ couple ○ comfort ○ least ● no mistake

27

Dictation

Reinforce correct spelling by using current and previous words in context.

Listen as I read each sentence and then write it in your Worktext. Remember to use correct capitalization and punctuation. (Slowly read each sentence twice. Sentences are found in the Student Worktext to the left.)

Proofreading

Familiarize students with standardized test format and reinforce recognition of misspelled words.

Look at each set of words. If a word is misspelled, fill in the oval by that word. If all the words are spelled correctly, fill in the oval by **no mistake**.

3 Hide and Seek

Reinforce correct spelling of current spelling words. Repeat this activity from Day 2. (A reproducible master is provided in Appendix A as shown on the inset page to the right.)

4 Other Word Forms

Have your students complete this activity to strengthen spelling ability and expand vocabulary.

1 Posttest

Visit the **A Reason For** website to download free, printable Posttest pages.

I will say the word once, use it in a sentence, then say it again. Write your words on a separate sheet of paper.

Progress Chart

Students may record scores. (Appendix B)

Personal Dictionary

Students may add any words they have misspelled to their personal dictionaries. (Appendix B)

Lesson 4 | Other Word Forms

Hide and Seek

Play Hide and Seek with your words. Create a bar graph by filling in a box (left to right) for each word you spell correctly.

Other Word Forms

Prefixes and Suffixes

Circle the correct prefix or suffix to make a new word, write the word correctly on the line. Remember, when a base word ends with a long vowel sound spelled with **y**, change the **y** to **i** when adding the ending. When words have the consonant-vowel-consonant-silent **e** pattern (CVCe), drop the **e** when adding an ending that begins with a vowel.

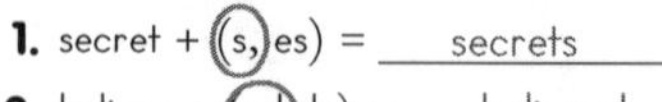

1. secret + (s, es) = secrets
2. believe + (ed, ly) = believed
3. (mis, dis) + agree = disagree
4. behave + (ior, ion) = behavior
5. freight + (er, ior) = freighter
6. jelly + (ing, ed) = jellied
7. lazy + (or, er) = lazier
8. agree + (able, ible) = agreeable
9. freight + (ness, ing) = freighting
10. (dis, mis) + belief = disbelief
11. fail + (ed, er) = failed
12. lean + (iest, est) = leanest
13. lay + (ing, est) = laying
14. cane + (ing, able) = caning
15. (un, mis) + believe + (able, ible) = unbelievable
16. (dis, un) + become + (ing, ness) = unbecoming
17. (mis, dis) + agree + (able, tion) = disagreeable
18. agree + (ness, ment) = agreement
19. fail + (ure, es) = failure

328

1. **cave** Mr. Burton's white van carried the students to the **cave.**
2. **freight** A **freight** train brought the early spelunkers to Whispering Winds Cave.
3. **least** Tony guessed Mr. Davis had been a park ranger for at **least** ten years.
4. **behave** The kids knew they must **behave** well and listen to Mr. Davis.
5. **station** There was an information **station** at the entrance to the park.
6. **cane** You could buy a **cane** or walking stick for hiking the park's nature trails.
7. **cape** Mr. Davis' big smile shone from under the hood of his yellow **cape.**
8. **lazy** "Park rangers and spelunkers can't be **lazy,**" he teased.
9. **chief** A picture of a Native American **chief** was drawn on the wall at the cave entrance.
10. **fail** Christopher got nervous when his flashlight batteries began to **fail.**
11. **laid** Thorny fell right where Christopher had **laid** his flashlight.
12. **became** Thorny imagined the tunnel **became** narrower each second.
13. **believe** "I **believe** I am suffering from claustrophobia!" squeaked Thorny.
14. **agree** "I **agree** with your view that we are in need of assistance," he said.
15. **secret** Christopher told Thorny about his **secret** fear of the dark.
16. **tray** Mr. Burton brought out a **tray** of cookies with small cartons of milk.
17. **jelly** Mrs. Burton had baked **jelly**–centered sugar cookies for the spelunkers.
18. **lean** It is good to know that we can **lean** on Jesus when we are afraid.

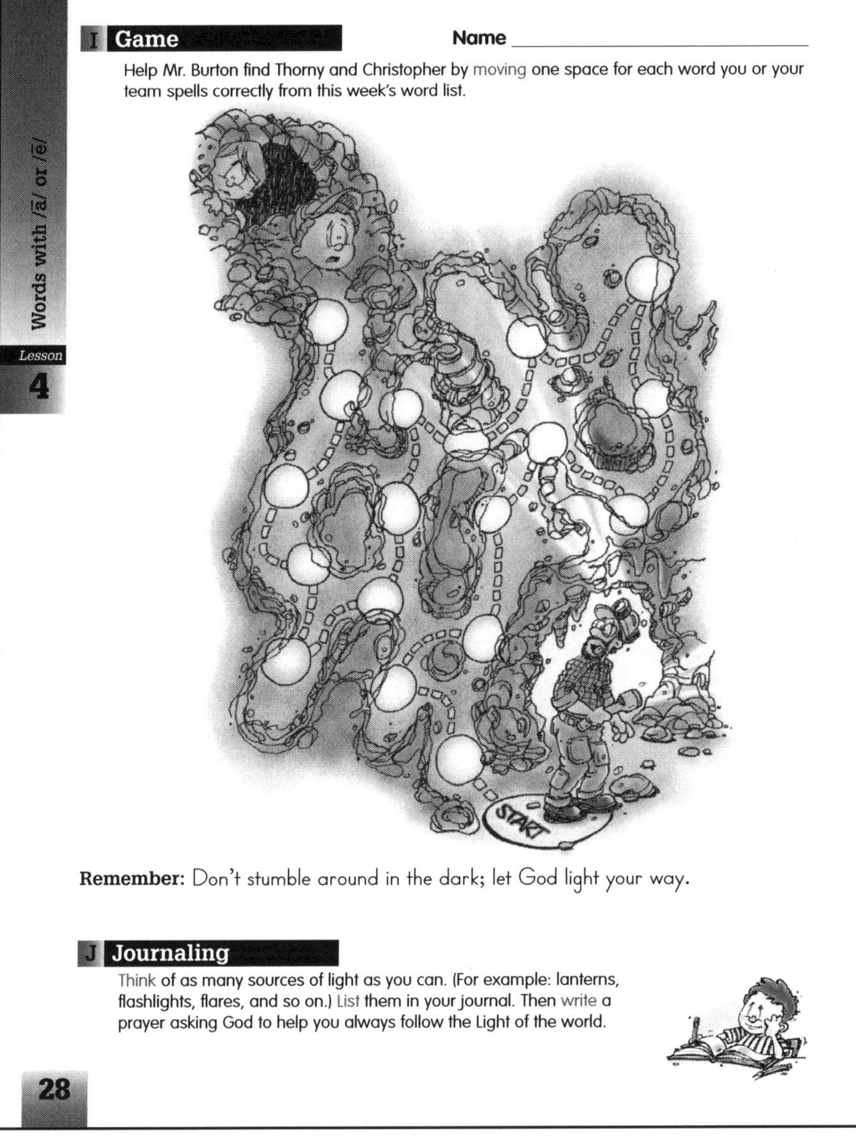

Words with /ā/ or /ē/

Lesson 4

I Game Name ____________________

Help Mr. Burton find Thorny and Christopher by moving one space for each word you or your team spells correctly from this week's word list.

Remember: Don't stumble around in the dark; let God light your way.

J Journaling

Think of as many sources of light as you can. (For example: lanterns, flashlights, flares, and so on.) List them in your journal. Then write a prayer asking God to help you always follow the Light of the world.

28

How to Play:

- Divide students into two teams.
- Have each student place his/her game piece on Start.
- Have a student from team A go to the board.
- Say the spelling word.
- Have the student write the word on the board.
- If correct, instruct each member of team A to move their game piece forward one space.
- Alternate between teams A and B as you go down the word list.
- The team to reach Thorny and Christopher first is the winner.

Small Group Option: Students may play this game without teacher direction in small groups of two or more.

2 Game

Reinforce spelling skills and provide motivation and interest.

Materials

- game page (from Student Worktext)
- game pieces (1 per child)
- game word list

Game Word List

1. **cane**
2. **cape**
3. **cave**
4. **became**
5. **behave**
6. **fail**
7. **laid**
8. **lazy**
9. **station**
10. **tray**
11. **freight**
12. **lean**
13. **least**
14. **agree**
15. **secret**
16. **jelly**
17. **believe**
18. **chief**

3 Journaling

Provide a meaningful reason for correct spelling through personal writing.

Review the story using discussion leads provided on the following page. Encourage students to apply the Scriptural value in their journaling.

Journaling (continued)

- Have you ever been in a cave? Tell about it.
- What did Tony mean by "stag nights" and "stack tights?" (Stalagmites are rock formations on cave floors formed by dripping water. Stalactites are formed in the same way and hang from the cave ceiling like icicles.)
- Who was Mr. Davis? (A park ranger who knew a lot about the cave and guided the students through it.)
- What did Mr. Davis tell the students to do if they got lost? (Stay exactly where they were and wait for help to come to them.)
- What had the cave been used for in the past? (Native tribes had used it for shelter and robbers had used it for a hideout.)
- Why was the cave especially scary for Christopher? (He was afraid of the dark.)
- Why do you need a good light when you go into a cave? (It's totally dark in caves. You can get lost very easily and possibly hurt badly if you don't have a light to see where you're going.)
- Why is God called the Light of the World? (Because if we follow His way we won't get lost as easily in things we shouldn't do which could hurt us badly. Following Him is like a light keeping us headed the right direction.)

The word "karate" means "empty hand."

1 **Literature Connection**
Topic: Following Directions
Theme Text: John 14:6

Messing with Models

Christopher assembles a model rocket without instructions – and reaps the consequences.

"Do all of you have your seat belts buckled?" Mrs. Wright glanced around the car at her four children before putting the car into gear.

"Just a second." Eight-year-old Cathy grabbed her seat belt. "Guess what Tim Sinclair did during science class today, Mom?" Cathy snapped the seat belt closed and went on, "Mrs. Morgan gave us some big beans that she'd soaked in water so they were soft, you know. We were supposed to take them apart and look at the inside where the little plant is. Tim ate his!"

Mom smiled and shook her head. "That doesn't sound like following directions very well." She checked the traffic and pulled the car out of the school parking lot onto the main road. "How was your day, Kristin?"

"We had a timed multiplication drill and I did pretty well. I got everything up to the sixes right, but I missed a couple on the sevens and eights."

"I'm proud of you, Kristin! You remembered a lot from last year and you'll get those sevens and eights." She turned onto another street. "What about you, Christopher? How did your day go?"

"It was okay. Where are we going, Mom? This isn't the way home."

"Mrs. Morgan asked me to make a costume for the play Cathy's class is going to put on. I need to stop by the store to get a pattern and material."

Cathy and Kristin perched on stools and looked at pattern books while their mother shopped. Five-year-old Cory hid in the bolts of cloth and knocked a bunch of them down. Christopher turned the button racks around and around. Finally the clerk cut the last piece of fabric and the family headed toward the cashier.

"Mom, look!" Christopher grabbed his mother's arm as they passed the toy section. "These model rockets are on sale!"

Mrs. Wright took the box Christopher handed her. "Yes, that does look like a good price." She turned the box over to read the back while the other Wright children spotted toys to look at.

"Can I get one, Mom?" Christopher selected another box. "Look, this one has three stages!"

Mom looked thoughtfully at the models. "Well, Christopher, I think it would be all right for you to buy a rocket if you want to spend your own money for it. But," she held up one hand as Christopher started to put the three-stage rocket in the shopping cart, "I think you should choose one that isn't quite as complicated."

She pointed at the small print. "See, this one's marked as 'Skill Level 1' and that one you're holding is marked 'Skill Level 3.' Since you've never put a rocket together by yourself, it seems wise to start with the first skill level."

Christopher took the Level 1 rocket from his mother and held the two model boxes side by side. "Could I get this one after I put the easy one together?"

"Probably. But let's see how one goes before making any other decisions."

"Okay." Christopher put the 'Skill Level 1' box in the cart and returned the three-stage rocket to the shelf. "I like this one anyway—the Sidewinder. It's supposed to twist as it goes up and make a smoke trail. That'll be cool!"

On the way home Christopher held the box and admired the sleek red and blue rocket pictured on the front. As soon as the car came to a halt, Christopher jumped out and headed to his room. He opened the box and laid out all the rocket pieces. There seemed to be quite a lot. The long tubes were the body of the rocket, but what were those rings and metal hooks and things for?

"Mom!" Christopher stuck his head out into the hall and called again, "Mom!"

"In the kitchen, Son."

"Mom, will you help me put my rocket together?" Christopher bounced into the kitchen.

"I can't, Christopher." She put some salt into the pot simmering on the stove. "Maybe after supper Dad will be able to help you, but I need to get started making the costume."

Christopher wandered out of the kitchen. Cathy and Kristin were playing in their room. Cory was in the living room, zooming and roaring as he drove his cars around the floor. Christopher ended up in his own room staring at the pieces of Sidewinder scattered across his desk. The red and blue picture on the front of the box didn't look that complicated.

"Sidewinder. Flying Model Rocket. 'Skill Level 1.'" Christopher read the writing on the box. "I can't wait to see it all put together like that picture, but Dad may not have time to help me tonight. It can't be that hard to do since it's 'Skill Level 1.' I'll just do it myself!" Christopher reached for the glue.

"Wonderful meal, as usual, Maggie." Dad leaned back in his chair after supper and rubbed his stomach. He turned to Christopher. "I hear you've got a project for us this evening. Since it's not your night to clean up the kitchen, let's go take a look at that rocket after you carry your dishes to the sink."

"Uh, are you sure you have time tonight?" Christopher carefully stacked his dishes and silverware.

"Sure, I'm sure." Dad raised his eyebrows at Christopher's lack of enthusiasm. "C'mon, Son. Let's get that rocket ready to

Story (continued)

fly!" He followed his oldest son across the kitchen.

Christopher slowly led the way to his room. He stood back as Dad looked at the stuff on his desk. Dad picked up the rocket Christopher had already put together by himself. He turned it in his hands and looked at it from every angle. Then he picked up several pieces of neatly folded paper that had come with the rocket.

Dad sat on the edge of Christopher's bed. "Well, Son, want to tell me what happened to your Sidewinder?"

"I, um, I thought I could put it together," Christopher mumbled toward the carpet at his feet. "I mean, it does say it's a 'Skill Level 1' and the picture on the box front doesn't look complicated."

He spoke faster once he got going. "But after I glued the main tubes together and the nose cone on, I couldn't figure out how to get the parachute inside, so I used that metal hook thingy to make it stay in. But it tore the parachute and now I don't know how it's supposed to come out when the rocket's in the air. And I sort of forgot to paint the rocket till after I put the decals on. Then I tried to take them off again and that tore the cardboard tube, so I just painted around the stickers."

Christopher paused. "And I can't get the engine to stay inside. It just keeps falling out. And I don't know where those rings and things go. And..."

"I get the picture."

Christopher noticed that his dad looked kind of red and he seemed to be biting his lip.

"Are you okay, Dad?" Christopher walked over to the bed.

Mr. Wright burst out laughing. Christopher stared at his dad as he howled with laughter. "It's okay, Christopher," Mr. Wright choked out as soon as he could control his voice. "I'm not making fun of you." He picked up the funny-looking Sidewinder and chuckled again. "But this is one rocket that'll never fly."

Christopher's mouth twitched into a grin as he looked at the rocket in his dad's hand. "It does look a lot different from the picture on the box," he giggled. "Maybe I should call it the Sad-winder."

Dad put his arm around Christopher's shoulders. "Did you use the directions, Son?"

When Christopher shook his head and muttered, "No," Dad unfolded the sheets of paper he held. "I think you'd have ended up with a very different rocket if you had."

Dad smoothed the pages across his knee and pulled Christopher down to sit beside him. "These instructions tell what each piece is for and where it goes." He pointed at the illustrations printed by each step. "The pictures show exactly what should be done and in what order to do them. See, there's even a box by each step so you can check it off when you've finished it. It helps you keep track of where you are."

Dad folded the rocket instructions into a paper airplane. "Following instructions is important, Son. Mom couldn't make that costume without following the instructions on the pattern. Without following these, there won't be a rocket to fly." He threw the instruction-sheet airplane and it landed amid the rocket stuff on Christopher's desk.

Dad took the kids' Bible off the bookshelf. "God gave us this set of instructions for a reason, too." He ran his hand over the smooth surface of the Scriptures. "Without following them, we cannot know God."

He opened the Bible to John 14. "Read verse six, Son." He handed the book to Christopher and stood up. At the door he turned and pointed at the strange looking Sidewinder on Christopher's desk. "You know, if that rocket helps you learn to follow the instructions in the Book, then it was worth any price, although it'll never fly!"

Christopher read the verse aloud after his dad left the room. "I am the Way—yes, and the Truth and the Life. No one can get to the Father except by means of Me."

And right then, Christopher decided to keep the grounded Sidewinder to remind him to follow instructions—including the one in John 14:6.

2 Discussion Time

Check understanding of the story and development of personal values.

- How did Cathy's classmate, Tim Sinclair, not follow directions?
- Where did Mrs. Wright stop on the way home from school?
- Why did Mrs. Wright need to buy a pattern and material?
- What did Christopher buy at the store?
- What did Mrs. Wright look at to find out what other supplies the rocket would need?
- Why did Christopher think he could put the rocket together all by himself?
- What was the rocket called?
- How was the rocket supposed to fly?
- Why wasn't Christopher eager to show his dad the rocket after supper?
- What could Christopher have done differently so the rocket would have turned out right?

A Preview
Name
Write each word as your teacher says it.
1. tiger
2. crow
3. lonely
4. notice
5. alike
6. reply
7. supply
8. chose
9. rose
10. dive
11. pile
12. hollow
13. oak
14. iron
15. pine
16. stove
17. coach
18. tied
Scripture
John 14:6
Words with /ī/ or /ō/
Lesson 5
29

3 Preview

Test for knowledge of the correct spellings of these words.

Customize Your List

On a separate sheet of paper, additional words of your choice may be tested.

I will say each word once, use the word in a sentence, then say the word again. Write the words on the lines in your Worktext.

Correct Immediately!

Let's correct our Preview. I will spell each word out loud. If you spelled a word incorrectly, rewrite it correctly.

Progress Chart

Students may record scores. (Reproducible master provided in Appendix B.)

1.	tiger	Cory knocked over a bolt of fabric with **tiger** print all over it.
2.	crow	Christopher saw a button shaped like a **crow.**
3.	lonely	He picked up a **lonely** card of buttons from the floor.
4.	notice	Christopher did **notice** the models on sale.
5.	alike	The rocket models were not all **alike.**
6.	reply	Mrs. Wright did not **reply** until she had read the box carefully.
7.	supply	"Check the **supply** list for other things you might need," said his mom.
8.	chose	Christopher **chose** the Sidewinder since it was marked 'Skill Level One.'
9.	rose	He imagined how neat it would look as it **rose** high in the air, trailing smoke!
10.	dive	He could just see it taking a sharp **dive** back toward earth.
11.	pile	Christopher stared at the **pile** of model pieces.
12.	hollow	He was sure the **hollow** cardboard tubes were the body of the rocket.
13.	oak	Models usually include pieces made of balsa wood, not **oak.**
14.	iron	The little metal rings in the kit were not made of **iron.**
15.	pine	He planned to make a base out of **pine** to display his model.
16.	stove	Mom was adding salt to the pot simmering on the **stove** top.
17.	coach	"Your dad can **coach** you as you put together your model," she said.
18.	tied	He **tied** the parachute strings to one of the metal rings.

Word Shapes

Help students form a correct image of whole words.

Look at each word and think about its shape. Now, write the word in the correct Word Shape Boxes. You may check off each word as you use it.

(In many words, the sound of **/ī/** is spelled with **i** at the end of a syllable, or with **ie**, or **i-consonant-e**. It is sometimes spelled with **y** at the end of a word. In many words, the sound of **/ō/** is spelled with **o-consonant-e**, **oa**, or **ow**.)

In the Word Shape Boxes, fill in the boxes containing the letter or letters that spell the sound of **/ī/** or **/ō/** in each word.

Take a minute to memorize...

John 14:6

Words with /ī/ or /ō/ — Lesson 5

B Word Shapes Name ____________

Write each word in the correct Word Shape Boxes. Next, in the Word Shape Boxes, shade in the boxes containing the letter or letters that spell the sound of **/ī/** or **/ō/** in each word.

	Word	Word Shape Answer
1.	alike	pine
2.	dive	tiger
3.	pile	tied
4.	pine	crow
5.	iron	reply
6.	tiger	pile
7.	tied	supply
8.	reply	coach
9.	supply	alike
10.	coach	iron
11.	oak	oak
12.	chose	dive
13.	lonely	notice
14.	rose	chose
15.	stove	hollow
16.	notice	lonely
17.	crow	rose
18.	hollow	stove

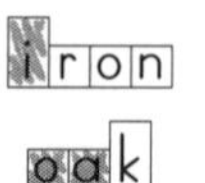

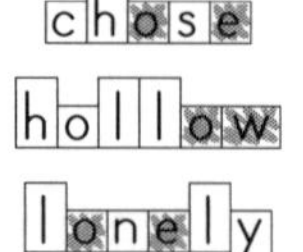

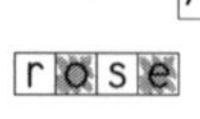

30

Answers may vary for duplicate word shapes.

Be Prepared For Fun

Check these supply lists for **Fun Ways to Spell** - presented **Day 2**.
Purchase and/or gather these items ahead of time!

General
- Pencil
- 3 X 5 Cards cut in half (18 per child)
- Spelling List

Auditory
- Pencil
- Notebook Paper
- Spelling List

Visual
- Black Construction Paper (1 sheet per child)
- Lemon Juice
- Cotton Swabs
- Spelling List

Tactile
- Pipe Cleaners (cut in an assortment of lengths)
- Spelling List

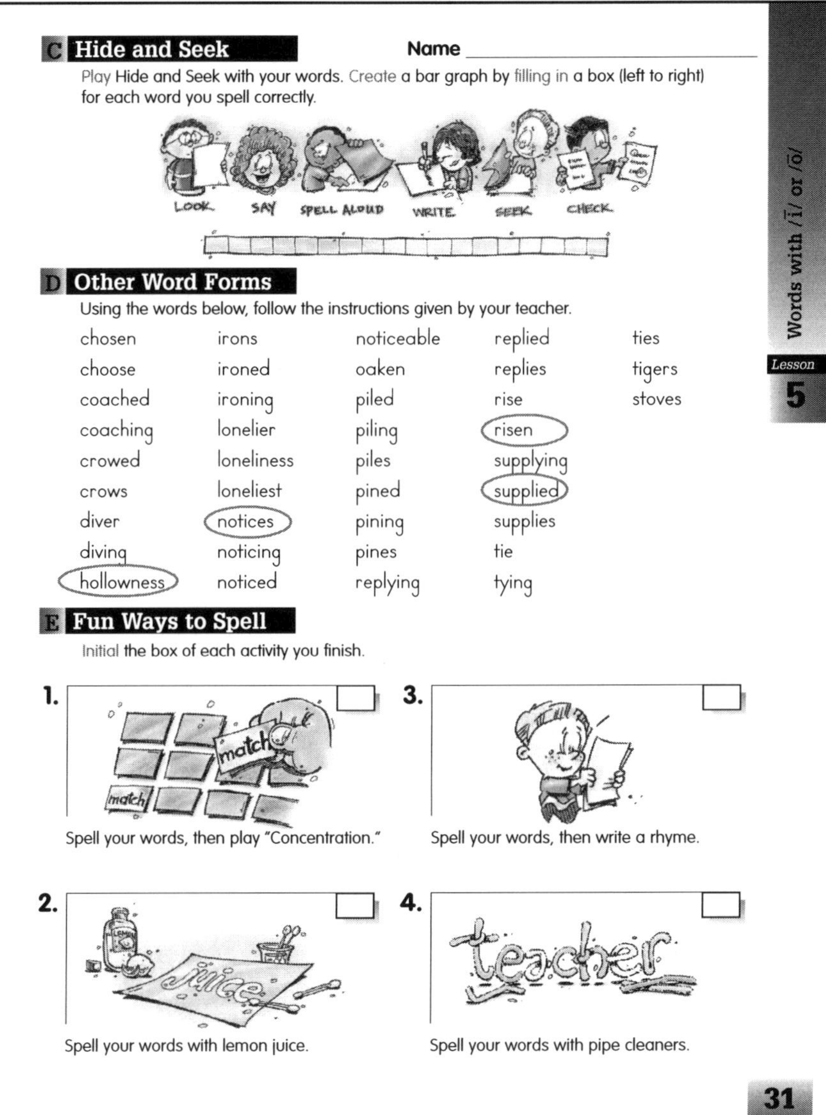

C Hide and Seek

Name ____________________

Play Hide and Seek with your words. Create a bar graph by filling in a box (left to right) for each word you spell correctly.

D Other Word Forms

Using the words below, follow the instructions given by your teacher.

chosen	irons	noticeable	replied	ties
choose	ironed	oaken	replies	tigers
coached	ironing	piled	rise	stoves
coaching	lonelier	piling	risen	
crowed	loneliness	piles	supplying	
crows	loneliest	pined	supplied	
diver	notices	pining	supplies	
diving	noticing	pines	tie	
hollowness	noticed	replying	tying	

E Fun Ways to Spell

Initial the box of each activity you finish.

1. Spell your words, then play "Concentration."

2. Spell your words with lemon juice.

3. Spell your words, then write a rhyme.

4. Spell your words with pipe cleaners.

Words with /ī/ or /ō/

Lesson 5

31

1 Hide and Seek

Reinforce spelling by using multiple styles of learning.

On a white board, Teacher writes each word — one at a time. **Have students:**

- **Look** at the word.
- **Say** the word out loud.
- **Spell** the word out loud.
- **Hide** (teacher erases word.)
- **Write** the word on paper.
- **Seek** (teacher rewrites word.)
- **Check** spelling. If incorrect, rewrite word correctly.

2 Other Word Forms

This activity is optional. Have students find and circle the Other Word Forms that are antonyms of the following:

fullness
ignores
fallen
withheld

3 Fun Ways to Spell

Four activities are provided. Use one, two, three, or all of the activities. Have students initial the box for each activity they complete.

Options:

- assign activities to students according to their learning styles
- set up the activities in learning centers for students to do throughout the day
- divide students into four groups and assign one activity per group
- do one activity per day

General

Spell your words; then play Concentration...
Write each spelling word on a card. Mix your cards and a classmate's cards together. Arrange them face down in six rows of six. Pick up two cards. If the cards match, play again. If the cards do not match, turn them back over. It is your classmate's turn. Continue taking turns until all the cards are matched. The player with the most cards wins!

Auditory

To spell your words and write a rhyme...

- Write a rhyming verse for each word on your list.
- Example:
  My little brother could dive.
  When he was barely five.
- Underline your spelling words.

Visual

To spell your words with lemon juice...

- Dip a cotton swab in lemon juice.
- With the swab, write each of your spelling words on black construction paper.
- Check your spelling before your writing disappears!

Tactile

To spell your words with pipe cleaners...

- Choose a word from your spelling list.
- Shape the pipe cleaners to spell the word.
- Check your spelling.
- Do this for each word on your list.

Working with Words

Familiarize students with word meaning and usage.

Dictionary Skills

Explain that guide words are the two words in boldface type at the top of each dictionary page. Guide words make it easy to find a word. The first guide word is the same as the first entry word on the page. The second guide word is the same as the last entry word on that page. Other words come in between in alphabetical order. Write the guide words **dollar - doorway** on the board. Beside those, write the words **domino**, **dolphin**, **dove**, **donate**, **doughnut**, **doll**, and **doodle**. Have students tell you which words would be on this dictionary page. Write the words under the guide words.

Pretend the words in each group are guide words on a dictionary page. Using your word bank, write the spelling words that would be found on a page with these guide words.
Then, match each pair of guide words to the spelling word that would be on that dictionary page by writing the letter of the spelling word on the line in front of the guide words.

Take a minute to memorize...

John 14:6

Words with /ī/ or /ō/ — Lesson 5

F Working with Words Name ______

Dictionary Skills

Pretend the words in each group are guide words on a dictionary page. Write the spelling words that would be found on the page between these guide words.

1. chorus – crown	2. holiday – look	3. nothing – pink
chose	hollow	notice
coach	iron	oak
crow	lonely	pile
		pine

4. repent – straight	5. supper – tile
reply	supply
rose	tied
stove	tiger

Using the word bank below, write the correct spelling word on the line in front of the guide words.

1.	coach	clue – cobra	10.	stove	stout – supper
2.	dive	disturb – divide	11.	oak	nurse – ocean
3.	chose	choir – Christ	12.	pile	pigtail – pinch
4.	lonely	logic – long	13.	tiger	tide – toast
5.	iron	invite – island	14.	supply	style – swap
6.	alike	alibi – alligator	15.	pine	pilgrim – pinto
7.	crow	cross – crumb	16.	reply	rent – roller
8.	notice	north – noun	17.	tied	thumb – tier
9.	hollow	holiday – home	18.	rose	room – rotate

Word Bank

alike	pine	tied	coach	lonely	notice
dive	iron	reply	oak	rose	crow
pile	tiger	supply	chose	stove	hollow

32

G Dictation

Name ____________________

Write each sentence as your teacher dictates. Use correct punctuation.

1. The coach helped me learn to dive.
2. He tied his shoe, then rose to play football.
3. A hollow pine tree is next to a tall oak.

Words with /ī/ or /ō/

Lesson 5

H Proofreading

If a word is misspelled, fill in the oval by that word. If all the words are spelled correctly, fill in the oval by **no mistake**.

1.
- ○ jelly
- ○ chief
- ○ alike
- ● no mistake

2.
- ● crowe
- ○ believe
- ○ dive
- ○ no mistake

3.
- ○ agree
- ● piel
- ○ secret
- ○ no mistake

4.
- ● notiss
- ○ least
- ○ pine
- ○ no mistake

5.
- ○ lean
- ● roze
- ○ iron
- ○ no mistake

6.
- ○ tray
- ○ freight
- ● tiegir
- ○ no mistake

7.
- ○ lazy
- ○ station
- ● tiede
- ○ no mistake

8.
- ● loanly
- ○ reply
- ○ laid
- ○ no mistake

9.
- ○ behave
- ○ fail
- ● supplie
- ○ no mistake

10.
- ○ cave
- ○ became
- ○ coach
- ● no mistake

11.
- ○ cape
- ● oke
- ○ stove
- ○ no mistake

12.
- ○ cane
- ○ hollow
- ○ chose
- ● no mistake

33

Dictation

Reinforce correct spelling by using current and previous words in context.

Listen as I read each sentence and then write it in your Worktext. Remember to use correct capitalization and punctuation. (Slowly read each sentence twice. Sentences are found in the Student Worktext to the left.)

Proofreading

Familiarize students with standardized test format and reinforce recognition of misspelled words.

Look at each set of words. If a word is misspelled, fill in the oval by that word. If all the words are spelled correctly, fill in the oval by **no mistake**.

3 Hide and Seek

Reinforce correct spelling of current spelling words. Repeat this activity from Day 2. (A reproducible master is provided in Appendix A as shown on the inset page to the right.)

4 Other Word Forms

Have your students complete this activity to strengthen spelling ability and expand vocabulary.

1 Posttest

Visit the **A Reason For** website to download free, printable Posttest pages.

I will say the word once, use it in a sentence, then say it again. Write your words on a separate sheet of paper.

Progress Chart

Students may record scores. (Appendix B)

Personal Dictionary

Students may add any words they have misspelled to their personal dictionaries. (Appendix B)

Hide and Seek

Play Hide and Seek with your words. Create a bar graph by filling in a box (left to right) for each word you spell correctly.

Other Word Forms

Synonyms

Use the synonyms to write the words. Remember, a synonym is a word that means the same or nearly the same as another word.

1. aloneness — loneliness
2. Asian cats — tigers
3. black birds — crows
4. elevated — risen
5. frogman — diver
6. providing — supplying
7. visible — noticeable
8. made of wood — oaken
9. answered — replied
10. been selected — chosen
11. directs athletics — coaches
12. emptiness — hollowness
13. heaped — piled
14. removing wrinkles — ironing
15. yearning — pining
16. binding — tying

Syllables

A syllable is a unit of sound in a word containing a vowel and possibly one or more consonants. Count how many syllables each word has and write the number on the line.

1. 2 chosen
2. 2 risen
3. 2 diver
4. 3 loneliness
5. 3 replying
6. 2 pining
7. 2 tigers
8. 2 coaches
9. 3 hollowness
10. 4 noticeable
11. 1 stoves
12. 2 replied
13. 3 supplying
14. 1 crowed
15. 2 ironing
16. 1 piled
17. 1 coached
18. 1 ties

Word Bank

chosen	diver	loneliness	piled	risen	tigers
coaches	hollowness	noticeable	pining	supplying	tying
crows	ironing	oaken	replied		

Other Word Forms — Lesson 5 — 329

1. **oak**	Mrs. Wright parked the car in the shade of a huge **oak** tree.
2. **pile**	She smiled as her children began to **pile** into the car.
3. **supply**	There was a sewing **supply** list on the back of each pattern.
4. **alike**	Some of the costume patterns were very much **alike.**
5. **chose**	She **chose** a pattern, several pieces of fabric, and two spools of thread.
6. **tiger**	Cathy picked up a stuffed **tiger** and gave it a big hug.
7. **crow**	Cory pressed the stomach of a toy **crow** and it cawed loudly!
8. **pine**	Christopher dumped all the pieces out on his **pine** desktop.
9. **hollow**	He counted three **hollow** cardboard tubes and five metal rings.
10. **notice**	Christopher took no **notice** of the model's instructions.
11. **dive**	He decided to **dive** right in and put it together by himself.
12. **iron**	"I can't **iron** the wrinkles out of this plastic parachute," he thought.
13. **tied**	Christopher **tied** a double knot in the thin string.
14. **stove**	Mom served the delicious hot stew from the pot on the **stove.**
15. **coach**	"I'd love to **coach** you as you build your model," said his dad.
16. **lonely**	Christopher scooted a **lonely** carrot around his plate with his fork.
17. **reply**	He did not **reply** right away.
18. **rose**	He **rose** slowly from the kitchen table.

Words with /ī/ or /ō/

Lesson 5

I Game

Name ______________________

Play a game of tic-tac-toe by marking the grid each time you or your team spells a word correctly from this week's word list.

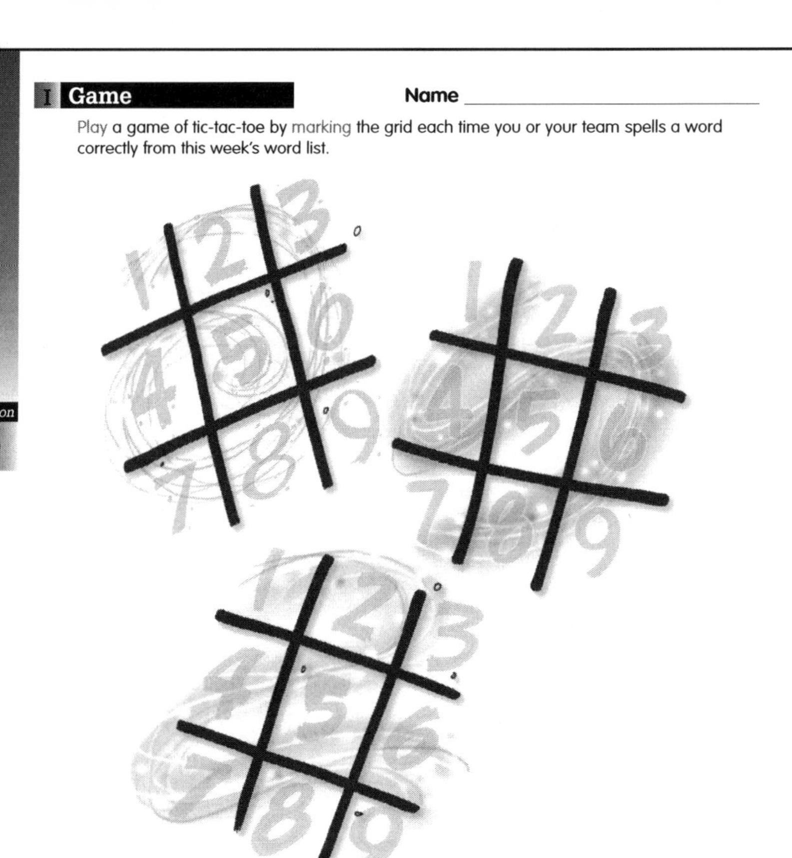

Remember: The only way to truly experience fun living is by getting to know Jesus and following His instructions.

J Journaling

In your journal, write directions so that someone starting at the school could get to your home. Remember to make your directions clear and in the correct order.

34

How to Play:

- Divide students into two teams (the X's and the O's).
- Have a student from team X choose a number from 1 to 9.
- Say the word that matches that number from the Game Word List (Game 1).
- Have the student write the word on the board.
- If correct, have each member of both teams put an X on that number.
- Alternate between teams X and O.
- The first team to score three marks in a row (up, down, across, or diagonally) is the winner.
- Word lists and tic-tac-toe grids are provided for two additional games.

Small Group Option: Students may play this game without teacher direction in groups of two.

2 Game

Reinforce spelling skills and provide motivation and interest.

Materials

- game page (from Student Worktext)
- pencils (1 per child)
- game word list

Game 1 Word List

1. **dive**
2. **coach**
3. **pine**
4. **chose**
5. **notice**
6. **tied**
7. **reply**
8. **hollow**
9. **supply**

Game 2 Word List

1. **pile**
2. **alike**
3. **iron**
4. **oak**
5. **lonely**
6. **tiger**
7. **rose**
8. **stove**
9. **crow**

Game 3 Word List

1. **pile**
2. **iron**
3. **reply**
4. **tied**
5. **supply**
6. **coach**
7. **lonely**
8. **notice**
9. **hollow**

3 Journaling

Provide a meaningful reason for correct spelling through personal writing.

Review the story using discussion leads provided on the following page. Encourage students to apply the Scriptural value in their journaling.

Journaling (continued)

- Is following directions important?
- When are directions important? (Brainstorm and write responses on the board. Driving somewhere new. Flying a plane. Building a house. Cooking from a recipe. Making clothes. Using chemicals. Taking medicine, etc.)
- Why do you think Christopher didn't follow the directions for putting the Sidewinder together? (It looked easy. He thought he could figure it out by himself.)
- Who do you think knew more about building the rocket, the people that designed it or Christopher? Why? (The people that designed it. They made it the way it was. They had worked with it and tested it enough to know exactly what to do to make it fly right.)
- Did God give us directions for how to live? (Yes.)
- Where are these directions found? (In the Scriptures.)
- Who do you think knows more about the best way to live and to know God, Jesus or us? Why? (Jesus. He made us the way we are. He knows exactly what we need to do to live right.)
- Do you think Christopher wished he'd followed the directions? Shouldn't we follow God's directions and spend time getting to know Jesus?

The most commonly used words in the English language are: the, and, a, that, I, of, to, in, is, it.

1 **Literature Connection**
Topic: Obedience
Theme Text: John 20:29

Street Skating Headache

Laney ignores her stepfather's advice about wearing a helmet, and learns a painful lesson.

"We're going skateboarding on the sidewalks and parking lot over by my house, Coach." Tony turned the wide deck of his purple skateboard on end and spun a small urethane wheel with his thumb. "Stephen's papa is going to help us."

"Would you like to go, Laney?" Coach Larkin pushed open the screen door and put his big hands on Laney's shoulders.

Laney leaned back against her stepfather and looked up into his blue eyes. "Uh huh. It'd be fun. Maybe he can teach me how to ollie. I've never been able to jump over things with my board."

"Stephen does ollies—and he's good at flatland tricks, too. He can spin his board all around under his feet. Mr. Wilson calls it 'freestyle skating.'" Tony sat down cross-legged in the grass and flipped his skateboard over. "Mr. Wilson used to compete in freestyle skating competitions when he was younger. He knows a bunch of tricks. He teaches us lots of cool stuff."

"I'll go get my board." Laney disappeared into the house.

"How long are you guys going to skate, Tony?" Coach asked.

"Oh, I don't know—probably an hour or so. It depends when the Wilsons eat dinner."

Coach sat down in a white wicker chair on the porch. "So, have you learned to ollie, Tony?"

Tony started all four wheels on his board spinning before he answered. "I can jump up onto the curb, but not much higher than that. Mr. Wilson ollies over handrails and steps. I'm good at wheelies though."

Laney came out on the porch a few minutes later with her blue board. Bright graphics covered the underside of the wooden deck. She sat down on the first step to lace up her high-top shoes and put on her elbow and knee pads.

"Don't forget your helmet, Laney." Coach Larkin smiled and leaned back in the chair. "It's in the garage near your bike."

Laney frowned. "I'm pretty good. I used to practice a lot at the skate park in New York."

"Believe me, Laney, you'll be glad you have a helmet on if your head ever hits cement. Ask Stephen if you can see the helmet he was wearing when he had his bike accident a few years ago. He broke both legs, but his head was okay."

Laney let the screen door slam as she ran back through the house to get the helmet. *I never hit my head when I fall—just elbows and knees.* She grabbed the helmet off the shelf beside her bike. *I can't believe he bought this for me. I don't like this thing! My hair looks awful after stuffing it into this Styrofoam and plastic.* She frowned as she stepped back out onto the front porch.

"Have a good time! We'll go get ice cream when you get back. Tony, you're welcome to come with us if you like." Coach smiled. "That helmet will be more useful on your head, Laney."

"He's such a safety nut." Laney followed Tony across the road to Mason Springs Park, her helmet under her arm. "He bought this for me right after we moved here. He said it was the best money could buy. I have to wear it rollerblading, biking, and skateboarding. He always makes me fasten my seat belt and sit in the back seat of the car because it's safer. I have to wear a life jacket when we go out in the boat, too."

"Be glad he cares." Tony looked down at the ground. "Hey! There are the Wilsons! Hi, Stephen! Hi, Mr. Wilson!"

Laney put her helmet down while she tightened the Velcro straps on her knee pads.

"Watch this!" Stephen yelled as he whizzed by. He expertly jumped his board over a baseball bat in the middle of the parking lot, did a kick turn, then a nose slide along the edge of a nearby curb.

"He's good." Laney looked at Tony and raised her eyebrows. "I can't believe the way he slides the tail of his board across the curb like that."

"I like the way he changes direction with a kick turn." Tony put his board down on the pavement. "He just kicks down on the tail and the nose of his board shoots up in the air and twists in the other direction. His papa taught him everything. He'll help us, too."

Laney carried her skateboard to the other end of the gently sloping parking lot and hopped on. "Ollie over that bat, Stephen. I want to watch you one more time before I try."

"Place your feet on your board like this," Stephen instructed. "Right before you get to the bat, shift your weight to your back foot and push down hard on the tail. Quickly slide your front foot from the middle of the board to the nose—and fly." Stephen laughed and took off across the parking lot, ollieing over all the obstacles in his path.

Laney shifted her weight to the tail of her board, and the front end popped up into the air.

"Just swivel it around now. You could do a flip turn first if you want," Stephen yelled.

"Helmet, Laney. Where's your helmet?" Mr. Wilson called from across the parking lot.

Laney lost her concentration, and the front of her skateboard slammed onto the cement. Her weight shifted forward, and she nosedived into the pavement.

"Are you okay?" Tony

Story Continued

and Stephen came skating over to her at the same time.

Laney sat up, opened her eyes and felt her throbbing head.

Stephen screamed, "Dad, come quick! Laney's hurt!"

"Lie down, Laney," Tony directed.

"Don't move." Mr. Wilson puffed. "Stephen, go call 911. Hurry!"

Laney's hands felt wet and sticky. She was shocked to see that they were covered with blood.

"Head wounds bleed a lot, Laney. You have a gash on your forehead. Just lie still." Mr. Wilson put a hand on her shoulder.

Laney closed her eyes, but she couldn't stop her thoughts from spinning. *Helmet. Helmet would have helped here. Why didn't I wear my helmet? I'm going to get killed when I get home. Dad told me to wear my helmet. I'll be grounded for a month. He'll never trust me again. I'm just the baggage that came along when he married my mom. He won't like me any more. I'm just a big expense. He bought me a helmet and I didn't even wear it.*

An hour later Laney was sitting on the edge of the emergency room examining table, swinging her legs back and forth. "Come see me in a week and we'll take those stitches out of your forehead, Little Lady." The doctor patted her knee. "A helmet would have protected your head, Laney. You really should wear one when you're skateboarding."

Laney nodded but didn't say a word. *Mom's husband will probably make me pay the ambulance bill,* she thought. *The emergency room bill and the doctor bill too. I won't have an allowance forever.*

Mom squeezed Laney's hand and smiled sympathetically. "Edward will pick you up. I'm already late for a meeting."

"Can't you just take me home, Mom?"

"Well, I guess I could, but your dad said something about taking you, Tony, and Stephen out for ice cream."

"After what I did? He told me to wear a helmet, Mom. He even made me go back in the house and get it."

"Laney, how are you feeling, Sweetheart?" Edward Larkin rushed into the examining room and scooped his daughter up in his arms.

Laney looked up into her dad's face. She thought he looked like he had tears in his eyes. Laney reached up and wiped the drops away as they trickled down his face.

"I'm just glad you're okay, Sweetheart. I'm just glad you're okay. You ready for ice cream?" Edward Larkin smiled down at his stepdaughter.

"Aren't you mad at me?" Laney searched his eyes for a trace of anger or resentment.

"I was too worried about you to be angry." Dad ran his hand across his forehead. "Head injuries can be very serious."

"But I didn't obey you." Laney frowned. "I never even put my helmet on!"

"Laney, it was wrong for you to disobey, and I'm sorry you chose not to listen. But sometimes all of us insist on learning things the hard way. We don't want to listen because we think we know better."

"I thought I knew more about skateboarding than you do." Laney glanced at her dad's face.

"You're probably right about that," Dad chuckled. "But I wish you'd believed me when I said you needed to wear a helmet."

Laney put her hand up to her bandaged forehead. "I wish I had, too!"

"Laney, we haven't been a family for very long, but I want you to know I'll always tell you the truth. I'll tell you important things I want you to obey—to protect you. If you do what I say, you won't need another gash on your forehead to convince you I know what I'm talking about. Sound like a good plan?"

"Yeah, but you don't need to get me ice cream. I don't deserve it."

"Laney, I didn't say I'd give you ice cream if you made good choices or if you didn't cost me a lot of money or even if you obeyed. I said I'd give you ice cream because I enjoy doing things to make you happy—and that's what we're going to do. I love you no matter what you do, Laney."

"I believe you, Dad. And thanks. It's nice to be loved by someone like you."

2 Discussion Time

Check understanding of the story and development of personal values.

- When was the last time you went skate boarding or watched someone else skate?
- What tricks can you do with your skateboard?
- How did Laney feel about wearing a helmet?
- Why did Laney say her dad was a "safety nut?"
- What did Laney think her dad would do to her for not obeying?
- Did Laney think her dad would buy her ice cream after she had disobeyed him?
- What did her dad say that helped Laney believe she would get the ice cream, even though she had made a bad mistake by not wearing her helmet?

A Test-Words

Name ______

Write each spelling word on the line as your teacher says it.

1.	shove	8.	believe
2.	depend	9.	instead
3.	pleasant	10.	tied
4.	laid	11.	practice
5.	plastic	12.	couple
6.	coach	13.	lean
7.	chose	14.	notice

Review Lesson 6

B Test-Sentences

Write the sentences on the lines below, correcting each misspelled word, as well as all capitalization and punctuation errors. There are two misspelled words in each sentence.

the large frate train backed into the dirty staeshen

1. The large freight train backed into the dirty station.

I bought musterd and a pakige of hot dogs,

2. I bought mustard and a package of hot dogs.

stone steps led from the dok to the rige above?

3. Stone steps led from the dock to the ridge above.

mom made fresh pumken muffins for brekfist

4. Mom made fresh pumpkin muffins for breakfast.

35

4 Test-Sentences

Reinforce recognizing misspelled words.

Read each sentence carefully. Write the sentences on the lines in your Worktext. There are two misspelled words in each sentence. Correct each misspelled word, as well as all capitalization and punctuation errors.

Take a minute to memorize...

John 20:29

Day 1 | Review 6

3 Test-Words

Test for knowledge of the correct spellings of these words.

I will say each word once, use the word in a sentence, then say the word again. Write the words on the lines in your Worktext.

1.	**shove**	"Do you **shove** off with your left or right foot?" asked Coach Larkin.
2.	**depend**	"When we leave will **depend** on when the Wilsons plan to eat dinner," said Tony.
3.	**pleasant**	Coach Larkin sat on the front porch to enjoy the **pleasant** weather.
4.	**laid**	Laney had **laid** her helmet on the garage shelf by her bike.
5.	**plastic**	Parts of Laney's helmet are made of a tough **plastic**.
6.	**coach**	Mr. Larkin is Laney's stepfather and a **coach**.
7.	**chose**	Laney **chose** to disobey him and not wear her helmet.
8.	**believe**	She did not really **believe** that he knew what was best for her.
9.	**instead**	Laney disobeyed her dad **instead** of trusting that he knew best.
10.	**tied**	Tony **tied** his shoe laces in double knots before they began skateboarding.
11.	**practice**	Tony and Stephen **practice** lots of flatland tricks.
12.	**couple**	Mr. Wilson won more than a **couple** of awards in freestyle competitions.
13.	**lean**	"I'll just **lean** here against the car and watch you kids practice," he said.
14.	**notice**	Mr. Wilson did **notice** that Laney was not wearing her helmet.

Day 2

Review 6

1 Test-Dictation

Reinforce correct spelling by using current and previous words in context.

Listen as I read each sentence, then write it in your Worktext. Remember to use correct capitalization and punctuation. (Slowly read each sentence twice. Sentences are found in the Student Worktext at right. The words **cabbage**, **chief**, **attic**, and **oak** are found in this unit.)

2 Test-Proofreading

Familiarize students with standardized test format and reinforce recognizing misspelled words.

Look at each set of words. If a word is misspelled, fill in the oval by that word. If all the words are spelled correctly, fill in the oval by **no mistake**.

Review Lesson 6

C Test-Dictation

Name ______________________

Write each sentence as your teacher dictates. Use correct punctuation.

1. Today my grandmother will plant cabbage.
2. The fire chief came to our class.
3. We found twelve old song books in the attic.
4. Can a giraffe be taller than an oak tree?

D Test-Proofreading

If a word is misspelled, fill in the oval by that word. If all the words are spelled correctly, fill in the oval by **no mistake**.

1. ○ swept ○ done ○ depend ● no mistake
2. ● arest ○ pleasant ○ laid ○ no mistake
3. ○ plastic ○ coach ● swet ○ no mistake
4. ○ chose ○ believe ○ became ● no mistake
5. ○ instead ● leest ○ tied ○ no mistake
6. ○ practice ● mezure ○ couple ○ no mistake
7. ○ lean ○ notice ● welth ○ no mistake
8. ● jellie ○ dive ○ hollow ○ no mistake
9. ● reaply ○ dust ○ sink ○ no mistake
10. ○ blood ● ahed ○ against ○ no mistake
11. ○ supply ○ damage ● behaev ○ no mistake
12. ○ tray ● krowe ○ bandage ○ no mistake

36

E Test-Table Name ______________

If a word is misspelled, shade in that box.

past	flock	ded (shaded)	ment (shaded)			
self	hung	laed (shaded)	comfert (shaded)			
fist	nothing	leather	cuzin (shaded)	cane	cape	fale (shaded)

Review Lesson 6

F Writing Assessment

Write about what you believe heaven will be like.

____

____

____

____

____

____

____

____

Scripture

John 20:29

37

The combination "ough" can be pronounced in eight different ways. The following sentence contains them all: "A rough-coated, dough-faced ploughman strode through the streets of Scarborough, coughing and hiccoughing thoughtfully."

Test-Table

Test mastery of words in this unit.

If a word is misspelled, fill in the space on the grid.

Writing Assessment

Assess student's spelling, grammar, and composition skills through personal writing.

- How did Coach Larkin feel about Laney skateboarding with her friends? (He was happy to let her go.)
- Why did Laney's dad want her to wear a helmet? (He loved her and didn't want her to get hurt.)
- Did Laney believe her dad when he said she needed to wear a helmet? (No. She thought she only needed to wear her knee and elbow pads.)
- Jesus said, "You believe because you have seen Me. But blessed are those who haven't seen Me and believe anyway." You haven't seen Jesus, but do you believe He was raised from the dead and is coming back to take us to heaven?

1 Test-Sentences

Reinforce recognizing misspelled words.

Read each sentence carefully. Write the sentences on the lines in your Worktext, correcting each misspelled word, as well as all capitalization and punctuation errors.

G Test-Sentences

Name ____________________

Write the sentences on the lines below, correcting each misspelled word, as well as all capitalization and punctuation errors. There are two misspelled words in each sentence.

the city just bilt a new publik library,

1. The city just built a new public library.

he will colect an obgekt of interest from each site"

2. He will collect an object of interest from each site.

we swam every day this week exsept yestirday?

3. We swam every day this week except yesterday.

the tieger paced back and forth behind the irn bars

4. The tiger paced back and forth behind the iron bars.

H Test-Words

Write each spelling word on the line as your teacher says it.

1.	dive	8.	supply
2.	hollow	9.	tray
3.	dust	10.	bandage
4.	sink	11.	arrow
5.	blood	12.	trust
6.	against	13.	accept
7.	damage	14.	trouble

2 Test-Words

Test for knowledge of the correct spellings of these words.

I will say the word once, use the word in a sentence, then say the word again. Write the word on the lines in your Worktext.

1.	dive	Laney took a **dive** forward toward the hard, gray cement.
2.	hollow	Her stomach felt **hollow** and queasy after she fell.
3.	dust	Her face was covered with **dust** and gravel from the hard pavement.
4.	sink	Laney allowed her head to **sink** back against Mr. Wilson's arm.
5.	blood	A lot of **blood** ran from the gash in her forehead.
6.	against	He put pressure **against** the head wound with Tony's jacket.
7.	damage	A severe head injury can cause brain **damage**.
8.	supply	The nurse handed the doctor a syringe out of the **supply** cabinet.
9.	tray	Needle, thread, and medicines lay on a metal **tray** by the bed.
10.	bandage	The doctor put a flesh-colored **bandage** over Laney's stitches.
11.	arrow	The bright red **arrow** pointed the way to the emergency room.
12.	trust	"I know I need to **trust** you and obey your instructions," Laney said to her dad.
13.	accept	It is sometimes hard to **accept** instruction from our parents.
14.	trouble	Not obeying God and our parents can get us into a lot of **trouble**.

I Test-Editing

Name ________________

If a word is spelled correctly, fill in the oval under **Correct**. If the word is misspelled, fill in the oval under **Incorrect**, and write the word correctly on the blank.

		Correct	Incorrect	
1.	lazie	○	●	lazy
2.	branch	●	○	
3.	brand	●	○	
4.	caev	○	●	cave
5.	laonly	○	●	lonely
6.	pebel	○	●	pebble
7.	reptile	●	○	
8.	seacrit	○	●	secret
9.	touch	●	○	
10.	agrea	○	●	agree
11.	alike	●	○	
12.	pile	●	○	
13.	pien	○	●	pine
14.	roze	○	●	rose
15.	stove	●	○	

Review Lesson 6

39

3 Test-Editing

Reinforce recognizing and correcting misspelled words.

4 Action Game

Reinforce spelling skills and provide motivation and interest.

Materials

- Two sets of 26 alphabet cards—one letter on each card.
- Four cards with a picture of a vehicle

TRAFFIC JAM

How to Play:

Divide students into two teams. Give each team 26 alphabet cards and two cards with pictures of cars or trucks on them. Divide the cards evenly among the team members. Call out the first spelling word to be reviewed. The players holding the letters of the word arrange themselves to spell the word. (If a letter is used more than once, a player holding a vehicle card substitutes it for the duplicate letter.) When a team has the letters in the correct order, they yell **Traffic Jam**! Both teams freeze. Check the word. If the word is spelled correctly, then the team gets one point, and the game continues on to the next word. If the word is spelled incorrectly, the players from the other team may complete their arrangement and score a point if their word is spelled correctly. When all the words have been spelled, the team with the most points wins!

Game

Reinforce spelling skills and provide motivation and interest.

Materials

- game pages (from Student Worktext)
- stickers (13 per child)
- game word list

J Game Name ____________

Stephen, Tony, and Laney practiced several techniques on their skateboards. Two of those will be your team names for this game. Place a sticker on the game board each time you or your team spells a review word correctly.

Remember: Jesus gives a special blessing to those who trust Him "sight unseen."

Review Lesson 6

40

Game Word List

Check off each word lightly in pencil as it is used.

The Ollies	The Kickturns
1. **swept**	1. **self**
2. **arrest**	2. **fist**
3. **sweat**	3. **flock**
4. **became**	4. **hung**
5. **least**	5. **nothing**
6. **measure**	6. **dead**
7. **wealth**	7. **lead**
8. **jelly**	8. **leather**
9. **reply**	9. **meant**
10. **ahead**	10. **comfort**
11. **behave**	11. **cousin**
12. **crow**	12. **cane**
13. **past**	13. **fail**

How to Play:

- Divide students into two teams. Name one team **The Kickturns**, one **The Ollies**. (Optional: If you have an even number of students, you may wish to pair students from opposing teams and have them share a game page.)
- Read the instructions from the student game page aloud.
- Have a student from the first team choose a number from 1 to 13.
- Say the word that matches that number from the team's word list.
- Have the student write the word on the board.
- If correct, have each member of that team put a sticker on that number by his/her team name. If the word is misspelled, have him/her put an X through that number. That number may not be chosen again.
- Repeat this process with the second team.
- When the words from both lists have been used, the team with the most stickers is the winner.

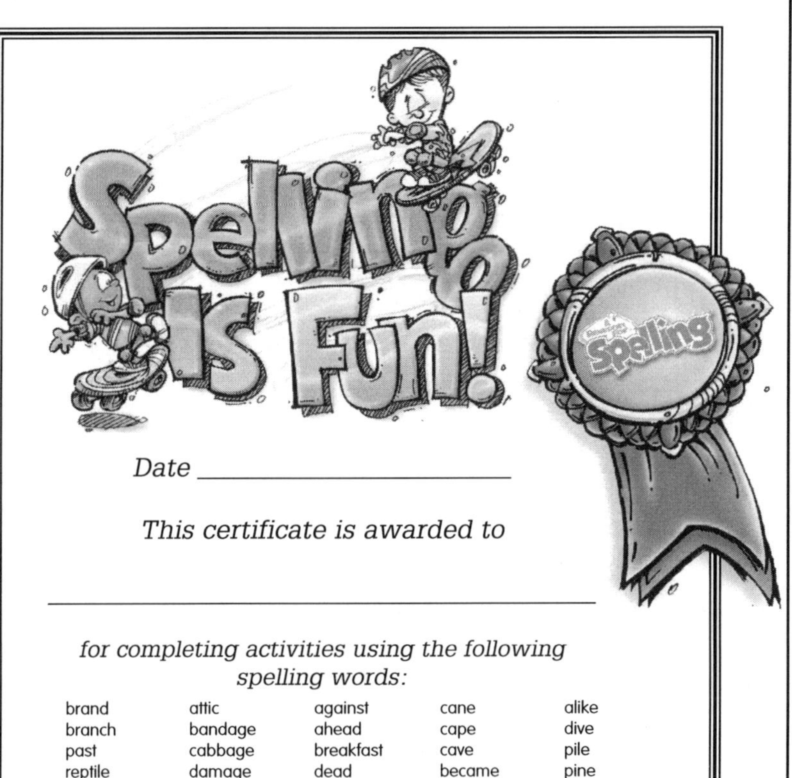

Date ______________________

This certificate is awarded to

____

for completing activities using the following spelling words:

brand	attic	against	cane	alike
branch	bandage	ahead	cape	dive
past	cabbage	breakfast	cave	pile
reptile	damage	dead	became	pine
pebble	package	yesterday	behave	iron
self	plastic	instead	fail	tiger
swept	practice	lead	laid	tied
fist	accept	leather	lazy	reply
ridge	arrest	meant	station	supply
sink	arrow	measure	tray	coach
dock	collect	pleasant	freight	oak
flock	depend	sweat	lean	chose
shove	except	wealth	least	lonely
dust	object	built	agree	rose
touch	mustard	comfort	secret	stove
hung	nothing	couple	jelly	notice
blood	public	cousin	believe	crow
trust	pumpkin	trouble	chief	hollow

2 Certificate

Provide an opportunity for parents or guardians to encourage and assess their child's progress.

Fill in today's date and your name on your certificate.

Take a minute to memorize...

John 20:29

3

Letter

Provide the parent or guardian with the spelling word lists for the next unit.

Give your parents or guardian this letter that lists your spelling words for the next unit. Put it where you will remember to practice the words together.

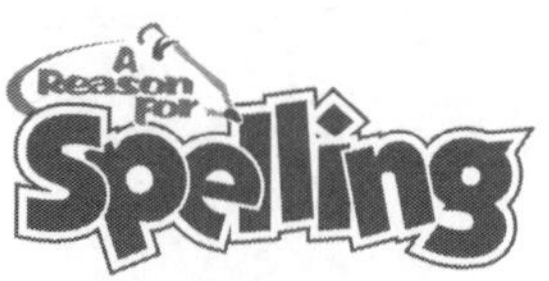

Dear Parent,

We are about to begin a new spelling unit containing five weekly lessons. A set of eighteen words will be studied each week. All the words will be reviewed in the sixth week. Values based on the Scriptures listed below will be taught in each lesson.

Lesson 7	Lesson 8	Lesson 9	Lesson 10	Lesson 11
bloom	blade	slippery	mild	climb
broom	blanket	smash	belt	bomb
roof	clear	spill	legend	comb
movie	flour	spirit	pretend	dumb
whom	flow	split	remind	limb
movement	plank	spray	understand	reign
dew	bridge	steady	among	although
flute	crack	stool	wrong	delight
pollute	cream	style	blank	ought
tune	dream	strap	apartment	thorough
avenue	drum	stretch	bent	thoughtful
clue	fry	strike	government	folks
due	grave	stroke	merchant	knife
glue	smoke	struck	moment	knob
rescue	snap	thread	forward	unknown
human	groan	thrill	guard	whose
usual	speak	throat	crust	wreath
beautiful	stew	true	frost	wren
Matthew 6:8	John 15:4	John 15:10	Luke 16:10	Luke 9:58

1 **Literature Connection**
Topic: God's Tender Care
Theme Text: Matthew 6:8

Boxes of Blessings

Setsuko notices Sarah's needs and comes up with a plan to help.

"Sarah, over here!" Setsuko waved at Sarah. "Come join me. Mrs. Burton said we could sit with a friend during lunch today."

Setsuko moved her lunch box and juice bottle to make room for Sarah's lunch on her desk. A blob of mayonnaise from her sandwich stuck on one of the puppies frolicking on her shiny new lunch box. "I like this puppy best." Setsuko rubbed the smudge of mayonnaise off the white puppy's ear as Sarah pulled her chair up. "She looks a lot like my dog, Chimi. Do you have a dog, Sarah?"

"No." Sarah put a brown paper bag on Setsuko's desk. She pointed at another puppy on Setsuko's lunch box. "I think this brown one's the cutest! He almost looks real with that ball in his mouth."

"Chimi really loves her ball!" Setsuko reached into the lunch box for her bag of chips, her cookies, and the carrot and celery sticks. "I was SO hungry after recess! It seemed to take forever for lunch time to get here." She spread everything out on her desk. "Uh, Sarah? Is that all of your lunch?"

"I've got some apple, too." Sarah reached back into the rumpled paper bag and pulled out half an apple and laid it on the desk beside two slices of bread and butter.

Sarah changed the subject when she noticed Setsuko still looking at her small lunch. "Our neighbors have a dog. I don't know what kind he is, but he's big. If he jumped up he'd be as tall as I am, but he's really gentle. I think he likes me because he comes over a lot and I play with him and pretend he's mine."

"Hey!" Setsuko set her bottle down so hard the apple juice almost splashed out. "I've got an idea. My mother has to work late at the store on Wednesday and Thursday. They're having a sale or something. Anyway, my father will be out of town and I was supposed to stay with our neighbors. But what if I could come to your house after school instead?" Setsuko bounced in her chair. "We'd have all afternoon to play and I could see your house and your neighbors' dog and everything! We could practice our parts for the program together. Wouldn't that be fun?"

"You can't come." Sarah shook her head. "It would be fun, but...you can't come to my house." She bent her head and carefully picked the tiny crumbs of bread off the napkin she'd spread on Setsuko's desk. "Momma has to work... or something." Setsuko could hardly hear the last two words Sarah mumbled.

"Okay." Setsuko crunched a carrot stick and held the bag out to Sarah. "Here, have some. I'm getting full." She shoved one of her cookies over toward Sarah. "Maybe you can come to my house next week. You've gotta meet Chimi. She can sit and lie down and stuff, but she doesn't like to stay. She whines and acts like she's miserable when you tell her to stay."

Sarah giggled. "She sounds spoiled."

"My father says she is!" Setsuko dropped a few of her chips onto Sarah's napkin. "She gets really upset when any other animal gets in her yard. One time the Wiederman's cat..."

"Where-sh the trash?!" Daniel started slowly across the room from his desk, weaving and staggering. Classmates stared as he bumped into desks, then stopped at Stephen's empty desk. "Where'd you trash the put?" He asked the empty desk as if Stephen was sitting right there. Everyone laughed.

"Hey, Daniel!" Christopher called out. "What'd you have to drink in your lunch today?"

Daniel stared at Christopher as if he couldn't understand the question. "D'you want thish trush?" He held up his empty milk carton and food wrappers.

"He's pretending to be drunk like a man I saw in a movie once." Setsuko picked up her cookie. "Can you eat this last celery stick? I'm full." Her smile disappeared when she glanced at Sarah. While the rest of the kids were laughing and joking about Daniel's performance, Sarah was staring at the floor, her face red and her lower lip trembling.

"Mrs. Burton," Thorny called from his seat by the window, "Daniel appears to be quite an accomplished actor, does he not? Perhaps he should utilize his acting abilities in our upcoming program."

Mrs. Burton smiled. "He is a good actor." She leaned against the front edge of her desk. "Let's just remember to use all our talents in good ways." Daniel grinned sheepishly and returned to his seat—without clowning around.

"About the program, Mrs. Burton," Rosa asked from her spot at Kristin's desk. "What are we supposed to wear?"

"Well, it's our first program of the year. Many community people will be there, along with all of your families. I think it would be nice for the girls to wear dresses and the boys to wear slacks. Something nice like you'd wear to church." She took her whistle out of the drawer and slipped its cord over her head. "But right now, it's time for recess."

Dresses! That evening Sarah Johansen stood in front of the closet in the room she shared with her older sister. *A nice dress! What am I going to wear?*

"Sarah!" Nellie called from the kitchen. "Since I don't know when Momma might come home, I'm going to start supper. Do you want to... Why do you have a

Story (continued)

dress on?" Nellie exclaimed as she stopped in the doorway.

Sarah flopped down on Nellie's bed. "We're supposed to wear nice dresses for our program next week."

"Well, that one won't work—it's way too small." Nellie glanced at the other clothes hanging in the closet and shook her head. "Maybe there's something that I've outgrown."

Nellie rummaged through the box in the corner of the closet. Sarah could hear her muttering, "If Momma didn't drink all the time, you could get a new dress and maybe I could take flute lessons. It sure would be nice to have food all the time, too." Nellie emerged from the closet holding a wrinkled blue dress. "Here, try this one! I always liked it."

But it was too big. Tears pricked in Sarah's eyes as she stared at the drooping sleeves. Nellie crossed her arms and tipped her head as she studied the dress hanging on her little sister. "Well," she sighed, "the program's not till next week. We'll think of something."

Across town, Setsuko perched on a tall stool, her elbows propped on the kitchen bar, her chin resting in her hands. "Setsuko, you've been sitting there quietly for almost 10 minutes!" Mrs. Noma turned from the kitchen sink and stepped over to her daughter. "Is something bothering you? Is there a problem?"

"What should you do when you think maybe someone else has a problem, but she won't tell you anything about it?" Setsuko raised troubled eyes to her mother's face.

"Well, that depends." Mother sat on the stool next to Setsuko. "Why don't you tell me who you are thinking of and what you think the problem might be?"

"It's Sarah. I think maybe her mother drinks too much. See, she never will say anything about her mother and she doesn't want anyone to come to her house and she doesn't ever have very much food or new clothes or any other new stuff and she got really upset today when Daniel acted drunk and she…"

"Just a minute, please!" Mrs. Noma touched her finger to Setsuko's lips. "Slow down a little, Suzi-Q. Now, what's this about Daniel?"

Setsuko and her mother discussed it all with Mr. Noma at the dinner table that evening. Before supper was over, they had a plan.

The program is tomorrow! Sarah stared out the window of Mrs. Bentley's car as it turned onto Piney Street. The school secretary always waited to see if the Johansen girls needed a ride home after school. *Since Momma didn't show up to get us after school today, she'll probably be out till late. What am I going to wear for that program? Dear God, please help me. I need something to wear for our program.* Sarah wound a finger through her light brown hair.

"Well, girls." Mrs. Bentley stopped in front of the little gray house. "I'll see you tomorrow."

As the car pulled away, the girls stared at their home. The grass was cut, the bushes were trimmed. The window shutter that had been swinging from one nail was straight and tight. The screen door was repaired. Two large boxes were sitting on the small front porch. The sisters looked at each other and ran up the walk.

Nellie spotted the note taped to the side of one box. "We hope you can use these things. We just wanted to share a little of what God has given us." Nellie read the note and then turned it over. That was all.

The girls tugged the boxes inside and dug into them. Food—lots of it. And clothes. Exactly the right sizes for Nellie and Sarah. Maybe not brand new, but very nice. And a lovely green dress for Sarah that fit perfectly and looked just right with her light brown hair and hazel eyes.

The next evening Sarah stood with her classmates in front of the crowded auditorium. After group songs, poems, and solos, the whole class repeated together Scriptures they'd learned. Sarah concentrated on getting the words just right. "Remember, your Father knows exactly what you need even before you ask Him!" Matthew 6:8.

God really does know and care! Sarah thought as she fingered the soft green skirt of her new dress. She stood up straighter next to Setsuko and smiled brightly at Nellie sitting by their momma in the audience. *After all, He helped someone think of giving me this dress before I even thought about asking Him for help.*

2 Discussion Time

Check understanding of the story and development of personal values.

- What did Sarah have for lunch?
- How did Sarah act when Daniel pretended to be drunk?
- What did Mrs. Burton ask the students to wear for the program?
- Why was this a problem for Sarah?
- What surprises did Sarah and Nellie find when Mrs. Bentley took them home one day?
- How did this surprise help Sarah understand what Matthew 6:8 meant when it says, "Your Father knows exactly what you need even before you ask Him?"

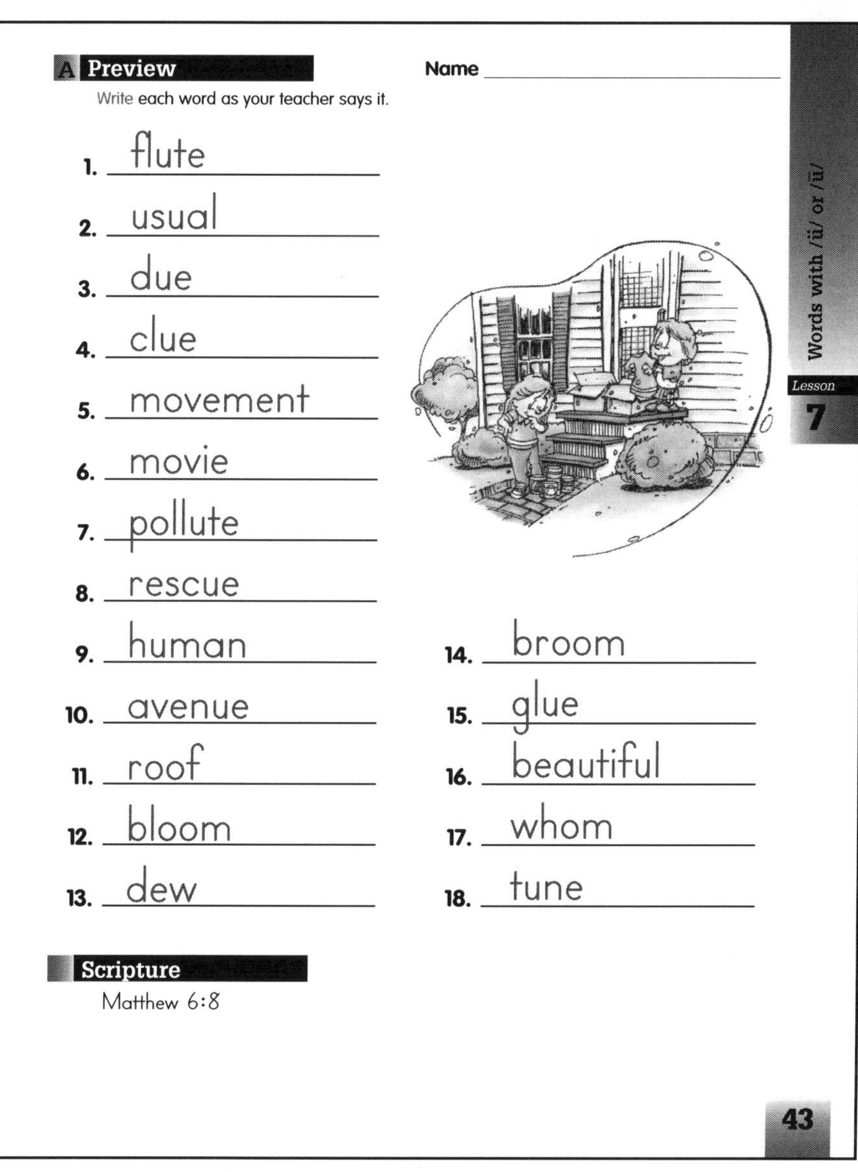

A Preview Name ______________

Write each word as your teacher says it.

1. flute
2. usual
3. due
4. clue
5. movement
6. movie
7. pollute
8. rescue
9. human
10. avenue
11. roof
12. bloom
13. dew
14. broom
15. glue
16. beautiful
17. whom
18. tune

Scripture

Matthew 6:8

Words with /ü/ or /ū/

Lesson 7

43

3 Preview

Test for knowledge of the correct spellings of these words.

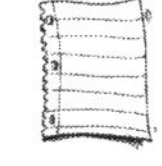

Customize Your List

On a separate sheet of paper, additional words of your choice may be tested.

I will say each word once, use the word in a sentence, then say the word again. Write the words on the lines in your Worktext.

Correct Immediately!

Let's correct our Preview. I will spell each word out loud. If you spelled a word incorrectly, rewrite it correctly.

Progress Chart

Students may record scores. (Reproducible master provided in Appendix B.)

1.	flute	"I'd like to take **flute** lessons," dreamed Nellie.
2.	usual	It was a **usual** thing for Sarah's clothes to be old and too small.
3.	due	The girls have a lot of problems **due** to their mom's alcoholism.
4.	clue	The look on Sarah's face gave Setsuko a **clue** that there was a problem.
5.	movement	The **movement** of her eyes downward showed Sarah was embarrassed.
6.	movie	Sarah does not have money to go see a **movie.**
7.	pollute	We should not **pollute** the world God created.
8.	rescue	God sent Setsuko's family to Nellie and Sarah's **rescue.**
9.	human	God wants us to show His love to other **human** beings.
10.	avenue	Mr. and Mrs. Noma drove down the **avenue** toward Piney Street.
11.	roof	Sarah's house has a gray **roof.**
12.	bloom	There was one **bloom** on a gnarled rose bush by the front door.
13.	dew	The **dew** drops looked really pretty on it.
14.	broom	Setsuko's mom took a **broom** to sweep the sidewalks.
15.	glue	Her dad used a little wood **glue** to repair the door facing.
16.	beautiful	Sarah and Nellie thought the house and yard looked almost **beautiful.**
17.	whom	The girls did not know from **whom** the groceries and clothes came.
18.	tune	Sarah hummed a **tune** as she put the groceries away.

Lesson **7** | Day 1

4 Word Shapes

Help students form a correct image of whole words.

Look at each word and think about its shape. Now, write the word in the correct Word Shape Boxes. You may check off each word as you use it.

(In most words, the sound of **/ü/** is usually spelled with the letters **oo** or **u**. However, the sound of **/ü/** can also be spelled with **o**, **ew**, **u-consonant-e**, or **ue**. The sound of **/ū/** can be spelled with **u-consonant-e**, **ue**, **ew**, or **eau**.)

In the Word Shape Boxes, fill in the boxes containing the letter or letters that spell the sound of **/ü/ or /ū/** in each word.

Take a minute to memorize...

Matthew 6:8

Words with /ü/ or /ū/ — Lesson 7

B Word Shapes

Name ____________________

Write each word in the correct Word Shape Boxes. Next, in the Word Shape Boxes, shade in the boxes containing the letter or letters that spell the sound of **/ü/** or **/ū/** in each word.

1. bloom
2. broom
3. roof
4. movie
5. whom
6. movement
7. dew
8. flute
9. pollute
10. tune
11. avenue
12. clue
13. due
14. glue
15. rescue
16. human
17. usual
18. beautiful

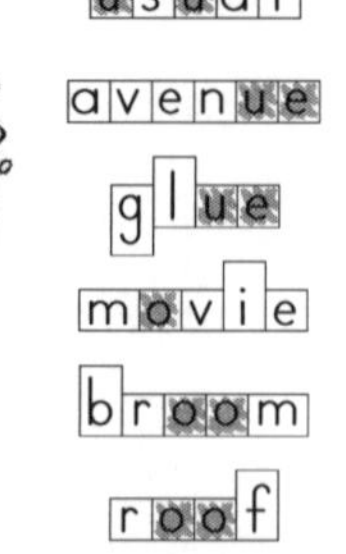

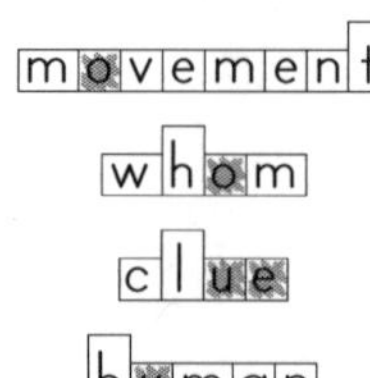

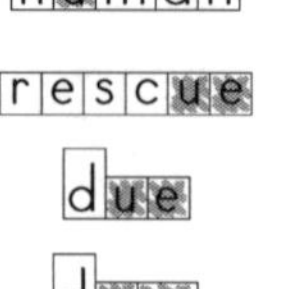

pollute
usual
avenue
glue
movie
broom
roof
beautiful
tune
bloom
flute
movement
whom
clue
human
rescue
due
dew

44

Answers may vary for duplicate word shapes.

Be Prepared For Fun

Check these supply lists for **Fun Ways to Spell** - presented **Day 2**. Purchase and/or gather these items ahead of time!

General
- Pencil
- Graph Paper (1 sheet per child)
- Spelling List

Auditory
- Voice Recorder
- Spelling List

Visual
- Water Color Paint Box (1 per child)
- Paint Brush (1 per child)
- Art Paper (3 or 4 sheets per child)
- Spelling List

Tactile
- Soccer Ball, Basketball, Tennis Ball, or 4-Square Ball
- Spelling List

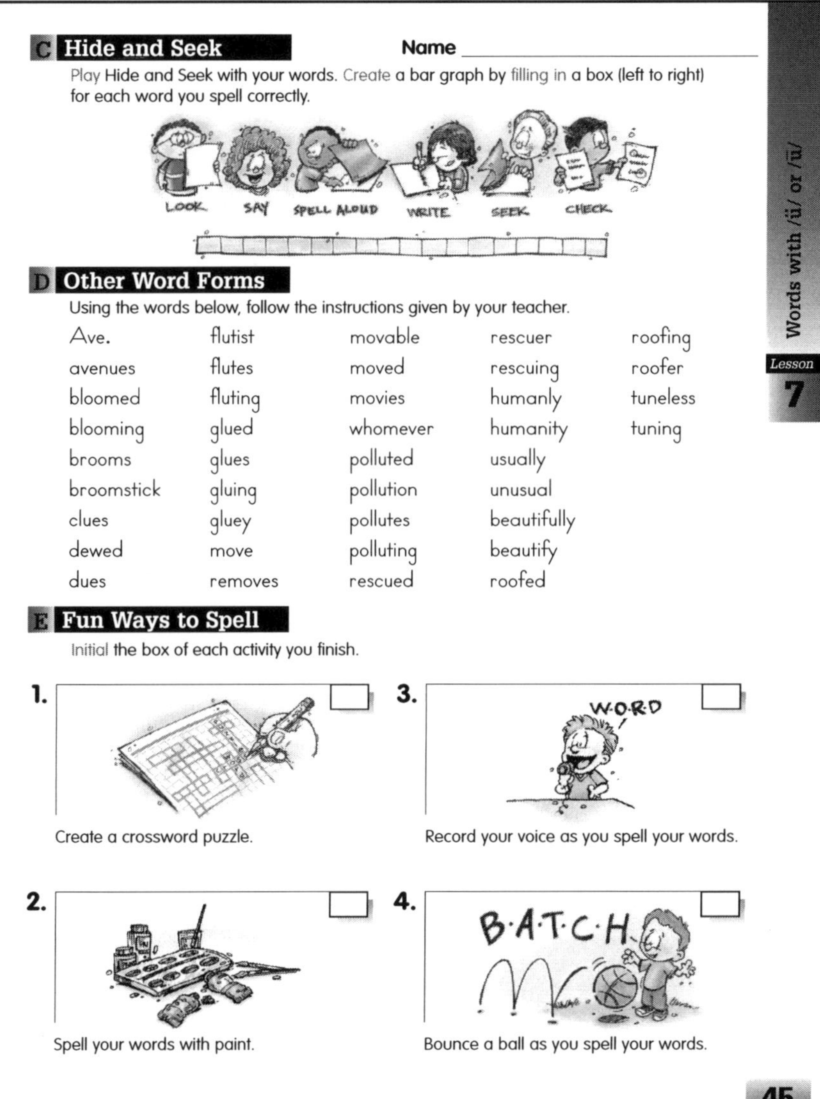

C Hide and Seek Name ____________

Play Hide and Seek with your words. Create a bar graph by filling in a box (left to right) for each word you spell correctly.

D Other Word Forms

Using the words below, follow the instructions given by your teacher.

Ave.	flutist	movable	rescuer	roofing
avenues	flutes	moved	rescuing	roofer
bloomed	fluting	movies	humanly	tuneless
blooming	glued	whomever	humanity	tuning
brooms	glues	polluted	usually	
broomstick	gluing	pollution	unusual	
clues	gluey	pollutes	beautifully	
dewed	move	polluting	beautify	
dues	removes	rescued	roofed	

E Fun Ways to Spell

Initial the box of each activity you finish.

1. Create a crossword puzzle.

3.
Record your voice as you spell your words.

2. Spell your words with paint.

4.
Bounce a ball as you spell your words.

Words with /ü/ or /ū/

Lesson 7

45

1 Hide and Seek

Reinforce spelling by using multiple styles of learning.

On a white board, Teacher writes each word — one at a time. **Have students:**

- **Look** at the word.
- **Say** the word out loud.
- **Spell** the word out loud.
- **Hide** (teacher erases word.)
- **Write** the word on paper.
- **Seek** (teacher rewrites word.)
- **Check** spelling. If incorrect, rewrite word correctly.

2 Other Word Forms

This activity is optional. Have students write original sentences using these Other Word Forms:

dues
bloomed
roofer
tuning

3 Fun Ways to Spell

Four activities are provided. Use one, two, three, or all of the activities. Have students initial the box for each activity they complete.

Options:

- assign activities to students according to their learning styles
- set up the activities in learning centers for students to do throughout the day
- divide students into four groups and assign one activity per group
- do one activity per day

General

To create a crossword puzzle…
- Use a pencil to arrange your words on graph paper.
- Overlap words where letters are shared.
- Don't create any new words.
- Outline each word with a marker and number them.
- Write a clue for each word.
- Erase your words.
- Trade with a classmate and work each other's puzzles.

Auditory

To spell your words using a voice recorder...
- Record yourself as you say and spell each word on your spelling list.
- Listen to your recording and check your spelling.

Visual

To spell your words with paint…
- Paint each spelling word on your paper.
- Trade papers with a classmate and check each other's spelling.

Tactile

To bounce a ball as you spell your words…
- Look at the first word on your list.
- Bounce the ball as you say each letter of the word aloud.
- Do this with each word on your list.

1 Working with Words

Familiarize students with word meaning and usage.

Missing Letters

The sound of /ü/ is usually spelled with the letters **oo** or **u**. However, the sound of /ü/ can also be spelled with **o, ew, u-consonant-e,** or **ue**. The sound of /ū/ can be spelled with **u-consonant-e, ue, ew**, or **eau**. Fill in the missing letter or letters that spell the sound of /ü/ or /ū/ to complete each word.

Nouns and Verbs

Write the word **dust** on the board. Read these sentences and ask students whether **dust** is being used as a noun or verb.

The car is covered with dust. (noun)

Please dust the table. (verb)

Decide whether the boldfaced word is used as a noun or verb in the sentence. Write **n** if it is a noun or **v** if it is a verb.

Take a minute to memorize...

Matthew 6:8

Words with /ü/ or /ū/ — Lesson 7

F Working with Words Name ____________

Missing Letters

Fill in the missing letter or letters that spell the sound of /ü/ or /ū/.

1. aven u e	7. b e a u tiful	13. bl o o m
2. br o o m	8. cl u e	14. d e w or ue
3. d u e or ew	9. fl u t e	15. gl u e
4. h u man	10. m o vement	16. m o vie
5. poll u t e	11. resc u e	17. r o o f
6. t u n e	12. u s u al	18. wh o m

Nouns and Verbs

A **noun** is a word that names a person, place, thing, or idea. A **verb** is a word that shows action or state of being. Decide whether the bold-faced word is used as a noun or a verb in the sentence. Write **n** if it is a **noun** or **v** if it is a **verb**.

1. v The dogwood tree will **bloom** in April.
   n There is one red **bloom** on the rose bush.
2. n We needed a new **roof** after the hail storm.
   v The men can **roof** the house in two days.
3. v Let's **clue** Dad in on the surprise for Mom.
   n The first **clue** in the treasure hunt was easy.
4. n The fourth-graders played a lovely **tune** on their flutes.
   v Please **tune** the radio in the car to my favorite station.
5. n This **glue** is sticky, but it dries fast.
   v Dad will **glue** this broken airplane back together.

Word Bank

avenue	broom	due	human	pollute	tune
beautiful	clue	flute	movement	rescue	usual
bloom	dew	glue	movie	roof	whom

46

G Dictation

Name ______________________

Write each sentence as your teacher dictates. Use correct punctuation.

1. The went down the avenue as usual.

2. She played a beautiful tune on the flute.

3. There is no clue from whom the boxes came.

Words with /ü/ or /ū/

Lesson 7

H Proofreading

If a word is misspelled, fill in the oval by that word. If all the words are spelled correctly, fill in the oval by **no mistake**.

1. ○ alike ○ dive ○ bloom ● no mistake
2. ○ pile ○ pine ○ broom ● no mistake
3. ○ iron ○ tiger ○ roof ● no mistake
4. ○ tied ○ glue ● muvie ○ no mistake
5. ● butifull ○ whom ○ reply ○ no mistake
6. ○ crow ○ hollow ● moovment ○ no mistake
7. ○ notice ○ human ● fluet ○ no mistake
8. ○ due ○ rose ● paloot ○ no mistake
9. ○ stove ● reskew ○ tune ○ no mistake
10. ○ lonely ● avinue ○ chose ○ no mistake
11. ○ coach ○ oak ● cloo ○ no mistake
12. ○ dew ○ usual ○ supply ● no mistake

47

Dictation

Reinforce correct spelling by using current and previous words in context.

Listen as I read each sentence and then write it in your Worktext. Remember to use correct capitalization and punctuation. (Slowly read each sentence twice. Sentences are found in the Student Worktext to the left.)

Proofreading

Familiarize students with standardized test format and reinforce recognition of misspelled words.

Look at each set of words. If a word is misspelled, fill in the oval by that word. If all the words are spelled correctly, fill in the oval by **no mistake**.

3 Hide and Seek

Reinforce correct spelling of current spelling words. Repeat this activity from Day 2. (A reproducible master is provided in Appendix A as shown on the inset page to the right.)

4 Other Word Forms

Have your students complete this activity to strengthen spelling ability and expand vocabulary.

1 Posttest

Visit the **A Reason For** website to download free, printable Posttest pages.

I will say the word once, use it in a sentence, then say it again. Write your words on a separate sheet of paper.

Progress Chart

Students may record scores. (Appendix B)

Personal Dictionary

Students may add any words they have misspelled to their personal dictionaries. (Appendix B)

Hide and Seek

Play Hide and Seek with your words. Create a bar graph by filling in a box (left to right) for each word you spell correctly.

LOOK SAY HIDE WRITE SEEK CHECK

Other Word Forms

Sentence Fun

Circle the word that correctly completes each sentence.

1. A piano (tuning, tuner) has come to work on our piano.
2. Have you paid the (dews, dues) to join the stamp club?
3. I carefully (gluey, glued) all the pieces, but it fell apart!
4. I like this game with all the little (moves, movable) objects.
5. Our class is going to help clean up that (pollution, polluted) river.
6. It will be fun to help (beautify, beauty) our town.
7. My dad went to help with a (roofing, roofs) project.
8. My grandmother really likes this recording of a (flutist, fluting) playing.
9. Some of the (clueing, clues) for this treasure hunt are difficult.
10. The emergency team (rescues, rescued) several people last year.
11. I love June when the roses are (bloomed, blooming).
12. We (unusual, usually) have spaghetti on Friday nights.
13. What kind of (moving, movies) do you watch at home?
14. Dad is busy (tuning, tuned) his favorite guitar.
15. My hands are all (gluing, gluey) from making a toothpick tower.
16. His sprained ankle hurt whenever he (move, moved) it.
17. The vet did all that was (humanness, humanly) possible to save the bird.
18. This car is burning oil and needs a (tune-up, tuneful).
19. That is a very (usualness, unusual) kind of plant.
20. Her address is 32261 Maple (Av., Ave.).

330

1.	clue	Sarah's meager lunch gave Setsuko a **clue** that she needed help.
2.	movement	Setsuko saw the quick **movement** of Sarah's eyes toward the floor.
3.	flute	Sarah's sister Nellie would like to take **flute** lessons.
4.	whom	"About **whom** are you thinking?" asked Setsuko's mother.
5.	due	They don't have a stable home life **due** to their mother's alcoholism.
6.	pollute	Chemicals can **pollute** the air and water around us.
7.	rescue	God often sends special people to our **rescue**.
8.	avenue	Piney Street is just off of a long wooded **avenue**.
9.	broom	Setsuko's mom used the **broom** to sweep the front walk.
10.	roof	Her dad got an old dead tree branch off the **roof**.
11.	glue	The wood **glue** held the trim on the door in place.
12.	movie	They put a funny **movie** in one of the boxes for the girls to watch.
13.	human	God's love can be shown by one **human** to another.
14.	usual	The yard was not in its **usual** unkempt state.
15.	bloom	Sarah smiled down at the pretty little **bloom** on the rose bush.
16.	dew	The next morning the **dew** sparkled on the freshly cut grass.
17.	beautiful	In the box there was a **beautiful** green dress for Sarah.
18.	tune	Sarah hummed a **tune** as she tried on the new dress.

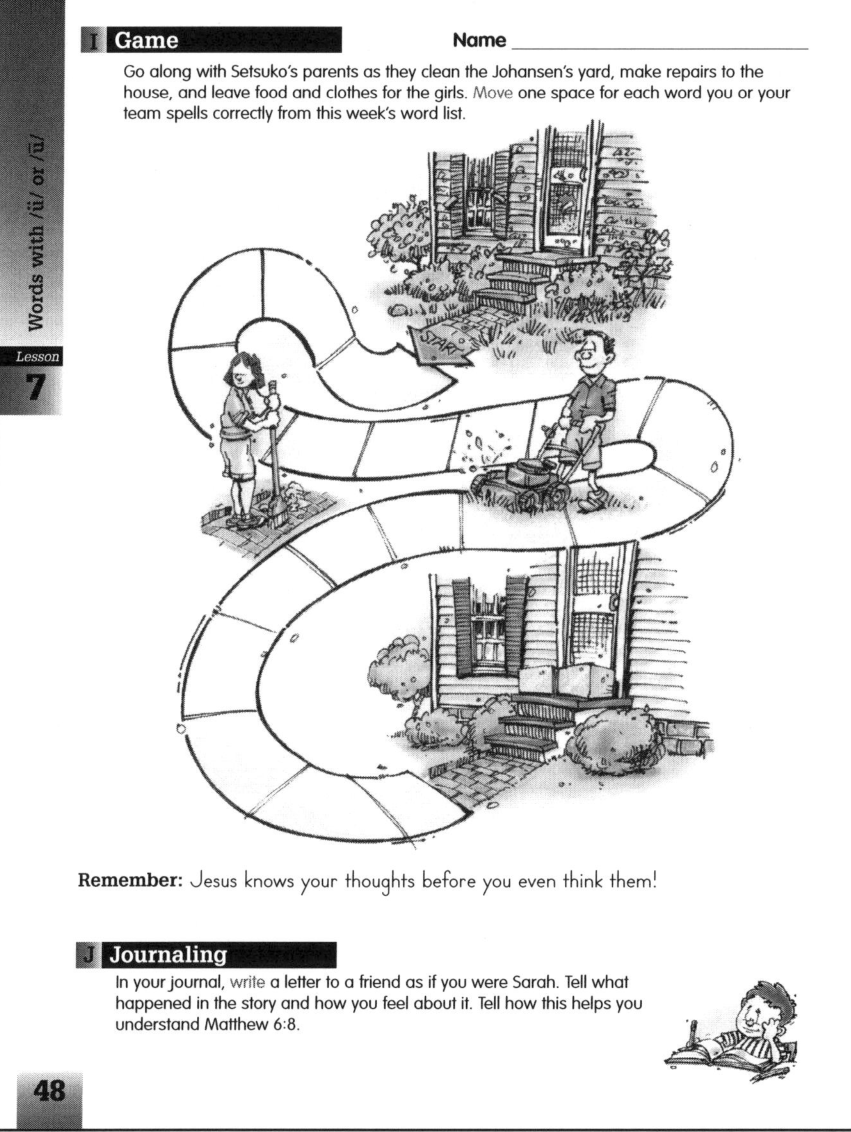

Words with /ü/ or /ū/

Lesson 7

I Game Name ____________________

Go along with Setsuko's parents as they clean the Johansen's yard, make repairs to the house, and leave food and clothes for the girls. Move one space for each word you or your team spells correctly from this week's word list.

Remember: Jesus knows your thoughts before you even think them!

J Journaling

In your journal, write a letter to a friend as if you were Sarah. Tell what happened in the story and how you feel about it. Tell how this helps you understand Matthew 6:8.

48

2 Game

Reinforce spelling skills and provide motivation and interest.

Materials

- game page (from Student Worktext)
- game pieces (1 per child)
- game word list

Game Word List

1. **bloom**
2. **broom**
3. **roof**
4. **movie**
5. **whom**
6. **movement**
7. **dew**
8. **flute**
9. **pollute**
10. **tune**
11. **avenue**
12. **clue**
13. **due**
14. **glue**
15. **rescue**
16. **human**
17. **usual**
18. **beautiful**

How to Play:

- Divide students into two teams.
- Have each student place his/her game piece on Start.
- Have a student from team A go to the board.
- Say the spelling word.
- Have the student write the word on the board.
- If correct, instruct each member of team A to move his/her game piece forward one space.
- Alternate between teams A and B as you go down the word list.
- The team to reach the Johansen's house first is the winner.

Small Group Option: Students may play this game without teacher direction in small groups of two or more.

3 Journaling

Provide a meaningful reason for correct spelling through personal writing.

Review the story using discussion leads provided on the following page. Encourage students to apply the Scriptural value in their journaling.

Journaling (continued)

- What things did Setsuko notice that made her wonder if Sarah's mother was an alcoholic? (Sarah never talks about her mother and doesn't want anyone to come to her house. She often doesn't have a lot to eat. She doesn't have many new things. Her clothes are usually old and often too small. She got very upset when Daniel pretended to be drunk.)
- Why was Sarah worried about the class program? (She didn't have a dress to wear.)
- Have you ever been somewhere and been dressed differently than everyone else was? How did you feel or how do you think you'd feel if that happened to you?
- How did Setsuko and her parents help Sarah? (They cut the grass, trimmed the bushes, and fixed the shutter and the screen on the door. They gave them lots of food and clothes.)
- Sarah realized that God really does know what we need even before we ask him. What things has God done for you without your asking? (Good parents, home, health, etc. Students may have more specific answers, as well, from their personal experiences.)

"Madam, I'm Adam" is a palindrome.

Out on a Limb

Rachel struggles with Scripture study and keeping focused.

"I give up! This is too hard to understand." Rachel closed the big black Bible and picked up her baby sister, who was crying on the floor beside her. "I can't concentrate with you screaming in my ear." She made a face at Leah.

"Life's rough, isn't it?" Rachel glared at Leah. "It's hard eating and sleeping all day. I know. I know." She laid the baby back down and just watched her scream.

Five-month-old Benjamin rolled toward Leah and bumped his head on the leg of the white crib. His eyes got big; then he started wailing with his twin.

"Great! Now you're both crying. I've had enough babysitting for a while!" Rachel stood up and put her hands on her hips. "Anything else I can do for you two while you wait for your dinner?"

"Sorry I took so long." Mom stood in the doorway with a bottle in each hand. "Would you be willing to help babysit this Saturday night? Mrs. Hill called and invited us out for dinner. Your father and I haven't gone out with friends for a long time. I'd really appreciate it if you four older girls would watch the twins for us. Would you be willing to help?"

"Do I have a choice?" Rachel frowned.

"Yes," Mom picked the fussing Leah up and offered her the warm bottle. "You can say, 'No.'"

Rachel didn't respond.

"Mrs. Hill also wanted to know if you'd like to go over to their farm tomorrow after school. They're picking apples. She thought you might have fun watching and helping some with the harvest."

"Yes!" Rachel smiled, took Benjamin's bottle, and offered it to her baby brother. "Are you hungry, Benjie? Maybe this will keep you quiet for a while."

After school the next afternoon Rachel climbed into the back seat of the Hills' pickup behind Beth. "Hi, girls," Mrs. Hill said. "You ready to pick apples?" The girls nodded. "The pickers have been working all day in the orchard. They should be done with this first picking by sundown. I've saved a tree close to the house for you to pick."

"Have you ever picked apples before, Rachie?" Beth's younger brother turned around in the front seat and looked at the two girls.

"No, there weren't any apple orchards around Dallas. And I've never had a chance since we moved up here. This should be fun!"

"Well, ya don't pick the ones that are green," seven-year-old Luke instructed.

"I think she knows that, Luke!" Beth laughed. "Nobody likes to eat green apples."

"Do you have to check every side of an apple for green before you pick it?" Rachel asked.

"No; you just lift the apple up into the palm of your hand and twist gently. It's ready for picking if it's easy to pull from the tree and the stem stays on the apple." Beth looked out the window at the passing fields. "That's what my grandpa taught me."

"What about the ones at the top of the trees?" Rachel asked.

"We use nets." Luke pointed to the bed of the pickup. "We've got some right back there."

"So, you put a net on the ground and then shake the tree to get the ripe ones to fall?" Rachel raised her eyebrows.

Luke laughed. "No one would want to eat those apples. They'd be all bruised and yucky in no time."

"The nets are on bamboo poles." Mrs. Hill turned the truck off the pavement onto their dirt driveway. "We push the frame of the net against the apple stem. If the apple is ripe, it will drop into the little net."

"Grandpa used to tell me that we should handle the apples like they're eggs. We put the apples in a crate lined with soft stuff to keep them from getting bruised." Beth smiled at her friend.

"Here we are, girls. Take those two crates in the back of the pickup and I'll bring the ladder over to the tree. Luke, you can carry the apple pickers," Mom directed.

Luke hurried ahead to the apple tree carrying the long bamboo poles with nets on their ends. "This is how you do it, Rachie." He expertly demonstrated the proper use of the apple picker and gently laid the apple he picked in the crate.

"That's neat. Can I try?" Rachel reached for another bamboo pole.

"I need to go in the house and make some phone calls before it gets too late." Mrs. Hill set the small ladder up under the tree. "Use the ladder if you need to, but don't climb around on the branches. They're heavy with fruit—they could break with your added weight. I don't want anyone to get hurt." Mrs. Hill hurried toward the house. "Don't worry about apples you can't reach," she said over her shoulder, "the pickers will get 'em! Just have a good time!"

Everyone worked silently for a while. Rachel tried to figure out how to use the apple picker. The apples didn't seem to want to drop into her net.

"I'm thirsty." Luke put an apple gently in the crate. "I'm going inside."

The two girls watched him run to the house. "He didn't last long." Beth picked a big red apple.
"Picking's not his favorite

Story (continued)

job. He likes sorting and packing apples better."

"It's not as easy as it looks," Rachel observed. "Like, I can't get this apple off. It looks ripe to me, but it just won't come off."

Beth climbed up the ladder behind Rachel. "Here, let me try. She put her foot over on a branch to steady herself. "It's being a little stubborn, isn't it. Maybe if I…"

"Beth! Don't climb out on that branch! You know what your mom said."

"I'll just stand on it long enough to pick these few apples. I'm not very heavy."

"Okay, scoot over. Let me help." Rachel stepped out on the big branch beside Beth.

CRACK! The wood splintered under the girls' weight. They held on tightly to the branch above their heads and stepped back onto the ladder. "Uh oh! Mom isn't going to be very happy."

"Can't we just put it back together? It didn't break off all the way," Rachel suggested.

"We can try, but it probably won't work—and it'll be easy to see from the driveway."

The girls picked the ripe apples off the branch and then pushed it back into place. They propped it up with a couple of sticks and stood back to survey their handiwork. Rachel tipped her head to one side. "I can hardly tell. Maybe it will grow back together."

"It does look pretty good," added Beth. "Maybe no one will ever know."

After sorting and packing their apples, the girls checked the branch. It still looked healthy. "It just might work!" Rachel said.

The next afternoon Helen called Rachel into the nursery where she was folding a pile of clean baby things. The house was unusually quiet because Rebecca had the twins out for a ride in their stroller. "Rachel, did you have a good time at the Hills' yesterday?"

"Yeah, but Luke can pick apples better than I can."

"Luke has grown up on a farm." Mrs. Jacobson folded two matching shirts and put them on the dresser. "Most things people do well take a lot of practice and work. You can't give up every time things start getting hard."

Mom worked silently for a few minutes before she said, "Did you also find out how much weight a certain branch could not hold?"

Rachel studied the pattern in the rug and felt her face getting hot. "Yeah, but we thought we'd fixed it. How'd you know?"

"Broken branches don't graft well, Rachel. Mrs. Hill said the leaves have already wilted."

"I'm sorry." Rachel looked down. "I was trying to get a stubborn apple off the tree."

Helen Jacobson picked up the big black Bible off the floor where Rachel had left it the day before. "John says, 'Take care to live in Me, and let Me live in you. For a branch can't produce fruit when severed from the vine. Nor can you be fruitful apart from Me.' What do you think that verse means, Rachel?"

"Well, I think it means branches don't grow fruit if they're broken, and we won't be fruitful away from Jesus. But what does Jesus mean when He says to 'live in Me?'"

"'Live in Me and let Me live in you.' What do you think?"

"Well, my teacher says learning what a special friend Jesus can be is the most important thing she has to teach us. She says we need to have our own quiet time, but I have a hard time reading my Bible every day. The twins are noisy and make it hard for me to think—and some of it just isn't very interesting."

Mom put the sleepers in the second drawer of the white dresser. "What happens to the branch when it's broken from the tree?"

"No more fruit." Rachel took the tiny folded socks off the bed and put them in the basket on top of the dresser.

"What will happen if you don't spend time with Jesus?" Mom slowly folded Leah's green blanket.

Rachel shrugged her shoulders and didn't say anything. Mom put an arm around her daughter. "The less time we spend with Jesus, the fewer good choices we make. I've got some books that may help you discover some interesting things in the Scriptures."

"Thanks," Rachel said softly.

"And Jesus loves to help us. Why don't we ask Him?" Rachel nodded her head and Mom gave her a squeeze. "Lord, we want You to live in our lives. Help our branches not to get broken off from You. Be with my special girl, Rachel. Amen."

"Mom?"

"Yes, Rachel."

"I'll babysit for you Saturday night."

"Thanks!" Mom smiled. "I think breaking that branch may be teaching you how to be fruitful!"

2 Discussion Time

Check understanding of the story and development of personal values.

- Why were Benjamin and Leah crying?
- How did Rachel feel about the fussy twins?
- How would you feel if you were asked to help take care of a brother or sister?
- How did Rachel feel about reading her Bible?
- What did Rachel decide to do about helping her parents with the twins?
- What do you think Rachel could do about concentrating during her quiet time?
- What have you enjoyed for your quiet time?

A Preview Name ____________

Write each word as your teacher says it.

1. groan
2. snap
3. bridge
4. flow
5. cream
6. flour
7. fry
8. clear
9. blade
10. plank
11. smoke
12. crack
13. speak
14. dream
15. drum
16. stew
17. blanket
18. grave

Scripture

John 15:4

Words with Consonant Clusters

Lesson 8

49

3 Preview

Test for knowledge of the correct spellings of these words.

Customize Your List

On a separate sheet of paper, additional words of your choice may be tested.

I will say each word once, use the word in a sentence, then say the word again. Write the words on the lines in your Worktext.

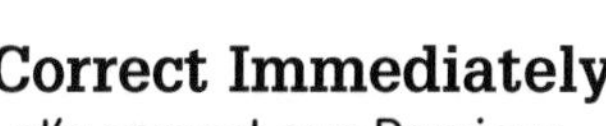

Correct Immediately!

Let's correct our Preview. I will spell each word out loud. If you spelled a word incorrectly, rewrite it correctly.

Progress Chart

Students may record scores. (Reproducible master provided in Appendix B.)

1.	groan	Beth let out a **groan** as she closed her Bible to pick up Leah.
2.	snap	She felt like her nerves would **snap** when Benjamin rolled over and hit his head.
3.	bridge	They crossed a short **bridge** before Mrs. Hill turned down their road.
4.	flow	"I never saw a creek **flow** so swiftly," said Rachel.
5.	cream	"You can save the **cream** of the crop for yourselves," said Mrs. Hill.
6.	flour	"I have the **flour** and other stuff to make pie crusts," she continued.
7.	fry	"We can **fry** some apple rings in butter," said Beth with a smile.
8.	clear	The sky above the orchard was a beautiful **clear** blue.
9.	blade	Luke chewed on a long **blade** of grass.
10.	plank	The kids set the crates on a long **plank** to keep the bottoms dry.
11.	smoke	The kids could see **smoke** rising from the chimney of the house.
12.	crack	The limb began to **crack** and splinter under the girls' weight.
13.	speak	Beth was the first to **speak.**
14.	dream	"I didn't **dream** it would break that easily!" she said.
15.	drum	Rachel's heart beat hard and loud like a **drum.**
16.	stew	She tried not to let herself **stew** over the broken branch.
17.	blanket	Mrs. Jacobson folded Leah's green **blanket.**
18.	grave	She looked **grave** as she asked Beth about the branch.

4 Word Shapes

Help students form a correct image of whole words.

Look at each word and think about its shape. Now, write the word in the correct Word Shape Boxes. You may check off each word as you use it.

(Initial clusters are practiced in this lesson. Unlike a digraph, in which two letters combine to form a single sound, the letters that make up a consonant cluster keep their sounds when pronounced in words. These clusters are often found at the beginning of words.)

In the Word Shape Boxes, fill in the boxes containing the letters that spell the initial consonant cluster in each word.

Take a minute to memorize...

John 15:4

B Word Shapes Name ______________________

Write each word in the correct Word Shape Boxes. Next, in the Word Shape Boxes, shade in the boxes containing the letters that spell the initial consonant cluster in each word.

1. blade
2. blanket
3. clear
4. flour
5. flow
6. plank
7. bridge
8. crack
9. cream
10. dream
11. drum
12. fry
13. grave
14. smoke
15. snap
16. groan
17. speak
18. stew

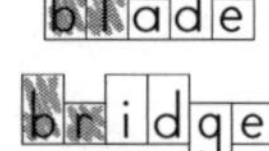

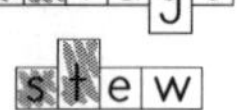

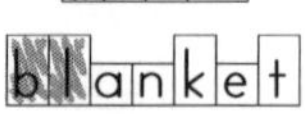

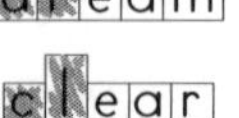

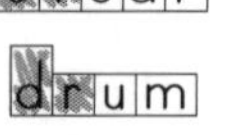

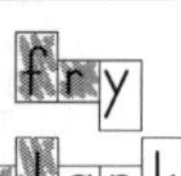

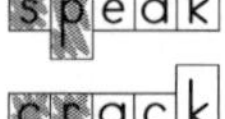

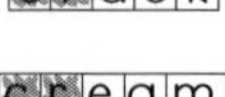

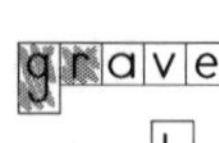

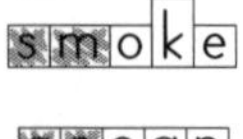

snap, flour, flow, blade, bridge, stew, blanket, dream, clear, drum, fry, plank, speak, crack, cream, grave, smoke, groan

Answers may vary for duplicate word shapes.

Be Prepared For Fun

Check these supply lists for **Fun Ways to Spell** - presented **Day 2**. Purchase and/or gather these items ahead of time!

General
- Pencil
- Notebook Paper
- Spelling List

Auditory
- Spelling List

Visual
- Pencil
- Paper
- Spelling List

Tactile
- Thick Pile Carpet Samples
- Spelling List

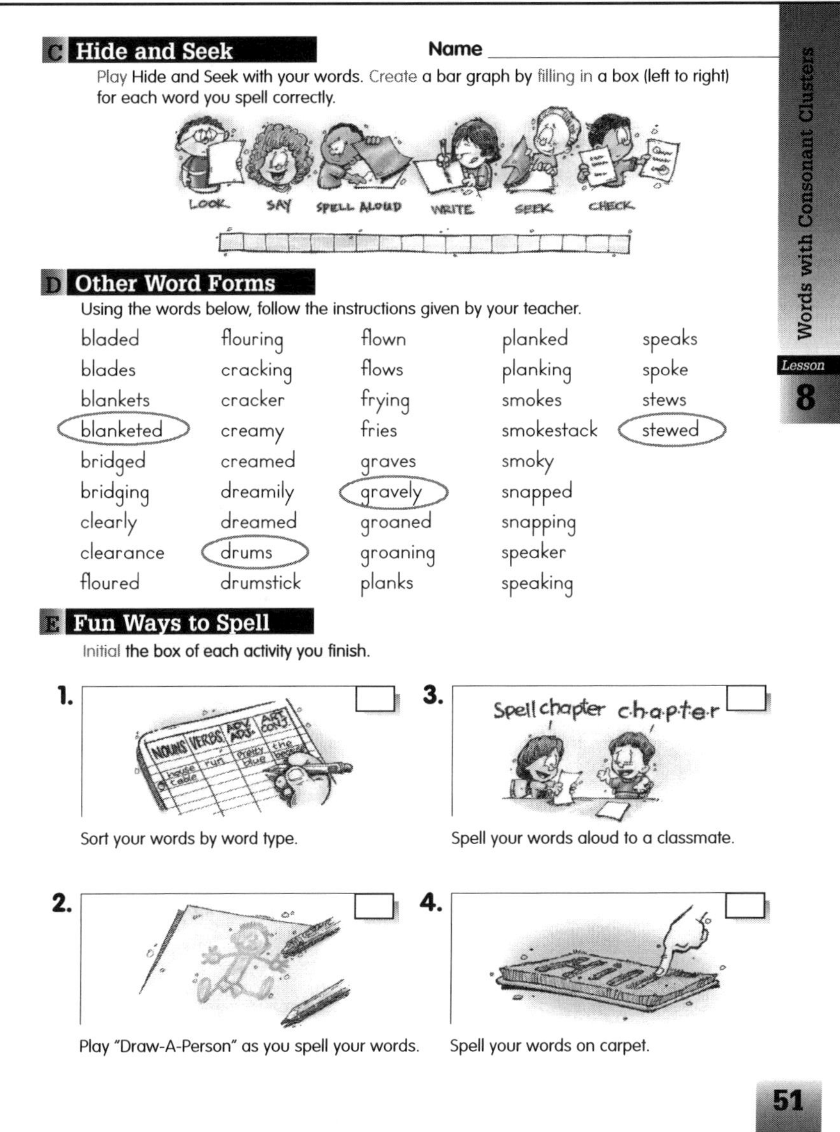

C Hide and Seek

Name ______________________

Play Hide and Seek with your words. Create a bar graph by filling in a box (left to right) for each word you spell correctly.

D Other Word Forms

Using the words below, follow the instructions given by your teacher.

bladed	flouring	flown	planked	speaks
blades	cracking	flows	planking	spoke
blankets	cracker	frying	smokes	stews
blanketed	creamy	fries	smokestack	stewed
bridged	creamed	graves	smoky	
bridging	dreamily	gravely	snapped	
clearly	dreamed	groaned	snapping	
clearance	drums	groaning	speaker	
floured	drumstick	planks	speaking	

E Fun Ways to Spell

Initial the box of each activity you finish.

1. Sort your words by word type.

2. Play "Draw-A-Person" as you spell your words.

3. Spell your words aloud to a classmate.

4. Spell your words on carpet.

Words with Consonant Clusters

Lesson 8

51

1 Hide and Seek

Reinforce spelling by using multiple styles of learning.

On a white board, Teacher writes each word — one at a time. **Have students:**

- **Look** at the word.
- **Say** the word out loud.
- **Spell** the word out loud.
- **Hide** (teacher erases word.)
- **Write** the word on paper.
- **Seek** (teacher rewrites word.)
- **Check** spelling. If incorrect, rewrite word correctly.

2 Other Word Forms

This activity is optional. Have students find and circle the Other Word Forms that are synonyms of the following:

seethed
solemnly
covered
percussion

3 Fun Ways to Spell

Four activities are provided. Use one, two, three, or all of the activities. Have students initial the box for each activity they complete.

Options:

- assign activities to students according to their learning styles
- set up the activities in learning centers for students to do throughout the day
- divide students into four groups and assign one activity per group
- do one activity per day

General

To sort your words by word type...

- Make four columns on your paper.
- Label the columns: Nouns, Verbs, Adjectives/Adverbs, and Articles/Conjunctions.
- Write each of your spelling words in the appropriate column.

Auditory

To spell your words aloud to a classmate...

- Ask a classmate to read a word from your spelling list.
- Spell the word aloud to your classmate.
- Ask your classmate to check your spelling.
- Read a word to your classmate and continue taking turns.
- The person to spell the most words right wins!

Visual

To play "Draw-A-Person" when you spell your words...

- Ask a classmate to read a word from your spelling list to you.
- Write the word on your paper. Check your spelling.
- If you misspell the word, draw one part of a person on your paper.
- Read a word to a classmate and continue taking turns.
- The last one to finish drawing a person wins!

Tactile

To spell your words on carpet...

- Use fingertip to write a spelling word on carpet.
- Check your spelling.
- Smooth the word out with your hand and write another word.

Working with Words

Familiarize students with word meaning and usage.

Alphabetical Order

Write the words **east**, **easy**, **Easter**, and **easel** on the board. Remind the students that when words begin with the same letter, they need to look at the second letter to put the words in alphabetical order. If the first two letters are the same, look at the third letter, fourth letter, and so on. Guide the students in putting these four words in alphabetical order.

Look at each set of words. Write them in alphabetical order on the lines.

Dictionary Skills

Explain that some entry words in a dictionary have more than one meaning, or definition.

Read the definitions for each word. Write the word that matches both meanings.

Take a minute to memorize...

John 15:4

Words with Consonant Clusters — Lesson 8

F Working with Words Name ____________________

Alphabetical Order

Dictionary words are listed in **alphabetical order**. Words beginning with **a** come first, then words beginning with **b**, and so on. It is simple to find a word in the dictionary if you know about **alphabetical order.** Remember, when words begin with the same letter, look at the second letter. If the first two letters are the same, look at the third letter.
Write the words in each group in alphabetical order.

1. dream cream crack drum
   crack cream dream drum
2. flow flour clear blade
   blade clear flour flow
3. bridge blanket plank snap smoke
   blanket bridge plank smoke snap
4. speak fry stew groan grave
   fry grave groan speak stew

Dictionary Skills

Some dictionary entries have more than one meaning or definition. Read the definitions. Write the word that matches both meanings.

1. The cutting part on a knife.
   A single piece of grass. blade
2. To say that someone is not guilty of a crime.
   To move things that are blocking a space. clear
3. A place of burial.
   To be dignified and solemn. grave
4. To boil slowly.
   To be in a state of agitation and worry. stew

Word Bank

flow	smoke	bridge	dream	fry	snap
blanket	flour	crack	blade	cream	groan
clear	plank	stew	drum	grave	speak

52

G Dictation

Name ______________________

Write each sentence as your teacher dictates. Use correct punctuation.

1. She finished her stew, then cleared the table.
2. The girls gave a groan as they saw the branch crack.
3. Did you walk over the plank bridge?

H Proofreading

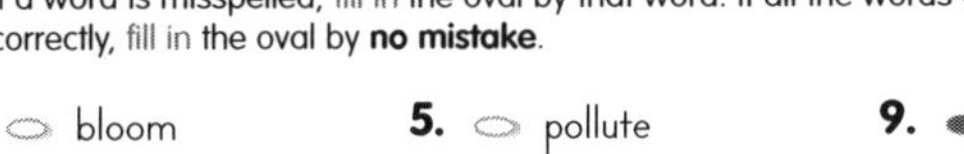

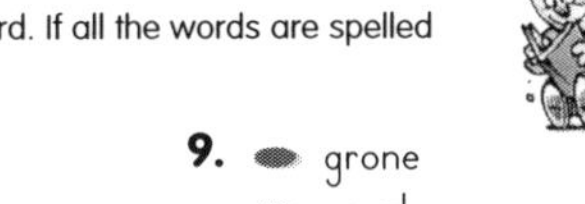

If a word is misspelled, fill in the oval by that word. If all the words are spelled correctly, fill in the oval by **no mistake**.

1.	5.	9.
○ bloom	○ pollute	● grone
○ broom	○ tune	○ usual
○ blade	○ flow	○ cream
● no mistake	● no mistake	○ no mistake

2.	6.	10.
● blankit	○ avenue	○ smoke
○ roof	○ clue	○ snap
○ movie	○ plank	● dreem
○ no mistake	● no mistake	○ no mistake

3.	7.	11.
○ whom	○ due	○ beautiful
○ movement	○ glue	● speek
● cleer	● brige	○ drum
○ no mistake	○ no mistake	○ no mistake

4.	8.	12.
○ dew	● stue	○ human
● flowr	○ rescue	● graev
○ flute	○ crack	○ fry
○ no mistake	○ no mistake	○ no mistake

Words with Consonant Clusters

Lesson 8

53

1 Dictation

Reinforce correct spelling by using current and previous words in context.

Listen as I read each sentence and then write it in your Worktext. Remember to use correct capitalization and punctuation. (Slowly read each sentence twice. Sentences are found in the Student Worktext to the left.)

2 Proofreading

Familiarize students with standardized test format and reinforce recognition of misspelled words.

Look at each set of words. If a word is misspelled, fill in the oval by that word. If all the words are spelled correctly, fill in the oval by **no mistake**.

3 Hide and Seek

Reinforce correct spelling of current spelling words. Repeat this activity from Day 2. (A reproducible master is provided in Appendix A as shown on the inset page to the right.)

4 Other Word Forms

Have your students complete this activity to strengthen spelling ability and expand vocabulary.

1 Posttest

Visit the **A Reason For** website to download free, printable Posttest pages.

I will say the word once, use it in a sentence, then say it again. Write your words on a separate sheet of paper.

Progress Chart

Students may record scores. (Appendix B)

Personal Dictionary

Students may add any words they have misspelled to their personal dictionaries. (Appendix B)

Hide and Seek

Play Hide and Seek with your words. Create a bar graph by filling in a box (left to right) for each word you spell correctly.

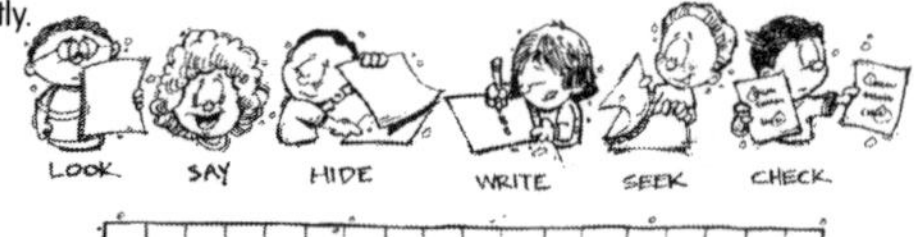

Other Word Forms

Suffixes

Add each suffix to the word in each row to make a new word. Remember, normally when a one-syllable word ends in one vowel followed by one consonant, double the consonant before adding an ending that begins with a vowel.

	+ ed	+ ing	+ s
1. snap	snapped	snapping	snaps
2. blanket	blanketed	blanketing	blankets
3. cream	creamed	creaming	creams
4. flour	floured	flouring	flours
5. dream	dreamed	dreaming	dreams
6. drum	drummed	drumming	drums
7. bridge	bridged	bridging	bridges
8. clear	cleared	clearing	clears
9. crack	cracked	cracking	cracks
10. groan	groaned	groaning	groans
11. smoke	smoked	smoking	smokes
12. plank	planked	planking	planks

When words have the consonant-vowel-consonant-**e** pattern, drop the **e** when adding an ending that begins with a vowel. Add the suffix to make a new word. Write it on the line.

1. smoky − y + i + er = smokier
2. snappy − y + i + ly = snappily
3. grave − e + en = graven
4. clear + ness = clearness
5. bridge + able = bridgeable
6. crack + er = cracker

331

---

1. groan	Beth let out a **groan** as Leah and Benjamin wailed loudly.
2. blanket	Benjamin rolled off his **blanket** and against the leg of the crib.
3. dream	"I feel like I'm in the middle of a bad **dream**," complained Beth.
4. clear	"Maybe some time at the orchard will **clear** your head," suggested Helen.
5. bridge	The **bridge** was just a few yards before the road that leads to Beth's house.
6. flow	The girls saw the water **flow** under the bridge.
7. stew	"I'll have a big pot of **stew** ready for your supper," said Mrs. Hill.
8. flour	"I bought some **flour** to make pie crusts, too," she said with a grin.
9. fry	"We can **fry** apple rings in butter for our dessert," offered Beth.
10. cream	"They taste great with hot cocoa and whipped **cream**!" said Luke.
11. blade	Luke spit out the **blade** of grass and reached for a net.
12. smoke	The **smoke** curled up from the chimney of Beth and Luke's house.
13. grave	Rachel knew that **grave** consequences often come from disobeying.
14. crack	She and Beth heard the limb **crack**.
15. snap	The girls stepped back onto the ladder as they felt the branch **snap**.
16. drum	Beth felt her heart pounding like a **drum**.
17. plank	The girls stood on the **plank** as they propped up the broken branch.
18. speak	Beth did not **speak** when Helen mentioned the branch.

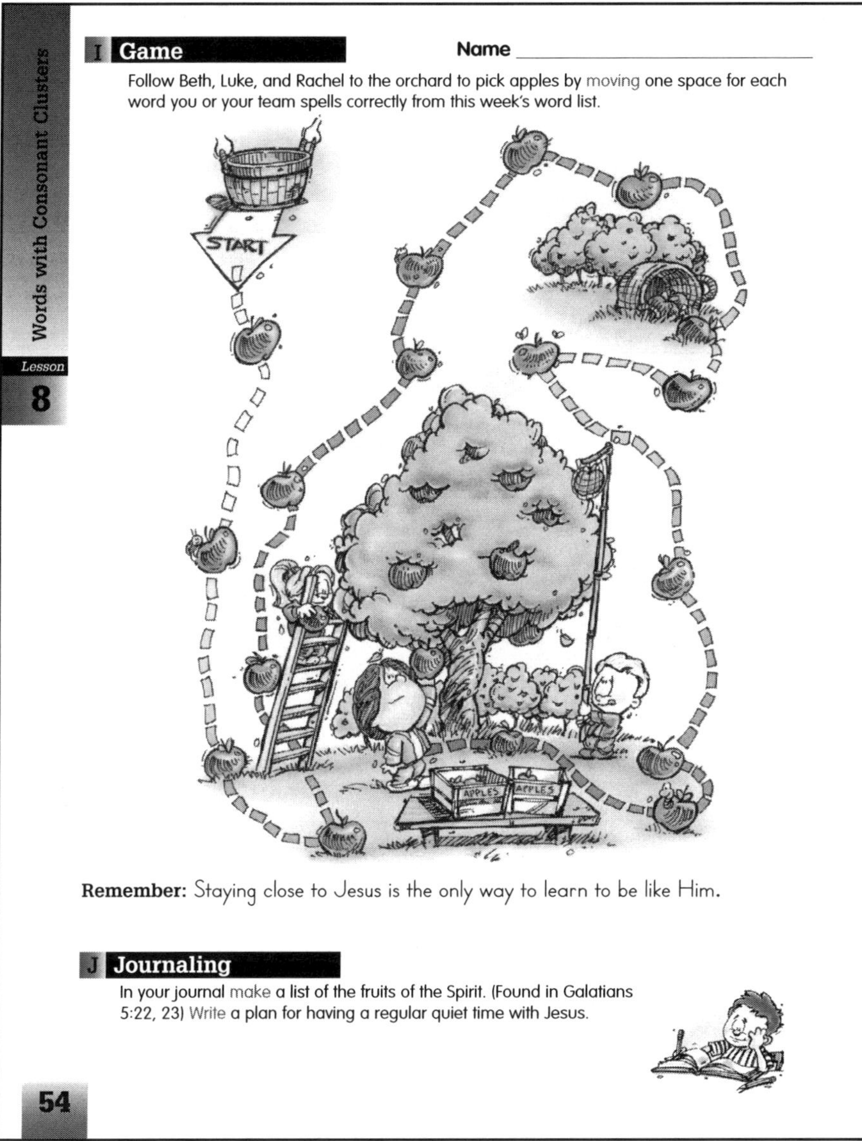

Words with Consonant Clusters

Lesson 8

I Game

Name ______________________

Follow Beth, Luke, and Rachel to the orchard to pick apples by moving one space for each word you or your team spells correctly from this week's word list.

Remember: Staying close to Jesus is the only way to learn to be like Him.

J Journaling

In your journal make a list of the fruits of the Spirit. (Found in Galatians 5:22, 23) Write a plan for having a regular quiet time with Jesus.

54

How to Play:

- Divide students into two teams.
- Have each student place his/her game piece on Start.
- Have a student from team A go to the board.
- Say the spelling word.
- Have the student write the word on the board.
- If correct, instruct each member of team A to move his/her game piece forward one space.
- Alternate between teams A and B as you go down the word list.
- The team to reach the apple tree first is the winner.

Small Group Option: Students may play this game without teacher direction in small groups of two or more.

2 Game

Reinforce spelling skills and provide motivation and interest.

Materials

- game page (from Student Worktext)
- game pieces (1 per child)
- game word list

Game Word List

1. **blade**
2. **blanket**
3. **clear**
4. **flour**
5. **flow**
6. **plank**
7. **bridge**
8. **crack**
9. **cream**
10. **dream**
11. **drum**
12. **fry**
13. **grave**
14. **smoke**
15. **snap**
16. **groan**
17. **speak**
18. **stew**

3 Journaling

Provide a meaningful reason for correct spelling through personal writing.

Review the story using discussion leads provided on the following page. Encourage students to apply the Scriptural value in their journaling.

Journaling (continued)

- What did Rachel's mom want her to do on Saturday night? (Babysit the twins.)
- Why did Rachel not feel like babysitting the twins? (She was tired of listening to them both scream. She couldn't concentrate on what she was reading.)
- What happened to Rachel at Beth's house that helped her understand branches and being fruitful? (The girls broke a branch and all the leaves were wilted by the next afternoon.)
- Jesus says we can't be fruitful apart from Him. What does He mean? (When we don't spend time with Jesus we make more bad choices.)
- What are the fruits of the Spirit? (Galatians 5:22, 23 says, "The fruit of the Spirit is love, joy, peace, patience, kindness, goodness, faithfulness, gentleness, and self control.")

The word "girl" appears only once in the King James version of the Bible.

Word Wow!

1 **Literature Connection**
Topic: Obedience
Theme Text: John 15:10

The Computer Crash

Rosa learns that Dad's rules are based on what's best for her.

"Rosa! Rosa!" Maria called from the back door. "Come here! A package came in the mail for you!"

"I'm coming!" Rosa jumped down from her special place in the barn and ran toward the house. "What—pff pff—is it?" She panted as she got close to Maria. "Pff—who's it from? Pff, pff."

"It's from Uncle Mario and Aunt Mimi." Eleven-year-old Maria grabbed Rosa's arm and dragged her into the house. "I bet it's a late birthday present. C'mon!"

A brown package sat on the kitchen table. "Open it!" Carlos picked up the package and shook it near his ear.

"Give me a chance!" Rosa grabbed her package and tugged at the packing tape.

"Maybe this would help." Dad held out his pocket knife. "But be careful, no telling what Uncle Mario might have wrapped up."

"Yeah!" Carlos snapped his fingers. "Maybe it's a New Mexico rattlesnake!"

"I bet it's some new books." Maria sat in one of the kitchen chairs. "It's a pretty heavy package and Rosa loves to read."

Rosa cut the last bit of tape and reached into the box. "It's a..." She pulled out a black plastic cylinder several inches long. "What is it, Dad?"

"Let's see." Mr. Vasquez reached for papers that came with the strange object. "This says it's a computer for your bike, Rosita. It'll tell you how fast you're going and how far you've gone on each trip. It's got a horn that you can set to sound four different ways. And it has an alarm you can set when you stop. Then, if anyone tries to move the bike without putting in the correct code, it'll make a loud noise and say 'STOLEN BIKE.'"

"Cool!" Carlos picked up the shiny bike computer. "I could use this on my bike, Rosa."

"No, you can't." Rosa took the computer and handed it to her dad. "It's mine! Can you put it on my bike right now, Dad?"

"Sure." Mr. Vasquez glanced at the instruction sheet again. "We just need a Phillips screw driver and pliers."

Soon Dad tightened the last screw and checked that all the buttons worked properly. "You're all set, Rosita." Dad picked up his tools and stood. "Be sure you put your bike away in the garage when you're done riding it—and have fun!" He waved as Rosa sped down the driveway with Maria and Carlos in hot pursuit on their bikes.

They raced, and Rosa let Maria and Carlos take turns on her bike to see how fast they could go. They laughed when Rosa forgot the code and the computer started shrieking, "STOLEN BIKE! STOLEN BIKE!" They clocked the distance from the big tree to the wild rose bush and how far it was to the Andersons' house. They showed their "adopted" grandparents all the things Rosa's bike computer could do. Even after Carlos and Maria got tired and went inside, Rosa rode up and down the road until it was almost too dark to see and Dad called her inside.

After supper, Rosa sat at her desk and started a thank-you note. "Dear Uncle Mario and Aunt Mimi, I think the bike computer you sent me for my tenth birthday is one of the best presents I've ever gotten. Thank you! Thank you! Thank you! I can go 15 miles an hour..."

"Rosa." Dad stood in the doorway. "Did you put your bike away when you came in this evening?"

"I meant, uh, I was going to. Um, I...I was..." Rosa twisted her pen in her fingers. "No," she finally answered.

Oh, no! What's Dad going to do? He looks pretty upset. But I was going to put it away. It's just that I had to go feed the dogs and then I forgot. It's really no big deal, Rosa thought.

"Rosa, I ask you to do certain things because I love you and want what's best for you." Mr. Vasquez came into the room and sat on the corner of Rosa's bed. "It's important for you to obey. Because you disobeyed by leaving your bike on the driveway, you won't be able to ride it for a week. Do you understand?"

Rosa nodded and stared at a white thread on the carpet. Dad sat still for a minute, then sighed. As he walked toward the door Rosa muttered, "I don't see why putting my bike away is so important."

Dad turned and rested a hand against the door jamb. "It's important to learn to put things away where they belong. If I hadn't noticed your bike on the driveway tonight, I might have hit it when I backed out in the morning." He glanced at the clock on the wall. "It's getting late. Please go put your bike away and then get ready for bed."

Finally Rosa got to ride her bike again. She glided down the road enjoying the wind through her hair. *If I pedal really fast down this little hill I bet I can go faster than I've gone before.* Rosa pedaled furiously and checked her speed on the gentle slope. *Yes! That's my fastest speed yet! I might even be faster if I'd been able to ride all this time. Wouldn't you know, the weather was perfect for bike riding when my dad wouldn't let me ride! Then, when I can ride again, it gets all rainy and yucky 'til today.*

Rosa beeped her horn. *I wonder how far it is from here to the Andersons' mailbox?* She pushed a button on the bike computer and pedaled off to find out. When she

Story (continued)

turned around at the mailbox, she spotted a familiar green vehicle parked in the driveway of her own house. *Hey, that's the Wrights' car! I wonder if Kristin's here?* In minutes, Rosa was home and rushing into the house.

"Rosa!" Kristin was in the living room trying to play with Nipper, the feisty red squirrel. "Dad said I could come with him when he brought some papers and stuff over to your dad." Kristin put her hand over her pocket. "Where's Chipper? I brought pecans, and Nipper's trying to get all of them for herself."

Rosa grabbed the greedy squirrel. "Come on. He's probably asleep in one of the bedrooms." He was curled up in one of his favorite places, among the stuffed animals in Maria's room. He woke up when Kristin offered him pecans. Nipper tried to steal them, so the girls shut her out in the hall and dressed Chipper in doll clothes.

"Kristin! Time to go!" Mr. Wright called.

"See you later, Rosa." Kristin followed her dad to the door.

"Yeah, bye!" Rosa waved from the front door as Kristin and her dad climbed into their car. "See you tomorrow!"

SCRUNCH! Mr. Wright stopped the car and jumped out. Mr. Vasquez rushed past Rosa to see what had happened. Rosa followed him and stopped short when she reached the back of the car. Her bike! Rosa stared, her hand clamped over her mouth.

"I'm so sorry, Rafael." Mr. Wright ran his hands through his hair. "I just didn't see it there. I'm sorry."

"No need to apologize." Mr. Vasquez knelt and looked at the back of the Wrights' car. "I'm afraid there are a few scratches on your car here, just above the bumper." He stood and pulled the wrecked bike out of the way. "Let me know how much it costs to fix them and anything else that was damaged. It wasn't your fault. The bike shouldn't have been left right behind your car like that."

Rosa stood like a statue until the Wrights' car drove away. Then she slowly walked over to what remained of her bike. The front wheel was bent in half. The shiny red body was twisted out of shape. Pieces of the new bike computer were scattered across the driveway. Rosa didn't realize she was crying until Dad gathered her into a gentle hug. He rubbed her back as she gulped and cried harder.

"I'm s-s-s-sorry." Rosa hung her head after the worst of the crying was over. Dad continued to hold her gently and silently. "I shouldn't have left my bike there. If I'd put it away when I was done riding like you said, then it wouldn't be ruined. And Mr. Wright's car wouldn't be messed up." Rosa sniffed and cried. "I didn't think it mattered, but it did." She peeked up into her father's face. "Aren't you mad?"

"No, Rosita. I'm not mad." Mr. Vasquez wiped the tears off Rosa's cheeks with his thumb. "I'm just sad. Sad that you learned this lesson the hard way."

Dad gave Rosa a big squeeze. "You see, Rosita, that's what John 15:10 is all about. It says, 'When you obey Me you are living in My love, just as I obey My Father and live in His love.'"

Dad squatted down and picked up a piece of black plastic that used to be part of Rosa's "cool" bike computer. "I ask you to obey me because I love you and want what's best for you." He held up the chip of plastic. "God asks us to obey Him because He loves us and knows what's best for us." Dad looked into Rosa's face. "We need to learn to obey, even in things that don't seem that important to us. Obedience to God gives us the best possible life on this earth."

Dad handed the piece of plastic to Rosa. "Run get a trash bag, and we'll clean up this mess together."

"Okay, Dad." Rosa managed a small smile. "And, Dad? Thanks!" He winked, and she started off for the trash bag with a lighter heart. *I think it'll be a long, long time before I forget this lesson about obeying, the lesson I learned the hard way.*

2 Discussion Time

Check understanding of the story and development of personal values.

- What did Rosa's uncle and aunt send her for her birthday?
- What kind of things could the bike computer do?
- What did Rosa's dad remind her to do when she was done riding her bike?
- Why wasn't Rosa allowed to ride her bike for a week?
- Where did Rosa leave her bike when Kristin came over with her dad?
- What happened to the bike?
- Why does God ask us to obey Him?

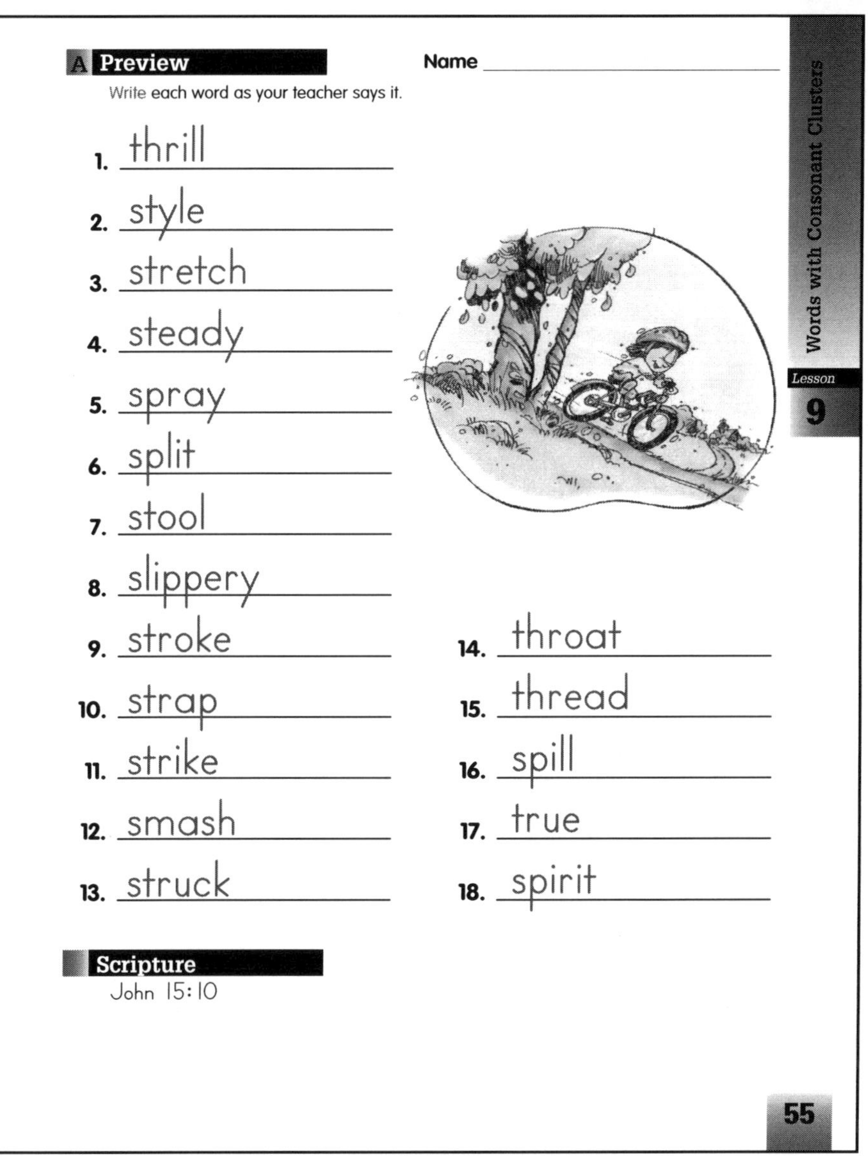

A Preview Name ____________

Write each word as your teacher says it.

1. thrill
2. style
3. stretch
4. steady
5. spray
6. split
7. stool
8. slippery
9. stroke
10. strap
11. strike
12. smash
13. struck
14. throat
15. thread
16. spill
17. true
18. spirit

Scripture
John 15:10

Words with Consonant Clusters

Lesson 9

55

3 Preview

Test for knowledge of the correct spellings of these words.

Customize Your List

On a separate sheet of paper, additional words of your choice may be tested.

I will say each word once, use the word in a sentence, then say the word again. Write the words on the lines in your Worktext.

Correct Immediately!

Let's correct our Preview. I will spell each word out loud. If you spelled a word incorrectly, rewrite it correctly.

Progress Chart

Students may record scores. (Reproducible master provided in Appendix B.)

1.	thrill	Rosa felt a **thrill** as she opened the birthday package.
2.	style	Her gift was a cool **style** of bike computer.
3.	stretch	Rosa timed her speed on the long **stretch** of road.
4.	steady	She pedaled at a **steady** pace.
5.	spray	She liked to feel the **spray** of the wind-blown rain against her face.
6.	split	Nipper and Chipper can **split** open peanuts with their claws.
7.	stool	Kristin sat on a small **stool** in Rosa's bedroom.
8.	slippery	Nipper almost felt **slippery** when she moved so fast.
9.	stroke	Kristin likes to **stroke** Chipper's soft, silky coat.
10.	strap	She slipped the **strap** of a doll's hat under his chin.
11.	strike	Rosa heard the car **strike** her bike with a loud CRUNCH!
12.	smash	She did not want a car to **smash** her bike.
13.	struck	The back bumper of Mr. Wright's car **struck** Rosa's bike.
14.	throat	Rosa had a big lump in her **throat** and tears in her eyes.
15.	thread	She twisted a loose **thread** at the bottom of her sweatshirt.
16.	spill	The tears began to **spill** down her cheeks.
17.	true	It was **true** that she had not taken care of her responsibility.
18.	spirit	Rosa has a happy **spirit**!

Word Shapes

Help students form a correct image of whole words.

Look at each word and think about its shape. Now, write the word in the correct Word Shape Boxes. You may check off each word as you use it.

(Initial clusters that begin with **s** or **t** are practiced in this lesson. Unlike a digraph, in which two letters combine to form a single sound, the letters that make up a consonant cluster keep their sounds when pronounced in words. These clusters are often found at the beginning of words.)

In the Word Shape Boxes, fill in the boxes containing the letters that spell the initial consonant cluster in each word.

Take a minute to memorize...
John 15:10

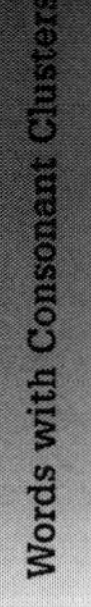

Words with Consonant Clusters — Lesson 9

B Word Shapes Name ____________________

Write each word in the correct Word Shape Boxes. Next, in the Word Shape Boxes, shade in the boxes containing the letters that spell the initial consonant cluster in each word.

1. slippery
2. smash
3. spill
4. spirit
5. split
6. spray
7. steady
8. stool
9. style
10. strap
11. stretch
12. strike
13. stroke
14. struck
15. thread
16. thrill
17. throat
18. true

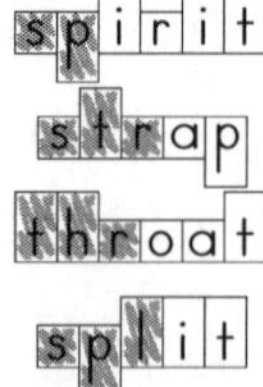

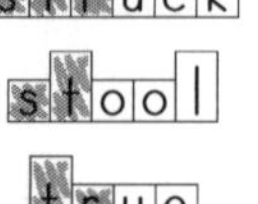

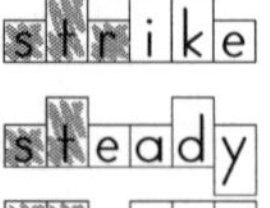

56

Answers may vary for duplicate word shapes.

Be Prepared For Fun

Check these supply lists for **Fun Ways to Spell** - presented **Day 2**. Purchase and/or gather these items ahead of time!

General
- Pencil
- Notebook Paper
- Spelling List

Auditory
- Spelling List

Visual
- Pencil
- Scissors
- 3 X 5 cards (18 per child)
- Spelling List

Tactile
- Toothpicks
- Art Paper (3 sheets per child)
- Glue
- Spelling List

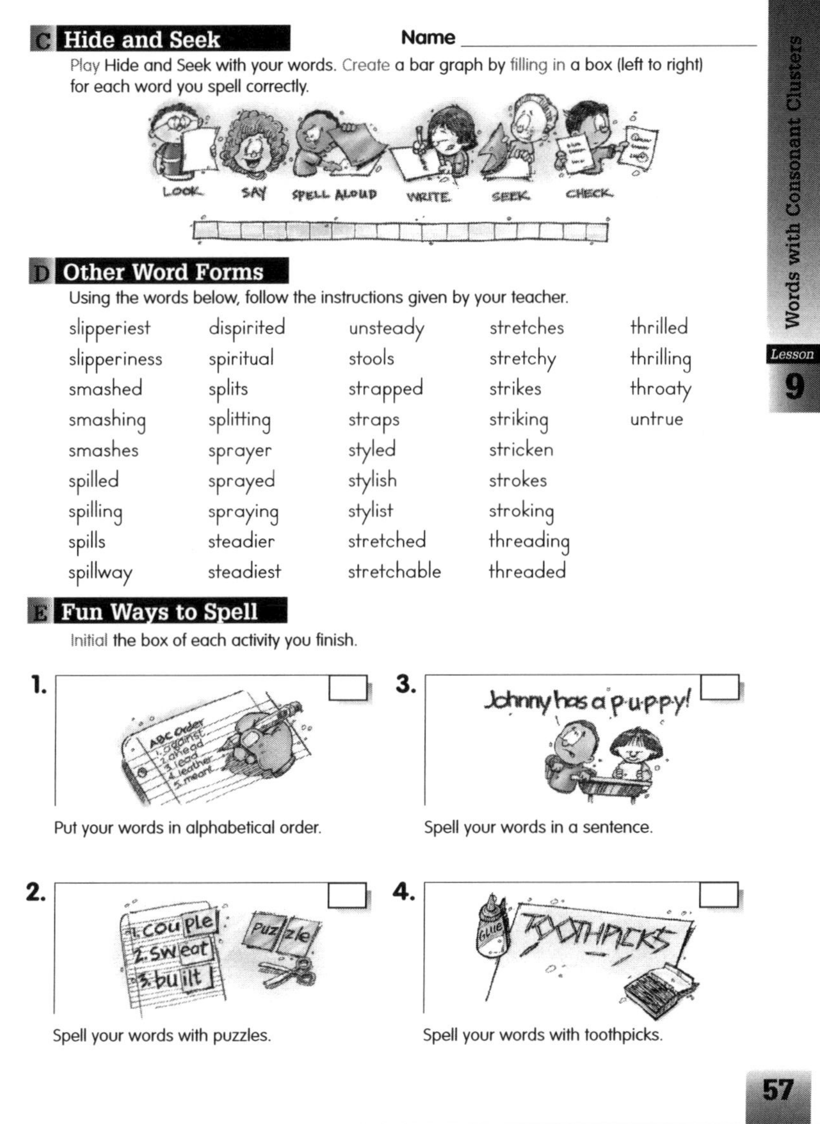

C Hide and Seek

Name ______________________

Play Hide and Seek with your words. Create a bar graph by filling in a box (left to right) for each word you spell correctly.

D Other Word Forms

Using the words below, follow the instructions given by your teacher.

slipperiest	dispirited	unsteady	stretches	thrilled
slipperiness	spiritual	stools	stretchy	thrilling
smashed	splits	strapped	strikes	throaty
smashing	splitting	straps	striking	untrue
smashes	sprayer	styled	stricken	
spilled	sprayed	stylish	strokes	
spilling	spraying	stylist	stroking	
spills	steadier	stretched	threading	
spillway	steadiest	stretchable	threaded	

E Fun Ways to Spell

Initial the box of each activity you finish.

1. Put your words in alphabetical order.

2. Spell your words with puzzles.

3. Spell your words in a sentence.

4. Spell your words with toothpicks.

Words with Consonant Clusters

Lesson 9

57

1 Hide and Seek

Reinforce spelling by using multiple styles of learning.

On a white board, Teacher writes each word — one at a time. **Have students:**

- **Look** at the word.
- **Say** the word out loud.
- **Spell** the word out loud.
- **Hide** (teacher erases word.)
- **Write** the word on paper.
- **Seek** (teacher rewrites word.)
- **Check** spelling. If incorrect, rewrite word correctly.

2 Other Word Forms

This activity is optional. Have students write these Other Word Forms in alphabetical order:

spiritual
throaty
spillway
slipperiness

3 Fun Ways to Spell

Four activities are provided. Use one, two, three, or all of the activities. Have students initial the box for each activity they complete.

Options:

- assign activities to students according to their learning styles
- set up the activities in learning centers for students to do throughout the day
- divide students into four groups and assign one activity per group
- do one activity per day

General

To put your words in alphabetical order...

- Write all the words in alphabetical order.
- Remember to look at the second, third, or fourth letters of the words when the first letters are the same.

Auditory

To spell your words in a sentence...

- Have a classmate read a spelling word to you.
- Say a sentence with that spelling word to your classmate.
- Ask your classmate to spell the word.
- Check your classmate's spelling.
- Read a word to your classmate, continue taking turns until you have each spelled all the words.

Visual

To spell your words with puzzles...

- Write each word on a card.
- Ask a classmate to cut each word apart between two letters.
- Arrange half of each word on your desk.
- Write the missing part of the word on a piece of paper.
- Do it again with the other half of your cards.
- Check your spelling.

Tactile

To spell your words with toothpicks...

- Choose a word from your spelling list.
- Arrange toothpicks to represent each letter of the word.
- Glue them to a piece of art paper.

Working with Words

Familiarize students with word meaning and usage.

Sentence Skills

Remember, there are four kinds of sentences: **imperative**, **declarative**, **exclamatory**, and **interrogative**.

Rewrite the sentences in your Worktext, correcting the misspelled word. Then, circle the word that tells which kind of sentence it is.

Take a minute to memorize...

John 15:10

Words with Consonant Clusters — Lesson 9

F Working with Words Name ______________________

Sentence Skills

An **imperative sentence** is a command and ends with a period or an exclamation point.
Get me a bandage for my knee. Give me that!
A **declarative sentence** tells something and ends with a period.
My knee has a bandage on it.
An **exclamatory sentence** shows strong feelings and ends with an exclamation point.
My knee really hurts!
An **interrogative sentence** asks something and ends with a question mark.
Do you think my knee needs stitches?

Write the sentences below, correcting the misspelled word. Circle the word that tells what kind of sentence it is.

1. Chipper likes to strecth out for a nap.
   Chipper likes to stretch out for a nap.
   imperative (declarative) exclamatory interrogative
2. The car struk Rosa's bike hard!
   The car struck Rosa's bike hard!
   imperative declarative (exclamatory) interrogative
3. Hold the computer stedy while I bolt it on the frame.
   Hold the computer steady while I bolt it on the frame.
   (imperative) declarative exclamatory interrogative
4. The girls like to stroak Chipper's soft fur.
   The girls like to stroke Chipper's soft fur.
   imperative (declarative) exclamatory interrogative
5. Is it trew that you have not put your bike away?
   Is it true that you have not put your bike away?
   imperative declarative exclamatory (interrogative)

Word Bank

slippery	spirit	steady	strap	stroke	thrill
smash	split	stool	stretch	struck	throat
spill	spray	style	strike	thread	true

58

G Dictation

Name ______________________

Write each sentence as your teacher dictates. Use correct punctuation.

1. She held it steady so Dad could tie the strap.
2. The gift would be smashed if a car struck it hard.
3. She held her bicycle steady on the slippery road.

H Proofreading

If a word is misspelled, fill in the oval by that word. If all the words are spelled correctly, fill in the oval by **no mistake**.

1. ○ stew ○ stroke ● slippry ○ no mistake
2. ○ groan ○ speak ○ smash ● no mistake
3. ○ smoke ● spil ○ snap ○ no mistake
4. ○ grave ○ struck ○ spirit ● no mistake
5. ○ dream ○ thrill ○ spray ● no mistake
6. ● steddy ○ crack ○ cream ○ no mistake
7. ● troo ○ stool ○ plank ○ no mistake
8. ○ drum ○ fry ○ split ● no mistake
9. ○ style ○ bridge ● throte ○ no mistake
10. ○ flour ○ flow ○ strap ● no mistake
11. ○ blanket ● strech ○ clear ○ no mistake
12. ● thred ○ blade ○ strike ○ no mistake

1 Dictation

Reinforce correct spelling by using current and previous words in context.

Listen as I read each sentence and then write it in your Worktext. Remember to use correct capitalization and punctuation. (Slowly read each sentence twice. Sentences are found in the Student Worktext to the left.)

2 Proofreading

Familiarize students with standardized test format and reinforce recognition of misspelled words.

Look at each set of words. If a word is misspelled, fill in the oval by that word. If all the words are spelled correctly, fill in the oval by **no mistake**.

3 Hide and Seek

Reinforce correct spelling of current spelling words. Repeat this activity from Day 2. (A reproducible master is provided in Appendix A as shown on the inset page to the right.)

4 Other Word Forms

Have your students complete this activity to strengthen spelling ability and expand vocabulary.

1 Posttest

Visit the **A Reason For** website to download free, printable Posttest pages.

I will say the word once, use it in a sentence, then say it again. Write your words on a separate sheet of paper.

Progress Chart

Students may record scores. (Appendix B)

Personal Dictionary

Students may add any words they have misspelled to their personal dictionaries. (Appendix B)

Lesson 9 | Other Word Forms

Hide and Seek

Play Hide and Seek with your words. Create a bar graph by filling in a box (left to right) for each word you spell correctly.

Other Word Forms

Code Words

Use the code to write each other word form.

0 = h 1 = l 2 = n 3 = p 4 = r 5 = s 6 = t

1. 6 0 4 i 1 1 5 thrills
2. 5 6 e a d i e 4 steadier
3. 5 6 4 e 6 c 0 y stretchy
4. 5 3 1 i 6 6 i 2 g splitting
5. 6 0 4 o a 6 5 throats
6. 5 3 4 a y e d sprayed
7. 5 m a 5 0 e 5 smashes
8. 5 6 4 o k i 2 g stroking
9. 5 6 4 u c k struck
10. 5 1 i 3 3 e 4 i 2 e 5 5 slipperiness
11. 5 1 i 3 5 slips
12. 5 6 4 a 3 5 straps
13. 6 0 4 e a d 5 threads
14. 6 4 u e 5 6 truest

332

1.	steady	With a **steady** hand, Mr. Vasquez cut the packing tape.
2.	stool	Christopher sat on a tall **stool** near the kitchen table.
3.	thrill	Rosa felt a **thrill** as she opened the gift from her aunt and uncle.
4.	style	Rosa liked the sleek **style** of the bike computer.
5.	smash	"A car won't **smash** your bike if you put it away," said her dad.
6.	true	Rosa knew that what her dad had told her was **true.**
7.	stroke	Chipper liked Kristin to **stroke** him under the chin.
8.	thread	Chipper chewed on a loose **thread** on the doll's dress.
9.	strap	He pulled at the hat **strap** with his little claws.
10.	spray	Nipper liked to play with the **spray** bottle used to water the plants.
11.	slippery	She chattered as her claws slid across the **slippery** plastic.
12.	struck	There was an awful noise when the bumper **struck** the bike.
13.	split	The computer **split** and broke apart when the car hit the bike.
14.	spill	Rosa felt the hot tears **spill** down her cheeks.
15.	strike	Rosa forgot Mr. Wright's car might **strike** her bicycle.
16.	stretch	She saw her dad **stretch** out his arms to hug her.
17.	spirit	Rosa asked God to give her an obedient **spirit.**
18.	throat	Rosa's head and **throat** ached from crying.

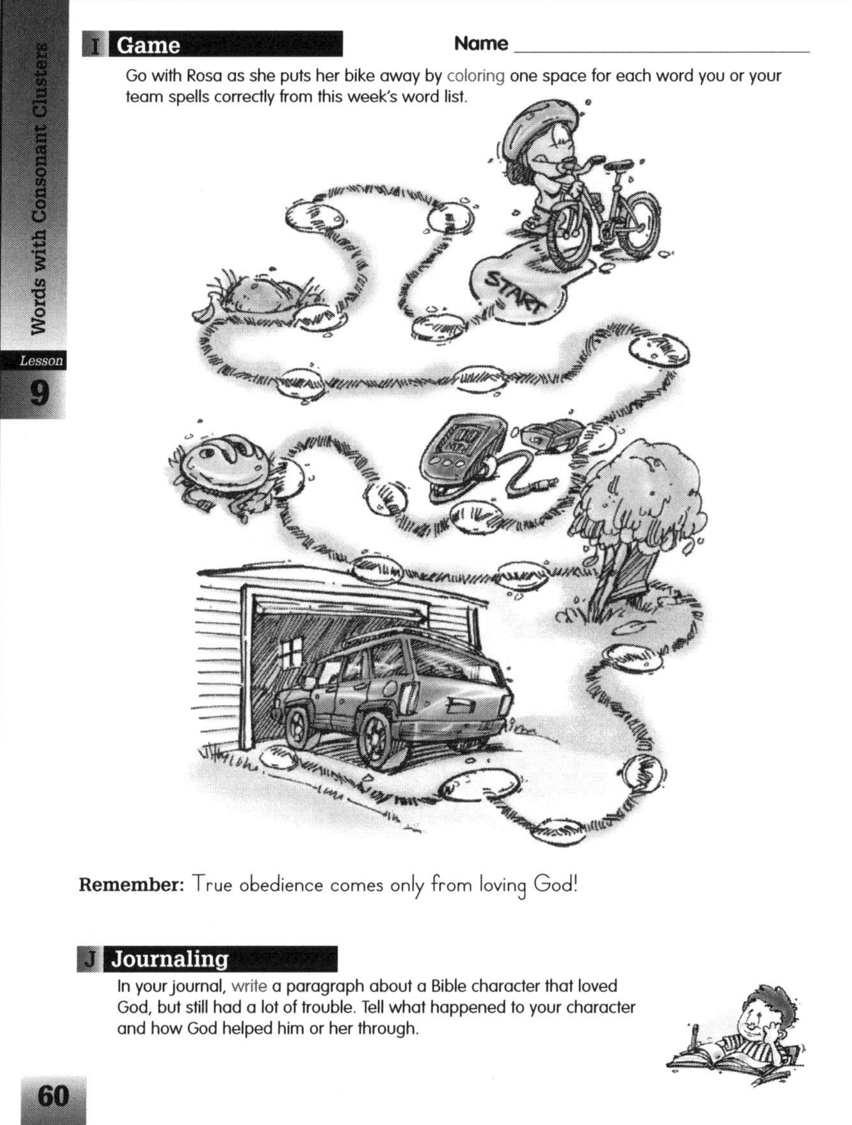

Words with Consonant Clusters

Lesson 9

I Game Name ______________________

Go with Rosa as she puts her bike away by coloring one space for each word you or your team spells correctly from this week's word list.

Remember: True obedience comes only from loving God!

J Journaling

In your journal, write a paragraph about a Bible character that loved God, but still had a lot of trouble. Tell what happened to your character and how God helped him or her through.

60

How to Play:

- Divide students into two teams.
- Have a student from team A go to the board.
- Say the spelling word.
- Have the student write the word on the board.
- If correct, instruct each member of team A to color one space, beginning at Start.
- Alternate between teams A and B as you go down the word list.
- The team to reach the garage first is the winner.

Small Group Option: Students may play this game without teacher direction in small groups of two or more.

2 Game

Reinforce spelling skills and provide motivation and interest.

Materials

- game page (from Student Worktext)
- crayons or colored pencils (1 per child)
- game word list

Game Word List

1. **slippery**
2. **smash**
3. **spill**
4. **spirit**
5. **split**
6. **spray**
7. **steady**
8. **stool**
9. **style**
10. **strap**
11. **stretch**
12. **strike**
13. **stroke**
14. **struck**
15. **thread**
16. **thrill**
17. **throat**
18. **true**

3 Journaling

Provide a meaningful reason for correct spelling through personal writing.

Review the story using discussion leads provided on the following page. Encourage students to apply the Scriptural value in their journaling.

Journaling (continued)

- What are some of the best birthday presents you've ever gotten? (Allow time for responses.)
- Why do you think Rosa really liked the bike computer her uncle and aunt sent? (It was fun to see how fast she was going, to check how far she'd gone, to be able to honk the horn, and to make it sound different ways. She also enjoyed setting the alarm so no one else could move the bike without the computer making a loud noise and saying, "STOLEN BIKE!")
- How did Rosa learn that it is important to be obedient even when it doesn't seem like a big deal? (She left her bike out in the driveway when her dad had told her to always put it away. Mr. Wright ran over it accidentally and ruined the bike and the bike computer.)
- Why did Rosa's dad make the rule about always putting away her bike? (Because he loved Rosa and wanted what was best for her.)
- Why does God give us rules that we should obey? (Because He loves us and knows what is best for us.)
- What do we call the list of rules found in Exodus 20 that God gave us? (The Ten Commandments.)

"Corduroy" comes from the French, "cord du roi" or "cloth of the king."

1 Literature Connection

Topic: Honesty
Theme Text: Luke 16:10

A Matter of Math

Matthew finds out that being dishonest only makes him cheat himself.

"Here's my milk money," said Heather as she handed Matthew some money. Matthew carefully counted the bills and put a check mark by Heather's name.

Tommy walked up behind Heather and put his money down on the desk by the classroom door. "Here's my money for the week." Matthew smiled and looked at the change Tommy handed him. "You need to give me another quarter, Tommy."

Tommy dug into his pocket. "Here it is. Sorry. I didn't mean to keep any. Honest."

Matthew carefully put a check mark in the box after Tommy's name.

"You're lucky to get this job, Matthew." Tommy plopped down on the desk where Matthew was sitting. "I have to clean the sink. I'm not very good at math, so Mrs. Burton will never give me the milk-money job."

"She'll let you, Tommy. You just have to do it with a partner, like Heather did." Matthew took Rosa's money and put a check beside her name.

"I don't think so." Tommy frowned. "I'm too slow and I make mistakes."

The loud ringing of the morning bell interrupted the conversation. Matthew picked up the cash box and headed toward Mrs. Burton's desk. "You could be my partner. I'll ask Mrs. Burton."

Right after lunch recess, Mrs. Burton asked everyone to get out their math books. She walked to the front of the classroom holding a big bag of M&M®'s. She dumped the candy in a jar. "Daniel, I would like you to take 18 pieces and divide them into equal groups."

"Tommy, you divide these." Mrs. Burton looked around the room at the waving hands, "I need another volunteer."

"Okay, Kristin, you may divide some." Mrs. Burton counted out eighteen M&M®'s on Kristin's desk.

She waited until everyone had separated their candy into little piles or rows. "How many do you have in each group, Daniel?"

"Six." Daniel pointed to his three rows of candy.

Mrs. Burton smiled. "Good job!"

"I have two groups of nine." Tommy looked up at Mrs. Burton.

"I have eight groups of two because I'm going to eat these." Kristin held two pieces close to her lips.

Mrs. Burton shook her head. "We're going to use these for a few minutes. You'll get to eat them when we're finished." She started spooning piles of M&M®'s on each student's desk. "We're starting a chapter about division today. Division is all about dividing things into groups."

Matthew groaned. "I hate division," he whispered to Stephen.

"So do I—but I like chocolate."

"When you're finished with the problems on page 100, you may check your answers in my answer book," Mrs. Burton instructed a few minutes later. "Be sure to use the red pen at the grading table to mark the ones you missed—and correct those before class time tomorrow."

Matthew got out a piece of notebook paper and put it beside his math book. "I hate division. I hate division," he whispered.

His friend overheard his muttering and turned to Matthew. "You always get good grades in math," Stephen said. "You never even study."

"I'm just not very fast at division and I always miss some." Matthew slowly numbered his paper.

It was just before break when he finished the last problem. *I think I'll grade this really quick. I don't want any homework and we have science class after this break. I'll hurry and get it graded.*

Matthew rushed over to the grading table and picked up the red pen. After checking the first two wrong, he groaned. *I missed a lot of these! I'm going to be doing division tonight after my stamp collector's club meeting.*

"Hurry, Matthew. We need you for our goalie in soccer." Tommy grabbed the soccer ball and ran out the door.

Matthew checked all the ones he'd gotten wrong. He looked around the room and realized he was the only one left. Mrs. Burton stuck her head back in the door. "Come on Matthew." Matthew jumped at the sound of her voice. "It's break time; you can do that later." She smiled at Matthew.

"I'll be there in a minute; I just need to finish this." He grabbed his regular pencil and lightly wrote in the correct answers for the ones he'd missed. *This isn't really cheating,* Matthew thought, *because I checked them all wrong. I'm just writing down the answers so I won't have to correct and redo so many times.*

After Matthew came home from his stamp collector's meeting that evening, he plopped down on his bed and looked at his math book. There just wasn't time to figure out all those division problems he'd missed. He erased his old answers and wrote down the ones he'd copied from the answer key. *I did them once,* he thought. *I know how to divide. It just takes me a long time to do. I don't have time tonight.*

Matthew had a lot of interests. Homework wasn't one of them. Usually he didn't have homework because he easily got his work done at school. But Matthew didn't like to divide. He liked to read detective books. He had fun doing science

Story (continued)

Lesson 10 | Day 1

experiments. He enjoyed building things. He had a stamp collection. He liked to try out different food combinations in the kitchen. As days went by there was always something more interesting to do than correct the problems he missed every day in math class.

The end of the chapter on division came much sooner than Matthew expected. Mrs. Burton put the division test on his desk and he wasn't ready! *How do I do these that have something left over?* he thought. *I know I'll miss lots!* He couldn't remember which was the divisor and which was the dividend on the fill-in-the-blank section. Sweat started dripping down his forehead when he saw the long division problems at the end of the test. He spent so much time working and reworking the problems he didn't finish the test in the allotted time. He felt miserable! Worst of all, he knew it was his own fault he hadn't done well.

The next day Mrs. Burton asked him to stay after school for a few minutes. "Division isn't easy for you is it, Matthew?" She looked him straight in the eye and said, "You failed your math test. Are you surprised?"

Matthew shook his head slowly.

"Your daily work has been good. You've missed more than you usually do, but you corrected them all without asking for help. I assumed you understood division quite well." She raised her eyebrows as she looked at him. "What happened. Were you sick yesterday?"

Matthew looked down at his teacher's desk to avoid her eyes. "I'm sorry, Mrs. Burton." Matthew bit his lower lip and scuffed the toe of his shoe across the carpet. "I've been cheating. I hate division. It takes me a long time to do. I just copied the answers to the ones I missed every day."

"I see." Mrs. Burton looked sad. "I forgive you, Matthew, but I'm sorry that you cheated. You only hurt yourself. But I'm also sorry that you broke my trust in you. I think I need to give the milk-money job to someone who can handle such a big responsibility. Will you please bring me the check sheet?"

Matthew nodded and got the check sheet for the milk money from his desk.

The next morning, Matthew trudged into the classroom. Tommy sat at the little desk by the door. "Do you have any money for milk?"

Matthew shook his head. *I wonder what my new job will be?* he thought. He walked over to the job chart to see. "Emptying the trash." He frowned as he shuffled across the classroom to get the trash liners out of the cupboard. As he passed the board he read the text from spelling class for the week. "Unless you are honest in small matters, you won't be in large ones. If you cheat even a little, you won't be honest with greater responsibilities."

He put the fresh liner in the trash can beside Mrs. Burton's desk. He noticed there was still some candy in the jar beside her stapler. "I haven't learned division in math class—but I've learned a lot about being honest," he said to no one in particular. "Responsibility, too."

Discussion Time

Check understanding of the story and development of personal values.

- What subject in school is the hardest for you?
- Why did Matthew not like the new chapter in math?
- What did Matthew do at the grading table that wasn't honest?
- How did he do on the chapter test over division?
- Why did Mrs. Burton think he'd cheated on his homework?
- Why do you think Mrs. Burton gave the special milk money job to Tommy?

A Preview Name ______________

Write each word as your teacher says it.

1. mild
2. frost
3. wrong
4. belt
5. among
6. bent
7. apartment
8. forward
9. government
10. crust
11. merchant
12. blank
13. legend
14. pretend
15. moment
16. understand
17. remind
18. guard

Scripture

Luke 16:10

3 Preview

Test for knowledge of the correct spellings of these words.

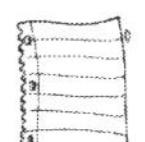

Customize Your List

On a separate sheet of paper, additional words of your choice may be tested.

I will say each word once, use the word in a sentence, then say the word again. Write the words on the lines in your Worktext.

Correct Immediately!

Let's correct our Preview. I will spell each word out loud. If you spelled a word incorrectly, rewrite it correctly.

Progress Chart

Students may record scores. (Reproducible master provided in Appendix B.)

1. **mild** — The weather was warm and **mild** at break time.
2. **frost** — There was no **frost** on the ground yet.
3. **wrong** — "Mark the ones you got **wrong** with the red pen," said Mrs. Burton.
4. **belt** — Mrs. Burton wore a bright yellow **belt** with her navy blue dress.
5. **among** — She walked **among** her students passing out papers.
6. **bent** — Matthew **bent** over the grading table as he penciled in the correct answers.
7. **apartment** — Matthew's family does not live in an **apartment**.
8. **forward** — He was looking **forward** to his stamp collectors' club meeting.
9. **government** — Matthew's class is not studying **government** this year.
10. **crust** — He loves the **crust** of his Mom's homemade pies.
11. **merchant** — A businessman or **merchant** should have good math skills.
12. **blank** — Matthew's mind went **blank** when he saw the test paper.
13. **legend** — There was a **legend** in the corner of the map on the math test.
14. **pretend** — Matthew did not **pretend** he had been honest.
15. **moment** — Mrs. Burton was quiet for a **moment**.
16. **understand** — "You **understand** I can't trust you to take milk money?" she asked.
17. **remind** — The punishment will **remind** Matthew how important honesty is.
18. **guard** — We must be on **guard** against the temptation to cheat and lie.

Word Shapes

Help students form a correct image of whole words.

Look at each word and think about its shape. Now, write the word in the correct Word Shape Boxes. You may check off each word as you use it.

(In many words, a consonant cluster starts with **l**, **n** or **r**. These clusters are never at the beginning of a word.)

In the Word Shape Boxes, fill in the boxes containing the consonant cluster at the end of each word.

Take a minute to memorize...

Luke 16:10

B Word Shapes Name ______________________

Write each word in the correct Word Shape Boxes. Next, in the Word Shape Boxes, shade in the boxes containing the consonant cluster at the end of each word.

Word	Word Shape Boxes
1. remind	mild
2. frost	belt
3. bent	legend
4. pretend	pretend
5. blank	remind
6. apartment	understand
7. crust	among
8. wrong	wrong
9. government	blank
10. merchant	apartment
11. legend	bent
12. belt	government
13. moment	merchant
14. forward	moment
15. understand	forward
16. guard	guard
17. mild	crust
18. among	frost

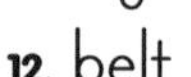

62

Answers may vary for duplicate word shapes.

Be Prepared For Fun

Check these supply lists for **Fun Ways to Spell** - presented **Day 2**. Purchase and/or gather these items ahead of time!

General
- Pencil
- Graph Paper (1 sheet per child)
- Spelling List

Auditory
- Pencil
- 3 X 5 Cards Cut in half lengthwise (18 per child)
- Spelling List

Visual
- Glitter
- Glue
- Art Paper (2 sheets per child)
- Spelling List

Tactile
- ABC Macaroni
- Art Paper (1 sheet per child)
- Glue
- Spelling List

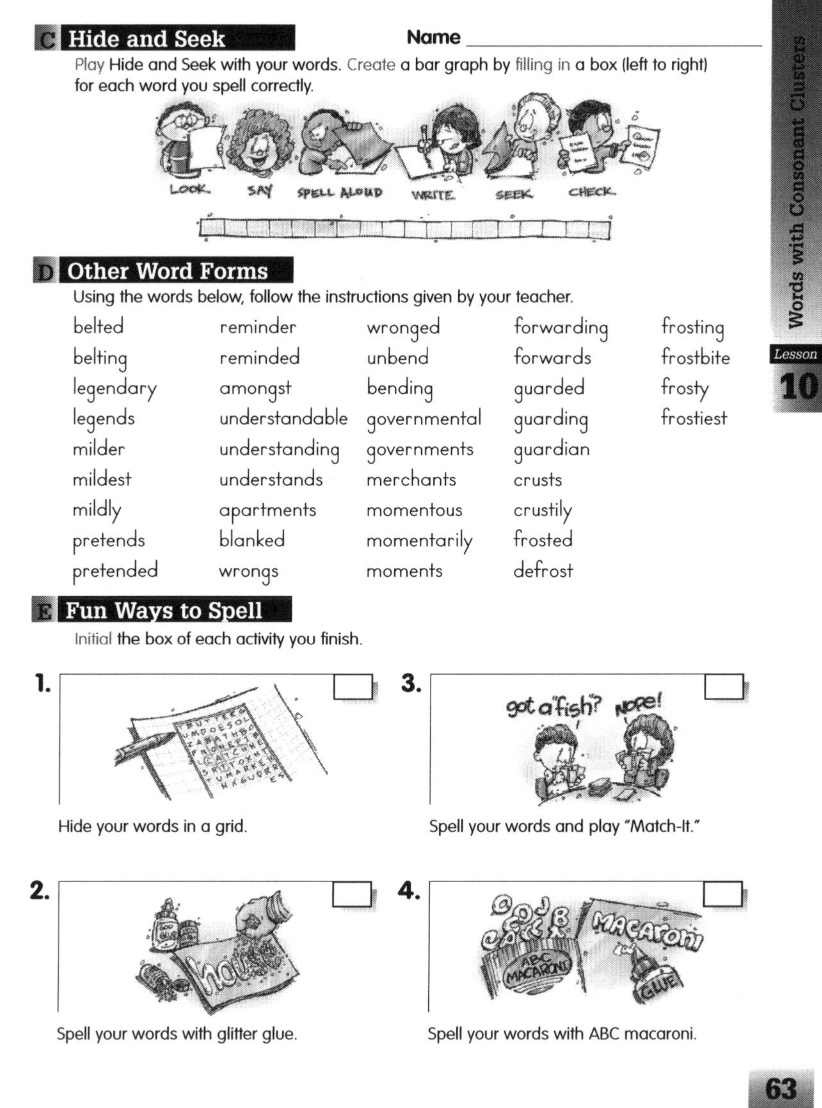

C Hide and Seek Name ____________________

Play Hide and Seek with your words. Create a bar graph by filling in a box (left to right) for each word you spell correctly.

D Other Word Forms

Using the words below, follow the instructions given by your teacher.

belted	reminder	wronged	forwarding	frosting
belting	reminded	unbend	forwards	frostbite
legendary	amongst	bending	guarded	frosty
legends	understandable	governmental	guarding	frostiest
milder	understanding	governments	guardian	
mildest	understands	merchants	crusts	
mildly	apartments	momentous	crustily	
pretends	blanked	momentarily	frosted	
pretended	wrongs	moments	defrost	

E Fun Ways to Spell

Initial the box of each activity you finish.

1. Hide your words in a grid.

2. Spell your words with glitter glue.

3.
Spell your words and play "Match-It."

4.
Spell your words with ABC macaroni.

Words with Consonant Clusters — Lesson 10

63

1 Hide and Seek

Reinforce spelling by using multiple styles of learning.

On a white board, Teacher writes each word — one at a time. **Have students:**

- **Look** at the word.
- **Say** the word out loud.
- **Spell** the word out loud.
- **Hide** (teacher erases word.)
- **Write** the word on paper.
- **Seek** (teacher rewrites word.)
- **Check** spelling. If incorrect, rewrite word correctly.

2 Other Word Forms

This activity is optional. Have students write variations of this sentence using these Other Word Forms:

The officer could understand her concern.
understands
understanding
understandable

3 Fun Ways to Spell

Four activities are provided. Use one, two, three, or all of the activities. Have students initial the box for each activity they complete.

Options:

- assign activities to students according to their learning styles
- set up the activities in learning centers for students to do throughout the day
- divide students into four groups and assign one activity per group
- do one activity per day

General

To hide your words on a grid...
- Arrange your words on a piece of graph paper.
- Put one letter of each word in a square.
- Words may be written backwards, forwards, or diagonally.
- Outline your puzzle.
- Hide your words by filling in all the spaces inside the puzzle with random letters.
- Trade grids with a classmate and find the hidden words.

Auditory

To spell your words and play "Match-It"...

Write each spelling word on a card. Mix your word cards and a classmate's together. Deal six cards per player; put the rest face down between you. Ask classmate for a word-card that matches one in your hand. If the classmate has the word-card, take it and play again. If not, draw from the remaining stack, then it is your classmate's turn. Continue taking turns until all the cards are matched. Player with most cards wins!

Visual

To spell your words with glitter glue...
- Write each of your spelling words on your paper with glue.
- Sprinkle with glitter.

Tactile

To spell your words with ABC macaroni...
- Choose a word from your spelling list.
- Spell the word with macaroni letters.
- Glue the macaroni word to art paper.
- Do this for each word on your list.

Working with Words

Familiarize students with word meaning and usage.

Clues

Students will be using context clues and a dictionary in selecting correct words in sentences.

Remember, context clues are words in the sentence that help explain the meaning of a word. Look at the context clue in each sentence and choose the word from the word bank that completes the sentence. Write the word on the line.

Take a minute to memorize...

Luke 16:10

Words with Consonant Clusters — Lesson 10

F Working with Words Name ____________________

Clues

Write a spelling word for each clue.

1. Something that is not right is ___wrong___.
2. A set of rooms used as a home is called an ___apartment___.
3. Weather that is moderate and not too harsh is ___mild___.
4. To ___frost___ a cake is to spread icing on it.
5. Words written beside a map to explain it are called the ___legend___.
6. To look ___forward___ is to look ahead to the future.
7. A strip of leather worn around the waist is a ___belt___.
8. To make believe is to ___pretend___.
9. The earth's ___crust___ is its hard outer layer.
10. Something that is ___bent___ is crooked or curved.
11. ___Government___ is the control and administration of a country.
12. To protect, defend, or watch over a person or place is to ___guard___ it.
13. A ___moment___ is a very short period of time.
14. To ___remind___ someone is to help them remember something.
15. Someone who sells goods for profit is known as a ___merchant___.
16. Something that is ___blank___ has nothing on it.
17. To divide something with several people is to share it ___among___ them.
18. To know what something means is to ___understand___.

Word Bank

among	bent	forward	guard	mild	remind
apartment	blank	frost	legend	moment	understand
belt	crust	government	merchant	pretend	wrong

64

G Dictation

Name ____________________

Write each sentence as your teacher dictates. Use correct punctuation.

1. Matthew got some words wrong since he did not understand.
2. He bent down to write in the blank.
3. I will remind you to look at the map legend.

H Proofreading

If a word is misspelled, fill in the oval by that word. If all the words are spelled correctly, fill in the oval by **no mistake**.

1.	● fowerd ○ mild ○ slippery ○ no mistake	**5.**	○ struck ○ crust ○ true ● no mistake	**9.**	○ strike ○ stretch ● rong ○ no mistake
2.	○ smash ○ thrill ○ belt ● no mistake	**6.**	○ spray ○ split ○ remind ● no mistake	**10.**	○ strap ● merchent ○ blank ○ no mistake
3.	○ spill ○ thread ● lejend ○ no mistake	**7.**	● goverment ○ stool ○ understand ○ no mistake	**11.**	○ throat ○ steady ● apartmint ○ no mistake
4.	○ spirit ● gard ○ pretend ○ no mistake	**8.**	○ stroke ○ style ● amung ○ no mistake	**12.**	○ moment ○ frost ○ bent ● no mistake

Words with Consonant Clusters

Lesson 10

65

1 Dictation

Reinforce correct spelling by using current and previous words in context.

Listen as I read each sentence and then write it in your Worktext. Remember to use correct capitalization and punctuation. (Slowly read each sentence twice. Sentences are found in the Student Worktext to the left.)

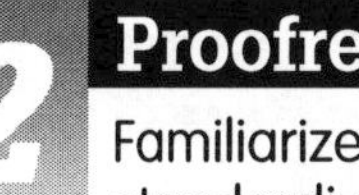

2 Proofreading

Familiarize students with standardized test format and reinforce recognition of misspelled words.

Look at each set of words. If a word is misspelled, fill in the oval by that word. If all the words are spelled correctly, fill in the oval by **no mistake**.

3 Hide and Seek

Reinforce correct spelling of current spelling words. Repeat this activity from Day 2. (A reproducible master is provided in Appendix A as shown on the inset page to the right.)

4 Other Word Forms

Have your students complete this activity to strengthen spelling ability and expand vocabulary.

1 Posttest

Visit the **A Reason For** website to download free, printable Posttest pages.

I will say the word once, use it in a sentence, then say it again. Write your words on a separate sheet of paper.

Progress Chart

Students may record scores. (Appendix B)

Personal Dictionary

Students may add any words they have misspelled to their personal dictionaries. (Appendix B)

Hide and Seek

Play Hide and Seek with your words. Create a bar graph by filling in a box (left to right) for each word you spell correctly.

Other Word Forms

Scrambled Words

Use the sentence clue to help you unscramble each word. Write the unscrambled word in the sentence.

adeeglnry	**1.** We read a book about a legendary man.
deilmts	**2.** This is the mildest weather we have had.
ddeeenprt	**3.** Matthew pretended to correct his math problems.
fginorst	**4.** I like to lick the frosting out of the bowl.
ceirssttu	**5.** I like the crustiest part of the bread best.
aeilmmnorty	**6.** I momentarily forgot to watch the ball.
bdeelt	**7.** Dad asked if everyone was belted in his seat belt.
ddeeimnr	**8.** Mom reminded me to take my homework to school.
aabddelnnrstuy	**9.** He was understandably tired after the 5k run.
dgginnoorw	**10.** Matthew was sorry for his wrongdoing.
abdekln	**11.** His mind blanked out when he took the math test.
agmnost	**12.** Mrs. Burton divided the candy amongst the students.
emmnoostu	**13.** Choosing to follow Christ is a momentous decision.
addeforrw	**14.** The post office forwarded the letter to his new address.

Prefixes and Suffixes

Add the prefixes or suffixes to make new words. Write the words on the lines.

1. guard + ian = guardian	**5.** frosty – y + i + er = frostier
2. frost + y = frosty	**6.** understand + able = understandable
3. mild + ness = mildness	**7.** crusty – y + i + ly = crustily
4. pretend + ing = pretending	**8.** mis + understand = misunderstand

333

Lesson 10 | Other Word Forms

1.	mild	The weather was still **mild** and pleasant.
2.	frost	The first **frost** had not come.
3.	belt	Mrs. Burton knew her funny yellow **belt** made the students smile.
4.	understand	"I don't **understand** division very well," Matthew told Tommy.
5.	among	Mrs. Burton walked **among** the students as they worked.
6.	government	Many **government** jobs require strong math skills.
7.	merchant	A **merchant** uses his math skills every day in his work.
8.	bent	Matthew **bent** over the grading table.
9.	wrong	"I got a lot of these **wrong**," he groaned.
10.	moment	Matthew thought for a **moment** before he copied down the answers.
11.	guard	We must **guard** against the temptation to cheat.
12.	forward	He was looking **forward** to seeing new stamps at the club meeting.
13.	apartment	His family lives in a house, not an **apartment**.
14.	crust	Matthew's favorite part of a pie is the **crust**.
15.	legend	The **legend** on the map gave information needed for the word problem.
16.	blank	He felt his mind go **blank**!
17.	pretend	Mrs. Burton was glad Matthew didn't **pretend** he hadn't cheated.
18.	remind	"I don't need to **remind** you that cheating is like lying," she said.

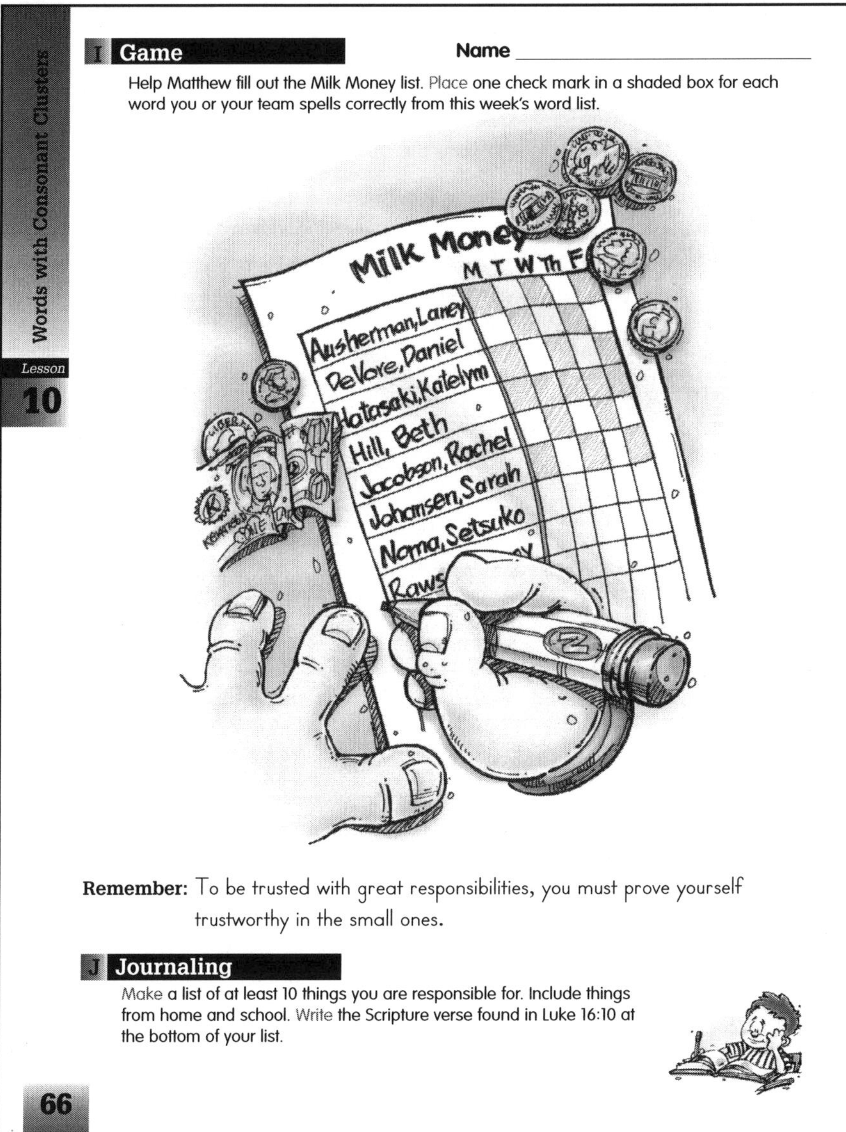

Words with Consonant Clusters

Lesson 10

I Game Name ______________________

Help Matthew fill out the Milk Money list. Place one check mark in a shaded box for each word you or your team spells correctly from this week's word list.

Remember: To be trusted with great responsibilities, you must prove yourself trustworthy in the small ones.

J Journaling

Make a list of at least 10 things you are responsible for. Include things from home and school. Write the Scripture verse found in Luke 16:10 at the bottom of your list.

66

2 Game

Reinforce spelling skills and provide motivation and interest.

Materials

- game page (from Student Worktext)
- pencils (1 per child)
- game word list

Game Word List

1. **mild**
2. **belt**
3. **legend**
4. **pretend**
5. **remind**
6. **understand**
7. **among**
8. **wrong**
9. **blank**
10. **apartment**
11. **bent**
12. **government**
13. **merchant**
14. **moment**
15. **forward**
16. **guard**
17. **crust**
18. **frost**

How to Play:

- Divide students into two teams.
- Have a student from team A go to the board.
- Say the spelling word.
- Have the student write the word on the board.
- If correct, Instruct each member of team A to check one shaded space on the milk money check sheet.
- Alternate between teams A and B as you go down the word list.
- The team with the most check marks when you have gone through the word list once is the winner.

Small Group Option: Students may play this game without teacher direction in small groups of two or more.

3 Journaling

Provide a meaningful reason for correct spelling through personal writing.

Review the story using discussion leads provided on the following page. Encourage students to apply the Scriptural value in their journaling.

Journaling (continued)

- How did Matthew feel about division? (He hated division.)
- Why do you think Matthew cheated on his math assignment every day? (It wasn't usual for him to spend so much time on his schoolwork. He was frustrated because he missed so many every day and correcting them took too much time.)
- What responsibilities do you have in your classroom or at home?
- What job did Matthew do every day for Mrs. Burton? (He collected the milk money and kept track of how much each student brought in.)
- Why did Mrs. Burton take Matthew's job of collecting milk money away? (She couldn't trust him anymore.)
- What is the greatest responsibility you have?

One of the three longest words in the English language is "floccinaucinihilipilification," which means "the action or habit of estimating something as worthless." There are 29 letters in the word.

Word Wow!

1 **Literature Connection**
Topic: Possessions
Theme Text: Luke 9:58

Air Mail to Africa

Kristin's pen pal helps her discover what's truly valuable in life.

August 12

Dear Diane,

Well, summer's almost over. You and your family are probably on your way back to Africa by now. Maybe this letter will get there before you do! I'm glad you got to spend some time in the United States this summer so I could meet you. We had so much fun together at Camp Stillwater. Remember the time we went canoeing to the island and lost our paddles? And remember how Jessica's snoring kept everyone in the cabin awake that one night?

You're so lucky to live in Africa. I wish my dad was a mission doctor. Send me some pictures of where you live when you write, okay?

What's it like to fly in a huge jet over the whole ocean? Can you see the waves or any ships? Someday maybe I'll get a chance to fly in a plane. My dad took another business trip last week. We took him to the airport and waited to watch his plane take off. You know those checkpoints at airports that you have to walk through to make sure you're not carrying a knife or gun or something? Well, the man in front of us had to walk through about five times before they let him board.

School starts in a few days. I bet you'd like our school. Mrs. Burton is going to be my teacher this year. She seems really nice. Mom had to get a lot of new clothes for Christopher and me. She says we've grown too much this summer.

Mom's taking us all to town this afternoon to get the rest of our school supplies. I already got a new notebook. It's got zebras and those antelope things on it. You know, those spring something-or-others that you've got in Africa? Anyway, it reminds me of you and the stories you told me at camp.

Gotta go! Write back soon!

Love,

Kristin

September 25

Dear Diane,

Wow! Have we been busy! School started a few weeks ago. We've got some new kids in our class this year. One is a cousin of one of the boys in my class. She loves insects, and it's amazing how well she plays the piano. Anyway, the other one's a boy. He's tall and kind of thin and uses big words all the time. He's a foster kid.

Were you glad to get back to Africa? You must have been busy lately, too, because I haven't gotten any letters from you yet! One of the kids in my class (Matthew) collects stamps. When he heard I had a friend in Africa, he begged for the stamps off your letters. So, WRITE!

I like our teacher, Mrs. Burton, or Mrs. B. She talked to us about having our own time every day to read the Scriptures and pray. I've been trying to do that, but it's hard to have your own time when you share a room with your little sister! Cathy's always bugging me. She wants help with her homework. She wants me to comb her hair. She wants me to play some silly games with her. I guess you know how it is since you've got a little sister, too. Do you have to share a room with Pamela?

Cathy's class put on a play a few days ago. Mom made Cathy a special costume. Our class is giving a program in a week or so. I've got a poem to repeat. Remember the skit we did at camp? Linda was supposed to be Zacchaeus, but she couldn't climb the tree in her costume. She looked so funny when she finally tucked that long robe into her shorts!

Hey, Diane, WRITE to me! I can't wait to hear all about Africa and everything you're doing.

Bye for now.

Love,

Kristin

October 12

Dear Diane,

I'm so tired of sharing my room with Cathy I'm about to explode! She leaves her things all over the room—and she won't leave my stuff alone. Christopher has his own room, and even Cory has a room of his own. It's just not fair. I asked my mom if I could move into the study or the attic or part of the garage, or somewhere. She said she'd think about it and talk to Dad.

So, why haven't you written me yet, Diane? It's been almost three months since camp and you promised you'd write. I double checked the address you gave me. I even had my mom make sure I wrote the address right. What's going on?

I bought a scrapbook the other night. I'd been saving my allowance to get a really nice one. This afternoon I spread all the pictures I took at camp out on my bed and arranged them before putting them inside. That picture of you riding Samson is great. You can tell by the expression on your face you'd never ridden such a big horse so fast!

I guess I should finish my math. I hate long division, don't you?

WRITE TO ME!!!!

Love,

Kristin

November 3

Dear Kristin,

Sorry it took me so long to write. Actually, I just now got all of your letters. It's kind of a long story.

Story (continued)

Our flight back was fine, but I slept a lot of the way. Not long after we got back home to Africa, things began to change. It's not like it is in the USA. The people here don't get to elect their leaders and vote for new ones if they don't do a good job. In this country, the government is whoever has the most power.

Six years ago my folks felt God calling them to Africa. The government that was in power for these six years was glad to have mission doctors. But right about the time we got back from our trip to the United States, a new group became more powerful. They don't like people who believe in Jesus Christ. They say that believing in Jesus means you're against the government, and you are enemies of the country. Of course, that's not true, but as this group got more powerful, they started making things hard for anyone they thought might believe in Jesus.

A lot of the Christians we know were forced out of their homes. Some lost their jobs. Some had their children taken away. Some were beaten. Lots of other bad stuff happened to them—all because they love Jesus.

Well, it got dangerous for my dad. He's pretty well known, and everyone knows he teaches about Jesus. When it looked sure that this group would force the old government out and take over, friends managed to get our family out of the country.

We had to leave at night and we couldn't take anything with us, but we're okay. Right now we're staying with some missionaries in another country in Africa. They cleared out one room so that our family could live in it. There are a lot of other refugees here besides us, so everyone's pretty crowded.

I don't know when, or if, we'll get to go home or if we'll get all of our things that we left behind. My father misses his books. He loves books and has collected special ones ever since I've been alive. My mother says what she misses most are the photos she had there. Some were really old, taken years ago when she and my father were young, and there were albums full of photos of things our family's done over the years. Pamela misses her stuffed animals and toys.

I miss our dog Dough Boy most. And the rock wall behind the house where you can sit and watch the sunset. And my wooden animal collection. And, well, lots of stuff. We all miss our African friends and hope things get better for them soon.

Anyway, someone at our old mission managed to get your letters to me and I finally did write! I've still got my Camp Stillwater T-shirt. In fact, I have it on right now. Write me again soon at this new address, okay?

Love,
Diane

P. S. I'll use a different kind of stamp on each letter so Matthew can have a bunch of different ones.

November 30

Dear Diane,

Your letter sure made me stop and think. Here I am complaining about having to share a room with Cathy—and your family loses everything you own because you love Jesus. I hope you don't mind, but I took your letter to school and read it to everybody. We're all praying for you, your family, and your friends.

Mrs. B reminded us that Jesus never said choosing to love and follow Him would be easy. She showed us Luke 9:58 where Jesus says He has no earthly home at all. He was telling someone who wanted to follow Him what to expect. But the good thing is, Jesus also said He'd be right there to help us through the hard times.

Remember when we spent hours just talking at camp? You told me about the lions' roaring waking you up in the night and how Pamela talks in another language more than she does in English. I told you how I felt when I said something mean about another girl. You became a special friend. I feel close to you even when you're on the other side of the world.

Maybe that's what Mrs. B's talking about when she says we should spend time with God every day. Maybe that's how we get to be special friends with Him.

Anyway, I'm so glad you're okay! Do you think you'll be coming back to the United States—or staying there? It sure would be neat if you could move here!

Love,
Kristin

P. S. Matthew says THANK YOU for the cool stamp.

2 Discussion Time

Check understanding of the story and development of personal values.

- To whom was Kristin writing letters?
- Where did Kristin meet Diane?
- Where did Diane live and why?
- What reasons did Kristin give for being upset about sharing a room with Cathy?
- Why did it take a long time for Diane to write back to Kristin?
- Does following God make life easier? Why or why not?

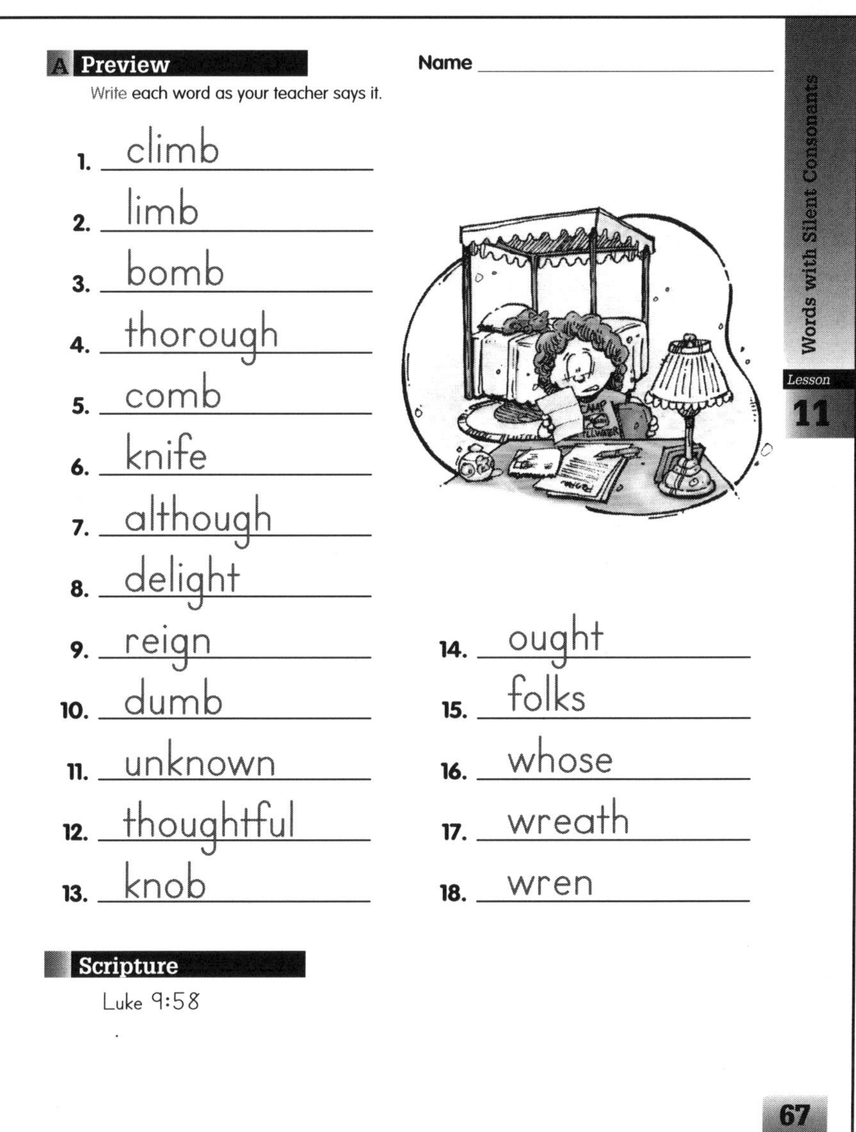
A Preview

Name ______________________

Write each word as your teacher says it.

1. climb
2. limb
3. bomb
4. thorough
5. comb
6. knife
7. although
8. delight
9. reign
10. dumb
11. unknown
12. thoughtful
13. knob
14. ought
15. folks
16. whose
17. wreath
18. wren

Scripture

Luke 9:58

Words with Silent Consonants

Lesson 11

67

3 Preview

Test for knowledge of the correct spellings of these words.

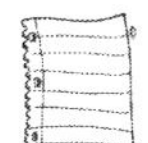

Customize Your List

On a separate sheet of paper, additional words of your choice may be tested.

I will say each word once, use the word in a sentence, then say the word again. Write the words on the lines in your Worktext.

Correct Immediately!

Let's correct our Preview. I will spell each word out loud. If you spelled a word incorrectly, rewrite it correctly.

Progress Chart

Students may record scores. (Reproducible master provided in Appendix B.)

1.	climb	Kristin remembered how Linda had to **climb** up the tree.
2.	limb	She had played the part of Zacchaeus as she sat on the **limb**.
3.	bomb	A **bomb** could be detected by airport security.
4.	thorough	They make a **thorough** search of passengers' luggage.
5.	comb	Even a metal **comb** could set off the security alarm.
6.	knife	A passenger may not carry a **knife** onto a plane.
7.	although	Kristin was anxious to hear from Diana **although** she tried to be patient.
8.	delight	It was a **delight** for Kristin to find Diana's letter in the mailbox!
9.	reign	The new group in power will **reign** over the people harshly.
10.	dumb	Many of the terrified people were struck **dumb** with fear.
11.	unknown	"The future of the country is **unknown**," wrote Diana.
12.	thoughtful	Kristin was very **thoughtful** after she read the letter.
13.	knob	Kristin looked at her pretty new book bag hanging on the door **knob**.
14.	ought	She realized she **ought** not complain about her situation.
15.	folks	Diana and her **folks** had to leave their home and possessions behind.
16.	whose	They are grateful to the family in **whose** home they are now living.
17.	wreath	The stamp on her letter had a small **wreath** of purple flowers on it.
18.	wren	Matthew has a valuable, old stamp with a tiny **wren** on it.

4 Word Shapes

Help students form a correct image of whole words.

Look at each word and think about its shape. Now, write the word in the correct Word Shape Boxes. You may check off each word as you use it.

(A silent letter occurs when two letters spell the sound of only one letter or when one or two letters stand for a completely silent sound.)

In the Word Shape Boxes, fill in the boxes containing the silent consonant or consonants in each word.

Take a minute to memorize...

Luke 9:58

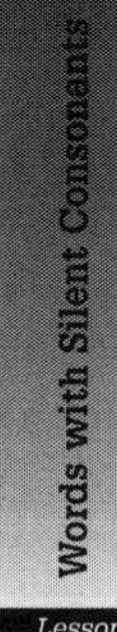

Words with Silent Consonants

Lesson 11

B Word Shapes Name ______________

Write each word in the correct Word Shape Boxes. Next, in the Word Shape Boxes, shade in the boxes containing the silent consonant or consonants in each word.

Word	Word Shape Boxes
1. climb	thorough
2. bomb	ought
3. comb	limb
4. dumb	reign
5. limb	delight
6. reign	wreath
7. although	whose
8. delight	climb
9. ought	dumb
10. thorough	thoughtful
11. thoughtful	folks
12. folks	bomb
13. knife	although
14. knob	comb
15. unknown	knife
16. whose	unknown
17. wreath	knob
18. wren	wren

68

Answers may vary for duplicate word shapes.

Be Prepared For Fun

Check these supply lists for **Fun Ways to Spell** - presented **Day 2**. Purchase and/or gather these items ahead of time!

General
- Pencil
- 3 X 5 Cards cut in half (18 per child)
- Spelling List

Auditory
- Pencil
- Notebook Paper
- Spelling List

Visual
- Black Construction Paper (1 sheet per child)
- Lemon Juice
- Cotton Swabs
- Spelling List

Tactile
- Pipe Cleaners (cut in an assortment of lengths)
- Spelling List

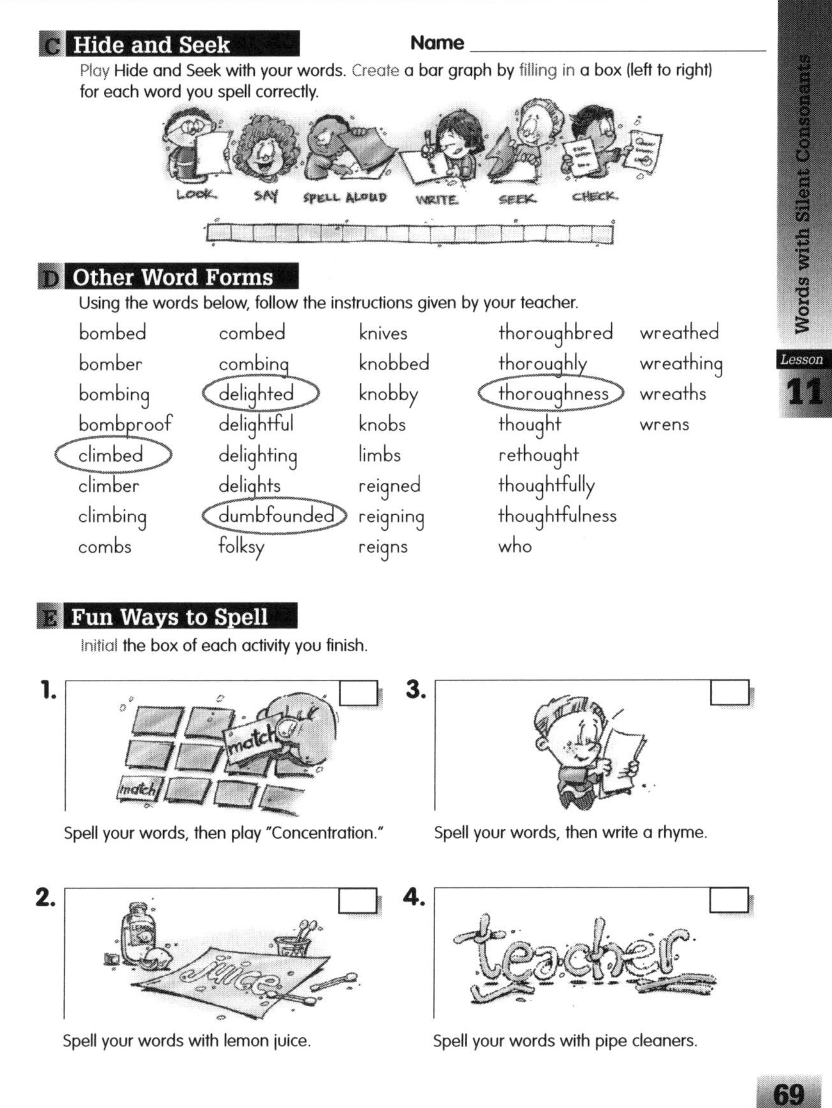

C Hide and Seek Name ______________________

Play Hide and Seek with your words. Create a bar graph by filling in a box (left to right) for each word you spell correctly.

D Other Word Forms

Using the words below, follow the instructions given by your teacher.

bombed	combed	knives	thoroughbred	wreathed
bomber	combing	knobbed	thoroughly	wreathing
bombing	delighted	knobby	thoroughness	wreaths
bombproof	delightful	knobs	thought	wrens
climbed	delighting	limbs	rethought	
climber	delights	reigned	thoughtfully	
climbing	dumbfounded	reigning	thoughtfulness	
combs	folksy	reigns	who	

E Fun Ways to Spell

Initial the box of each activity you finish.

1. Spell your words, then play "Concentration."

2. Spell your words with lemon juice.

3. Spell your words, then write a rhyme.

4. Spell your words with pipe cleaners.

Words with Silent Consonants

Lesson 11

69

1 Hide and Seek

Reinforce spelling by using multiple styles of learning.

On a white board, Teacher writes each word — one at a time. **Have students:**

- **Look** at the word.
- **Say** the word out loud.
- **Spell** the word out loud.
- **Hide** (teacher erases word.)
- **Write** the word on paper.
- **Seek** (teacher rewrites word.)
- **Check** spelling. If incorrect, rewrite word correctly.

2 Other Word Forms

This activity is optional. Have students find and circle the Other Word Forms that are synonyms of the following:

elated
meticulousness
flabbergasted
scaled

3 Fun Ways to Spell

Four activities are provided. Use one, two, three, or all of the activities. Have students initial the box for each activity they complete.

Options:

- assign activities to students according to their learning styles
- set up the activities in learning centers for students to do throughout the day
- divide students into four groups and assign one activity per group
- do one activity per day

General

Spell your words; then play Concentration…

Write each spelling word on a card. Mix your cards and a classmate's cards together. Arrange them face down in six rows of six. Pick up two cards. If the cards match, play again. If the cards do not match, turn them back over. It is your classmate's turn. Continue taking turns until all the cards are matched. The player with the most cards wins!

Auditory

To spell your words and write a rhyme…

- Write a rhyming verse for each word on your list.
- Example:
  My little brother could dive.
  When he was barely five.
- Underline your spelling words.

Visual

To spell your words with lemon juice…

- Dip a cotton swab in lemon juice.
- With the swab, write each of your spelling words on black construction paper.
- Check your spelling before your writing disappears!

Tactile

To spell your words with pipe cleaners…

- Choose a word from your spelling list.
- Shape the pipe cleaners to spell the word.
- Check your spelling.
- Do this for each word on your list.

Working with Words

Familiarize students with word meaning and usage.

Secret Words

The boxed letters in the acrostic are a phrase from the Scripture verse for this week. Use the clues to write the words in the puzzle, then write the boxed letters on the lines to find the secret phrase.

Take a minute to memorize...

Luke 9:58

Lesson 11 | Day 3

Words with Silent Consonants — Lesson 11

F **Working with Words** Name ____________________

Secret Words

Use the clues to write the words in the puzzle. Then use the boxed letters to fill in the lines below to find the secret words from this week's Scripture.

1. large branch of a tree
2. should
3. circle of flowers, leaves or branches
4. to rule as a king or queen
5. handle on a door or drawer
6. a toothed tool for fixing hair
7. pleasure or joy
8. a small songbird
9. in spite of
10. used to ask to whom something belongs
11. to go up a slope or stairway
12. to do a job carefully and completely
13. people
14. not able to speak
15. tool with a sharp blade used for cutting

1. limb
2. ought
3. wreath
4. reign
5. knob
6. comb
7. delight
8. wren
9. although
10. whose
11. climb
12. thorough
13. folks
14. dumb
15. knife

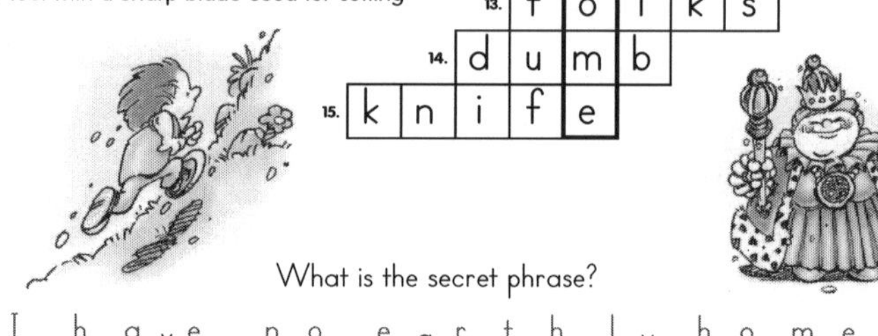

What is the secret phrase?

I have no earthly home.

Word Bank

although	comb	folks	limb	thorough	whose
bomb	delight	knife	ought	thoughtful	wreath
climb	dumb	knob	reign	unknown	wren

70

G Dictation

Name ____________________

Write each sentence as your teacher dictates. Use correct punctuation.

1. She climbed on the limb although she should not have.
2. Those are the folks whose homes burned.
3. She was thoughtful as she heard the wren sing.

Words with Silent Consonants

Lesson 11

H Proofreading

If a word is misspelled, fill in the oval by that word. If all the words are spelled correctly, fill in the oval by **no mistake**.

1. ○ frost ● reeth ○ climb ○ no mistake
2. ○ crust ● whoze ○ bomb ○ no mistake
3. ● nife ○ guard ○ comb ○ no mistake
4. ○ moment ○ forward ● dum ○ no mistake
5. ○ government ○ merchant ○ limb ● no mistake
6. ○ wren ○ bent ● riegn ○ no mistake
7. ○ apartment ●althogh ○ blank ○ no mistake
8. ○ among ○ wrong ● delite ○ no mistake
9. ○ understand ○ unknown ● owght ○ no mistake
10. ○ remind ● therogh ○ pretend ○ no mistake
11. ● thotful ○ belt ○ legend ○ no mistake
12. ○ mild ● nob ○ folks ○ no mistake

71

1 Dictation

Reinforce correct spelling by using current and previous words in context.

Listen as I read each sentence and then write it in your Worktext. Remember to use correct capitalization and punctuation. (Slowly read each sentence twice. Sentences are found in the Student Worktext to the left.)

2 Proofreading

Familiarize students with standardized test format and reinforce recognition of misspelled words.

Look at each set of words. If a word is misspelled, fill in the oval by that word. If all the words are spelled correctly, fill in the oval by **no mistake**.

3 Hide and Seek

Reinforce correct spelling of current spelling words. Repeat this activity from Day 2. (A reproducible master is provided in Appendix A as shown on the inset page to the right.)

4 Other Word Forms

Have your students complete this activity to strengthen spelling ability and expand vocabulary.

1 Posttest

Visit the **A Reason For** website to download free, printable Posttest pages.

I will say the word once, use it in a sentence, then say it again. Write your words on a separate sheet of paper.

Progress Chart

Students may record scores. (Appendix B)

Personal Dictionary

Students may add any words they have misspelled to their personal dictionaries. (Appendix B)

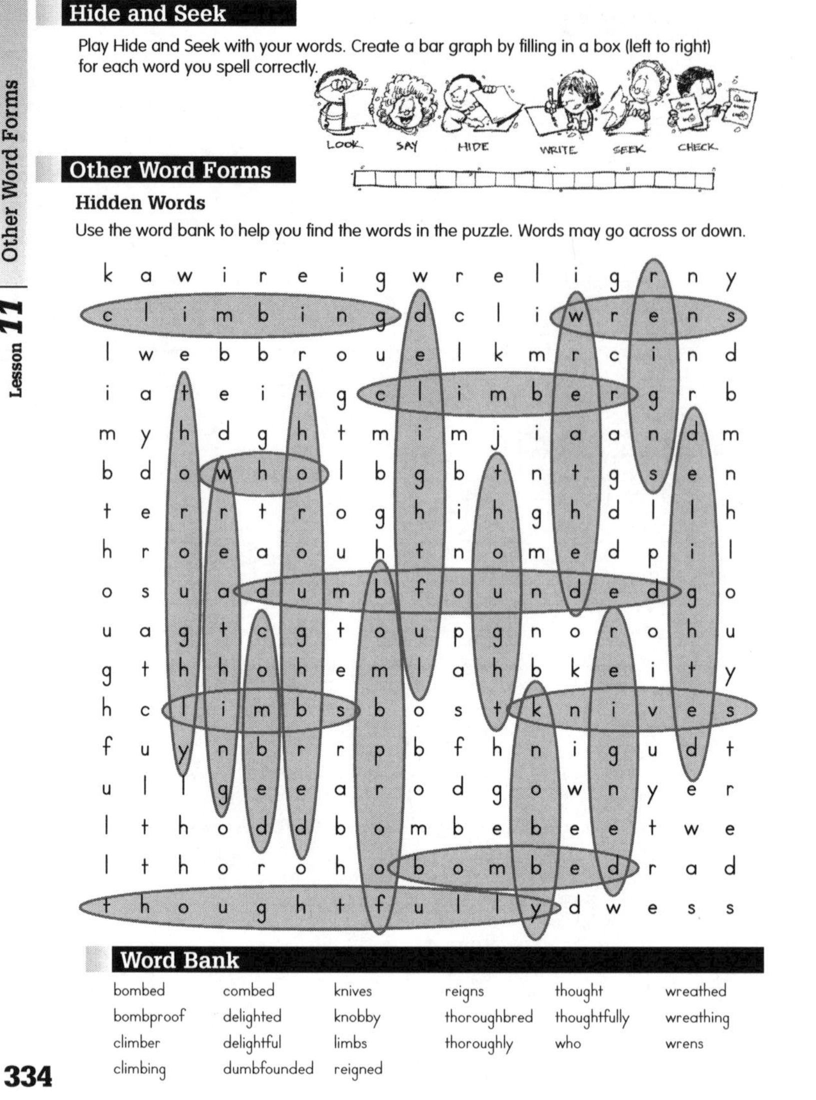

Other Word Forms

Lesson 11

Hide and Seek

Play Hide and Seek with your words. Create a bar graph by filling in a box (left to right) for each word you spell correctly.

LOOK SAY HIDE WRITE SEEK CHECK

Other Word Forms

Hidden Words

Use the word bank to help you find the words in the puzzle. Words may go across or down.

k a w i r e i g w r e l i g r n y
c l i m b i n g d c l i w r e n s
l w e b b r o u e l k m r c i n d
i a t e i t g c l i m b e r g r b
m y h d g h t m i m j i a a n d m
b d o w h o l b g b t n t g s e n
t e r r t r o g h i h g h d l l h
h r o e a o u h t n o m e d p i l
o s u a d u m b f o u n d e d g o
u a g t c g t o u p g n o r o h u
g t h h o h e m l a h b k e i t y
h c l i m b s b o s t k n i v e s
f u y n b r r p b f h n i g u d t
u l l g e e a r o d g o w n y e r
l t h o d d b o m b e b e e t w e
l t h o r o h o b o m b e d r a d
t h o u g h t f u l l y d w e s s

Word Bank

bombed	combed	knives	reigns	thought	wreathed
bombproof	delighted	knobby	thoroughbred	thoughtfully	wreathing
climber	delightful	limbs	thoroughly	who	wrens
climbing	dumbfounded	reigned			

334

1. **thorough** Airport security may make a **thorough** search of a passenger's luggage.
2. **unknown** The contents of many packages are **unknown.**
3. **knob** Kristin turned the **knob** of the front door and ran out to the mailbox.
4. **comb** Kristin had bought a pretty blue **comb** to keep in her book bag.
5. **thoughtful** She was in a **thoughtful** mood after reading Diana's letter.
6. **climb** She and Diana liked to **climb** trees together at camp.
7. **bomb** Diana said the people were afraid because of the many **bomb** threats.
8. **dumb** Some of them are **dumb**, or speechless, with fear and worry.
9. **folks** Lots of **folks** fled from their homes because of the persecution.
10. **reign** "A king does not **reign** in this country," explained Diana.
11. **although** They had enjoyed religious freedom before, **although** there were regulations.
12. **limb** Many Christians are willing to risk life and **limb** for Jesus' sake.
13. **ought** We **ought** to be very thankful for our religious freedom.
14. **delight** Jesus will always **delight** in our choice to follow Him.
15. **knife** They cannot allow a passenger to carry a **knife** on the plane.
16. **whose** I'm not sure **whose** handwriting is on the outside of the envelope.
17. **wreath** Matthew really appreciated the stamp with the **wreath** on it.
18. **wren** He put it in his book next to the stamp with the **wren.**

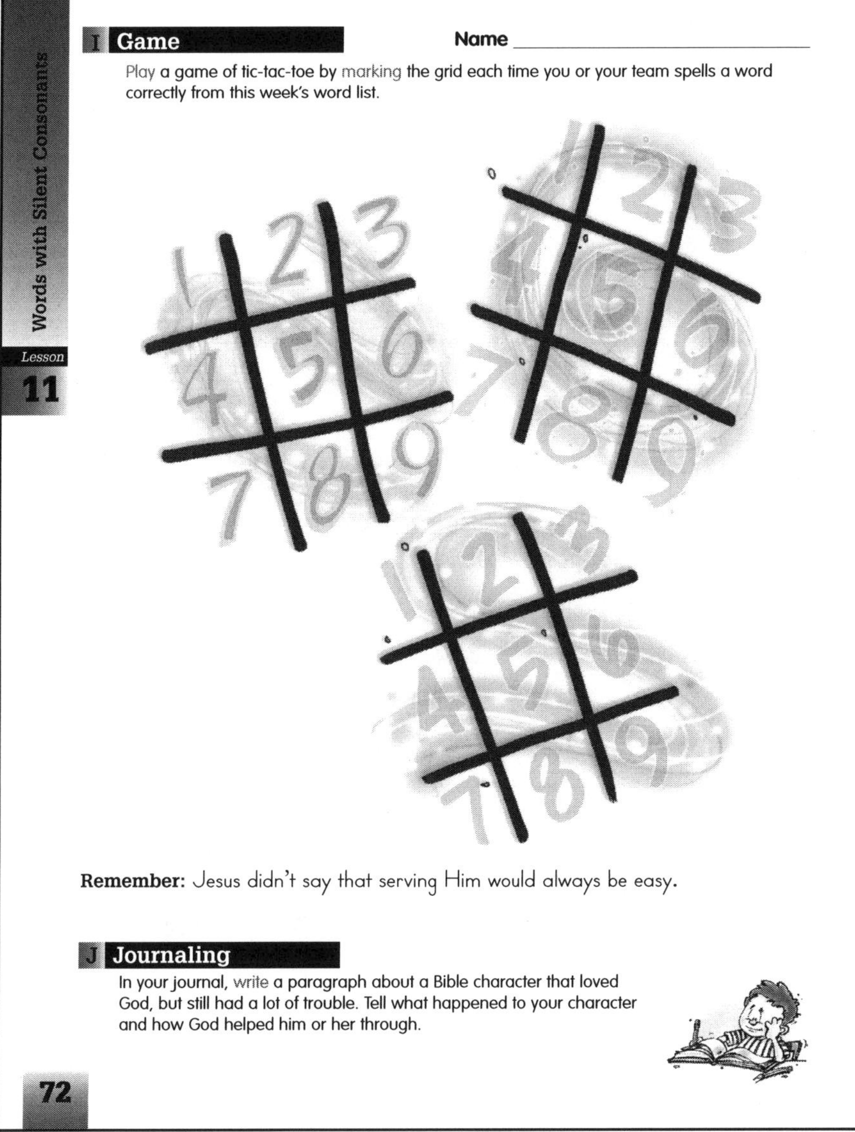

Words with Silent Consonants

Lesson 11

I Game Name ____________________

Play a game of tic-tac-toe by marking the grid each time you or your team spells a word correctly from this week's word list.

Remember: Jesus didn't say that serving Him would always be easy.

J Journaling

In your journal, write a paragraph about a Bible character that loved God, but still had a lot of trouble. Tell what happened to your character and how God helped him or her through.

72

How to Play:

- Divide students into two teams (the X's and the O's).
- Have a student from team X choose a number from 1 to 9.
- Say the word that matches that number from the Game Word List (Game 1).
- Have the student write the word on the board.
- If correct, have each member of both teams put an X on that number.
- Alternate between teams X and O.
- The first team to score three marks in a row (up, down, across, or diagonally) is the winner.
- Word lists and tic-tac-toe grids are provided for two additional games.

Small Group Option: Students may play this game without teacher direction in groups of two.

2 Game

Reinforce spelling skills and provide motivation and interest.

Materials

- game page (from Student Worktext)
- pencils (1 per child)
- game word list

Game 1 Word List

1. **climb**
2. **thorough**
3. **comb**
4. **folks**
5. **limb**
6. **knife**
7. **although**
8. **whose**
9. **ought**

Game 2 Word List

1. **bomb**
2. **thoughtful**
3. **dumb**
4. **reign**
5. **knob**
6. **unknown**
7. **delight**
8. **wreath**
9. **wren**

Game 3 Word List

1. **thorough**
2. **although**
3. **climb**
4. **whose**
5. **thoughtful**
6. **bomb**
7. **unknown**
8. **reign**
9. **delight**

3 Journaling

Provide a meaningful reason for correct spelling through personal writing.

Review the story using discussion leads provided on the following page. Encourage students to apply the Scriptural value in their journaling.

Journaling (continued)

- Have you ever had a pen pal? (Allow time for student responses.)
- In our country, we choose our government by voting for the people we want to lead us. In the country Diane lived in, how was the government chosen? (It wasn't really chosen. Whichever group was most powerful just took over the country and did whatever they wanted to do.)
- Why did Diane and her family have to leave their home in Africa? (A new government came into power that did not like people to believe in Jesus Christ. They said that those who believed in Jesus were against the government and enemies of the country.)
- What did this new government do to the people who loved Jesus? (They forced them out of their homes, took their jobs away, beat some of them, and even took their children away from some of them.)
- What does Scripture say about our lives when we follow God? (Following God won't necessarily make our lives easy. We may have lots of trouble, but we have God's promise to always be right there to help us through the hard times.)
- The Scriptures tell about many people who loved God but still had troubles in their lives. Name some of them. (Joseph, Noah, Paul, John the Baptist, Abraham, David, etc.)

The only fifteen letter words that can be spelled without repeating a letter are "uncopyrightable" and "dermatoglyphics" (the study of fingerprints).

Word Wow!

1 **Literature Connection**
Topic: Criticism
Theme Text: Matthew 7:1, 2

Embarrassing Episodes

An asthma attack helps Katelynn learn a lesson about others' feelings.

Katelynn took a notepad out of her desk and put it beside her handwriting book. There were pictures of horses around the edge of the unlined paper. "Dear Laney," she wrote. "Can you come over tomorrow? I got the riding outfit for my doll. I almost have enough saved for the horse. What did Heather do to her hair?" She signed her name beside the picture of the brown mare, folded the note and handed it across the aisle to her friend.

Mrs. Burton was busy reading with a small group. Everyone else was supposed to be doing handwriting. Laney read the note, then ripped a piece of paper from her own notepad. She looked over at Heather, who was sitting beside Mrs. Burton. She quickly wrote, "Katelynn, Heather's hair? What do you mean? I think I can come after my piano lesson." She signed her name at the bottom of the paper and dropped it on Katelynn's desk on her way to the pencil sharpener.

"Her bangs—" Katelynn wrote back, "look at her bangs." Katelynn drew a stick person with very short bangs and sent it across the aisle to Laney.

Laney wadded the note and walked to the trash can beside Mrs. Burton's desk. On the way back to her seat she sauntered past the group reading so she could see Heather's bangs. Heather looked up as Laney passed. Their eyes locked for an instant before Heather looked back at the book in her lap. She wiggled uncomfortably and put her hand over the too-short bangs.

When Laney reached her seat she glanced at Katelynn and made a face. "Mower was set too low?" she wrote on her little pad. Laney drew a picture of Heather and a lawn mower. She traced short lines all over the paper with her marker to represent flying hair.

Katelynn giggled when she saw the drawing. It looked a lot like Heather. Mrs. Burton frowned in their direction but didn't stop the discussion about reptiles.

Katelynn risked one more note. "Laney," she wrote. "I wonder who cut her bangs? Maybe her cousin Tony?"

Laney smiled and nodded as she read the note. Another frown from Mrs. Burton coaxed her to concentrate on the row of D's she was supposed to be writing.

After lunch Mrs. Burton led the class to the gym. When everyone was seated on the blue mats she smiled. "We're going to be focusing on physical fitness this year for PE. The events include a mile run, shuttle run, pull-ups, stretching exercises, and sit-ups. This will be harder for some of you than for others—just like math and spelling. In the spring, we'll have a school-wide track and field day. If you place in the top three, you'll get a trophy."

Kids were getting restless, so Mrs. Burton wrapped up her speech, "We're going to go outside for the mile run—four times around the track." Mrs. Burton checked her clipboard. "Today, our goal is to make it in nine and one-half minutes."

Katelynn didn't hear any more. *I'll never do it that fast!*

The class lined up on the track. When Mrs. Burton yelled "Go!" everyone took off. After the first lap, Beth, Tony, and Stephen were way out in front. Katelynn and Heather were last.

Laney jogged along beside Rachel. "What's with Katelynn? She's back there with Heather."

Rachel shrugged her shoulders. "Asthma, maybe. Beth told me she has it."

Katelynn slowed to a walk when she felt her chest tightening. Heather fell in step beside her. "How long have you had asthma?"

"Who says…whee-eee…I have asthma?" Katelynn snapped.

"My best friend at my old school had asthma. Sometimes she would breathe like you are right now. She always carried an inhaler. Don't you have one?"

Katelynn fingered the small aerosol bottle in her pocket. "I just don't want everyone feeling sorry for me. Most of the time," she noisily sucked in another breath of air, "I can exercise without…whh-eeee…an episode. It depends. Whhhh-eee! I just have to slow down before it gets bad. Whhh-eee. Then I'm okay."

"It's not your fault." Heather touched Katelynn's shoulder. Katelynn thought about the note she'd written that morning. The girls walked on in silence. As she relaxed, Katelynn's breathing became less labored.

When the girls finished, Katelynn hurried past Beth, Stephen, and Tony. She heard Tony say her name. But she didn't look to the right or the left as she headed to the bathroom. She felt like everyone was staring at her… whispering. Rachel and Laney burst out laughing. An hour ago she would have plopped down beside them and begged to know what was so funny—but now she knew…they were laughing at how long it took her to do the mile.

As soon as the bathroom door swung shut behind her, Katelynn leaned against the cool tiled wall and took a couple of slow, deep breaths. She walked slowly to the sink and splashed water on her hot face. She cupped her hands and slurped a quick drink before she rejoined her classmates in the gym.

Mrs. Burton put an arm around her, "Katelynn, do you feel like you can do sit-ups today?" Katelynn nodded. "Well, don't push

Story Continued

yourself too hard. I don't want you to have an episode." Katelynn nodded, but she was worried about the sit-ups. Even walking is hard today, she thought.

Mrs. Burton held up the black stopwatch. "Let's do some sit-ups now. Find a partner to hold your feet and count how many you do. Then you'll trade places. Let's go!"

"Will you be my partner?" Laney sat down beside Katelynn.

"I'm sure I won't be able to do enough." Katelynn looked down at her hands.

"I'll go first. You count." Laney crossed her arms across her chest and put her hands on her shoulders. She put her feet flat on the floor and bent her knees.

After 35 sit-ups Laney fell back on the mat exhausted.

"Stop! Time to switch!" Mrs. Burton yelled. "Remember how many you did."

Katelynn lay on the mat and looked at the ceiling. *I've never told Laney I have asthma,* she thought. *I just always take my medicine and stop exercising when my chest feels tight or it's hard for me to breathe.* She felt the inhaler in her pocket.

"Go!" Mrs. Burton yelled.

Katelynn sat up slowly. She tried to keep her rhythm even. Up, down, up, down, up. After the tenth sit-up, her face was red and she was puffing. She could feel her chest tightening, and it was harder and harder for her to get her breath. After 15 she flopped back down on her back. "I just can't…whhh-eee… do any more…whhh-eee."

Laney jumped up. "I'll be right back."

Katelynn felt the inhaler in her pocket again as she watched Laney sit down beside Rachel and whisper something in her ear. Both girls giggled, then looked toward Katelynn.

Katelynn jumped up and walked quickly to the bathroom. When the door swung shut she gave herself a dose of medication.

"Your inhaler will work out there, you know."

Katelynn jumped at the sound of Heather's voice. "You don't have to go hide in the bathroom to use it," Heather said.

"I don't want…whhh-eee… everyone staring at me. It's too… whhhh-eee…embarrassing."

"So are my bangs." Heather covered them up with her hand. "My mom baby-sits some little neighbor kids," Heather said in a rush. "I was reading my snake book last night and the littlest girl turned around and cut a big hunk out of my hair. One minute she was cutting out a snowman—the next she was whacking my bangs. Mom had to even them out."

"They'll grow." Katelynn thought of the notes again. "It's not your fault."

The next morning Mrs. Burton called another group of students up to the table to discuss reptile books they'd read. Katelynn's row would be the next group. She got out the book she'd read and put it on the corner of her desk; then she opened her handwriting book. Laney's picture of Heather's hair and the lawn mower was tucked between the pages. She glanced at the text and read it slowly to herself. "Don't criticize, and then you won't be criticized. For others will treat you as you treat them."

Katelynn's face turned red with shame. *I sure did think it was funny to poke fun at Heather's hair,* she thought. *But when it was me that was being laughed at…Heather was really nice to me. She didn't laugh at me at all. She did what God says to do in that verse and I didn't.*

Katelynn wadded the thoughtless picture into a ball. She got out another piece of paper and wrote, "Dear Laney, A little girl cut a hunk out of Heather's bangs. It's not her fault. Sorry I said those mean things about her. Katelynn." She folded the note and quickly passed it across the aisle.

Laney looked at Katelynn with an I'm-sorry-too look, then drew a picture of three girls—one with black hair, one with red hair, and one with short blond hair—all smiling. She labeled the picture "Friends."

Mrs. Burton called Katelynn's group up to the table. As she headed toward the front, she laid the drawing on Heather's desk. "Laney draws neat pictures, doesn't she?"

Heather smiled, "It's great. This really looks like us."

"Heather," Katelynn whispered, "thanks for being nice to me yesterday in PE. I really needed a friend. And your bangs aren't so bad. They even look like they might have grown some."

2 Discussion Time

Check understanding of the story and development of personal values.

- What does criticize mean?
- What did Katelynn's first notes say about Heather's bangs?
- What did Laney draw on her note about Heather's hair cut?
- Raise your hand if you think the girls were being critical?
- How do you feel when someone criticizes you?

A Test-Words Name ____________

Write each spelling word on the line as your teacher says it.

1.	whom	8.	dream
2.	comb	9.	stretch
3.	whose	10.	blanket
4.	wrong	11.	movement
5.	broom	12.	strap
6.	knob	13.	stool
7.	usual	14.	spirit

Review Lesson 12

B Test-Sentences

Write the sentences on the lines below, correcting each misspelled word, as well as all capitalization and punctuation errors. There are two misspelled words in each sentence.

the little girl played a lovely toon on her floot:

1. The little girl played a lovely **tune** on her **flute.**

a nearby rose bush flaunted a butiful blume

2. A nearby rose bush flaunted a **beautiful bloom.**

Were you careful not to spil the creem.

3. Were you careful not to **spill** the **cream?**

the blaid of that nife is very sharp

4. The **blade** of that **knife** is very sharp**.**

73

4 Test-Sentences

Reinforce recognizing misspelled words.

Read each sentence carefully. Write the sentences on the lines in your Worktext. There are two misspelled words in each sentence. Correct each misspelled word, as well as all capitalization and punctuation errors.

Take a minute to memorize...

Matthew 7:1,2

3 Test-Words

Test for knowledge of the correct spellings of these words.

I will say each word once, use the word in a sentence, then say the word again. Write the words on the lines in your Worktext.

1. whom	About **whom** were Katelynn and Laney writing?
2. comb	Heather tried to **comb** her bangs down flat.
3. whose	Do you remember **whose** fault it was that Heather's bangs were so short?
4. wrong	Katelynn knew that making fun of Heather was **wrong.**
5. broom	The janitor used a large **broom** to sweep the gym floor.
6. knob	There is a long chrome bar on the gym door, not a **knob.**
7. usual	This was not a **usual** class day.
8. dream	"It's a **dream** of mine to get a trophy," said Tony.
9. stretch	Mrs. Burton showed the class how to **stretch** their muscles.
10. blanket	Katelynn sat on a blue mat, not a **blanket,** to exercise.
11. movement	"Make a curling **movement** forward," instructed Mrs. Burton.
12. strap	She wore a silver whistle on a **strap** around her wrist.
13. stool	Mrs. Burton sat on a tall **stool** as the students ran their laps.
14. spirit	"You can do it! That's the **spirit!**" encouraged Mrs. Burton.

Test-Dictation

Reinforce correct spelling by using current and previous words in context.

Listen as I read each sentence, then write it in your Worktext. Remember to use correct capitalization and punctuation. (Slowly read each sentence twice. Sentences are found in the Student Worktext at right. The words **roof**, **crust**, **thread**, and **wren** are found in this unit.)

Test-Proofreading

Familiarize students with standardized test format and reinforce recognizing misspelled words.

Look at each set of words. If a word is misspelled, fill in the oval by that word. If all the words are spelled correctly, fill in the oval by **no mistake**.

C Test-Dictation

Name ______________________

Write each sentence as your teacher dictates. Use correct punctuation.

1. Her husband climbed a tall ladder to get on the roof.
2. Should we bake the crust, then add the fruit?
3. Grandmother bought thread at the store.
4. A wren made a nest in that tree.

D Test-Proofreading

If a word is misspelled, fill in the oval by that word. If all the words are spelled correctly, fill in the oval by **no mistake**.

1. ● reskew ○ whom ○ comb ○ no mistake
2. ○ whose ○ wrong ● movey ○ no mistake
3. ● polute ○ broom ○ knob ○ no mistake
4. ○ usual ○ avenue ○ dream ● no mistake
5. ○ stretch ○ blanket ● blaid ○ no mistake
6. ● humin ○ movement ○ strap ○ no mistake
7. ● glew ○ stool ○ spirit ○ no mistake
8. ○ throat ● fluor ○ speak ○ no mistake
9. ○ groan ○ folks ● slipery ○ no mistake
10. ○ smoke ○ climb ○ due ● no mistake
11. ○ moment ● crak ○ dumb ○ no mistake
12. ● stroak ○ steady ○ understand ○ no mistake

E Test-Table

Name ______________________

If a word is misspelled, shade in that box.

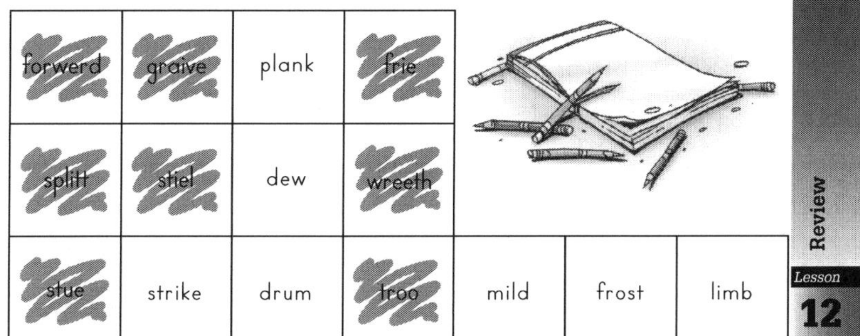

forwerd	graive	plank	frie
splitt	stiel	dew	wreeth

stue	strike	drum	troo	mild	frost	limb

Review

Lesson 12

F Writing Assessment

Write a note to one of your friends. Tell him or her why you're glad you are friends. Talk about the things you like to do together and why he or she is fun to be around.

____

____

____

____

____

____

____

____

Scripture

Matthew 7:1, 2

75

Level, deed, eye, bib, ewe, pip, noon, tot, sis, pop, nun, mom, and pup are palindromes, along with the names Bob, Otto, Nan, Ana, Lil and Tut.

1 Test-Table

Test mastery of words in this unit.

If a word is misspelled, fill in the space on the grid.

2 Writing Assessment

Assess student's spelling, grammar, and composition skills through personal writing.

- Did Katelynn run the mile very fast? (No.) Why? (She has asthma.)
- How did Katelynn feel when she heard her name as she walked past Tony, Stephen, and Beth? (She was embarrassed. She thought they were talking about how slowly she'd done the mile.)
- How did Heather treat Katelynn during PE class? (She walked with her around the track. She encouraged her not to be embarrassed about the asthma she couldn't help.)
- What did Katelynn do when she first noticed Heather's short bangs? (She wrote a note to Laney and they talked about how it looked like her bangs had been mowed with a lawn mower.)
- How did Heather's bangs get cut so short? (A little neighbor girl cut a big hunk out of them. Her mom had to even them up.)
- How did Heather feel about her short bangs? (She was embarrassed.)
- Raise your hand if you would like to have a friend like Heather?

1 Test-Sentences

Reinforce recognizing misspelled words.

Read each sentence carefully. Write the sentences on the lines in your Worktext, correcting each misspelled word, as well as all capitalization and punctuation errors.

G Test-Sentences Name ____________

Write the sentences on the lines below, correcting each misspelled word, as well as all capitalization and punctuation errors. There are two misspelled words in each sentence.

rumind dad to lock the apartmunt door?

1. Remind Dad to lock the apartment door.

The map,s lejind showed the symbol for a brij;

2. The map's legend showed the symbol for a bridge.

the guverment pays him to gard the president

3. The government pays him to guard the President.

the small boy felt a thril as his bat struk the ball

4. The small boy felt a thrill as his bat struck the ball!

H Test-Words

Write each spelling word on the line as your teacher says it.

1. throat
2. speak
3. groan
4. folks
5. climb
6. due
7. moment
8. dumb
9. steady
10. understand
11. thoughtful
12. pretend
13. clear
14. ought

Review Lesson 12

76

2 Test-Words

Test for knowledge of the correct spellings of these words.

I will say the word once, use the word in a sentence, then say the word again. Write the word on the lines in your Worktext.

1. **throat** Katelynn's **throat** felt dry and sore.
2. **speak** It was difficult for her to **speak.**
3. **groan** She let out a **groan** as she felt her chest tighten.
4. **folks** Many **folks** suffer from asthma.
5. **climb** Sometimes when they try to run or **climb,** they begin to wheeze.
6. **due** She found it hard to continue **due** to her asthma.
7. **moment** "I just need to rest for a **moment,**" she explained.
8. **dumb** She felt **dumb** using her inhaler in front of her classmates.
9. **steady** Katelynn leaned against the bathroom wall to **steady** herself.
10. **understand** "I **understand** now how it feels to be criticized," she muttered.
11. **thoughtful** Heather was very **thoughtful** and kind to Katelynn.
12. **pretend** "Why do you **pretend** you don't have asthma?" she asked.
13. **clear** The verse made it **clear** to Katelynn that she had done wrong.
14. **ought** We **ought** not criticize and make fun of others.

I Test-Editing Name ____________

If a word is spelled correctly, fill in the oval under **Correct**. If the word is misspelled, fill in the oval under **Incorrect**, and write the word correctly on the blank.

	Correct	Incorrect	
1. snap	●	○	
2. spray	●	○	
3. flowe	○	●	flow
4. belt	●	○	
5. amung	○	●	among
6. blank	●	○	
7. bint	○	●	bent
8. merchant	●	○	
9. bom	○	●	bomb
10. reign	●	○	
11. alltho	○	●	although
12. delite	○	●	delight
13. theroe	○	●	thorough
14. smash	●	○	
15. ren	○	●	wren

Review Lesson 12

77

3 Test-Editing

Reinforce recognizing and correcting misspelled words.

4 Action Game

Reinforce spelling skills and provide motivation and interest.

Materials

- Two Bells

PROOF RINGING

How to Play:

Divide students into two teams. Each team sits around their game bell. Say a word aloud then slowly spell it. (Spell most words incorrectly.) When a word is spelled incorrectly, teams compete to ring their bell first. If the student who rings the bell first can correct the mistake, his/her team receives a point. If a student rings the bell when a mistake has not been made, his/her team loses a point. Repeat this process until all the words have been spelled. The team with the most points wins!

Game

Reinforce spelling skills and provide motivation and interest.

Materials

- game pages (from Student Worktext)
- stickers (13 per child)
- game word list

J Game Name ____________________

Mrs. Burton's class prepared for the fitness challenge this week. Use these winning words as team names for this game. Place a sticker on the game board each time you or your team spells a review word correctly.

Remember: Say the kinds of things about others you would like to have said about you.

Review Lesson 12

78

Game Word List

Check off each word lightly in pencil as it is used.

The Champions	The Conquerors
1. **rescue**	1. **movie**
2. **pollute**	2. **split**
3. **human**	3. **drum**
4. **glue**	4. **forward**
5. **flour**	5. **dew**
6. **crack**	6. **smoke**
7. **stroke**	7. **slippery**
8. **stew**	8. **avenue**
9. **grave**	9. **wreath**
10. **style**	10. **plank**
11. **strike**	11. **fry**
12. **true**	12. **frost**
13. **mild**	13. **limb**

How to Play:

- Divide students into two teams. Name one team **The Champions**, one **The Conquerors**. (Optional: If you have an even number of students, you may wish to pair students from opposing teams and have them share a game page.)
- Read the instructions from the student game page aloud.
- Have a student from the first team choose a number from 1 to 13.
- Say the word that matches that number from the team's word list.
- Have the student write the word on the board.
- If correct, have each member of that team put a sticker on that number by his/her team name. If the word is misspelled, have him/her put an X through that number. That number may not be chosen again.
- Repeat this process with the second team.
- When the words from both lists have been used, the team with the most stickers is the winner.

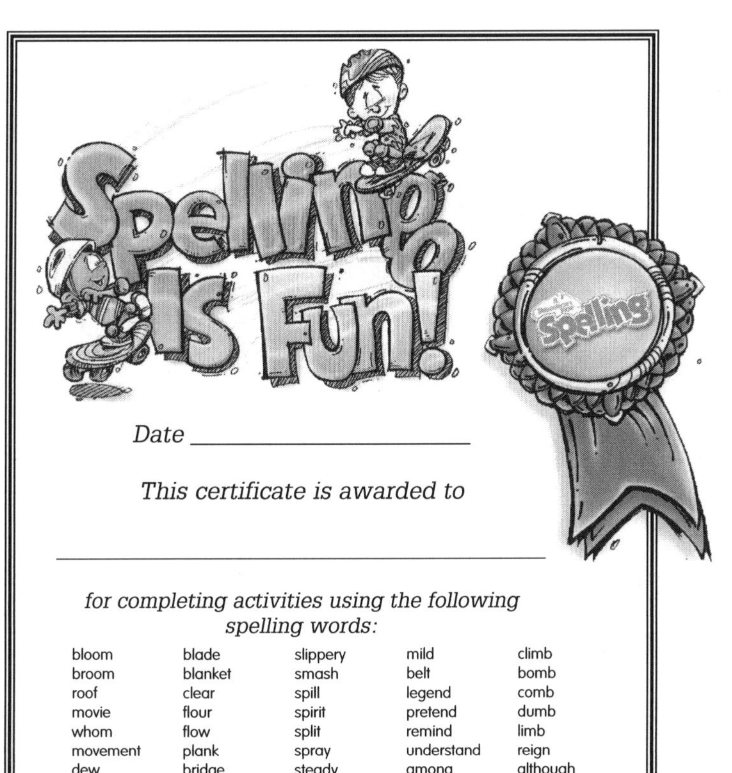

Date ____________________

This certificate is awarded to

____

for completing activities using the following spelling words:

bloom	blade	slippery	mild	climb
broom	blanket	smash	belt	bomb
roof	clear	spill	legend	comb
movie	flour	spirit	pretend	dumb
whom	flow	split	remind	limb
movement	plank	spray	understand	reign
dew	bridge	steady	among	although
flute	crack	stool	wrong	delight
pollute	cream	style	blank	ought
tune	dream	strap	apartment	thorough
avenue	drum	stretch	bent	thoughtful
clue	fry	strike	government	folks
due	grave	stroke	merchant	knife
glue	smoke	struck	moment	knob
rescue	snap	thread	forward	unknown
human	groan	thrill	guard	whose
usual	speak	throat	crust	wreath
beautiful	stew	true	frost	wren

2 Certificate

Provide an opportunity for parents or guardians to encourage and assess their child's progress.

Fill in today's date and your name on your certificate.

Take a minute to memorize...

Matthew 7:1,2

3 Letter

Provide the parent or guardian with the spelling word lists for the next unit.

Give your parents or guardian this letter that lists your spelling words for the next unit. Put it where you will remember to practice the words together.

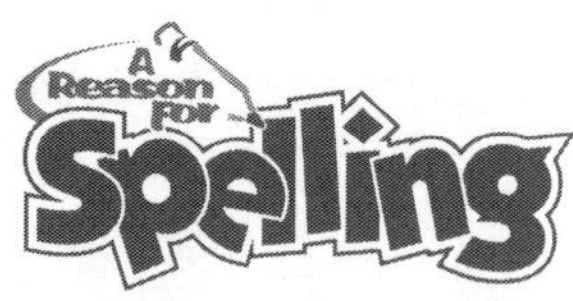

Dear Parent,

We are about to begin a new spelling unit containing five weekly lessons. A set of eighteen words will be studied each week. All the words will be reviewed in the sixth week. Values based on the Scriptures listed below will be taught in each lesson.

Lesson 13	Lesson 14	Lesson 15	Lesson 16	Lesson 17
cough	cellar	aloud	all right	barber
enough	chance	bounce	almost	barnyard
laugh	citizen	county	already	cardboard
rough	decide	household	false	carnival
tough	exciting	noun	quarrel	carpet
alphabet	fence	outdoors	toward	cart
elephant	glance	pound	applause	farmer
graph	peace	scout	author	farther
orphan	police	stout	fault	garbage
photograph	scene	trout	haul	garden
bluff	science	underground	pause	hardly
stuff	across	frown	sauce	harm
office	press	gown	awful	harsh
chef	recess	growl	hawk	marbles
loaf	beast	owl	fog	scarf
craft	else	however	offer	spark
drift	famous	powder	cord	starve
swift	son	tower	forest	yarn
Luke 6:27, 28	John 10:14, 15	Luke 11:9	Mark 9:37	John 3:16

1 **Literature Connection**

Topic: Loving Enemies
Theme Text: Luke 6:27, 28

The Candy Snatcher

Tony faces a difficult challenge when a bully steals his candy.

Tony pulled the collar of his green jacket up around his ears and stuffed his hands into his dark blue gloves. "It's cold out here today. Let's warm up playing tag." His eyes swept across the playground. "No base—and you're 'It' first!" He took a giant step backwards and danced around Stephen and Beth.

Stephen ignored Tony and rubbed his hands together. He looked down at his brown boots, then stomped his feet. "It's freezing." He reached out and touched Tony. "I wasn't 'It' for long!" he laughed. "No touch-backs!" Tony lunged for Beth, barely missing her.

"Nice try," she grinned and ran toward the lone pine tree in the middle of the playground. "Better luck next time," she called over her shoulder.

Stephen pulled his striped wool hat over his ears. He watched Tony try unsuccessfully to catch Beth. Her blond hair swirled around her face as she quickly changed directions and out-maneuvered Tony. Stephen smiled and stuffed his hands deep into the pockets of his coat. His fingers touched something unexpected. "What in the world?" he said out loud. He pulled a golden package out of his right pocket. He turned it over and read "Milkduds®" in brown letters. *My favorite! I wonder how these got in my pocket?* He pulled out a folded note that read, "Dear Stephen, You're special. Love, Gram."

Stephen smiled. *I wish she lived closer,* he thought. *She's the best grandma in the world.*

Beth grabbed the pole of the swing set. "Base! Pfff...Pfff...Pfff! This is base," she panted.

Tony stopped chasing her when she touched the pole. He walked the remaining distance between them and touched Beth's shoulder. "There's no base. You're 'It.' We said no base, didn't we, Stephen?"

Stephen put a piece of candy in his mouth before he nodded his agreement.

"Where'd you get those? Can I have some?" Tony held out a hand.

"Sure." Stephen dumped several pieces of the chocolate-covered caramel candy into Tony's hand. Beth held out her hand, too.

Tony tagged her. "You're 'It' for sure now—you're not even touching the pole."

Beth grinned. "Mmm. Where'd you get these? You finished your lunch inside a few minutes ago."

"I found them in my coat pocket. Gram is visiting us. She loves to surprise me. It's a game we've played since I was little. Here. You want some more?"

"Yeah, hand over the rest." A big hand grabbed the package. Stephen looked up into the face of Brutus, an eighth-grade boy. Brutus didn't smile. His eyes were squinting in the bright noon sun. His forehead was wrinkled. He looked angry and BIG. Brutus's friends laughed as the huge eighth-grader poured the rest of the candy into his mouth.

"I wouldn't go tattling to Miz Burton." Brutus wadded up the wrapper and threw it on the ground. "If you want to stay in one piece, you'd better keep your mouths shut. Understand, you little runts?"

Beth, Tony, and Stephen looked at each other and nodded their heads. They didn't say a word until Brutus and company were out of earshot.

"What creeps!" Beth put her hands on her waist.

"Is Brutus his real name?" Stephen pointed at the back of the obnoxious eighth-grader.

"He's new this year." Tony leaned against the pole of the swing set and crossed his arms. "I don't know if it's his real name or not, but it sure fits him, doesn't it?"

"That was my special candy from Gram." Stephen clenched and unclenched his fists as his fear turned to rage. "He has no right to take it from me!" He felt his face grow hot. "He just can't do this to us!"

"He could really hurt us," Tony observed. "We can't even think of telling Mrs. Burton. He could torture us for the rest of the year."

At noon recess the next day the three friends joined the line to play four-square. A brisk wind was blowing from the north. Thick clouds covered the sun. Stephen flipped up the hood of his jacket—and a bright red package of Skittles® fell to the ground.

"I like having Gram here. She played dominoes with me until bedtime last night—and now this. You guys want some?" Stephen ripped open the package and dumped some of the brightly colored candy pieces into their outstretched hands. A note taped to the package fluttered to the ground.

"Quick, hide the candy! Here comes Rudest Brutus!" Beth put all the candy in her mouth at once.

Stephen nonchalantly put the candy in his coat pocket, but he felt sweat trickle down the back of his neck. "Are you guys going to the party at the church Sunday night?"

"Not this time." Brutus bumped into Stephen hard and knocked him off balance. The candy in his hand scattered across the pavement.

"Brought me more candy today, I see." The bully reached into Stephen's pocket and pulled out the red package.

Stephen ignored Brutus. He bent over to pick up his note. Brutus' big boot stomped down on Stephen's fingers. Stephen yelped in pain. Big tears came to his

Story (continued)

eyes and rolled down his cheeks. He didn't want anyone to see the tears—especially Rudest Brutus.

"I don't want to hear about this from Miz Burton or more than a few fingers will be hurting," Brutus sneered. He ground the spilled candy into the pavement with his boot before he sauntered off.

Stephen grabbed his note and unfolded it. He kept looking down hoping no one would notice his tears. "Dear Stephen," he read, "I'm looking forward to going shopping with you after school today. Maybe we can find some of those little cars you like. Love Gram." He wanted to scream at Brutus, "I hate you! I hate you! I hate you!" He didn't—mostly because he didn't want to draw attention to his tear-stained cheeks. He clenched his fists in frustration.

"I think we should eat your candy inside tomorrow," Beth declared.

Stephen wiped his eyes with the back of his hand. "I would, but Gram keeps hiding it in different places. On Monday I found some in my striped hat before first recess. Yesterday I found Milkduds® in my coat pocket. Today the Skittles® fell out of the hood of my coat. No telling where she'll put it tomorrow."

The next day Stephen discovered a package of Sweet-Tarts® in his big notebook. He shared them with his friends before they went out for noon recess. Mrs. Burton organized a game of dodge ball. Stephen quickly joined the game. He hoped Rudest Brutus would leave them alone if Mrs. Burton was close. Stephen didn't really want to know what Rudest Brutus would do if no one had any candy to give him.

Friday morning Stephen carefully wrote the Scripture verse on his border sheet for handwriting class. "Love your enemies. Do good to those who hate you. Pray for the happiness of those who curse you; implore God's blessing on those who hurt you." *Yuck! This verse can't mean Rudest Brutus,* Stephen thought. *I'm supposed to pray for Brutus to be happy and ask God to bless him? I'll never be able to love Brutus! He hates me. He stepped on my fingers on purpose.* Stephen carefully colored the border sheet and turned it in, but he couldn't get the words of the verse they'd studied all week out of his mind.

Stephen tossed and turned in his bed that night. He kept thinking of the verse and Rudest Brutus. Gram poked her head into his room at 10 o'clock. "You still not asleep, my boy?" She came in and sat down on the edge of Stephen's bed and pulled the blanket up under his chin. "I love you, Stephen. You're growing up so quickly. I wish I lived closer so I could see you more often."

"Why don't you move here, Gram?" Stephen patted her arm. "Then I could see you every day."

"I'd like to, Stephen, but Grandpa's job is in Maryland. We have to have a way to make a livin.' Maybe we can move here when we retire." She squeezed Stephen's hand. I'll be happy when we all live in heaven and I can see you every day—forever."

Stephen was quiet for a minute. "Gram, you know that verse about enemies?"

"You mean the one your mom hung on the fridge this afternoon? In Luke 6?"

"Yeah, that's the one." Stephen squirmed under the covers. "Why does God want us to love our enemies? Why does He want us to ask Him to bless people who hurt us?"

It was Gram's turn to be quiet. Finally she answered, "That's a good question, Stephen. What do you think?"

"Well, I've been thinking about it all week. I'm not sure. If we love our enemies they wouldn't be enemies any more. Maybe God wants to get rid of enemies."

"That's a good thought, my boy." Gram patted his hand.

"But it takes two people, doesn't it, Gram? You can't make a friend out of someone who doesn't want to be friends."

"Maybe that's where the prayin' part comes in, Stephen. You have an enemy we need to be prayin' for tonight? Is that why you're havin' trouble sleepin?'"

Stephen nodded his head in the dark.

"Who should I pray for, Stephen?"

There was a long silence. Finally Gram said, "You just let me know if you want to talk about it. Sometimes talkin' helps. Why don't we pray? God will know who we mean without names."

"You pray, Gram—you've known God longer than I have." Stephen smiled in the dark.

"Lord, change my boy's heart. Help him not to hate. Hatin' and anger can tear you up inside. Give him strength to do good—even to his enemy. Amen."

"Thanks, Gram." Stephen rolled over and was soon fast asleep.

2 Discussion Time

Check understanding of the story and development of personal values.

- What surprise did Stephen find in his pocket?
- How did Stephen feel when he found the candy and note from Gram?
- Who grabbed Stephen's candy?
- If Brutus took your candy, what would you do?
- What did Brutus do to Stephen the next day?
- What Scripture verse was Stephen learning in school?
- Why do you think it is important to "do good to those who hate you?"

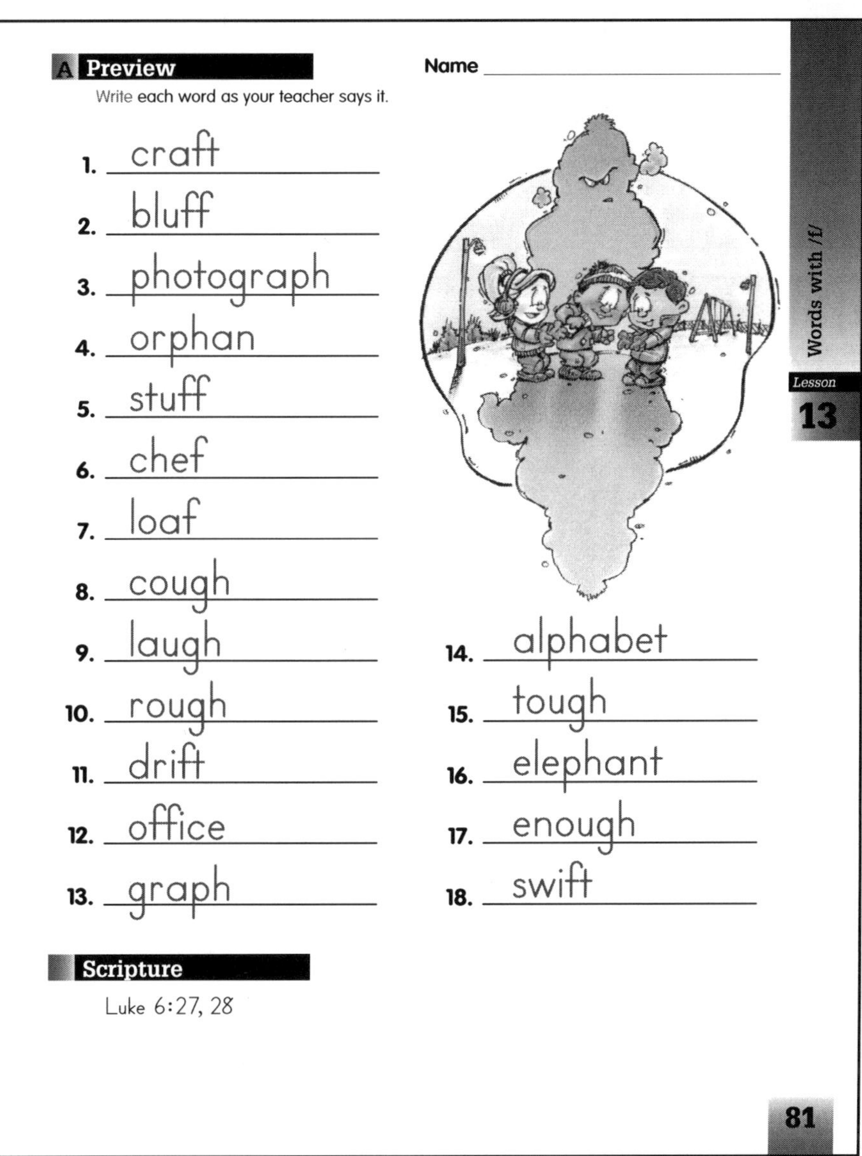

A **Preview** Name ______________

Write each word as your teacher says it.

1. craft
2. bluff
3. photograph
4. orphan
5. stuff
6. chef
7. loaf
8. cough
9. laugh
10. rough
11. drift
12. office
13. graph
14. alphabet
15. tough
16. elephant
17. enough
18. swift

Scripture

Luke 6:27, 28

Words with /f/

Lesson 13

81

3 Preview

Test for knowledge of the correct spellings of these words.

Customize Your List

On a separate sheet of paper, additional words of your choice may be tested.

I will say each word once, use the word in a sentence, then say the word again. Write the words on the lines in your Worktext.

Correct Immediately!

Let's correct our Preview. I will spell each word out loud. If you spelled a word incorrectly, rewrite it correctly.

Progress Chart

Students may record scores. (Reproducible master provided in Appendix B.)

1.	craft	"There will be a **craft** time after recess," said Mrs. Burton.
2.	bluff	Beth ran in a zigzag pattern to **bluff** Tony.
3.	photograph	Stephen has a **photograph** of Gram in his room.
4.	orphan	Stephen's grandmother was an **orphan**.
5.	stuff	"Gram has put special **stuff** in my coat or backpack each day," he said.
6.	chef	"My mom says Gram is a master **chef**," he informed his friends.
7.	loaf	"She makes an awesome **loaf** of sweetbread," Stephen said with a smile.
8.	cough	Brutus' rough **cough** startled Stephen and his friends.
9.	laugh	Brutus gave a short, harsh **laugh** as he grabbed Stephen's candy.
10.	rough	"I'll make it **rough** for you if you tell Mrs. Burton," warned Brutus.
11.	drift	"Do you get my **drift**?" he sneered.
12.	office	If Mrs. Burton finds out, Brutus will be sent to the principal's **office**.
13.	graph	Stephen completed the **graph** in his math Worktext before bed.
14.	alphabet	He also practiced writing the **alphabet** in cursive.
15.	tough	It is **tough** to love your enemies without God's help.
16.	elephant	Stephen plopped on his bed like a weary **elephant**.
17.	enough	Gram understood **enough** to know they needed to pray about it.
18.	swift	Be **swift** to pray for those who hurt you.

Word Shapes

Help students form a correct image of whole words.

Look at each word and think about its shape. Now, write the word in the correct Word Shape Boxes. You may check off each word as you use it.

(In many words, the sound of **/f/** is spelled with **f**, **ff**, **gh**, or **ph**. The **ff** and **gh** spellings are never found at the beginning of a word.)

In the Word Shape Boxes, fill in the boxes containing the letter or letters that spell the **/f/** sound in each word.

B Word Shapes Name ____________

Write each word in the correct Word Shape Boxes. Next, in the Word Shape Boxes, shade in the boxes containing the letter or letters that spell the **/f/** sound in each word.

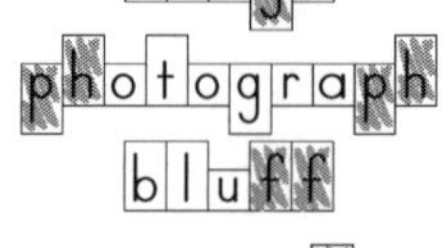

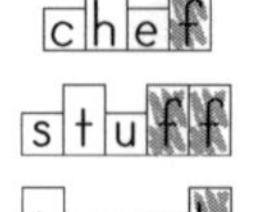

Word	Word Shape Boxes
1. cough	craft
2. enough	elephant
3. laugh	graph
4. rough	loaf
5. tough	office
6. alphabet	cough
7. elephant	alphabet
8. graph	orphan
9. orphan	swift
10. photograph	drift
11. bluff	rough
12. stuff	photograph
13. office	bluff
14. chef	enough
15. loaf	laugh
16. craft	chef
17. drift	stuff
18. swift	tough

82

Answers may vary for duplicate word shapes.

Take a minute to memorize...

Luke 6:27, 28

Be Prepared For Fun

Check these supply lists for **Fun Ways to Spell** - presented **Day 2**. Purchase and/or gather these items ahead of time!

General
- Pencil
- Graph Paper (1 sheet per child)
- Spelling List

Auditory
- Voice Recorder
- Spelling List

Visual
- Water Color Paint Box (1 per child)
- Paint Brush (1 per child)
- Art Paper (3 or 4 sheets per child)
- Spelling List

Tactile
- Soccer Ball, Basketball, Tennis Ball, or 4-Square Ball
- Spelling List

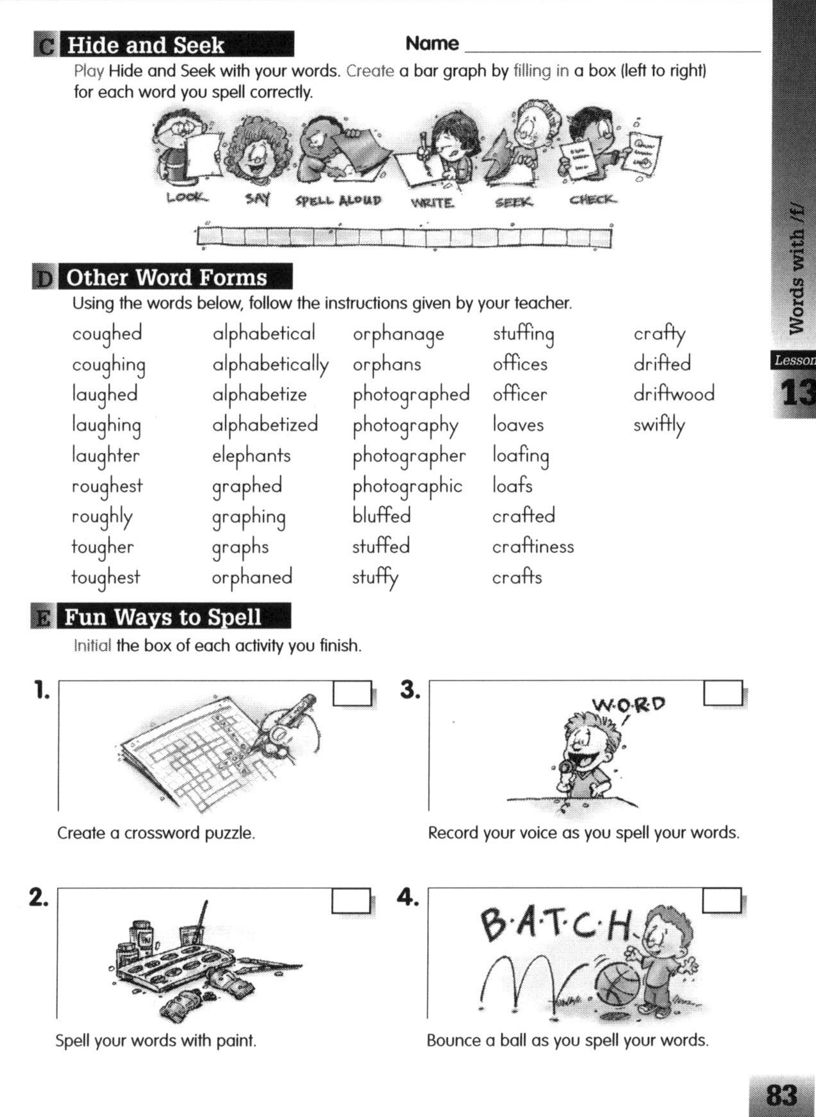

C Hide and Seek

Name ______________________

Play Hide and Seek with your words. Create a bar graph by filling in a box (left to right) for each word you spell correctly.

D Other Word Forms

Using the words below, follow the instructions given by your teacher.

coughed	alphabetical	orphanage	stuffing	crafty
coughing	alphabetically	orphans	offices	drifted
laughed	alphabetize	photographed	officer	driftwood
laughing	alphabetized	photography	loaves	swiftly
laughter	elephants	photographer	loafing	
roughest	graphed	photographic	loafs	
roughly	graphing	bluffed	crafted	
tougher	graphs	stuffed	craftiness	
toughest	orphaned	stuffy	crafts	

E Fun Ways to Spell

Initial the box of each activity you finish.

1. Create a crossword puzzle.

3.
Record your voice as you spell your words.

2. Spell your words with paint.

4.
Bounce a ball as you spell your words.

Words with /f/

Lesson 13

83

1 Hide and Seek

Reinforce spelling by using multiple styles of learning.

On a white board, Teacher writes each word — one at a time. **Have students:**

- **Look** at the word.
- **Say** the word out loud.
- **Spell** the word out loud.
- **Hide** (teacher erases word.)
- **Write** the word on paper.
- **Seek** (teacher rewrites word.)
- **Check** spelling. If incorrect, rewrite word correctly.

2 Other Word Forms

This activity is optional. Have students write original sentences using these Other Word Forms:

graphed
tougher
alphabetized
stuffy

3 Fun Ways to Spell

Four activities are provided. Use one, two, three, or all of the activities. Have students initial the box for each activity they complete.

Options:

- assign activities to students according to their learning styles
- set up the activities in learning centers for students to do throughout the day
- divide students into four groups and assign one activity per group
- do one activity per day

General

To create a crossword puzzle…
- Use a pencil to arrange your words on graph paper.
- Overlap words where letters are shared.
- Don't create any new words.
- Outline each word with a marker and number them.
- Write a clue for each word.
- Erase your words.
- Trade with a classmate and work each other's puzzles.

Auditory

To spell your words using a voice recorder...
- Record yourself as you say and spell each word on your spelling list.
- Listen to your recording and check your spelling.

Visual

To spell your words with paint…
- Paint each spelling word on your paper.
- Trade papers with a classmate and check each other's spelling.

Tactile

To bounce a ball as you spell your words…
- Look at the first word on your list.
- Bounce the ball as you say each letter of the word aloud.
- Do this with each word on your list.

Working with Words

Familiarize students with word meaning and usage.

Dictionary Skills

Explain that a verb is a word that expresses action or a state of being. Write these examples on the board:

action - run, fish, swim, laugh

state of being - is, are, were, seems, looks

Each group of words contains one or two verbs. Several of these can also be used as nouns or adjectives. Use a dictionary to help you write the verb or verbs from each group of words.

Proofing

Write this sentence on the board:

the bithday cake all gon.

Ask the students to find the misspelled words. Demonstrate the editing mark used in proofreading to show that a word is misspelled. Next, ask students if any words are missing. Draw the editing mark used to show that a word is missing. Now, show the mark that indicates a letter should be capitalized.

You will be using these editing marks to show the errors in the paragraph at the bottom of your page. After editing, write the misspelled words correctly on the lines.

Take a minute to memorize...

Luke 6:27, 28

F **Working with Words** Name ____________________

Dictionary Skills

A **verb** is a word that shows action or state of being. In a dictionary, this is shown by a **v** following the entry word. Use a dictionary to help you write the verb or verbs from each group of words below.

1. alphabet tough cough — cough, tough
2. laugh rough elephant — laugh, rough
3. swift chef photograph — photograph
4. office drift stuff — drift, stuff
5. craft enough graph — craft, graph
6. loaf bluff orphan — loaf, bluff

Proofing

Use the **proofreading marks** to show the errors in the paragraph below. Write the misspelled words correctly on the lines.

◯ word is misspelled	^ word is missing	≡ capitalize letter

dad had the day off from the offise and we to the zoo. i had packed my camera and other stough. I got a great photograft of an elefant and her calf. they had such rouph skin. There also a little orfan bear that the zoo cheff was fixing lunch for. It so funny, i had to lagh. Looking very tugh, the gorillas sat on a bluph by a swift creek. The tigers had seen enouph visitors and just lay the shade to lofe. Too soon, it was time go home. what a fun day we had!

1. office
2. stuff
3. photograph
4. elephant
5. rough
6. orphan
7. chef
8. laugh
9. tough
10. bluff
11. enough
12. loaf

Word Bank

alphabet	cough	elephant	laugh	orphan	stuff
bluff	craft	enough	loaf	photograph	swift
chef	drift	graph	office	rough	tough

84

G Dictation

Name ______________________

Write each sentence as your teacher dictates. Use correct punctuation.

1. Stephen did not stuff the candy out of sight quickly enough.
2. He gave a rough laugh and kicked the note.
3. He always loafs around and looks so tough!

Words with /f/

Lesson 13

H Proofreading

If a word is misspelled, fill in the oval by that word. If all the words are spelled correctly, fill in the oval by **no mistake**.

1.	○ climb ○ drift ● cawf ○ no mistake	**5.**	○ dumb ● tuf ○ craft ○ no mistake	**9.**	○ folks ● lofe ○ orphan ○ no mistake
2.	○ bomb ○ wren ○ enough ● no mistake	**6.**	○ unknown ○ limb ○ alphabet ● no mistake	**10.**	○ thoughtful ○ delight ○ photograph ● no mistake
3.	○ comb ○ wreath ● lauf ○ no mistake	**7.**	○ limb ○ reign ● elephent ○ no mistake	**11.**	○ ought ○ chef ○ bluff ● no mistake
4.	● ruf ○ whose ○ swift ○ no mistake	**8.**	○ knob ○ knife ● graff ○ no mistake	**12.**	● offise ○ stuff ○ thorough ○ no mistake

85

Dictation

Reinforce correct spelling by using current and previous words in context.

Listen as I read each sentence and then write it in your Worktext. Remember to use correct capitalization and punctuation. (Slowly read each sentence twice. Sentences are found in the Student Worktext to the left.)

2 Proofreading

Familiarize students with standardized test format and reinforce recognition of misspelled words.

Look at each set of words. If a word is misspelled, fill in the oval by that word. If all the words are spelled correctly, fill in the oval by **no mistake**.

3 Hide and Seek

Reinforce correct spelling of current spelling words. Repeat this activity from Day 2. (A reproducible master is provided in Appendix A as shown on the inset page to the right.)

4 Other Word Forms

Have your students complete this activity to strengthen spelling ability and expand vocabulary.

1 Posttest

Visit the **A Reason For** website to download free, printable Posttest pages.

I will say the word once, use it in a sentence, then say it again. Write your words on a separate sheet of paper.

Progress Chart

Students may record scores. (Appendix B)

Personal Dictionary

Students may add any words they have misspelled to their personal dictionaries. (Appendix B)

Hide and Seek

Play Hide and Seek with your words. Create a bar graph by filling in a box (left to right) for each word you spell correctly.

Other Word Forms

Sentence Fun

Circle the word that correctly completes each sentence.

1. Brutus (laughing, laughed) as he took Stephen's candy.
2. We began (crafting, craftily) a cabin with the sticks and pebbles.
3. Who is the (swiftest, swiftness) runner in our class?
4. We had to put our spelling words in (alphabetize, alphabetical) order.
5. Brutus is the (toughest, toughen) kid to pray for.
6. He choked on the candy and began (coughing, coughed).
7. In math, we are (graphed, graphing) the colors of M&M®s.
8. These baby raccoons have been (orphaned, orphanage).
9. The (photographer, photographic) is coming to take school pictures.
10. Stephen (stuffing, stuffed) the candy in his pocket.
11. The police (offices, officer) is directing traffic.
12. Mom made several (loaves, loafs) of bread for the neighbors.
13. Our tubes began (drifted, drifting) downstream with the current.
14. We tried (bluffing, bluffed) so Brutus wouldn't know we had candy.
15. This trail is (rougher, roughest) than the one we hiked last week.
16. It was hard to keep from (laughs, laughing) when he tripped.
17. This test seems (tougher, toughens) than the last one.
18. We opened the windows because the room felt hot and (stuffy, stuffily).
19. My brother is taking a (photographed, photography) class.
20. We watched a (craftsman, crafty) carving wood.

Lesson 13 | Other Word Forms

335

1.	laugh	Stephen's grandmother has a gentle **laugh** and cheerful eyes.
2.	photograph	A **photograph** of Stephen and Gram was taken at the zoo.
3.	elephant	There was a big, gray **elephant** in the background.
4.	craft	Being a bully was Brutus's **craft**, or area of expertise.
5.	tough	Brutus acted **tough** to scare the younger children.
6.	cough	His rough **cough** made them jump.
7.	orphan	Stephen wondered if Brutus was an **orphan.**
8.	bluff	Brutus' tough act is just a **bluff** for his feelings of insecurity.
9.	enough	Stephen felt he had had quite **enough** of Brutus's bullying!
10.	office	He was too scared to go to the school **office** or to Mrs. Burton.
11.	loaf	A **loaf** of sweetbread was cooling on the counter when he got home.
12.	chef	"You are a terrific **chef**!" complimented Stephen.
13.	stuff	"Gram, you do all sorts of special **stuff** for me," he said.
14.	graph	Stephen completed the **graph** and put his Worktext away.
15.	alphabet	He still needed to practice writing the **alphabet** in cursive.
16.	rough	Gram could tell that Stephen had had a **rough** time at school.
17.	drift	After praying with Gram, Stephen was able to **drift** off to sleep.
18.	swift	Jesus wants us to be **swift** to pray for those who hurt us.

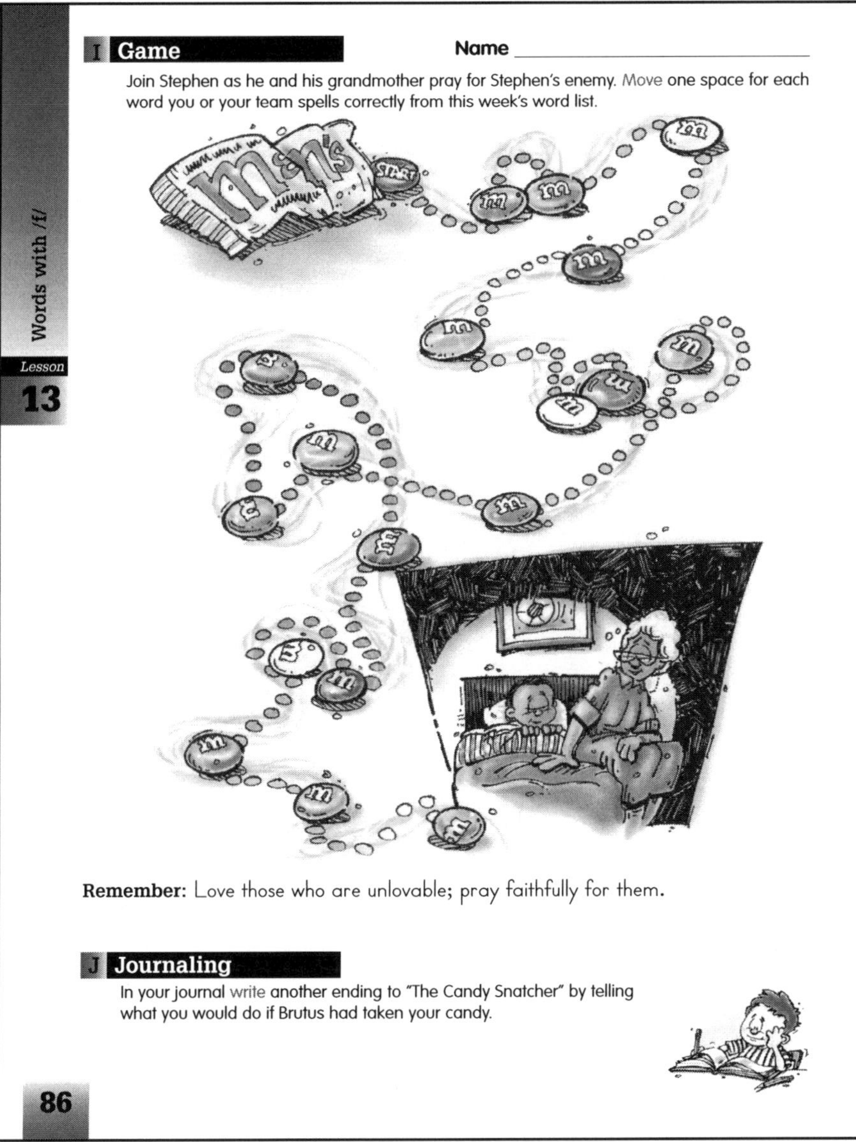

Words with /f/

Lesson 13

I **Game** Name ____________________

Join Stephen as he and his grandmother pray for Stephen's enemy. Move one space for each word you or your team spells correctly from this week's word list.

Remember: Love those who are unlovable; pray faithfully for them.

J **Journaling**

In your journal write another ending to "The Candy Snatcher" by telling what you would do if Brutus had taken your candy.

86

How to Play:

- Divide students into two teams.
- Have each student place his/her game piece on Start.
- Have a student from team A go to the board.
- Say the spelling word.
- Have the student write the word on the board.
- If correct, instruct each member of team A to move his/her game piece forward one space.
- Alternate between teams A and B as you go down the word list.
- The team to reach Stephen and Gram first is the winner.

Small Group Option: Students may play this game without teacher direction in small groups of two or more.

2 Game

Reinforce spelling skills and provide motivation and interest.

Materials

- game page (from Student Worktext)
- game pieces (1 per child)
- game word list

Game Word List

1. **cough**
2. **enough**
3. **laugh**
4. **rough**
5. **tough**
6. **alphabet**
7. **elephant**
8. **graph**
9. **orphan**
10. **photograph**
11. **bluff**
12. **stuff**
13. **office**
14. **chef**
15. **loaf**
16. **craft**
17. **drift**
18. **swift**

3 Journaling

Provide a meaningful reason for correct spelling through personal writing.

Review the story using discussion leads provided on the following page. Encourage students to apply the Scriptural value in their journaling.

Journaling (continued)

- Raise your hand if a bigger kid has ever been mean to you.
- What happened?
- Why did Stephen have trouble falling asleep? (He didn't want to love Brutus. He didn't want to do good to Brutus. He didn't want to pray for Brutus. The Scripture he learned said he should do all of those things.)
- Why didn't Stephen want to tell anyone about what Brutus did? (Brutus told him not to tell and Stephen was scared Brutus would hurt him if he told.)
- Who noticed Stephen had not fallen asleep? (Gram.)
- What did Gram suggest Stephen should do? (Talk to her when he was ready. Pray.)

The longest English words without regular vowels are: rhythm, spryly, sylphy, and syzygy.

Word Wow!

1 **Literature Connection**
Topic: Knowing God
Theme Text: John 10:14, 15

Directions from the Dugout

Thorny begins to understand the wonder of having a Heavenly Father.

"Yes!" Tommy Rawson raised his fist in the air and brought it down quickly, elbow bent as if he were making a muscle.

"May I inquire as to the source of your obvious pleasure?" Hubert Thornton Remington, III—Thorny for short—stopped beside Tommy in the busy school hallway.

Tommy grinned up at Thorny. "You know, it's scary when I actually understand you!" He jabbed a finger against the glass of the bulletin board where announcements were posted. "There. Isn't that great?"

Thorny shrugged and stepped closer. "I see you've left a rather nice print of your right index finger on the glass, but I hardly think that is sufficient cause for such excitement."

Tommy wiped at the fingerprint with his sleeve and shook his head. "Read that announcement, Thorny."

Thorny began, "Father/Son Baseball Day to be held at the city ball fields on…"

Tommy broke in, "Isn't that great? I didn't think I'd get to play any more baseball 'til next spring when baseball season rolls around again. Let's see, this is going to be next week. I've gotta let my dad know when it is so we can make plans. Hey, you want us to pick you guys up that day and all come together?"

"Pick who up, Tommy? Have you suffered a memory lapse? I don't HAVE a father."

"But you've got a foster dad, and I bet he'd like to come with you to Baseball Day." Thorny didn't look convinced. "At least ask him, Thorny. It'll be a lot of fun. Rich Delaney's going to be there to give batting tips and stuff. You can't miss him, Thorny. He's a pro!" Tommy thumped the glass once more, leaving another fingerprint or two.

Thorny grabbed Tommy's shoulder, turning him in the direction of the boys' classroom. "I can see you feel quite strongly that it's an event of great importance, but right now it's important that we endeavor to arrive at our classroom in a timely manner."

Tommy glanced at the large clock on the wall as the boys hurried down the deserted hallway. "Yikes! C'mon, Thorny, we're gonna be late if we don't hurry!"

"Precisely my point." The boys rushed down the hall, squeezing through the classroom door together. They made it on time—just barely.

"So, what'd he say?" Tommy was waiting for Thorny the next morning by the school's front doors.

"What did who say?" Thorny pulled open one of the glass doors.

"Mr. Simmons—your foster dad!" Tommy stopped suddenly in the middle of the hallway, causing the crowd of incoming kids to go around him like water around a rock. "Don't tell me you didn't ask him about the Baseball Day?"

Thorny grabbed Tommy's arm to get him moving again. "Actually, as a matter of fact…What I mean to say, is…"

"What?" Tommy lightly thumped Thorny's arm with his fist. "Did you ask him—or didn't you?"

"I did."

"Well, is he coming or not?" Tommy pulled him out of the way so the other kids could get through the door.

"Amazingly enough, yes." Thorny shook his head. "He appeared to be quite pleased that I had approached him about attending the Father/Son event with me. In fact, he even canceled previous plans."

It was Tommy's turn to shake his head. "Thorny, for all your brains, you're nuts. Of course he'd want to go with you—he's your foster dad and that's how dads are."

Tommy watched weather reports over the next few days and drove his mother crazy asking if she thought it would be nice on Baseball Day. When the day dawned the air was crisp and quite cold, but without rain, snow or wind.

When Mr. Rawson turned into the parking area, boys of all ages were already swarming toward the fields with their fathers. A crowd had gathered around Rich Delaney. There were tables for each age group where participants signed up. Each boy got a baseball signed by Rich Delaney himself.

The city leagues' coaches sorted boys into age groups and showed them to the proper ball fields, where fathers and sons got to practice batting, catching, and fielding. There was even a game-show-like quiz about the rules of baseball. Rich Delaney went from one group to another, demonstrating and encouraging.

The day ended with a real game for each age level. After watching the players all day, the coaches had divided them pretty evenly for the games. The scoreboard at Tommy and Thorny's field flashed a score of 6 to 7, with their team trailing. It was the bottom of the ninth inning, the bases were loaded, and Tommy was up to bat.

"STRIKE!" Tommy tensed at the umpire's call.

Gotta relax. Keep it loose. Tommy stepped out of the batter's box and wriggled his shoulders before stepping back up to the plate. *Feet apart, left one at the back line of home plate. Bend the knees slightly, keep the right elbow up.* Tommy recited to

Story (continued)

himself some of the tips he'd heard that day. *Keep your eyes on the ball. Here it comes!* Tommy stepped into the pitch and swung with all his might.

"STRIKE TWO!"

It's okay. I can do this. Tommy thumped the bat on home plate and prepared for the next pitch. *I CAN hit this ball.* SMACK! As soon as the bat cracked against the ball, Tommy was off toward first base as fast as he could move. He had no idea where the ball was, but the first-base coach was motioning him on toward second base, so on he went. Now he could see the fielders scrambling for the ball. On to third base. Everyone was shouting.

"Where's the third base coach?" Tommy's thoughts spun. "Do I run for home or not?"

Tommy couldn't slow down and look around. The noise was deafening, everyone yelling their own bit of advice to the boy running toward third. Then Tommy heard his dad. "Home, Son! Run on home!"

Tommy steamed through third and headed home running flat out. He slid into home plate just before the ball thunked into the catcher's mitt. His team roared—they won 10 to 7.

The next afternoon after school Thorny and Tommy played catch in Tommy's backyard. "You know, Tommy, that Father/Son Baseball Day was quite enjoyable indeed." Thorny caught the ball and tossed it back to Tommy.

"Told you so. Mr. Simmons is a good ball player. Remember that ball he whacked way out in right field? And that catch he made in the second inning was awesome."

"It's truly amazing." Thorny trotted after a ball he missed.

"What's amazing?" Tommy pounded his fist into his glove. "That the day was fun or that Mr. Simmons is good at baseball?"

"Neither." Thorny threw the ball in a high arc. "While I hate to disillusion you, Tommy, not all fathers want to do things of that nature with their sons. From my considerable experience, I can safely say that this is particularly true of many—if not most—foster fathers."

"Now wait a minute." Tommy held the ball in his glove and propped his other hand on his hip. "Are you telling me none of your foster dads ever played ball or did anything special like that with you?"

"That is correct." Thorny walked over and sat on one of the swings. "None until Mr. Simmons, to be exact. That is what's truly amazing. He appeared to genuinely enjoy spending the day playing ball—with me!" Thorny pushed the swing gently and stared at the ground. "Last night he, um, hugged me, uh, and said that he was proud to be my foster dad."

"Well, maybe the other foster dads were more foster and Mr. Simmons is more dad. You know?" Tommy tossed the ball up and caught it.

"As you said, Tommy, it is truly frightening that I find myself actually understanding what you mean even though at face value your statement makes little sense! Ooomph!" He caught the fastball Tommy hurled at him. "By the way, what factors influenced your decision to run through to home plate at the end of the game yesterday?"

"Dad told me to." Tommy took a couple steps to the right to catch the ball and tossed it back to Thorny. Thorny caught it and stared into his glove like he'd never seen a baseball before. Tommy grinned. "Okay, Thorny. What're you analyzing now?"

"Thirty, probably more, men and boys are yelling at once and you actually hear the advice of one man?" Thorny took the ball out of his glove and turned it over and over in his hand.

"Hey, he's my dad." Tommy waved his glove to get Thorny to throw the ball. "It was easy to tell his voice from everybody else's...I guess 'cause I know him so well."

"Are you referring to the Scripture we wrote at school today?" Thorny still held the ball.

"Huh? Oh, the one about the Shepherd knowing the sheep? Well, I guess it does fit. I know my dad so well that I recognize his voice and trust him to tell me what to do; that is a lot like knowing God so well that we recognize His leading."

"Well, I'm beginning to reach the conclusion that having a father—even a foster father—who cares enough to want to spend time with me is quite pleasant." Thorny tossed a low ball to Tommy. "Having a heavenly Father who cares for me is certainly a nice thought."

Tommy nabbed the ball. "It's more than that, Thorny. It's real. If you just ask God to be your Father, He will. He already knows you and loves you so much He died for you." Tommy let the ball fly in a straight pitch. "And it's a lot of fun getting to know Him!"

2 Discussion Time

Check understanding of the story and development of personal values.

- Where did Tommy see the notice about the Father/Son Baseball Day?
- What special guest was going to be at the Baseball Day?
- Why wasn't Thorny excited?
- Why didn't Thorny think Mr. Simmons would want to go with him?
- What did Mr. Simmons do when Thorny asked about it?
- What kinds of things did the boys and their dads do during the Baseball Day?
- How was the game going when Tommy was up to bat?
- How did Tommy know that he should keep running around third for home?
- How can we get to know and trust God very much, like Tommy knew and trusted his dad?

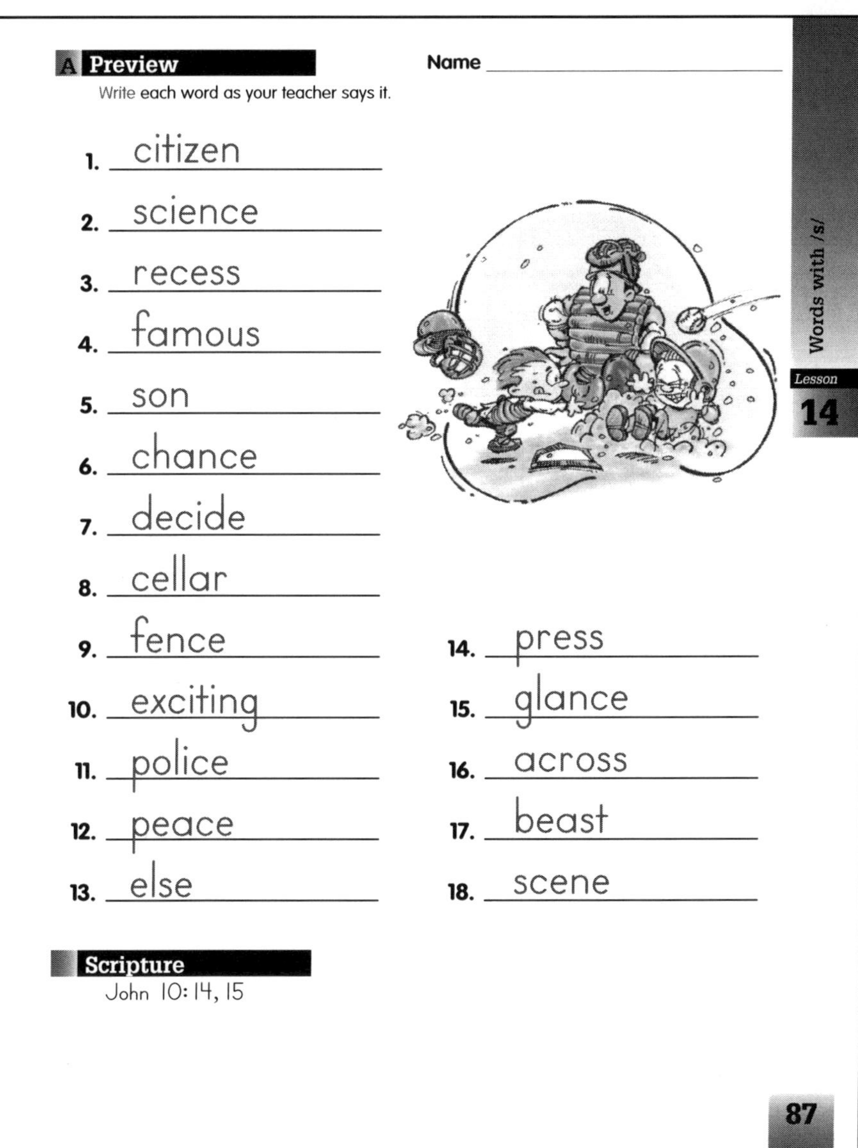

A Preview Name ______________

Write each word as your teacher says it.

1. citizen
2. science
3. recess
4. famous
5. son
6. chance
7. decide
8. cellar
9. fence
10. exciting
11. police
12. peace
13. else
14. press
15. glance
16. across
17. beast
18. scene

Words with /s/

Lesson 14

Scripture

John 10:14, 15

87

3 Preview

Test for knowledge of the correct spellings of these words.

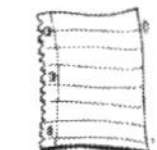

Customize Your List

On a separate sheet of paper, additional words of your choice may be tested.

I will say each word once, use the word in a sentence, then say the word again. Write the words on the lines in your Worktext.

Correct Immediately!

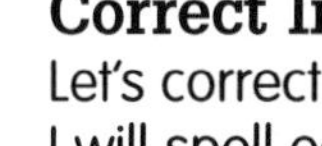

Let's correct our Preview. I will spell each word out loud. If you spelled a word incorrectly, rewrite it correctly.

Progress Chart

Students may record scores. (Reproducible master provided in Appendix B.)

1.	citizen	Thorny is a **citizen** of the United States of America.
2.	science	He especially looks forward to **science** class.
3.	recess	During the fall, the boys enjoyed playing ball at **recess**.
4.	famous	"Rich Delaney is a **famous** batter!" exclaimed Tommy.
5.	son	Thorny is Mr. Simmons's foster **son**.
6.	chance	"Did you have a **chance** to ask Mr. Simmons?" he inquired.
7.	decide	"Yes, I did **decide** to broach the subject with him," replied Thorny.
8.	cellar	Tommy got the cooler out of the **cellar**, or basement.
9.	fence	He set the cooler full of drinks by the **fence** at the ball park.
10.	exciting	Baseball Day was very **exciting** for the boys and their dads.
11.	police	The **police** department sent officers to patrol the area.
12.	peace	They made sure no one was disturbing the **peace**.
13.	else	Above all **else**, Tommy wanted to hear his dad's advice.
14.	press	He didn't know whether to **press** on to home, or to stay safe on third.
15.	glance	Tommy threw a swift **glance** to his right.
16.	across	His dad shouted **across** the field to him.
17.	beast	Tommy ran fast, like a wild **beast**, toward home plate.
18.	scene	It was a joyful **scene** as the boys and dads cheered their victory.

4 Word Shapes

Help students form a correct image of whole words.

Look at each word and think about its shape. Now, write the word in the correct Word Shape Boxes. You may check off each word as you use it.

(In many words, the sound of **/s/** is spelled with **s**, or **sc**, and it is often spelled this way when it is at the beginning of a word. The **/s/** sound can also be spelled with **c** when followed by **i**, or **e**. The spelling **ss** is usually used in the middle, or at the end of a word.)

In the Word Shape Boxes, fill in the boxes containing the letter or letters that spell the sound of **/s/** in each word.

Take a minute to memorize...

John 10:14, 15

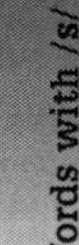

Words with /s/ — Lesson 14

B Word Shapes Name ______________________

Write each word in the correct Word Shape Boxes. Next, in the Word Shape Boxes, shade in the boxes containing the letter or letters that spell the sound of **/s/** in each word.

1. cellar
2. chance
3. citizen
4. decide
5. exciting
6. fence
7. glance
8. peace
9. police
10. scene
11. science
12. across
13. press
14. recess
15. beast
16. else
17. famous
18. son

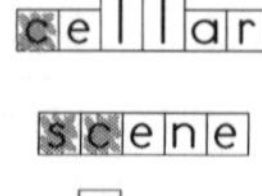

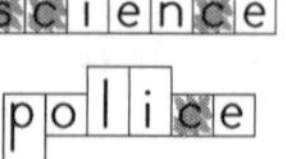

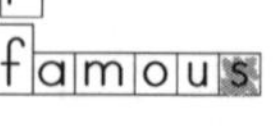

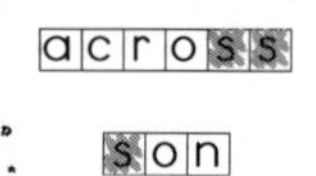

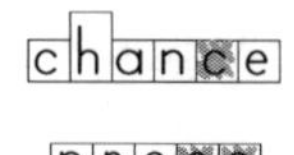

peace
citizen
fence
decide
cellar
scene
science
police
famous
recess
beast
glance
exciting
across
son
chance
press
else

88

Answers may vary for duplicate word shapes.

Be Prepared For Fun

Check these supply lists for **Fun Ways to Spell** - presented **Day 2**.
Purchase and/or gather these items ahead of time!

General
- Pencil
- Notebook Paper
- Spelling List

Auditory
- Spelling List

Visual
- Pencil
- Paper
- Spelling List

Tactile
- Thick Pile Carpet Samples
- Spelling List

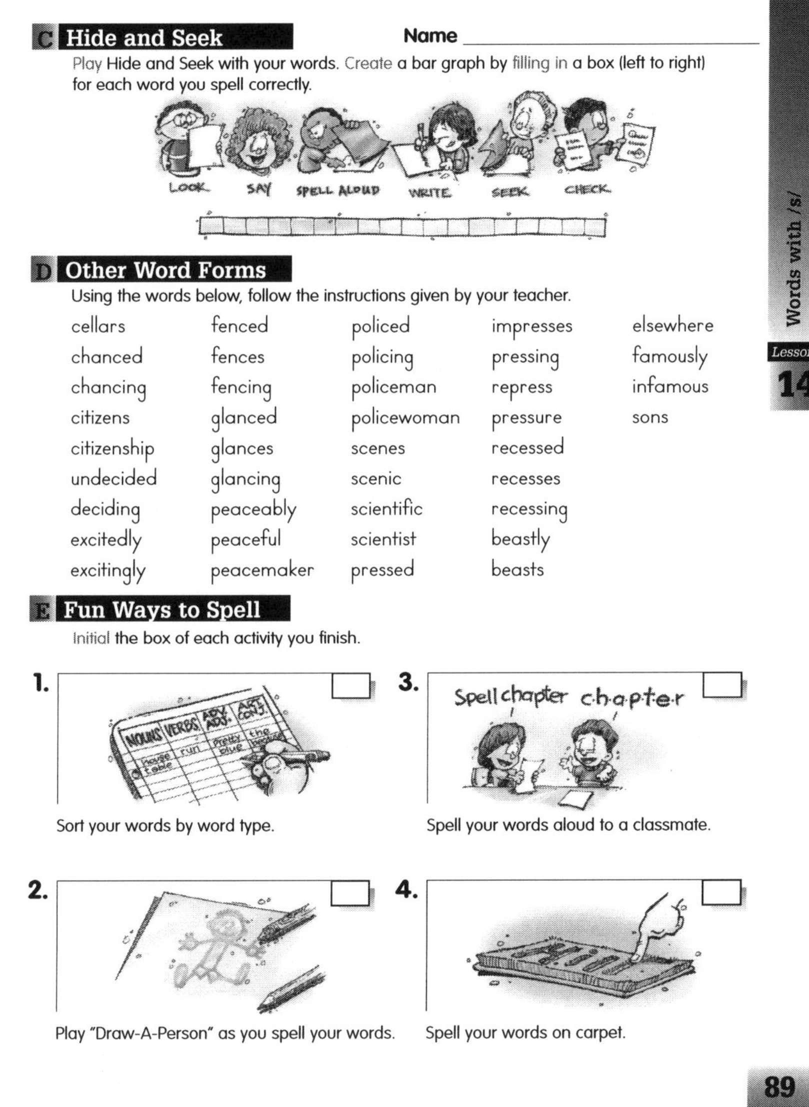

1 Hide and Seek

Reinforce spelling by using multiple styles of learning.

On a white board, Teacher writes each word — one at a time. **Have students:**

- **Look** at the word.
- **Say** the word out loud.
- **Spell** the word out loud.
- **Hide** (teacher erases word.)
- **Write** the word on paper.
- **Seek** (teacher rewrites word.)
- **Check** spelling. If incorrect, rewrite word correctly.

2 Other Word Forms

This activity is optional. Have students write these Other Word Forms in alphabetical order:

scientific
excitingly
scenic
excitedly

3 Fun Ways to Spell

Four activities are provided. Use one, two, three, or all of the activities. Have students initial the box for each activity they complete.

Options:

- assign activities to students according to their learning styles
- set up the activities in learning centers for students to do throughout the day
- divide students into four groups and assign one activity per group
- do one activity per day

General

To sort your words by word type...
- Make four columns on your paper.
- Label the columns: Nouns, Verbs, Adjectives/Adverbs, and Articles/Conjunctions.
- Write each of your spelling words in the appropriate column.

Auditory

To spell your words aloud to a classmate...
- Ask a classmate to read a word from your spelling list.
- Spell the word aloud to your classmate.
- Ask your classmate to check your spelling.
- Read a word to your classmate and continue taking turns.
- The person to spell the most words right wins!

Visual

To play "Draw-A-Person" when you spell your words...
- Ask a classmate to read a word from your spelling list to you.
- Write the word on your paper. Check your spelling.
- If you misspell the word, draw one part of a person on your paper.
- Read a word to a classmate and continue taking turns.
- The last one to finish drawing a person wins!

Tactile

To spell your words on carpet...
- Use finger tip to write a spelling word on carpet.
- Check your spelling.
- Smooth the word out with your hand and write another word.

Working with Words

Familiarize students with word meaning and usage.

Missing Letters

Be sure students understand that the sound of **/s/** is spelled with **s** or **sc**, or with **c** when followed by **i** or **e**. The spelling **ss** is usually used in the middle, or at the end of a word.

Fill in the missing letter or letters that spell the sound of **/s/** to complete each word.

Nouns and Verbs

Remind students that a word can often be used as more than one part of speech. Write the word **equal** on the board. Read these sentences and ask students whether **equal** is being used as a noun or verb.

We met with a group of our equals to discuss the problem. (noun)

I think I can equal his broad jump record. (verb)

Decide whether the bolded word is used as a noun or verb in the sentence. Write **n** if it is a noun, **v** if it is a verb.

Take a minute to memorize...

John 10:14, 15

Words with /s/ — Lesson 14

F Working with Words Name ______________________

Missing Letters

Fill in the missing letter or letters that spell the sound of **/s/**.

1. de _c_ ide	7. chan _c_ e	13. ex _c_ iting
2. bea _s_ t	8. poli _c_ e	14. glan _c_ e
3. _s_ on	9. _s_ _c_ ene	15. famou _s_
4. _c_ ellar	10. el _s_ e	16. _s_ _c_ ien _c_ e
5. fen _c_ e	11. _c_ itizen	17. pea _c_ e
6. pre _s_ _s_	12. acro _s_ _s_	18. re _c_ e _s_ _s_

Nouns and Verbs

Remember, a noun is a word that names a person, place, thing, or idea. A verb is a word that shows action or state of being. Decide whether the underlined word is used as a noun or a verb in the sentence. Write **n** if it is a **noun** or **v** if it is a **verb**.

1. _v_ The judge said the court would **recess** until Monday.
   _n_ It is time to go out for **recess**.
2. _v_ We'll **chance** a picnic even though the sky is cloudy.
   _n_ Tommy had a **chance** to make a home run.
3. _n_ Mr. Simmons hit the ball clear to the **fence**.
   _v_ We had to **fence** the garden to keep out deer.
4. _n_ People from the **press** reported on Rich Delaney's visit.
   _v_ Mom had to **press** Dad's new shirt.
5. _v_ We heard the ball **glance** off the bat, before going foul.
   _n_ Thorny gave the bulletin board a quick **glance**.
6. _v_ We had to **police** the park and pick up litter.
   _n_ The **police** kept order around the scene of the accident.

Word Bank

across	chance	else	fence	police	scene
beast	citizen	exciting	glance	press	science
cellar	decide	famous	peace	recess	son

90

G Dictation

Name ______________________

Write each sentence as your teacher dictates. Use correct punctuation.

1. The game at recess was exciting.
2. He had a chance to play ball with his son.
3. Dad's voice from across the field helped him decide.

Words with /s/

Lesson 14

H Proofreading

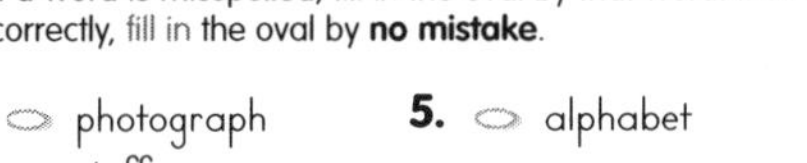

If a word is misspelled, fill in the oval by that word. If all the words are spelled correctly, fill in the oval by **no mistake**.

1. ○ photograph ○ stuff ● famus ○ no mistake
2. ● sellar ○ bluff ○ chance ○ no mistake
3. ○ orphan ● citizin ○ graph ○ no mistake
4. ○ son ○ elephant ● deside ○ no mistake
5. ○ alphabet ○ press ● exsiting ○ no mistake
6. ● beest ○ fence ○ craft ○ no mistake
7. ○ else ○ glance ○ loaf ● no mistake
8. ● peece ○ chef ○ office ○ no mistake
9. ○ cough ○ swift ○ police ● no mistake
10. ○ enough ● resess ○ scene ○ no mistake
11. ● sience ○ laugh ○ rough ○ no mistake
12. ○ tough ● acros ○ drift ○ no mistake

91

1 Dictation

Reinforce correct spelling by using current and previous words in context.

Listen as I read each sentence and then write it in your Worktext. Remember to use correct capitalization and punctuation. (Slowly read each sentence twice. Sentences are found in the Student Worktext to the left.)

2 Proofreading

Familiarize students with standardized test format and reinforce recognition of misspelled words.

Look at each set of words. If a word is misspelled, fill in the oval by that word. If all the words are spelled correctly, fill in the oval by **no mistake**.

3 Hide and Seek

Reinforce correct spelling of current spelling words. Repeat this activity from Day 2. (A reproducible master is provided in Appendix A as shown on the inset page to the right.)

4 Other Word Forms

Have your students complete this activity to strengthen spelling ability and expand vocabulary.

1 Posttest

Visit the **A Reason For** website to download free, printable Posttest pages.

I will say the word once, use it in a sentence, then say it again. Write your words on a separate sheet of paper.

Progress Chart

Students may record scores. (Appendix B)

Personal Dictionary

Students may add any words they have misspelled to their personal dictionaries. (Appendix B)

Hide and Seek

Play Hide and Seek with your words. Create a bar graph by filling in a box (left to right) for each word you spell correctly.

Other Word Forms

Prefixes and Suffixes

Circle the correct prefix or suffix to make a new word, then write the word correctly on the line. Remember, when words have the consonant-vowel-consonant-**e** pattern, drop the **e** when adding an ending that begins with a vowel.

1. decide + (s, ly) = decides
2. peace + (ing, ably) = peaceably
3. recess + (s, es) = recesses
4. chance + (ing, er) = chancing
5. police + (ing, ment) = policing
6. fence + (ably, ing) = fencing
7. excite + (ment, ness) = excitement
8. (de, un) + excite + (ed, ly) = unexcited
9. (im, ir) + press + (ied, ion) = impression
10. glance + (ed, ness) = glanced
11. beast + (ly, ably) = beastly
12. citizen + (ment, ship) = citizenship
13. scene + (ic, ish) = scenic
14. peace + (ing, ful) = peaceful
15. press + (ure, ful) = pressure
16. (il, in) + famous = infamous

336

1.	recess	Thorny and Tommy like to practice pitching during **recess.**
2.	science	The boys saw the announcement on their way to **science** class.
3.	son	Mr. Simmons is very glad to have Thorny as his foster **son.**
4.	chance	Thorny did have a **chance** to ask him about Baseball Day.
5.	famous	He wanted to meet Rich Delaney, the **famous** ball player.
6.	citizen	Delaney is a patriotic **citizen** and a great ball player!
7.	exciting	"Today is going to be really **exciting,**" beamed Tommy.
8.	cellar	"Please get the cooler out of the **cellar,**" his dad requested.
9.	fence	The boys stood by the **fence** drinking cold soft drinks.
10.	beast	Tommy hit the ball and ran like a wild **beast.**
11.	decide	He needed help to **decide** what to do.
12.	glance	Tommy gave a quick **glance** around for his dad.
13.	else	He trusts his dad's advice above all **else.**
14.	across	His dad yelled loudly **across** the field.
15.	press	He encouraged Tommy to **press** on toward home.
16.	police	The **police** officers enjoyed watching the ball game.
17.	scene	Sometimes people make a **scene** when they see someone famous.
18.	peace	No one disturbed the **peace** during the event.

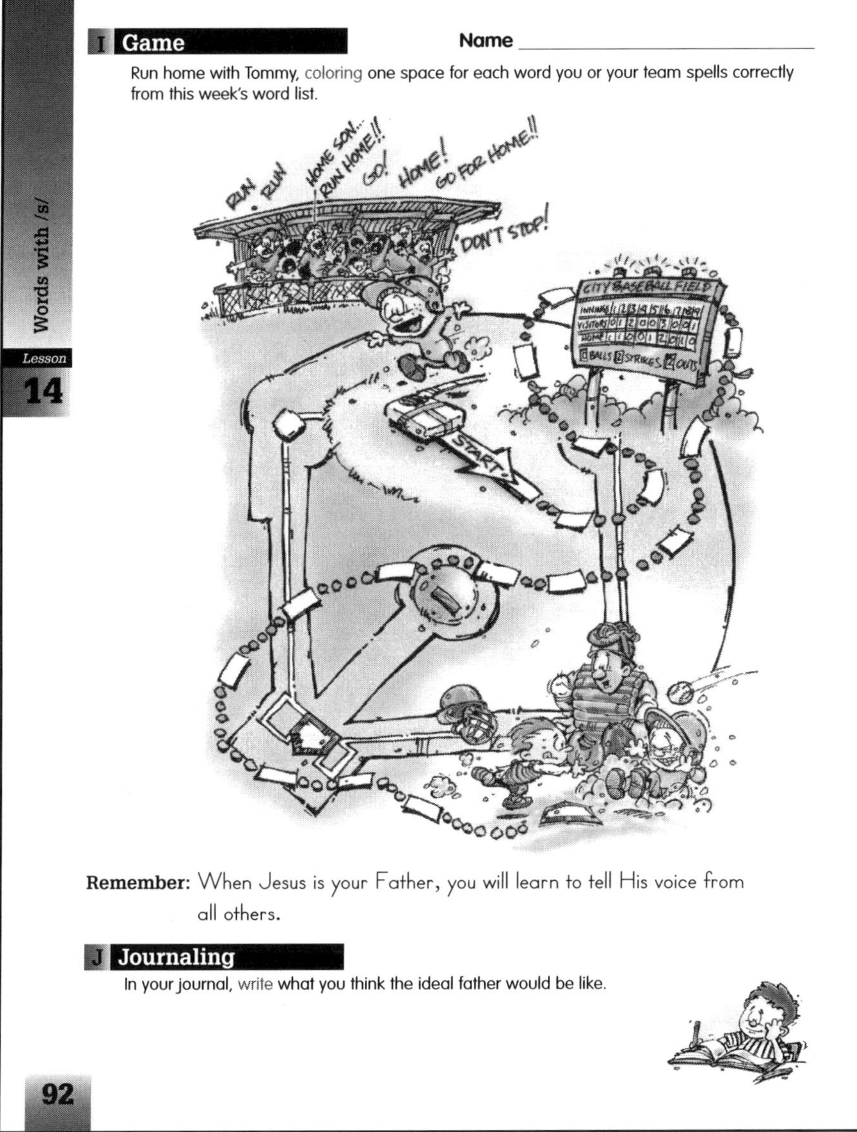
I **Game** Name ______________________

Run home with Tommy, coloring one space for each word you or your team spells correctly from this week's word list.

Remember: When Jesus is your Father, you will learn to tell His voice from all others.

J **Journaling**

In your journal, write what you think the ideal father would be like.

Words with /s/ Lesson 14

92

2 Game

Reinforce spelling skills and provide motivation and interest.

Materials

- game page (from Student Worktext)
- crayons or colored pencils (1 per child)
- game word list

Game Word List

1. **cellar**
2. **chance**
3. **citizen**
4. **decide**
5. **exciting**
6. **fence**
7. **glance**
8. **peace**
9. **police**
10. **scene**
11. **science**
12. **across**
13. **press**
14. **recess**
15. **beast**
16. **else**
17. **famous**
18. **son**

How to Play:

- Divide students into two teams.
- Have a student from team A go to the board.
- Say the spelling word.
- Have the student write the word on the board.
- If correct, instruct each member of team A to color one space, beginning at Start.
- Alternate between teams A and B as you go down the word list.
- The team to reach home plate first is the winner.

Small Group Option: Students may play this game without teacher direction in small groups of two or more.

3 Journaling

Provide a meaningful reason for correct spelling through personal writing.

Review the story using discussion leads provided on the following page. Encourage students to apply the Scriptural value in their journaling.

Journaling (continued)

- What are some special things you and your dad like to do together? (You may wish to list your students' responses on the board.)
- Have you ever played in a baseball league — or any baseball game where something interesting happened?
- Do you think Mr. Simmons cared about Thorny? Why? (Yes. Because he canceled his previous plans in order to go to the Father/Son Baseball Day with him.)
- How do you think Thorny felt when Mr. Simmons was happy and proud to go with him? (Surprised, special, happy, excited, etc.)
- How do you feel when your father takes time to spend doing fun things with you?
- Why was Thorny surprised that Tommy heard his father tell him to run past third base? (Because there was a lot of noise. Everyone was yelling at once.)
- How did Tommy hear his dad? (He knew him well and recognized his voice.)
- How can you get to know God, your Heavenly Father, so well that you can recognize His leading? (Spending time with Him. Reading the Scriptures, praying, thinking about Him, etc.)

"Polish" is the only word in the English language that, when capitalized, is changed from a noun or a verb to a nationality.

Word Wow!

1 **Literature Connection**
Topic: Prayer
Theme Text: Luke 11:9

Getting What You Ask For

Stephen learns some important lessons about prayer answers.

"Look at this one!" Tony held up a miniature black Ferrari.

Stephen pointed to another shiny sports car and said, "I like the blue one better."

Mr. Wilson folded his arms and rocked back on his heels. He smiled as he watched the two boys carefully look over the big display of miniature cars in the toy store. They searched for missing cars in the series they were collecting and discussed collecting new series. They wondered if their cars would make them rich in a few years because they had so many complete sets in good condition.

Stephen finally narrowed his selection down to two cars. He slipped them off the hooks and brought them over to his father. "Which one do you like best, Dad?"

Mr. Wilson took the packages from Stephen. "This one has good aerodynamic lines. I haven't seen it before. This other one would complete your techno bits series, wouldn't it?" Stephen nodded. "You buy the one you like though, my boy." Dad handed the cars back to him and strolled up the aisle of the store.

Stephen looked at the bright green price tag on the display. "I only have enough money for one of these. But I like them both."

Tony looked down at the four cars he'd picked out. "Remember the text in spelling about prayer? It starts out, 'Keep on asking and you will keep on getting.' Why don't you ask God? The verse says you'll get it." Tony headed up to the front of the store to pay for his cars.

Stephen arched his eyebrows and replied, "I guess it can't hurt to try." He lowered his eyes and silently asked God for both cars.

"Mom, have you seen my track shoes?" Beth lifted her bedspread and checked under her bed.

"I saw them yesterday morning in the garage." Mrs. Hill bent down and scratched behind the dog's ears. "I hope Eagle didn't get them." The dog's tail started thumping the carpet when he heard his name.

Beth frowned. "I wore them to Katelynn's last night. I just don't remember where I put them when I got home." Beth checked under the pile of dirty clothes on her bedroom floor. "We're going to practice track & field today at school. I can't run in my boots."

Luke swished some water around in his mouth and then spat it into the sink. "What are you looking for, Beth?"

"I can't find my track shoes. I've looked everywhere for them."

"Have you looked in your closet?" Luke checked the mirror, then wiped the toothpaste and water off his face.

Beth flung open her closet door. A pair of black dress shoes tumbled out—along with her soccer ball and some papers. The spelling preview page she'd done the day before floated down from the shelf and landed on top of her brown boots. She picked it up and looked at the score—10/18. *I missed underground, bounce, county, and five other "ou" words. I need to study,* she thought. Her eyes lingered on the verse at the bottom of the spelling paper. "So it is with prayer—keep on looking and you will keep on finding." She shoved the pile back into the closet. "Lord," she prayed, "I'm looking for my track shoes. Will You help me find them?"

Tony ran down the street to Stephen's duplex. "Help him to be there, Lord," he prayed. "I need to get my math book out of their car. We have a test tomorrow and I need to study. I can't believe I left it in the net pocket on the back of the seat." Tony took the steps two at a time and knocked on the front door. He rang the doorbell, then knocked on the blue door again. He looked up and down the street and shifted his weight from one foot to the other. He shaded his eyes with his hand and peeked in the front window. Then he knocked one last time. "Please, Lord, let them be home. I need to do that review page."

The next day Stephen flopped into the swing beside Tony. "How'd you do on the math test?"

"Okay, I think." Tony twirled the swing in a circle, winding up the chains. "I left my math book in your car when we went to the mall. I came over to get it, but you weren't there last night. I was afraid I'd flunk if I didn't do the review. I prayed you'd answer my knock. I guess God said, 'No.'"

"Sorry. Mom called from work and wanted us to meet her at the taco place." Stephen stood up and pulled his new toy car out of his coat pocket.

Tony lifted his feet and let the swing unwind. "It's okay. I borrowed Rachel's."

Beth ran up and slid to a stop between the two boys. "You guys wanna play tag?"

"Sure, you're 'It.'" Tony lunged toward Beth. She darted to the left, but not before Tony tagged her shoulder. She laughed and took off after Stephen, who was headed toward the fence on the other side of the playground. She couldn't catch up with him, but she followed at a distance so he couldn't rest. After a long chase he finally flopped on the ground, exhausted.

"I thought...pff, pff, pff...you might not be able to...pff, pff, pff...catch me...pff,

Story (continued)

pff…in those heavy boots."

"It…pff, pff, pff…just took longer…pff, pff." Beth sat down beside Stephen and leaned against the fence. The two friends were quiet while they caught their breath. "I looked everywhere for my track shoes this morning. I prayed, too, but I guess God said, 'No.' I've got to wear these boots for the mile run in PE this afternoon, too."

Tony jogged across the playground and sat down beside Beth and Stephen. "Did you show her your new car, Stephen?"

Stephen took the tiny car out of his coat pocket. The paint sparkled in the bright sunshine. "It's the last one I needed for the techno series I'm collecting. It's fast!"

Brutus stepped out from behind some shrubs and grabbed the purple car. "Techno series," he sneered. "I bet it can fly, too." The big eighth-grader laughed loudly and flung the car onto the cement play area beside him. It rolled end-over-end across the rough surface. Brutus strolled off but paused after a few steps and turned around. "Don't even think of telling on me. Or you'll be the ones flying across the cement." Still laughing, he sauntered over to talk to a couple of the eighth-grade girls.

Stephen groaned. "I think I need to pray more—lots more." He kicked the brown grass and headed over to retrieve his not-so-shiny car. He thought about his grandma and wished she hadn't returned to her home in Maryland the week before.

"I think the projectile of this car should be calculated to ensure a landing on a more pliable surface." Thorny handed the battered car to Stephen. "Rotating across cement does not enhance the appearance of any vehicle."

"Thanks for the info." Stephen smiled weakly and took the car.

Later that evening Stephen sat on the floor of his room and lined up all his techno series cars that were still shiny.

"Stephen, the phone's for you." Dad came into Stephen's room and handed him the phone, "It's Gram."

Stephen took the phone and smiled at the voice he heard. "Hi, Gram. No, I'm not fine. My enemy isn't getting any better. I prayed but he's still mean to me. You should see what he did to my new miniature car today. He demolished it by throwing it across the cement. No. . .for no reason."

"I wonder if God even listens to kids. I asked Him for TWO toy cars last night at the mall, and the ONE I got is trashed today. Beth looked for her track shoes and didn't find them after she prayed. She had to run the mile in her boots. Tony prayed about the math book he left at our house yesterday but we weren't home to answer his knock." Stephen took a deep breath and rushed on. "The Scriptures say 'Keep on asking and you will keep on getting; keep on looking and you will keep on finding; knock and the door will be opened.' Maybe it's just not true for kids."

Stephen paused in his tirade and listened to the love and care coming over the phone from thousands of miles away. "Stephen, my boy, that verse is about how Jesus will give us peace when we ask. When we look for Him, we will find out how to live a life like His."

Grandma sensed Stephen was comprehending what she was saying, so she continued to explain the verse. "If we knock, Jesus is always waiting to open the door. He invites us to make wise choices with His help and strength. Pray, Stephen. There is power in prayer. Jesus sometimes says 'No' to prayers for stuff we think we need—and He doesn't always fix the messes we make. But He always, always, always says 'Yes' to prayers asking Him to come into our lives and change our hearts."

Stephen talked for a few more minutes before he hung up the phone. He thought about the wrecked car.

"Lord," he prayed, "change my heart. Help me to love my enemy. Amen."

Discussion Time

Check understanding of the story and development of personal values.

- What are some prayers you have prayed?
- How did God answer your prayers?
- Did God say yes to Stephen's prayer about getting two toy cars?
- Did God help Beth find her track shoes when she was looking for them?
- Did God have someone ready to open the door at Stephen's house when Tony knocked?
- What prayer does God always answer with a yes?
- Who helped Stephen understand God's willingness to change his heart and give him peace?

A Preview Name ______

Write each word as your teacher says it.

1. growl
2. tower
3. bounce
4. pound
5. outdoors
6. scout
7. county
8. aloud
9. owl
10. noun
11. trout
12. frown
13. underground
14. household
15. stout
16. gown
17. powder
18. however

Words with /ou/

Lesson 15

Scripture

Luke 11:9

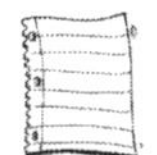

3 Preview

Test for knowledge of the correct spellings of these words.

Customize Your List

On a separate sheet of paper, additional words of your choice may be tested.

I will say each word once, use the word in a sentence, then say the word again. Write the words on the lines in your Worktext.

Correct Immediately!

Let's correct our Preview. I will spell each word out loud. If you spelled a word incorrectly, rewrite it correctly.

Progress Chart

Students may record scores. (Reproducible master provided in Appendix B.)

1. **growl** — Stephen heard something like a **growl** as Brutus stepped out of the bushes.
2. **tower** — Brutus tends to **tower** over Stephen because he is older and taller.
3. **bounce** — Stephen saw his car **bounce** as Brutus flung it across the cement.
4. **pound** — "I'll **pound** on you if you tell on me!" threatened Brutus.
5. **outdoors** — Tony ran **outdoors** to meet Stephen and his dad.
6. **scout** — They went to the store to **scout** for new miniature cars.
7. **county** — Both boys live in the same **county.**
8. **aloud** — "Will You help me find my track shoes?" Beth prayed **aloud.**
9. **owl** — An **owl** prefers to live in the forest, not the city.
10. **noun** — Mrs. Burton reviewed with her class how to identify a **noun.**
11. **trout** — Stephen's dad especially likes to fish for **trout.**
12. **frown** — Beth's forehead wrinkled in a **frown.**
13. **underground** — She had misspelled the word "**underground**" on the preview.
14. **household** — Stephen's grandmother does not live in their **household.**
15. **stout** — Gram is not **stout,** but rather tall and thin.
16. **gown** — She was ready for bed in her pink **gown.**
17. **powder** — She wears **powder** that smells like lilacs.
18. **however** — Stephen was sad; **however,** he was glad that Gram called.

Word Shapes

Help students form a correct image of whole words.

Look at each word and think about its shape. Now, write the word in the correct Word Shape Boxes. You may check off each word as you use it.

(A diphthong is two vowel sounds that are sounded together in the same syllable. In many words, the diphthong **/ou/** is spelled **ow** if it is at the end of a word or syllable, or comes before **l** or **n**. The **/ou/** sound is spelled **ou** in most other words.)

In the Word Shape Boxes, fill in the boxes containing the letters that spell the sound of **/ou/** in each word.

Take a minute to memorize...

Luke 11:9

Words with /ou/ — Lesson 15

B Word Shapes Name ____________________

Write each word in the correct Word Shape Boxes. Next, in the Word Shape Boxes, shade in the boxes containing the letters that spell the sound of **/ou/** in each word.

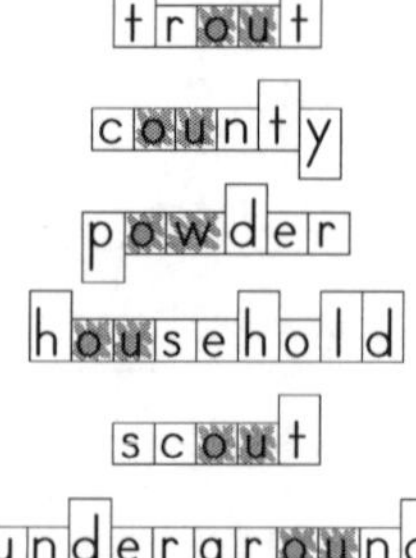

Word	Word Shape Boxes
1. aloud	trout
2. bounce	county
3. county	powder
4. household	household
5. noun	scout
6. outdoors	underground
7. pound	outdoors
8. scout	pound
9. stout	aloud
10. trout	tower
11. underground	noun
12. frown	frown
13. gown	stout
14. growl	gown
15. owl	bounce
16. however	growl
17. powder	owl
18. tower	however

94

Answers may vary for duplicate word shapes.

Be Prepared For Fun

Check these supply lists for **Fun Ways to Spell** - presented **Day 2**.
Purchase and/or gather these items ahead of time!

General
- Pencil
- Notebook Paper
- Spelling List

Auditory
- Spelling List

Visual
- Pencil
- Scissors
- 3 X 5 cards (18 per child)
- Spelling List

Tactile
- Toothpicks
- Art Paper (3 sheets per child)
- Glue
- Spelling List

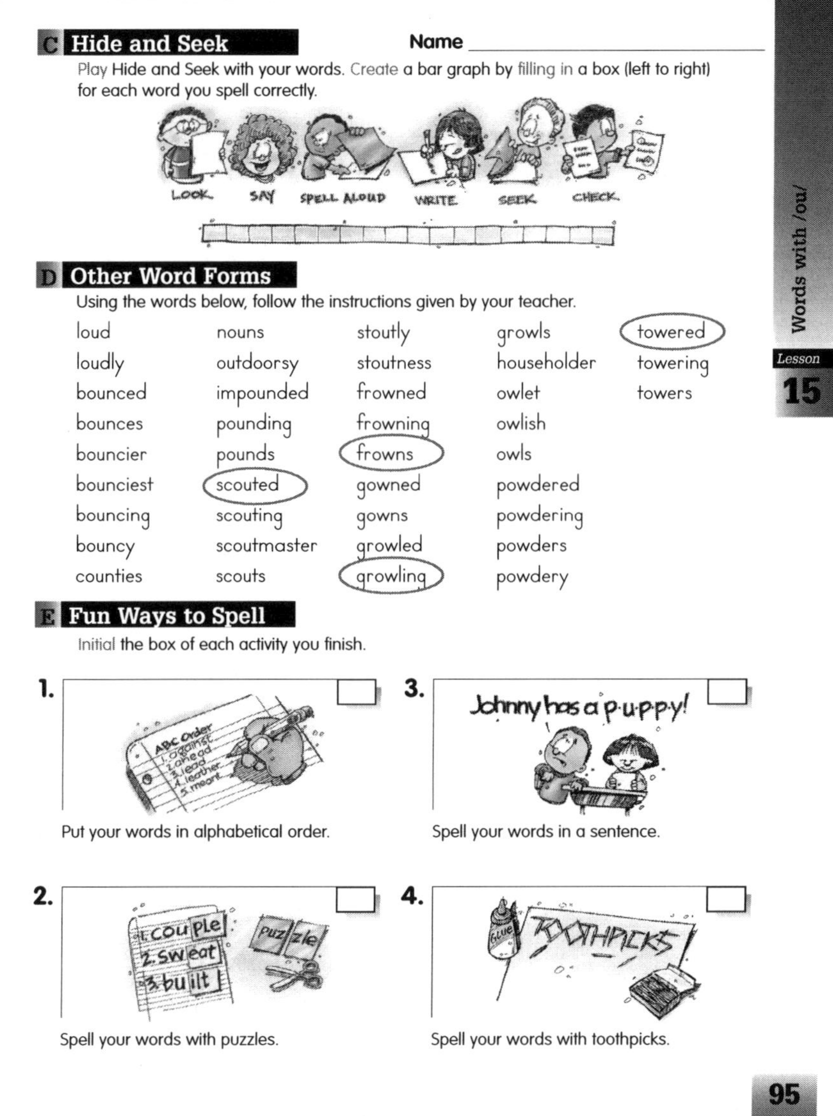

C Hide and Seek

Name ______________________

Play Hide and Seek with your words. Create a bar graph by filling in a box (left to right) for each word you spell correctly.

D Other Word Forms

Using the words below, follow the instructions given by your teacher.

loud	nouns	stoutly	growls	(towered)
loudly	outdoorsy	stoutness	householder	towering
bounced	impounded	frowned	owlet	towers
bounces	pounding	frowning	owlish	
bouncier	pounds	(frowns)	owls	
bounciest	(scouted)	gowned	powdered	
bouncing	scouting	gowns	powdering	
bouncy	scoutmaster	growled	powders	
counties	scouts	(growling)	powdery	

E Fun Ways to Spell

Initial the box of each activity you finish.

1. Put your words in alphabetical order.

2. Spell your words with puzzles.

3. Spell your words in a sentence.

4. Spell your words with toothpicks.

Words with /ou/

Lesson 15

95

1 Hide and Seek

Reinforce spelling by using multiple styles of learning.

On a white board, Teacher writes each word — one at a time. **Have students:**

- **Look** at the word.
- **Say** the word out loud.
- **Spell** the word out loud.
- **Hide** (teacher erases word.)
- **Write** the word on paper.
- **Seek** (teacher rewrites word.)
- **Check** spelling. If incorrect, rewrite word correctly.

2 Other Word Forms

This activity is optional. Have students find and circle the Other Word Forms that are synonyms of the following:

explored
scowls
loomed
snarling

3 Fun Ways to Spell

Four activities are provided. Use one, two, three, or all of the activities. Have students initial the box for each activity they complete.

Options:

- assign activities to students according to their learning styles
- set up the activities in learning centers for students to do throughout the day
- divide students into four groups and assign one activity per group
- do one activity per day

General

To put your words in alphabetical order…
- Write all the words in alphabetical order.
- Remember to look at the second, third, or fourth letters of the words when the first letters are the same.

Auditory

To spell your words in a sentence…
- Have a classmate read a spelling word to you.
- Say a sentence with that spelling word to your classmate.
- Ask your classmate to spell the word.
- Check your classmate's spelling.
- Read a word to your classmate, continue taking turns until you have each spelled all the words.

Visual

To spell your words with puzzles…
- Write each word on a card.
- Ask a classmate to cut each word apart between two letters.
- Arrange half of each word on your desk.
- Write the missing part of the word on a piece of paper.
- Do it again with the other half of your cards.
- Check your spelling.

Tactile

To spell your words with toothpicks…
- Choose a word from your spelling list.
- Arrange toothpicks to represent each letter of the word.
- Glue them to a piece of art paper.

Working with Words

Familiarize students with word meaning and usage.

Pronunciation

It will be helpful for students to look at a pronunciation key as you explain this lesson. (Pronunciations vary slightly between sources.) Show students that a dictionary lists pronunciation for each entry, written in phonetic symbols as a guide to how the word is pronounced.

In your Worktext, write the group of words in alphabetical order. Now, look up each word in the dictionary and write the pronunciation beside each word. Then, at the bottom, using the pronunciation key, write the spelling word each pronunciation stands for.

F **Working with Words** Name ____________

Words with /ou/ — Lesson 15

Pronunciation

A dictionary lists a pronunciation for each entry word. This pronunciation is written in phonetic symbols as a guide to how the word is pronounced. Place the following group of words in alphabetical order. Then look up each word in the dictionary and write the pronunciation beside each word.

scout however bounce growl county

1. bounce — Answers will vary
2. county — Answers will vary
3. growl — Answers will vary
4. however — Answers will vary
5. scout — Answers will vary

Pronunciation Key

/ô/ collar /ou/ out, town /ə/ water, fund /ôr/ floor

Using the **Pronunciation Key** above, write the spelling word each of these pronunciations stands for.

1. /tou′ ər/	tower	10. /ən′ dər ground/	underground
2. /ə loud′/	aloud	11. /pound/	pound
3. /out dôrz′/	outdoors	12. /froun/	frown
4. /pou′ dər/	powder	13. /stout/	stout
5. /hous′ hold/	household	14. /bouns/	bounce
6. /noun/	noun	15. /scout/	scout
7. /oul/	owl	16. /groul/	growl
8. /trout/	trout	17. /koun′ tē/	county
9. /goun/	gown	18. /hou ev′ ər/	however

Word Bank

aloud	frown	household	outdoors	powder	tower
bounce	gown	however	owl	scout	trout
county	growl	noun	pound	stout	underground

96

Take a minute to memorize...

Luke 11:9

G Dictation

Name ____________________

Write each sentence as your teacher dictates. Use correct punctuation.

1. With a frown he saw his new car bounce.
2. He gave a growl and began to pound the ground.
3. Outdoors on the porch, he prayed aloud.

Words with /ou/

Lesson 15

H Proofreading

If a word is misspelled, fill in the oval by that word. If all the words are spelled correctly, fill in the oval by **no mistake**.

1. ○ cellar ○ chance ● alowd ○ no mistake
2. ○ powder ● bownce ○ citizen ○ no mistake
3. ○ decide ○ exciting ○ county ● no mistake
4. ● groul ○ owl ○ household ○ no mistake
5. ○ famous ○ son ○ noun ● no mistake
6. ○ else ○ tower ● outdors ○ no mistake
7. ○ recess ○ beast ○ pound ● no mistake
8. ○ across ○ press ○ scout ● no mistake
9. ○ science ○ however ● stowt ○ no mistake
10. ○ police ○ trout ○ scene ● no mistake
11. ○ peace ○ glance ○ underground ● no mistake
12. ○ fence ○ gown ● froun ○ no mistake

97

1 Dictation

Reinforce correct spelling by using current and previous words in context.

Listen as I read each sentence and then write it in your Worktext. Remember to use correct capitalization and punctuation. (Slowly read each sentence twice. Sentences are found in the Student Worktext to the left.)

2 Proofreading

Familiarize students with standardized test format and reinforce recognition of misspelled words.

Look at each set of words. If a word is misspelled, fill in the oval by that word. If all the words are spelled correctly, fill in the oval by **no mistake**.

3 Hide and Seek

Reinforce correct spelling of current spelling words. Repeat this activity from Day 2. (A reproducible master is provided in Appendix A as shown on the inset page to the right.)

4 Other Word Forms

Have your students complete this activity to strengthen spelling ability and expand vocabulary.

1 Posttest

Visit the **A Reason For** website to download free, printable Posttest pages.

I will say the word once, use it in a sentence, then say it again. Write your words on a separate sheet of paper.

Progress Chart

Students may record scores. (Appendix B)

Personal Dictionary

Students may add any words they have misspelled to their personal dictionaries. (Appendix B)

Hide and Seek

Play Hide and Seek with your words. Create a bar graph by filling in a box (left to right) for each word you spell correctly.

LOOK SAY HIDE WRITE SEEK CHECK

Other Word Forms

Synonyms

Use the synonyms to write the words. Remember, a synonym is a word that means the same or nearly the same as another word.

1. banging pounding
2. dusting powdering
3. exploring scouting
4. lofty towering
5. kennels pounds
6. rural divisions counties
7. snarling growling
8. parts of speech nouns
9. fine grains powders
10. stubbornly stoutly
11. countrified outdoorsy
12. evening dresses gowns
13. inhabitant householder
14. noisily loudly
15. clothed gowned
16. scowling frowning
17. springiest bounciest
18. plumpness stoutness
19. skyscrapers towers
20. young bird of prey owlet

Syllables

Count how many syllables each word has and write the number on the line.

1. 3 powdery
2. 2 bouncy
3. 2 loudly
4. 2 owlish
5. 3 impounded
6. 3 scoutmaster
7. 2 stoutness
8. 1 nouns
9. 3 towering
10. 3 powdering
11. 1 pounds
12. 1 growled
13. 1 frowned
14. 3 bouncier
15. 2 scouted

Word Bank

bounciest	gowns	nouns	pounds	stoutly
counties	growling	outdoorsy	powdering	stoutness
frowning	householder	owlet	powders	towering
gowned	loudly	pounding	scouting	towers

Lesson 15 Other Word Forms

337

---

1. noun	Mrs. Burton had her students underline each **noun** in the sentence.
2. outdoors	The students enjoy it when Mrs. Burton has class **outdoors.**
3. scout	The boys like to **scout** the stores for new models of collector cars.
4. trout	Stephen's dad has a huge **trout** mounted on a plaque.
5. frown	Beth's **frown** showed she was not pleased with her score.
6. underground	She needed to practice spelling the word "**underground.**"
7. gown	Her spelling book was not under her **gown,** either.
8. aloud	Beth read **aloud** the verse for the week.
9. owl	It would be difficult to find an **owl** in a city.
10. tower	He did not like it when Brutus stood like a **tower** over him.
11. growl	Brutus's laugh was more like a nasty **growl.**
12. pound	Stephen's heart began to **pound** very hard!
13. however	He was angry; **however,** he was too scared to speak.
14. bounce	His heart sank as he saw his new car **bounce** across the concrete.
15. powder	Stephen's car landed beside the **powder** from the sidewalk chalk.
16. stout	Gram is tall and thin, not **stout.**
17. household	Stephen's gram does not live in his **household.**
18. county	She doesn't even live in the same **county** or state.

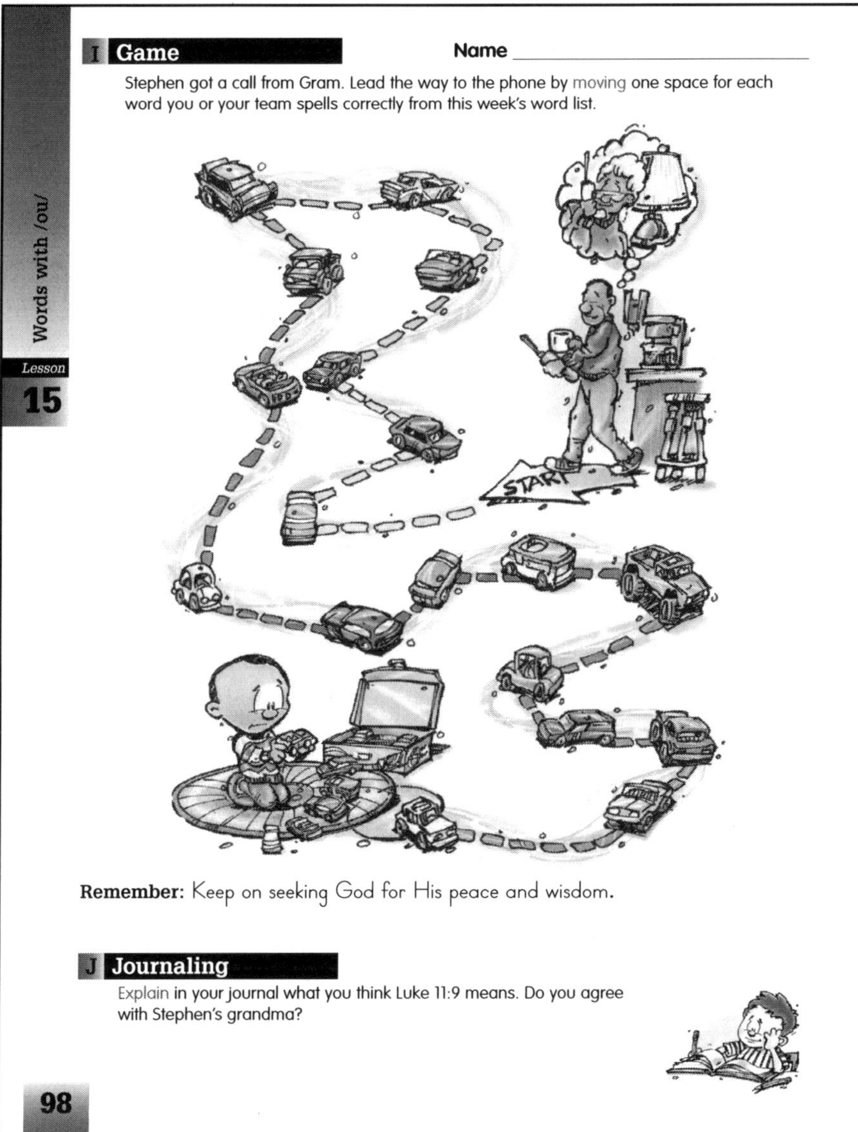

Words with /ou/

Lesson 15

I Game

Name ________________________

Stephen got a call from Gram. Lead the way to the phone by moving one space for each word you or your team spells correctly from this week's word list.

Remember: Keep on seeking God for His peace and wisdom.

J Journaling

Explain in your journal what you think Luke 11:9 means. Do you agree with Stephen's grandma?

98

How to Play:

- Divide students into two teams.
- Have each student place his/her game piece on Start.
- Have a student from team A go to the board.
- Say the spelling word.
- Have the student write the word on the board.
- If correct, instruct each member of team A to move his/her game piece forward one space.
- Alternate between teams A and B as you go down the word list.
- The team to reach Stephen first is the winner.

Small Group Option: Students may play this game without teacher direction in small groups of two or more.

2 Game

Reinforce spelling skills and provide motivation and interest.

Materials

- game page (from Student Worktext)
- game pieces (1 per child)
- game word list

Game Word List

1. **aloud**
2. **bounce**
3. **county**
4. **household**
5. **noun**
6. **outdoors**
7. **pound**
8. **scout**
9. **stout**
10. **trout**
11. **underground**
12. **frown**
13. **gown**
14. **growl**
15. **owl**
16. **however**
17. **powder**
18. **tower**

3 Journaling

Provide a meaningful reason for correct spelling through personal writing.

Review the story using discussion leads provided on the following page. Encourage students to apply the Scriptural value in their journaling.

Journaling (continued)

- What did Stephen ask God for in the toy store? (Two miniature cars.)
- What did Beth ask God to help her find? (Her track shoes.)
- Why was Tony hoping Stephen would be home? (He'd left his Math book in Stephen's car.)
- Did God answer the kids' prayers the way Stephen expected? (No.)
- What Scripture verse was Stephen talking about when he said, "It's just not true for kids." (Luke 11:9)
- What did Gram tell Stephen God was always willing to give us? (Peace and a change of heart.)

The word for "dog" in the Australian aboriginal language Mbabaran happens to be "dog."

Word Wow!

1 Literature Connection

Topic: Kindness
Theme Text: Mark 9:37

Derailment at DeVore Mtn.

Milli helps Daniel show kindness to an energetic young visitor.

"Daniel." Millicent Dunlap's call sounded loud in the wide upstairs hallway of the DeVore home. The new maid's feet sunk into the plush carpet as she walked toward the open door halfway down the hall. "Daniel?"

Millicent—Milli for short—glanced around the large bedroom. No Daniel. She raised her voice. "Daniel! It's be'n time to leave for your school, Lad!"

"Okay! Just a minute. I'm coming." Daniel DeVore emerged from the door leading off his bedroom to a large playroom. He grabbed a leather bookpack from his desk. "D'you know anything about model trains, Milli? I'm having trouble with one of my HO engines."

"Sure'n I know they run on tracks, but that's aboot all I'd be a-knowin.'" Milli crossed the bedroom to reach into the playroom and flip off the light switch. "Now we'd best be a-gettin' you off to school."

"Is my mother up yet?" Daniel stopped in the hall and looked toward the double doors at the end of the hallway.

"'Fraid not, Lad." Milli shook her head and guided him toward the staircase. "You be a-knowin' she had that big charity ball over in Fayetteville last night 'til real late. Just tired out, she is."

"Well, I'm just about finished putting together the coal train and all the new track in the train room." Daniel followed the maid past the laundry room toward the garage. "I want to get it running along with the rest 'cause James is coming to visit next week and I want to have Tommy and him over to see it all."

"Sure'n that room off the playroom turned into a right nice place for all of them trains your father's been a-gettin' for you." Milli pushed the button to open the garage doors and started the car. "You got a town, a mountain, a river with a train bridge over it, and a whole passel of trains now, I be a-thinkin.'"

"Yes." Daniel rubbed a finger over a little spot on the car window. "It's just that, well, it doesn't look real nice like it's supposed to. You know, that diorama stuff is kind of hard to do and it'd be nice to have someone to help me do it all."

Milli flashed Daniel her ready smile. "It may be that your father will be a-spendin' more time at home once this big deal he's a-workin' on now goes through."

"Hmmmph!" Daniel snorted and then laughed. "Not my dad, Milli. You haven't been around long enough yet or you wouldn't even think that! He's always working on some big deal." Daniel glanced at the maid out of the corner of his eye. "Too bad you don't know more about trains."

"Don't you be a-thinkin' I can't learn, young Daniel! Sure'n I can learn more about lots of things and trains seem right interestin!'"

She pulled into the drive at Knowlton Elementary and reached across the seat to pat Daniel's shoulder. "You be a-havin' a good day now Lad, y'hear?"

"Yes'm!" Daniel grinned as he climbed out of the car. "You too, Milli!"

"Before we begin our handwriting practice today, is there someone who would like to read this week's Scripture verse for us?" Mrs. Burton held up her open ***A Reason For Handwriting***® Worktext and pointed to page 40. "How about you, Sarah?"

Daniel noticed that Sarah's face turned a little pink as it always did when she had to say something in front of the whole class, but she read the words clearly. "Anyone who welcomes a little child like this in My name is welcoming Me, and anyone who welcomes Me is welcoming My Father who sent Me! Mark 9:37"

I wonder why Sarah always turns red? Daniel's thoughts wandered as the discussion continued.

"Thank-you, Sarah." Mrs. Burton smiled. "Who's saying these words that Sarah just read to us? Katelynn?"

"Jesus. He was talking to His disciples."

"That's true, Katelynn, but were these words meant only for the twelve disciples?"

"No." Katelynn pointed to the first word. "It says 'anyone' right at the first, so it's for all people. For us, too."

Mrs. Burton nodded. "Good point. Now what do you think the message is for us, Daniel?"

Uh-oh. What's she talking about? Daniel's thoughts jerked back to the present. *What did that verse say?*

"Uh, it means that everyone should be nice to us kids." Daniel grinned when everyone laughed. Mrs. Burton smiled and shook her head.

"Mrs. B." Kristin spoke up. "Doesn't it mean that when we're kind to everyone—especially kids or people that aren't real important—that we're, like, being kind to God or something?"

"Good thinking, Kristin." Mrs. Burton leaned against her desk. "When we welcome Jesus into our lives, our love for Him causes us to treat all people well because He loves them. That means even small children and those people who can't do anything for us. Welcoming Jesus and accepting what He's done to save us is the only way we get to know God, to welcome Him into our lives."

Story (continued)

"Bye, Tommy! Don't forget James will be here next week, so ask your mom if you can come over after school Monday!" Daniel called across the parking area to his friend. "See you tomorrow!" He hopped into the shiny car his parents kept for the maid to use. "Hi, Milli!" He started to toss his book bag into the back seat and stopped. "What's this?"

"Hi, yourself, Lad." Milli pulled carefully out into the stream of cars leaving the school. "That be shoppin' for your mother."

"Hmmmm." Daniel reached into one of the bags resting on the floor behind the driver's seat. "My mother wanted this?" He grinned and held up the book he'd pulled out, *Everything You Need to Know About Model Trains*.

Milli shrugged. "Now that be somethin' I was a-needin.' Sure'n how else was I a-goin' to be a-helpin' you with that train room of yours?"

Daniel swallowed the sudden lump in his throat. "Really? You're really going to help me with the train?"

"Help or hinder, we'll be a-seein' which it be." As they neared the DeVore's sprawling white brick home, Milli pointed to a red Cadillac parked in the half-circle drive. "Seems there be company."

Mrs. Fitzsimmons had come to talk with Daniel's mother about a women's society luncheon. She'd brought her three-year-old boy, Dalton, who was happily destroying Daniel's room, the playroom, and the train room!

"MY TRAINS!" Daniel ignored the mess in his bedroom and the playroom. He stared at the little train village he'd worked so hard to lay out. It looked like a tornado—or two or three—had hit it. The river was full of coal from the mining mountain that had come down when Dalton yanked out the train bridge and moved it to the top of the mountain. Train cars were scattered. Dalton sat in the middle of the model train diorama and pulled at the wheels of Daniel's newest HO engine.

"Hi." Dalton grinned up at Daniel.

"You! You…" Daniel sputtered. He stared at the little boy's happy face. "Anyone who welcomes a little child like this in My name is welcoming Me." Sarah's clear voice reading the Scripture repeated itself in Daniel's mind. He remembered how nice Milli was to him. He swallowed hard and spoke as kindly as he could. "Hi, Dalton. Can I play with you?"

Milli saw the mess when she came to tell Dalton it was time to leave. Her eyebrows rose clear up under her bangs.

"You're my bestest friend, Daniel." Dalton flung his arms around the surprised boy, and Milli had to gently pull him away.

When the toddler was gone, Daniel sank back against the wall and groaned. "My train, Milli. Look at my train room. James is coming to visit in five days and I wanted it to be perfect."

"Why, Daniel Rocklin DeVore! Just look at this mess!" Daniel's mother stood in the doorway frowning. "You must learn to take better care of your things!"

"But, Mom, I…" Daniel stood up.

"No excuses! Now get this cleaned up right away." Mrs. DeVore turned to the maid. "I'll be out this evening, Millicent. Please see that Daniel cleans this up and is in bed at the proper time." She turned and left the room. Daniel sank down into his spot against the wall.

Milli picked up an armload of toys.

"Milli, why are you helping me?" Daniel started sorting through the mixed-up game pieces on the carpet. "It's not part of your job."

"Because I be a-wantin' to." Milli returned a load of stuffed animals to the shelves. "And because I was a-seein' how kind you be to that bit of a boy, Dalton."

Daniel carried the games to the closet. "I was only nice to him because I was supposed to be. I really didn't feel like it, but we talked about a Scripture at school today and I remembered it. You know the one that says, 'Anyone who welcomes a little child like this in My name is welcoming Me.'"

"Aye. I know it."

"That, and I thought about how nice you've been to me ever since you came to work here." Daniel fiddled with a matchbox car. "I can tell you love God because you're so nice to me and I'm just a kid. I want to be like that, Milli, but I'm usually not very nice."

Milli dumped a load of books onto the top of the bookshelf. "You and I just need to be a-welcomin' Jesus into our hearts every day, Lad. Sure'n He'll be a-changin' us to do the kind things we ought." Daniel was surprised when she gave him a quick hug. "Now, we'd best be a-gettin' some dinner into us before we be a-startin' on that train room!"

2 Discussion Time

Check understanding of the story and development of personal values.

- Who is Milli?
- From whom did Daniel get all the model train things?
- Where did Daniel set up the train track and the models that went with it?
- Why did Daniel want to get the rest of the model train set up before the next week?
- Who was at Daniel's house when he got home from school?
- What had Dalton done to Daniel's things?
- How did Daniel react to the terrible mess Dalton had made?
- What two things made Daniel choose to be kind to Dalton?

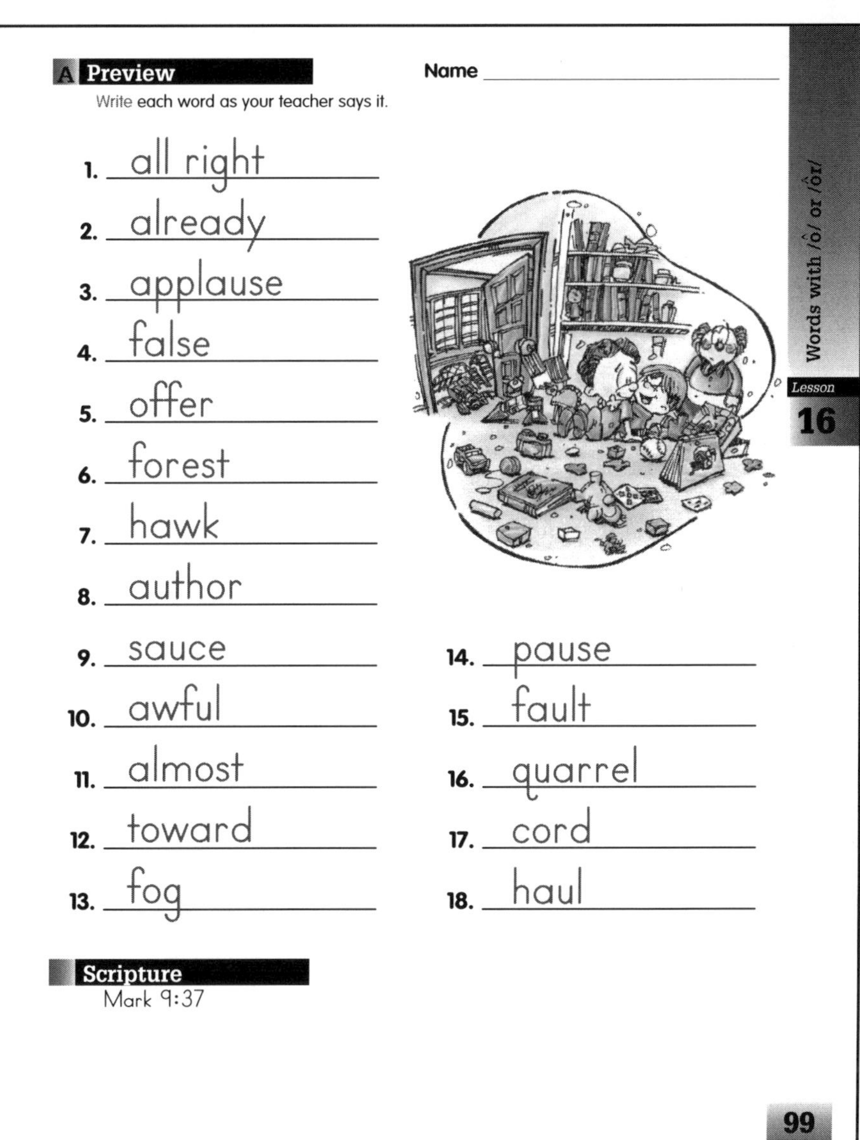

A Preview Name ______________

Write each word as your teacher says it.

1. all right
2. already
3. applause
4. false
5. offer
6. forest
7. hawk
8. author
9. sauce
10. awful
11. almost
12. toward
13. fog
14. pause
15. fault
16. quarrel
17. cord
18. haul

Words with /ô/ or /ôr/

Lesson 16

Scripture
Mark 9:37

99

3 Preview

Test for knowledge of the correct spellings of these words.

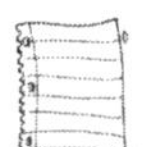

Customize Your List

On a separate sheet of paper, additional words of your choice may be tested.

I will say each word once, use the word in a sentence, then say the word again. Write the words on the lines in your Worktext.

Correct Immediately!

Let's correct our Preview. I will spell each word out loud. If you spelled a word incorrectly, rewrite it correctly.

Progress Chart

Students may record scores. (Reproducible master provided in Appendix B.)

1. **all right** — "It is **all right** if you talk quietly for a few minutes," said Mrs. Burton.
2. **already** — Sarah **already** had her handwriting book open to the correct lesson.
3. **applause** — Daniel enjoys the class's laughter and **applause.**
4. **false** — Mrs. Burton gave the class a brief true-or-**false** quiz before lunch.
5. **offer** — It was kind of Milli to **offer** to help Daniel with his train diorama.
6. **forest** — He planned to put a perfectly scaled **forest** beside the painted river.
7. **hawk** — Daniel may put a miniature **hawk** in one of the trees on the mountain.
8. **author** — Daniel recognized the name of the **author** on the book Milli bought.
9. **sauce** — Milli made a delicious spaghetti **sauce** for dinner.
10. **awful** — When he walked into his room, an **awful** sight met his eyes.
11. **almost** — He **almost** yelled at Dalton for the mess he had made.
12. **toward** — Instead he chose to show kindness **toward** the little boy.
13. **fog** — Seeing his model scattered about his room put his mind in a momentary **fog.**
14. **pause** — During the short **pause,** Daniel remembered the verse he learned at school.
15. **fault** — It was Dalton's **fault** that Daniel's room was a mess.
16. **quarrel** — God was very happy that Daniel did not **quarrel** with Dalton.
17. **cord** — Milli pulled the **cord** to lower the blind in Daniel's playroom.
18. **haul** — She helped **haul** the toys back to their proper places.

Word Shapes

Help students form a correct image of whole words.

Look at each word and think about its shape. Now, write the word in the correct Word Shape Boxes. You may check off each word as you use it.

(In some words **/ô/** is spelled with **a**, and it is often spelled this way when it is followed by **l** or **ll**. In some words **/ô/** is spelled with **aw**, **o**, or **au**.)

In the Word Shape Boxes, fill in the boxes containing the letter or letters that spell the sound of **/ô/** in each word.

Take a minute to memorize...

Mark 9:37

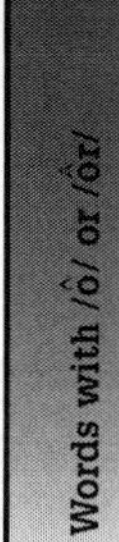

Name ____________________

Write each word in the correct Word Shape Boxes. Next, in the Word Shape Boxes, shade in the boxes containing the letter or letters that spell the sound of **/ô/** or **/ôr/** in each word.

1. all right
2. almost
3. already
4. false
5. quarrel
6. toward
7. applause
8. author
9. fault
10. haul
11. pause
12. sauce
13. awful
14. hawk
15. fog
16. offer
17. cord
18. forest

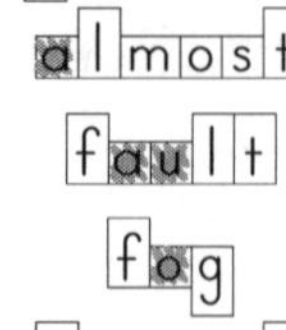

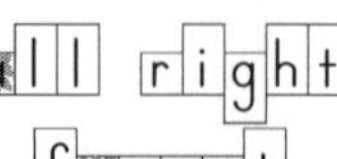

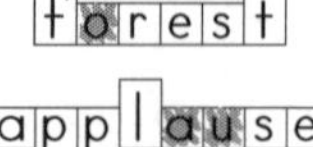

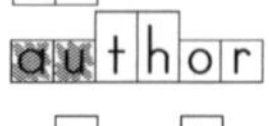

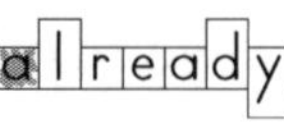

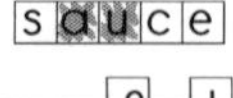

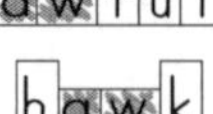

100

Answers may vary for duplicate word shapes.

Be Prepared For Fun

Check these supply lists for **Fun Ways to Spell** - presented **Day 2**. Purchase and/or gather these items ahead of time!

General
- Pencil
- Graph Paper (1 sheet per child)
- Spelling List

Auditory
- Pencil
- 3 X 5 Cards Cut in half lengthwise (18 per child)
- Spelling List

Visual
- Glitter
- Glue
- Art Paper (2 sheets per child)
- Spelling List

Tactile
- ABC Macaroni
- Art Paper (1 sheet per child)
- Glue
- Spelling List

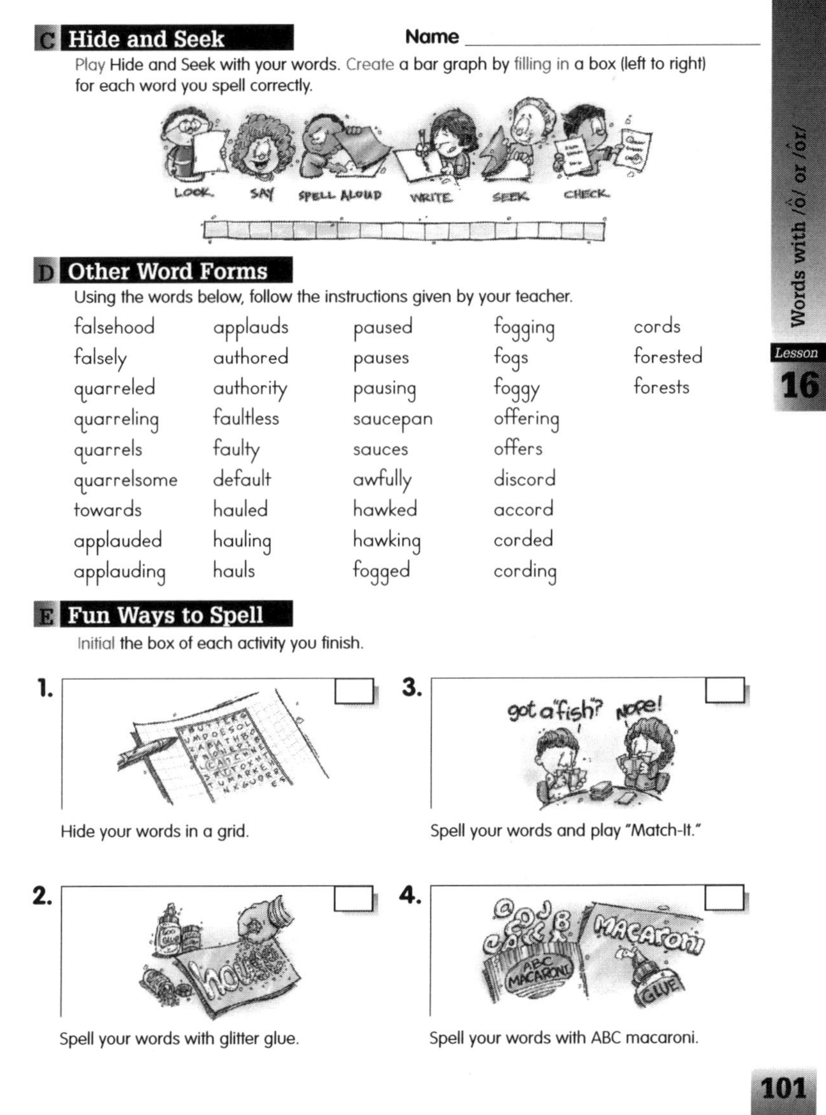

C Hide and Seek Name ____________________

Play Hide and Seek with your words. Create a bar graph by filling in a box (left to right) for each word you spell correctly.

D Other Word Forms

Using the words below, follow the instructions given by your teacher.

falsehood	applauds	paused	fogging	cords
falsely	authored	pauses	fogs	forested
quarreled	authority	pausing	foggy	forests
quarreling	faultless	saucepan	offering	
quarrels	faulty	sauces	offers	
quarrelsome	default	awfully	discord	
towards	hauled	hawked	accord	
applauded	hauling	hawking	corded	
applauding	hauls	fogged	cording	

E Fun Ways to Spell

Initial the box of each activity you finish.

1. Hide your words in a grid.

3. Spell your words and play "Match-It."

2. Spell your words with glitter glue.

4. Spell your words with ABC macaroni.

Words with /ô/ or /ôr/

Lesson 16

101

1 Hide and Seek

Reinforce spelling by using multiple styles of learning.

On a white board, Teacher writes each word — one at a time. **Have students:**

- **Look** at the word.
- **Say** the word out loud.
- **Spell** the word out loud.
- **Hide** (teacher erases word.)
- **Write** the word on paper.
- **Seek** (teacher rewrites word.)
- **Check** spelling. If incorrect, rewrite word correctly.

2 Other Word Forms

This activity is optional. Have students write variations of this sentence using these Other Word Forms:

The applause was deafening.
applauds
applauded
applauding

3 Fun Ways to Spell

Four activities are provided. Use one, two, three, or all of the activities. Have students initial the box for each activity they complete.

Options:

- assign activities to students according to their learning styles
- set up the activities in learning centers for students to do throughout the day
- divide students into four groups and assign one activity per group
- do one activity per day

General

To hide your words on a grid...
- Arrange your words on a piece of graph paper.
- Put one letter of each word in a square.
- Words may be written backwards, forwards, or diagonally.
- Outline your puzzle.
- Hide your words by filling in all the spaces inside the puzzle with random letters.
- Trade grids with a classmate and find the hidden words.

Auditory

To spell your words and play "Match-It"...
Write each spelling word on a card. Mix your word cards and a classmate's together. Deal six cards per player; put the rest face down between you. Ask classmate for a word-card that matches one in your hand. If the classmate has the word-card, take it and play again. If not, draw from the remaining stack, then it is your classmate's turn. Continue taking turns until all the cards are matched. Player with most cards wins!

Visual

To spell your words with glitter glue...
- Write each of your spelling words on your paper with glue.
- Sprinkle with glitter.

Tactile

To spell your words with ABC macaroni...
- Choose a word from your spelling list.
- Spell the word with macaroni letters.
- Glue the macaroni word to art paper.
- Do this for each word on your list.

Working with Words

Familiarize students with word meaning and usage.

Riddles in Rhyme

Say this riddle and have students complete it with a rhyming word.

Our new scoutmaster, makes us hike ________.
Elicit the answer **faster**.

Read each of the riddles in your Worktext. Write the spelling word that completes each rhyme.

Spelling Clues

Recognizing that many words are made up of common letter patterns and/or shorter words can help students spell better. Write **sentence** on the board. Have a volunteer circle the shorter word **ten**, and the common letter pattern of **en**, which is used twice. Now, write the word **consonant**. Have a volunteer circle the shorter words **on** and **ant**.

Find the spelling word that contains the shorter word and write it on the line.

Take a minute to memorize...

Mark 9:37

Words with /ô/ or /ôr/ — Lesson 16

F **Working with Words** Name ________________

Riddles in Rhyme

Write the spelling word that completes each rhyme.

1. Milli and Daniel went to the mall
And found a tank-car for his train to haul.
2. Around the track the train did coast
With a clickety-clack you could hear — almost.
3. But Dalton tried to pull the cord
And knocked some pieces off the board.
4. The little bridge fell out of sight,
And Daniel hoped it was all right.
5. The roads were bad, the hills the poorest;
The trees had fallen in the forest.
6. He viewed the mess, his mind in a whirl,
But Dalton determined he wouldn't quarrel.
7. In dashed Mom, to a sudden halt.
She thought the mess was Daniel's fault!

Spelling Clues

Write the correct spelling word on the line.

1. The short word **off** is in what longer word? offer
2. The short word **read** is in what longer word? already
3. The short word **ward** is in what longer word? toward
4. The short word **use** is in what longer words? applause pause
5. The short word **or** is in what longer words? author forest cord

Word Bank

all right	applause	cord	fog	hawk	quarrel
almost	author	false	forest	offer	sauce
already	awful	fault	haul	pause	toward

102

G Dictation

Name

Write each sentence as your teacher dictates. Use correct punctuation.

1. It was his fault that the room looked awful.
2. He already started to haul out the stuff.
3. Her offer to help almost made him drop the train.

Words with /ô/ or /ôr/

Lesson 16

H Proofreading

If a word is misspelled, fill in the oval by that word. If all the words are spelled correctly, fill in the oval by **no mistake**.

1. ● alright ○ county ○ household ○ no mistake
2. ○ aloud ○ bounce ● all most ○ no mistake
3. ○ cord ○ noun ● alredy ○ no mistake
4. ○ outdoors ○ pound ○ false ● no mistake
5. ● quarel ○ scout ○ tower ○ no mistake
6. ● ofer ○ toward ○ stout ○ no mistake
7. ○ trout ○ underground ● aplause ○ no mistake
8. ○ fog ○ frown ● auther ○ no mistake
9. ○ gown ● forrest ○ fault ○ no mistake
10. ○ growl ○ owl ○ haul ● no mistake
11. ○ however ○ hawk ○ pause ● no mistake
12. ○ powder ● sause ○ awful ○ no mistake

103

1 Dictation

Reinforce correct spelling by using current and previous words in context.

Listen as I read each sentence and then write it in your Worktext. Remember to use correct capitalization and punctuation. (Slowly read each sentence twice. Sentences are found in the Student Worktext to the left.)

Day 4 | Lesson 16

2 Proofreading

Familiarize students with standardized test format and reinforce recognition of misspelled words.

Look at each set of words. If a word is misspelled, fill in the oval by that word. If all the words are spelled correctly, fill in the oval by **no mistake**.

NOTE: Some dictionaries and websites now say that **(alright)** is a correct spelling option for **(all right)**.

3 Hide and Seek

Reinforce correct spelling of current spelling words. Repeat this activity from Day 2. (A reproducible master is provided in Appendix A as shown on the inset page to the right.)

4 Other Word Forms

Have your students complete this activity to strengthen spelling ability and expand vocabulary.

1 Posttest

Visit the **A Reason For** website to download free, printable Posttest pages.

I will say the word once, use it in a sentence, then say it again. Write your words on a separate sheet of paper.

Progress Chart

Students may record scores. (Appendix B)

Personal Dictionary

Students may add any words they have misspelled to their personal dictionaries. (Appendix B)

Lesson 16 | Other Word Forms

Hide and Seek

Play Hide and Seek with your words. Create a bar graph by filling in a box (left to right) for each word you spell correctly.

Other Word Forms

Sentence Fun

Circle the word that correctly completes each sentence.

1. Milli bought a book by an (authoring, **authority**) on model trains.
2. The vegetables simmered in a (**saucepan**, sauces).
3. The audience (applauding, **applauded**) after the recital.
4. Usually one (falsely, **falsehood**) leads to another.
5. Daniel could have (**quarreled**, quarrels) with Dalton.
6. The switch on the train set seems to be (faulted, **faulty**).
7. Daniel's train ran through a little (forests, **forested**) section.
8. Daniel (**paused**, pausing) in the doorway of the playroom.
9. Mom is (awfulness, **awfully**) tired after staying up late.
10. The mirror (fogging, **fogged**) up when I took a shower.
11. This money is my (**offering**, offers) for church.
12. The (**cords**, corded) on the computer are tangled.
13. She is feeling tired and (**quarrelsome**, quarreler).
14. A man stood by the road (hawker, **hawking**) his fruits and vegetables.
15. We began (hauled, **hauling**) bags of groceries in from the car.
16. It does not feel good to be (false, **falsely**) accused of something.
17. We drove carefully through the (fogging, **foggy**) streets.

338

---

1. almost	Daniel was **almost** ready for school when Milli called him.
2. already	Milli **already** had his lunch packed.
3. author	Daniel had read several train books by his favorite **author**.
4. offer	Milli was glad to **offer** to help Daniel with his diorama.
5. hawk	Daniel found a miniature **hawk** at the hobby store.
6. forest	There were a variety of trees with which to build a **forest**.
7. false	Daniel did well on the true-or-**false** quiz Mrs. Burton gave the class.
8. quarrel	Daniel does not **quarrel** at school as much as he used to.
9. applause	Daniel likes to hear laughter and **applause** at his jokes.
10. fault	It was the three-year-old's **fault** that Daniel's room was a mess.
11. fog	Daniel was so shocked, he felt like his head was in a **fog**.
12. toward	Daniel's choice to show kindness **toward** Dalton pleased God.
13. cord	Milli gently lowered the big blind with the thin **cord**.
14. all right	"It'll be **all right**, now," comforted Milli.
15. haul	Daniel quietly began to **haul** the scattered toys back to the shelves.
16. pause	It was good for Daniel to **pause** and think before he spoke.
17. awful	It took a while to clean up the **awful** mess.
18. sauce	Milli served him a double dip of ice cream with hot fudge **sauce**.

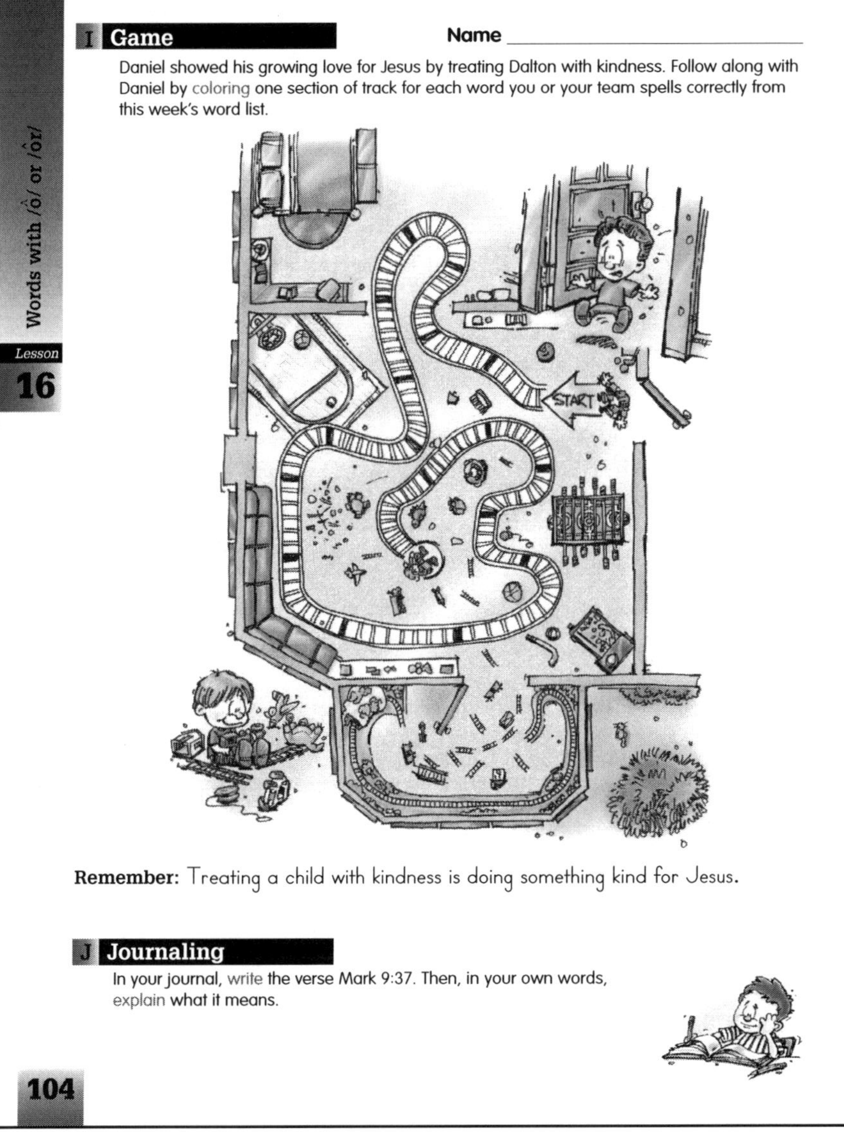

Words with /ô/ or /ôr/

Lesson 16

I Game Name ______________________

Daniel showed his growing love for Jesus by treating Dalton with kindness. Follow along with Daniel by coloring one section of track for each word you or your team spells correctly from this week's word list.

Remember: Treating a child with kindness is doing something kind for Jesus.

J Journaling

In your journal, write the verse Mark 9:37. Then, in your own words, explain what it means.

104

How to Play:

- Divide students into two teams.
- Have a student from team A go to the board.
- Say the spelling word.
- Have the student write the word on the board.
- If correct, instruct each member of team A to color one section of track, beginning at Start.
- Alternate between teams A and B as you go down the word list.
- The team to reach Dalton first is the winner.

Small Group Option: Students may play this game without teacher direction in small groups of two or more.

2 Game

Reinforce spelling skills and provide motivation and interest.

Materials

- game page (from Student Worktext)
- crayons or colored pencils (1 per child)
- game word list

Game Word List

1. **all right**
2. **almost**
3. **already**
4. **false**
5. **quarrel**
6. **toward**
7. **applause**
8. **author**
9. **fault**
10. **haul**
11. **pause**
12. **sauce**
13. **awful**
14. **hawk**
15. **fog**
16. **offer**
17. **cord**
18. **forest**

3 Journaling

Provide a meaningful reason for correct spelling through personal writing.

Review the story using discussion leads provided on the following page. Encourage students to apply the Scriptural value in their journaling.

Journaling (continued)

- Where did Daniel set up the HO train models his dad sent him? (In a room off the playroom.)
- What kinds of things did he have to go with the trains? (A town, a mountain, a river with a train bridge over it, and lots of train cars.)
- Have you ever built a model of any kind? Describe your experience.
- Why was it hard for Daniel to put everything together? (Building the diorama, or setting, for the tracks was difficult. Daniel didn't have anyone to help him or show him what to do.)
- Where was Daniel's dad? (Always working.)
- What did Milli do that let Daniel know she was interested in helping him? (Bought a book about model trains.)
- How did Daniel put Mark 9:37 into practice? (He was kind to Dalton even though Dalton had wrecked his room.)
- In what ways can you put Mark 9:37 in practice in your life?

Spoonerisms are an unintentional interchange of sounds, usually initial sounds, in two or more words. They were named after Reverend W. A. Spooner who was famous for such slips. For example, "a well-boiled icicle" for "a well-oiled bicycle."

Word Wow!

Midnight Alarm!

Tommy learns about God's care watching his mother care for an Alzheimer's patient.

The baseball came sailing through the clear sky like a comet. Tommy knew it was going to be too far away for him to catch. Straining to reach it before it hit the ground, Tommy found himself flying through the air effortlessly. He reached out as he flew close to the ball. It flashed like lightning in the air and changed directions. Just before he could close his glove over the escaping ball, Tommy began falling. He wasn't afraid. After all, there was a huge trampoline under him now. His baseball glove disappeared as his feet touched the surface with a CRASH!

Tommy's eyes flew open. He stared about his room, not quite awake yet. BUMP! SLAM! Tommy raised his head and looked toward the open door of his bedroom. He shook his head, trying to clear his sleepy mind as it awoke from the dream. Tommy heard a scraping sound. He squeezed the button that lighted his wristwatch. Two-thirty in the morning. Bump! Those noises had to be coming from somewhere downstairs.

Cautiously Tommy crept out of bed and peeked into the hallway. Total darkness. The rest of the family appeared to be sleeping soundly. Who—or what—was making those noises downstairs?

Tommy located his baseball bat and moved carefully across the upstairs landing to the door of his parents' room. Clunk. Scrape. The noises below continued. Tommy tiptoed across the darkened room to the edge of their bed. "Dad." His whisper sounded loud in the stillness. What if "they" could hear him downstairs?

A sudden snore made him jump. "Dad." Tommy tapped the blankets where the snore came from. "Dad, wake up." He tried a little louder. "Dad!" He thumped the blankets again.

Suddenly the figure in the bed reached out and grabbed Tommy! "Dad! It's me!"

"Tommy?" Mr. Rawson sat up and reached for the lamp.

"Don't, Dad." Tommy urged. "There's someone downstairs. Listen!" Sure enough, they all heard another bump from somewhere below.

"What is it, Bob?" Tommy's mother sat up and pushed the hair out of her face.

"I'm not sure." Mr. Rawson stood up. "You and Tommy stay right here. I'll go see what's going on."

"But, Bob. . ." Mrs. Rawson reached for the phone. "If you're not back in two minutes, I'm calling the police."

"You can call them if I'm not back in one minute." Mr. Rawson whispered.

"Here, Dad." Tommy held up the bat, "Take this with you."

With a firm grip on the bat, Dad tiptoed out the door. Tommy sat on the edge of the bed and held his breath. Scrape. Thud, thud, thud, thud. That noise was Tommy's heart beating wildly. Mom picked up the phone and pushed the "9."

Suddenly they could hear Dad's voice. What was he saying? A louder crash than the others made Tommy jump. Mom pushed the "1" on the phone.

"It's okay, Carolyn." Dad came up the stairs two at a time. Mom dropped the phone and slumped over. "It's okay." Dad repeated as he walked around the bed and gave her a hug. "But I need your help downstairs. It's Grandma."

"Oh!" Mom jumped up. "Is she all right? She didn't fall or anything, did she?" She was already pulling on her robe and stuffing her feet into slippers.

"She's fine physically, Carolyn." Dad handed the bat back to Tommy. "You'd better head back to bed, Son. Morning's going to come too soon."

"But, Dad, what's wrong with Grandma?" Tommy's insides filled with a new fear.

"Son, she's really okay. She just decided it was time to scrub the kitchen floor. You know, it's the Alzheimer's that causes her to get confused. She moved all the chairs and bar stools and got out a bucket and the mop. We've got a bit of a mess to clean up and we need to make sure Grandma gets back to bed." Dad ran a hand through Tommy's already messed up hair. "Hey, get some rest. You've earned it!"

Tommy hugged his dad and stumbled back to his room. He sure was sleepy. Being scared out of your wits could really wear a fellow out.

Ten-thirty in the morning. That's what the clock said. Tommy yawned and squinted at the clock on the classroom wall once more. Yep. Only 10:30! He rubbed his tired eyes and drew a squiggle down the side of his paper.

After Dad sent him back to bed, Tommy had tossed and turned, trying to get back to sleep. Although Dad and Mom had tried to be quiet, Grandma argued loudly about going back to bed.

Life just isn't fair. Tommy decided. *Lisa slept through the whole thing! Even Grandma's protests!* Tommy could still hear Grandma's voice in his mind. "What's the world coming to! Why, plumb strangers come walking into my house, telling me what to do. I tell you this, if my Georgie were here he'd stop you, he would! A woman just can't abide not being able to take care of her own home!"

"Tommy, is something bothering you?" Mrs. Burton's light touch on his shoulder startled

Story (continued)

Tommy so much he dropped his pencil and it bounced off his desk onto the floor.

"Uh, no." Tommy leaned over and grabbed the pencil. "Well, um, yes. I guess so." He felt his face heat up in embarrassment. "My grandma. She, well, you know she lives with us and all." Tommy darted a quick glance around to see if his classmates were staring at him. He breathed easier when he saw that those near him were either at centers across the room or concentrating on the work they were doing.

"Did something happen to her?" Mrs. Burton pulled Rachel's empty desk chair a little closer and sat facing Tommy. "Is she getting worse?"

"Not really. I mean, she can walk around and all that." Tommy drew some stars on his paper. "It's her mind that's worse. She doesn't even recognize my dad any more, and he's her only son. She wanders away and gets lost or does stuff that's dangerous. Someone has to stay with her all the time. My mom and dad never have time to go places with Lisa and me or do stuff all together as a family."

Tommy continued when he saw the understanding look on his teacher's face. "It's hardest for my mom. Even though Grandma doesn't remember who Mom is, she's always calmer when Mom's there, so Mom hardly ever leaves to go to the store—or any place—anymore."

Mrs. Burton's response surprised Tommy. He expected her to say how sorry she was for his family, especially his mom. Instead, she smiled at him and said, "Why Tommy, what a wonderful modern day parable that is!"

"Huh?" Tommy looked blank.

"I know it's difficult for you all right now." Mrs. Burton rose and straightened Rachel's chair at her desk. "We'll continue to pray for your mother and the rest of your family. But, Tommy, what your mother is doing for your grandma is an example of what Jesus did for all of us." Mrs. Burton glanced at the clock on the wall. "It reminds me of a story I heard once. Maybe I'll share it with everyone after lunch today."

The long day finally ended and Tommy was happy to crawl into his bed that night. "Sweet dreams, Son." Mrs. Rawson sat on the edge of his bed and rubbed his back the way he liked. "Maybe you'll be able to catch up on a little sleep tonight."

"Mom?" Tommy rolled over so he could see his mother. "Did you know you're a, um, a 'modern day parable'?"

"A what?" Mom straightened the covers around Tommy.

"Mrs. Burton said that the way you're giving up so much to take care of Grandma is a little like how Jesus gave up stuff for us." Tommy yawned. "You know, how you spend all your time making sure Grandma's okay even though she doesn't even know you anymore. You don't get to do anything BUT take care of Grandma anymore. See, it's kind of like Jesus giving up His life in heaven for us when lots of us don't even know Him or care about Him. 'Cept He gave up a lot more for us. Even His life."

Another yawn split Tommy's face. "Mrs. Burton told us about a little boy a long time ago whose brother was hurt and needed blood to get better. The little brother had the right kind of blood and said he'd give blood for his brother. I guess nobody had much time to explain things to the little brother, 'cause after it was all over he was lying there real still. After the big brother started to get better, someone asked the little brother how he felt. Real quietly he asked when he was going to die. See, he thought giving the blood to help his big brother live would kill him, but he was willing to give it anyway!"

"That's a beautiful story." In the lamplight Mrs. Rawson's eyes sparkled with unshed tears. "Dad and I love Grandma, Tommy, even though the Alzheimer's has changed her. We'll continue to do our best to take care of her. We love you, too, Son. But Mrs. Burton's right. As much as we love our family and would do anything we could for each of you, God loves all of us even more."

Mom leaned over and gave her sleepy boy a hug and goodnight kiss. "Remember, Tommy, your heavenly Father loves you enough that He was willing to die for you. But now He's living for you. Isn't that a wonderful thought?" She stood and turned out the lamp. "Sweet dreams, Son."

"'Night, Mom." Tommy snuggled into his covers. His last thought before his tired mind slipped into restful sleep was, *I'm glad God loves me that much.*

2 Discussion Time

Check understanding of the story and development of personal values.

- What woke Tommy up in the middle of the night?
- What was Mrs. Rawson going to do if Dad didn't come back upstairs very soon?
- Whom did Mr. Rawson find downstairs and what was causing all the noise?
- What's a "modern day parable"?
- How was Mrs. Rawson acting out a modern day parable according to Mrs. Burton?
- What story did Mrs. Burton tell the class?
- How do you know God loves you?

A Preview

Name ____________________

Write each word as your teacher says it.

1. carpet
2. farther
3. spark
4. cart
5. harsh
6. hardly
7. harm
8. starve
9. barber
10. carnival
11. farmer
12. garden
13. barnyard
14. scarf
15. yarn
16. marbles
17. cardboard
18. garbage

Words with /är/

Lesson 17

Scripture

John 3:16

105

3 Preview

Test for knowledge of the correct spellings of these words.

Customize Your List
On a separate sheet of paper, additional words of your choice may be tested.

I will say each word once, use the word in a sentence, then say the word again. Write the words on the lines in your Worktext.

Correct Immediately!
Let's correct our Preview. I will spell each word out loud. If you spelled a word incorrectly, rewrite it correctly.

Progress Chart
Students may record scores. (Reproducible master provided in Appendix B.)

1. **carpet** — Tommy heard someone scuffing across the **carpet** downstairs.
2. **farther** — Tommy leaned a little **farther** over the banister to listen.
3. **spark** — A **spark** of fear started his heart pounding furiously.
4. **cart** — Grandma often got the **cart** before the horse, so to speak.
5. **harsh** — Sometimes she says **harsh** things she doesn't really mean.
6. **hardly** — Tommy's mom **hardly** ever goes out because of Grandma.
7. **harm** — Their family is careful not to allow any **harm** to come to Grandma.
8. **starve** — They serve Grandma nutritious meals so she won't **starve.**
9. **barber** — Mom always stays with Grandma while dad goes to the **barber.**
10. **carnival** — Grandma would not enjoy going to a **carnival.**
11. **farmer** — Grandpa, Grandma's husband, was a **farmer** when he was alive.
12. **garden** — He also had a huge **garden** just for their family.
13. **barnyard** — Tommy would have liked visiting their **barnyard.**
14. **scarf** — Grandma's favorite **scarf** is bright orange.
15. **yarn** — Sometimes Grandma likes to wind **yarn** into a big ball.
16. **marbles** — Holding a few smooth, glass **marbles** often makes her feel better.
17. **cardboard** — Tommy likes to look at her **cardboard** box of keepsakes.
18. **garbage** — One of Tommy's chores is to take out the **garbage.**

4 Word Shapes

Help students form a correct image of whole words.

Say: Look at each word and think about its shape. Now, write the word in the correct Word Shape Boxes. You may check off each word as you use it.

(In most words, the letters **ar** spell the sound of **/är/**, whether it is at the beginning, middle, or end of a word. There are very few exceptions.)

Say: In the Word Shape Boxes, fill in the boxes containing the letters that spell the sound of **/är/** in each word.

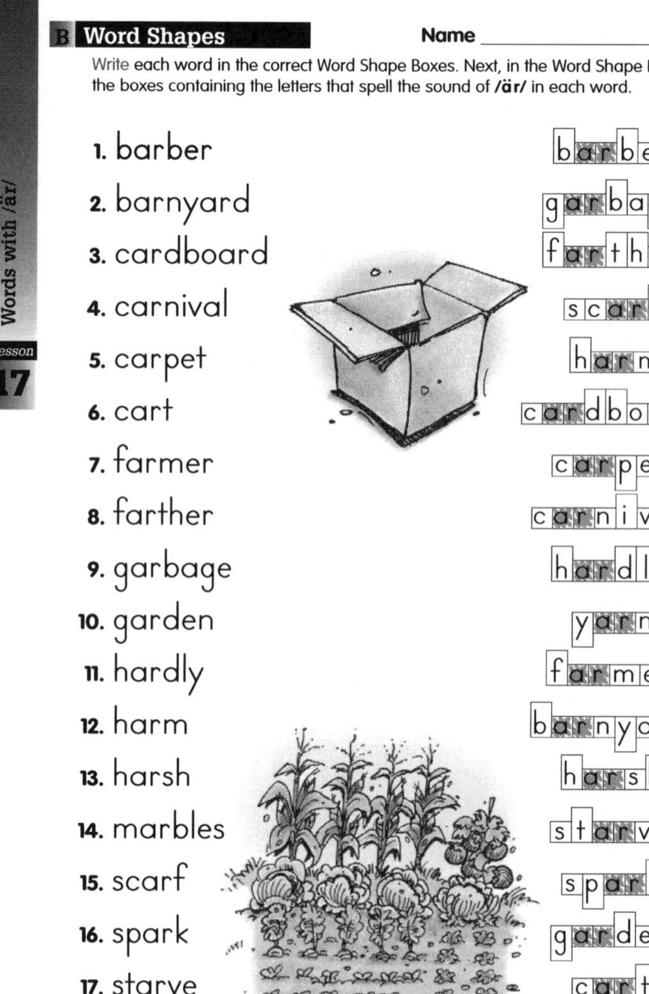

Take a minute to memorize...

John 3:16

Words with /är/ — Lesson 17

B Word Shapes Name ____________

Write each word in the correct Word Shape Boxes. Next, in the Word Shape Boxes, shade in the boxes containing the letters that spell the sound of **/är/** in each word.

1. barber	barber
2. barnyard	garbage
3. cardboard	farther
4. carnival	scarf
5. carpet	harm
6. cart	cardboard
7. farmer	carpet
8. farther	carnival
9. garbage	hardly
10. garden	yarn
11. hardly	farmer
12. harm	barnyard
13. harsh	harsh
14. marbles	starve
15. scarf	spark
16. spark	garden
17. starve	cart
18. yarn	marbles

106

Answers may vary for duplicate word shapes.

Be Prepared For Fun

Check these supply lists for **Fun Ways to Spell** - presented **Day 2**.
Purchase and/or gather these items ahead of time!

General
- Pencil
- 3 X 5 Cards cut in half (18 per child)
- Spelling List

Auditory
- Pencil
- Notebook Paper
- Spelling List

Visual
- Black Construction Paper (1 sheet per child)
- Lemon Juice
- Cotton Swabs
- Spelling List

Tactile
- Pipe Cleaners (cut in an assortment of lengths)
- Spelling List

C Hide and Seek

Name ______________________

Play Hide and Seek with your words. Create a bar graph by filling in a box (left to right) for each word you spell correctly.

D Other Word Forms

Using the words below, follow the instructions given by your teacher.

barbered	carting	gardens	harshly	sparks
barbering	carts	hard	harshness	starved
barbers	farm	harmed	marble	starving
barbershop	farming	harmful	marbled	starves
carpeted	farmed	harmless	marbling	yarns
carpeting	gardened	harming	scarves	
carpets	gardener	harsher	sparked	
carted	gardening	harshest	sparking	

E Fun Ways to Spell

Initial the box of each activity you finish.

1.

Spell your words, then play "Concentration."

3.

Spell your words, then write a rhyme.

2.

Spell your words with lemon juice.

4.

Spell your words with pipe cleaners.

Words with /är/

Lesson 17

107

1 Hide and Seek

Reinforce spelling by using multiple styles of learning.

On a white board, Teacher writes each word — one at a time. **Have students:**

- **Look** at the word.
- **Say** the word out loud.
- **Spell** the word out loud.
- **Hide** (teacher erases word.)
- **Write** the word on paper.
- **Seek** (teacher rewrites word.)
- **Check** spelling. If incorrect, rewrite word correctly.

2 Other Word Forms

This activity is optional. Have students find and circle the Other Word Forms that are antonyms of the following:

helpful
nourished
gently
tender

3 Fun Ways to Spell

Four activities are provided. Use one, two, three, or all of the activities. Have students initial the box for each activity they complete.

Options:

- assign activities to students according to their learning styles
- set up the activities in learning centers for students to do throughout the day
- divide students into four groups and assign one activity per group
- do one activity per day

General

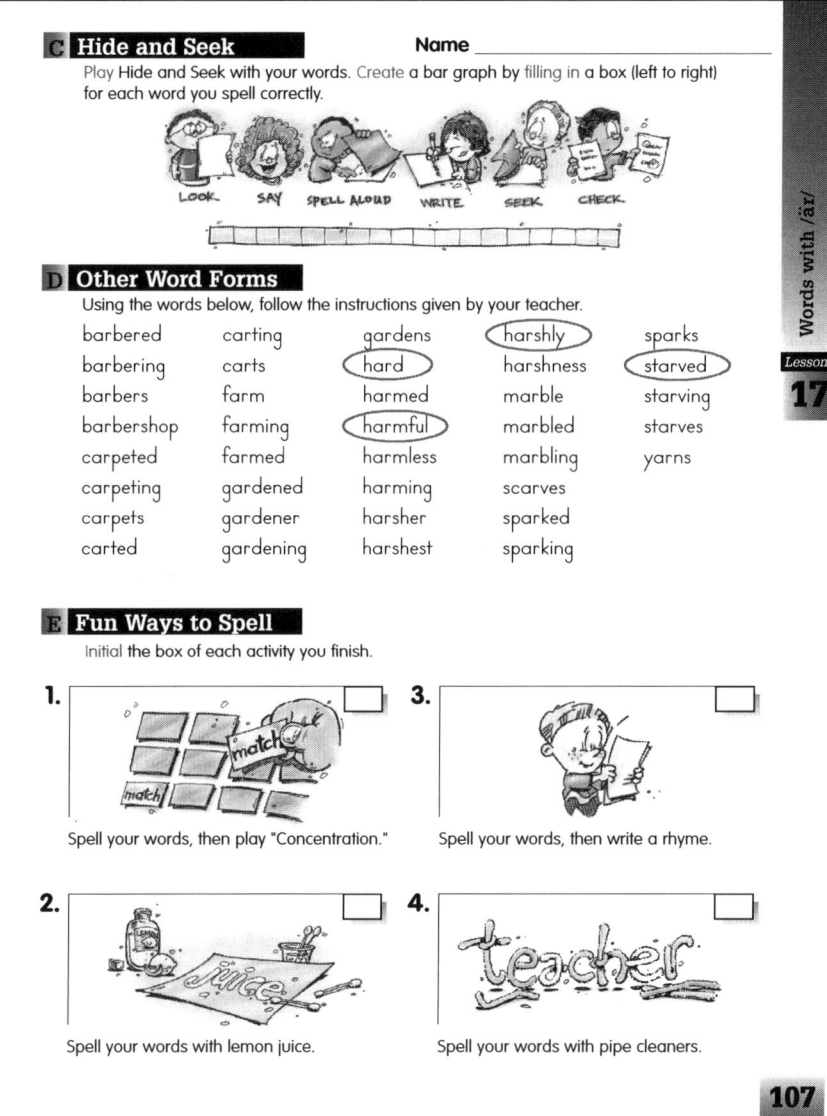

Spell your words; then play Concentration…
Write each spelling word on a card. Mix your cards and a classmate's cards together. Arrange them face down in six rows of six. Pick up two cards. If the cards match, play again. If the cards do not match, turn them back over. It is your classmate's turn. Continue taking turns until all the cards are matched. The player with the most cards wins!

Auditory

To spell your words and write a rhyme…
- Write a rhyming verse for each word on your list.
- Example:
  My little brother could dive.
  When he was barely five.
- Underline your spelling words.

Visual

To spell your words with lemon juice…
- Dip a cotton swab in lemon juice.
- With the swab, write each of your spelling words on black construction paper.
- Check your spelling before your writing disappears!

Tactile

To spell your words with pipe cleaners…
- Choose a word from your spelling list.
- Shape the pipe cleaners to spell the word.
- Check your spelling.
- Do this for each word on your list.

Working with Words

Familiarize students with word meaning and usage.

Crossword Puzzle

Using the synonyms and clues, write the spelling words in the crossword puzzle.

Take a minute to memorize...

John 3:16

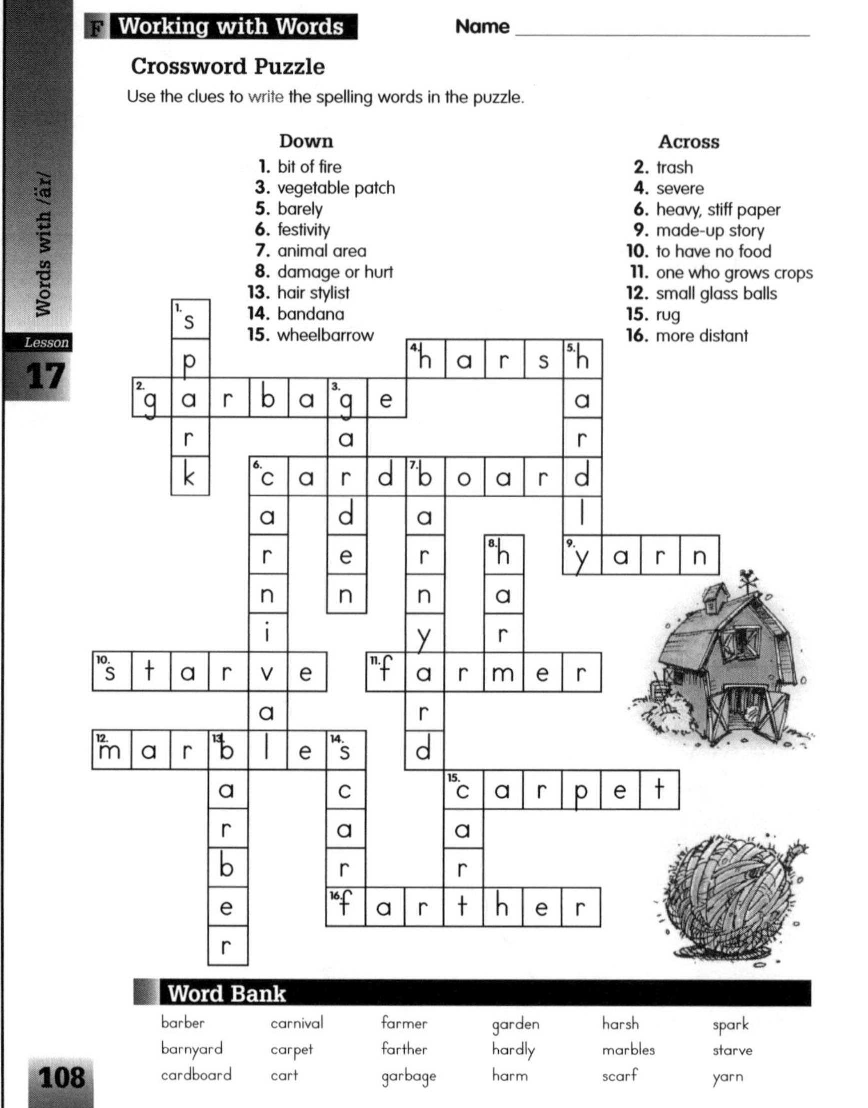

Words with /är/

Lesson 17

F **Working with Words** Name ______________________

Crossword Puzzle

Use the clues to write the spelling words in the puzzle.

Down
1. bit of fire
3. vegetable patch
5. barely
6. festivity
7. animal area
8. damage or hurt
13. hair stylist
14. bandana
15. wheelbarrow

Across
2. trash
4. severe
6. heavy, stiff paper
9. made-up story
10. to have no food
11. one who grows crops
12. small glass balls
15. rug
16. more distant

Word Bank

barber	carnival	farmer	garden	harsh	spark
barnyard	carpet	farther	hardly	marbles	starve
cardboard	cart	garbage	harm	scarf	yarn

108

G Dictation

Name ____________________

Write each sentence as your teacher dictates. Use correct punctuation.

1. He crossed the carpet with hardly a sound.

2. She used bright yarn to make the scarf.

3. Grandmother planted a garden by the barnyard.

H Proofreading

If a word is misspelled, fill in the oval by that word. If all the words are spelled correctly, fill in the oval by **no mistake**.

1. ● starv ○ barber ○ almost ○ no mistake
2. ○ offer ○ fog ○ barnyard ● no mistake
3. ○ forest ○ cord ● cardbord ○ no mistake
4. ○ spark ● carnnivel ○ all right ○ no mistake
5. ○ yarn ○ already ● carpit ○ no mistake
6. ○ harsh ○ cart ● suace ○ no mistake
7. ○ quarrel ○ toward ○ farmer ● no mistake
8. ○ haul ○ hawk ● scarff ○ no mistake
9. ○ farther ● garbige ○ awful ○ no mistake
10. ● gardin ○ applause ○ author ○ no mistake
11. ● hardley ○ fault ○ pause ○ no mistake
12. ○ harm ○ false ● marlbes ○ no mistake

Words with /är/

Lesson 17

109

1 Dictation

Reinforce correct spelling by using current and previous words in context.

Listen as I read each sentence and then write it in your Worktext. Remember to use correct capitalization and punctuation. (Slowly read each sentence twice. Sentences are found in the Student Worktext to the left.)

2 Proofreading

Familiarize students with standardized test format and reinforce recognition of misspelled words.

Look at each set of words. If a word is misspelled, fill in the oval by that word. If all the words are spelled correctly, fill in the oval by **no mistake**.

3 Hide and Seek

Reinforce correct spelling of current spelling words. Repeat this activity from Day 2. (A reproducible master is provided in Appendix A as shown on the inset page to the right.)

4 Other Word Forms

Have your students complete this activity to strengthen spelling ability and expand vocabulary.

1 Posttest

Visit the **A Reason For** website to download free, printable Posttest pages.

I will say the word once, use it in a sentence, then say it again. Write your words on a separate sheet of paper.

Progress Chart

Students may record scores. (Appendix B)

Personal Dictionary

Students may add any words they have misspelled to their personal dictionaries. (Appendix B)

Hide and Seek

Play Hide and Seek with your words. Create a bar graph by filling in a box (left to right) for each word you spell correctly.

Other Word Forms

Prefixes and Suffixes

Add each suffix to the word in each row to make a new word. Remember, when words have the consonant-vowel-consonant-**e** pattern, drop the **e** when adding an ending that begins with a vowel.

	+ ed	+ ing	+ s
1. spark	sparked	sparking	sparks
2. garden	gardened	gardening	gardens
3. carpet	carpeted	carpeting	carpets
4. starve	starved	starving	starves
5. harm	harmed	harming	harms
6. barber	barbered	barbering	barbers
7. cart	carted	carting	carts
8. farm	farmed	farming	farms
9. marble	marbled	marbling	marbles

Add the prefixes and suffixes to make new words. Write the words on the lines.

1. barber + shop = barbershop
2. harm + ful = harmful
3. yarn + s = yarns
4. harsh + ness = harshness
5. farm + er = farmer
6. harsh + er = harsher
7. un + harm + ed = unharmed
8. garden + er = gardener
9. harsh + ly = harshly
10. harm + less = harmless
11. scarf − f + ves = scarves
12. hard + est = hardest
13. un + carpet + ed = uncarpeted
14. harsh + est = harshest

Other Word Forms | Lesson 17

339

1.	carpet	Tommy thought a burglar was scuffing across the **carpet.**
2.	farther	He leaned a little **farther** over the banister to see who it was.
3.	spark	A **spark** of fear made Tommy's knees began to shake.
4.	hardly	His dad **hardly** knew what to think when Tommy woke him.
5.	barber	Dad gave Grandma a kiss before he went to the **barber.**
6.	farmer	Grandpa was a good **farmer** many, many years ago.
7.	barnyard	Grandma used to love tending the animals in their **barnyard.**
8.	garden	She also enjoyed working in their big vegetable **garden.**
9.	cardboard	In her **cardboard** box of keepsakes, there are photos of Grandpa.
10.	carnival	A **carnival** would make Grandma very nervous.
11.	garbage	Tommy takes out the **garbage** every day after school.
12.	cart	He uses a special **cart** to wheel the big trash cans to the curb.
13.	harm	His family takes precautions to keep Grandma from **harm.**
14.	starve	Grandma would **starve** if Tommy's mom did not help her eat.
15.	harsh	When Grandma gets upset, she sometimes says **harsh** things.
16.	marbles	Tommy gave her some smooth **marbles** to hold to calm her.
17.	scarf	Grandma likes to wear her orange **scarf** every day.
18.	yarn	She often sits and winds **yarn** into a ball for hours at a time.

Words with /är/

Lesson 17

I Game

Name ______________________

Play a game of tic-tac-toe by marking the grid each time you or your team spells a word correctly from this week's word list.

Remember: God loves you so much He sent Jesus to save you.

J Journaling

In your journal, rewrite the story Mrs. Burton told her class in your own words. Who needed help, and why? Who helped, and how? Tell how this story is an example of God's great love.

110

How to Play:

- Divide students into two teams (the X's and the O's).
- Have a student from team X choose a number from 1 to 9.
- Say the word that matches that number from the Game Word List (Game 1).
- Have the student write the word on the board.
- If correct, have each member of both teams put an X on that number.
- Alternate between teams X and O.
- The first team to score three marks in a row (up, down, across, or diagonally) is the winner.
- Word lists and tic-tac-toe grids are provided for two additional games.

Small Group Option: Students may play this game without teacher direction in groups of two.

2 Game

Reinforce spelling skills and provide motivation and interest.

Materials

- game page (from Student Worktext)
- pencils (1 per child)
- game word list

Game 1 Word List

1. **cart**
2. **barber**
3. **farmer**
4. **harsh**
5. **cardboard**
6. **garbage**
7. **harm**
8. **carpet**
9. **scarf**

Game 2 Word List

1. **barnyard**
2. **carnival**
3. **farther**
4. **garden**
5. **hardly**
6. **marbles**
7. **spark**
8. **yarn**
9. **starve**

Game 3 Word List

1. **cardboard**
2. **carnival**
3. **barber**
4. **farther**
5. **carpet**
6. **marbles**
7. **scarf**
8. **starve**
9. **garbage**

3 Journaling

Provide a meaningful reason for correct spelling through personal writing.

Review the story using discussion leads provided on the following page. Encourage students to apply the Scriptural value in their journaling.

Journaling (continued)

- Why did Tommy think someone was downstairs? (The bumps and scraping sounds woke him up.)
- What did Dad find downstairs? (Grandma was up and moving stuff around in order to scrub the kitchen floor.)
- What is Alzheimer's disease? (A sickness that causes people to forget people and things they know — even their own families. The illness causes them to use poor judgment sometimes, and do things they normally wouldn't do.)
- In what way was Tommy's mom an example of God? (Because of love, she was giving up so much of her life to take care of her mother-in-law, even though her mother-in-law didn't even know her anymore. God gave so much, including His life, for people, even though some don't care to know Him at all.)
- What story did Mrs. Burton tell that gave another example of God's great love? (A story about a little brother who was willing to give his life to save his older brother.)

"A Man, a Plan, a Canal—Panama!" is a palindrome.

Word Wow!

1 **Literature Connection**
Topic: Time Management
Theme Text: Mark 12:29, 30

Detectives' Discoveries

Beth discovers there are more important things in life than reading.

Beth looked down at the stack of corrected papers Mrs. Burton put on her desk. She picked up the one on top. One, two, three, four. She counted the red check marks in the test-words section. *Uhhh! Enough! I spelled 'enough' with a ph. There are too many ways to spell the /f/ sound. You can spell it with a ph. You can spell it with a gh—and an f. I can never remember which letters make the /f/ sound in which words!* Beth hadn't done much better on the rest of the page either. *Ugh! I don't like reviews! I need to study! Maybe Mom will help me. She always thinks of funny ways to remember how to spell words.*

Beth looked at the rest of the graded papers on her desk, folded them in half, and tucked them into the zippered pocket of her backpack. She thought about the book she knew was in the big pocket—*Detective Zack and the Red Hat Mystery.*

I wonder who the man in the red hat is? He's been following Zack and the tour group. I think I have time to start the next chapter and at least find out who the man is. I already finished math and it isn't time for science yet. Beth opened the paperback to the second chapter, "Clues From an Old Letter." She was soon so absorbed in figuring out the clues with the young detective that she didn't hear Mrs. Burton tell everyone it was time to work on their science reports. An hour later the dismissal bell jarred her back to reality.

"Are you done with your report?" Katelynn asked as she stopped at Beth's desk.

"No. I only have one page written." Beth quickly closed the mystery and slipped it into her backpack.

Katelynn frowned, "Then why aren't you working on it?"

"I'll work on it at home." Beth rummaged through the stacks of papers and books in her desk.

After the dismissal prayer, Beth met her younger brother, Luke, in the hallway and walked with him toward the parking lot. "Let's play dominoes when we get home, Bethy. Maybe Mom will pop some popcorn and we can eat while we play. I'm starved." Luke chattered as they walked, "Do you want apples with our popcorn or not? It's kinda cold. Mom and Dad might play dominoes with us. Should we play train or double sixes? Which do you want to play, Beth? Beth!"

"Uh huh." Beth dug through her backpack until she found *Detective Zack.* She climbed into the car and opened the book to where she'd left off.

Luke clambered up into the seat beside his sister. "Which do you want to play, Beth?" he asked again.

Beth didn't look up from her book, "I don't care."

"Hi, Mom." Luke continued to chatter, "Will you play dominoes with us tonight? I bet Eagle will be happy to see us. Poor dog. He doesn't have anyone to play with while we're at school. Mom, can I give Eagle a treat when we get home?"

Beth tuned out the conversation and concentrated on Zack and Mitchell Roberts, the man in the red hat. *I've just got to find out if Mr. Roberts is the thief who tried to steal stuff from Zack's car,* she thought before she turned the page.

Later that evening Beth's mom came in and sat on the edge of her daughter's bed. "Are you almost finished with your book, Beth?"

"I'm on chapter nine. The thief who stole Zack's clothes bag got away. I bet the man in the red hat is the thief. Can I read for a while?" Beth pleaded.

"You've read since you got home from school, Bethy. You didn't play dominoes with us or take Eagle for a walk. That must really be a good book." Mom patted Beth's arm.

"It is. Can I at least finish the chapter before I turn out the light?" Beth closed the book but held her place with her finger.

Mom leaned over and kissed Beth on the forehead. "Don't read too long. You need to get some sleep. You have school tomorrow."

School. Oops! I forgot to ask Mom to help me study my spelling words, Beth thought. *And I didn't work on my science report, but I have to find out what happens to Zack and his friends, Steph and Achmed.* She found her spelling list and put it right under her lamp so she wouldn't forget in the morning. *I'll study my words before breakfast. And I'll work really hard at school on my report,* she reasoned with herself. Beth snuggled down under the covers and opened her book.

The next morning Beth turned on the lamp beside her bed and reached for her Bible. She moved *Detective Zack and the Red Hat Mystery* aside, before she found the Bible under her spelling list. She glanced at the cover of the mystery. Steph and Achmed were laughing at Zack, who had his hands over his ears because a donkey was braying loudly in his face. Beth picked up the book and thumbed through the pages until she came to chapter ten. *I think I'll read my book this morning instead of my Bible. On his tour through the Middle East, Zack is looking for clues about why the Bible stories are true. Maybe he'll figure out who took his clothes bag out of the car, too.*

Mom's voice brought Beth back to reality. "Time for breakfast. Come on, Beth."

She looked at the clock and gasped. *How did I read*

Story Continued

for so long? She jumped out of bed and pulled her hair back into a ponytail. "Coming," she yelled down the stairs. Beth put on an old shirt and a pair of pants she didn't like. There wasn't time to search for her favorite clothes in the stack of clean laundry on the dresser. She ran down the stairs and slid into her place at the table. Everyone else was already eating.

Dad smiled at his daughter. "Are you in a little bit of a hurry this morning, Bethy?"

"I didn't know it was so late."

"Your shirt's wrong side out, Bethy," Luke laughed. "Your hair's a mess too!"

Beth slowly wiped her mouth with her napkin. She didn't look up as she pushed herself away from the table.

By the time she was really ready for school, there wasn't time to eat breakfast or study the spelling words. She was hungry, so she grabbed a piece of cold toast on the way out the door.

Beth took seconds of everything at dinner that evening—even the green beans and salad. After dessert she helped clear the table, then quietly retrieved her backpack from the laundry room where she'd dropped it. *I'll finish the book, then work on my science report and study my spelling words.* She tucked a quilt around her and snuggled down on one end of the flowered couch with *Detective Zack and the Red Hat Mystery*.

I'm finally going to find out how Detective Zack traps the thief! Beth smiled to herself and flipped to the next-to-last chapter.

"Beth," Mom stood in the doorway and called her daughter, "it's time for worship. Come on into the family room."

"Can't we skip worship tonight?" Beth held up the book, "I'm almost finished."

Mom came into the living room and sat down beside Beth on the couch. "Beth, there's a text in the Scriptures that says, 'The Lord our God is the one and only God. And you must love Him with all your heart and soul and mind and strength.' What do you think that means?"

Beth looked down and studied Zack's face on the cover of her book. She shrugged her shoulders.

"Beth, the verse says to love God with all your heart, soul, mind, and strength. Anytime something besides God becomes the most important thing in our lives, we have a problem."

"But Detective Zack books are good. This one teaches me why the Bible stories are true and stuff."

"I didn't say there was a problem with the book—just a problem with how important it is to you. Balance is good, Bethy. By the looks of the paper you brought home yesterday, you need to study your spelling words harder. I think you have a science report due soon, too." Mom continued her list of Beth's oversights, "You ignored me and Luke yesterday and didn't join us for dominoes last night. You went to sleep late and looked awful when you came down for breakfast this morning. You didn't brush your teeth or make your bed today. Your room is trashed! And you're still reading! I'd say that book is a pretty important thing to you right now." Mom stood up. "Is that what you want?"

Beth and her mom joined the rest of the family. Beth didn't say much. After worship she straightened her room, got ready for bed and then finished the last chapter of the book. Zack figured out that the man in the red hat was also trying to catch the thief. He discovered that the best evidence the Bible is true is in the lives of people. Zack told his father in the plane on the way home, "If the Bible is true, if God is real, then we should be different too. Other people should be able to see God's footprints on us."

Whew! I think Zack's footprints—instead of God's—are all over me. Beth smiled to herself. She picked up the next book in the Detective Zack series—*Detective Zack and the Mystery at Thunder Mountain*. She'd borrowed it from Rachel the day before. She looked at her watch. *I'm going to read this book differently because reading a book—even a good book—is not the most important thing.* Beth smiled and reached for her Bible.

2 Discussion Time

Check understanding of the story and development of personal values.

- What is your favorite thing to do?
- What is Beth's favorite thing to do?
- How did Beth's mom know how important reading had become to Beth?
- Why would a mother not want her child to read?
- Raise your hand if you think keeping busy doing good things can become more important to you than God.
- How could Beth read another Detective Zack book differently?
- What are some things you should include in your life to keep it in balance?

A Test-Words Name ______

Write each spelling word on the line as your teacher says it.

1. enough
2. rough
3. toward
4. hardly
5. already
6. bounce
7. exciting
8. fault
9. glance
10. science
11. author
12. scene
13. recess
14. else

Review Lesson 18

B Test-Sentences

Write the sentences on the lines below, correcting each misspelled word, as well as all capitalization and punctuation errors. There are two misspelled words in each sentence.

the polees have a photagraf of the escaped prisoner,

1. The police have a photograph of the escaped prisoner.

an enormous hauk stole a large trowt from the bear:

2. An enormous hawk stole a large trout from the bear.

the italian shef is famus for his delicious pastas?

3. The Italian chef is famous for his delicious pastas.

one scowt stood watch in the touwer of the old fort

4. One scout stood watch in the tower of the old fort.

111

4 Test-Sentences

Reinforce recognizing misspelled words.

Read each sentence carefully. Write the sentences on the lines in your Worktext. There are two misspelled words in each sentence. Correct each misspelled word, as well as all capitalization and punctuation errors.

Take a minute to memorize...

Mark 12:29, 30

3 Test-Words

Test for knowledge of the correct spellings of these words.

I will say each word once, use the word in a sentence, then say the word again. Write the words on the lines in your Worktext.

1. **enough** Beth misspelled the word "**enough**" on her spelling test.
2. **rough** She had a **rough** time remembering how to spell many of the words.
3. **toward** Beth and Luke walked **toward** their mom who was parked nearby.
4. **hardly** Beth **hardly** paid any attention to what her brother was asking her.
5. **already** She was **already** engrossed in her book again.
6. **bounce** She did not like it when Luke began to **bounce** on the seat.
7. **exciting** He thought it would be **exciting** for their family to play dominoes.
8. **fault** It was Beth's own **fault** that she was not prepared for her test.
9. **glance** She did not take the time to even **glance** over her spelling words.
10. **science** She forgot to work on her **science** project, too.
11. **author** The writer of this series was her favorite **author**.
12. **scene** The **scene** illustrated on the front of the book made Beth smile.
13. **recess** She even ignored her friends at **recess** so she could read her book.
14. **else** Beth had put her reading for pleasure above all **else**.

Test-Dictation

Reinforce correct spelling by using current and previous words in context.

Listen as I read each sentence, then write it in your Worktext. Remember to use correct capitalization and punctuation. (Slowly read each sentence twice. Sentences are found in the Student Worktext at right. The words **outdoors**, **cellar**, **gown**, and **county** are found in this unit.)

Test-Proofreading

Familiarize students with standardized test format and reinforce recognizing misspelled words.

Look at each set of words. If a word is misspelled, fill in the oval by that word. If all the words are spelled correctly, fill in the oval by **no mistake**.

Review Lesson 18

C Test-Dictation

Name ____________________

Write each sentence as your teacher dictates. Use correct punctuation.

1. We went outdoors and caught three tiny bugs.
2. Mom brought soap and butter from the cellar.
3. Grandmother wore her long gown to bed last night.
4. The county has plans to paint yellow lines on this road.

D Test-Proofreading

If a word is misspelled, fill in the oval by that word. If all the words are spelled correctly, fill in the oval by **no mistake**.

1. ○ rough ○ enough ● kwarrel ○ no mistake

2. ○ powder ○ glance ○ science ● no mistake

3. ● orfin ○ toward ○ hardly ○ no mistake

4. ○ already ● citisen ○ bounce ○ no mistake

5. ○ exciting ○ fault ○ garbage ● no mistake

6. ○ else ○ recess ● nown ○ no mistake

7. ○ author ○ starve ○ scene ● no mistake

8. ○ harm ● carnivle ○ loaf ○ no mistake

9. ○ however ○ sauce ○ swift ● no mistake

10. ○ son ○ frown ○ across ● no mistake

11. ○ chance ● fense ○ harsh ○ no mistake

12. ● pres ○ carpet ○ drift ○ no mistake

112

E Test-Table

Name ____________________

If a word is misspelled, shade in that box.

kraft	forrest	marbels	offer			
pound	yarn	farther	cart			
alright	houshold	growl	false	stuff	tuff	stowt

Review Lesson 18

F Writing Assessment

Write a letter to a friend. Pretend there is a new student in your class who does things all the time that show how important God is in his/her life. Tell your friend about this student.

____

____

____

____

____

____

____

____

Scripture

Mark 12:29, 30

113

The words "facetious" and "abstemious" (along with 190 others in the English language) contain all the vowels in ABC order.

Test-Table

Test mastery of words in this unit.

If a word is misspelled, fill in the space on the grid.

Writing Assessment

Assess student's spelling, grammar, and composition skills through personal writing.

- What was Beth doing at school instead of her science report? (Reading her book.)
- While Luke was chattering about the day what was Beth doing? (Reading her book.)
- What did Beth do while Luke and Mom played dominoes and took Eagle for a walk? (Read her book.)
- What did Beth want to do instead of going to sleep? (Read her book.)
- What did Beth decide to read for her quiet time the next morning? (Her book.)
- What did Beth want to skip so she could finish her book? (Family worship.)
- What was the most important thing to Beth? (Reading her book.)
- What could Beth do to make God a more important part of her life again? (Pray, read the Scriptures, participate in family worship.)

Test-Sentences

Reinforce recognizing misspelled words.

Read each sentence carefully. Write the sentences on the lines in your Worktext, correcting each misspelled word, as well as all capitalization and punctuation errors.

Review Lesson 18

G Test-Sentences Name ____________________

Write the sentences on the lines below, correcting each misspelled word, as well as all capitalization and punctuation errors. There are two misspelled words in each sentence.

The old farmmer called the chickens into the baryard;

1. The old **farmer** called the chickens into the **barnyard.**

a dense fogg made it allmost impossible to see the road

2. **A** dense **fog** made it **almost** impossible to see the road**.**

the comedian knew just when to pauze for aplauze?

3. **The** comedian knew just when to **pause** for **applause.**

mom wears a skarf when she works in the gardin

4. **Mom** wears a **scarf** when she works in the **garden.**

H Test-Words

Write each spelling word on the line as your teacher says it.

1. harm	8. harsh
2. loaf	9. carpet
3. sauce	10. drift
4. swift	11. awful
5. frown	12. decide
6. across	13. bluff
7. chance	14. owl

114

2 Test-Words

Test for knowledge of the correct spellings of these words.

I will say the word once, use the word in a sentence, then say the word again. Write the word on the lines in your Worktext.

1. harm — "It won't do any **harm** to read this instead of my Bible," she muttered.
2. loaf — Mom placed the freshly baked **loaf** of French bread on the table.
3. sauce — Beth ladled a double helping of **sauce** over her spaghetti.
4. swift — She ate her dinner at a **swift** pace so she could have more time to read.
5. frown — Mrs. Hill's forehead wrinkled in a **frown.**
6. across — She walked **across** the room towards Beth.
7. chance — "You are reading every **chance** you get," she commented.
8. harsh — Mom was not **harsh** with Beth, but she was very firm.
9. carpet — Beth scuffed her slippers across the **carpet** as she joined her family.
10. drift — During family devotions, Beth let her thoughts **drift** back to her book.
11. awful — She felt **awful** when she realized she had put her reading before God.
12. decide — Beth knew she had to **decide** what was most important to her.
13. bluff — She could not **bluff** her way through this science report.
14. owl — You can't stay up all night like an **owl** and still be rested for school.

I Test-Editing

Name ______________________

If a word is spelled correctly, fill in the oval under **Correct**. If the word is misspelled, fill in the oval under **Incorrect**, and write the word correctly on the blank.

	Correct	Incorrect	
1. spark	●	○	
2. cardbord	○	●	cardboard
3. graff	○	●	graph
4. aloud	●	○	
5. undergrownd	○	●	underground
6. cord	●	○	
7. barber	●	○	
8. cawf	○	●	cough
9. peace	●	○	
10. laf	○	●	laugh
11. beast	●	○	
12. ofice	○	●	office
13. elaphant	○	●	elephant
14. haul	●	○	
15. alfabet	○	●	alphabet

Review Lesson 18

115

3 Test-Editing

Reinforce recognizing and correcting misspelled words.

4 Action Game

Reinforce spelling skills and provide motivation and interest.

Materials

- Two Word Lists
- Tennis Ball or Sponge Ball

SPELL TOSS

How to Play:

Divide students into two teams. Choose a "Caller" for each team and provide them with a list of spelling words to be reviewed. Instruct each team to sit in a circle. The Callers begin the game by saying a spelling word aloud and tossing the ball to a teammate. When the teammate catches the ball, he/she must say the first letter of the spelling word. The student then throws the ball to another teammate who must say the second letter of the word. Continue tossing the ball until the word is correctly spelled. The first team to correctly spell all the words on their caller's list wins!

Game

Reinforce spelling skills and provide motivation and interest.

Materials

- game pages (from Student Worktext)
- stickers (13 per child)
- game word list

Game Word List

Check off each word lightly in pencil as it is used.

The Secret Agents

1. **quarrel**
2. **powder**
3. **orphan**
4. **citizen**
5. **garbage**
6. **noun**
7. **starve**
8. **carnival**
9. **however**
10. **fence**
11. **press**
12. **craft**
13. **pound**

1. **all right**
2. **forest**
3. **yarn**
4. **household**
5. **marbles**
6. **farther**
7. **growl**
8. **offer**
9. **cart**
10. **false**
11. **stuff**
12. **tough**
13. **stout**

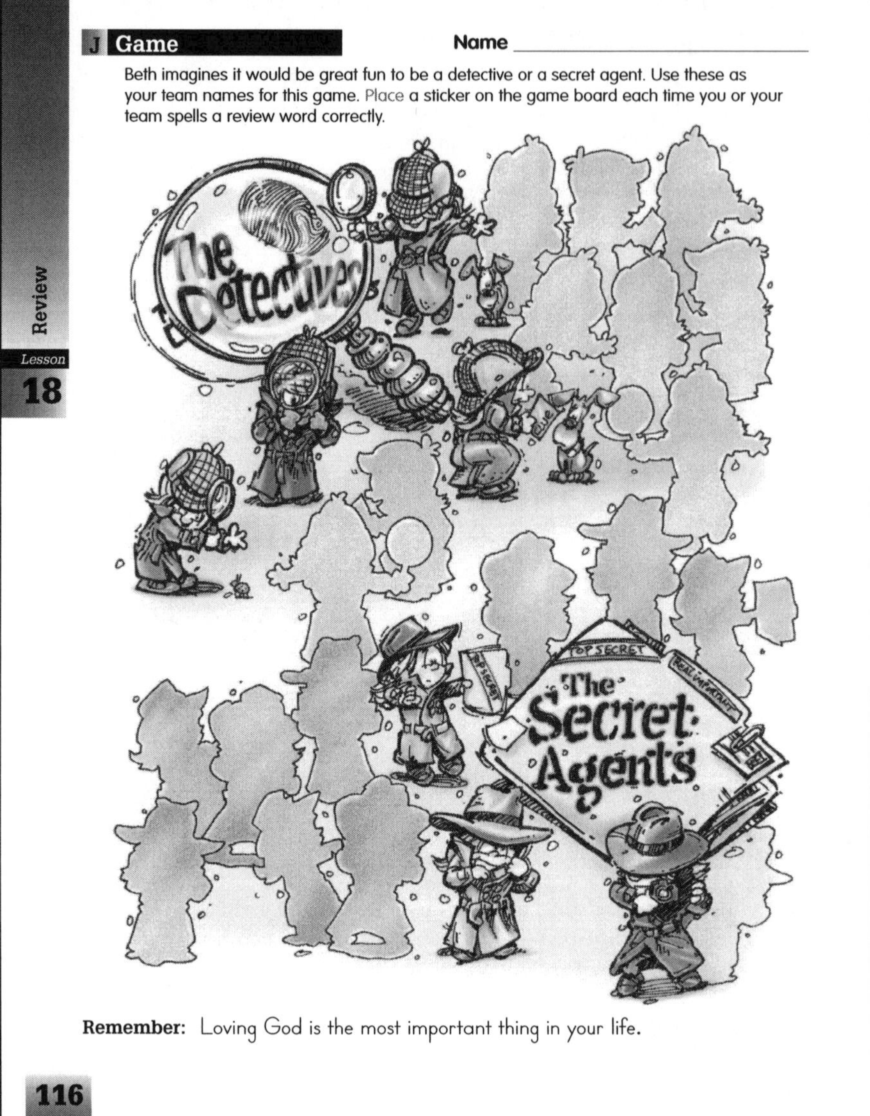

Review Lesson 18

J Game Name ______________________

Beth imagines it would be great fun to be a detective or a secret agent. Use these as your team names for this game. Place a sticker on the game board each time you or your team spells a review word correctly.

Remember: Loving God is the most important thing in your life.

116

How to Play:

- Divide students into two teams. Name one team **The Secret Agents**, one **The Detectives**. (Optional: If you have an even number of students, you may wish to pair students from opposing teams and have them share a game page.)
- Read the instructions from the student game page aloud.
- Have a student from **The Secret Agents** go to the board.
- Say the spelling word.
- Have the student write the word on the board.
- If correct, have each member of that team put a sticker on one silhouette by his/her team name. If the word is misspelled, have him/her put an X on one silhouette. That word may not be given again.
- Repeat this process with **The Detectives**.
- When the words from both lists have been used, the team with the most stickers is the winner.

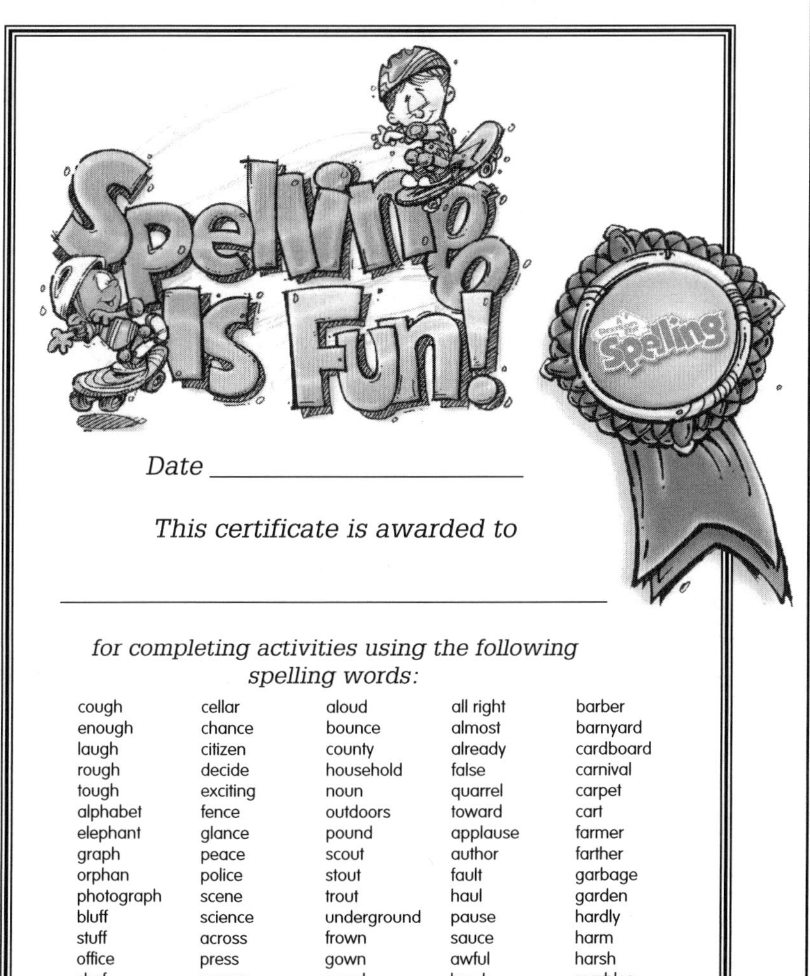

Spelling Is Fun!

Date ______________________

This certificate is awarded to

____

for completing activities using the following spelling words:

cough	cellar	aloud	all right	barber
enough	chance	bounce	almost	barnyard
laugh	citizen	county	already	cardboard
rough	decide	household	false	carnival
tough	exciting	noun	quarrel	carpet
alphabet	fence	outdoors	toward	cart
elephant	glance	pound	applause	farmer
graph	peace	scout	author	farther
orphan	police	stout	fault	garbage
photograph	scene	trout	haul	garden
bluff	science	underground	pause	hardly
stuff	across	frown	sauce	harm
office	press	gown	awful	harsh
chef	recess	growl	hawk	marbles
loaf	beast	owl	fog	scarf
craft	else	however	offer	spark
drift	famous	powder	cord	starve
swift	son	tower	forest	yarn

2 Certificate

Provide an opportunity for parents or guardians to encourage and assess their child's progress.

Fill in today's date and your name on your certificate.

Take a minute to memorize...

Mark 12:29, 30

3 Letter

Provide the parent or guardian with the spelling word lists for the next unit.

Give your parents or guardian this letter that lists your spelling words for the next unit. Put it where you will remember to practice the words together.

Dear Parent,

We are about to begin a new spelling unit containing five weekly lessons. A set of eighteen words will be studied each week. All the words will be reviewed in the sixth week. Values based on the Scriptures listed below will be taught in each lesson.

Lesson 19	Lesson 20	Lesson 21	Lesson 22	Lesson 23
dessert	crooked	appointment	danger	festival
germ	footprint	avoid	donor	final
perfect	goodness	choice	either	general
birth	overlook	disappoint	enter	hospital
firm	wooden	joint	feather	several
sir	tourist	moist	finger	total
skirt	bulldozer	oily	neither	label
worry	bulletin	point	owner	level
worst	fully	rejoice	rather	model
worth	handful	topsoil	favor	evil
burst	cure	annoy	honor	battle
curl	curious	destroy	humor	castle
curve	during	employ	motor	gentle
furniture	furious	enjoyment	visitor	jungle
further	plural	loyal	capture	possible
nurse	pure	royalty	nature	puddle
purpose	sure	soybean	pasture	simple
turkey	butcher	voyage	picture	uncle
Matthew 7:24	Luke 12:15	Luke 9:48	Mark 9:50	Luke 6:38

The Blistering Blunder

Christopher discovers the importance of building on a firm foundation.

"Mom, look!" Christopher waved a sheet of paper in front of her face. "Can we go? Please? It's taken such a long time to get built! We can go, can't we?"

"Go where?" Mom tried to capture the half sheet of blue paper to see what Christopher was talking about.

"Mrs. Burton said our whole class could go, but you've gotta sign this paper first."

"Here, Mom." Kristin handed an identical blue paper to her mother. "The ice skating place is open now, and Mrs. B's taking all of us if we get permission slips signed by our parents." Mrs. Wright took the paper and glanced at the information on it. "We can go, can't we?" Kristin repeated her twin's question.

Mom smiled down into two matching pairs of eager green eyes. "Wel-l-l-l-l, let's see now," she teased.

Kristin relaxed, but Christopher missed the twinkle in his mother's eyes. "Mom!" He waved his permission slip in the air. "We've got our own ice skates that Paw Paw sent us, so we won't have to rent skates and it won't cost quite as much. Please?"

Mom winked at Kristin. "Yes, you may both go, but you'll…" Her words trailed off when Christopher gave her a giant squeeze.

Mrs. Wright laughed at the twin grins. "Thanks, Mom!" they echoed at the same instant in voices so much alike.

"Thanks for what?" Cathy grabbed a glass off the counter and filled it with water for Cory, who trailed behind her.

"We get to go ice skating with our class at the new ice skating place!" Kristin leaned over her mother's shoulder as Mrs. Wright sat down at the dinette table to sign the two permission slips.

"Hey, I want to go, too." Cathy came over to the table.

"Me, too." Cory climbed onto Mrs. Wright's lap.

"Maybe your class will go sometime, Cathy." Christopher stood at his mother's elbow. "It's going to be great! I can't believe it's finally open and we can use our new ice skates. Those builders sure seemed to take forever pushing dirt around with big machines and stuff before they even started on the building. You'd think they'd hurry up."

"Now, listen up, you two." Mrs. Wright held up the signed permission slips. "You must be sure to wear wool socks over your regular socks. Those ice skates your grandfather sent you are brand new and stiff, besides being a little large. You'll need the wool socks to keep from getting blisters. Got it?"

"Got it." Kristin took the permission slip her mom handed her. "C'mon, Cathy, help me get my skates out. Maybe Mom and Dad will take our family skating some time if your class doesn't go soon."

Christopher went to his closet and got out the brand new black skates. As he admired them he could picture himself gliding gracefully over the ice. It was going to be great!

"Hurry up, Christopher!" Kristin called from down the hall. "It's almost time to go."

"Just a minute!" Christopher stuck his foot into a boot and started tying it.

"Mom said to wear wool socks." Cory looked up from the block building he was designing.

"They're prickly and make my legs itch." Christopher tied the lace and grabbed the other boot. "I'll be all right this way. These hiking boots I'm wearing now never gave me blisters, even when they were new, and I didn't wear wool socks."

"But Mom said…" Cory insisted.

"Oh, mind your own business!" Christopher jumped up and grabbed his coat. "What're you doing in my room, anyway?" He grabbed the ice skates and slung them over his shoulder. "And why are you trying to build something on a rug? That's a stupid place to build anything with blocks!" Christopher dashed out into the hall without waiting for an answer.

The ice rink wasn't very crowded. Some skaters twirled and glided gracefully. Some tottered and fell. Christopher was one of those. But he kept trying, ignoring the discomfort of the new ice skates. As the minutes ticked by, he fell less often and skated more easily.

"Hey, Christopher!" Tommy waved from one end of the ice. "C'mon and race with Thorny and me!"

Christopher joined them. Just as he arrived, Daniel came to a swishing halt right beside him. "I'll race you guys." Daniel leaned over to adjust his skate.

Thorny grinned at Daniel. "I believe, in the interest of fair play, that you should allow the rest of us a significant head start before you commence the race. I've observed your skill, particularly in maneuvering through turns."

"Okay." Daniel agreed easily enough. "I'll give you a half-lap head start. How many laps are we racing?"

"Well, we were just racing from one end to the other." Tommy waved his hand toward the opposite end of the skating rink. "But I guess we can go around the whole thing, maybe, twice?" He looked to Christopher for his agreement.

"Sure." Christopher knelt with one knee on the ice to

Story (continued)

tighten his right skate. It didn't seem to fit right. Maybe if he made it real tight it wouldn't be rubbing on his heel like it was now. "Okay, ready." He jumped up and joined the three boys at the starting line.

Tommy called, "On your mark, get set…GO!"

For a while Thorny kept up with Daniel. By the second lap there was no doubt who would win. Or who would lose. Christopher gave it all he had and wasn't too far behind Tommy, though. "Next time," Tommy panted, "we'll give you a closer race, Daniel."

"Anytime!" Daniel called over his shoulder as he skated away easily.

"Not anytime soon, I sincerely hope." Thorny pushed the hair out of his face. Christopher echoed that thought. He didn't say anything out loud—he needed all the air he could get for breathing right then. And his feet hurt. Especially the right one.

Moving carefully, he skated to the exit off the ice. Sitting on a bench by the lockers, he took off his right skate. Christopher winced when he pulled the sock off. No wonder his foot hurt—a large blister was broken open and oozing on his heel. The skin around his leg where the top of the leather ended was rubbed red and raw looking. His left foot wasn't in much better shape.

Christopher didn't enjoy the rest of the afternoon. Time dragged as he sat and watched everyone else having a great time. It didn't help his feelings each time Kristin skated by, long brown curls flying behind her—and wool socks peeking out above her pretty white skates. It didn't improve his mood each time someone asked why he wasn't skating.

Mrs. Wright didn't make any comment that evening while she tended to Christopher's poor feet. But Cory did. "Mom said to wear wool socks." He peered at Christopher's blisters.

"Don't you have a castle to build or something?" Christopher muttered.

"Nope." Cory rearranged the bandage and the antibiotic ointment on the table. "It fell down."

"I told you that was a stupid place to build something out of blocks!" Christopher snapped.

"Cory, why don't you go see what the girls are doing?" Mrs. Wright replaced the cap on the peroxide and picked up the ointment. "Christopher, remember the other day when you said it seemed to take forever for the builders working on the new ice skating place to even get started on the building? They moved the dirt with big machines and worked on the foundation for a long time. They probably spent as much time on it as they did on all the rest of the building."

"Uh-huh." Christopher winced when Mom gently spread the ointment over his broken blisters. "Why?"

"Have you ever wondered why builders spend so long on the foundation when you don't ever see that part of the building?" Mom wiped her fingers and picked up a bandage.

"No, I guess not." Christopher picked up another bandage and opened it. "Why?"

"Because it's very important. Perhaps the most important part of the whole building. If the foundation isn't strong, the building will fall, no matter how lovely it is." Mom placed the bandage gently across Christopher's heel.

"Like Cory's block castle!" Christopher tried to balance the bandage box on the top of the peroxide bottle. "It had a terrible foundation and it fell!"

"That's right." Mom smoothed on the last bandage and sat down in a dinette chair by her son. "You see, the Scriptures say 'All who listen to My instructions and follow them are wise, like a man who builds his house on solid rock.' That's in Matthew 7. I'm afraid you didn't listen very well to instructions, did you, Son?"

Christopher scooted the bandage wrappers around on the table and shook his head.

"I don't want you to be like Cory's castle. I don't want you to build your character on such a shaky foundation, Christopher. When you listen to and obey your parents or teachers, it helps you learn to listen to and obey God. That will help you build a strong character, to be someone who will do what's right even when it's hard to do."

"I'm sorry, Mom." Christopher blinked rapidly. "I'm sorry I didn't obey you. I really am. Not just because I got hurt, but because I want to be strong enough to do what's right."

"I forgive you, Christopher." Mom stood up and squeezed his shoulder.

Christopher gathered up the first aid supplies and limped down the hall to put them away in the medicine cabinet. As he passed the living room he noticed Cory busily constructing a new block castle. This time he was building it at one end of the brick hearth—a much better foundation!

2 Discussion Time

Check understanding of the story and development of personal values.

- Where was Mrs. Burton taking her class?
- Why did Mrs. Wright tell the twins to wear wool socks?
- Did the twins obey?
- Who won the ice skating race?
- What happened to Christopher's feet?
- Why had the builders taken so long to work on the foundation of the new skating rink?
- Is a solid foundation important for people, too?

A Preview Name ______

Write each word as your teacher says it.

1. burst
2. dessert
3. birth
4. curl
5. perfect
6. further
7. curve
8. sir
9. turkey
10. worst
11. worth
12. purpose
13. worry
14. firm
15. skirt
16. furniture
17. nurse
18. germ

Scripture

Matthew 7:24

Words with /er/

Lesson 19

119

3 Preview

Test for knowledge of the correct spellings of these words.

Customize Your List

On a separate sheet of paper, additional words of your choice may be tested.

I will say each word once, use the word in a sentence, then say the word again. Write the words on the lines in your Worktext.

Correct Immediately!

Let's correct our Preview. I will spell each word out loud. If you spelled a word incorrectly, rewrite it correctly.

Progress Chart

Students may record scores. (Reproducible master provided in Appendix B.)

1. burst — Christopher **burst** through the door waving a blue permission slip.
2. dessert — Mrs. Wright was making **dessert** when the kids came home.
3. birth — Christopher has had brown hair since **birth.**
4. curl — Kristin does not have to **curl** her hair with rollers.
5. perfect — "These skates are a **perfect** fit," Christopher decided.
6. further — He gave no **further** thought to Mom's instructions.
7. curve — Daniel took the **curve** of the rink in smooth, easy strides.
8. sir — When asked if he was ready to skate, Christopher said, "Yes, **sir**!"
9. turkey — Everyone laughed during the **turkey** race.
10. worst — It was the **worst** blister Christopher had ever had!
11. worth — It would have been **worth** it for him to have worn the wool socks.
12. purpose — There was a **purpose** in Mrs. Wright's instructions.
13. worry — "I didn't even **worry** that you wouldn't obey," she said.
14. firm — Mother's voice was soft but **firm.**
15. skirt — She laid Christopher's leg across her soft, denim **skirt.**
16. furniture — He was careful not to bump his heel on any **furniture.**
17. nurse — "Mom is a good **nurse,**" Christopher said to himself.
18. germ — The antibiotic ointment is a **germ**–preventive medicine.

Word Shapes

Help students form a correct image of whole words.

Look at each word and think about its shape. Now, write the word in the correct Word Shape Boxes. You may check off each word as you use it.

(The sound of **/ər/** can be spelled with **er**, **ir**, **or**, or **ur**. Because spellers cannot rely on a phonetic way of remembering the various spellings, this sound is often difficult.)

In the Word Shape Boxes, fill in the boxes containing the letters that spell the sound of **/ər/** in each word.

Take a minute to memorize...

Matthew 7:24

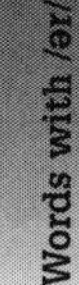

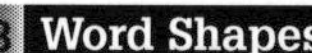

B Word Shapes Name ____________________

Write each word in the correct Word Shape Boxes. Next, in the Word Shape Boxes, shade in the boxes containing the letters that spell the sound of **/ər/** in each word.

1. dessert
2. germ
3. perfect
4. birth
5. firm
6. sir
7. skirt
8. worry
9. worst
10. worth
11. burst
12. curl
13. curve
14. furniture
15. further
16. nurse
17. purpose
18. turkey

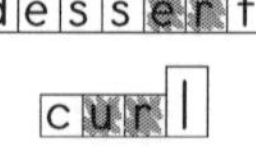

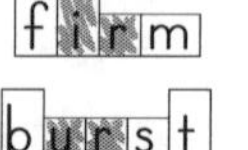

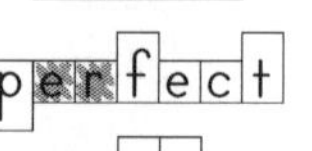

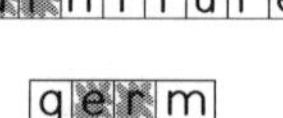

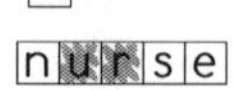

curl

firm

burst

perfect

furniture

germ

nurse

worry

further

curve

120

Answers may vary for duplicate word shapes.

Be Prepared For Fun

Check these supply lists for **Fun Ways to Spell** - presented **Day 2**.
Purchase and/or gather these items ahead of time!

General

- Pencil
- Graph Paper (1 sheet per child)
- Spelling List

Auditory

- Voice Recorder
- Spelling List

Visual

- Water Color Paint Box (1 per child)
- Paint Brush (1 per child)
- Art Paper (3 or 4 sheets per child)
- Spelling List

Tactile

- Soccer Ball, Basketball, Tennis Ball, or 4-Square Ball
- Spelling List

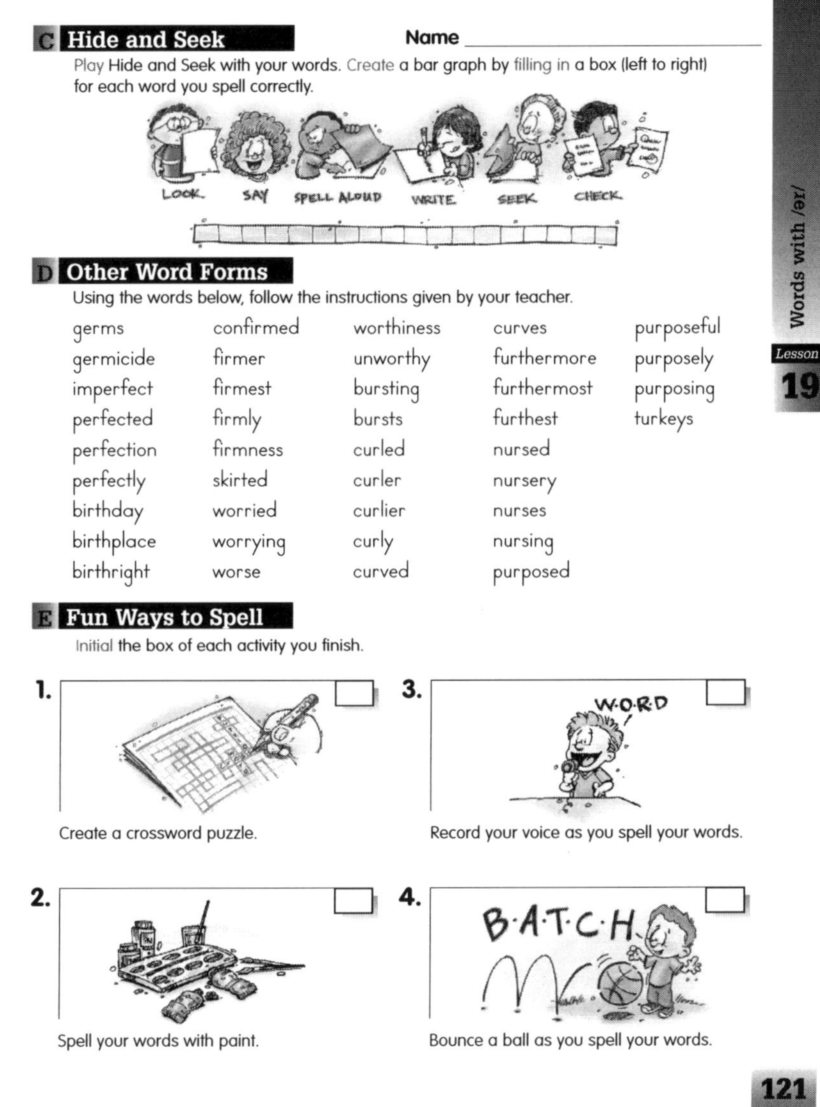

Words with /er/

Lesson 19

C Hide and Seek Name ______________________

Play Hide and Seek with your words. Create a bar graph by filling in a box (left to right) for each word you spell correctly.

D Other Word Forms

Using the words below, follow the instructions given by your teacher.

germs	confirmed	worthiness	curves	purposeful
germicide	firmer	unworthy	furthermore	purposely
imperfect	firmest	bursting	furthermost	purposing
perfected	firmly	bursts	furthest	turkeys
perfection	firmness	curled	nursed	
perfectly	skirted	curler	nursery	
birthday	worried	curlier	nurses	
birthplace	worrying	curly	nursing	
birthright	worse	curved	purposed	

E Fun Ways to Spell

Initial the box of each activity you finish.

1. Create a crossword puzzle.

2. Spell your words with paint.

3.
Record your voice as you spell your words.

4.
Bounce a ball as you spell your words.

121

1 Hide and Seek

Reinforce spelling by using multiple styles of learning.

On a white board, Teacher writes each word — one at a time. **Have students:**

- **Look** at the word.
- **Say** the word out loud.
- **Spell** the word out loud.
- **Hide** (teacher erases word.)
- **Write** the word on paper.
- **Seek** (teacher rewrites word.)
- **Check** spelling. If incorrect, rewrite word correctly.

2 Other Word Forms

This activity is optional. Have students write original sentences using these Other Word Forms:

birthplace
perfected
purposely
curled

3 Fun Ways to Spell

Four activities are provided. Use one, two, three, or all of the activities. Have students initial the box for each activity they complete.

Options:

- assign activities to students according to their learning styles
- set up the activities in learning centers for students to do throughout the day
- divide students into four groups and assign one activity per group
- do one activity per day

General

To create a crossword puzzle…
- Use a pencil.
- Arrange your words on graph paper.
- Overlap words where letters are shared.
- Don't create any new words.
- Outline each word with a marker.
- Erase your words.
- Trade with a classmate and work each other's puzzles.

Auditory

To spell your words using a voice recorder…
- Record yourself as you say and spell each word on your spelling list.
- Listen to your recording and check your spelling.

Visual

To spell your words with paint…
- Paint each spelling word on your paper.
- Trade papers with a classmate and check each other's spelling.

Tactile

To bounce a ball as you spell your words…
- Look at the first word on your list.
- Bounce the ball as you say each letter of the word aloud.
- Do this with each word on your list.

1 Working with Words

Familiarize students with word meaning and usage.

Missing Letters

The sound of **/ər/** can be spelled with **er**, **ir**, **or**, or **ur**. Fill in the missing letter or letters that spell the sound of **/ər/**.

Nouns and Verbs

Remind students that a word can often be used as more than one part of speech. Write the word **battle** on the board. Read these sentences and ask students whether **battle** is being used as a noun or verb.

The soldiers engaged in a fierce battle. (noun)

We had to battle the ants in our yard. (verb)

Decide whether the underlined word is used as a noun or verb in the sentence. Write **n** if it is a noun or **v** if it is a verb.

Take a minute to memorize...

Matthew 7:24

Lesson 19 — Words with /ər/

F Working with Words Name ____________________

Missing Letters

Fill in the missing letter or letters that spell the sound of **/ər/**.

1. p _e_ _r_ fect	**7.** dess _e_ _r_ t	**13.** f _i_ _r_ m
2. sk _i_ _r_ t	**8.** b _i_ _r_ th	**14.** w _o_ _r_ st
3. w _o_ _r_ th	**9.** w _o_ _r_ ry	**15.** c _u_ _r_ ve
4. b _u_ _r_ st	**10.** c _u_ _r_ l	**16.** p _u_ _r_ pose
5. f _u_ _r_ th _e_ _r_	**11.** n _u_ _r_ se	**17.** s _i_ _r_
6. t _u_ _r_ key	**12.** g _e_ _r_ m	**18.** f _u_ _r_ nit _u_ _r_ e

Nouns and Verbs

Remember, a noun is a word that names a person, place, thing, or idea. A verb is a word that shows action or state of being. Decide whether the bold-faced word is used as a noun or a verb in the sentence. Write **n** if it is a noun or **v** if it is a verb.

1. _n_ Kristin twisted a brown **curl** around her fingers.
   _v_ The hamster likes to **curl** up in a corner of the cage.
2. _n_ Christopher thought Mom was a good **nurse**.
   _v_ Someone had to **nurse** Grandma when she got sick.
3. _v_ Christopher tried to **skirt** around the wool sock question.
   _n_ Kristin wore her new corduroy **skirt**.
4. _n_ With a **burst** of energy, Thorny almost passed Daniel.
   _v_ Water could flood the house if the pipes **burst**.
5. _n_ Tommy raced around the **curve** just ahead of Christopher.
   _v_ Kristin began to **curve** pipe cleaners to spell her words.
6. _n_ Christopher's **worry** over his foot made him have a bad day.
   _v_ Christopher did not want to **worry** about wearing wool socks.

Word Bank

birth	curve	furniture	nurse	sir	worry
burst	dessert	further	perfect	skirt	worst
curl	firm	germ	purpose	turkey	worth

122

G Dictation

Name ______________________

Write each sentence as your teacher dictates. Use correct punctuation.

1. This good dessert was worth the wait.
2. Her skirt is the perfect color of her curls.
3. The curved legs on the furniture look beautiful.

Words with /er/

Lesson 19

H Proofreading

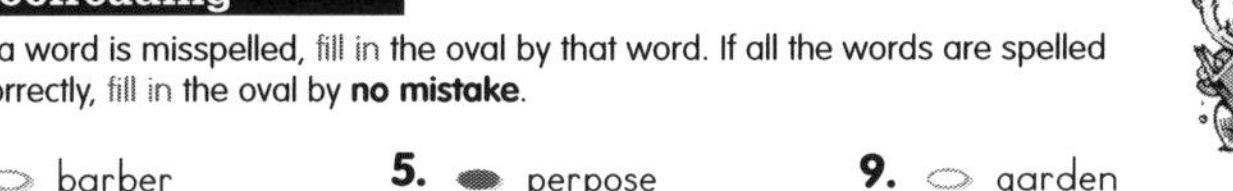

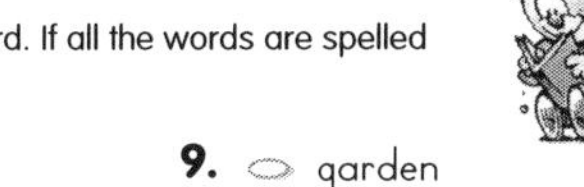

If a word is misspelled, fill in the oval by that word. If all the words are spelled correctly, fill in the oval by **no mistake**.

1. ○ barber ● deasert ○ barnyard ○ no mistake	**5.** ● perpose ○ farmer ○ firm ○ no mistake	**9.** ○ garden ○ curve ● werst ○ no mistake
2. ○ cardboard ○ nurse ● jerm ○ no mistake	**6.** ○ yarn ○ starve ● sirr ○ no mistake	**10.** ○ turkey ○ hardly ○ worth ● no mistake
3. ○ carnival ● perfict ○ carpet ○ no mistake	**7.** ● furnitere ○ skirt ○ farther ○ no mistake	**11.** ○ harm ● berst ○ scarf ○ no mistake
4. ● ferther ○ cart ○ birth ○ no mistake	**8.** ○ spark ● worrey ○ garbage ○ no mistake	**12.** ● cirl ○ harsh ○ marbles ○ no mistake

123

1 Dictation

Reinforce correct spelling by using current and previous words in context.

Listen as I read each sentence and then write it in your Worktext. Remember to use correct capitalization and punctuation. (Slowly read each sentence twice. Sentences are found in the Student Worktext to the left.)

2 Proofreading

Familiarize students with standardized test format and reinforce recognition of misspelled words.

Look at each set of words. If a word is misspelled, fill in the oval by that word. If all the words are spelled correctly, fill in the oval by **no mistake**.

Lesson 19 | Day 4

3 Hide and Seek

Reinforce correct spelling of current spelling words. Repeat this activity from Day 2. (A reproducible master is provided in Appendix A as shown on the inset page to the right.)

4 Other Word Forms

Have your students complete this activity to strengthen spelling ability and expand vocabulary.

1 Posttest

Visit the **A Reason For** website to download free, printable Posttest pages.

I will say the word once, use it in a sentence, then say it again. Write your words on a separate sheet of paper.

Progress Chart

Students may record scores. (Appendix B)

Personal Dictionary

Students may add any words they have misspelled to their personal dictionaries. (Appendix B)

Other Word Forms | Lesson 19

Hide and Seek

Play Hide and Seek with your words. Create a bar graph by filling in a box (left to right) for each word you spell correctly.

LOOK SAY HIDE WRITE SEEK CHECK

Other Word Forms

Scrambled Words

Use the sentence clue to help you unscramble each word. Write the unscrambled word in the sentence.

egmrs	1.	Mrs. Wright used peroxide to kill the germs.
limrfy	2.	Christopher laced his skates firmly on his feet.
deikrst	3.	Daniel skirted around the boy who had fallen.
cgilnru	4.	I like curling up by the fire with a good book.
denrsu	5.	Christopher felt better after Mom nursed his hurt foot.
ceeflprty	6.	Cory's castle stood up perfectly on the hearth.
abdhirty	7.	I invited the whole class to my birthday party.
deiorrw	8.	Cory was worried because Christopher disobeyed Mom.
brsstu	9.	When a blister bursts it hurts more.
cginruv	10.	The curving sidewalk is a fun place to ride bikes.
eloprsuy	11.	He purposely chose not to wear wool socks.
hortwy	12.	We are not worthy, but God forgives our sins.
bginrstu	13.	Kristin was bursting with excitement about the field trip.
eorsw	14.	He felt worse about disobeying than about his blister.
efhrsttu	15.	Thorny rounded the furthest corner of the ice rink.
ceilrstu	16.	Kristin has the curliest hair in her class.
abhikmrrt	17.	There is a birthmark on my right ankle.
eedrsst	18.	There were five yummy desserts at my birthday party.

340

1.	dessert	Mom put **dessert** in the oven just as the kids came in from school.
2.	burst	The twins were about to **burst** with excitement.
3.	curl	Kristin pulled at a brown **curl** as she looked at Mom expectantly.
4.	worry	"Don't **worry**; you may go," Mom said with a smile.
5.	firm	Mom was **firm** in her instructions to wear wool socks.
6.	perfect	Daniel's skating style seemed **perfect** and effortless.
7.	curve	He took the **curve** of the rink at high speed.
8.	turkey	The **turkey** race was great fun for the whole class.
9.	birth	Kristin's **birth** occurred just a few minutes before Christopher's.
10.	skirt	Kristin wore her new corduroy **skirt** on the skating field trip.
11.	sir	"May I have change for this dollar to rent a locker, **sir**?" she asked.
12.	worst	"This is the **worst** blister I've ever had," groaned Christopher.
13.	germ	"This will kill any **germ** or bacteria in the blister," Mom explained.
14.	worth	"It surely wasn't **worth** it to disobey," he moaned.
15.	nurse	"You're a good **nurse**, Mom," said Christopher gratefully.
16.	furniture	He walked slowly between the **furniture** so as not to bump his heel.
17.	further	Christopher did not say anything **further** about Cory's building.
18.	purpose	We must **purpose** in our hearts to obey our parents and God.

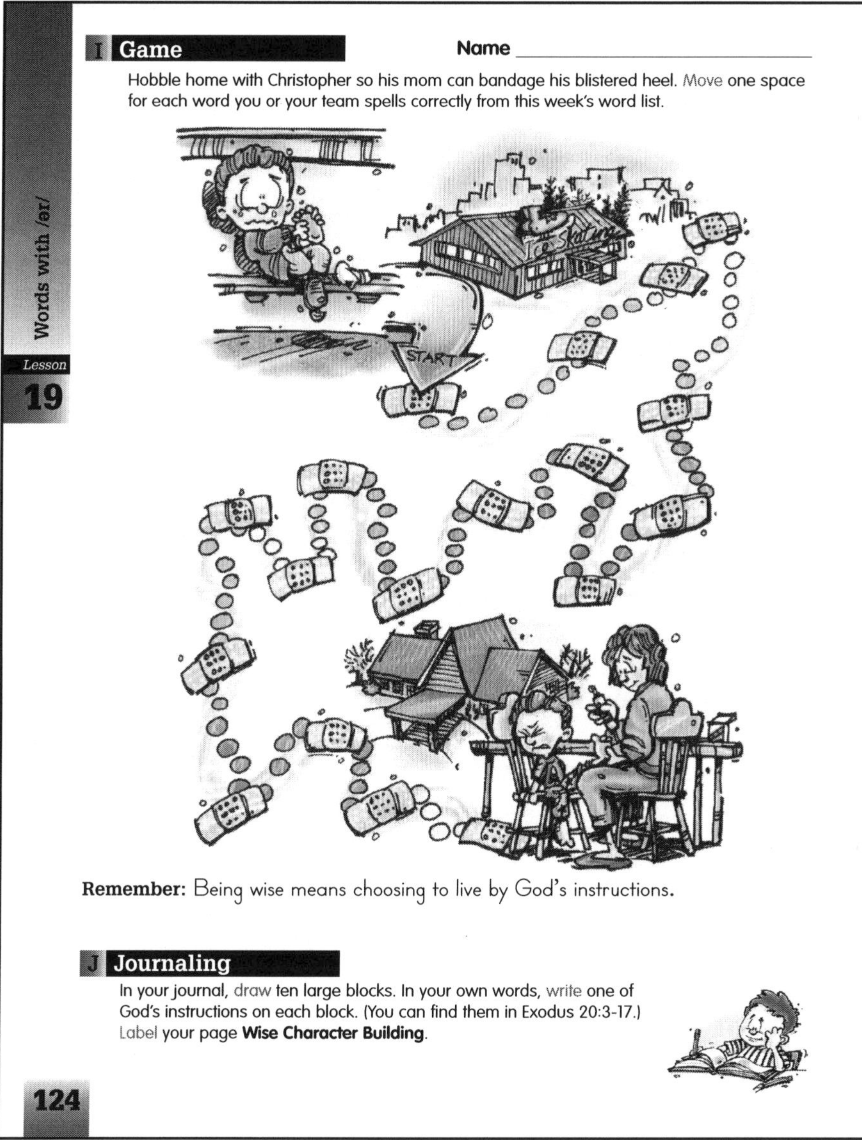

Lesson 19

Words with /er/

I Game

Name ______________________

Hobble home with Christopher so his mom can bandage his blistered heel. Move one space for each word you or your team spells correctly from this week's word list.

Remember: Being wise means choosing to live by God's instructions.

J Journaling

In your journal, draw ten large blocks. In your own words, write one of God's instructions on each block. (You can find them in Exodus 20:3-17.) Label your page **Wise Character Building**.

124

2 Game

Reinforce spelling skills and provide motivation and interest.

Materials

- game page (from Student Worktext)
- game pieces (1 per child)
- game word list

Game Word List

1. **dessert**
2. **germ**
3. **perfect**
4. **birth**
5. **firm**
6. **sir**
7. **skirt**
8. **worry**
9. **worst**
10. **worth**
11. **burst**
12. **curl**
13. **curve**
14. **furniture**
15. **further**
16. **nurse**
17. **purpose**
18. **turkey**

How to Play:

- Divide students into two teams.
- Have each student place his/her game piece on Start.
- Have a student from team A go to the board.
- Say the spelling word.
- Have the student write the word on the board.
- If correct, instruct each member of team A to move his/her game piece forward one space.
- Alternate between teams A and B as you go down the word list.
- The team to reach Christopher and his mom first is the winner.

Small Group Option: Students may play this game without teacher direction in small groups of two or more.

3 Journaling

Provide a meaningful reason for correct spelling through personal writing.

Review the story using discussion leads provided on the following page. Encourage students to apply the Scriptural value in their journaling.

Journaling (continued)

- Why did the twins want Mrs. Wright to sign their permission slips? (So they could go with their class to the new ice skating rink.)
- Where did the twins' ice skates come from? (Their grandfather, Paw-Paw, had sent them all new ice skates.)
- Why didn't Christopher want to wear wool socks like his mother asked him to? (He said they were prickly and made his legs itch. He thought it wouldn't matter since he hadn't worn wool socks when his hiking boots were new.)
- How did Christopher learn that following instructions is wise? (Because he didn't obey, his feet got very bad blisters and raw places. He didn't have a very good time.)
- Which of Cory's block buildings do you think would be stronger, and why? The one built on the rug or the one built on the brick hearth?

No word in the English language rhymes with "month," "orange," "silver," or "purple."

Word Wow!

Weathering the Storm

Sarah's situation helps Setsuko see the difference between wants and needs.

"It's still snowing," Setsuko reported from her spot by the front window. "I can't even see the mailbox."

"The weatherman said we'd be getting a major winter storm soon. This must be it." Mrs. Noma glanced up from the couch where she was reading the mail in the warm glow of the lamp.

"Just look at all that snow." Setsuko ran her finger down the window and left a streak in the frost."

"Listen to this, Setsuko." Her mother held up the letter she'd been reading. "Your Aunt Miyako and Uncle Taku took the children to Vail for a skiing holiday. They were there for five days and even little Yoko learned to ski quite well."

Setsuko let the curtain drop over the window, shutting out the gloomy day outside. "That sounds like fun. Why can't we go on a skiing trip?" She plopped down on the other end of the couch.

"That's not possible right now, Setsuko." Mrs. Noma carefully refolded the letter from her sister and put it back in the envelope. "Perhaps we'll take a vacation this summer." She laid the letter on the lamp table and stood up. "It's time to start supper—want to help? We're having tempura."

Setsuko shook her head and stayed right where she was. She could hear her mother moving about in the kitchen, and it wasn't long before delicious smells began wafting through the duplex.

"We never go anywhere or do anything fun. Daniel went to the Bahamas last summer. Kristin and Christopher's family went on a two-week camping trip to Yellowstone. Rachel's family got to fly on a plane to Dallas at Christmas—and there's a bunch of them in that family. Even my own cousins got to go skiing!" Setsuko sulked.

She picked up the big book from the coffee table and propped it on her lap. Turning the pages slowly, she gazed at colored pictures of interesting spots to visit. There was a two-page photograph of the Grand Canyon. The cars in the Indy 500 picture looked like they could race right off the page. The waters surrounding a Caribbean island were true blue. Setsuko dreamed of visiting such far-off spots until Mother called her for supper.

The duplex was cozy and warm in spite of the snowstorm. The rice was hot, the tempura crisp, and the sweet-sour sauce yummy. But Setsuko was restless.

"All right, Suzy-Q." Mr. Noma laid his chopsticks across his plate and leaned back in his chair. "What's bothering you?"

"Nothing." Setsuko stuffed another bite into her mouth.

"I see." Mr. Noma reached for the tempura platter. "You haven't said two words during supper—and you're eating one of your favorite foods with as much enthusiasm as you'd eat cardboard—but I'm glad nothing is bothering you."

"I just want to go somewhere or do something!" Setsuko waved her chopsticks in the air. "Why don't we ever fly somewhere exciting or take a cruise or something? Uncle Taku and Aunt Miyako went skiing. Why can't we? We never do anything fun and exciting."

Mr. and Mrs. Noma looked at each other across the table. "Well, Setsuko." Father cleared his throat, "All those things cost money. While your mother and I both have good jobs, we don't have money to spend on trips and things like that right now. You know we're saving money to buy a house. We thought you wanted a house with a bigger yard and..."

"I do! I do want a real house with a big yard for Chimi and some big trees for a treehouse and a bedroom with a big closet and a bay window. But I want to do things, too! Some kids live in big houses and have lots of things and go on fun vacations. Why can't we?" Setsuko slumped in her chair. "We live in this little old duplex and never go anywhere."

"Now, Setsuko, I think..." Mr. Noma began when the lights suddenly blinked, then went out. It was quiet and dark. Very dark. "Well, I guess the snow knocked out the power lines somewhere. You stay put—I'll get a flashlight." Setsuko could hear her father carefully making his way across the kitchen. He rattled things in a drawer. "Here it is. I'll get the kerosene camping lantern and be right back."

Setsuko held her hand up in front of her face. She couldn't see it. "Okasan? What will happen to us now?"

"We'll be fine, Setsuko. We've got the lantern and some candles for light. We can cook on the camp stove and we've got plenty of kerosene for it and the lantern. I'm just very glad that this 'little old duplex' has a 'little old' fireplace." It sounded like mother was smiling as she quoted the words Setsuko had used to describe their home. "I feel sorry for those who don't have any other way to heat their homes. It could get very cold for them if the electricity doesn't come back on soon."

"What about Sarah?" Setsuko blinked in the brightness of the lantern Mr. Noma carried into the kitchen.

"What about Sarah, Suzi-Q?" Father set the lantern on the bar. It cast long funny shadows about the room.

"I don't think they have a fireplace."

"I didn't see any chimney

Story (continued)

when I was working on their house." Mr. Noma opened a box of candles. "After I get a fire going I'll run over and make sure they're all right. Most of the roads weren't too bad when I came home from the hospital, and the van's four-wheel-drive, so driving shouldn't be a problem."

"May I go?" Setsuko asked as Mr. Noma pulled on his warm coat and heavy gloves.

"No. You keep your mother company." The cold air swooshed in when Mr. Noma opened the door to the carport. "I'll be back soon."

It didn't seem soon. Since the dishwasher wouldn't run without electricity, Setsuko helped her mother wash and dry the dishes. The fire snapped and crackled, warming the small living room and kitchen. The snow kept falling—and the electricity stayed off.

Setsuko wandered to the front window again and peered down the darkened street. "Okasan, I see lights coming down the street. I think it's father!" Mother joined her at the window and they peered through the falling snow. Sure enough, the vehicle came slowly down the street and turned into their driveway.

Setsuko rushed to meet her father. "How's S-Sarah?...Oh, hi, Sarah."

"Let's get these girls warmed up." Mr. Noma led Sarah and her sister, Nellie, over to the fire. "The electricity was off at their house, too. It was already quite cold when I got there, and they didn't have any heat. Since Mrs. Johansen wasn't home, I thought it would be best to bring them here." Father held his hands near the fire to warm them. "We left a note with our address so she'll know where the girls are if she gets home."

"Why, you girls must be practically frozen! I'll heat some water on the camp stove for hot chocolate to help warm you up."

"Thank you." Nellie started to follow Mrs. Noma into the kitchen. "We're sorry to put you all to such trouble. May I help?"

"Nonsense!" Mother gave Nellie a hug. "We're very glad to have you here, and it's no trouble at all. Now, you girls just make yourselves at home."

They played games and told stories. They popped corn over the flames and drank hot chocolate. They sang silly songs and told jokes. "Oh, my." She glanced at her watch. "I didn't realize it was getting so late. We must get you all to bed right..." She stopped and blinked in the sudden glare of overhead lights. The heating system coughed and started humming. The electricity was on again.

When Setsuko snuggled into her warm bed it seemed kind of quiet even though the heating system hummed and the stereo played softly. Father had taken Sarah and Nellie back home. Their mother was home and their electricity was on again. Everything was back to normal, but things didn't seem quite the same to Setsuko.

Instead of dreaming of visiting exotic places, she remembered what Sarah had said just before she left. "Thank you for everything. It was wonderful!"

Setsuko had to smile. It had been a wonderful evening. Excellent, really, and they'd been right here in this "little old duplex" the whole time.

What was that verse Mrs. Burton had them all repeat together at school yesterday? "Don't wish...No, that's not right." Setsuko thought a moment and spoke the words aloud slowly. "Don't always be wishing for what you don't have. For real life and real living are not related to how rich we are."

"Do you need something, Setsuko-chan?" Mother stood in the doorway to Setsuko's room. "I heard you talking, but couldn't understand what you were saying."

Setsuko shook her head and yawned. "No, I've got everything I need. G'night."

2 Discussion Time

Check understanding of the story and development of personal values.

- Where did Setsuko's aunt and uncle go for their holiday?
- What did Setsuko want to do?
- Why did the electricity go off?
- Why did Mr. Noma bring Sarah and Nellie to the Noma's house?
- What did they do while the power was out?
- What did Setsuko learn about real life and real living?

A Preview Name ______________

Write each word as your teacher says it.

1. furious
2. sure
3. tourist
4. crooked
5. bulletin
6. wooden
7. footprint
8. during
9. bulldozer
10. cure
11. curious
12. butcher
13. plural
14. handful
15. pure
16. fully
17. overlook
18. goodness

Words with /ů/ or /yü/

Lesson 20

Scripture

Luke 12:15

125

3 Preview

Test for knowledge of the correct spellings of these words.

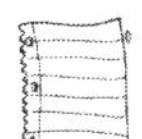

Customize Your List

On a separate sheet of paper, additional words of your choice may be tested.

I will say each word once, use the word in a sentence, then say the word again. Write the words on the lines in your Worktext.

Correct Immediately!

Let's correct our Preview. I will spell each word out loud. If you spelled a word incorrectly, rewrite it correctly.

Progress Chart

Students may record scores. (Reproducible master provided in Appendix B.)

1. furious — Although she did not feel **furious**, Setsuko was very frustrated.
2. sure — She wasn't exactly **sure** where she wanted to travel.
3. tourist — Travel agencies often offer **tourist** packages with special rates.
4. crooked — Setsuko drew a **crooked** line in the frost on the window.
5. bulletin — The National Weather Service issued a weather **bulletin**.
6. wooden — Mr. Noma took his coat from a **wooden** peg in the hallway.
7. footprint — Each **footprint** left by his boot was quickly filled with new snow.
8. during — He did not want Sarah and Nellie to be alone **during** the storm.
9. bulldozer — A piece of equipment like a **bulldozer** will clear the roads of snow.
10. cure — Hot chocolate was the perfect **cure** for Sarah's and Nellie's chills.
11. curious — They were **curious** about the Noma's home.
12. butcher — The electricity was out at the **butcher** shop.
13. plural — The Japanese language does not have **plural** words.
14. handful — Sarah smiled as she scooped up a **handful** of popcorn.
15. pure — Setsuko saw the look of **pure** delight on the girls' faces.
16. fully — She had not **fully** realized how blessed she really was.
17. overlook — We often **overlook** the things for which we should be most thankful.
18. goodness — Setsuko thanked the Lord for His **goodness** to her.

Word Shapes

Help students form a correct image of whole words.

Look at each word and think about its shape. Now, write the word in the correct Word Shape Boxes. You may check off each word as you use it.

(In many words, the sound of **/ù/** or **/yù/** is spelled with **oo**, **ou**, or **u**.)

In the Word Shape Boxes, fill in the boxes containing the letter or letters that spell the sound of **/ù/** or **/yù/** in each word.

Take a minute to memorize...

Luke 12:15

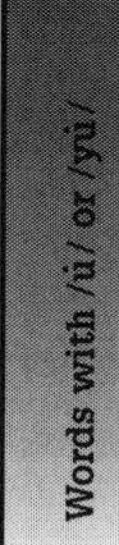

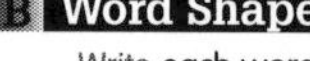

B Word Shapes Name ____________________

Write each word in the correct Word Shape Boxes. Next, in the Word Shape Boxes, shade in the boxes containing the letter or letters that spell the sound of **/ù/** or **/yù/** in each word.

Word	Word Shape Boxes
1. crooked	wooden
2. footprint	curious
3. goodness	overlook
4. overlook	tourist
5. wooden	bulldozer
6. tourist	sure
7. bulldozer	pure
8. bulletin	footprint
9. fully	plural
10. handful	fully
11. cure	handful
12. curious	goodness
13. during	cure
14. furious	crooked
15. plural	during
16. pure	bulletin
17. sure	butcher
18. butcher	furious

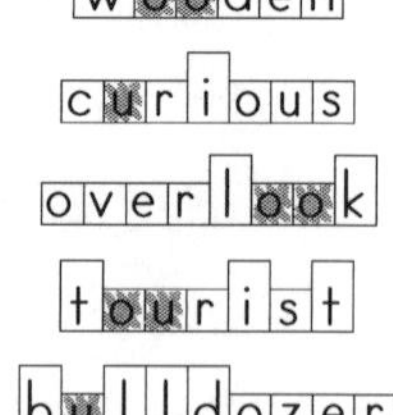

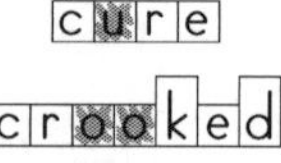

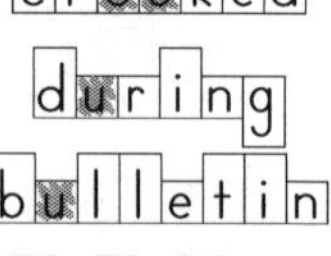

126

Answers may vary for duplicate word shapes.

Be Prepared For Fun

Check these supply lists for **Fun Ways to Spell** - presented **Day 2**. Purchase and/or gather these items ahead of time!

General
- Pencil
- Notebook Paper
- Spelling List

Auditory

- Spelling List

Visual
- Pencil
- Paper
- Spelling List

Tactile
- Thick Pile Carpet Samples
- Spelling List

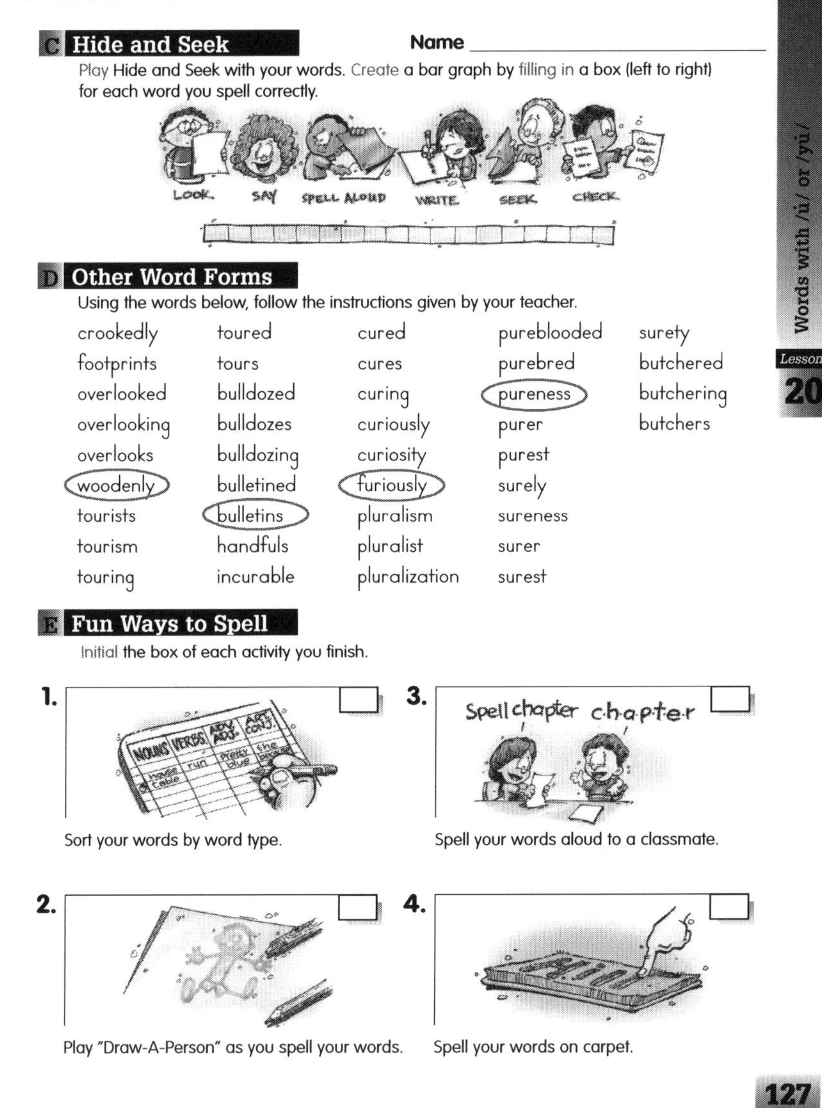

C Hide and Seek Name ____________________

Play Hide and Seek with your words. Create a bar graph by filling in a box (left to right) for each word you spell correctly.

D Other Word Forms

Using the words below, follow the instructions given by your teacher.

crookedly	toured	cured	pureblooded	surety
footprints	tours	cures	purebred	butchered
overlooked	bulldozed	curing	(pureness)	butchering
overlooking	bulldozes	curiously	purer	butchers
overlooks	bulldozing	curiosity	purest	
(woodenly)	bulletined	(furiously)	surely	
tourists	(bulletins)	pluralism	sureness	
tourism	handfuls	pluralist	surer	
touring	incurable	pluralization	surest	

E Fun Ways to Spell

Initial the box of each activity you finish.

1. Sort your words by word type.

2. Play "Draw-A-Person" as you spell your words.

3.

Spell your words aloud to a classmate.

4. Spell your words on carpet.

Words with /ü/ or /yü/

Lesson 20

127

1 Hide and Seek

Reinforce spelling by using multiple styles of learning.

On a white board, Teacher writes each word — one at a time. **Have students:**

- **Look** at the word.
- **Say** the word out loud.
- **Spell** the word out loud.
- **Hide** (teacher erases word.)
- **Write** the word on paper.
- **Seek** (teacher rewrites word.)
- **Check** spelling. If incorrect, rewrite word correctly.

2 Other Word Forms

This activity is optional. Have students find and circle the Other Word Forms that are synonyms of the following:

notices
stiffly
cleanness
frantically

3 Fun Ways to Spell

Four activities are provided. Use one, two, three, or all of the activities. Have students initial the box for each activity they complete.

Options:

- assign activities to students according to their learning styles
- set up the activities in learning centers for students to do throughout the day
- divide students into four groups and assign one activity per group
- do one activity per day

General

To sort your words by word type...

- Make four columns on your paper.
- Label the columns: Nouns, Verbs, Adjectives/Adverbs, and Articles/Conjunctions.
- Write each of your spelling words in the appropriate column.

Auditory

To spell your words aloud to a classmate...

- Ask a classmate to read a word from your spelling list.
- Spell the word aloud to your classmate.
- Ask your classmate to check your spelling.
- Read a word to your classmate and continue taking turns.
- The person to spell the most words right wins!

Visual

To play "Draw-A-Person" when you spell your words...

- Ask a classmate to read a word from your spelling list to you.
- Write the word on your paper. Check your spelling.
- If you misspell the word, draw one part of a person on your paper.
- Read a word to a classmate and continue taking turns.
- The last one to finish drawing a person wins!

Tactile

To spell your words on carpet...

- Use fingertip to write a spelling word on carpet.
- Check your spelling.
- Smooth the word out with your hand and write another word.

Working with Words

Familiarize students with word meaning and usage.

Sentence Fun

Using context clues in each sentence, decide which word best completes the sentence. Write the word in the blank.

Take a minute to memorize...

Luke 12:15

Words with /ü/ or /yü/ — Lesson 20

F **Working with Words** Name ______________________

Sentence Fun

Write the spelling word that best completes each sentence.

1. The rabbit tracks in the snow made a __crooked__ path.
2. Because of God's __goodness__, we have everything we need.
3. Sarah made a __footprint__ in the fresh snow.
4. Mr. and Mrs. Noma had to __overlook__ Setsuko's grumbling.
5. The Nomas liked to eat around a small, __wooden__ table.
6. Setsuko looked at pictures of places that were __tourist__ attractions.
7. She was __curious__ about other parts of the country.
8. The county soon had tractors and a __bulldozer__ cleaning the streets.
9. Sarah and Nellie were __fully__ clothed in coats, hats, and mittens.
10. The weather __bulletin__ said to expect several inches of snow.
11. Nellie tossed a __handful__ of snow at Setsuko.
12. Sarah and Setsuko had fun __during__ the power outage.
13. The happy evening seemed to __cure__ Setsuko's complaining.
14. Mr. Noma filled the lantern with __pure__ kerosene.
15. Sarah was not __sure__ when her mom would get home.
16. The wind blew around the house with a __furious__ sound.
17. To make a word __plural__, you usually add **s** or **es**.
18. Setsuko read that pioneer families had to __butcher__ their own hogs.

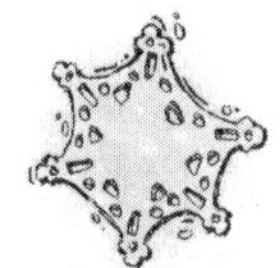

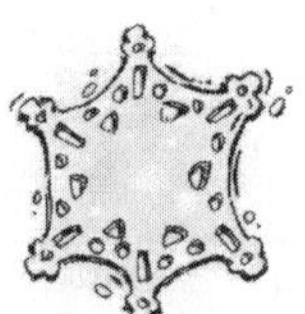

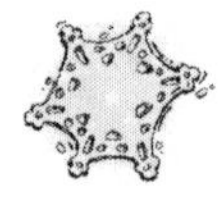

Word Bank

bulldozer	crooked	during	furious	overlook	sure
bulletin	cure	footprint	goodness	plural	tourist
butcher	curious	fully	handful	pure	wooden

128

G Dictation

Name ______________________

Write each sentence as your teacher dictates. Use correct punctuation.

1. The tourist stood at an overlook.

2. We saw the news bulletin during the storm.

3. The bulldozer plowed a crooked road.

Words with /ü/ or /yü/

Lesson 20

H Proofreading

If a word is misspelled, fill in the oval by that word. If all the words are spelled correctly, fill in the oval by **no mistake**.

1.
- ○ dessert
- ● crookid
- ○ germ
- ○ no mistake

2.
- ○ perfect
- ○ birth
- ○ footprint
- ● no mistake

3.
- ● bucher
- ○ goodness
- ○ firm
- ○ no mistake

4.
- ○ sure
- ○ sir
- ○ overlook
- ● no mistake

5.
- ○ skirt
- ● plurall
- ○ wooden
- ○ no mistake

6.
- ○ worry
- ○ turkey
- ○ tourist
- ● no mistake

7.
- ○ worst
- ○ purpose
- ○ bulldozer
- ● no mistake

8.
- ○ pure
- ○ nurse
- ● bullitin
- ○ no mistake

9.
- ○ worth
- ● fuly
- ○ burst
- ○ no mistake

10.
- ● furyious
- ○ curl
- ○ handful
- ○ no mistake

11.
- ○ furniture
- ○ further
- ○ cure
- ● no mistake

12.
- ○ during
- ● cureius
- ○ curve
- ○ no mistake

129

Dictation

Reinforce correct spelling by using current and previous words in context.

Listen as I read each sentence and then write it in your Worktext. Remember to use correct capitalization and punctuation. (Slowly read each sentence twice. Sentences are found in the Student Worktext to the left.)

2 Proofreading

Familiarize students with standardized test format and reinforce recognition of misspelled words.

Look at each set of words. If a word is misspelled, fill in the oval by that word. If all the words are spelled correctly, fill in the oval by **no mistake**.

3 Hide and Seek

Reinforce correct spelling of current spelling words. Repeat this activity from Day 2. (A reproducible master is provided in Appendix A as shown on the inset page to the right.)

4 Other Word Forms

Have your students complete this activity to strengthen spelling ability and expand vocabulary.

1 Posttest

Visit the **A Reason For** website to download free, printable Posttest pages.

I will say the word once, use it in a sentence, then say it again. Write your words on a separate sheet of paper.

Progress Chart
Students may record scores. (Appendix B)

Personal Dictionary
Students may add any words they have misspelled to their personal dictionaries. (Appendix B)

Hide and Seek

Play Hide and Seek with your words. Create a bar graph by filling in a box (left to right) for each word you spell correctly.

Other Word Forms

Code Words

Use the code to write each other word form.

0 = a 1 = e 2 = i 3 = o 4 = u 5 = r 6 = s 7 = t

1. c 4 5 2 3 6 2 7 y — curiosity
2. b 4 7 c h 1 5 2 n g — butchering
3. 3 v 1 5 l 3 3 k 1 d — overlooked
4. p l 4 5 0 l 2 6 7 — pluralist
5. 6 4 5 1 6 7 — surest
6. w 3 3 d 1 n l y — woodenly
7. f 3 3 7 p 5 2 n 7 6 — footprints
8. c 4 5 2 n g — curing
9. 7 3 4 5 2 n g — touring
10. 6 4 5 1 n 1 6 6 — sureness
11. p 4 5 1 b 5 1 d — purebred
12. c 5 3 3 k 1 d l y — crookedly
13. 7 3 4 5 2 6 m — tourism
14. b 4 l l 1 7 2 n 6 — bulletins

Other Word Forms Lesson 20

341

1. bulldozer	A **bulldozer** is parked on the empty lot at the end of their street.
2. crooked	A bead of water made a **crooked** path down the window pane.
3. tourist	Setsuko sometimes dreamed of being a **tourist** in an exotic land.
4. furious	Although she was not **furious**, she did feel aggravated and grumpy.
5. fully	Her parents did not **fully** understand why Setsuko was gloomy.
6. bulletin	The radio repeated the weather **bulletin** every few minutes.
7. footprint	Each of Sarah and Nellie's steps left a deep **footprint** in the snow.
8. wooden	Mr. Noma hung the girls' coats on the **wooden** pegs in the hall.
9. during	**During** the storm, they enjoyed the warmth of Setsuko's home.
10. handful	Setsuko dumped another **handful** of popcorn into Nellie's bowl.
11. curious	Sarah and Nellie were **curious** about Setsuko's family.
12. sure	They weren't **sure** they would be safe in their own house.
13. butcher	Electricity was out everywhere, including the pet store and **butcher** shop.
14. plural	There are no **plural** words in the Japanese language.
15. pure	It was **pure** joy to the girls to share this time with Setsuko's family.
16. goodness	Sarah and Nellie appreciated the **goodness** of the Noma family.
17. cure	Seeing their thankfulness was a good **cure** for Setsuko's ungratefulness.
18. overlook	She realized it was wrong to **overlook** God's wonderful blessings.

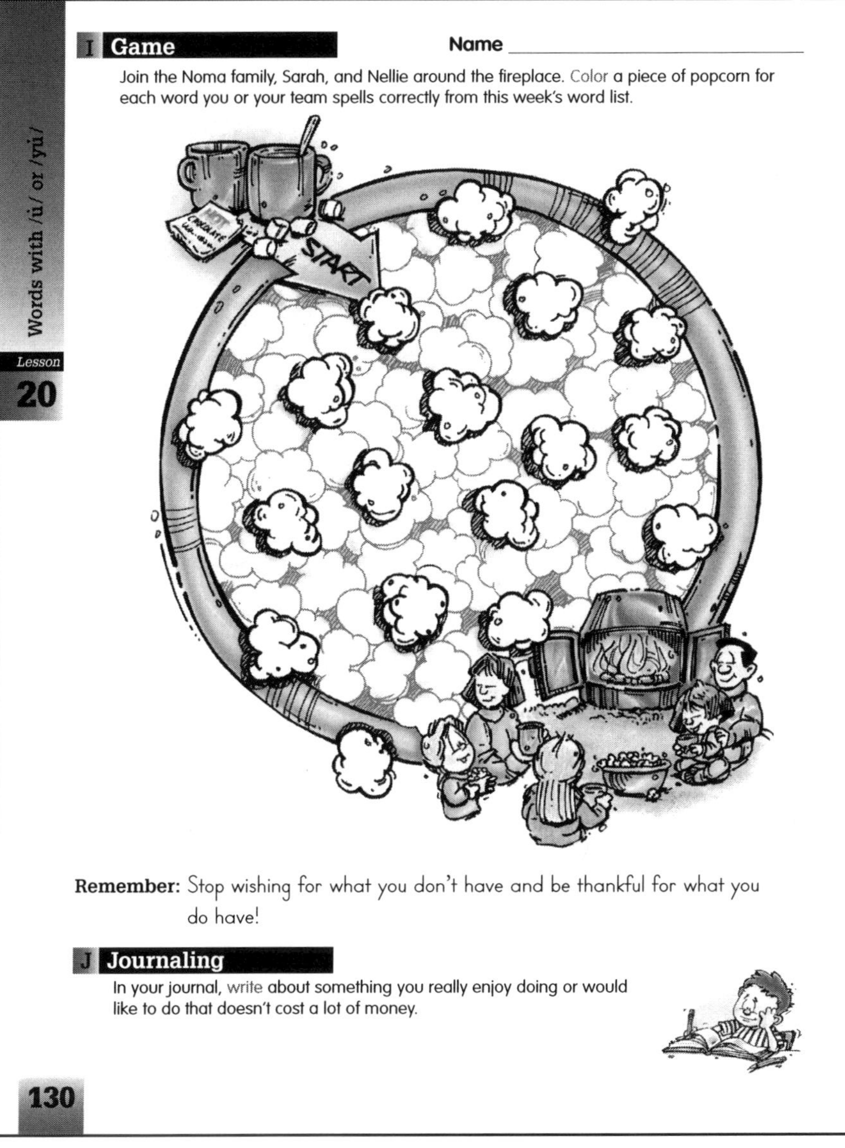

Words with /ü/ or /yü/

Lesson 20

I Game Name ______________________

Join the Noma family, Sarah, and Nellie around the fireplace. Color a piece of popcorn for each word you or your team spells correctly from this week's word list.

Remember: Stop wishing for what you don't have and be thankful for what you do have!

J Journaling

In your journal, write about something you really enjoy doing or would like to do that doesn't cost a lot of money.

130

How to Play:

- Divide students into two teams.
- Have a student from team A go to the board.
- Say the spelling word.
- Have the student write the word on the board.
- If correct, instruct each member of team A to color one piece of popcorn, beginning at Start.
- Alternate between teams A and B as you go down the word list.
- The team to reach the fireplace first is the winner.

Small Group Option: Students may play this game without teacher direction in small groups of two or more.

2 Game

Reinforce spelling skills and provide motivation and interest.

Materials

- game page (from Student Worktext)
- crayons or colored pencils (1 per child)
- game word list

Game Word List

1. **crooked**
2. **footprint**
3. **goodness**
4. **overlook**
5. **wooden**
6. **tourist**
7. **bulldozer**
8. **bulletin**
9. **fully**
10. **handful**
11. **cure**
12. **curious**
13. **during**
14. **furious**
15. **plural**
16. **pure**
17. **sure**
18. **butcher**

3 Journaling

Provide a meaningful reason for correct spelling through personal writing.

Review the story using discussion leads provided on the following page. Encourage students to apply the Scriptural value in their journaling.

Journaling (continued)

- Do you get a lot of snow each winter where you live?
- What are some things you can't do when the electricity is off?
- What things did Sarah, Nellie, and Setsuko's family do while the power was out? (Played games, told stories, popped corn over the fire, drank hot chocolate, sang silly songs, and told jokes.)
- Why didn't things seem the same to Setsuko after the electricity came back on? (She realized they had a wonderful evening right there at home. She learned that things can't make people happy. It isn't necessary to have everything, like trips to faraway places, to be happy.)
- Remember, real living doesn't have anything to do with how rich we are, but with our attitude.
- What are some things you like to do that aren't expensive? (Allow time for ideas.)

Without rearranging any letters, the word "therein" can be broken into ten different words: the, there, he, in, rein, her, here, ere, therein, herein.

Word Wow!

1 Literature Connection

Topic: Caring for Others
Theme Text: Luke 9:48

Heather's Hectic Day

Heather deals with a frightening emergency while babysitting.

Heather carefully pulled the white eyelet comforter up over her blankets. She tugged on the left side until the part hanging down was even with the other side. *Those Jensen kids better stay out of my room today,* she said to herself as she arranged her bright yellow throw pillows and finished by lining up her bean-bag animals on the bed. Finished! Heather stepped back to admire her work.

"Time for breakfast," Mom called.

"I'll be there in a second!" Heather tossed her pajamas into the dirty clothes basket. Her collection of insect identification cards was in 41 stacks on the floor where she'd been sorting them the night before. *I'm going to leave these here. I'll finish tonight,* she said to herself. Grabbing her coat off the hook beside the door, she headed toward the kitchen. Heather stopped in the hall and looked back at her room. *What have I forgotten? It seems like I need to do one more thing.*

"Heather, have you seen my rollerblades?" Collin brushed by his sister on the way back to his room.

"They were in the car the last time I saw them." Heather put her coat on the chair beside the front door. "Can I go skating with you?"

"No, it's Blake's birthday today. His mom rented the whole rink just for the seventh-grade class. Last year they say he invited everyone to Locomotion. They got to ride the bumper cars and go carts as many times as they wanted." Collin came back into the kitchen and sat down at the table.

When the Stark family had finished breakfast, Heather practiced the piano for 30 minutes. Collin searched for his blades until he finally found them in the garage where he'd left them.

Later that afternoon Tony slid to a stop beside Heather on the steps of Knowlton Elementary and said, "You're riding with us today, Cuz. Grandma Miller said she's taking you home. The Jensen kids are still asleep and your mom doesn't want to wake them all up."

Heather followed Tony to the car. "Where's Collin?"

"Grandma Miller said I didn't have to find him because he's going to Blake Edwards' birthday party." Tony opened the door of Grandma Miller's little car and jumped in.

"Oh, yeah. I forgot. Collin gets to eat cake—and I get stuck with the Jensens." Heather slammed the car door.

"Heather! That isn't the proper way to talk about the children your mother takes care of." Grandma Miller pulled out into the line of cars leaving the parking lot.

"They need to be taught some manners." Heather frowned. "They get into my stuff without asking. My bangs are just now growing back after Betsy chopped them off. Bryson used my bug collection jar and broke the lid. Brandon pulls all my books off the shelf."

Grandma Miller looked at Heather in the rearview mirror. "They're just small children...not even in school yet. How old is Brandon—four and a half? Betsy just turned three and wouldn't that make Bryson almost two?"

"Yeah, we have a box of baby toys for them in the garage. Mom said Collin and I could lock our rooms if we didn't want them to go in there." Heather snapped her fingers. "Oh! No! That's what I forgot! I didn't lock my room this morning."

Heather jumped out of the car as soon as Grandma Miller pulled up to the curb. Mom waved at Grandma from the front door. Heather pushed by her mother and rushed to her room. She groaned and then stamped her foot on the wood floor. "Mom, just look at my room. All my cards are in one big pile now. It looks like someone jumped on my bed. See the footprints?" Heather's voice got louder and louder.

Mom gently put her hand over Heather's mouth. "Don't wake them up, Heather. Let them sleep as long as they will."

"I can't believe this, Mom. Why do you have to babysit the Jensen kids?"

"It puts food on the table, Heather. It's something I can do at home to supplement the money Dad makes driving trucks. I'm sorry your room got messed up. I said you could lock it. Did you forget?"

Heather nodded and went out into the garage to get the box of toys. "Maybe these toys will distract them long enough for me to get my room back in order. Then I will lock my door," she mumbled to herself.

Heather peeked into her parents' room where the Jensen children were still sleeping. *They're cute when they're asleep,* Heather smiled to herself. Bryson had her stuffed butterfly toy hanging over the edge of his playpen. Betsy had the lady bug and caterpillar clutched tightly in her hands. Heather giggled. Brandon must have found all of Collin's stuffed animals, because he had them snaking across the big bed. He must have played with them until he fell asleep. Heather sighed and returned to straighten up her room.

"Heather, I'm going to vacuum the car while they're still sleeping." Mom stuck her head in the door and whispered. "Will you listen for them, please?"

Heather nodded and continued sorting through the big pile of insect cards on the floor. She was so absorbed in arranging the cards again she didn't hear Bryson go down the hall and into the living room.

Story (continued)

Suddenly there was a piercing scream from the front room! Heather dashed down the hall. Bryson stood by the toy box rubbing his eyes. Heather knelt down in front of the little boy and grabbed his hands. They felt greasy and smelled like gasoline. Heather knew he shouldn't be rubbing his eyes no matter what he'd gotten in them. She picked up the little boy and rushed to the kitchen sink. His screams intensified as she sprayed water into his face.

Out of the corner of her eye she caught a movement in the living room doorway. Brandon and Betsy were sleepily watching. "Go get my mom," she yelled to Betsy. "She's in the garage. Brandon, dial '911' or just give me the phone." Heather continued to spray Bryson's eyes with the black kitchen sprayer. She finally thought to add a little warm water so the water hitting his body wasn't so icy.

Mom rushed in and grabbed the baby. "What happened?" she asked Heather.

Heather handed Bryson to Mom. "I don't know. He got some gasoline-smelling stuff in his eyes." Mom took the little guy into the bathroom and ran a warm bath. She shampooed his hair with tearless baby shampoo and let the suds run down his face. His eyelids were swelling so quickly she could hardly see his eyes.

Brandon brought the cordless phone into the bathroom and gave it to Mrs. Stark. Mom explained the situation to the 911 dispatcher and asked for her advice. She suggested rinsing his eyes with sterile saline solution and putting on ice packs to decrease the swelling. Then the poison control operator suggested Benadryl to counteract the allergic reaction and told Mom to continue rinsing Bryson's eyes with the saline until paramedics arrived.

"Bring me a bag of frozen peas, Heather," Mom said as she wrapped Bryson in a towel and cradled him in her arms. Mrs. Stark grabbed a bottle of the saline solution she used with her contacts and squirted it into Bryson's eyes.

"Here, Mom." Heather handed her the bag of peas.

Mrs. Stark put the bag of cold vegetables across Bryson's face and headed to the locked medicine cabinet for the Benadryl. She squirted the proper dosage down his throat with a dropper and then collapsed on the couch, clutching the crying baby tightly.

Late that night Dad came in off the road and sat down on the edge of Heather's bed. She was still awake, staring at the ceiling. "I hear you had a rough day, girl," he said softly.

"Yeah." A tear slipped down Heather's cheek.

"Mom said that you did just the right thing or Bryson might have damaged his eyes permanently." Dad smiled in the dark.

"Yeah. I guess Collin knocked the weed-eater over on the toy box this morning when he was looking for his rollerblades. Some of the gasoline and oil mixture in it spilled onto the toys. Bryson got it on his hands and then rubbed his eyes."

"Heather, I know it's hard for you having the Jensen kids here every afternoon, but we really need the money Mom earns for babysitting. They've messed with your stuff and cut your hair. They take up a lot of Mom's time and energy."

Dad pondered the situation. "You know, Heather, the Scriptures say, 'Anyone who takes care of a little child like this is caring for Me!' It goes on to say, 'Your care for others is the measure of your greatness.' I want you to know I'm proud of you. You took good care of Bryson today. The paramedics said they couldn't have done a better job themselves."

Dad bent over and kissed the tip of Heather's nose. "I'm glad you're my daughter. You're a great kid!"

2 Discussion Time

Check understanding of the story and development of personal values.

- Raise your hand if you have ever dialed 911 in an emergency?
- What happened?
- How did Heather feel about the Jensen children?
- How did Heather feel about her mom babysitting?
- How did Heather care for Bryson in the emergency?
- How did Mr. Starks feel about how Heather handled the situation?
- Did you know your care for others is the measure of your greatness?

A Preview Name ______

Write each word as your teacher says it.

1. enjoyment
2. appointment
3. soybean
4. royalty
5. employ
6. annoy
7. choice
8. topsoil
9. avoid
10. joint
11. point
12. destroy
13. voyage
14. disappoint
15. oily
16. moist
17. rejoice
18. loyal

Get Mom! call 911!!

Scripture

Luke 9:48

Words with /oi/

Lesson 21

131

3 Preview

Test for knowledge of the correct spellings of these words.

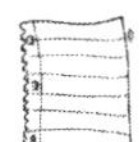

Customize Your List

On a separate sheet of paper, additional words of your choice may be tested.

I will say each word once, use the word in a sentence, then say the word again. Write the words on the lines in your Worktext.

Correct Immediately!

Let's correct our Preview. I will spell each word out loud. If you spelled a word incorrectly, rewrite it correctly.

Progress Chart

Students may record scores. (Reproducible master provided in Appendix B.)

Lesson 21 | Day 1

1. **enjoyment** — Heather finds great **enjoyment** in playing the piano.
2. **appointment** — She will make an **appointment** to get her hair trimmed.
3. **soybean** — Heather's mom made delicious **soybean** burgers.
4. **royalty** — Heather and her family do not live like **royalty**.
5. **employ** — Heather's dad is in the **employ** of a large trucking company.
6. **annoy** — The Jensen kids could really **annoy** Heather sometimes.
7. **choice** — It was her mom's **choice** to watch the Jensen kids for extra money.
8. **topsoil** — Her mom let the kids turn over the **topsoil** with big spoons.
9. **avoid** — Heather wanted to lock her room to **avoid** more messes.
10. **joint** — Collin and Heather made a **joint** effort to protect their things.
11. **point** — At one **point** Heather realized she had forgotten to lock her room.
12. **destroy** — She hoped they would not **destroy** her room today.
13. **voyage** — Heather dreams of taking a **voyage** to study exotic insects.
14. **disappoint** — It will **disappoint** Heather to find her insect indentification cards messed up.
15. **oily** — Bryson had rubbed something **oily** into his eyes.
16. **moist** — Heather patted the area around his eyes with a cold, **moist** cloth.
17. **rejoice** — The heavens **rejoice** when we do what God wants us to do.
18. **loyal** — Heather is **loyal** or faithful to what God has asked her to do.

Word Shapes

Help students form a correct image of whole words.

Look at each word and think about its shape. Now, write the word in the correct Word Shape Boxes. You may check off each word as you use it.

(In many words, the sound of **/oi/** is spelled with **oi**, or **oy**. The spelling **oy** is often used at the end of a word or syllable.)

In the Word Shape Boxes, fill in the boxes containing the letters that spell the sound of **/oi/** in each word.

Lesson 21 — Words with /oi/

B Word Shapes Name ____________________

Write each word in the correct Word Shape Boxes. Next, in the Word Shape Boxes, shade in the boxes containing the letters that spell the sound of **/oi/** in each word.

Word	Word Shape Boxes
1. appointment	moist
2. avoid	voyage
3. choice	employ
4. disappoint	rejoice
5. joint	avoid
6. moist	appointment
7. oily	joint
8. point	choice
9. rejoice	oily
10. topsoil	soybean
11. annoy	point
12. destroy	royalty
13. employ	destroy
14. enjoyment	disappoint
15. loyal	topsoil
16. royalty	enjoyment
17. soybean	loyal
18. voyage	annoy

132

Answers may vary for duplicate word shapes.

Take a minute to memorize...

Luke 9:48

Be Prepared For Fun

Check these supply lists for **Fun Ways to Spell** - presented **Day 2**. Purchase and/or gather these items ahead of time!

General
- Pencil
- Notebook Paper
- Spelling List

Auditory
- Spelling List

Visual
- Pencil
- Scissors
- 3 X 5 cards (18 per child)
- Spelling List

Tactile
- Toothpicks
- Art Paper (3 sheets per child)
- Glue
- Spelling List

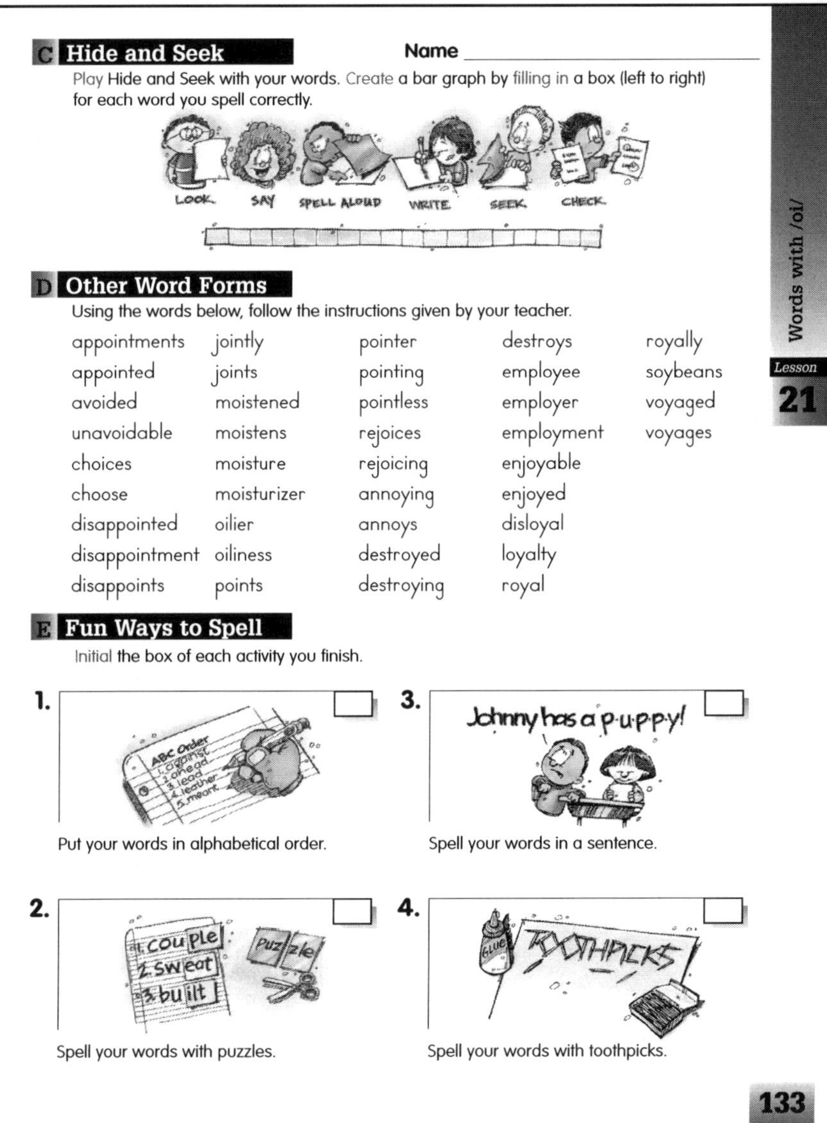

C Hide and Seek

Name ____________________

Play Hide and Seek with your words. Create a bar graph by filling in a box (left to right) for each word you spell correctly.

D Other Word Forms

Using the words below, follow the instructions given by your teacher.

appointments	jointly	pointer	destroys	royally
appointed	joints	pointing	employee	soybeans
avoided	moistened	pointless	employer	voyaged
unavoidable	moistens	rejoices	employment	voyages
choices	moisture	rejoicing	enjoyable	
choose	moisturizer	annoying	enjoyed	
disappointed	oilier	annoys	disloyal	
disappointment	oiliness	destroyed	loyalty	
disappoints	points	destroying	royal	

E Fun Ways to Spell

Initial the box of each activity you finish.

1. Put your words in alphabetical order.

3. Spell your words in a sentence.

2. Spell your words with puzzles.

4. Spell your words with toothpicks.

Words with /oi/

Lesson 21

133

1 Hide and Seek

Reinforce spelling by using multiple styles of learning.

On a white board, Teacher writes each word — one at a time. **Have students:**

- **Look** at the word.
- **Say** the word out loud.
- **Spell** the word out loud.
- **Hide** (teacher erases word.)
- **Write** the word on paper.
- **Seek** (teacher rewrites word.)
- **Check** spelling. If incorrect, rewrite word correctly.

2 Other Word Forms

This activity is optional. Have students write these Other Word Forms in alphabetical order:

pointless
points
pointing
joints

3 Fun Ways to Spell

Four activities are provided. Use one, two, three, or all of the activities. Have students initial the box for each activity they complete.

Options:

- assign activities to students according to their learning styles
- set up the activities in learning centers for students to do throughout the day
- divide students into four groups and assign one activity per group
- do one activity per day

General

To put your words in alphabetical order...
- Write all the words in alphabetical order.
- Remember to look at the second, third, or fourth letters of the words when the first letters are the same.

Auditory

To spell your words in a sentence...
- Have a classmate read a spelling word to you.
- Say a sentence with that spelling word to your classmate.
- Ask your classmate to spell the word.
- Check your classmate's spelling.
- Read a word to your classmate, continue taking turns until you have each spelled all the words.

Visual

To spell your words with puzzles...
- Write each word on a card.
- Ask a classmate to cut each word apart between two letters.
- Arrange half of each word on your desk.
- Write the missing part of the word on a piece of paper.
- Do it again with the other half of your cards.
- Check your spelling.

Tactile

To spell your words with toothpicks...
- Choose a word from your spelling list.
- Arrange toothpicks to represent each letter of the word.
- Glue them to a piece of art paper.

Lesson 21 | Day 3

1 Working with Words

Familiarize students with word meaning and usage.

Dictionary Skills

Explain that pronunciations in a dictionary tell how to pronounce a word. An accent mark (′) is a part of this guide. It tells which syllable of a word is spoken with more emphasis or stress. Write the words **beaver** and **condense** on the board. Have a volunteer mark the accented syllable.

Using the words at the top of your Worktext page, fill in the answers for numbers one and two. Then, decide which pronunciation stands for a spelling word. Write the word and circle the correct pronunciation.

Take a minute to memorize...

Luke 9:48

Words with /oi/ | Lesson 21

F Working with Words

Name ______________________

Dictionary Skills

Pronunciations in a dictionary tell how to pronounce a word. An accent mark (′) is a part of this guide. It tells which syllable of a word is spoken with more emphasis or stress.

avoid /ə void′/	loyal /loi′ əl/	annoy /ə noi′/
topsoil /top′ soil/	rejoice /ri jois′/	employ /em ploi′/

1. Write the words that have the accent on the first syllable.
   topsoil, loyal
2. Write the words that have the accent on the second syllable.
   avoid, rejoice, annoy, employ

Decide which pronunciation stands for a spelling word. Then circle the correct pronunciation and write the word on the blank.

3. (/moist/) /moirst/ moist
4. (/joint/) /joi nt′/ joint
5. /choice/ (/chois/) choice
6. /po′ int/ (/point/) point
7. /oi′ le/ (/oi′ lē/) oily
8. (/di stroi′/) /di′ stroi/ destroy
9. /soi ben′/ (/soi′ bēn/) soybean
10. /voi oj′/ (/voi′ ij/) voyage

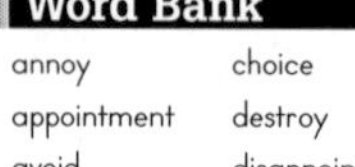

Word Bank

annoy	choice	employ	loyal	point	soybean
appointment	destroy	enjoyment	moist	rejoice	topsoil
avoid	disappoint	joint	oily	royalty	voyage

134

G Dictation

Name ______________________

Write each sentence as your teacher dictates. Use correct punctuation.

1. She employs my mom to take care of the kids.

2. The moist oily stuff got in his eyes.

3. She made the choice to help, even though the kids annoy her.

Words with /oi/

Lesson 21

H Proofreading

If a word is misspelled, fill in the oval by that word. If all the words are spelled correctly, fill in the oval by **no mistake**.

1. ○ soybean ○ crooked ○ rejoice ● no mistake
2. ○ footprint ● apointment ○ goodness ○ no mistake
3. ○ overlook ○ voyage ○ avoid ● no mistake
4. ○ wooden ○ loyal ● choise ○ no mistake
5. ○ tourist ● roylty ○ joint ○ no mistake
6. ○ butcher ○ moist ○ bulldozer ● no mistake
7. ○ bulletin ○ enjoyment ● oilly ○ no mistake
8. ○ fully ○ handful ○ point ● no mistake
9. ○ plural ○ pure ○ topsoil ● no mistake
10. ○ cure ○ sure ● disapoint ○ no mistake
11. ○ employ ● anoy ○ curious ○ no mistake
12. ○ furious ○ during ○ destroy ● no mistake

135

1 Dictation

Reinforce correct spelling by using current and previous words in context.

Listen as I read each sentence and then write it in your Worktext. Remember to use correct capitalization and punctuation. (Slowly read each sentence twice. Sentences are found in the Student Worktext to the left.)

2 Proofreading

Familiarize students with standardized test format and reinforce recognition of misspelled words.

Look at each set of words. If a word is misspelled, fill in the oval by that word. If all the words are spelled correctly, fill in the oval by **no mistake**.

Lesson 21 | Day 4

3 Hide and Seek

Reinforce correct spelling of current spelling words. Repeat this activity from Day 2. (A reproducible master is provided in Appendix A as shown on the inset page to the right.)

4 Other Word Forms

Have your students complete this activity to strengthen spelling ability and expand vocabulary.

1 Posttest

Visit the **A Reason For** website to download free, printable Posttest pages.

I will say the word once, use it in a sentence, then say it again. Write your words on a separate sheet of paper.

Progress Chart

Students may record scores. (Appendix B)

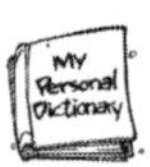

Personal Dictionary

Students may add any words they have misspelled to their personal dictionaries. (Appendix B)

Lesson 21 — Other Word Forms

Hide and Seek

Play Hide and Seek with your words. Create a bar graph by filling in a box (left to right) for each word you spell correctly.

Other Word Forms

Prefixes and Suffixes

Circle the correct prefix or suffix to make a new word, then write the word correctly on the line. Remember, sometimes base words change when adding a suffix.

1. choice + (est, ness) = choicest
2. joint + (ly, er) = jointly
3. moist + (ed, en) = moisten
4. point + (er, ment) = pointer
5. royal + (en, ist) = royalist
6. (dis, il) + loyal = disloyal
7. enjoy + (er, able) = enjoyable
8. destroy + (ed, ty) = destroyed
9. appoint + (ed, er) = appointed
10. (mis, dis) + jointed = disjointed
11. disappoint + (ly, ment) = disappointment
12. loyal + (ty, ed) = loyalty
13. oily + (ness, mess) = oiliness
14. rejoice + (ship, ing) = rejoicing
15. soybean + (ed, s) = soybeans
16. voyage + (er, ly) = voyager
17. employ + (ment, ance) = employment
18. avoid + (er, ance) = avoidance
19. annoy + (able, ing) = annoying
20. (un, dis) + employment = unemployment

342

1.	appointment	Heather has an **appointment** for a hair trim on Wednesday.
2.	royalty	She and her family live simply, not like **royalty.**
3.	soybean	Her favorite meal is **soybean** burgers with gravy and mashed potatoes.
4.	employ	The trucking company was glad to **employ** Heather's dad.
5.	enjoyment	Heather plays the piano for the **enjoyment** of the whole family.
6.	topsoil	The Jensen kids like to play in the **topsoil** with cups and spoons.
7.	joint	Collin and Heather made a **joint** effort to child-proof their things.
8.	avoid	To **avoid** future problems, their mom said they could lock their rooms.
9.	destroy	Heather did not want them to **destroy** her insect card collection.
10.	voyage	She studies exotic species and hopes to one day take a **voyage** to see their habitat.
11.	rejoice	Heather did not **rejoice** when she remembered her unlocked room.
12.	annoy	Bryson and Betsy did not really mean to **annoy** Heather.
13.	point	Their presence was still sometimes a sore **point** with her.
14.	disappoint	She did not want to **disappoint** her mother by having a bad attitude.
15.	oily	The **oily** fuel made Bryson's eyes burn and swell.
16.	moist	Heather held the **moist**, cold cloth over his eyes.
17.	choice	Heather's **choice** to lovingly help Bryson pleased God.
18.	loyal	Heather wants to be **loyal** to the things God has called her to do.

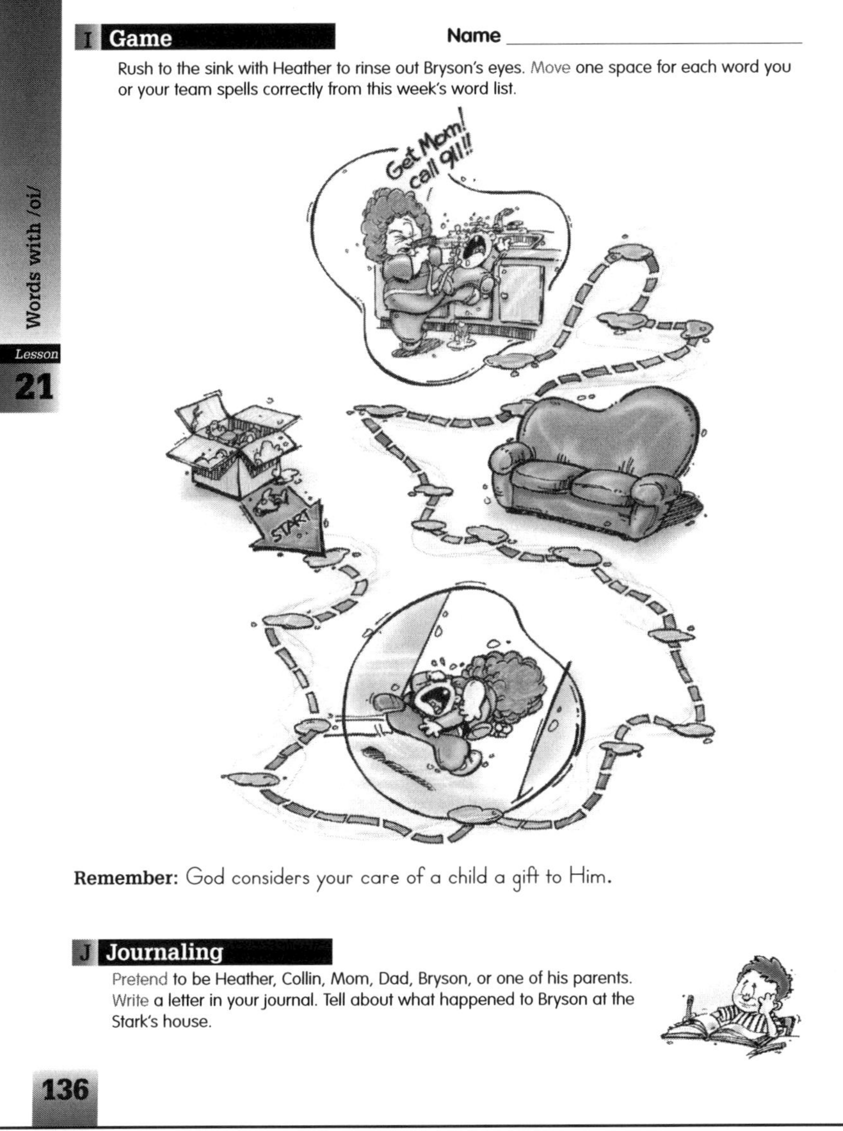

I Game
Name
Rush to the sink with Heather to rinse out Bryson's eyes. Move one space for each word you or your team spells correctly from this week's word list.
Get Mom! call 911!!
START
Remember: God considers your care of a child a gift to Him.
J Journaling
Pretend to be Heather, Collin, Mom, Dad, Bryson, or one of his parents. Write a letter in your journal. Tell about what happened to Bryson at the Stark's house.
Words with /oi/
Lesson 21
136

How to Play:

- Divide students into two teams.
- Have each student place his/her game piece on Start.
- Have a student from team A go to the board.
- Say the spelling word.
- Have the student write the word on the board.
- If correct, instruct each member of team A to move his/her game piece forward one space.
- Alternate between teams A and B as you go down the word list.
- The team to reach the kitchen sink first is the winner.

Small Group Option: Students may play this game without teacher direction in small groups of two or more.

2 Game

Reinforce spelling skills and provide motivation and interest.

Materials

- game page (from Student Worktext)
- game pieces (1 per child)
- game word list

Game Word List

1. **appointment**
2. **avoid**
3. **choice**
4. **disappoint**
5. **joint**
6. **moist**
7. **oily**
8. **point**
9. **rejoice**
10. **topsoil**
11. **annoy**
12. **destroy**
13. **employ**
14. **enjoyment**
15. **loyal**
16. **royalty**
17. **soybean**
18. **voyage**

3 Journaling

Provide a meaningful reason for correct spelling through personal writing.

Review the story using discussion leads provided on the following page. Encourage students to apply the Scriptural value in their journaling.

Journaling (continued)

- What is the Scripture this week? ("Luke 9:48")
- Why did Mrs. Stark ask Heather to watch the Jensen children? (She was going to be in the garage vacuuming the car.)
- How does Heather feel about the Jensen children? (She wishes her mom did not have to babysit them.)
- How did Heather handle the emergency? (She figured out what the problem was and immediately rinsed Bryson's eyes. She asked Betsy to call Mom. She told Brandon to dial 911. She got the peas out of the freezer for her mom.)
- How did the paramedics think Heather handled the emergency? (They said they couldn't have done a better job themselves.)
- Why did Heather's dad say she was a great kid? (Heather took good care of Bryson even though she really didn't like having him around.)

The word "robot" was created by Karel Capek. It came from Czech/Slovak "robota," which means "forced labor."

Word Wow!

1 Literature Connection
Topic: Witnessing
Theme Text: Mark 9:50

Sharin' the Salt

Daniel shares God's love with a troublesome child.

"G-o-o-d space." Daniel leaned over the desk in his bedroom and wrote the letters carefully as he said them aloud. "S-a-l-t space i-s space w-o-r. Uh, oh." He flipped the pencil over to erase the last couple of letters. "That won't work. That 'o' looked like an 'a.' Gotta make sure the line from the top of the 'o' doesn't go down too far. There."

Daniel finished the word and read what he'd written out loud. "'Good salt is worthless.' I wonder what that's supposed to mean?" He leaned back in his chair. A neighbor's dog barked. The grandfather clock chimed four times and the doorbell rang. Probably someone to see his mother. Daniel picked up his pencil and continued the handwriting practice page.

"Daniel!" Milli, the DeVores' maid, stood in the doorway.

"Milli, what does this mean?" Daniel held up the paper he was writing on. "'Good salt is worthless if it loses its saltiness; it can't season anything. So don't lose your flavor! Live in peace with each other.'" He waved the practice paper. "That last part makes sense—to live in peace with each other. But what's that part about salt talking about?"

"Well, now, I be a-thinkin' a smart lad like yourself can be a-figurin' on that and a-comin' up with some answers of your own. Least ways right now you need to be a-comin' downstairs." She motioned with one hand. "C'mon, lad. Somethin's arrived for you."

"What is it, Milli?" Daniel followed her down the curving staircase.

"They'll be a-bringin' it in. Soon enough you'll be a-seein' with your own eyes." Millicent Dunlap opened the double front doors for two men carrying a long cardboard box. "Mr. DeVore said to put it upstairs in the lad's room. Right this way, please."

Daniel followed at a safe distance. When the men went back downstairs Daniel peeked into one end of the box. Whatever it was, it was made of smooth, finished wood. "Tell me what it is, Milli." Daniel tried to open a flap on the box.

"You'll soon be a-seein' for yourself." Milli looked at the box and then around Daniel's room. "Help me move this chair so there'll be room along this wall for it."

The men carried in boxes of assorted sizes and shapes. It wasn't until they brought in another long box about the same size as the first that Daniel figured out what it was. There, big letters across the side of the box said, "100-gallon aquarium." The men placed the wooden base against the wall with the glass aquarium sitting on it. As they opened all the other boxes and set things up, they started explaining how everything worked.

"Now this is crushed coral," the tall man said as he arranged the stuff in the bottom of the dry tank. "Although other things—such as silica sand, river gravel or live rock—can be used for the substrate, most saltwater aquarium owners choose the crushed coral."

"Uh, all right." Daniel looked to Milli for help. Milli just shrugged and grinned.

"The filtration system is a trickle filter with bioballs. The trickle filter is an acrylic water reservoir with a series of bioballs, and a fiberfloss filter," the other man explained as he installed the filter in the aquarium. The men talked for several minutes about heaters, light sources, test kits and gravel vacuums. Daniel didn't understand any of it.

"Now, since this is a saltwater aquarium, it is very important to regulate the balance of salt in the water." The tall man held up another device. "That's what this hydrometer does by reading the specific gravity of the saltwater. By using a hydrometer, you can accurately maintain the salinity of the aquarium, which is important in a saltwater system."

"You mean I've gotta be sure the fish have the right amount of salt in their water or they'll die?" Daniel ran his hand through his hair.

"That's right." The tall man picked up another box. "Salt levels are very important. Salt's even good for freshwater fish. But it's not as hard as it sounds. We'll get everything set up for you and if you have any questions or need help, all you have to do is call us."

That night Daniel lay in his bed and watched the brightly colored fish swimming in their new tank across the room. The different colored damsels, blennies, and tangs flashed all the colors of the rainbow. Daniel liked the clown fish best.

He was almost asleep when his mother came home from a fancy dinner she'd attended. She came into his room and stood watching the fish. "Mom, when will Dad be home?" Daniel turned over on his side to see the tank better.

"Oh! I didn't know you were still awake. It's quite late, Daniel." Mrs. DeVore sank into the chair by the aquarium. She straightened the skirt of her evening dress before she answered. "I don't really know. He'll probably be gone for another week at least. But isn't it nice that he ordered this saltwater aquarium for you? It's a very valuable gift." She got up and walked over to his bed.

"Yeah. It's real nice." Daniel returned her hug, careful not to mess up her hair.

"Well, goodnight, Daniel." She patted his head and left the room.

"Yeah, it's a valuable gift." Daniel spoke to the

Story (continued)

clown fish. "But what I'd really like Dad to do is to be here sometimes. I guess his time is too valuable to give to me."

Daniel dropped tiny pieces of food into the tank and watched the fish go after them. "Whatcha doing?" Daniel jumped and almost dropped the fish food when Dalton spoke right behind him.

"Feeding these fish." He closed the cap and replaced the container of food in one of the drawers in the aquarium base. "I didn't know you were here."

"I am." Three-year-old Dalton stared wide-eyed at the bright fish. "Can I hold one?"

"No. Holding it would hurt the fish." Daniel caught Dalton's hand as the little boy started to bang his fist on the glass. "We don't tap on their tank either. They don't like it."

"What do we do with them?" Dalton's forehead wrinkled into a frown.

"See how pretty they are?" Daniel pointed at the clown fish. "We watch them."

"Why?" Dalton demanded.

"Well, because that's what fish like this are for," Daniel shrugged. "To watch."

"What's that?" Dalton jabbed a finger at a creature moving along the bottom of the tank.

"That's a shrimp. He helps keep the tank clean." Daniel captured Dalton's little hand again before he could touch the glass.

"Oh." Since he couldn't touch the aquarium, Dalton quickly lost interest in it. "Let's go play." He headed for the playroom and Daniel's trains.

"Hey, Dalton!" Daniel quickly moved in front of the little boy. "Why don't we, uh, why don't we pretend we're animals?"

Dalton stared at Daniel for a few seconds. Daniel tried to think of something else that would interest the three-year-old, other than his trains. They couldn't go outside—it was too cold.

"R-r-r-r-O-A-R!" Dalton dropped to all fours and became a lion. Daniel was a deer. The lion was hunting the deer. Daniel found out that three-year-olds have a lot of energy. Finally he convinced Dalton that even pretend deer have to rest sometimes.

"Is that fish resting, too?" Dalton sat on Daniel's stomach where he lay on the carpet.

"Huh? Which one? It's not the clown fish, is it?" Daniel struggled to move Dalton so he could get up. "Oh, it's okay!" He sank back down on the carpet. "That kind of fish likes to sit near the bottom of the tank and, um… rest."

"Were you upset he was resting?" Dalton crawled back up on Daniel's crossed legs.

"No. I was afraid one of them was sick, or something. You see, Dalton, their water has salt in it and it has to have just the right amount or they get sick."

"I like salt." Dalton smacked his lips. "'Specially on corn-on-the-cob!"

"Yeah, me, too." Daniel noticed his handwriting paper on the floor by his desk. "You know, Dalton, we're supposed to be like salt."

"What?" Dalton frowned up into Daniel's face.

"It's true." Daniel tickled Dalton's ribs. "Just like the fish need salt in their water to keep them healthy and living, this world needs people in it who love and obey God. We're supposed to make the world a better place by the way we live. You know, like salt makes corn-on-the-cob taste better. And we're supposed to let other people know about God so they can have the chance to live forever."

Dalton spotted Milli leaning against the door frame behind Daniel. "Hi, me and Daniel are salt! Are you salt, too?"

"Sure'n I hope so." Milli stepped into the room. "Your mother be a-wantin' you, young Dalton."

"Bye, Daniel." Dalton almost toppled Daniel with a giant hug before he trotted out the door.

"Well, I be a-thinkin' you figured out two things for yourself today, Lad." Milli grinned down at Daniel.

"You mean about the salt?" Daniel stood up and walked over to pick up his handwriting paper. "How we're supposed to be like salt to help make the world a better place to live by letting people know about God? But what else? You said two things."

"That and how to keep Dalton from wreckin' your room." Milli started to leave, but turned back and winked. "But perhaps 'tis one thing after all. I be a-thinkin' you've been a-sharin' a bit of the salt with young Dalton today."

2 Discussion Time

Check understanding of the story and development of personal values.

- What gift did Daniel's father have delivered for him?
- Why was it important to keep the balance of salt in the water just right?
- Which was Daniel's favorite fish?
- What did Daniel wish his father would give him?
- How did Daniel treat Dalton?
- Why did Milli say that Daniel had learned two things that day?

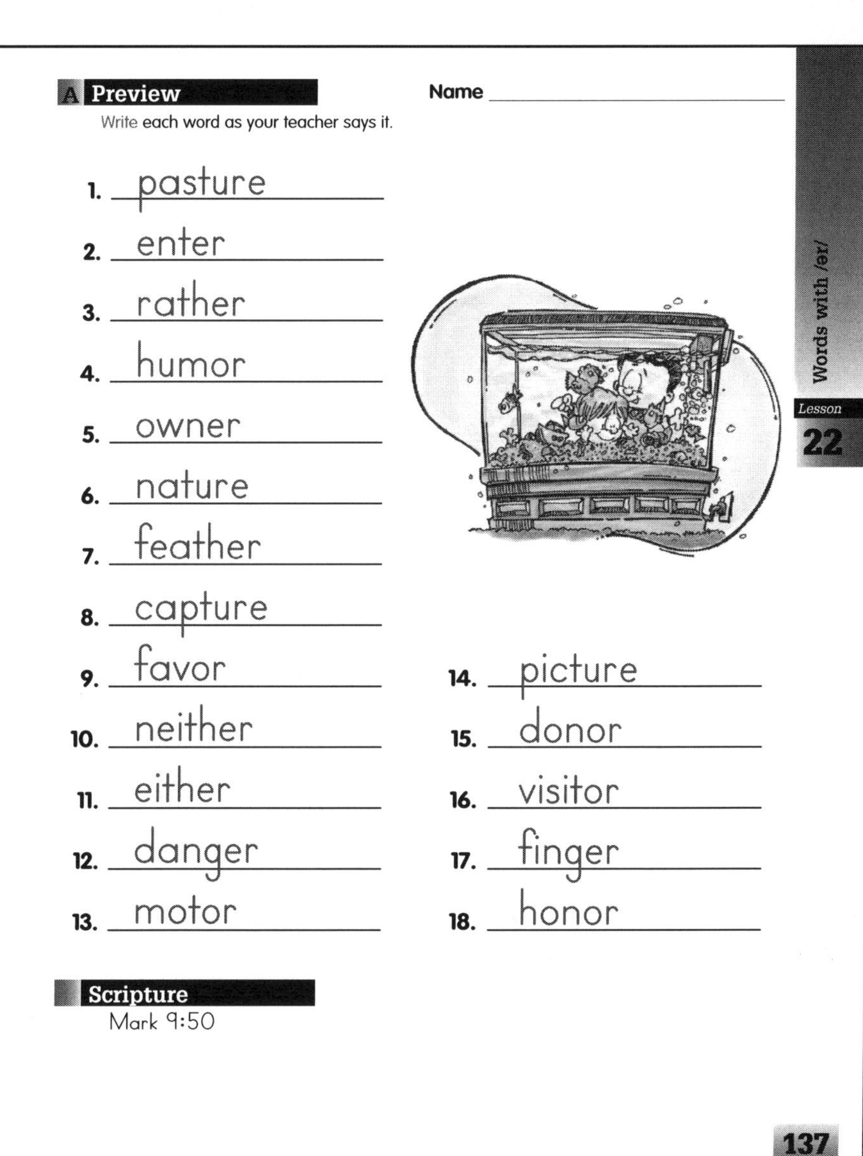

A Preview Name ______________

Write each word as your teacher says it.

1. pasture
2. enter
3. rather
4. humor
5. owner
6. nature
7. feather
8. capture
9. favor
10. neither
11. either
12. danger
13. motor
14. picture
15. donor
16. visitor
17. finger
18. honor

Scripture
Mark 9:50

Words with /ər/

Lesson 22

137

3 Preview

Test for knowledge of the correct spellings of these words.

Customize Your List
On a separate sheet of paper, additional words of your choice may be tested.

I will say each word once, use the word in a sentence, then say the word again. Write the words on the lines in your Worktext.

Correct Immediately!

Let's correct our Preview. I will spell each word out loud. If you spelled a word incorrectly, rewrite it correctly.

Progress Chart

Students may record scores. (Reproducible master provided in Appendix B.)

1. **pasture** Daniel's house is in a neighborhood, not a **pasture.**
2. **enter** The men delivering the tank could easily **enter** through the double doors.
3. **rather** He was **rather** skeptical about the contents of the large, long box.
4. **humor** Milli has a wonderful sense of **humor** and can make Daniel laugh.
5. **owner** Daniel found himself the proud new **owner** of a saltwater aquarium.
6. **nature** Saltwater fish are a beautiful part of **nature.**
7. **feather** Daniel moved his **feather** collection to make room for the supplies.
8. **capture** A special net will allow Daniel to **capture** a fish if necessary.
9. **favor** Daniel would **favor** his dad's time over expensive gifts.
10. **neither** They realized **neither** Daniel or Milli knew anything about the care of saltwater fish.
11. **either** They brought crushed coral or gravel; **either** can be used in the bottom of the tank.
12. **danger** There is a **danger** that the fish will die if the salt level is not correct.
13. **motor** A small **motor** pumps water through the trickle filter.
14. **picture** Daniel can take a **picture** of the tank and fish to show his class.
15. **donor** Dalton was not the **donor** of the fish.
16. **visitor** Milli called up the stairs to let Daniel know he had a **visitor.**
17. **finger** Daniel pulled Dalton's **finger** back from the glass.
18. **honor** We **honor** God when we show His love to others.

4 Word Shapes

Help students form a correct image of whole words.

Look at each word and think about its shape. Now, write the word in the correct Word Shape Boxes. You may check off each word as you use it.

(The sound of **/ər/** can be spelled with **er**, **or**, or **ure**. Because spellers cannot rely on a phonetic way of remembering the various spellings, this sound is often difficult.)

In the Word Shape Boxes, fill in the boxes containing the letters that spell the sound of **/ər/** in each word.

Take a minute to memorize...

Mark 9:50

B Word Shapes Name ____________

Write each word in the correct Word Shape Boxes. Next, in the Word Shape Boxes, shade in the boxes containing the letters that spell the sound of **/ər/** in each word.

Words with /ər/ — Lesson 22

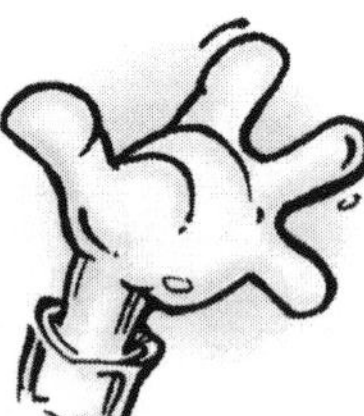

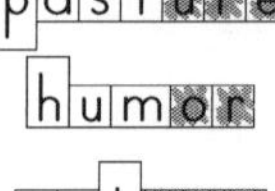

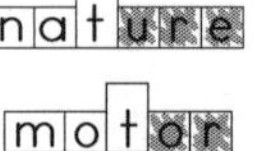

Word	Word Shape Boxes
1. danger	feather
2. donor	favor
3. either	donor
4. enter	picture
5. feather	enter
6. finger	danger
7. neither	finger
8. owner	visitor
9. rather	owner
10. favor	rather
11. honor	pasture
12. humor	humor
13. motor	nature
14. visitor	motor
15. capture	neither
16. nature	capture
17. pasture	honor
18. picture	either

138

Answers may vary for duplicate word shapes.

Be Prepared For Fun

Check these supply lists for **Fun Ways to Spell** - presented **Day 2**.
Purchase and/or gather these items ahead of time!

General
- Pencil
- Graph Paper (1 sheet per child)
- Spelling List

Auditory
- Pencil
- 3 X 5 Cards Cut in half lengthwise (18 per child)
- Spelling List

Visual
- Glitter
- Glue
- Art Paper (2 sheets per child)
- Spelling List

Tactile
- ABC Macaroni
- Art Paper (1 sheet per child)
- Glue
- Spelling List

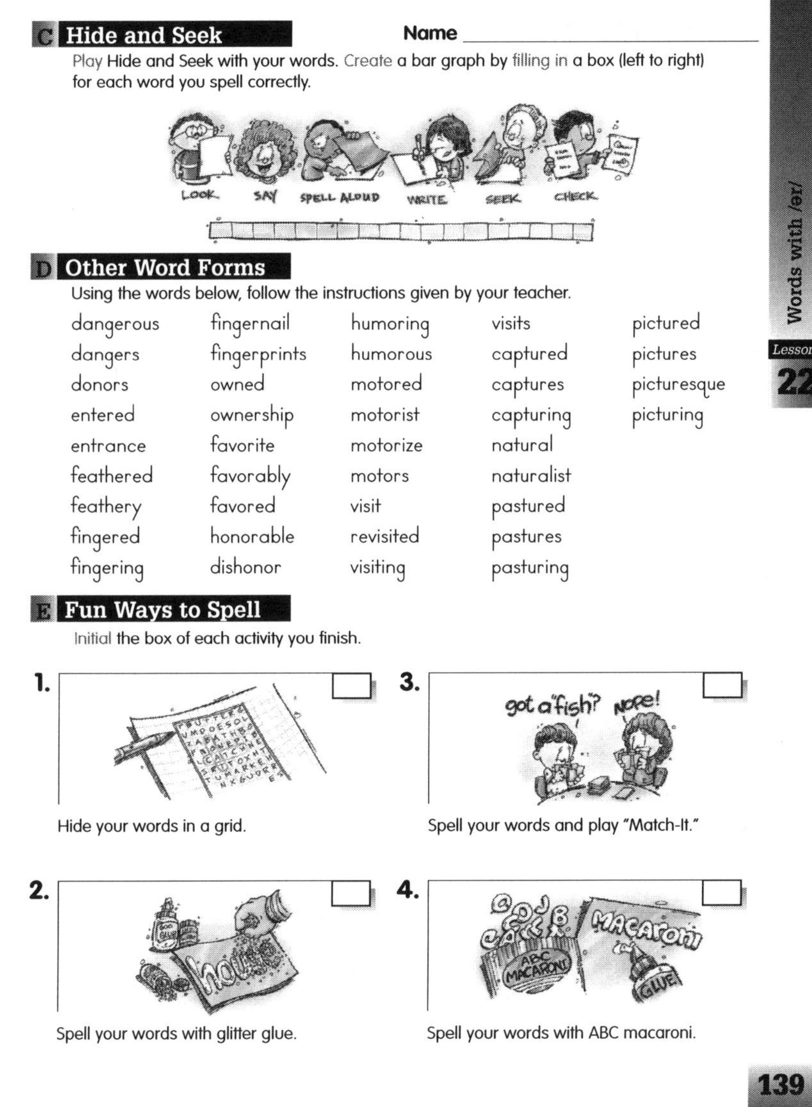

C Hide and Seek   Name ____________

Play Hide and Seek with your words. Create a bar graph by filling in a box (left to right) for each word you spell correctly.

D Other Word Forms

Using the words below, follow the instructions given by your teacher.

dangerous	fingernail	humoring	visits	pictured
dangers	fingerprints	humorous	captured	pictures
donors	owned	motored	captures	picturesque
entered	ownership	motorist	capturing	picturing
entrance	favorite	motorize	natural	
feathered	favorably	motors	naturalist	
feathery	favored	visit	pastured	
fingered	honorable	revisited	pastures	
fingering	dishonor	visiting	pasturing	

E Fun Ways to Spell

Initial the box of each activity you finish.

1. Hide your words in a grid.

3.
Spell your words and play "Match-It."

2.
Spell your words with glitter glue.

4.
Spell your words with ABC macaroni.

Words with /er/

Lesson 22

139

1 Hide and Seek

Reinforce spelling by using multiple styles of learning.

On a white board, Teacher writes each word — one at a time. **Have students:**

- **Look** at the word.
- **Say** the word out loud.
- **Spell** the word out loud.
- **Hide** (teacher erases word.)
- **Write** the word on paper.
- **Seek** (teacher rewrites word.)
- **Check** spelling. If incorrect, rewrite word correctly.

2 Other Word Forms

This activity is optional. Have students write variations of this sentence using these Other Word Forms:

The farmer found favor with the king.

favorably
favored
favorite

3 Fun Ways to Spell

Four activities are provided. Use one, two, three, or all of the activities. Have students initial the box for each activity they complete.

Options:

- assign activities to students according to their learning styles
- set up the activities in learning centers for students to do throughout the day
- divide students into four groups and assign one activity per group
- do one activity per day

General

To hide your words on a grid...
- Arrange your words on a piece of graph paper.
- Put one letter of each word in a square.
- Words may be written backwards, forwards, or diagonally.
- Outline your puzzle.
- Hide your words by filling in all the spaces inside the puzzle with random letters.
- Trade grids with a classmate and find the hidden words.

Auditory

To spell your words and play "Match-It"...

Write each spelling word on a card. Mix your word cards and a classmate's together. Deal six cards per player; put the rest face down between you. Ask classmate for a word-card that matches one in your hand. If the classmate has the word-card, take it and play again. If not, draw from the remaining stack, then it is your classmate's turn. Continue taking turns until all the cards are matched. Player with most cards wins!

Visual

To spell your words with glitter glue...
- Write each of your spelling words on your paper with glue.
- Sprinkle with glitter.

Tactile

To spell your words with ABC macaroni...
- Choose a word from your spelling list.
- Spell the word with macaroni letters.
- Glue the macaroni word to art paper.
- Do this for each word on your list.

Working with Words

Familiarize students with word meaning and usage.

Spelling Clues

Recognizing that many words are made up of common letter patterns and/or shorter words can help students spell better. Write **sentence** on the board. Have a volunteer circle the shorter word **ten**, and the common letter pattern of **en**, which is used twice. Now, write the word **consonant**. Have a volunteer circle the shorter words **on** and **ant**.

Find the spelling word or words that contain the shorter word and write it on the line.

Take a minute to memorize...

Mark 9:50

F Working with Words Name ____________

Spelling Clues

Write the correct spelling word on the line.

1. The short word **no** is found in the word honor.
2. The short word **nor** is found in the word donor.
3. The short word **eat** is found in the word feather.
4. The short word **anger** is found in the word danger.
5. The short word **hum** is found in the word humor.
6. The short word **fin** is found in the word finger.
7. The short word **on** is found in the word honor.
8. The short word **own** is found in the word owner.
9. The short word **visit** is found in the word visitor.
10. The short word **rat** is found in the word rather.
11. The short word **cap** is found in the word capture.
12. The short word **past** is found in the word pasture.
13. The short word **it** is found in the words either, neither, and visitor.
14. The short word **to** is found in the words motor and visitor.
15. The short word **the** is found in the words either, feather, neither, and rather
16. The short word **or** is found in the words favor, honor, humor, motor, and visitor.
17. Write the words which have the sound of /ch/.
    capture nature pasture picture

Word Bank

capture	either	feather	humor	neither	picture
danger	enter	finger	motor	owner	rather
donor	favor	honor	nature	pasture	visitor

G Dictation

Name ______________________

Write each sentence as your teacher dictates. Use correct punctuation.

1. We set things up and tested the motor.
2. There is a large nature picture in my room.
3. He is learning to honor God, rather than being unkind.

Words with /ər/

Lesson 22

H Proofreading

If a word is misspelled, fill in the oval by that word. If all the words are spelled correctly, fill in the oval by **no mistake**.

1. ○ appointment ○ avoid ○ danger ● no mistake
2. ○ choice ○ disappoint ○ donor ● no mistake
3. ● eather ○ capture ○ joint ○ no mistake
4. ○ enter ○ moist ○ oily ● no mistake
5. ● fether ○ point ○ rejoice ○ no mistake
6. ○ topsoil ○ annoy ○ finger ● no mistake
7. ● niether ○ destroy ○ employ ○ no mistake
8. ● pichter ○ enjoyment ○ loyal ○ no mistake
9. ○ owner ● vizitor ○ rather ○ no mistake
10. ○ royalty ○ pasture ● faver ○ no mistake
11. ● moter ○ soybean ○ honor ○ no mistake
12. ○ voyage ○ nature ● humer ○ no mistake

141

Dictation

Reinforce correct spelling by using current and previous words in context.

Listen as I read each sentence and then write it in your Worktext. Remember to use correct capitalization and punctuation. (Slowly read each sentence twice. Sentences are found in the Student Worktext to the left.)

2 Proofreading

Familiarize students with standardized test format and reinforce recognition of misspelled words.

Look at each set of words. If a word is misspelled, fill in the oval by that word. If all the words are spelled correctly, fill in the oval by **no mistake**.

Lesson 22 | Day 4

3 Hide and Seek

Reinforce correct spelling of current spelling words. Repeat this activity from Day 2. (A reproducible master is provided in Appendix A as shown on the inset page to the right.)

4 Other Word Forms

Have your students complete this activity to strengthen spelling ability and expand vocabulary.

1 Posttest

Visit the **A Reason For** website to download free, printable Posttest pages.

I will say the word once, use it in a sentence, then say it again. Write your words on a separate sheet of paper.

Progress Chart

Students may record scores. (Appendix B)

Personal Dictionary

Students may add any words they have misspelled to their personal dictionaries. (Appendix B)

Hide and Seek

Play Hide and Seek with your words. Create a bar graph by filling in a box (left to right) for each word you spell correctly.

Other Word Forms

Sentence Fun

Circle the word that correctly completes each sentence.

1. Dalton got (fingering, fingerprints) on the glass aquarium.
2. Daniel thought (owning, owned) the aquarium was exciting.
3. The clown fish was his (favorite, favoring).
4. That book I'm reading is (humored, humorous).
5. The (motored, motorist) drove carefully on the slick streets.
6. Mr. and Mrs. DeVore are (donor, donors) to many charities.
7. Mrs. Fitzsimmons is (visiting, visited) again.
8. The long box (captured, capturing) Daniel's attention.
9. All set up, the aquarium looked very (nature, natural).
10. These (pictured, pictures) are from our vacation.
11. The bridge is (dangerous, endangered) when it snows.
12. Milli stood in the (entering, entrance) of the playroom.
13. The (feathery, feathering) snowflakes floated softly down.
14. Mrs. DeVore was (honors, honored) at a special dinner.
15. Our neighbor (pasturing, pastures) his horses at a nearby farm.
16. The aquarium looked (picturesque, picturing) when it was set up.
17. Many kinds of animals are on the (dangers, endangered) species list.

Other Word Forms | Lesson 22

343

1. enter	Milli opened the double doors wide so the men could **enter** easily.
2. owner	Daniel was amazed to find himself the **owner** of a saltwater aquarium.
3. capture	One man gave Daniel a special net to **capture** the fish if need be.
4. danger	The lives of the fish are in **danger** if the salt level is too high or low.
5. either	Daniel was encouraged to ask **either** of the men any questions he had.
6. pasture	Saltwater fish could never survive in a **pasture**.
7. neither	It is sad that **neither** of Daniel's parents spend much time with him.
8. humor	Daniel enjoys Milli's kindness and her sense of **humor**.
9. rather	He would **rather** his parents gave him their time instead of presents.
10. donor	Mrs. DeVore is a generous **donor** to charitable causes.
11. nature	Clown fish add a lovely splash of color to saltwater **nature**.
12. visitor	Dalton was Daniel's **visitor** later that evening.
13. feather	He liked Daniel's **feather** collection and his new fish tank.
14. finger	"Don't touch the glass with your **finger**," Daniel instructed.
15. favor	Daniel finds **favor** with God each time he obeys Him.
16. motor	The hum of the small filter **motor** lulled Daniel to sleep.
17. honor	Daniel is learning to **honor** God with his actions and attitudes.
18. picture	He will take a **picture** of the tank to show Mrs. Burton.

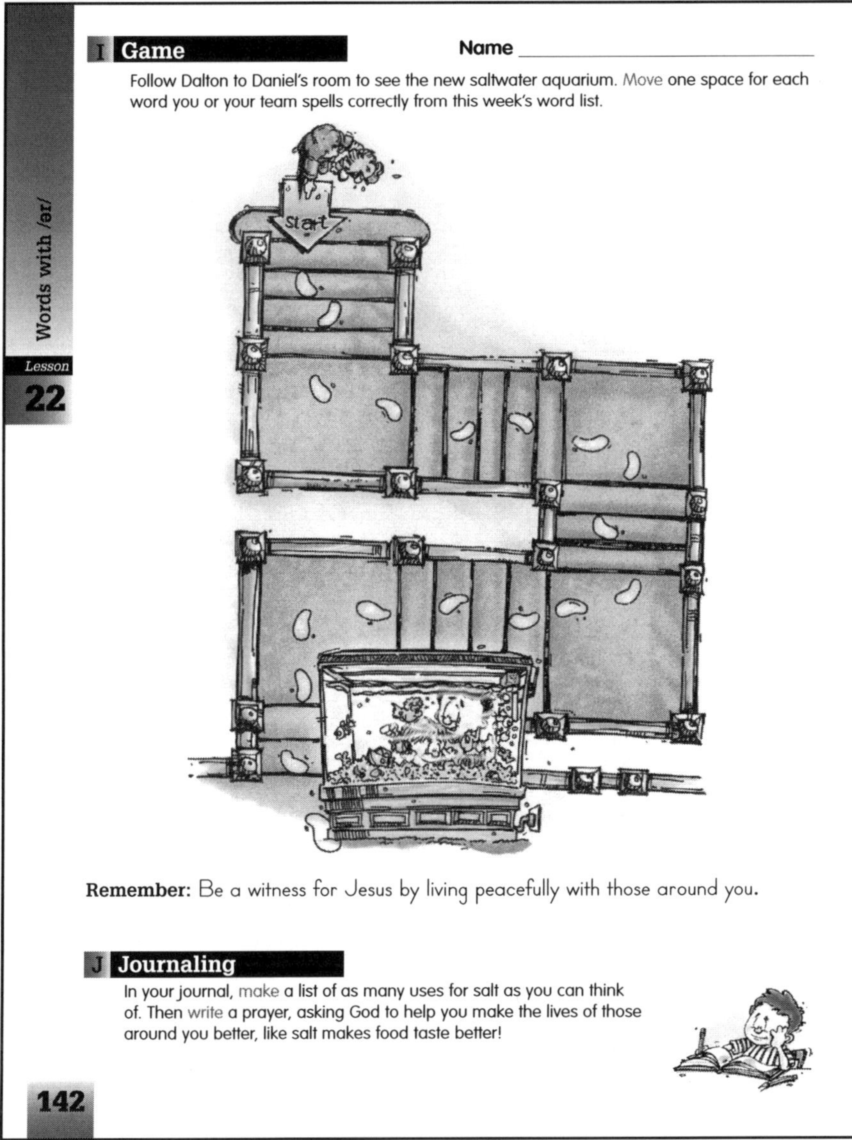

Words with /ər/

Lesson 22

I Game Name ____________________

Follow Dalton to Daniel's room to see the new saltwater aquarium. Move one space for each word you or your team spells correctly from this week's word list.

Remember: Be a witness for Jesus by living peacefully with those around you.

J Journaling

In your journal, make a list of as many uses for salt as you can think of. Then write a prayer, asking God to help you make the lives of those around you better, like salt makes food taste better!

142

How to Play:

- Divide students into two teams.
- Have each student place his/her game piece on Start.
- Have a student from team A go to the board.
- Say the spelling word.
- Have the student write the word on the board.
- If correct, instruct each member of team A to move his/her game piece forward one space.
- Alternate between teams A and B as you go down the word list.
- The team to reach the aquarium first is the winner.

Small Group Option: Students may play this game without teacher direction in small groups of two or more.

2 Game

Reinforce spelling skills and provide motivation and interest.

Materials

- game page (from Student Worktext)
- game pieces (1 per child)
- game word list

Game Word List

1. **danger**
2. **donor**
3. **either**
4. **enter**
5. **feather**
6. **finger**
7. **neither**
8. **owner**
9. **rather**
10. **favor**
11. **honor**
12. **humor**
13. **motor**
14. **visitor**
15. **capture**
16. **nature**
17. **pasture**
18. **picture**

3 Journaling

Provide a meaningful reason for correct spelling through personal writing.

Review the story using discussion leads provided on the following page. Encourage students to apply the Scriptural value in their journaling.

Journaling (continued)

- Have you ever had a fish tank? (Allow time for students to share experiences.)
- How is a salt-water tank different from a fresh-water tank? (It's for ocean fish and creatures. They have to have a certain amount of salt in their water to stay alive.)
- What did Daniel do to keep Dalton from tearing up his trains again? (He played with him. They played like they were wild animals. They talked about the fish.)
- How did Daniel explain to Dalton that we should be like salt? (That just like the fish need salt in their water to keep them healthy and living, this world needs people in it who love and obey God. We're supposed to make the world a better place by the way we live, like salt makes corn-on-the-cob taste better. We're supposed to let other people know about God so they can have the chance to live forever with Him in heaven.)

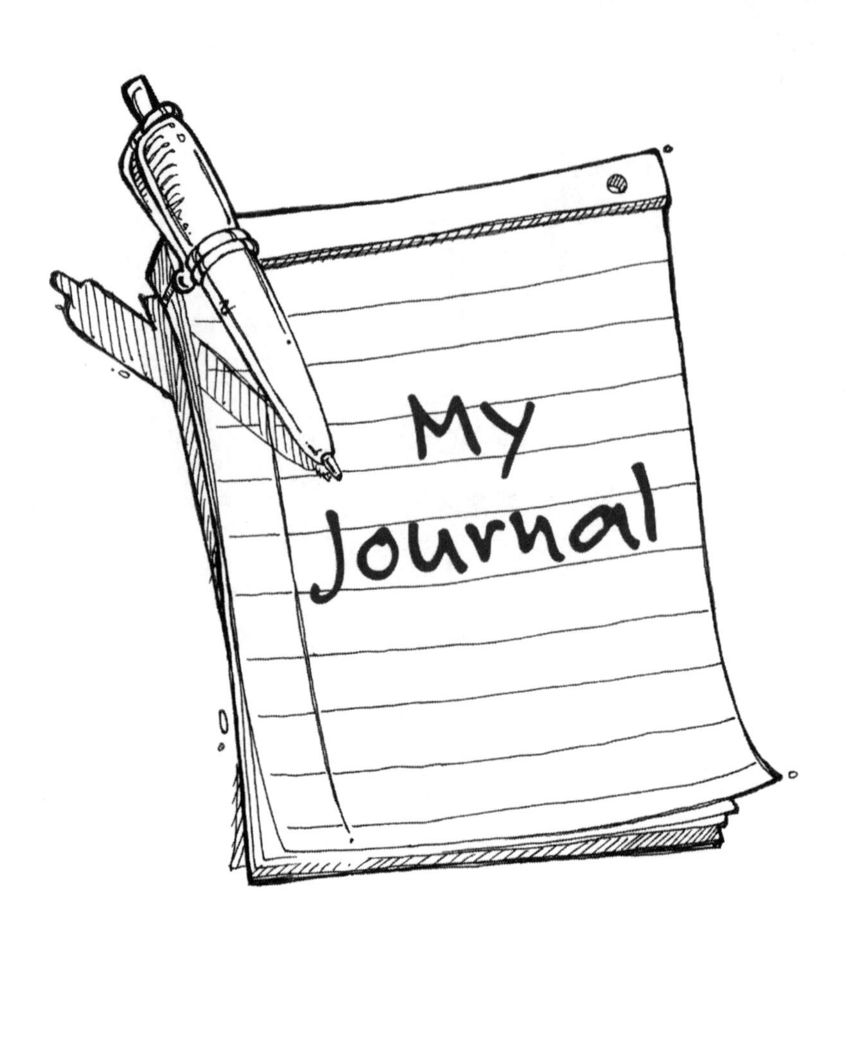

A rebus is a word or a phrase represented by pictures, letters, numbers or other words or phrases.

For example, *the address:*

Wood
John
Mass.

could mean: *John Underwood, Andover, Mass.*

Word Wow!

1 **Literature Connection**
Topic: Loving the Unlovely
Theme Text: Luke 6:38

Neighborly Nuisance

The Wrights interact with their obnoxious new neighbors.

"Hey, Kristin, look! There's a moving truck at the house next door."

"I wonder who bought it." Kristin peered out the window. "That house has been empty ever since the Petersons moved last fall. Did you see who's moving in?"

"No." Cathy wiped the condensation off the glass. "Just movers carrying in furniture and boxes. It's probably too cold for the family to be out there. Or maybe they haven't gotten here yet. Think they'll have girls our ages?"

The Wrights discussed their unknown new neighbors at the dinner table. "I'll bake some bread for them tomorrow morning to welcome them to our neighborhood," Mom said.

"As soon as they show up, I'll go over and see if they need help moving furniture around or unpacking." Mr. Wright shook parmesan cheese over his spaghetti.

"I remember how the Petersons helped us keep Treasure a secret till Mom's birthday." Cathy laughed when the canary chose that instant to start singing. "He knows I'm talking about him."

"It will be nice to have next-door neighbors again." Mom handed Cory another napkin to clean up the spaghetti sauce dribbling down his chin. Suddenly the door bell rang, followed by loud knocks on the front door.

"Who could that be?" Dad pushed his chair back and got up. "I'll see who's there."

"Hello, hello, hello!" A big voice boomed when Dad opened the front door. "We're your new neighbors!" Mrs. Wright and the children couldn't hear what Dad said, but suddenly the new neighbors were in the kitchen.

"Hello, hello, hello!" The man repeated as if he were talking to someone across the street. "We're the Pruitts. I'm Jimmy Joe, and this here's the wife, Bessie Mae." The small woman nodded her head up and down, setting her frizzy curls bouncing. "And these are the young'uns —Billy Ray, Jessie Lynn, and the baby's Sally Ann."

"We're pleased to meet you." Mrs. Wright stood and shook hands. Billy Ray was about five, Jessie Lynn probably three and the baby had just learned to walk. They stood around the table for several minutes and talked without saying a word about interrupting the Wrights' meal. Jessie Lynn grabbed a piece of garlic bread from the basket and started eating it. "Would you care to join us for dinner?" Mrs. Wright finally asked.

"Don't mind if we do!" Mr. Pruitt announced so loudly Kristin was sure the Jeffersons could hear clear across the street. Mom and Dad worked together fixing more spaghetti and salad while the Pruitts sat down at the table and ate. And ate.

They didn't seem to notice when Billy Ray left the room. They didn't pay any attention when Jessie Lynn stuffed spaghetti into her mouth with her hands. They acted like they didn't see her run both spaghetti-sauce-covered hands along the wall behind her. Sally Ann sat in the hallway and turned over her baby bottle of grape juice. It made a purple spot on the cream-colored carpet. She giggled and began making a circle of grape juice spots in the carpet around her. The Pruitts paid no attention whatsoever.

"So, have you lived in this area before or did you move here when you bought the house?" Mrs. Wright asked as she walked over to Sally Ann and traded the grape juice bottle for an old one of Cory's that she'd filled with water. Sally Ann bellowed when the bottle wouldn't make spots on the carpet, but the Pruitts ignored that, too.

"Oh, we didn't buy the house! We're just renting it until it sells. You know, you can get cheap rent that way, if you're willing to move out whenever a place sells. We've lived here for four years and moved nine times!" Mr. Pruitt announced.

"What kind of work do you do?" Dad asked as he quietly took a wet rag to the wall behind Jessie Lynn. Mom went to check on Billy Ray.

"I'm a salesman for Neumann's Electronics. We've got that new 10,000-square-foot store over near the mall." Kristin noticed that Mrs. Pruitt didn't say much, but she bobbed her head in agreement with just about everything Mr. Pruitt said. "Yep! I don't mean to brag, but I'm their top salesman. Sold more in December than any other salesman in this whole region! In the last year I bet I've sold more than any two of the other guys put together," Mr. Pruitt went on.

"I'm up for Salesman of the Year for this store." Mr. Pruitt shook his head. He helped himself to another piece of garlic bread, then continued. "Guess what the award is? Huh? Huh? Something you could use from the looks of your old stereo there. It's a complete entertainment center! Everything top-of-the-line! And I'm sure to get it."

"So, are you all settled?" Mom began to clear dirty plates off the table. Kristin got up to help her.

"Just about. We've gotten so good at moving we know just what to do." Mr. Pruitt laughed loudly.

"Who's this?" Jessie Lynn held up some photos from the basket in the living room where Mom kept those she hadn't yet put in albums.

The baby grabbed for the photographs. "ME!" She

Story (continued)

got a couple and stuffed them in her mouth.

"You can't have them!" Jessie Lynn yelled. She crammed the remaining photos under her shirt. "They're mine."

"Those two," Mr. Pruitt laughed, without stopping them. He changed the subject. "Hey, you ought to come out to the store sometime. I'll give you a good deal on just about anything you need. You know, since we're neighbors and all."

Mrs. Wright retrieved what was left of the photos by trading a piece of candy for them. "Please go gather things that might get messed up and lock them in my bedroom," she whispered to Kristin. Kristin slipped out of the kitchen and Cathy followed her.

"Oh, no!" Cathy moaned when they checked the living room. Photos had been dumped on the floor, walked on and torn. Mom's big ficus tree had been de-leafed as far up as Jessie Lynn could reach, and the crystal candy dish on the coffee table was empty and broken. The girls gathered up all the breakables they could carry to their parents' room. "We'd better check our room," Cathy whispered when they carried the last load down the hall.

But their door was already locked. Mom had locked Cory's and Christopher's doors as well. "I wonder what it's like in there," Kristin groaned. "It'll probably take us all night to clean up. I wish Mom and Dad would just tell these people to go away!"

Suddenly, the girls heard a crash. "What now?" Cathy rolled her eyes. It was Treasure—or at least Treasure's cage. Billy Ray couldn't figure out how to open the cage, so he knocked the whole thing on the floor. Mom rushed to right the cage, and Kristin put the cover over it to help calm the terrified canary.

The Pruitts finally went home, and the Wright family sat around the kitchen table. "Well." Dad propped his elbows on the table and rested his chin in his hands. "Well. So those are our new neighbors. Well."

"Why didn't you just tell them to leave?" Kristin put her hand down on her chair, then jerked it back. "Ugh—spaghetti sauce! It's everywhere!"

"They were awful!" Cathy sputtered. "So much for good neighbors. I hope the Petersons' house sells tomorrow!"

"Now, children." Mom ran a hand across her eyes. "We must remember the golden rule. We give kindness and courtesy because it's the thing to do, not because people deserve it. No matter what they do we must continue to be giving and kind."

"But that Billy Ray boy pulled the wheels off my favorite car!" Cory objected.

"Your mother's right, kids. We don't have to let them ruin things, but we must be kind and giving." Dad sighed. "Maybe the house will sell soon."

The days crept past. The Pruitt kids would appear without warning, and the Wrights would scramble to keep things out of their reach. Kristin was embarrassed one day when Billy Ray announced in front of his parents that the bedroom doors were always locked when they came over.

"Mom," Kristin opened her handwriting book on the way home from school one day. "Our Scripture this week says, 'If you give, you will get! Your gift will return to you in full and overflowing measure, pressed down, shaken together to make room for more, and running over.' Does that mean since we give and give and give to the Pruitts that we'll get a lot of stuff back?"

"Not necessarily 'stuff,' Kristin. But, yes, God has promised that all our actions have consequences, either good or bad. So when we give kindness to the Pruitts, we will be rewarded. Maybe not here or now, but certainly in heaven." She turned the car onto Appleby Road, their own familiar street.

"Look! There's a moving van at the Pruitts' house!" Christopher bounced on the seat. "And the sign says SOLD!"

"But what's that big box doing on our porch?" Cathy pointed out the window.

As soon as the car was parked, the Wright kids rushed to the box. Christopher was the first to spot the envelope taped to the top. Mom opened it and read:

"Told you I'd win Salesman of the Year! We're moving on, but we want our good friends and neighbors to have this. You wouldn't happen to need a new TV, would you? Your bud, Jimmy Joe Pruitt. P.S.—I'll win another one."

2 Discussion Time

Check understanding of the story and development of personal values.

- How did the Wright family feel when they saw the moving van at the house next door?
- How did the Wright family feel after their new neighbors came over to visit the first time?
- What did Mr. and Mrs. Wright say they should do even though the Pruitts were hard to put up with?
- What gift did the Wright family get after being kind to their neighbors?
- Do we always get things in return when we give?

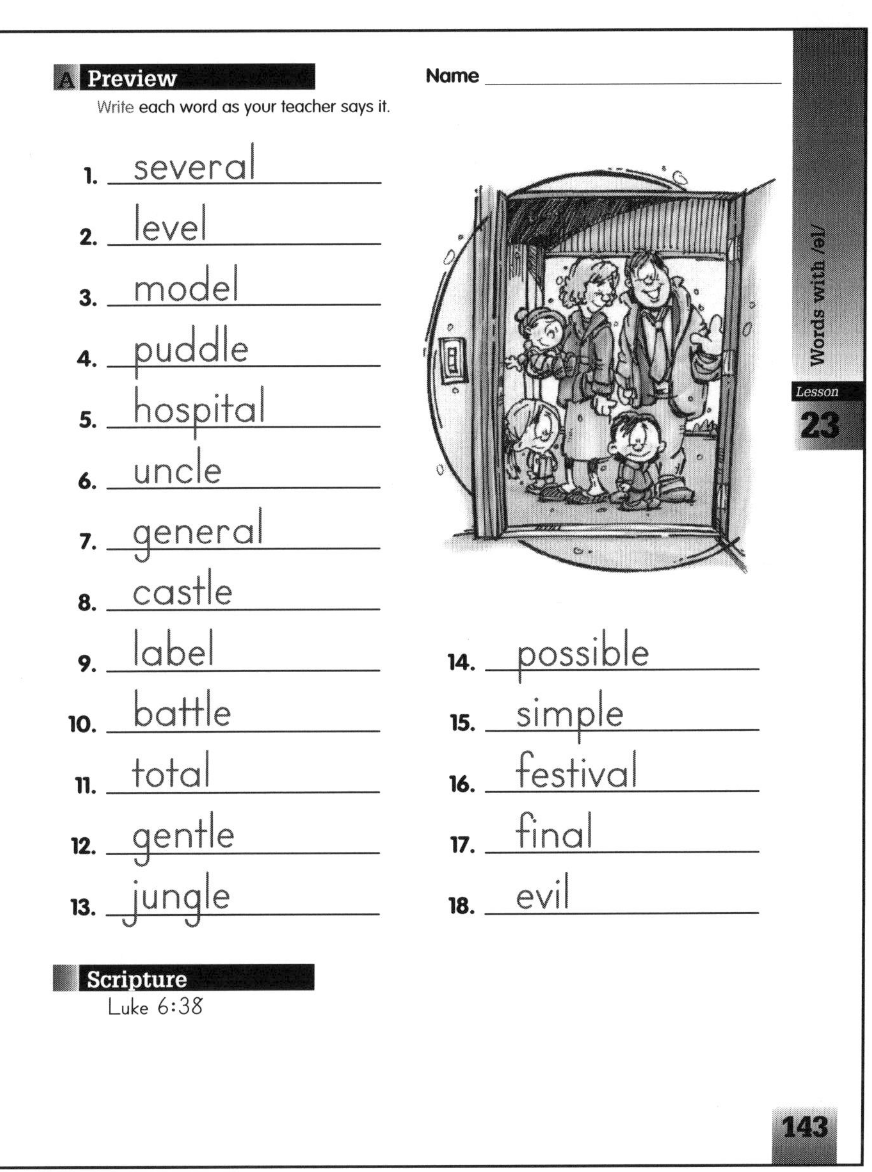

A Preview Name ______________

Write each word as your teacher says it.

1. several
2. level
3. model
4. puddle
5. hospital
6. uncle
7. general
8. castle
9. label
10. battle
11. total
12. gentle
13. jungle
14. possible
15. simple
16. festival
17. final
18. evil

Words with /əl/

Lesson 23

Scripture

Luke 6:38

143

3 Preview

Test for knowledge of the correct spellings of these words.

Customize Your List

On a separate sheet of paper, additional words of your choice may be tested.

I will say each word once, use the word in a sentence, then say the word again. Write the words on the lines in your Worktext.

Correct Immediately!

Let's correct our Preview. I will spell each word out loud. If you spelled a word incorrectly, rewrite it correctly.

Progress Chart

Students may record scores. (Reproducible master provided in Appendix B.)

1. **several** There were still **several** boxes in the moving van.
2. **level** "I've moved up to the fourth **level** in sales," he boasted.
3. **model** Mr. Pruitt won the latest **model** of television in a contest.
4. **puddle** There was a **puddle** of grape juice on the kitchen floor.
5. **hospital** The **hospital** is just down the highway from the electronic store.
6. **uncle** "You kids can just think of me as an **uncle**," said Mr. Pruitt loudly.
7. **general** Mrs. Pruitt's **general** response was to bob her head up and down.
8. **castle** Sally Ann knocked over Christopher's **castle** of blocks.
9. **label** Jessie Lynn began tearing each **label** off the canned goods.
10. **battle** It was a **battle** for Kristin not to groan out loud.
11. **total** Mr. Pruitt ate a **total** of five pieces of garlic bread.
12. **gentle** Mom's look was a firm but **gentle** reminder to be kind to the Pruitts.
13. **jungle** "It's a **jungle** out there at Neumann's Electronics!" joked Mr. Pruitt.
14. **possible** Was it **possible** for people to be so inconsiderate and not even know it?
15. **simple** The Pruitts seemed unaware of **simple** manners.
16. **festival** With all the noise from the Pruitt family it was like a rowdy **festival**.
17. **final** They were relieved when the Pruitts said their **final** good-bye for the night.
18. **evil** God does not want us to think **evil** thoughts about others.

Word Shapes

Help students form a correct image of whole words.

Look at each word and think about its shape. Now, write the word in the correct Word Shape Boxes. You may check off each word as you use it.

(In many words, the sound of **/əl/** is spelled with **le**, **al**, **el**, or **il**. Because spellers cannot rely on a phonetic way of remembering the various spellings, this sound is often difficult.)

In the Word Shape Boxes, fill in the boxes containing the letters that spell the sound of **/əl/** in each word.

B Word Shapes Name ____________________

Write each word in the correct Word Shape Boxes. Next, in the Word Shape Boxes, shade in the boxes containing the letters that spell the sound of **/əl/** in each word.

Words with /əl/ — Lesson 23

1. festival
2. final
3. general
4. hospital
5. several
6. total
7. label
8. level
9. model
10. evil
11. battle
12. castle
13. gentle
14. jungle
15. possible
16. puddle
17. simple
18. uncle

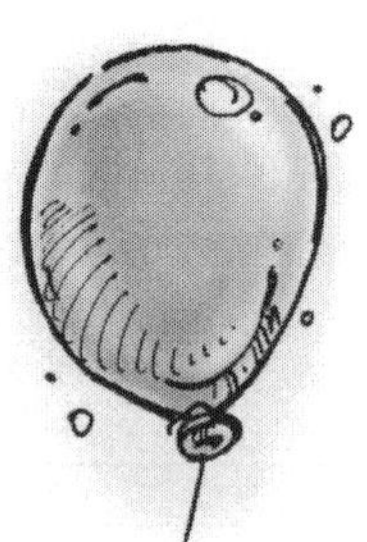

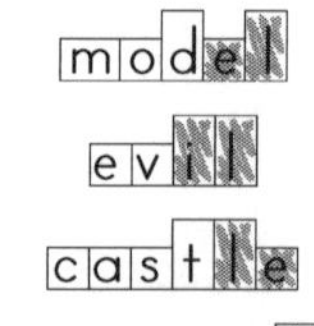

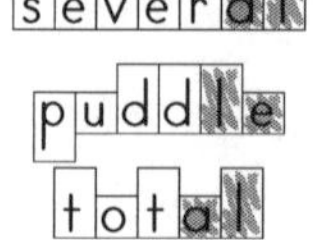

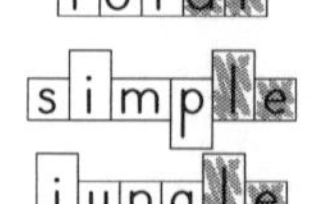

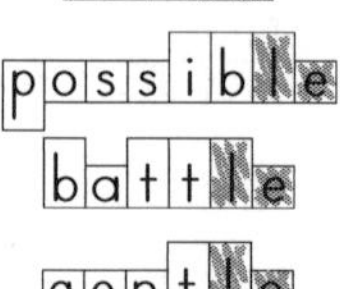

gentle

level

144

Answers may vary for duplicate word shapes.

Take a minute to memorize...

Luke 6:38

Be Prepared For Fun

Check these supply lists for **Fun Ways to Spell** - presented **Day 2**. Purchase and/or gather these items ahead of time!

General
- Pencil
- 3 X 5 Cards cut in half (18 per child)
- Spelling List

Auditory
- Pencil
- Notebook Paper
- Spelling List

Visual
- Black Construction Paper (1 sheet per child)
- Lemon Juice
- Cotton Swabs
- Spelling List

Tactile
- Pipe Cleaners (cut in an assortment of lengths)
- Spelling List

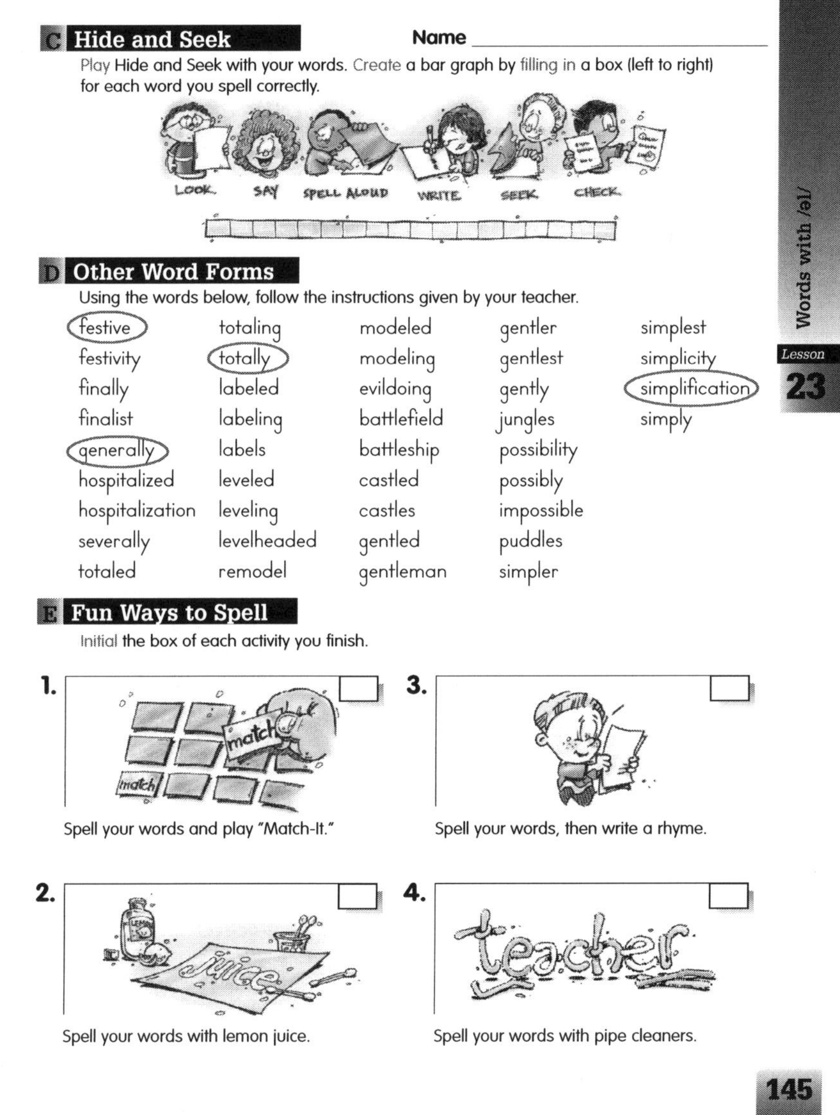

C **Hide and Seek** Name ____________

Play Hide and Seek with your words. Create a bar graph by filling in a box (left to right) for each word you spell correctly.

D **Other Word Forms**

Using the words below, follow the instructions given by your teacher.

festive	totaling	modeled	gentler	simplest
festivity	totally	modeling	gentlest	simplicity
finally	labeled	evildoing	gently	simplification
finalist	labeling	battlefield	jungles	simply
generally	labels	battleship	possibility	
hospitalized	leveled	castled	possibly	
hospitalization	leveling	castles	impossible	
severally	levelheaded	gentled	puddles	
totaled	remodel	gentleman	simpler	

E **Fun Ways to Spell**

Initial the box of each activity you finish.

1. Spell your words and play "Match-It."

3. Spell your words, then write a rhyme.

2. Spell your words with lemon juice.

4. Spell your words with pipe cleaners.

Words with /əl/

Lesson 23

145

1 Hide and Seek

Reinforce spelling by using multiple styles of learning.

On a white board, Teacher writes each word — one at a time. **Have students:**

- **Look** at the word.
- **Say** the word out loud.
- **Spell** the word out loud.
- **Hide** (teacher erases word.)
- **Write** the word on paper.
- **Seek** (teacher rewrites word.)
- **Check** spelling. If incorrect, rewrite word correctly.

2 Other Word Forms

This activity is optional. Have students find and circle the Other Word Forms that are antonyms of the following:

somber
complication
specifically
partially

3 Fun Ways to Spell

Four activities are provided. Use one, two, three, or all of the activities. Have students initial the box for each activity they complete.

Options:

- assign activities to students according to their learning styles
- set up the activities in learning centers for students to do throughout the day
- divide students into four groups and assign one activity per group
- do one activity per day

General

Spell your words; then play concentration…
Write each spelling word on a card. Mix your cards and a classmate's cards together. Arrange them face down in six rows of six. Pick up two cards. If the cards match, play again. If the cards do not match, turn them back over. It is your classmate's turn. Continue taking turns until all the cards are matched. The player with the most cards wins!

Auditory

To spell your words and write a rhyme…
- Write a rhyming verse for each word on list.
- Example:
  My little brother could dive.
  When he was barely five.
- Underline your spelling words.

Visual

To spell your words with lemon juice…
- Dip a cotton swab in lemon juice.
- With the swab, write each of your spelling words on black construction paper.
- Check your spelling before your writing disappears!

Tactile

To spell your words with pipe cleaners…
- Choose a word from your spelling list.
- Shape the pipe cleaners to spell the word.
- Check your spelling.
- Do this for each word on your list.

Working with Words

Familiarize students with word meaning and usage.

Dictionary Skills

Remind students that a word can often be used as more than one part of speech. Write the word **base** on the board. Read these sentences and ask students whether **base** is being used as a noun, verb, or adjective.

The rock is made of several base minerals. (adjective)

We had to find the length of the base of the triangle. (noun)

Be sure to base your decision on facts. (verb)

The spelling words in your Worktext can be **nouns**, **verbs**, or **adjectives**. Use the words to complete the sentences. Then circle **noun**, **verb**, or **adjective** to show how the word was used in the sentence.

Take a minute to memorize...

Luke 6:38

F Working with Words Name ____________

Words with /əl/ — Lesson 23

Dictionary Skills

An adjective is a word used to describe a noun or a pronoun. Words can often be used as more than one part of speech. The words below can be either nouns, verbs, or adjectives. Complete the sentences below using each word only one time. Then circle noun, verb, or adjective to show how the word was used in the sentence.

final general evil level gentle

1. A general is a high ranking officer in the army.
   (noun) verb adjective
2. If you work on a ranch you may learn how to gentle a horse.
   noun (verb) adjective
3. A bulldozer came to level the dirt around the new house.
   noun (verb) adjective
4. An evil-looking bolt of lightning lit up the sky.
   noun verb (adjective)
5. I studied hard before my science final.
   (noun) verb adjective

total label model battle

6. The Wright family wanted to model kindness to the Pruitts.
   noun (verb) adjective
7. Sally Ann made a total mess of the living room.
   noun verb (adjective)
8. Christopher had to battle his unkind feelings toward the Pruitts.
   noun (verb) adjective
9. The big box on the porch had a label that told what was inside.
   (noun) verb adjective

146

G Dictation

Name ______________________

Write each sentence as your teacher dictates. Use correct punctuation.

1. My uncle saw a tiger in the jungle.

2. Mom was as gentle as possible.

3. Cory built a model castle after breakfast.

Words with /əl/

Lesson 23

H Proofreading

If a word is misspelled, fill in the oval by that word. If all the words are spelled correctly, fill in the oval by **no mistake**.

1.	○ danger ● gentel ○ festival ○ no mistake	**5.**	● sevral ○ neither ○ owner ○ no mistake	**9.**	○ motor ● modle ○ visitor ○ no mistake
2.	● finall ○ donor ○ either ○ no mistake	**6.**	● tottal ○ rather ○ favor ○ no mistake	**10.**	● puddel ○ capture ○ nature ○ no mistake
3.	○ enter ○ jungle ● gennerel ○ no mistake	**7.**	○ honor ○ possible ● labell ○ no mistake	**11.**	○ pasture ○ evil ● batle ○ no mistake
4.	● hospitel ○ feather ○ finger ○ no mistake	**8.**	○ uncle ● levil ○ humor ○ no mistake	**12.**	○ picture ○ simple ● castel ○ no mistake

147

1 Dictation

Reinforce correct spelling by using current and previous words in context.

Listen as I read each sentence and then write it in your Worktext. Remember to use correct capitalization and punctuation. (Slowly read each sentence twice. Sentences are found in the Student Worktext to the left.)

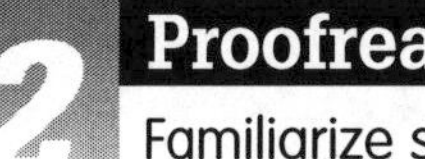

2 Proofreading

Familiarize students with standardized test format and reinforce recognition of misspelled words.

Look at each set of words. If a word is misspelled, fill in the oval by that word. If all the words are spelled correctly, fill in the oval by **no mistake**.

3 Hide and Seek

Reinforce correct spelling of current spelling words. Repeat this activity from Day 2. (A reproducible master is provided in Appendix A as shown on the inset page to the right.)

4 Other Word Forms

Have your students complete this activity to strengthen spelling ability and expand vocabulary.

1 Posttest

Visit the **A Reason For** website to download free, printable Posttest pages.

I will say the word once, use it in a sentence, then say it again. Write your words on a separate sheet of paper.

Progress Chart

Students may record scores. (Appendix B)

Personal Dictionary

Students may add any words they have misspelled to their personal dictionaries. (Appendix B)

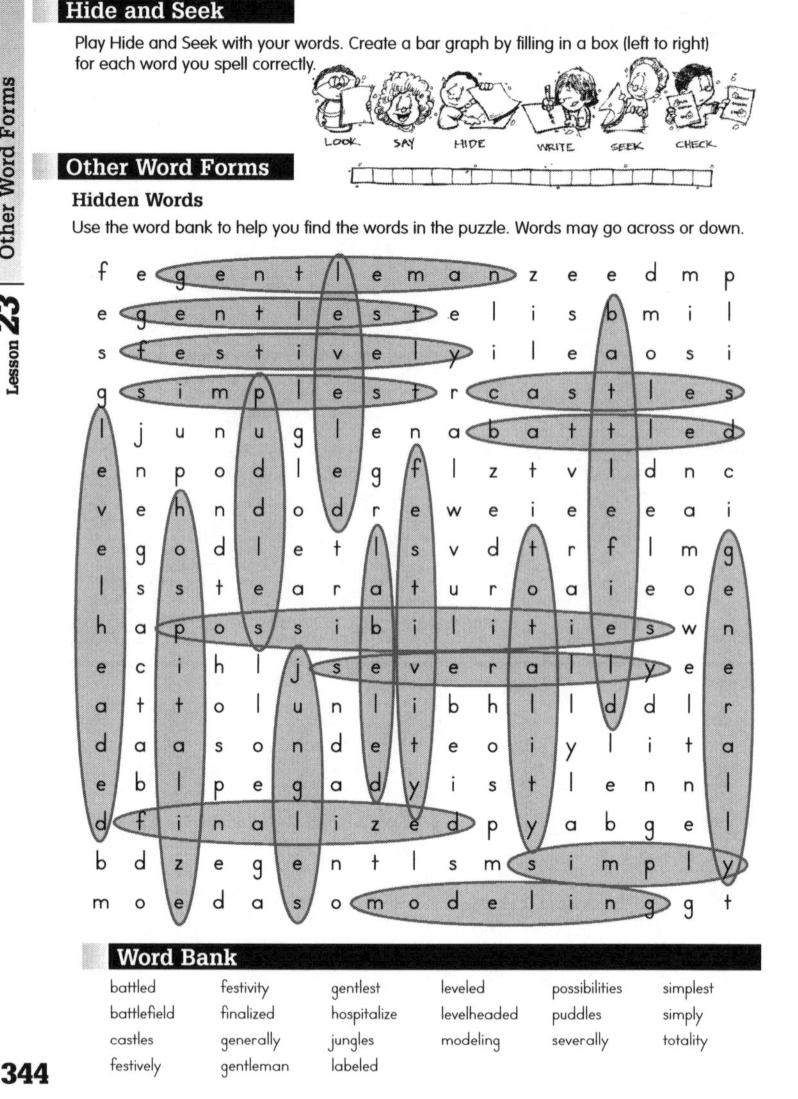

Other Word Forms

Lesson 23

Hide and Seek

Play Hide and Seek with your words. Create a bar graph by filling in a box (left to right) for each word you spell correctly.

Other Word Forms

Hidden Words

Use the word bank to help you find the words in the puzzle. Words may go across or down.

f e g e n t l e m a n z e e d m p
e g e n t l e s t e l i s b m i l
s f e s t i v e l y i l e a o s i
g s i m p l e s t r c a s t l e s
l j u n u g l e n a b a t t l e d
e n p o d l e g f l z t v l d n c
v e h n d o d r e w e i e e e a i
e g o d l e t l s v d t r f l m g
l s s t e a r a t u r o a i e o e
h a p o s s i b i l i t i e s w n
e c i h l j s e v e r a l l y e e
a t t o l u n l i b h l l d d l r
d a a s o n d e t e o i y l i t a
e b l p e g a d y i s t l e n n l
d f i n a l i z e d p y a b g e l
b d z e g e n t l s m s i m p l y
m o e d a s o m o d e l i n g g t

Word Bank

battled	festivity	gentlest	leveled	possibilities	simplest
battlefield	finalized	hospitalize	levelheaded	puddles	simply
castles	generally	jungles	modeling	severally	totality
festively	gentleman	labeled			

344

1. **uncle** "Just think of us as your aunt and **uncle**," instructed Mr. Pruitt.
2. **level** "I'm a top **level** salesman at Neumann's Electronics," he bragged.
3. **model** Mr. Pruitt's prize for top sales was a new **model** of TV.
4. **battle** It was a **battle** to keep a good attitude while they were there.
5. **castle** Sally Ann walked through Cory's **castle** scattering blocks everywhere.
6. **gentle** Mom spoke in **gentle** tones to the terrified canary.
7. **several** Kristin put **several** things in her parents' room and locked the door.
8. **jungle** Billy Ray ran through the house making sounds of **jungle** animals.
9. **total** The living room was a **total** mess when the Pruitts left.
10. **puddle** Kristin shrieked when she stepped in a **puddle** of spaghetti sauce.
11. **final** Stepping in the sauce was the **final** straw.
12. **evil** Kristin knew God did not want her to think **evil** thoughts.
13. **simple** "God wants us to show **simple** kindness and love to them," said Dad.
14. **festival** They invited the Pruitts to the winter **festival**.
15. **possible** With God's help it was **possible** to treat the Pruitts with kindness.
16. **hospital** Neumann's Electronics is near the **hospital**.
17. **label** The **label** on the box read "Fragile – This End Up."
18. **general** There was a **general** sense of excitement when they opened the box.

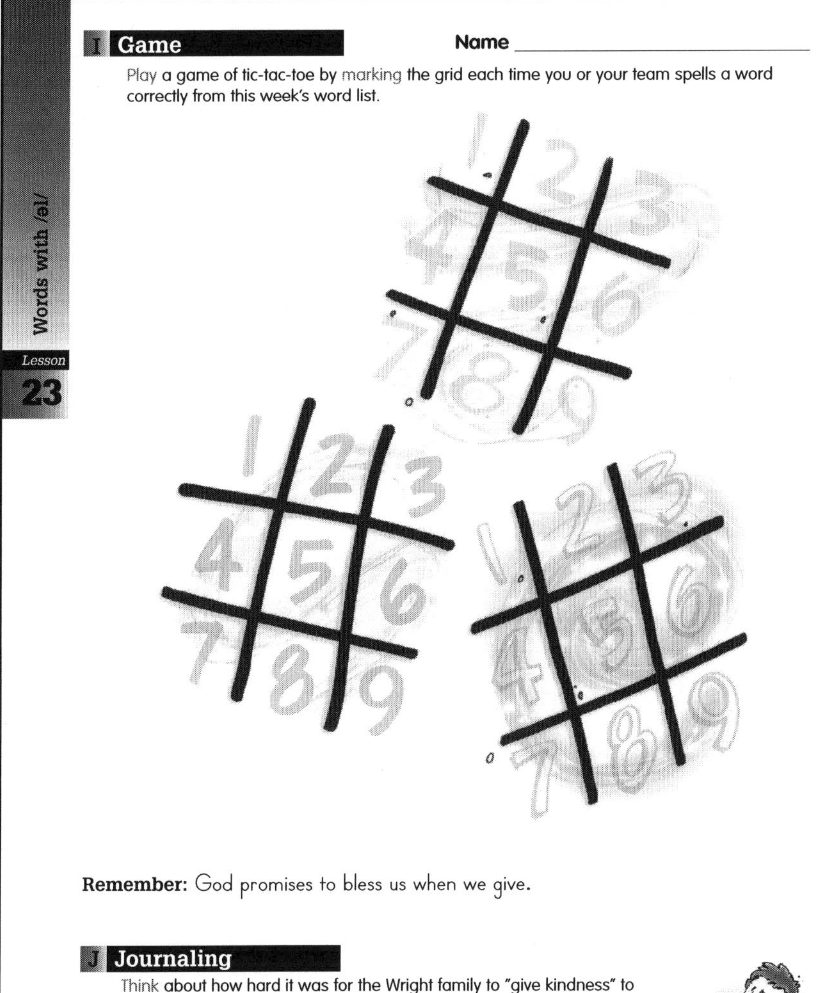

Words with /el/

Lesson 23

I **Game** Name ____________________

Play a game of tic-tac-toe by marking the grid each time you or your team spells a word correctly from this week's word list.

Remember: God promises to bless us when we give.

J **Journaling**

Think about how hard it was for the Wright family to "give kindness" to the Pruitts. In your journal, write about a time when you found it really hard to give.

148

How to Play:

- Divide students into two teams (the X's and the O's).
- Have a student from team X choose a number from 1 to 9.
- Say the word that matches that number from the Game Word List (Game 1).
- Have the student write the word on the board.
- If correct, have each member of both teams put an X on that number.
- Alternate between teams X and O.
- The first team to score three marks in a row (up, down, across, or diagonally) is the winner.
- Word lists and tic-tac-toe grids are provided for two additional games.

Small Group Option: Students may play this game without teacher direction in groups of two.

2 Game

Reinforce spelling skills and provide motivation and interest.

Materials

- game page (from Student Worktext)
- pencils (1 per child)
- game word list

Game 1 Word List

1. **festival**
2. **level**
3. **general**
4. **gentle**
5. **hospital**
6. **simple**
7. **total**
8. **model**
9. **possible**

Game 2 Word List

1. **uncle**
2. **final**
3. **puddle**
4. **label**
5. **several**
6. **castle**
7. **evil**
8. **battle**
9. **jungle**

Game 3 Word List

1. **festival**
2. **level**
3. **gentle**
4. **model**
5. **possible**
6. **label**
7. **several**
8. **jungle**
9. **final**

3 Journaling

Provide a meaningful reason for correct spelling through personal writing.

Review the story using discussion leads provided on the following page. Encourage students to apply the Scriptural value in their journaling.

Journaling (continued)

- What did the Wrights plan to do to welcome their new neighbors? (Mom was going to bake some bread and Dad was going to go help them move furniture or unpack.)
- What did the Pruitts and their children do when they came over that night? (Invited themselves to supper. Mr. Pruitt bragged and paid no attention to what his kids did. Billy Ray turned over Treasure's cage and broke Cory's car. Jessie Lynn smeared spaghetti sauce everywhere, ruined the photos, pulled the leaves off the plant, and ate the candy before breaking the candy dish. Sally Ann made grape juice spots on the carpet.)
- Why did the Wrights continue giving kindness to the Pruitts? (Because it was the right thing to do, what God asks us to do.)
- What does the Scripture mean that says, "If you give, you will get!?" (That there are consequences to all our actions. God will reward us for giving, but not necessarily with things and not necessarily right now.)

"Bookkeeper" and "bookkeeping" are the only non-hyphenated words in the English language with three consecutive double letters.

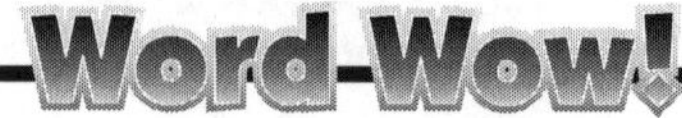

1 **Literature Connection**
Topic: Worry
Theme Text: Matthew 6:26

No Small Worries

Tony struggles with constant worrying about many things.

I'd better take this hat off before I go inside the house. Grandma Miller may still be here helping Mama. Grandma has this thing about boys wearing hats inside. She thinks a gentleman should take off his hat for three reasons—when he prays, when he meets a lady, or when he goes into a building. Everybody wears hats inside nowadays! I keep telling her, but somebody besides me will have to convince her.

I, for one, like hats for two reasons. They keep my ears warm when I'm outside in this cold wind. I know my ears won't be cold in the house. That brings me to the other reason I like hats. A hat covers up my hair when it's a mess. I want to leave my hat on now. I think once you put a hat on you should wear it the rest of the day!

Grandma and hats are one of the reasons I always carry this comb in my pocket. Mama said Mr. Hauth is coming over to help her with income tax tonight. Grandma's probably cleaning up the mess from dinner since I had soccer tryouts right after we ate. That will give Mama time to finish organizing the papers for Mr. Hauth. I can see my hair in the glass of the front window. I definitely look better with the hat on. Maybe Mr. Hauth won't be here yet.

"Hello," a deep voice booms as I open the front door, "you must be Tony."

I nod and scurry toward my room.

Grandma Miller blocks the hallway that leads to my bedroom. She bends down and whispers in my ear, "'Yes, sir,' would be an appropriate response to Mr. Hauth."

"Yes, sir," I blurt as I back around Grandma Miller. Mr. Hauth is a big man. He doesn't look like an accountant. He looks like a tackle from a football team. Maybe tax stuff is what he does at night. He sure doesn't look like he sits inside behind a desk all day.

Grandma Miller bends over and whispers in my ear again. "It's not polite to stare." Aloud she says, "Run along and get ready for bed, Tony-O." I don't know why she has to call me Tony-O in front of Mr. Hauth. It sounds like a name for a little kid. I wonder if I will ever be as big as Mr. Hauth?

Grandma supervises the bedtime stuff. She makes sure I brush my teeth. She has worship with me and tucks me in bed. I'm old enough to do all this by myself, but I don't want to hurt her feelings so I won't tell her she can go on home.

After she turns out the light, I lie in bed and think. I can't go to sleep. I think about how big Mr. Hauth is. Coach Larkin is big too. Papa is not a little man. He says I will grow. I wish I would start. I think I am one of the shortest kids in my class. I know all the girls are taller.

My alarm wakes me up at five-thirty. I wonder if I grew any? I need plenty of time to get ready for school. I have to take a shower, get dressed, eat, fix my hair, and polish my boots. I didn't have time to polish them last night because of soccer tryouts. Maybe I should sleep some more. Our science book says sleep is important for growing kids. Five-thirty is pretty early.

"Tony." Mama shakes me awake. I must have gone back to sleep. It's 6:30 now. That's when I usually get up. Maybe if I hurry, I'll still have time to polish my boots.

"Mama, do you think I'm going to grow any time soon?" I ask at breakfast. She says she doesn't know. Kids have growth spurts at different times.

"Your time will come," she says.

I hope it comes tomorrow. In soccer it's hard to outrun boys who are a foot taller. Grandma Miller beeps the horn in her car. I check my hair in the mirror before I run out the door for school. I'm not going to put my baseball cap on yet. Grandma will want me to take it off when I say good morning to her. It's not very cold out today. The sun is shining. It's getting close to spring. Everything is getting ready to grow again. I hope I'm getting ready to grow.

Grandma said someone told her we might have to wear uniforms at Knowlton Elementary next school year. I sure hope it's not true. I don't want to look like everyone else every day. Maybe I could wear my hat inside though. Grandma says that a gentleman does not have to take off his hat inside a building if it's part of his uniform.

Grandma says Mr. Hauth is coming back over tonight. I wish he wasn't. I need a haircut. I just got one last week but I like to look my best all the time.

Coach Larkin says he's going to put me in a new position this year. I wonder what it will be? I like being the striker. I bet he doesn't think I can outrun the tall boys. I'm not big enough to be the goalie and I'm not fast enough to be the striker. Those are the positions I like.

"What are you thinking about?" Grandma Miller smiles over at me, "You're awfully quiet this morning."

I don't want to tell her about how worried I am about growing. She'll just say my time will come like Mama did—so I'll ask her a question. "Do you think Mr. Hauth will finish the taxes with Mama tonight?"

"They're finished—but he may still come over. I think he and your Mama are getting to be good friends." Grandma stops to let me off at Knowlton Elementary before I can ask her what in the world she is talking about. This is just one

Story Continued

more thing to worry about.

Mrs. Burton likes to have class outside sometimes. Today is warm. The wind quit blowing and the sun is out. She says we'll have spelling beside the big pine tree on the playground.

We're talking about a new Scripture verse now. It says, "Look at the birds! They don't worry about what to eat—they don't need to sow or reap or store up food—for your Heavenly Father feeds them. And you are far more valuable to Him than they are." Maybe I should eat more. Then I would grow. I don't have to worry about my hair right now because even Grandma Miller says it's okay to wear caps on the playground.

I can't see over Stephen. He is a lot taller than I am. He's already had a growth spurt. His dad says he's stocky. If he's stocky, that makes me scrawny. He is both bigger and taller than I am. I start thinking about soccer. We finish the tryouts this afternoon. I might not even make the team.

Mrs. Burton wants us to memorize a certain Scripture verse every week. She likes us all to say it out loud together a couple of times on Monday. I think now is the time. "Look at the birds! They don't worry..." Don't worry. Don't worry. Don't worry. I can't get those words out of my head. I've been worried about a lot of things lately. I'm more valuable to God than a bird. I guess I should let God worry about when I will grow, how I look, and who Mom's friends are.

When we're finished saying the Scripture verse Mrs. Burton wants us to pray. I reach up and take off my hat. I wonder if my hair is standing straight up? Maybe it's all flat and smashed. Katelynn will notice. I reach up to feel what it looks like; then I look around at my classmates sitting on the grass that is just starting to turn green. They won't notice my hair—everyone is closing their eyes for prayer. I guess I don't need to worry!

Discussion Time

Check understanding of the story and development of personal values.

- How did Tony feel about his height?
- How did he feel about the way he looked?
- Why was he worried about Mr. Hauth?
- What are some things you worry about?
- How do you feel when you are worried?
- Do you think God wants us to worry?
- You are valuable to God. He wants you to feel secure in His love!

A Test-Words Name ____________________

Write each spelling word on the line as your teacher says it.

1. sure
2. sir
3. during
4. firm
5. overlook
6. possible
7. honor
8. curl
9. avoid
10. rather
11. dessert
12. either
13. germ
14. cure

Review Lesson 24

B Test-Sentences

Write the sentences on the lines below, correcting each misspelled word, as well as all capitalization and punctuation errors. There are two misspelled words in each sentence.

the angels did rejioce the night of Jesus' berth

1. The angels did rejoice the night of Jesus' birth.

a turist read the buletin at the theater box office;

2. A tourist read the bulletin at the theater box office.

the kind nerse told the girl not to wory

3. The kind nurse told the girl not to worry.

we studied the curius foutprint for a long time?

4. We studied the curious footprint for a long time.

149

4 Test-Sentences

Reinforce recognizing misspelled words.

Read each sentence carefully. Write the sentences on the lines in your Worktext. There are two misspelled words in each sentence. Correct each misspelled word, as well as all capitalization and punctuation errors.

Take a minute to memorize...

Matthew 6:26

3 Test-Words

Test for knowledge of the correct spellings of these words.

I will say each word once, use the word in a sentence, then say the word again. Write the words on the lines in your Worktext.

1. sure — Tony is not **sure** why Grandma Miller worries about manners so much.
2. sir — "'Yes, **sir**,' would be an appropriate response," Grandma Miller reminded.
3. during — She said Tony should take his hat off **during** prayer.
4. firm — Grandma Miller's voice is kind but **firm** when she instructs Tony.
5. overlook — She refuses to **overlook** bad manners.
6. possible — He wasn't sure it was **possible** to remember all her instructions.
7. honor — Tony will **honor** his grandmother by obeying her.
8. curl — Tony likes to **curl** his arm upward and check his muscles.
9. avoid — He wants to **avoid** seeing anyone when his hair is messed up.
10. rather — He was **rather** tired of being shorter than the other boys.
11. dessert — After **dessert** Tony went to change clothes for soccer tryouts.
12. either — When coughing, cover your mouth with **either** your hand or a tissue.
13. germ — If you do not, not just one **germ**, but many are spread.
14. cure — Putting your trust in God is the best **cure** for worry.

Test-Dictation

Reinforce correct spelling by using current and previous words in context.

Listen as I read each sentence, then write it in your Worktext. Remember to use correct capitalization and punctuation. (Slowly read each sentence twice. Sentences are found in the student text to the right. The words **voyage**, **furniture**, **point**, and **soybeans** are found in this unit.)

Test-Proofreading

Familiarize students with standardized test format and reinforce recognizing misspelled words.

Look at each set of words. If a word is misspelled, fill in the oval by that word. If all the words are spelled correctly, fill in the oval by **no mistake**.

Review Lesson 24

C Test-Dictation

Name ____________________

Write each sentence as your teacher dictates. Use correct punctuation.

1. Our voyage began in the early spring.
2. His grandfather makes beautiful furniture.
3. I made a point to say hello to her.
4. We must plow the soil and plant the soybeans.

D Test-Proofreading

If a word is misspelled, fill in the oval by that word. If all the words are spelled correctly, fill in the oval by **no mistake**.

1. ● leval ○ sure ○ sir ○ no mistake
2. ○ during ● berst ○ firm ○ no mistake
3. ○ overlook ○ possible ● wirst ○ no mistake
4. ○ honor ○ curl ○ plural ● no mistake
5. ○ avoid ○ rather ○ topsoil ● no mistake
6. ○ dessert ○ either ● choise ○ no mistake
7. ● royilty ○ germ ○ cure ○ no mistake
8. ○ handful ○ crooked ○ destroy ● no mistake
9. ● capcher ○ neither ○ enter ○ no mistake
10. ○ fully ○ oily ● genral ○ no mistake
11. ○ wooden ○ humor ○ joint ● no mistake
12. ○ enjoyment ○ nature ● finel ○ no mistake

150

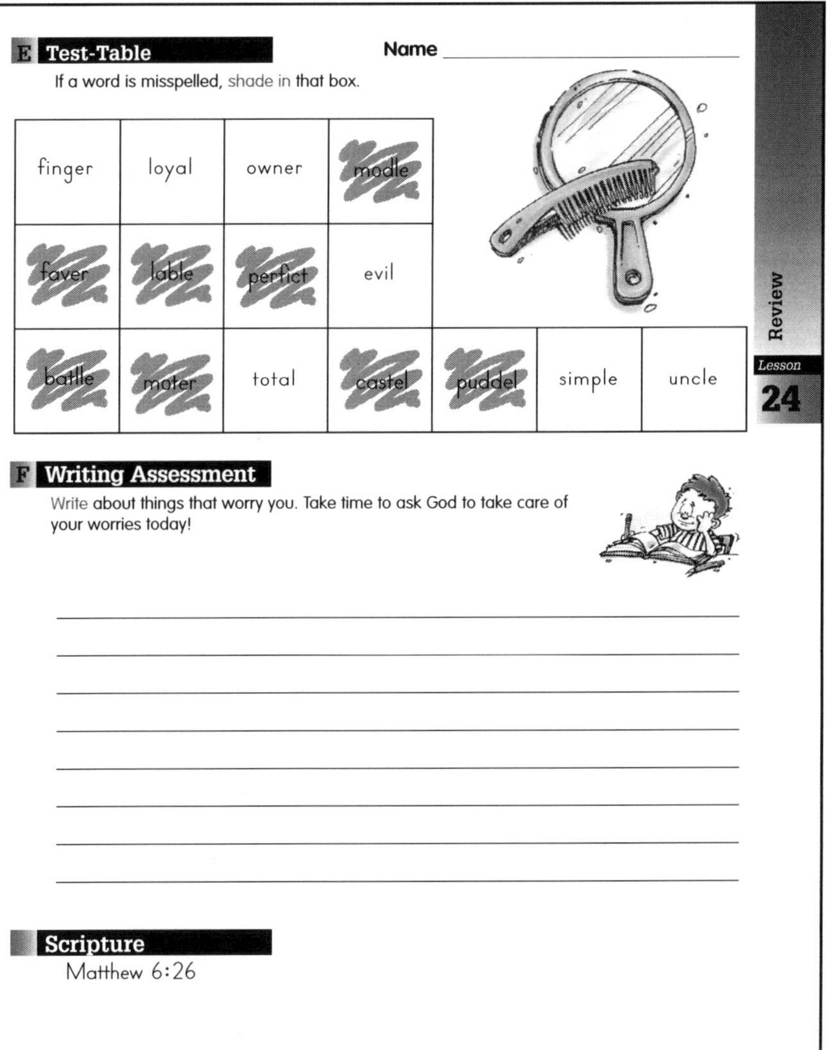

E **Test-Table** Name ______________________

If a word is misspelled, shade in that box.

finger	loyal	owner	modle			
faver	lable	perfict	evil			
batlle	moter	total	castel	puddel	simple	uncle

Review Lesson 24

F **Writing Assessment**

Write about things that worry you. Take time to ask God to take care of your worries today!

____

____

____

____

____

____

____

Scripture

Matthew 6:26

151

1 Test-Table

Test mastery of words in this unit.

If a word is misspelled, fill in the space on the grid.

2 Writing Assessment

Assess student's spelling, grammar, and composition skills through personal writing.

- How does God provide food for the birds? (He provides seeds, berries, meat, and flowers to feed the birds. People contribute food, too.)
- Raise your hand if you think the birds worry about what they are going to eat?
- How valuable are we to God compared to the birds? (We are far more valuable.)
- Why do you think God wants us to trust Him and not worry? (We are valuable to Him. He loves us and knows we are happiest when we feel secure in His love.)

The only word in the English language that consists of two letters, each used three times is the word "deeded."

Word Wow!

Test-Sentences

Reinforce recognizing misspelled words.

Read each sentence carefully. Write the sentences on the lines in your Worktext, correcting each misspelled word, as well as all capitalization and punctuation errors.

G Test-Sentences Name ____________

Write the sentences on the lines below, correcting each misspelled word, as well as all capitalization and punctuation errors. There are two misspelled words in each sentence.

The elderly bootcher plans to imploy an assistant
1. The elderly **butcher** plans to **employ** an assistant**.**

is this skert werth forty dollars
2. **Is** this **skirt worth** forty dollars**?**

the big terkey liked to anoy us with its gobbling'
3. **The** big **turkey** liked to **annoy** us with its gobbling**.**

our class had its pictere taken at the festivel
4. **Our** class had its **picture** taken at the **festival.**

H Test-Words

Write each spelling word on the line as your teacher says it.

1. handful
2. crooked
3. neither
4. enter
5. fully
6. oily
7. wooden
8. humor
9. enjoyment
10. nature
11. donor
12. moist
13. goodness
14. purpose

Test-Words

Test for knowledge of the correct spellings of these words.

Say: I will say the word once, use the word in a sentence, then say the word again. Write the word on the lines in your Worktext.

1. **handful** — Grandma Miller laughs and says Tony can be a **handful** sometimes.
2. **crooked** — Mama loves Tony's **crooked** grin.
3. **neither** — Tony knew that **neither** Mama nor Grandma Miller wanted him to worry.
4. **enter** — It's polite for a gentleman to allow a lady to **enter** a door before him.
5. **fully** — Tony does not always **fully** understand the importance of etiquette.
6. **oily** — Tony washed his hair every night so it wouldn't look **oily** and dirty.
7. **wooden** — He feels like a **wooden** soldier when he tries to have good posture.
8. **humor** — Mrs. Burton is a great teacher with a good sense of **humor**.
9. **enjoyment** — For the class's **enjoyment**, she had spelling under the pine tree.
10. **nature** — She likes her students to enjoy **nature** while they learn.
11. **donor** — Grandma Miller is a willing **donor** of advice on etiquette.
12. **moist** — Tony wiped his boots with a slightly **moist** cloth before polishing them.
13. **goodness** — The **goodness** of God is never-ending.
14. **purpose** — Tony must **purpose** in his heart to trust God and not worry.

I Test-Editing

Name ______________________

If a word is spelled correctly, fill in the oval under **Correct**. If the word is misspelled, fill in the oval under **Incorrect**, and write the word correctly on the blank.

	Correct	Incorrect	
1. curve	●	○	
2. fether	○	●	feather
3. jungel	○	●	jungle
4. pasture	●	○	
5. apointment	○	●	appointment
6. danger	●	○	
7. severel	○	●	several
8. visiter	○	●	visitor
9. buldozer	○	●	bulldozer
10. disapoint	○	●	disappoint
11. furious	●	○	
12. pure	●	○	
13. gentel	○	●	gentle
14. hospital	●	○	
15. ferther	○	●	further

Test-Editing

Reinforce recognizing and correcting misspelled words.

4 Action Game

Reinforce spelling skills and provide motivation and interest.

Materials

- Word Lists

SPELL FREEZE

How to Play:

Begin the game by establishing room or play area boundaries. Choose a student to be **IT**. If tagged by **IT**, the tagged student must freeze. While **IT** continues to chase and tag, the teacher moves among the frozen students giving each a review word to spell. If a student spells the word correctly, he/she is unfrozen. If the student is unable to spell a word, he/she may be given a copy of the word list to study while frozen. At any point the teacher may say, "Everybody freeze!" All the students stop where they are, including **IT**. Teacher selects new **IT** and then proceeds to unfreeze others by asking them to spell review words.

Game

Reinforce spelling skills and provide motivation and interest.

Materials

- game pages (from Student Worktext)
- stickers (13 per child)
- game word list

Review Lesson 24

J **Game** Name ______________________

Tony likes to wear his baseball cap. Use two baseball teams as your team names for this game. Place a sticker on the game board each time you or your team spells a review word correctly.

Remember: You are important to God. Don't waste time worrying!

154

Game Word List

Check off each word lightly in pencil as it is used.

The Green Sox	The Blue Sox
1. **level**	1. **loyal**
2. **burst**	2. **label**
3. **worst**	3. **motor**
4. **plural**	4. **owner**
5. **topsoil**	5. **perfect**
6. **choice**	6. **total**
7. **royalty**	7. **model**
8. **destroy**	8. **evil**
9. **capture**	9. **battle**
10. **general**	10. **castle**
11. **joint**	11. **puddle**
12. **final**	12. **simple**
13. **favor**	13. **uncle**

How to Play:

- Divide students into two teams. Name one team **The Green Sox**, one **The Blue Sox**. (Optional: If you have an even number of students, you may wish to pair students from opposing teams and have them share a game page.)
- Read the instructions from the student game page aloud.
- Have a student from the first team choose a number from 1 to 13.
- Say the word that matches that number from the team's word list.
- Have the student write the word on the board.
- If correct, have each member of that team put a sticker on that number by his/her team name. If the word is misspelled, have him/her put an X through that number. That number may not be chosen again.
- Repeat this process with the second team.
- When the words from both lists have been used, the team with the most stickers is the winner.

Date ____________________

This certificate is awarded to

____

for completing activities using the following spelling words:

dessert	crooked	appointment	danger	festival
germ	footprint	avoid	donor	final
perfect	goodness	choice	either	general
birth	overlook	disappoint	enter	hospital
firm	wooden	joint	feather	several
sir	tourist	moist	finger	total
skirt	bulldozer	oily	neither	label
worry	bulletin	point	owner	level
worst	fully	rejoice	rather	model
worth	handful	topsoil	favor	evil
burst	cure	annoy	honor	battle
curl	curious	destroy	humor	castle
curve	during	employ	motor	gentle
furniture	furious	enjoyment	visitor	jungle
further	plural	loyal	capture	possible
nurse	pure	royalty	nature	puddle
purpose	sure	soybean	pasture	simple
turkey	butcher	voyage	picture	uncle

2 Certificate

Provide an opportunity for parents or guardians to encourage and assess their child's progress.

Fill in today's date and your name on your certificate.

Take a minute to memorize...

Matthew 6:26

3 Letter

Provide the parent or guardian with the spelling word lists for the next unit.

Give your parents or guardian this letter that lists your spelling words for the next unit. Put it where you will remember to practice the words together.

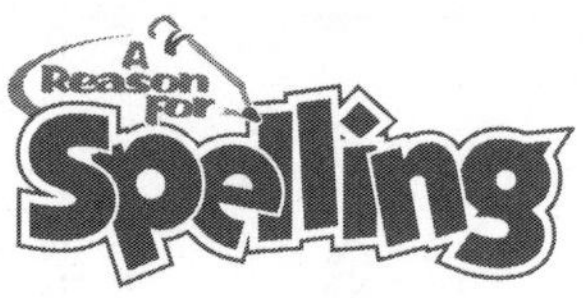

Dear Parent,

We are about to begin a new spelling unit containing five weekly lessons. A set of eighteen words will be studied each week. All the words will be reviewed in the sixth week. Values based on the Scriptures listed below will be taught in each lesson.

Lesson 25	Lesson 26	Lesson 27	Lesson 28	Lesson 29
curtain	bare	appear	he'd	anyway
fountain	compare	beard	I'd	backyard
chicken	dare	disappear	they'd	bathroom
kitchen	fare	fear	he'll	bathtub
listen	glare	gear	it'll	bedroom
oven	hare	near	she'll	bedspread
siren	scare	rear	couldn't	everybody
robin	share	spear	didn't	fireplace
ruin	stare	tear	hadn't	herself
champion	scarce	weary	weren't	homemade
lion	pear	cheer	wouldn't	homework
button	wear	deer	here's	newspaper
common	anywhere	steer	she's	yardstick
cotton	dairy	fierce	there's	playground
dragon	fair	cereal	what's	railroad
lemon	hair	period	where's	somewhere
reason	repair	sincerely	who's	sunshine
ribbon	upstairs	weird	we've	within
Mark 11:25	Matthew 6:6	John 15:13, 14	John 16:33	Luke 11:33

1 **Literature Connection**
Topic: Forgiveness
Theme Text: Mark 11:25

Tickets to Nowhere

Laney faces forgiveness issues when her Dad breaks a promise.

Mrs. Larkin handed her daughter a yellow envelope. Laney recognized the address she'd written on it the week before. Now the words Addressee Unknown were stamped in bright red ink across the front. "Dad, Suzanne, and Savanah must have moved." She looked up into her mother's eyes. "Dad hasn't called me in a long time—and now the handwriting border sheet I sent him just came back in the mail." Laney collapsed on the couch beside Coach Larkin.

"Laney, Laney, Laney!" Coach Larkin wrapped his stepdaughter in his big arms and squeezed. "There. I just called you three times. How often would you like me to do that?" he teased.

"You know who I mean—Dad Ausherman in New York, not you." Laney squirmed out of his arms and turned so she could see his face. "He hasn't called me in months. I thought he was just really busy representing all his clients. I'm supposed to spend next week in New York with him. I want to see my old friends. Now we can't even find him. I wanted to see Aunt Lorene, Uncle Howard, and Casey, too." Laney's shoulders slumped.

"I'm sorry, Laney." Elisa Larkin sat down on the other side of her daughter. "Your father and Suzanne probably moved to a new apartment. He's not hiding from you. I'm sure he will e-mail you or call when he gets settled again. I'll try his office tomorrow." Mom kissed Laney on the forehead.

"Why don't you see if Katelynn and Rachel would like to go with us to the mall?" Coach Larkin picked up the phone and handed it to Laney. "We can have supper at the food court, and then you women can shop."

The girls had fun. Rachel bought a new Detective Zack book for Beth's birthday that was coming up next week. Katelynn picked out some stickers she wanted. Laney found a pair of shoes and a church dress she really liked. Even though she talked and laughed a lot with her friends, a nagging thought in the back of her mind kept bothering Laney. *My own father has forgotten about me.*

The next day Elisa Larkin called her ex-husband's law firm. His secretary told her he was out of the country taking a deposition for an upcoming trial. He was supposed to be back Thursday. She was sure he would be back in New York Friday because he was scheduled to be in court.

When Laney heard the news she cried. "He probably doesn't even remember my spring break starts next week," she wailed. "He'll be too busy anyway. If his trial starts Friday, he'll be right in the middle of it when I'm there. I'll never see him even if he does remember his promise to buy plane tickets. I can't believe my own father has forgotten me." She wiped tears away with the back of her hand. "I may not go even if he does buy tickets. I'd like to make him feel like I feel right now," she sniffed.

It was a busy week. Laney had a history report to finish Tuesday night. Wednesday she went to a pool party at Daniel's house with the rest of her class. Thursday Stephen invited her over to skateboard. Tony came too and they skated until it was too dark to see. It was Friday before she knew it. Then no school for a whole week! Laney didn't talk about the tickets that didn't come. Her mom didn't mention them either. There was no use getting hysterical. They both knew Herald Ausherman did what Herald Ausherman wanted to do, and sometimes that didn't include his elder daughter.

The first morning of vacation Laney slept in. After a leisurely breakfast of blueberry waffles topped with whipped cream, she sat down in front of the TV. The phone rang while she was hunting for the remote. It was Tony. They discussed plans for the week.

Tony was thrilled Laney wasn't headed for New York. "We're going to have a lot of fun right here," Tony assured his friend. "We can ride our bikes in the park. We can skate. Stephen's going to his Aunt Bess's house for the week. It's a good time for him to visit since both his parents work all day. With Stephen gone, I'm sure glad you're going to be here. Even if you'd rather not be," he added.

"I'll be okay. It just makes me mad that Dad couldn't at least have let me know there was a scheduling conflict." Laney bit her lower lip.

"Can I go for ice cream, and then to Roller City with Tony?" Laney called from the couch a few minutes later.

"Who's going to take you? Doesn't Tony's mom work?" Elisa Larkin closed the door of the dishwasher.

"His mom." Laney called.

"When…" Mom started to ask.

"We'll leave right after supper and be back by 9:30…. Yes, his mom is going to stay there with us." Laney smiled. "This week may turn out okay after all."

The next morning Mom and Laney got up earlier. They straightened up the house and were ready to go to Fayetteville by 10 o'clock. "Where'd you like to go first?" Mom stopped at the mailbox on the way out the driveway.

"Oh, how about the mall?" Laney took the stack of mail her mom handed her and started thumbing through it.

She stopped at a thick, oversized envelope. It was addressed to Edward Larkin. "Who are

Story (continued)

Ken and Jean Rozell?"

Mom turned the car onto Mason Springs Drive. "Jean Rozell is Edward's sister who lives on the west coast. You haven't met them yet."

"But why is she sending Dad a card?" Laney looked out the window at the older couple walking their golden retriever on the trail in Mason Springs Park.

Mrs. Larkin smiled down at her daughter. "It's his birthday tomorrow! I'm sure it's a birthday card!"

"Oh, yeah. I almost forgot. I'd like to get him something special while we're shopping today. I was going to have Aunt Lorene help me when I was in New York, but I guess that's not going to happen. He's been so kind to me even though I'm not his real daughter." The car sped past the old couple and their dog.

All of a sudden Laney hit the palm of her hand to her forehead with a resounding smack. "I can't believe it! I can't believe it!" Mom looked at Laney and raised her eyebrows. "I forgot Beth's slumber party. It was last night. I thought I was going to be at Suzanne and Dad's. I didn't even get her a gift. I told her I was going to find something for her in New York. All the girls in our class were invited. Beth probably thinks I'm a snob or something," Laney ran her fingers through her hair.

"Rachel did call last night right after you left with Tony and his mom." Mrs. Larkin tuned the car on to Main Street.

"Yeah, she knew the tickets hadn't come. She probably wanted to know where I'd disappeared to. I hope Beth will forgive me. No telling what she thinks. Can I use your cell phone?"

Mrs. Larkin pulled the phone from her purse and handed it to Laney as they passed the Parks and Recreation building downtown. Edward Larkin was standing on the front steps talking to Mr. Jacobson. They both smiled and waved when she beeped the horn.

That evening Laney crawled between the cool sheets of her bed and pulled the blanket up under her chin. She could hear the TV downstairs and Mom's and Dad's voices occasionally as they laughed or made comments about the movie they were watching. Her eyes rested on the two carefully wrapped gifts sitting side by side on her dresser. Beth had been nice about her missing the party. She'd even asked if Laney would like to come out to her grandma's farm and ride horses Sunday.

Laney gazed at the ceiling. The Scripture she'd memorized the week before drifted through her brain as her eyelids grew heavy. "When you are praying, first forgive anyone you are holding a grudge against, so that your Father in heaven will forgive you your sins too."

"Oops! I forgot to pray!" she said out loud.

Laney slipped out from between the sheets and knelt beside her bed. "Father in heaven. Thank you for loving me. I'm sorry I forgot to pray and was so forgetful about Beth's birthday. I'm thankful she isn't mad. Thank you for bringing Edward Larkin to me and Mom. He's really a great stepdad. Please help me not to feel so angry at Dad. I'm sorry I wanted to hurt him when he forgot all about our plans for spring break. I love you. Amen."

2 Discussion Time

Check understanding of the story and development of personal values.

- What did Mr. Ausherman forget all about?
- How did Laney feel when her dad forgot about the spring break visit?
- What important event did Laney forget?
- What does "holding a grudge" mean?
- Did Beth hold a grudge when Laney forgot her birthday?
- Who's hurt the most when you hold a grudge?

Words with /ən/ or /in/

Lesson 25

A Preview Name ______________

Write each word as your teacher says it.

1. siren
2. curtain
3. button
4. kitchen
5. oven
6. lemon
7. chicken
8. robin
9. fountain
10. common
11. reason
12. dragon
13. lion
14. cotton
15. ruin
16. champion
17. ribbon
18. listen

Scripture

Mark 11:25

157

3 Preview

Test for knowledge of the correct spellings of these words.

Customize Your List

On a separate sheet of paper, additional words of your choice may be tested.

I will say each word once, use the word in a sentence, then say the word again. Write the words on the lines in your Worktext.

Correct Immediately!

Let's correct our Preview. I will spell each word out loud. If you spelled a word incorrectly, rewrite it correctly.

Progress Chart

Students may record scores. (Reproducible master provided in Appendix B.)

1.	siren	Laney could hear the wail of a **siren** in the distance.
2.	curtain	She pulled the **curtain** aside and looked forlornly out the window.
3.	button	She fiddled with a gold **button** on her vest.
4.	kitchen	Her mom called her to help in the **kitchen.**
5.	oven	Mrs. Larkin pulled a pan of lasagna out of the **oven.**
6.	lemon	Laney dropped slices of fresh **lemon** into the glasses of ice water.
7.	chicken	Laney's bird book had a picture of a **chicken** with an odd-shaped head.
8.	robin	A mother **robin** was pictured with her new hatchlings.
9.	fountain	At the water **fountain** Tony and Laney discussed their history reports.
10.	common	It was **common** for Laney's real dad to forget his promises.
11.	reason	The secretary explained the **reason** for Mr. Ausherman's absence.
12.	dragon	Laney stared at the silly **dragon** parading across the waffle box.
13.	lion	A funny cartoon **lion** was eating a big plate of waffles.
14.	cotton	As Laney prayed, teardrops fell on the cool **cotton** pillowcase.
15.	ruin	Laney knew that bitterness could **ruin** her relationship with God.
16.	champion	God wanted Laney to be a **champion** and have victory over bitterness.
17.	ribbon	Laney marked the spot in her Bible with a bright blue **ribbon.**
18.	listen	"I want to **listen** to You, Lord, and forgive my dad," she prayed.

Word Shapes

Help students form a correct image of whole words.

Look at each word and think about its shape. Now, write the word in the correct Word Shape Boxes. You may check off each word as you use it.

(In many words, the sound of **/ən/** is spelled with **en**, **ion**, or **on**. The sound of **/in/** is spelled with **ain** and **in**. Because spellers cannot rely on a phonetic way of remembering the various spellings, this sound is often difficult.)

In the Word Shape Boxes, fill in the boxes containing the letters that spell the sound of **/ən/** or **/in/** in each word.

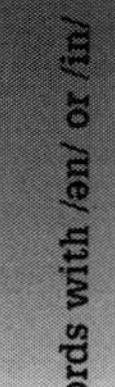

Words with /ən/ or /in/

Lesson 25

B Word Shapes Name ________________

Write each word in the correct Word Shape Boxes. Next, in the Word Shape Boxes, shade in the boxes containing the letters that spell the sound of **/ən/** or **/in/** in each word.

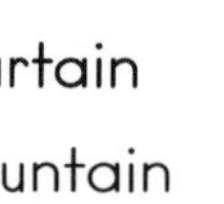

Word	Word Shape Boxes
1. curtain	cotton
2. fountain	oven
3. chicken	lion
4. kitchen	ruin
5. listen	chicken
6. oven	ribbon
7. siren	robin
8. robin	listen
9. ruin	curtain
10. champion	reason
11. lion	button
12. button	fountain
13. common	common
14. cotton	champion
15. dragon	dragon
16. lemon	kitchen
17. reason	siren
18. ribbon	lemon

158

Answers may vary for duplicate word shapes.

Take a minute to memorize...

Mark 11:25

Be Prepared For Fun

Check these supply lists for **Fun Ways to Spell** - presented **Day 2**. Purchase and/or gather these items ahead of time!

General
- Pencil
- Graph Paper (1 sheet per child)
- Spelling List

Auditory
- Voice Recorder
- Spelling List

Visual
- Water Color Paint Box (1 per child)
- Paint Brush (1 per child)
- Art Paper (3 or 4 sheets per child)
- Spelling List

Tactile
- Soccer Ball, Basketball, Tennis Ball, or 4-Square Ball
- Spelling List

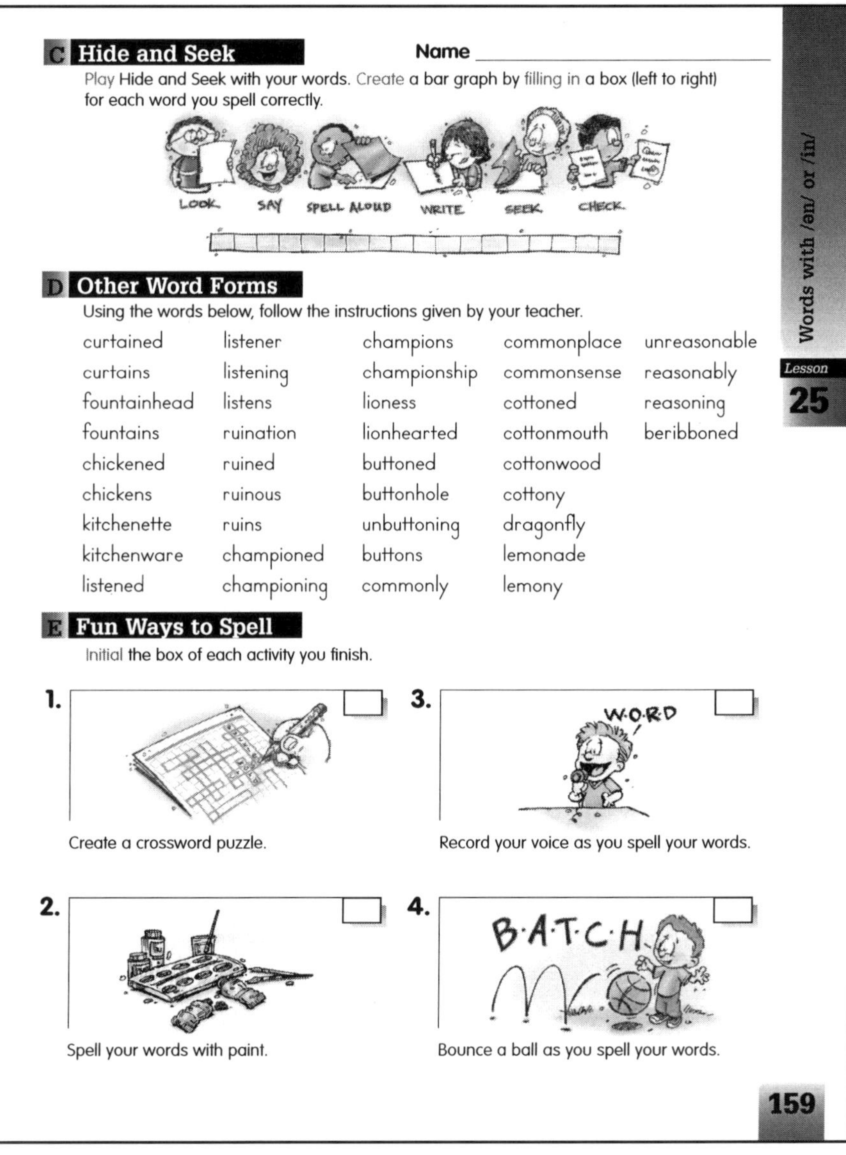

C Hide and Seek Name ______________________

Play Hide and Seek with your words. Create a bar graph by filling in a box (left to right) for each word you spell correctly.

D Other Word Forms

Using the words below, follow the instructions given by your teacher.

curtained	listener	champions	commonplace	unreasonable
curtains	listening	championship	commonsense	reasonably
fountainhead	listens	lioness	cottoned	reasoning
fountains	ruination	lionhearted	cottonmouth	beribboned
chickened	ruined	buttoned	cottonwood	
chickens	ruinous	buttonhole	cottony	
kitchenette	ruins	unbuttoning	dragonfly	
kitchenware	championed	buttons	lemonade	
listened	championing	commonly	lemony	

E Fun Ways to Spell

Initial the box of each activity you finish.

1. Create a crossword puzzle.

3.
Record your voice as you spell your words.

2. Spell your words with paint.

4.
Bounce a ball as you spell your words.

Words with /en/ or /in/

Lesson 25

159

1 Hide and Seek

Reinforce spelling by using multiple styles of learning.

On a white board, Teacher writes each word — one at a time. **Have students:**

- **Look** at the word.
- **Say** the word out loud.
- **Spell** the word out loud.
- **Hide** (teacher erases word.)
- **Write** the word on paper.
- **Seek** (teacher rewrites word.)
- **Check** spelling. If incorrect, rewrite word correctly.

2 Other Word Forms

This activity is optional. Have students write original sentences using these Other Word Forms:

ruinous
commonly
lionhearted
buttonhole

3 Fun Ways to Spell

Four activities are provided. Use one, two, three, or all of the activities. Have students initial the box for each activity they complete.

Options:

- assign activities to students according to their learning styles
- set up the activities in learning centers for students to do throughout the day
- divide students into four groups and assign one activity per group
- do one activity per day

General

To create a crossword puzzle…
- Use a pencil to arrange your words on graph paper.
- Overlap words where letters are shared.
- Don't create any new words.
- Outline each word with a marker and number them.
- Write a clue for each word
- Erase your words.
- Trade with a classmate and work each other's puzzles.

Auditory

To spell your words using a voice recorder…
- Record yourself as you say and spell each word on your spelling list.
- Listen to your recording and check spelling.

Visual

To spell your words with paint…
- Paint each spelling word on your paper.
- Trade papers with a classmate and check each other's spelling.

Tactile

To bounce a ball as you spell your words…
- Look at the first word on your list.
- Bounce the ball as you say each letter of the word aloud.
- Do this with each word on your list.

Working with Words

Familiarize students with word meaning and usage.

Sentence Skills

Remember, there are four kinds of sentences: **imperative**, **declarative**, **exclamatory**, and **interrogative**.

Rewrite the sentences in your Worktext, correcting the misspelled word. Then, circle the word that tells which kind of sentence it is.

Take a minute to memorize...

Mark 11:25

Words with /ən/ or /in/ — Lesson 25

F **Working with Words** Name ____________________

Sentence Skills

An **imperative sentence** is a command and ends with a period or an exclamation point.
Get me a bandage for my knee. Give me that!
A **declarative sentence** tells something and ends with a period.
My knee has a bandage on it.
An **exclamatory sentence** shows strong feelings and ends with an exclamation point.
My knee really hurts!
An **interrogative sentence** asks something and ends with a question mark.
Do you think my knee needs stitches?

Write the sentences below, correcting the misspelled word. Circle the word that tells what kind of sentence it is.

1. Laney pulled aside the cirtain to stare out the window.
   Laney pulled aside the curtain to stare out the window.
   imperative (declarative) exclamatory interrogative

2. Mom stood in the kichen to listin to Laney.
   Mom stood in the kitchen to listen to Laney.
   imperative (declarative) exclamatory interrogative

3. Dad's forgetfulness will not ruen my vacation!
   Dad's forgetfulness will not ruin my vacation!
   imperative declarative (exclamatory) interrogative

4. What is the reasen Dad forgot to send tickets?
   What is the reason Dad forgot to send tickets?
   imperative declarative exclamatory (interrogative)

5. Hurry and untie the ribon on the gift.
   Hurry and untie the ribbon on the gift.
   (imperative) declarative exclamatory interrogative

Word Bank

button	common	dragon	lemon	oven	robin
champion	cotton	fountain	lion	reason	ruin
chicken	curtain	kitchen	listen	ribbon	siren

160

G Dictation

Name ______________________

Write each sentence as your teacher dictates. Use correct punctuation.

1. She opened the kitchen curtain and saw a robin.
2. Mom pulled lemon cookies from the oven.
3. The champion of the race gets a blue ribbon.

H Proofreading

If a word is misspelled, fill in the oval by that word. If all the words are spelled correctly, fill in the oval by **no mistake**.

1. ○ evil ○ cotton ● curten ○ no mistake
2. ○ button ○ lemon ● founten ○ no mistake
3. ○ level ○ model ○ chicken ● no mistake
4. ● reeson ○ final ○ kitchen ○ no mistake
5. ○ battle ● ribon ○ uncle ○ no mistake
6. ○ gentle ○ festival ○ oven ● no mistake
7. ● comon ○ castle ○ siren ○ no mistake
8. ○ jungle ○ possible ● robbin ○ no mistake
9. ○ listen ○ simple ○ puddle ● no mistake
10. ● riun ○ total ○ label ○ no mistake
11. ○ several ○ champion ● draggon ○ no mistake
12. ○ general ○ hospital ○ lion ● no mistake

1 Dictation

Reinforce correct spelling by using current and previous words in context.

Listen as I read each sentence and then write it in your Worktext. Remember to use correct capitalization and punctuation. (Slowly read each sentence twice. Sentences are found in the Student Worktext to the left.)

2 Proofreading

Familiarize students with standardized test format and reinforce recognition of misspelled words.

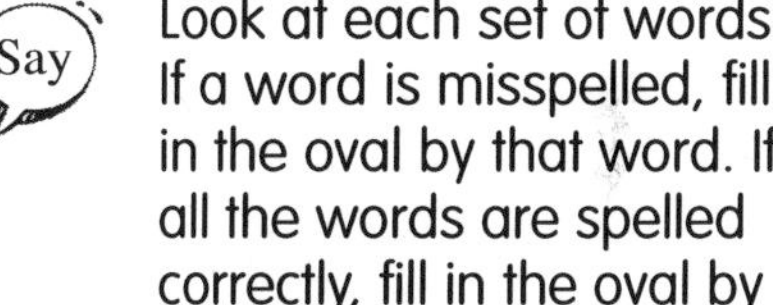

Say: Look at each set of words. If a word is misspelled, fill in the oval by that word. If all the words are spelled correctly, fill in the oval by **no mistake**.

3 Hide and Seek

Reinforce correct spelling of current spelling words. Repeat this activity from Day 2. (A reproducible master is provided in Appendix A as shown on the inset page to the right.)

4 Other Word Forms

Have your students complete this activity to strengthen spelling ability and expand vocabulary.

1 Posttest

Visit the **A Reason For** website to download free, printable Posttest pages.

I will say the word once, use it in a sentence, then say it again. Write your words on a separate sheet of paper.

Progress Chart

Students may record scores. (Appendix B)

Personal Dictionary

Students may add any words they have misspelled to their personal dictionaries. (Appendix B)

Hide and Seek

Play Hide and Seek with your words. Create a bar graph by filling in a box (left to right) for each word you spell correctly.

Other Word Forms

Synonyms

Use the synonyms to write the words. Remember, a synonym is a word that means the same or nearly the same as another word.

1. draperies curtains
2. sensible reasonable
3. jets of water fountains
4. hearing listening
5. African cat lioness
6. ordinarily commonly
7. like a citrus fruit lemony
8. thinking reasoning
9. ordinary commonplace
10. beyond repair ruined
11. was scared chickened
12. winners champions
13. fastening buttoning
14. poisonous snake cottonmouth
15. cowardly chickenhearted
16. kind of tree cottonwood
17. small place to cook kitchenette
18. covered with trimming beribboned

Syllables

Remember, a syllable is a unit of sound in a word. A syllable contains a vowel and possibly one or more consonants. Count how many syllables each word has and write the number on the line.

1. 3 fountainhead
2. 4 championship
3. 3 buttonhole
4. 3 listening
5. 5 unreasonable
6. 6 reasonability
7. 4 chickenhearted
8. 4 lionhearted
9. 3 commonsense
10. 3 dragonfly
11. 4 ruinously
12. 3 kitchenware
13. 4 ruination
14. 2 curtained
15. 3 cottony

Word Bank

beribboned	chickenhearted	cottonwood	lemony	reasonable
buttoning	commonly	curtains	lioness	reasoning
champions	commonplace	fountains	listening	ruined
chickened	cottonmouth	kitchenette		

345

---

1. ruin	Laney felt her vacation falling in **ruin** before her very eyes.
2. common	Although it was **common** for her dad to forget, she was still sad.
3. reason	It was hard to **reason** it all out in her mind.
4. robin	Laney showed Tony and Stephen the **robin** in her new bird book.
5. chicken	The **chicken** with the huge round head made them laugh.
6. fountain	At the water **fountain**, Stephen asked Laney over to skateboard.
7. curtain	Laney pulled back the **curtain** to watch for Stephen.
8. champion	Stephen's dad had been a **champion** in skateboard competition.
9. siren	When he heard a **siren**, Stephen's dad pulled to the curb.
10. dragon	Stephen's helmet has a fierce **dragon** decal along one side.
11. kitchen	Beth's grandma asked the girls to help her in the **kitchen**.
12. lemon	They cracked the eggs for a **lemon** meringue pie.
13. oven	Beth's grandma put the pie in the **oven** to brown the meringue.
14. lion	Laney bought Beth a figurine of a roaring **lion**.
15. button	Mrs. Larkin sewed a **button** on Laney's favorite blouse.
16. cotton	Laney wearily slipped between the cool **cotton** sheets.
17. ribbon	She tucked in her **ribbon** marker and closed her Bible thoughtfully.
18. listen	Laney is learning to **listen** to and obey God.

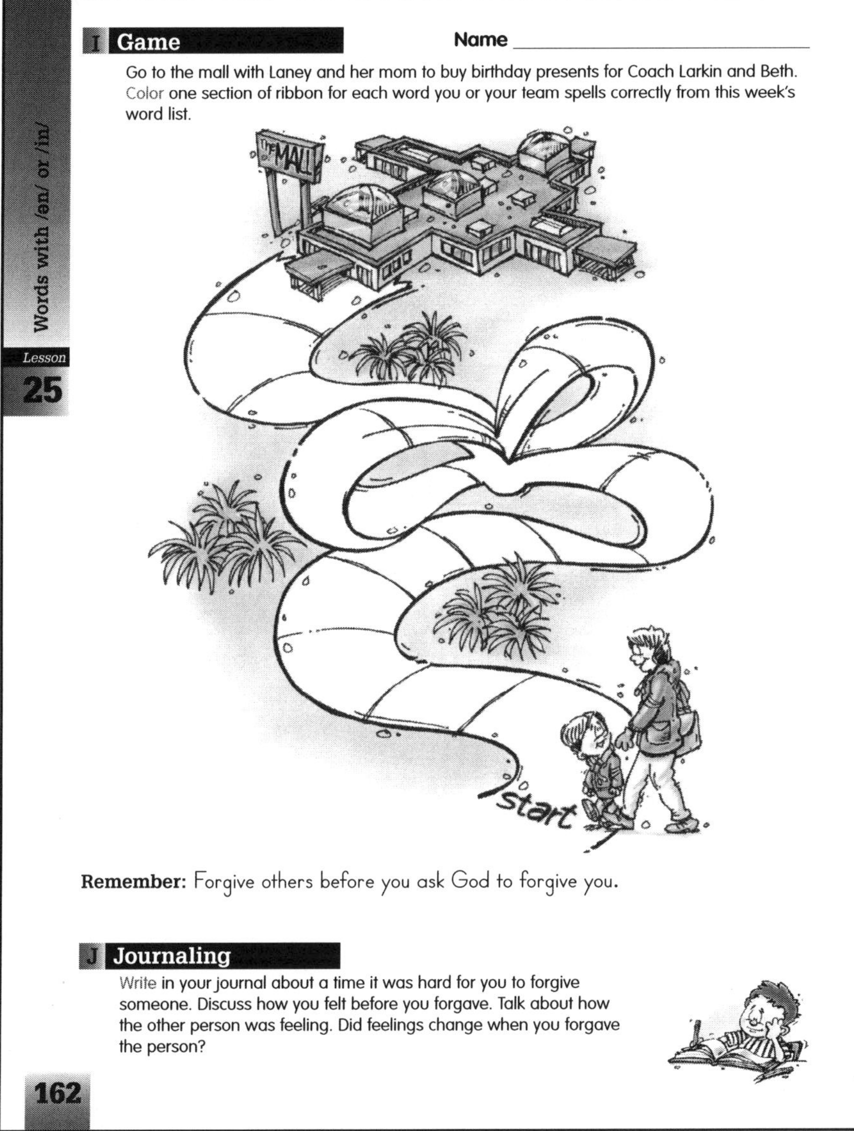

Words with /en/ or /in/

Lesson 25

I Game Name ____________________

Go to the mall with Laney and her mom to buy birthday presents for Coach Larkin and Beth. Color one section of ribbon for each word you or your team spells correctly from this week's word list.

Remember: Forgive others before you ask God to forgive you.

J Journaling

Write in your journal about a time it was hard for you to forgive someone. Discuss how you felt before you forgave. Talk about how the other person was feeling. Did feelings change when you forgave the person?

162

How to Play:

- Divide students into two teams.
- Have a student from team A go to the board.
- Say the spelling word.
- Have the student write the word on the board.
- If correct, instruct each member of team A to color one section of ribbon, beginning at Start.
- Alternate between teams A and B as you go down the word list.
- The team to reach the mall first is the winner.

Small Group Option: Students may play this game without teacher direction in small groups of two or more.

2 Game

Reinforce spelling skills and provide motivation and interest.

Materials

- game page (from Student Worktext)
- crayons or colored pencils (1 per child)
- game word list

Game Word List

1. **curtain**
2. **fountain**
3. **chicken**
4. **kitchen**
5. **listen**
6. **oven**
7. **siren**
8. **robin**
9. **ruin**
10. **champion**
11. **lion**
12. **button**
13. **common**
14. **cotton**
15. **dragon**
16. **lemon**
17. **reason**
18. **ribbon**

3 Journaling

Provide a meaningful reason for correct spelling through personal writing.

Review the story using discussion leads provided on the following page. Encourage students to apply the Scriptural value in their journaling.

Journaling (continued)

- How did Laney feel when her letter was returned stamped "Addressee Unknown?" (Angry because she couldn't reach her dad.)
- How do you think she felt when she found out her dad was going to be working all of spring break? (Angry, hurt. She wouldn't see her dad even if he did come through with the plane tickets.)
- How did she feel when the tickets never came? (Unimportant, angry, hurt.)
- Is it easy to forgive someone who hurts you? (No.)
- When did Laney remember she still needed to pray? (After she got in bed.)
- Raise your hand if you think prayer can help you forgive.

There are three commonly used words in the English language with the "uu" letter combination: muumuu, vacuum, and continuum.

Word Wow!

Sarah's Secret

Sarah prays for help when her mother and sister are both sick.

I wish I could write like Mrs. Burton does. Sarah Johansen sat quietly at her desk and watched her teacher write Matthew 6:6 on the board. *All of her letters look almost exactly like the letters in our handwriting book. Mine never do. Especially my capital letters like that 'F' in 'Father.'*

"Who would like to read this Scripture aloud for us?" Mrs. Burton smiled at her students. "Katelynn?"

"When you pray, go away by yourself, all alone, and shut the door behind you and pray to your Father secretly, and your Father, Who knows your secrets, will reward you." Katelynn read the words carefully.

Mrs. Burton picked up a colored marker and underlined some of the words in the text. "Lots of people had come to listen to Jesus that day, and He taught them many things which are recorded in the Scriptures. In this verse He was explaining how to talk to God. Why do you think He used these words?" She pointed at the words she'd underlined as she said them, "By yourself. All alone. Secretly. What do you think, Kristin?"

"Does it mean we're not supposed to pray in front of other people?" Kristin glared at Tommy when he snickered. "Well, isn't that what 'by yourself' and 'all alone' mean?"

"What do you think, Tommy?" Tommy squirmed when Mrs. Burton turned to him.

"Uh, well, I don't know." He fiddled with his pencil. "I guess it does say that, but we always pray in front of other people." He sat up straighter and laid the pencil down. "If it's wrong, why do families pray together and people pray up front at church? We even pray here at school every day."

"That's true." Mrs. Burton nodded. "Did you have something to add, Thorny?"

"Is it possible that there is information concerning this Scripture of which we are not aware?" Thorny pushed the hair out of his eyes.

"Good point, Thorny." Mrs. Burton picked up her Bible. "It's always a good idea to find out what comes before and after a Scripture passage. It's called the context, and it makes a difference in understanding what the Scripture means. Jesus was talking about how some of the people of that time liked to stand out on the street corner and pray out loud."

"Mrs. B, why would someone do that?" Kristin asked.

"They were showing off—just praying to make people think they were very good. Jesus explained that prayer isn't for impressing others. It's for talking to God. You can tell God how you feel, thank Him for things, or ask Him for help when you're with a group—or all by yourself. All alone. Secretly. He hears and will answer prayers that are sincere wherever they're prayed."

"Do You hear me, God, even when I just talk to You in my thoughts like this?" Sarah stared at the board without seeing any of the perfectly written letters.

Sarah waited and waited for Nellie in front of the school that afternoon. Finally Sarah spotted her older sister coming down the walk. "What took you so long?" she asked.

"I don't feel good," Nellie groaned. "I was lying down in the office till Mrs. Bentley was ready to go. She's coming now. Ohhhhh, my stomach feels so sick!"

Mrs. Bentley rushed toward the sisters. "Would you carry this for me, Sarah? We may need it if Nellie has to throw up." She handed a small plastic bucket to Sarah and wrapped an arm around Nellie's shoulders. "Let's get you settled in the car, Nellie."

Sarah bit her lip as Mrs. Bentley pulled out of the parking lot and turned the car toward the girls' home. Nellie slumped in the seat with her eyes closed.

Sarah met Mrs. Bentley's concerned gaze in the rearview mirror. "I'm afraid she has the stomach flu that's been going around. If so, she'll feel horrible for at least 24 hours," Mrs. Bentley said. "She had a fever of 102° about 2 o'clock. That's what concerns me—her fever may go higher this evening."

When she spotted the beat-up car parked in front of the Johansen house, Mrs. Bentley sighed with relief. "Oh, good—your mother's home." She pulled the car over to the curb and parked, then started to open her door.

"It's okay, Mrs. Bentley." Nellie pulled herself up. "Momma's here and Sarah can help me inside."

"Are you sure, dear?" Mrs. Bentley checked Nellie's forehead with her hand. Sarah jumped out and ran around to open the door on Nellie's side. "Just give me a call if you need anything, you hear?"

"Yes, ma'am." Sarah helped Nellie from the car. "Thank you, Mrs. Bentley." The school secretary didn't start her car until she saw that the girls were safely inside. When Sarah turned and waved, she finally pulled away.

"Sarah!" Nellie called from the kitchen. Sarah rushed in just in time with the plastic bucket. Nellie was violently sick. Her stomach heaved over and over. Sarah was afraid she would lose her own lunch as she tried to steady her sister. Finally, the spasms ended.

"Momma!" Sarah helped Nellie into a kitchen chair and grabbed a damp cloth to wipe her face and mouth. "Momma, Nellie's

Story (continued)

sick!" There was no answer. "Just a minute, Nellie." Sarah patted her older sister's shoulder. "You just lean on the table while I go get Momma." Nellie sagged onto the table and Sarah rushed into the living room. No momma. "Momma? Momma!" Sarah rushed into her mother's bedroom and stopped. "Oh, Momma."

Mrs. Johansen was lying across her bed, passed out from drinking too much. She'd been sick all over herself and the bed. Sarah leaned against the door frame. "Momma, no. Oh, Momma."

Sarah had seen her mother sick from too much alcohol, but Nellie had always cleaned things up. Now Nellie was sick. And Sarah didn't know how to take care of her if the fever went up. She shuddered.

Somehow she had to take care of both Nellie and her mother. Mrs. Bentley was gone. Mrs. Tucker in the house next door was at least 90, and Mr. Tanner on the other side worked the late shift. That left Mrs. Cosby across the street.

Sarah rushed to the front window and looked across the street. Mrs. Cosby's big dog guarded the porch, but her car wasn't in the driveway. *What do I do?* Sarah stared out the dirty window, feeling very much alone. *Alone. By yourself. Secretly. Those are the words Mrs. Burton underlined in the Scripture today.* "God, I'm all alone except for You. I really need Your help. Help me take care of Nellie and Momma. Help me know what to do and please help Nellie's temperature not to go up any higher."

Sarah squared her shoulders and went back to the kitchen. Seeing her sister looking so miserable, Sarah added another request to her prayer. "It sure would be nice if You could send someone to help."

"C'mon, Nellie." Sarah tried to sound cheerful. "Momma's not feeling well, either, so I'll help you to bed."

When Nellie was tucked in, Sarah went to dump the bucket and wash it out. When she brought it back to the bedroom, Nellie opened her eyes.

"Momma's unconscious again, isn't she, Sarah?" Nellie's eyes looked too bright and her skin was flushed instead of pale like it had been earlier.

Sarah nodded.

"I think my fever's getting worse." Nellie moved restlessly. "My head hurts a lot and I ache all over and my stomach is SO sick."

"I'll get you a cool damp cloth to put on your forehead like Momma does," Sarah said as she turned down the blanket.

"NO!" Nellie complained. "I'm freezing! Don't take the blanket away!"

"If your fever's getting higher, we've got to keep you as cool as we can." Sarah tried to sound calm.

Nellie groaned. "I'm going to see to Momma," Sarah said. "Call me if you need anything."

What do I need to get Momma cleaned up? Probably rags, some warm water….What's that? It sounded like a knock at the door. Sarah peeked out the window at the front door. *It's Mrs. Noma! Mrs. Noma is here!* Sarah rushed to open the door for her friend's mother.

"Hello, Sarah." Mrs. Noma's soft accent was so welcome. "I made cookies today and thought I'd share some with…" Sarah felt the tears spill over and down her cheeks. "Why, Sarah, what's the matter?" Setsuko's mother knelt down with her hands on Sarah's shoulders.

"N-Nellie's real sick and Momma's drunk and passed out and I didn't know what to do and I prayed for help and Jesus sent you." Sarah blurted it all out in one breath. Although she'd never told anyone before, she was surprised at how easy it was to admit that her mother was drunk. Mrs. Noma didn't seem surprised at the horrible secret. She just enfolded Sarah in a hug.

"There, there, Sarah." Mrs. Noma patted her back gently. "Everything will be just fine. Let's check on Nellie first, and then I'll take care of your mother."

The next day when Mrs. Burton asked everyone to get out their Worktexts for handwriting, Sarah read Matthew 6:6 again. "When you pray, go away by yourself, all alone, and shut the door behind you and pray to your Father secretly, and your Father, Who knows your secrets, will reward you."

"I'm glad You know everything, God, even the secret stuff no one else knows. Thank you for hearing me and sending Mrs. Noma to help us last night." Sarah took special care with her handwriting, and the letters looked almost exactly like the letters in the handwriting book, especially the capital 'F' in 'Father.'

2 Discussion Time

Check understanding of the story and development of personal values.

- Why was Nellie slow to come outside after school?
- What was Mrs. Bentley afraid might happen to Nellie?
- How come Nellie and Sarah's mother couldn't help take care of Nellie?
- Why couldn't Sarah get a neighbor to help?
- What did Sarah do when she was all alone and needed help?
- Who came and helped?

A Preview
Name
Write each word as your teacher says it.
1. compare
2. fare
3. glare
4. hare
5. share
6. dairy
7. upstairs
8. stare
9. bare
10. scarce
11. pear
12. wear
13. scare
14. hair
15. dare
16. anywhere
17. repair
18. fair
Scripture
Matthew 6:6
Words with /âr/
Lesson 26
163

3 Preview

Test for knowledge of the correct spellings of these words.

Customize Your List

On a separate sheet of paper, additional words of your choice may be tested.

I will say each word once, use the word in a sentence, then say the word again. Write the words on the lines in your Worktext.

Correct Immediately!

Let's correct our Preview. I will spell each word out loud. If you spelled a word incorrectly, rewrite it correctly.

Progress Chart

Students may record scores. (Reproducible master provided in Appendix B.)

1.	**compare**	Sarah knew that nothing could **compare** to God's love for her.
2.	**fare**	Sarah's mother could not afford the **fare** to have a driver pick up the girls after school.
3.	**glare**	The **glare** from the sun reflected dully off the dirty windows.
4.	**hare**	A long-legged **hare** bounded across the yard in front of them.
5.	**share**	Nellie and Sarah try to **share** the chores around the house.
6.	**dairy**	Cheddar cheese is Sarah's favorite **dairy** product.
7.	**upstairs**	There is not an **upstairs** in Sarah and Nellie's house.
8.	**stare**	Sarah did not just sit and **stare**; she worked hard to help her sister.
9.	**bare**	The cupboards were almost **bare** again.
10.	**scarce**	Money was **scarce** because of their mother's alcoholism.
11.	**pear**	Sarah ate a **pear** out of an open can in the refrigerator.
12.	**wear**	Sarah found a clean nightgown for Nellie to **wear**.
13.	**scare**	Nellie's rising temperature gave Sarah a **scare**.
14.	**hair**	She smoothed Nellie's **hair** back with the cool, damp cloth.
15.	**dare**	She did not **dare** leave the blanket on Nellie.
16.	**anywhere**	Sarah could not think of **anywhere** to turn for help but to God.
17.	**repair**	Mrs. Noma lovingly helped Sarah put the house back into good **repair**.
18.	**fair**	Even when life does not seem **fair**, God loves us and will hear our prayers.

Word Shapes

Help students form a correct image of whole words.

Look at each word and think about its shape. Now, write the word in the correct Word Shape Boxes. You may check off each word as you use it.

(In many words, the sound of **/âr/** is spelled with **are**, **ear**, **ere**, or **air**. Because spellers cannot rely on a phonetic way of remembering the various spellings, this sound is often difficult.)

In the Word Shape Boxes, fill in the boxes containing the letters that spell the sound of **/âr/** in each word.

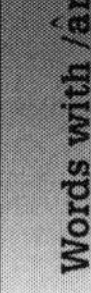

B Word Shapes Name ______________

Write each word in the correct Word Shape Boxes. Next, in the Word Shape Boxes, shade in the boxes containing the letters that spell the sound of **/âr/** in each word.

Word	Answer
1. bare	dairy
2. compare	stare
3. dare	dare
4. fare	fare
5. glare	wear
6. hare	repair
7. scare	hare
8. share	scare
9. stare	share
10. scarce	upstairs
11. pear	scarce
12. wear	pear
13. anywhere	hair
14. dairy	compare
15. fair	fair
16. hair	glare
17. repair	bare
18. upstairs	anywhere

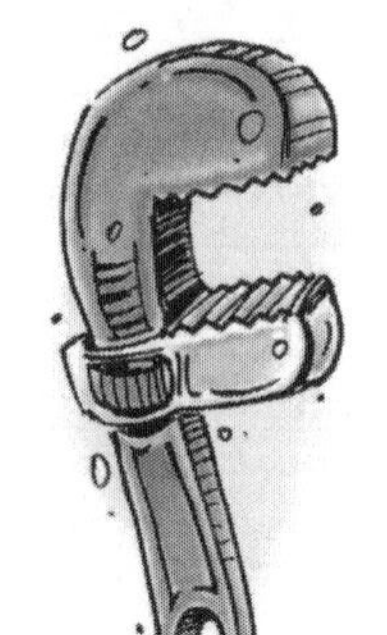

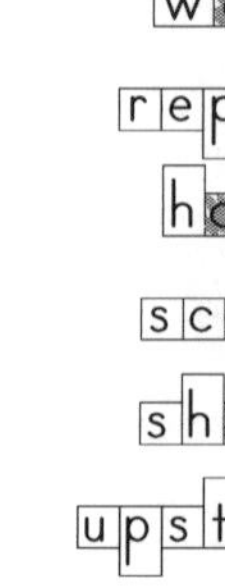

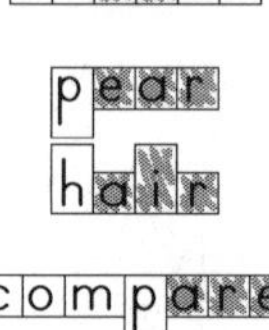

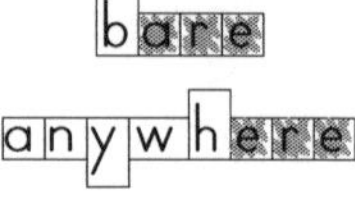

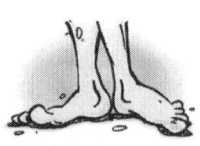

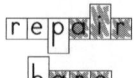

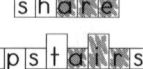

164

Answers may vary for duplicate word shapes.

Take a minute to memorize...

Matthew 6:6

Be Prepared For Fun

Check these supply lists for **Fun Ways to Spell** - presented **Day 2**. Purchase and/or gather these items ahead of time!

General
- Pencil
- Notebook Paper
- Spelling List

Auditory
- Spelling List

Visual
- Pencil
- Paper
- Spelling List

Tactile
- Thick Pile Carpet Samples
- Spelling List

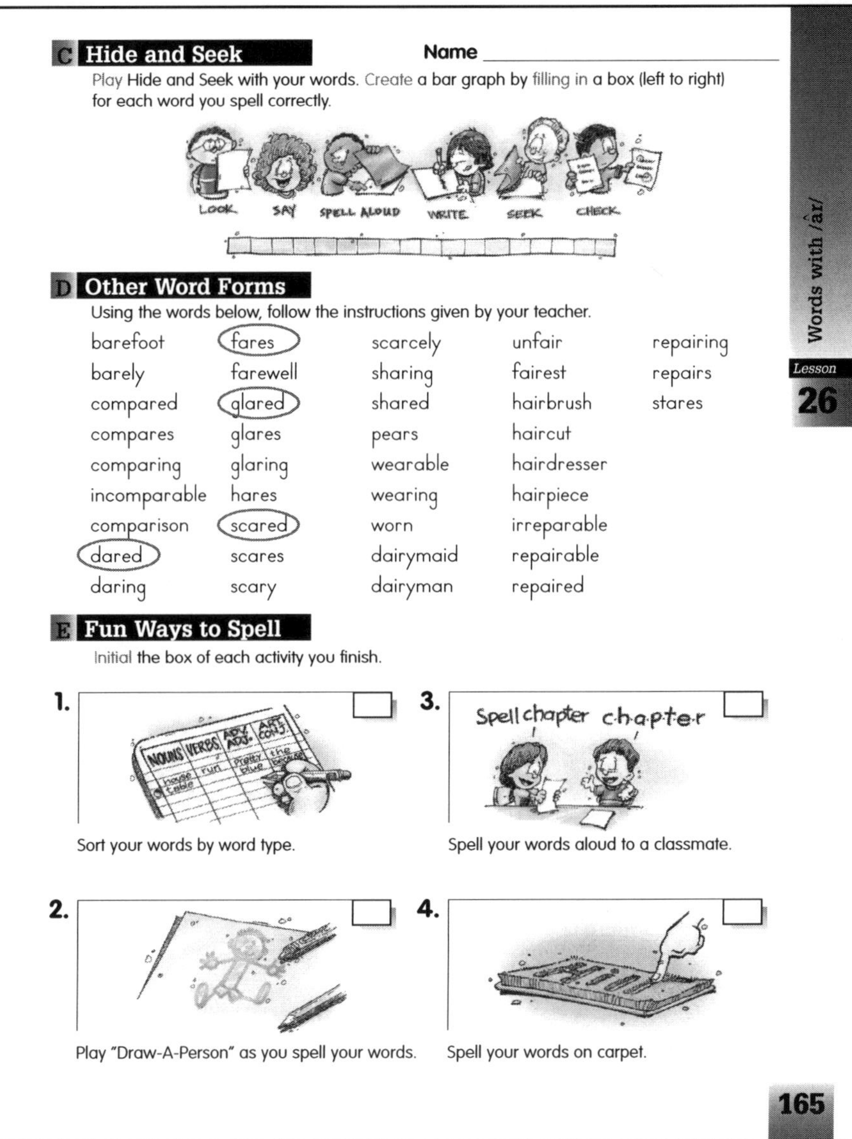

C Hide and Seek Name ____________

Play Hide and Seek with your words. Create a bar graph by filling in a box (left to right) for each word you spell correctly.

D Other Word Forms

Using the words below, follow the instructions given by your teacher.

barefoot	(fares)	scarcely	unfair	repairing
barely	farewell	sharing	fairest	repairs
compared	(glared)	shared	hairbrush	stares
compares	glares	pears	haircut	
comparing	glaring	wearable	hairdresser	
incomparable	hares	wearing	hairpiece	
comparison	(scared)	worn	irreparable	
(dared)	scares	dairymaid	repairable	
daring	scary	dairyman	repaired	

E Fun Ways to Spell

Initial the box of each activity you finish.

1. Sort your words by word type.

2. Play "Draw-A-Person" as you spell your words.

3. Spell your words aloud to a classmate.

4. Spell your words on carpet.

Words with /âr/ Lesson 26

165

1 Hide and Seek

Reinforce spelling by using multiple styles of learning.

On a white board, Teacher writes each word — one at a time. **Have students:**

- **Look** at the word.
- **Say** the word out loud.
- **Spell** the word out loud.
- **Hide** (teacher erases word.)
- **Write** the word on paper.
- **Seek** (teacher rewrites word.)
- **Check** spelling. If incorrect, rewrite word correctly.

2 Other Word Forms

This activity is optional. Have students find and circle the Other Word Forms that are synonyms of the following:

terrified
prospers
glowered
challenged

3 Fun Ways to Spell

Four activities are provided. Use one, two, three, or all of the activities. Have students initial the box for each activity they complete.

Options:

- assign activities to students according to their learning styles
- set up the activities in learning centers for students to do throughout the day
- divide students into four groups and assign one activity per group
- do one activity per day

General

To sort your words by word type...
- Make four columns on your paper.
- Label the columns: Nouns, Verbs, Adjectives/Adverbs, and Articles/Conjunctions.
- Write each of your spelling words in the appropriate column.

Auditory

To spell your words aloud to a classmate...
- Ask a classmate to read a word from your spelling list.
- Spell the word aloud to your classmate.
- Ask your classmate to check your spelling.
- Read a word to your classmate and continue taking turns.
- The person to spell the most words right wins!

Visual

To play "Draw-A-Person" when you spell your words...
- Ask a classmate to read a word from your spelling list to you.
- Write the word on your paper. Check your spelling.
- If you misspell the word, draw one part of a person on your paper.
- Read a word to a classmate and continue taking turns.
- The last one to finish drawing a person wins!

Tactile

To spell your words on carpet...
- Use fingertip to write a spelling word on carpet.
- Check your spelling.
- Smooth the word out with your hand and write another word.

Working with Words

Familiarize students with word meaning and usage.

Homophones

Homophones are words that are pronounced the same, but differ in meaning, origin, and sometimes spelling. Write the words **cents** and **sense** on the board. Explain that these words are homophones. Although they sound the same, they are spelled differently and have different meanings. Just for fun, ask this riddle:

Why didn't the quarter jump off the cliff after the dime?

Answer: because it had more cents or sense.

Circle the correct homophone to complete each sentence.

Clues

Using the context clues, write a spelling word in each blank.

Take a minute to memorize...

Matthew 6:6

Lesson 26 — Words with /âr/

F Working with Words Name ____________

Homophones

Words that sound alike but have different meanings and spellings are called homophones. Circle the correct homophones to complete the sentences.

1. Did you pay your (fair, **fare**) when you went to the (**fair**, fare)?
2. I like to (**pare**, pear) my apples before I eat them.
3. He took off his (**pair**, pear) of shoes and walked in his (**bare**, bear) feet.
4. A mammal like a large rabbit with strong back legs is a (hair, **hare**).
5. The (pair, **pear**) trees will (bare, **bear**) a good crop this year.
6. Why did the girl with long (**hair**, hare) sit on the (stare, **stair**) and (**stare**, stair) at me?

Clues

Write a spelling word for each clue.

1. To look at things to see how they are different is to <u>compare</u> them.
2. To choose which clothes to put on is to decide what to <u>wear</u>.
3. A farm that keeps cows to produce milk is a <u>dairy</u>.
4. To frighten or startle someone is to <u>scare</u> her.
5. To be bold and have enough courage to do something is to <u>dare</u>.
6. To not have plenty of something is to have a <u>scarce</u> supply.
7. The top floor of a house with more than one story is the <u>upstairs</u>.
8. To fix something and make it work well again is to <u>repair</u> it.
9. To use or enjoy something with others is to <u>share</u>.
10. To look fiercely or angrily at someone is to <u>glare</u> at them.
11. To stay home is to not go <u>anywhere</u>.
12. A variety of food provided for you to eat is called <u>fare</u>.

Word Bank

anywhere	dairy	fare	hare	scarce	stare
bare	dare	glare	pear	scare	upstairs
compare	fair	hair	repair	share	wear

166

G Dictation

Name ____________________

Write each sentence as your teacher dictates. Use correct punctuation.

1. She did not dare go anywhere for help.

2. Food was scarce so she ate a pear and cookies.

3. They shared clothes for her to wear.

Words with /âr/

Lesson 26

H Proofreading

If a word is misspelled, fill in the oval by that word. If all the words are spelled correctly, fill in the oval by **no mistake**.

1. ○ cotton ○ curtain ○ bare ● no mistake
2. ○ listen ○ kitchen ○ dare ● no mistake
3. ● repare ○ button ○ fare ○ no mistake
4. ○ ruin ○ fountain ● upstares ○ no mistake
5. ● fiar ○ glare ○ reason ○ no mistake
6. ○ ribbon ○ lemon ● haer ○ no mistake
7. ○ compare ○ champion ○ scare ● no mistake
8. ○ chicken ● dary ○ share ○ no mistake
9. ○ siren ○ lion ○ stare ● no mistake
10. ○ oven ○ hair ● scarse ○ no mistake
11. ○ common ○ pear ● anywere ○ no mistake
12. ○ robin ○ dragon ○ wear ● no mistake

167

1 Dictation

Reinforce correct spelling by using current and previous words in context.

Listen as I read each sentence and then write it in your Worktext. Remember to use correct capitalization and punctuation. (Slowly read each sentence twice. Sentences are found in the Student Worktext to the left.)

2 Proofreading

Familiarize students with standardized test format and reinforce recognition of misspelled words.

Look at each set of words. If a word is misspelled, fill in the oval by that word. If all the words are spelled correctly, fill in the oval by **no mistake**.

3 Hide and Seek

Reinforce correct spelling of current spelling words. Repeat this activity from Day 2. (A reproducible master is provided in Appendix A as shown on the inset page to the right.)

4 Other Word Forms

Have your students complete this activity to strengthen spelling ability and expand vocabulary.

Hide and Seek

Play Hide and Seek with your words. Create a bar graph by filling in a box (left to right) for each word you spell correctly.

Other Word Forms

Sentence Fun

Circle the word that correctly completes each sentence.

1. They decided to ride the horses (barely, bareback).
2. The (repairing, repairman) is downstairs fixing the dishwasher.
3. I got a stain on my shirt the first time I (wore, worn) it.
4. We used to buy milk from a (dairys, dairyman) who lives nearby.
5. Sarah and Nellie (shared, sharing) a bedroom.
6. Daniel (scary, scarcely) heard what his mom was saying.
7. We bought a bushel of (pears, pares) to can.
8. The little boy felt (daring, dares) as he climbed up the slide.
9. We enjoy going (barely, barefoot) in the summertime.
10. Our Pekingese dog is very (hairier, hairy) and bouncy.
11. Each autumn we go to the (fairgrounds, fairest) for the county fair.
12. The sun (glaring, glaringly) through the window makes me hot.
13. Mom is busy (comparison, comparing) prices in the grocery store.
14. I couldn't sleep after watching a (scared, scary) movie.
15. We will be (wearing, wearer) uniforms at my school next year.
16. Dad took me to the barber to get a (haircut, hairless).
17. I don't think her bike computer is (repairing, repairable).
18. Grandma waved (fared, farewell) when we took her to the airport.
19. This car doesn't look good, (compared, comparing) to our new one.
20. Sarah checked to see how her mother was (faring, fared).

346

1 Posttest

Visit the **A Reason For** website to download free, printable Posttest pages.

I will say the word once, use it in a sentence, then say it again. Write your words on a separate sheet of paper.

Progress Chart

Students may record scores. (Appendix B)

Personal Dictionary

Students may add any words they have misspelled to their personal dictionaries. (Appendix B)

1. scare — Nellie's fever gave Mrs. Bentley a **scare.**
2. fare — The girls could not pay **fare** for a ride home.
3. glare — The afternoon sun created a **glare** on Mrs. Bentley's windshield.
4. stare — Mrs. Bentley did not **stare** at the beat-up car.
5. bare — Sarah opened the cabinet doors and saw the shelves were **bare.**
6. dare — Sarah did not **dare** leave her sister alone in the house.
7. pear — Mrs. Noma brought some freshly baked cookies and **pear** preserves.
8. dairy — She had also stopped by the **dairy** store and purchased milk for the girls.
9. hair — Mrs. Noma hugged Sarah and smoothed her ruffled **hair.**
10. compare — Nothing can **compare** with God's solutions to our problems.
11. share — The Nomas are faithful to **share** what they have with Nellie and Sarah.
12. scarce — Because of their mom's alcoholism, money was often **scarce.**
13. wear — The Nomas often gave them good clothes to **wear.**
14. anywhere — Sarah did not have **anywhere** to turn for help but to the Lord.
15. fair — Life does not always seem **fair.**
16. repair — God wants to **repair** our broken hearts and answer our prayers.
17. hare — Sarah sometimes sees a wild **hare** leap across the yard.
18. upstairs — She is glad there is not an **upstairs** to clean, too.

Words with /âr/

Lesson 26

I Game Name ______________________

Follow along with Mrs. Noma to check on Sarah and her sister Nellie. Move one space for each word you or your team spells correctly from this week's word list.

Remember: God loves to hear your secret prayers.

J Journaling

In your journal, write a poem about prayer. (For example: I always talk to God above, I know He listens with real love.)

168

How to Play:

- Divide students into two teams.
- Have each student place his/her game piece on Start.
- Have a student from team A go to the board.
- Say the spelling word.
- Have the student write the word on the board.
- If correct, instruct each member of team A to move his/her game piece forward one space.
- Alternate between teams A and B as you go down the word list.
- The team to reach Sarah first is the winner.

Small Group Option: Students may play this game without teacher direction in small groups of two or more.

2 Game

Reinforce spelling skills and provide motivation and interest.

Materials

- game page (from Student Worktext)
- game pieces (1 per child)
- game word list

Game Word List

1. **bare**
2. **compare**
3. **dare**
4. **fare**
5. **glare**
6. **hare**
7. **scare**
8. **share**
9. **stare**
10. **scarce**
11. **pear**
12. **wear**
13. **anywhere**
14. **dairy**
15. **fair**
16. **hair**
17. **repair**
18. **upstairs**

3 Journaling

Provide a meaningful reason for correct spelling through personal writing.

Review the story using discussion leads provided on the following page. Encourage students to apply the Scriptural value in their journaling.

Journaling (continued)

- Which words did Mrs. Burton underline in the Scripture her class was discussing? (By yourself. All alone. Secretly.)
- Does this Scripture mean we shouldn't pray around anyone else? Explain its meaning. (No. It means we shouldn't pray to show off in front of others, but to talk to God sincerely. We can do that with others or all alone in secret.)
- What was wrong with Nellie? (She had the flu including a fever and a sick stomach.)
- What was wrong with Sarah's mother? (She was sick and had passed out from too much alcohol.)
- How was Sarah's prayer answered? (Mrs. Noma came to bring some cookies and stayed to help.)
- How do you think Sarah felt after sharing the secret of her mother's alcoholism with Mrs. Noma? (Relieved. Glad that someone she trusted knew about it and was there to help.)
- Remember, you can share your deepest secrets with God who loves you and is always there to help.

The naval rank of "Admiral" is derived from the Arabic phrase "amir al bahr," which means "commander of the sea."

Word Wow!

1 **Literature Connection**
Topic: Friendship
Theme Text: John 15:13, 14

Purple Hearts and Found Memories

Tommy learns about Grandpa's bravery in the war.

"It's never going to stop raining!" Tommy complained to no one in particular. In fact, no one was around to hear his complaint. "There's nothing to do." He wandered out of his bedroom and down the stairs. "Can't play baseball, can't go roller-blading, can't... Oh, hi, Grandma."

"It's time you got a haircut, Robert Nathaniel." Tommy's grandmother looked at him and scolded, "Just look at all that hair. Hair everywhere!" She turned her attention back to something she was holding and muttered on about hair.

Tommy moved closer to see what she was fussing with. He'd gotten used to being called by his dad's name, although it had bothered him at first. His grandmother never knew who he was anymore. She rarely recognized him as even being a part of her family, so it was nicer to be called Bob than to be treated as a stranger. "What's that, Grandma?" Tommy pointed at the object she was holding.

Grandma closed her eyes and leaned back in the comfortable recliner before answering. She rubbed one age-twisted finger over the bit of stuff in her hand. "You know your father loved your hair when you were a babe. He never wanted it cut—it was such a pretty color. He finally let me cut it so you wouldn't look like a girl. It was several inches long by then. He gathered up what was cut off and kept it in an envelope."

Grandma was silent. Tommy wondered if she'd fallen asleep again. He leaned over and touched the silky strawberry blonde strands resting in his grandmother's hand. His father's baby hair had been almost the same shade as his own. No wonder Grandma often called him Bob or Bobby. Grandma stirred at his touch. "Your father surely did love all of you children, Bobby. Did you know he took a lock of hair from each of you four with him when he left for the war?"

"No, I didn't know." Tommy settled on the carpet by his grandmother's box of keepsakes. "Tell me about the war, please, Grandma?" He leaned back against her special chair and looked at the variety of items his grandmother had treasured through the years.

"He was a fine man, your father. A fine man and a fine soldier." Grandma's eyes drifted closed again and she was lost in the past. "Of course, he didn't want to leave us all and go to war, but he was proud to serve his country. His letters told about the interesting places he saw and how bad he felt about the terrible damage the war was doing to those places and the people that lived there." Grandmother smiled and her head nodded. "He always ended each letter with a special bit just for each of you children. Wanted you to have something to remember him by, I suppose."

Tommy fingered a packet of yellowed envelopes tied together with a faded ribbon. "He used to say that when the war was over he wanted to take us all to visit so we could see the places he'd seen." All was silent for a few moments before Grandma spoke again. "And of course, he wrote about the other soldiers in his company, especially Barney and Frank, his buddies."

Grandma's eyes opened suddenly and she leaned forward to sort through the box, searching for something specific. "Look, Bobby, do you remember this?" She pulled out a battered blue velvet box and handed it to Tommy.

"Is that Grandpa's purple heart?" Tommy opened the box and ran his finger over the medal.

"It was supposed to be a simple mission that day." Grandmother settled back in her chair. "There weren't supposed to be any enemy soldiers near them, but there were. Frank came to see me after the war and told me all about it. They were walking along a country road when all of a sudden they were under attack. They fought back as best they could, dropping into the bushes and tall grass on one side of the road. Frank, Barney, your father and some of the others were close together. A grenade landed in the middle of the group, just inches from Frank. He glanced down and was sure he was going to die. But he didn't. Your father threw himself over that grenade and saved the lives of his buddies. Ten of them." A tear trickled down Grandma's wrinkled cheek.

Tommy sat silently listening to the rain drumming steadily on the roof. He held the medal and wondered what it would be like to have to fight in a war. How hard it must have been for his grandfather to make the choice he'd made, to give up everything—including the wife and children he adored—to save his buddies.

Grandma seemed to have fallen asleep. Tommy replaced the medal and laid the velvet box back in its place with Grandma's other mementos. He picked up the silver-framed picture he'd seen before. Three young men in army uniforms—their arms draped over each other's shoulders—grinned back at him. He studied the man in the middle, his grandfather.

"He was a fine man." Grandma wasn't asleep after all. She smiled at Tommy and patted his shoulder. "He would be proud to know he had such a wonderful grandson. You're very much like him, Tommy, and like your father. A good boy."

"She knew me, Dad." Tommy perched on a chair

Story (continued)

next to his dad in the study. "She called me Tommy and said I was like Grandfather."

Mr. Rawson turned the desk chair away from the computer to face Tommy. "That's great, Son. Moments like that are special. You can remember that on the days when she doesn't recognize any of us. It makes it a little easier."

"Yeah." Tommy picked up a pencil and fiddled with it. "Do you remember Grandpa much?"

Dad thought for a moment. "Not really. Not as much as I'd like. I was the baby of the family, of course, so I was pretty young when he left." Dad grinned and held out one arm, his hand in a fist. "I do remember he was very strong. We'd hold on to his arm with both hands and he'd pick us up that way. Even my oldest brother, Jerry."

"Do you remember his buddies, Frank and Barney?" Tommy persisted. "Grandma said Frank came to see her after the war."

"Sure. Barney lived clear across the country, but I remember Frank and Barney both. Good old Frank." Dad leaned back in the chair and linked his hands behind his neck. "Yes, I remember him. He sure looked out for us like family. Fact is, he and his wife, June, visited quite a bit through the years. They made sure mother had everything she needed to raise us all. We called him Uncle Frank."

Dad paused before he continued with his memories. "I don't think they ever had any children of their own, but we were their kids. Uncle Frank would play ball with us and tell us stories about the war and about our own dad whenever they came to see us."

Mr. Rawson stared absently into space. "I was probably about your age and feeling pretty sorry for myself because I didn't have a dad like everyone else. Frank sat me down and told me I'd had a special dad, a dad to be proud of. He said he'd do anything he could for me since my dad was gone, but he explained that I always had someone to turn to, even when he wasn't there."

"God?" Tommy questioned.

"Uh huh." Mr. Rawson propped his elbows on the desk and rested his chin on his folded hands. "I can still see Frank in my mind, sitting there on the front step, with tears in his eyes. 'Bobby,' he said. 'There never was a better friend than your father. He proved it by giving his life for his buddies. He truly knew how to love his family and friends because he loved God. And, Bobby, God loves you like that. He already gave His life. All you have to do is choose to be His buddy.'"

The rain was still falling steadily that evening when Dad called everyone to the living room for family devotions. Tommy looked around the lamp-lit room as the family gathered. Dad settled on the couch and looked for the right spot in the book. Mom was curled up comfortably in her favorite chair. Lisa sprawled across the carpet and Grandma dozed peacefully in her special chair. "God, help me to truly love You like Grandpa did. I want to be Your buddy, too!"

2 Discussion Time

Check understanding of the story and development of personal values.

- Why was Tommy bored?
- Who did Grandma often think Tommy was?
- What had Tommy's grandfather taken with him when he had to go to war?
- What happened to Tommy's grandfather?
- Who loves you so much that He gave His life for you?

A Preview Name ______________________

Write each word as your teacher says it.

1. cereal
2. appear
3. weary
4. beard
5. disappear
6. fear
7. period
8. gear
9. steer
10. deer
11. near
12. rear
13. spear
14. fierce
15. tear
16. cheer
17. sincerely
18. weird

Words with /ir/

Lesson 27

Scripture

John 15:13, 14

169

3 Preview

Test for knowledge of the correct spellings of these words.

Customize Your List
On a separate sheet of paper, additional words of your choice may be tested.

I will say each word once, use the word in a sentence, then say the word again. Write the words on the lines in your Worktext.

Correct Immediately!
Let's correct our Preview. I will spell each word out loud. If you spelled a word incorrectly, rewrite it correctly.

Progress Chart
Students may record scores. (Reproducible master provided in Appendix B.)

1. cereal	Tommy ate a bowl of **cereal** for an afternoon snack.
2. appear	It did not **appear** that Grandma recognized anyone in their family.
3. weary	Sometimes Tommy grew **weary** of not being recognized by her.
4. beard	Grandpa shaved his **beard** before he went to war.
5. disappear	He sometimes saw enemy soldiers **disappear** into the brush.
6. fear	The men had a **fear** of stepping on land mines.
7. period	For a **period** of time, Grandpa drove an army supply jeep.
8. gear	The **gear** stick in the jeep was sometimes hard to shift.
9. steer	He knew how to carefully **steer** the jeep down the treacherous road.
10. deer	There was a tiny porcelain **deer** in Grandma's box of keepsakes.
11. near	Grandpa bought it for her in a little town **near** where he was stationed.
12. rear	Tommy's grandpa did not hang back in the **rear** of his battalion.
13. spear	Grandpa's rifle had a bayonet on the end, which is like a small **spear**.
14. fierce	Grandpa wrote Grandma and said the war was **fierce**.
15. tear	A **tear** trickled down Grandma's cheek as she thought of Grandpa.
16. cheer	Tommy tried to **cheer** Grandma up by giving her a big hug.
17. sincerely	Tommy's grandpa **sincerely** cared for others.
18. weird	A lot of people think it's **weird** to give your life for someone else.

Word Shapes

Help students form a correct image of whole words.

Look at each word and think about its shape. Now, write the word in the correct Word Shape Boxes. You may check off each word as you use it.

(In many words, the sound of /îr/ is spelled with **ear**, **eer**, **ier**, **er**, **ere**, or **eir**. Because spellers cannot rely on a phonetic way of remembering the various spellings, this sound is often difficult.)

In the Word Shape Boxes, fill in the boxes containing the letters that spell the sound of /îr/ in each word.

Take a minute to memorize...

John 15:13, 14

B Word Shapes Name ____________________

Words with /îr/ — Lesson 27

Write each word in the correct Word Shape Boxes. Next, in the Word Shape Boxes, shade in the boxes containing the letters that spell the sound of /îr/ in each word.

Word	Word Shape Boxes
1. appear	gear
2. beard	steer
3. disappear	near
4. fear	weird
5. gear	sincerely
6. near	fear
7. rear	period
8. spear	appear
9. tear	rear
10. weary	spear
11. cheer	tear
12. deer	disappear
13. steer	cereal
14. fierce	weary
15. cereal	beard
16. period	cheer
17. sincerely	fierce
18. weird	deer

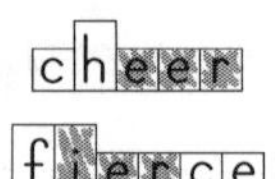

170

Answers may vary for duplicate word shapes.

Be Prepared For Fun

Check these supply lists for **Fun Ways to Spell** - presented **Day 2**. Purchase and/or gather these items ahead of time!

General
- Pencil
- Notebook Paper
- Spelling List

Auditory
- Spelling List

Visual
- Pencil
- Scissors
- 3 X 5 cards (18 per child)
- Spelling List

Tactile
- Toothpicks
- Art Paper (3 sheets per child)
- Glue
- Spelling List

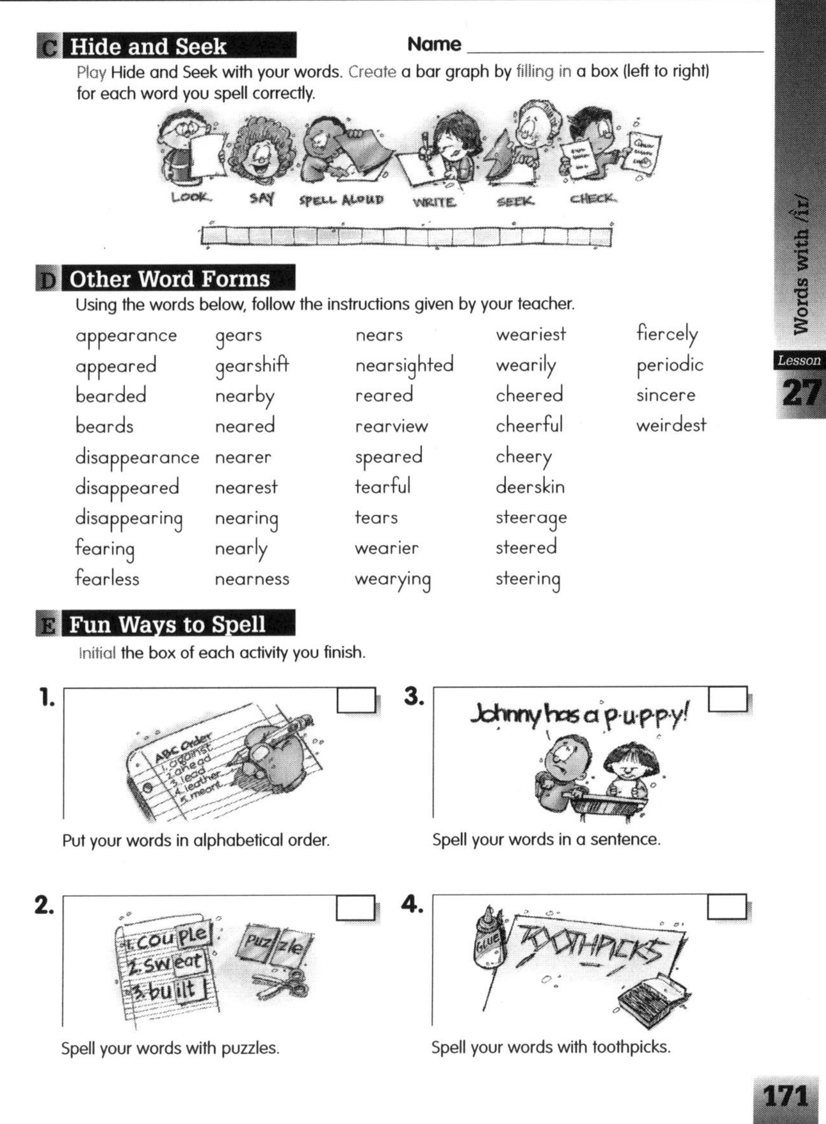

C Hide and Seek Name ______________________

Play Hide and Seek with your words. Create a bar graph by filling in a box (left to right) for each word you spell correctly.

D Other Word Forms

Using the words below, follow the instructions given by your teacher.

appearance	gears	nears	weariest	fiercely
appeared	gearshift	nearsighted	wearily	periodic
bearded	nearby	reared	cheered	sincere
beards	neared	rearview	cheerful	weirdest
disappearance	nearer	speared	cheery	
disappeared	nearest	tearful	deerskin	
disappearing	nearing	tears	steerage	
fearing	nearly	wearier	steered	
fearless	nearness	wearying	steering	

E Fun Ways to Spell

Initial the box of each activity you finish.

1. Put your words in alphabetical order.

3. Spell your words in a sentence.

2. Spell your words with puzzles.

4. Spell your words with toothpicks.

Words with /ir/

Lesson 27

171

1 Hide and Seek

Reinforce spelling by using multiple styles of learning.

On a white board, Teacher writes each word — one at a time. **Have students:**

- **Look** at the word.
- **Say** the word out loud.
- **Spell** the word out loud.
- **Hide** (teacher erases word.)
- **Write** the word on paper.
- **Seek** (teacher rewrites word.)
- **Check** spelling. If incorrect, rewrite word correctly.

2 Other Word Forms

This activity is optional. Have students write these Other Word Forms in alphabetical order:

wearying
wearily
weariest
wearier

3 Fun Ways to Spell

Four activities are provided. Use one, two, three, or all of the activities. Have students initial the box for each activity they complete.

Options:

- assign activities to students according to their learning styles
- set up the activities in learning centers for students to do throughout the day
- divide students into four groups and assign one activity per group
- do one activity per day

General

To put your words in alphabetical order...
- Write all the words in alphabetical order.
- Remember to look at the second, third, or fourth letters of the words when the first letters are the same.

Auditory

To spell your words in a sentence...
- Have a classmate read a spelling word to you from the list.
- Say a sentence with that spelling word.
- Ask your classmate to spell the word.
- Check your classmate's spelling.
- Read words aloud and continue taking turns until you have each spelled all words.

Visual

To spell your words with puzzles...
- Write each word on a card.
- Ask a classmate to cut each word apart between two letters.
- Arrange half of each word on your desk.
- Write the missing part of the word on a piece of paper.
- Do it again with the other half of your cards.
- Check your spelling.

Tactile

To spell your words with toothpicks...
- Choose a word from your spelling list.
- Arrange toothpicks to represent each letter of the word.
- Glue them to a piece of art paper.

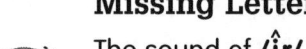

Working with Words

Familiarize students with word meaning and usage.

Missing Letters

The sound of /îr/ can be spelled with **ear, eer, ier, er, ere**, or **eir**. Fill in the missing letter or letters that spell the sound of /îr/.

Sentence Fun

Using context clues in each sentence, decide which word best completes the sentence. Write the word in the blank.

Take a minute to memorize...

John 15:13, 14

Lesson 27 | Day 3

Lesson 27 — Words with /îr/

F Working with Words Name ____________

Missing Letters

Fill in the missing letter or letters that spell the sound of /îr/.

1. app e a r	7. b e a r d	13. disapp e a r
2. f e a r	8. ch e e r	14. w e i r d
3. p e r iod	9. g e a r	15. sp e a r
4. d e e r	10. f i e r ce	16. n e a r
5. r e a r	11. t e a r	17. st e e r
6. c e r eal	12. w e a r y	18. sinc e r e ly

Sentence Fun

Write the spelling word for each sentence.

1. Tommy sat __near__ Grandma to hear about the war.
2. He felt kind of __weird__ when she called him Bobby.
3. A __tear__ escaped down Grandma's cheek as she talked.
4. The __weary__ men had been walking down a country road.
5. They were carrying their army __gear__.
6. Tommy's grandfather chose to ignore his feeling of __fear__.
7. He __sincerely__ loved his friends enough to give his life for them.
8. Frank has a thick, gray __beard__.
9. The rain storm seemed to __appear__ out of nowhere.
10. The sudden storm made the sun __disappear__.
11. I like to eat __cereal__, toast, and fruit for breakfast.
12. We have a history test next __period__.

Word Bank

appear	cheer	fear	near	sincerely	tear
beard	deer	fierce	period	spear	weary
cereal	disappear	gear	rear	steer	weird

172

G Dictation

Name ____________________

Write each sentence as your teacher dictates. Use correct punctuation.

1. He sat near Grandmother to cheer her up.
2. The man with the beard changed gears on his bicycle.
3. She does not appear to be weary.

Words with /ir/

Lesson 27

H Proofreading

If a word is misspelled, fill in the oval by that word. If all the words are spelled correctly, fill in the oval by **no mistake**.

1. ○ compare ○ dare ● apeer ○ no mistake	**5.** ○ fair ○ upstairs ● geer ○ no mistake	**9.** ● feirce ○ scarce ○ tear ○ no mistake
2. ● beerd ○ glare ○ fare ○ no mistake	**6.** ○ pear ○ hair ○ near ● no mistake	**10.** ● wiery ○ cereal ○ share ○ no mistake
3. ○ scare ● disapeer ○ hare ○ no mistake	**7.** ○ stare ○ rear ● peeriod ○ no mistake	**11.** ○ anywhere ○ steer ● chear ○ no mistake
4. ● wierd ○ bare ○ fear ○ no mistake	**8.** ● sincerly ○ spear ○ dairy ○ no mistake	**12.** ○ repair ○ wear ○ deer ● no mistake

173

Dictation

Reinforce correct spelling by using current and previous words in context.

Listen as I read each sentence and then write it in your Worktext. Remember to use correct capitalization and punctuation. (Slowly read each sentence twice. Sentences are found in the Student Worktext to the left.)

Proofreading

Familiarize students with standardized test format and reinforce recognition of misspelled words.

Look at each set of words. If a word is misspelled, fill in the oval by that word. If all the words are spelled correctly, fill in the oval by **no mistake**.

3 Hide and Seek

Reinforce correct spelling of current spelling words. Repeat this activity from Day 2. (A reproducible master is provided in Appendix A as shown on the inset page to the right.)

4 Other Word Forms

Have your students complete this activity to strengthen spelling ability and expand vocabulary.

1 Posttest

Visit the **A Reason For** website to download free, printable Posttest pages.

I will say the word once, use it in a sentence, then say it again. Write your words on a separate sheet of paper.

Progress Chart

Students may record scores. (Appendix B)

Personal Dictionary

Students may add any words they have misspelled to their personal dictionaries. (Appendix B)

Hide and Seek

Play Hide and Seek with your words. Create a bar graph by filling in a box (left to right) for each word you spell correctly.

LOOK SAY HIDE WRITE SEEK CHECK

Other Word Forms

Prefixes and Suffixes

Add each suffix to the word in each row to make a new word.

		+ ed	+ ing	+ s
1.	near	neared	nearing	nears
2.	cheer	cheered	cheering	cheers
3.	appear	appeared	appearing	appears
4.	fear	feared	fearing	fears
5.	gear	geared	gearing	gears
6.	spear	speared	spearing	spears
7.	rear	reared	rearing	rears
8.	tear	teared	tearing	tears
9.	steer	steered	steering	steers
10.	beard	bearded	bearding	beards
11.	disappear	disappeared	disappearing	disappears

Add the prefixes and suffixes to make new words. Write the words on the lines. Remember, when a base word ends with a long vowel sound spelled with **y**, change the **y** to **i** when adding the ending. Also, when words have the consonant-vowel-consonant-**e** pattern, drop the **e** when adding an ending that begins with a vowel.

1. tear + ful + ly = tearfully
2. fear + less = fearless
3. in + sincere = insincere
4. near + by = nearby
5. weird + est = weirdest
6. period + ic = periodic
7. cheery − y + i + ness = cheeriness
8. dis + appear + ance = disappearance
9. weary − y + i + some = wearisome
10. weary − y + i + ly = wearily
11. sincere − e + ity = sincerity
12. fierce + ly = fiercely

1.	cereal	Tommy's favorite afternoon snack is **cereal** and milk.
2.	beard	Grandpa wore a **beard** before he went into the war.
3.	deer	Tommy liked the porcelain **deer** in Grandma's keepsake box.
4.	near	In a faded photo, Tommy saw his grandpa standing **near** a jeep.
5.	period	For a **period** of six months, it was his job to drive the supply jeep.
6.	gear	Grandpa had to wiggle the stick to shift into third **gear**.
7.	steer	He would often **steer** the jeep off the road into the brush.
8.	disappear	He would camouflage the jeep so it would **disappear** from sight.
9.	rear	He would then crouch at the **rear** of the jeep and watch for the enemy.
10.	fear	Grandpa always took his **fear** to the Lord and trusted Him.
11.	spear	A bayonet is like a small **spear** on the end of a rifle.
12.	weary	Although Grandpa was very **weary**, he ran to save his friends.
13.	sincerely	Barney and the other men were **sincerely** grateful for his sacrifice.
14.	fierce	"It was a **fierce** war," Grandma remembered.
15.	tear	A **tear** rolled down her cheek as she looked at the medal.
16.	cheer	Tommy gave her a big hug to **cheer** her up.
17.	appear	For a moment it did **appear** that she recognized Tommy.
18.	weird	Lots of people think it's a **weird** idea to give your life for another.

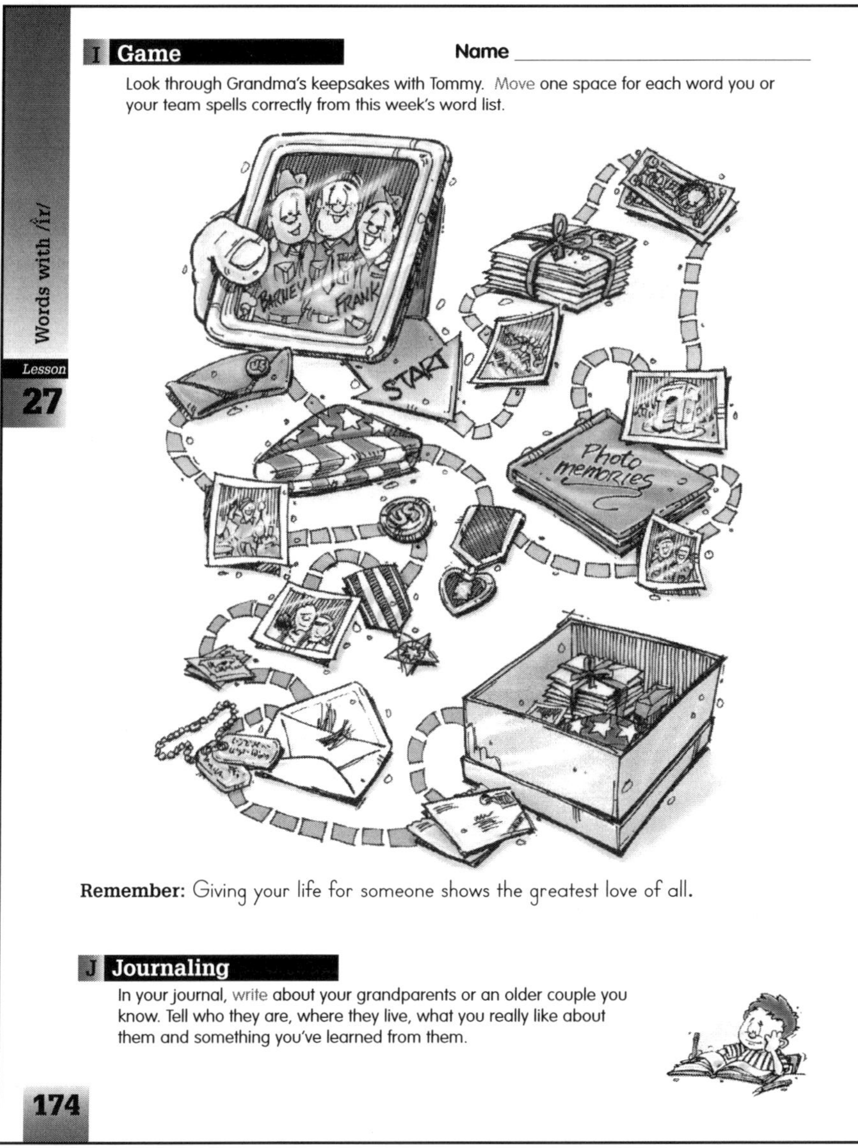

I Game

Name ______________________

Look through Grandma's keepsakes with Tommy. Move one space for each word you or your team spells correctly from this week's word list.

Remember: Giving your life for someone shows the greatest love of all.

J Journaling

In your journal, write about your grandparents or an older couple you know. Tell who they are, where they live, what you really like about them and something you've learned from them.

Words with /îr/

Lesson 27

174

How to Play:

- Divide students into two teams.
- Have each student place his/her game piece on Start.
- Have a student from team A go to the board.
- Say the spelling word.
- Have the student write the word on the board.
- If correct, instruct each member of team A to move his/her game piece forward one space.
- Alternate between teams A and B as you go down the word list.
- The team to reach Grandma's keepsake box first is the winner.

Small Group Option: Students may play this game without teacher direction in small groups of two or more.

2 Game

Reinforce spelling skills and provide motivation and interest.

Materials

- game page (from Student Worktext)
- game pieces (1 per child)
- game word list

Game Word List

1. **appear**
2. **beard**
3. **disappear**
4. **fear**
5. **gear**
6. **near**
7. **rear**
8. **spear**
9. **tear**
10. **weary**
11. **cheer**
12. **deer**
13. **steer**
14. **fierce**
15. **cereal**
16. **period**
17. **sincerely**
18. **weird**

3 Journaling

Provide a meaningful reason for correct spelling through personal writing.

Review the story using discussion leads provided on the following page. Encourage students to apply the Scriptural value in their journaling.

Journaling (continued)

- What did Grandma often call Tommy? (Bob or Bobby. His dad's name.)
- Why did Grandma usually not know who Tommy really was? (She had Alzheimer's.)
- What was in Grandma's box? (Keepsakes like letters, baby hair, pictures, and Grandpa's purple heart and silver star medals.)
- What did Grandpa do to save his buddies? (Threw himself over a grenade to save ten men.)
- Who told Grandma about it? (One of the men he'd saved, his buddy Frank.)
- What did Frank tell Tommy's dad? (That his dad had known how to truly love his family and friends because he'd loved God. That God loves us like that. He's already died for us and all we have to do is choose to be His "buddy" or friend.)
- Grandparents are very special! We can learn a lot from them. Think about the things you especially like about your own grandparents. (Or other relatives if a student in your class does not know any of his/her grandparents.)

"Canada" comes from the Huron-Iroquois word "kanata," meaning "village."

1 Literature Connection
Topic: Death
Theme Text: John 16:33

A Friend in Friscoe

The passing of a beloved pet leads Kristin's family to discuss death.

"Oh Mom, just look at those puppies in the window!" Kristin grabbed her mother's arm and pointed at the pet shop display window. "They're tiny! Surely a puppy that size wouldn't be too much to take care of. Can't we look? Please?"

"Well, okay." Mrs. Wright glanced at her watch. "For just a few minutes." She allowed Kristin to drag her through the stream of shoppers in the mall to the entrance of The Pet Place. "They are cute little dogs."

"Look at him, Mom." Kristin pointed to a tiny ball of brown and black fur in one corner. "Yorkshire Terrier," she read the sign on the pup's window. "He wouldn't grow big at all. Can we get him, Mom, please? Please!"

Mrs. Wright pointed to the part of the sign Kristin hadn't read. "$800.00. Do you have that much money, Kristin?"

"No, but couldn't you and Dad buy him?" Kristin watched the little fellow get up and trot over to lick the glass in front of her face. "See, he likes me already!"

"I'm afraid not, Kristin," Mrs. Wright said firmly. She smiled at the puppy's eager efforts to greet Kristin. "Anything else you want to look at here?"

"No." Kristin held her hand up to the glass. "Rosa has two dogs and two squirrels. We only have one canary and you can't pet it, or sleep with it, or take it for walks—or anything. It's not fair."

Mrs. Wright placed her hand on Kristin's shoulder and steered her gently back out into the mall. "Rosa lives in the country where the dogs can roam. We don't. We have close neighbors. Don't you remember how much the Thompson's dog bothered the whole neighborhood when he barked all the time? They finally gave him away and got Gypsy."

"Yes, but Gypsy doesn't bark and bother people." Kristin looked back at the pet shop.

"We'd have no way of knowing whether a dog would be a problem or not until we got it," Mom pointed out. "And I know a little girl who would have a very hard time giving away a dog once she got it." She reached over and tickled Kristin's ribs.

Kristin didn't even laugh. Mrs. Wright sighed. "Dogs are a big responsibility, Kristin. You know that. Now let's check out this sale." She turned into another store, and Kristin followed reluctantly.

The next Sunday afternoon Kristin was reading a book in the room she shared with Cathy when Mom called, "Kristin, come here, please."

"Coming!" Kristin answered while she looked for something to mark her place. Finally she stuffed Cathy's comb in to mark her spot and laid the book on her bed.

Mom introduced a smiling older woman when Kristin reached the living room, "Kristin, this is Mrs. Fitch."

"Hello." Kristin politely greeted the stranger, but she was puzzled. Why did Mom want her to come meet this woman? Dad patted the spot by him on the couch, and Kristin walked over to sit down beside him.

"Kristin, Mrs. Fitch worked at my company, but now she's moving," Dad said. Everyone in the room was smiling. Kristin couldn't figure out why. "She can't take something with her that she'd like to give to you." Kristin turned confused green eyes towards Mrs. Fitch.

"Here, dear," Mrs. Fitch beckoned with one hand. "Come and meet Friscoe." She reached into the rather large handbag resting by her feet and brought out a beautifully groomed Yorkshire Terrier.

"Friscoe!" In an instant Kristin was kneeling by the chair and the little dog was welcoming her with a friendly lick on the nose. "Is he for me?" Kristin could hardly believe it.

Mrs. Fitch smiled and handed the little dog to Kristin. "Yes, dear. I haven't had him very long, but since I'm moving to take care of my mother, I'm afraid he wouldn't get any attention if I took him with me. He's been as good as he could be in the apartment all day by himself, but I think he needs a little girl to play with and to take care of him." She laughed when Friscoe danced on his back feet in Kristin's lap and licked her nose again. "He seems to think so, too!"

"Oh, thank you, Mrs. Fitch! Thank you, Mom and Dad!" Kristin cuddled the wiggly little body close. "I'll take good care of him! He's just perfect!"

Kristin and Friscoe had so much fun together. Kristin fed him, brushed him, played with him, and tried to teach him tricks. Within a week he would respond to Kristin's commands: "Speak!" "Roll over!" "Stay!" When he had completed each trick, she'd give him a tiny treat.

Kristin took Friscoe for walks and introduced him to the neighborhood and all her friends. She warned him of the houses where big dogs and cats lived. At night he slept on the foot of her bed on her favorite old doll blanket. When she got home from school each day, he met her at the door, spinning in circles with excitement.

The week after she got him, Kristin spent all the money in her bank on things for Friscoe. At The Pet Place she bought him a bright red collar studded with rhinestones, a name tag engraved with his new

Story (continued)

address and telephone number, and a special two-section dish for food and water.

When Friscoe had been part of the family for a few months, Kristin started to feed him one evening and was surprised to find his bowl full of food already. "Mom, did you feed Friscoe today?" She carried the bowl to the kitchen to show her mother.

"No, dear. Maybe Cathy or Christopher did." Mom turned back to putting away groceries. But no one admitted to feeding Friscoe.

"Is he sick, Mom?" Kristin worried when Friscoe sniffed his favorite flavor of canned dog food, then walked slowly over to lie down on his pillow without taking a bite. "He hasn't eaten anything for a whole day."

"He's probably all right." Mrs. Wright watched the small dog for a few minutes. "He looks okay. We'll watch him and if he doesn't eat anything tomorrow we'll call the vet."

"Okay." Kristin sat on the floor by Friscoe and stroked his silky hair gently. Friscoe made a little sighing sound and snuggled close to his mistress. Kristin kept him by her side all evening.

The following day Friscoe still didn't eat. Dr. LeBlanc said they'd better bring him in to the animal hospital. The vet took him into an examining room and looked the little dog over carefully. He took his temperature and listened to his heart.

A few minutes later he came out to talk to Kristin and Mom. The vet explained that there wasn't anything he could do to make Friscoe well again. "Sometimes dogs just get sick and there's nothing that can be done to save them." Dr. LeBlanc's eyes looked serious under his bushy gray eyebrows. "It would be much easier for him—much less painful—if he were to be put to sleep now." He rested a gentle hand lightly on the little dog's head. "I know it's hard, but he won't get better. He's already in a lot of pain. I'm surprised he's acted as well as he has for this long."

Kristin cried all the way home from the animal hospital. She couldn't eat any supper, although Mom had fixed tacos just for her. She didn't want to do anything. She couldn't think of anything but poor little Friscoe. At worship time that evening she crawled into her mother's lap like she had when she was much smaller. Her brothers and sister were weepy, too. Even Mom's eyes looked a little red.

Dad opened the Scriptures and turned the pages until he found the verse he wanted. "In John 16 Jesus tells his disciples about the troubles that will come to them. He told them plainly that they would be sad and grieve. This world is just like that. Bad things happen, even to people who love and obey God. But listen to verse 33. This is the good part. 'I have told you all this so that you will have peace of heart and mind. Here on earth you will have many trials and sorrows; but cheer up, for I have overcome the world.'"

"We'll all miss little Friscoe." Dad cleared his throat. "He was a pretty special little dog and we'll be sad that he's gone, especially Kristin." He smiled at his older daughter. "But it's good to know that this sadness won't last forever. We can have peace inside even when we feel really awful, because God has overcome this old world."

Dad closed the Scriptures and laid the book on his knee. "And because of God, a time will come when bad things won't happen anymore. That's something to be glad about!"

2 Discussion Time

Check understanding of the story and development of personal values.

- What did Kristin want at the mall?
- Why did Mom say no?
- How did Kristin get a dog after all?
- What kind of dog was it and what was his name?
- What things did Kristin do with her new dog?
- How did the Wrights know that Friscoe needed to go to the vet?
- What happened to Friscoe?
- How can we be cheerful when bad things like that happen?

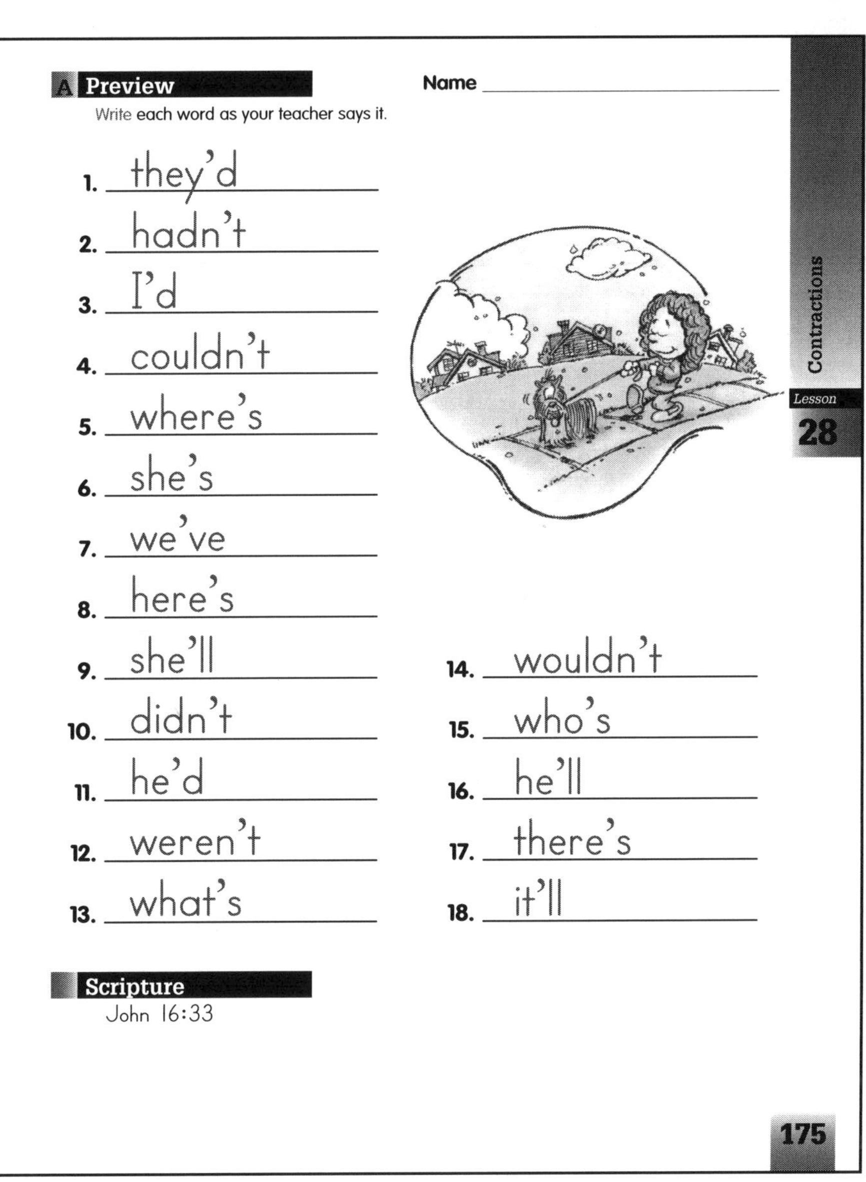
A Preview Name ______

Write each word as your teacher says it.

1. they'd
2. hadn't
3. I'd
4. couldn't
5. where's
6. she's
7. we've
8. here's
9. she'll
10. didn't
11. he'd
12. weren't
13. what's
14. wouldn't
15. who's
16. he'll
17. there's
18. it'll

Contractions

Lesson 28

Scripture

John 16:33

175

3 Preview

Test for knowledge of the correct spellings of these words.

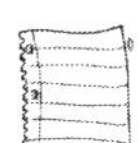

Customize Your List

On a separate sheet of paper, additional words of your choice may be tested.

I will say each word once, use the word in a sentence, then say the word again. Write the words on the lines in your Worktext.

Correct Immediately!

Let's correct our Preview. I will spell each word out loud. If you spelled a word incorrectly, rewrite it correctly.

Progress Chart

Students may record scores. (Reproducible master provided in Appendix B.)

1.	they'd	Kristin realized **they'd** just passed a pet store.
2.	hadn't	Kristin and Christopher **hadn't** ever had a dog.
3.	I'd	"**I'd** just love to have one of those darling puppies," she exclaimed.
4.	couldn't	She **couldn't** understand why she couldn't just pick a puppy.
5.	where's	"I wonder, **where's** your daughter now? I'd love to meet her," said Mrs. Fitch.
6.	she's	"I believe **she's** upstairs reading; I'll call her down," said Mrs. Wright.
7.	we've	"There is someone **we've** been wanting you to meet," said her parents.
8.	here's	"And **here's** Mrs. Fitch's dog, Friscoe," laughed Mr. Wright.
9.	she'll	"I am certain **she'll** take good care of Friscoe," Mrs. Wright assured Mrs. Fitch.
10.	didn't	Kristin **didn't** expect to be given a dog.
11.	he'd	Kristin just knew that **he'd** be happy with them.
12.	weren't	Mrs. Wright and Kristin **weren't** sure why Friscoe wouldn't eat.
13.	what's	"I don't know **what's** the matter with him!" said Kristin with concern.
14.	wouldn't	Friscoe **wouldn't** eat a bit of his food.
15.	who's	"Dr. LeBlanc is the vet **who's** going to look at Friscoe," said the assistant.
16.	he'll	"Do you think **he'll** be all right?" asked Kristin.
17.	there's	"I'm afraid **there's** nothing we can do to save him," said Dr. LeBlanc sadly.
18.	it'll	"You know, **it'll** be wonderful to have no tears in heaven," said Kristin's dad.

Word Shapes

Help students form a correct image of whole words.

Look at each word and think about its shape. Now, write the word in the correct Word Shape Boxes. You may check off each word as you use it.

(A contraction combines two words into one word by leaving out one or more letters. An apostrophe shows where the letters have been left out.)

In the Word Shape Boxes, shade each apostrophe that replaces more than one missing letter.

Name ______________________

Write each word in the correct Word Shape Boxes. Shade each apostrophe that replaces more than one missing letter.

Contractions — Lesson 28

1. he'd
2. I'd
3. they'd
4. he'll
5. it'll
6. she'll
7. couldn't
8. didn't
9. hadn't
10. weren't
11. wouldn't
12. here's
13. she's
14. there's
15. what's
16. where's
17. who's
18. we've

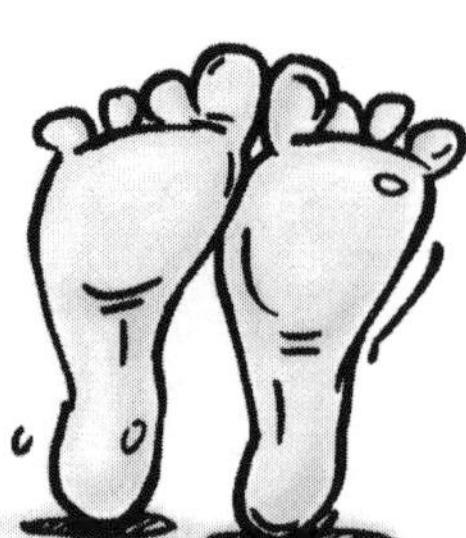

Word Shape Boxes (answers):

- wouldn't
- hadn't
- he'll
- here's
- couldn't
- he'd
- who's
- they'd
- weren't
- I'd
- she'll
- it'll
- where's
- she's
- there's
- we've
- didn't
- what's

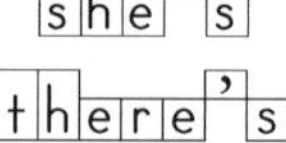
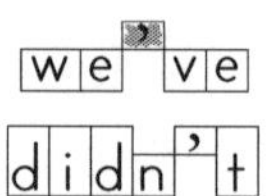

176

Answers may vary for duplicate word shapes.

Take a minute to memorize...

John 16:33

Be Prepared For Fun

Check these supply lists for **Fun Ways to Spell** - presented **Day 2**. Purchase and/or gather these items ahead of time!

General
- Pencil
- Graph Paper (1 sheet per child)
- Spelling List

Auditory
- Pencil
- 3 X 5 Cards Cut in half lengthwise (18 per child)
- Spelling List

Visual
- Glitter
- Glue
- Art Paper (2 sheets per child)
- Spelling List

Tactile
- ABC Macaroni
- Art Paper (1 sheet per child)
- Glue
- Spelling List

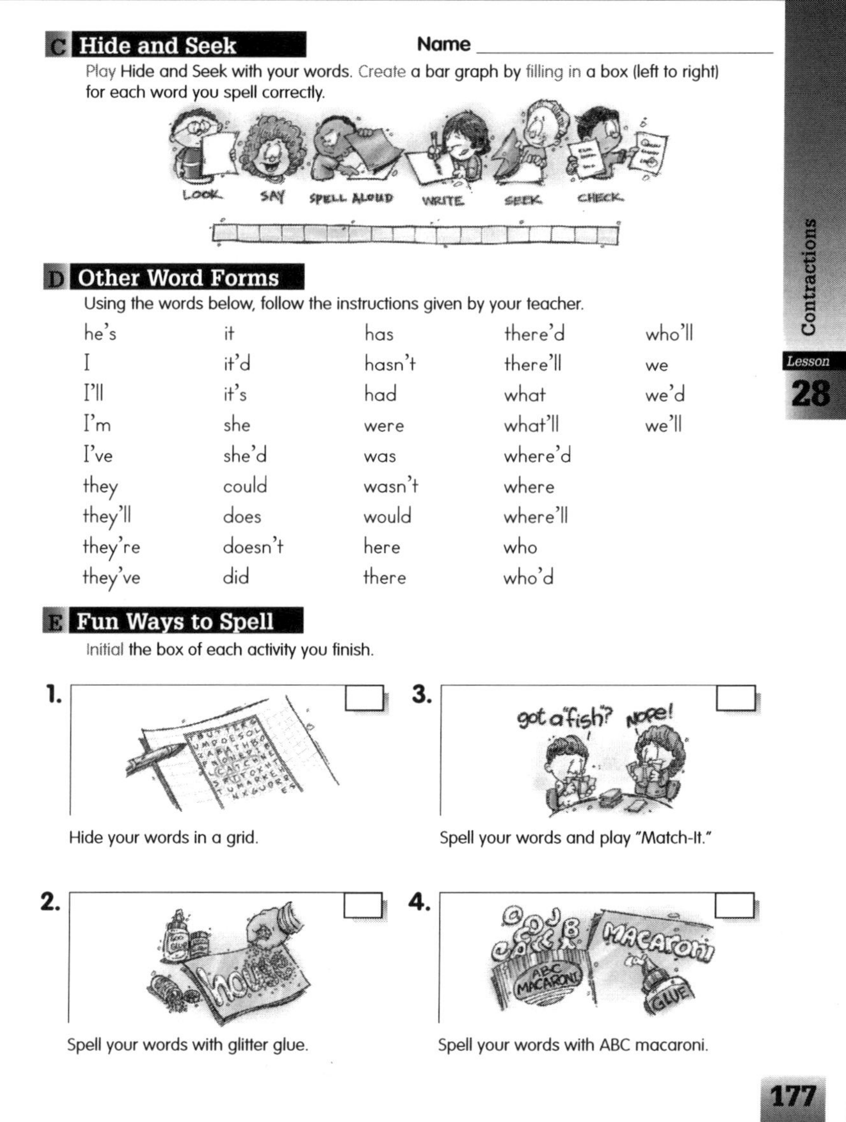

C Hide and Seek Name ____________

Play Hide and Seek with your words. Create a bar graph by filling in a box (left to right) for each word you spell correctly.

D Other Word Forms

Using the words below, follow the instructions given by your teacher.

he's	it	has	there'd	who'll
I	it'd	hasn't	there'll	we
I'll	it's	had	what	we'd
I'm	she	were	what'll	we'll
I've	she'd	was	where'd	
they	could	wasn't	where	
they'll	does	would	where'll	
they're	doesn't	here	who	
they've	did	there	who'd	

E Fun Ways to Spell

Initial the box of each activity you finish.

1. Hide your words in a grid.

2. Spell your words with glitter glue.

3.
Spell your words and play "Match-It."

4.
Spell your words with ABC macaroni.

Contractions

Lesson 28

177

1 Hide and Seek

Reinforce spelling by using multiple styles of learning.

On a white board, Teacher writes each word — one at a time. **Have students:**

- **Look** at the word.
- **Say** the word out loud.
- **Spell** the word out loud.
- **Hide** (teacher erases word.)
- **Write** the word on paper.
- **Seek** (teacher rewrites word.)
- **Check** spelling. If incorrect, rewrite word correctly.

2 Other Word Forms

This activity is optional. Have students write original sentences using these Other Word Forms:

she'd
there'll
what'll
who'll

3 Fun Ways to Spell

Four activities are provided. Use one, two, three, or all of the activities. Have students initial the box for each activity they complete.

Options:

- assign activities to students according to their learning styles
- set up the activities in learning centers for students to do throughout the day
- divide students into four groups and assign one activity per group
- do one activity per day

General

To hide your words on a grid…
- Arrange your words on a piece of graph paper.
- Put one letter of each word in a square.
- Words may be written backwards, forwards, or diagonally.
- Outline your puzzle.
- Hide your words by filling in all the spaces inside the puzzle with random letters.
- Trade grids with a classmate and find the hidden words.

Auditory

To spell your words and play "Match-It"…

Write each spelling word on a card. Mix your word cards and a classmate's together. Deal six cards per player; put the rest face down between you. Ask classmate for a word-card that matches one in your hand. If the classmate has the word-card, take it and play again. If not, draw from the remaining stack, then it is your classmate's turn. Continue taking turns until all the cards are matched. Player with most cards wins!

Visual

To spell your words with glitter glue…
- Write each of your spelling words on your paper with glue.
- Sprinkle with glitter.

Tactile

To spell your words with ABC macaroni…
- Choose a word from your spelling list.
- Spell the word with macaroni letters.
- Glue the macaroni word to art paper.
- Do this for each word on your list.

Working with Words

Familiarize students with word meaning and usage.

Proofing

Write the words **should + not, she + would, we + will,** and **they + have** on the board. Have volunteers come to the board and write the contraction for each set. Talk about which letters are being left out. Read the new words.

Look in your Worktext at the entry from Kristin's journal. She has misspelled the contractions. Write them correctly on the lines below. Then at the bottom, write the words each contraction stands for.

Take a minute to memorize...

John 16:33

F Working with Words Name ______________

Proofing

A contraction combines two words into one word by leaving out one or more letters. An apostrophe takes the place of the letters that have been left out. In her journal, Kristin wrote about wanting a dog. She has misspelled the contractions. Write them correctly on the lines below.

Monday evening: Mom took us to the mall today. We looked at puppies in The Pet Place. Thay'd be such fun to have. I wish they wern't so expensive. Mom said we coodn't get one, but I bet h'ed be good and wuoldn't be a problem.

Sunday afternoon: Mom is calling me. Whos'e that lady? Whats' she doing here? i'd better go see.

Later: Wow! She'z moving and shi'll give me her dog, Friscoe! He'l be so much fun. I did'ent expect something like that. She just said, "Hear's his toy ball. Take good care of him."

Months later: Their's still food in Friscoe's dish. Whare's Friscoe?

A week later: We'v been without Friscoe for a week now. It'il hurt for a long time when I think about him. I wish he had'ent gotten sick and died.

1.	They'd	**7.**	what's	**13.**	Here's
2.	weren't	**8.**	I'd	**14.**	There's
3.	couldn't	**9.**	She's	**15.**	Where's
4.	he'd	**10.**	she'll	**16.**	We've
5.	wouldn't	**11.**	He'll	**17.**	It'll
6.	who's	**12.**	didn't	**18.**	hadn't

Contractions

Write the two words each contraction stands for.

1.	they'd	they would	**3.**	didn't	did not	**5.**	we've	we have
2.	she'll	she will	**4.**	weren't	were not	**6.**	here's	here is

Word Bank

couldn't	he'd	I'd	she's	we've	where's
didn't	he'll	it'll	there's	weren't	who's
hadn't	here's	she'll	they'd	what's	wouldn't

G Dictation

Name ______________________

Write each sentence as your teacher dictates. Use correct punctuation.

1. Didn't Mom say he'd be too much trouble?
2. I'd like to have him if Mom wouldn't mind.
3. She hadn't had the dog long, but she couldn't keep him.

Contractions

Lesson 28

H Proofreading

If a word is misspelled, fill in the oval by that word. If all the words are spelled correctly, fill in the oval by **no mistake**.

1. ○ deer ○ it'll ○ he'd ● no mistake
2. ○ fear ● i'd ○ gear ○ no mistake
3. ○ disappear ○ cereal ○ they'd ● no mistake
4. ○ beard ○ she's ● he'l ○ no mistake
5. ○ period ○ weird ○ rear ● no mistake
6. ● hear's ○ near ○ she'll ○ no mistake
7. ● coudn't ○ weary ○ hadn't ○ no mistake
8. ○ didn't ● wern't ○ appear ○ no mistake
9. ○ steer ○ sincerely ○ where's ● no mistake
10. ○ wouldn't ○ tear ● who'se ○ no mistake
11. ● we'v ○ spear ○ fierce ○ no mistake
12. ○ cheer ○ what's ● ther's ○ no mistake

179

1 Dictation

Reinforce correct spelling by using current and previous words in context.

Listen as I read each sentence and then write it in your Worktext. Remember to use correct capitalization and punctuation. (Slowly read each sentence twice. Sentences are found in the Student Worktext to the left.)

Day 4

2 Proofreading

Familiarize students with standardized test format and reinforce recognition of misspelled words.

Look at each set of words. If a word is misspelled, fill in the oval by that word. If all the words are spelled correctly, fill in the oval by **no mistake**.

Lesson 28

3 Hide and Seek

Reinforce correct spelling of current spelling words. Repeat this activity from Day 2. (A reproducible master is provided in Appendix A as shown on the inset page to the right.)

4 Other Word Forms

Have your students complete this activity to strengthen spelling ability and expand vocabulary.

1 Posttest

Visit the **A Reason For** website to download free, printable Posttest pages.

I will say the word once, use it in a sentence, then say it again. Write your words on a separate sheet of paper.

Progress Chart

Students may record scores. (Appendix B)

Personal Dictionary

Students may add any words they have misspelled to their personal dictionaries. (Appendix B)

Lesson 28 | Other Word Forms

Hide and Seek

Play Hide and Seek with your words. Create a bar graph by filling in a box (left to right) for each word you spell correctly.

LOOK SAY HIDE WRITE SEEK CHECK

Other Word Forms

Code Words

Using the word plus the code word, write the contracted form on the line.

0 = am 1 = will 2 = is 3 = would

4 = not 5 = have 6 = are 7 = did

1. he + 2 = he's	**14.** she + 3 = she'd
2. I + 1 = I'll	**15.** they + 6 = they're
3. does + 4 = doesn't	**16.** there + 3 = there'd
4. who + 1 = who'll	**17.** I + 0 = I'm
5. they + 5 = they've	**18.** it + 3 = it'd
6. she + 1 = she'll	**19.** has + 4 = hasn't
7. there + 1 = there'll	**20.** where + 7 = where'd
8. we + 1 = we'll	**21.** I + 5 = I've
9. we + 3 = we'd	**22.** it + 2 = it's
10. they + 1 = they'll	**23.** was + 4 = wasn't
11. what + 1 = what'll	**24.** who + 3 = who'd
12. here + 2 = here's	**25.** where + 1 = where'll
13. we + 6 = we're	**26.** had + 4 = hadn't

348

---

1. she'll — "We know **she'll** be thrilled," assured Mr. and Mrs. Wright.
2. I'd — "**I'd** love to keep Friscoe!" exclaimed Kristin.
3. they'd — It was all right with her parents; **they'd** already talked it over with Mrs. Fitch.
4. he'd — Kristin just knew that **he'd** be a wonderful family pet.
5. didn't — Kristin **didn't** know Mrs. Fitch was going to give her a dog.
6. hadn't — She **hadn't** expected such a wonderful surprise.
7. wouldn't — When Friscoe **wouldn't** eat, Kristin began to worry.
8. what's — "Do you know **what's** the matter with Friscoe?" asked Cathy.
9. there's — "I don't know why **there's** still a lot of food left in his bowl," Kristin told her mom.
10. we've — "I know that **we've** got to take him to the vet today," her mom said.
11. who's — "I don't know **who's** going to examine Frisco,"said Mrs. Wright.
12. where's — "Where are they going? **Where's** Mom taking Friscoe?" asked Cathy.
13. she's — "I'm sure **she's** taking him to see the veterinarian," explained Christopher.
14. he'll — "Do you think **he'll** get well?" Kristin asked Dr. LeBlanc.
15. weren't — Mrs. Wright and Kristin **weren't** prepared for the bad news they received.
16. couldn't — Kristin **couldn't** seem to stop crying.
17. here's — "**Here's** a verse that might encourage you, Kristin," said her dad.
18. it'll — Kristin cried softly, "I'm so glad **it'll** be wonderful in heaven!"

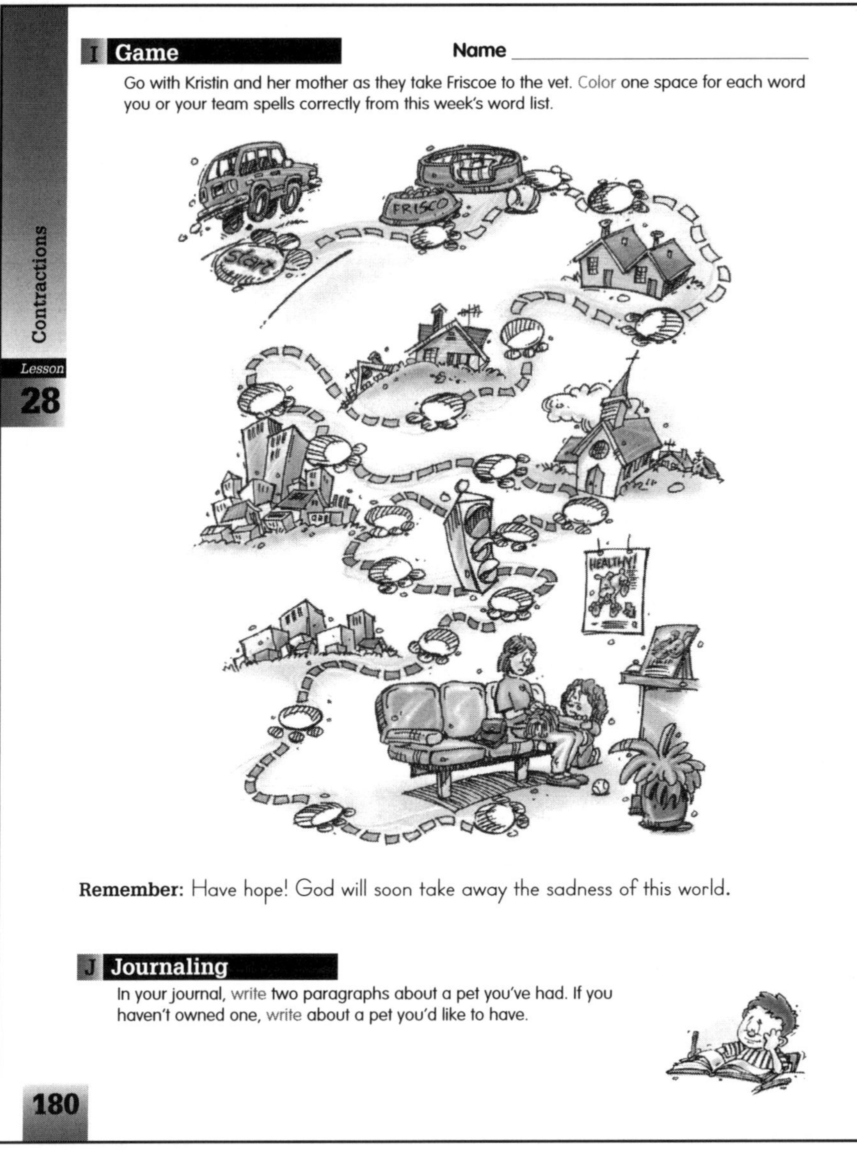

Contractions

Lesson 28

I Game

Name ______________________

Go with Kristin and her mother as they take Friscoe to the vet. Color one space for each word you or your team spells correctly from this week's word list.

Remember: Have hope! God will soon take away the sadness of this world.

J Journaling

In your journal, write two paragraphs about a pet you've had. If you haven't owned one, write about a pet you'd like to have.

180

How to Play:

- Divide students into two teams.
- Have a student from team A go to the board.
- Say the spelling word.
- Have the student write the word on the board.
- If correct, instruct each member of team A to color one space, beginning at Start.
- Alternate between teams A and B as you go down the word list.
- The team to reach the veterinarian's office first is the winner.

Small Group Option: Students may play this game without teacher direction in small groups of two or more.

2 Game

Reinforce spelling skills and provide motivation and interest.

Materials

- game page (from Student Worktext)
- crayons or colored pencils (1 per child)
- game word list

Game Word List

1. **he'd**
2. **I'd**
3. **they'd**
4. **he'll**
5. **it'll**
6. **she'll**
7. **couldn't**
8. **didn't**
9. **hadn't**
10. **weren't**
11. **wouldn't**
12. **here's**
13. **she's**
14. **there's**
15. **what's**
16. **where's**
17. **who's**
18. **we've**

3 Journaling

Provide a meaningful reason for correct spelling through personal writing.

Review the story using discussion leads provided on the following page. Encourage students to apply the Scriptural value in their journaling.

Journaling (continued)

- Do you have a dog? (Allow time for students to share stories about their dogs.)
- Why did Kristin want a dog? (To pet, play with, take for walks, and sleep with.)
- Why didn't Mrs. Fitch take Friscoe with her? (She was moving to take care of her mother and didn't think Friscoe would get enough attention. She wanted him to have someone to play with him and take good care of him.)
- Do you think Friscoe was a smart dog? Why? (Yes. He learned to "speak," "roll over," and "stay" within a week.)
- How did Kristin know that something was wrong with Friscoe? (He quit eating even his favorite food.)
- Do the Scriptures say bad things won't happen to good people? (No.)
- What do the Scriptures say about bad things happening? (That on this earth bad things will happen, but we can have peace anyway, because God has overcome the world.)

The letter "W" is the only letter in the alphabet that has more than one syllable. It has three.

Word Wow!

1 **Literature Connection**
Topic: Convictions
Theme Text: Luke 11:33

Reluctant to Shine

Rachel struggles to share her beliefs with Laney about entertainment choices.

Laney heard Wicker barking in the new kennel. She shined the flashlight across the backyard. The bright beam reflected off the shiny steel water bowl sitting on the ground beside the freshly painted doghouse. Her dog's barking stopped abruptly when he focused on the reflections of the light as they danced across the cement of the kennel.

Laney opened the gate and softly called the dog to her. "Are you lonely, Wicker? I bet you'd rather sleep with me. Come here, boy." The one-year-old Gordon Setter lifted his right front paw. His tail shot out straight as an arrow behind him and his nose pointed directly to the circle of light from the flashlight. Laney laughed. "Bird dogs are supposed to point at birds—not light. You silly dog."

She moved the beam around and watched the dog jump and leap trying to capture the light. She punched the switch on the flashlight. As soon the light disappeared, the dog came bounding over to her. Wicker nuzzled her face with his cold, wet nose. His tail whopped against the wire of the kennel and his whole body wiggled with the pleasure of seeing his new mistress. It was hard for Laney to leave him alone in the backyard, but at least she knew that he was safe. She was glad she'd gone out to check on her new pet.

Rachel eased the bedroom door open and tiptoed into the twins' room. She checked on the sleeping babies before clicking off the lamp on the dresser. Her eyes slowly adjusted to the glimmer from the night-light beside Leah's crib. Benjamin stirred and reached for his stuffed monkey. Rachel bent over and tucked the green blanket around her brother. *They are so cute when they're asleep,* Rachel mused as she tiptoed back out into the hall. She left the twins' door ajar and went to her own room to get ready for bed.

After school the next afternoon Rachel walked up Mason Springs Drive to Laney's house. She took the porch steps two at a time and rang the Larkins' doorbell. "I can hardly wait to see this crazy dog."

Laney's mom opened the door. "Come in, Rachel. Laney's in watching TV. She can't wait to show you her new dog." Mrs. Larkin stepped back and opened the door wider. "Laney, Rachel's here to see Wicker," she called.

Rachel went into the family room and sat down on the couch beside Laney. "So where's the awesome dog Coach got you from the pound?"

Laney didn't take her eyes off the characters on the big screen TV. She shook her head and put her index finger across her lips. "Shhhhhh. Just a sec."

Rachel watched the program for a few minutes before she realized it was one she wasn't allowed to see. She wasn't sure how to tell Laney about the Jacobson family TV rules, so she didn't say anything. *Maybe it's almost over*, she thought to herself.

Laney was totally absorbed. Rachel closed her eyes when the big man on the screen grabbed the woman forcefully and threatened her with a gun. Rachel couldn't drown out the woman's screams or the crude words spewing out of the man's mouth. When the noise subsided she peeked to see if the woman was hurt. It wasn't a pretty sight. "Ewwww!" she gasped.

Laney didn't appear bothered at all and didn't notice when Rachel got up and went into the bathroom. When the door was shut, Rachel sat down on the edge of the tub and put her hand across her eyes. *That was awful,* she thought. Images of the graphic scene she had seen flashed through her brain. *Laney seems to like it! My parents would never let me watch that. Well, if I keep my mouth shut maybe she won't even notice I'm here in the bathroom. The program's got to be over soon—almost everyone is dead!*

The credits started to spool down the screen of the TV. Laney stood up, hit the off button on the remote and called, "Rachel!" When her friend didn't answer, she said, "Mom, where did Rachel go?"

"I thought she was in there with you, Laney." Mrs. Larkin wiped her hands on a kitchen towel.

"No. She got up and left. I don't know where she went." Laney opened the back door and looked out at Wicker's kennel.

"Maybe she went on outside." Mom put the towel down and walked into the family room.

"I'm right here," Rachel joined her friend at the back door. "Where's Wicker? I need to see the dog who plays with light."

"Where'd you go? You missed the best part." Laney led the way to Wicker's kennel.

Rachel changed the subject. "Coach got this dog at the pound?"

"Yeah, he says Gordon Setters love to romp and play. His master was moving to an apartment in the city where pets aren't allowed. Can you imagine giving up this guy?"

"You're lucky. He's a beautiful dog." Rachel reached through the wire and scratched Wicker's nose.

The Jacobson girls sat with their mother on the rug in the twins' room. "I think they'll walk any day now," Rebecca said as she held out her arms to Leah.

Rachel smiled as

Story (continued)

Benjamin let go of the crib and reached for her hand that was just beyond his fingertips. He slowly let go of the crib and took one step toward his sister. "I think you're right, Rebecca. Did you see that? Do it again Benjamin!"

The girls helped the twins and cheered their progress. Mom finally called a halt to the walking lessons and suggested they have worship right there in the nursery.

"Sing!" Benjamin took two steps and then plopped down on his well-padded bottom.

"Light! Little light!" Leah smiled and held up her index finger.

"I think she wants 'This Little Light of Mine,'" Vanessa interpreted.

Leah let go of the dresser to clap her hands and fell forward onto the thick rug. The family had fun singing all the verses. Benjamin and Leah loved the motions and were delighted that their sisters sang with them.

After a story and good night prayers, Rachel picked up Benjamin and put him in his crib. She gave him his monkey and tucked the green blanket up under his chin. He looked up into Rachel's face with pleading eyes, "Light shine."

Rachel pointed her finger toward the ceiling and made it go in a circle. "All around the neighborhood, Benjamin. Good night." She reached over to turn out the lamp. Benjamin immediately sat up in his crib and said, "Light shine."

"We already sang that song, Benjamin. Good night," Rachel said firmly as she flipped off the lamp. Rebecca turned off the overhead light.

Benjamin stood up in his crib. "No! Light shine!"

"I think he wants the lamp on," Rebecca said from the doorway. Benjamin nodded and sat back down in his crib. Rachel turned the lamp back on and its small bulb softly lit the cozy nursery.

Rachel brushed her teeth, put on her pajamas and went out on the front porch swing. She loved spring evenings. The tune of "This Little Light of Mine" kept replaying through her head. It reminded her of the verse they were memorizing in spelling class: "No one lights a lamp and hides it! Instead, he puts it on a lampstand to give light to all who enter the room." *Benjamin likes his lamp on at night. It makes his room seem safe.*

Up the street she heard Wicker bark in the Larkins' backyard. *Wicker loves light—but I didn't let my light shine very well today at Laney's. I kind of hid it under a bushel like Benjamin's song says. I should have told her why I left. I was afraid Laney would laugh at me for being shocked at what the people were saying and doing on the TV show, so I didn't say anything.*

Rachel hummed the melody of the children's song. She tried to remember all of the verses. *'All around the neighborhood...Don't let Satan blow it out...Hide it under a bushel—No!...Let it shine 'til Jesus comes!' There's one more. Oh yeah, the first one. 'This little light of mine, I'm gonna let it shine! Let it shine. Let it shine!' I needed to hear that song tonight.*

Rachel tucked her feet up under her and hugged her knees. She heard Wicker bark again and smiled to herself. "No one lights a lamp and hides it! Instead, he puts it on a lampstand to give light to all who enter the room." Luke 11:33

2 Discussion Time

Check understanding of the story and development of personal values.

- What did Wicker do at night when Laney came out to check on him?
- What song did Benjamin and Leah love to sing?
- What are some of the verses of "This Little Light of Mine?"
- What does it mean to "Let your light shine?"
- What was Laney doing that made Rachel feel uncomfortable?
- What did Rachel do when she realized the TV show Laney was watching wasn't one she was allowed to see?
- Did Rachel let her light shine?

A Preview

Name ____________________

Write each word as your teacher says it.

1. playground
2. yardstick
3. homework
4. bedroom
5. bedspread
6. fireplace
7. railroad
8. homemade
9. within
10. everybody
11. newspaper
12. herself
13. bathroom
14. bathtub
15. anyway
16. backyard
17. sunshine
18. somewhere

Compound Words

Lesson 29

Scripture

Luke 11:33

181

3 Preview

Test for knowledge of the correct spellings of these words.

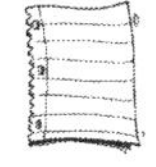

Customize Your List
On a separate sheet of paper, additional words of your choice may be tested.

I will say each word once, use the word in a sentence, then say the word again. Write the words on the lines in your Worktext.

Correct Immediately!
Let's correct our Preview. I will spell each word out loud. If you spelled a word incorrectly, rewrite it correctly.

Progress Chart
Students may record scores. (Reproducible master provided in Appendix B.)

1.	playground	On the **playground**, Laney invited Rachel to her house to see her new dog.
2.	yardstick	Rachel put away the **yardstick** she used for her math assignment.
3.	homework	After finishing her **homework** she was allowed to go to Laney's house.
4.	bedroom	Laney has a beautiful **bedroom**.
5.	bedspread	She got to choose the **bedspread** herself.
6.	fireplace	A huge **fireplace** covered one wall of the family room.
7.	railroad	The **railroad** does not run near Laney's house.
8.	homemade	Mrs. Larkin made **homemade** chocolate chip cookies for the girls.
9.	within	Rachel realized **within** minutes that this was a show she was not allowed to watch.
10.	everybody	In the Jacobson family, **everybody** knew their TV rules.
11.	newspaper	Uncomfortable, Rachel leafed through the **newspaper**.
12.	herself	"Maybe it's almost over," Rachel said to **herself**.
13.	bathroom	Rachel got up quietly and went into the **bathroom**.
14.	bathtub	She sat on the edge of the **bathtub** to think.
15.	anyway	Although the show was violent, Laney continued watching it **anyway**.
16.	backyard	The girls went out into the **backyard** to see Wicker.
17.	sunshine	The beautiful dog romped and played in the **sunshine**.
18.	somewhere	Rachel knew of **somewhere** she needed to let her light shine brighter.

Word Shapes

Help students form a correct image of whole words.

Look at each word and think about its shape. Now, write the word in the correct Word Shape Boxes. You may check off each word as you use it.

(Compound words are words that are made up of two words.)

In the Word Shape Boxes, circle the two words in each compound word.

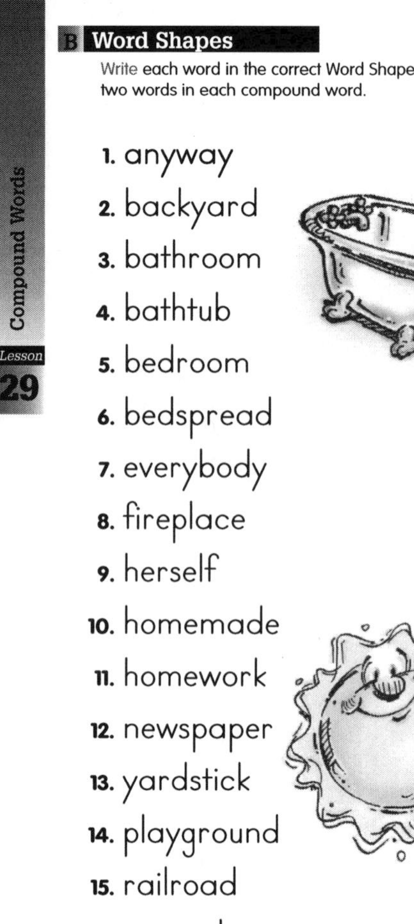

Compound Words

Lesson 29

B Word Shapes Name ____________________

Write each word in the correct Word Shape Boxes. Next, in the Word Shape Boxes, circle the two words in each compound word.

1. anyway
2. backyard
3. bathroom
4. bathtub
5. bedroom
6. bedspread
7. everybody
8. fireplace
9. herself
10. homemade
11. homework
12. newspaper
13. yardstick
14. playground
15. railroad
16. somewhere
17. sunshine
18. within

bathtub
bedspread
within
bathroom
herself
everybody
fireplace
sunshine
backyard
homework
newspaper
railroad
playground
bedroom
yardstick
somewhere
anyway
homemade

182

Answers may vary for duplicate word shapes.

Take a minute to memorize...

Luke 11:33

Be Prepared For Fun

Check these supply lists for **Fun Ways to Spell** - presented **Day 2**. Purchase and/or gather these items ahead of time!

General
- Pencil
- 3 X 5 Cards cut in half (18 per child)
- Spelling List

Auditory
- Pencil
- Notebook Paper
- Spelling List

Visual
- Black Construction Paper (1 sheet per child)
- Lemon Juice
- Cotton Swabs
- Spelling List

Tactile
- Pipe Cleaners (cut in an assortment of lengths)
- Spelling List

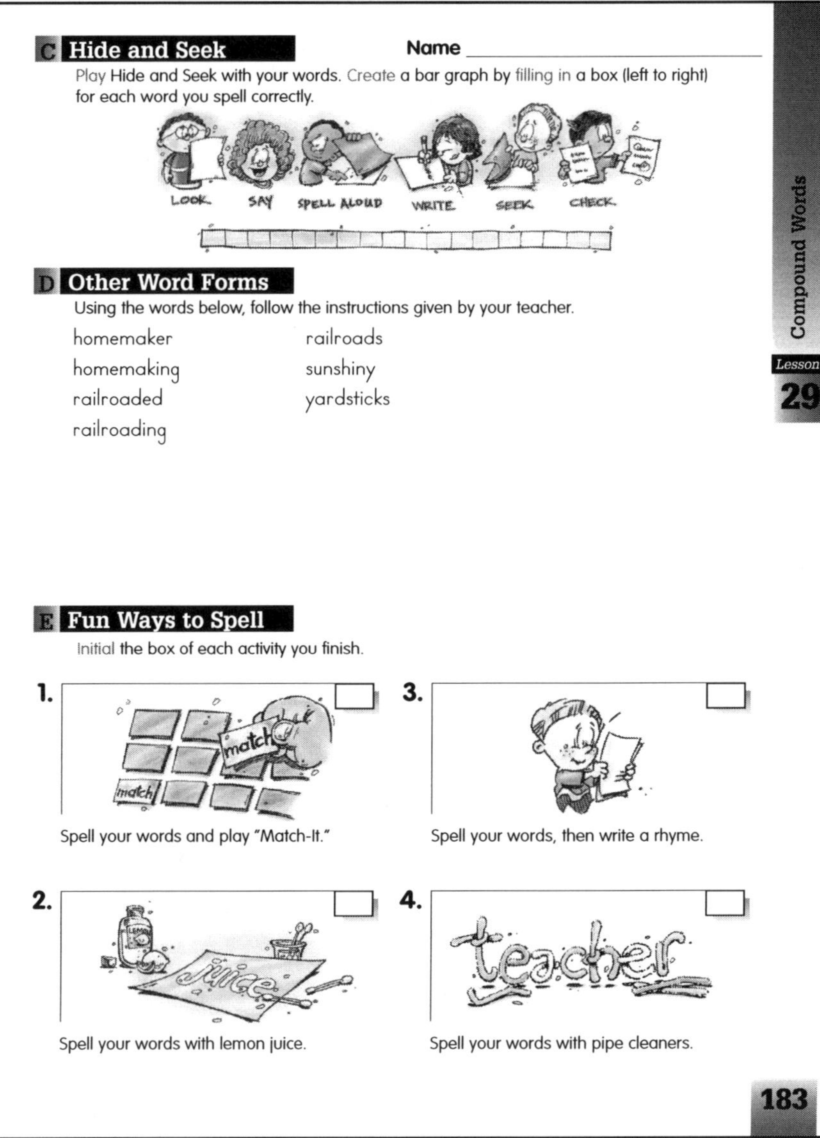

C Hide and Seek Name ____________

Play Hide and Seek with your words. Create a bar graph by filling in a box (left to right) for each word you spell correctly.

D Other Word Forms

Using the words below, follow the instructions given by your teacher.

homemaker	railroads
homemaking	sunshiny
railroaded	yardsticks
railroading	

E Fun Ways to Spell

Initial the box of each activity you finish.

1. Spell your words and play "Match-It."
2. Spell your words with lemon juice.
3. Spell your words, then write a rhyme.
4. Spell your words with pipe cleaners.

Compound Words

Lesson 29

183

1 Hide and Seek

Reinforce spelling by using multiple styles of learning.

On a white board, Teacher writes each word — one at a time. **Have students:**

- **Look** at the word.
- **Say** the word out loud.
- **Spell** the word out loud.
- **Hide** (teacher erases word.)
- **Write** the word on paper.
- **Seek** (teacher rewrites word.)
- **Check** spelling. If incorrect, rewrite word correctly.

2 Other Word Forms

This activity is optional. Have students write variations of this sentence using these Other Word Forms:

Grandpa worked for the railroad many years ago.

railroaded
railroads
railroading

3 Fun Ways to Spell

Four activities are provided. Use one, two, three, or all of the activities. Have students initial the box for each activity they complete.

Options:

- assign activities to students according to their learning styles
- set up the activities in learning centers for students to do throughout the day
- divide students into four groups and assign one activity per group
- do one activity per day

General

Spell your words; then play Concentration...
Write each spelling word on a card. Mix your cards and a classmate's cards together. Arrange them face down in six rows of six. Pick up two cards. If the cards match, play again. If the cards do not match, turn them back over. It is your classmate's turn. Continue taking turns until all the cards are matched. The player with the most cards wins!

Auditory

To spell your words and write a rhyme...
- Write a rhyming verse for each word on your list.
- Example:
  My little brother could dive.
  When he was barely five.
- Underline your spelling words.

Visual

To spell your words with lemon juice...
- Dip a cotton swab in lemon juice.
- With the swab, write each of your spelling words on black construction paper.
- Check your spelling before your writing disappears!

Tactile

To spell your words with pipe cleaners...
- Choose a word from your spelling list.
- Shape the pipe cleaners to spell the word.
- Check your spelling.
- Do this for each word on your list.

Working with Words

Familiarize students with word meaning and usage.

Secret Words

Two words that can be combined to make a new word are called compound words. Draw a line to make two columns on the board. In the first column write the words **sea**, **rain**, **base**, **oat**, **bull**, and **pea**. Number these words **1-6**. In the second column write the words **ball**, **nut**, **weed**, **dog**, **meal**, and **coat**. Have volunteers make compound words by writing the number of a word in the first column in front of a word in the second column. Read the new words.

In your Worktext, make compound spelling words by drawing a line from the word in the first column to a word in the second column. Next, write the words in order in the puzzle. Then, write the boxed letters on the lines below to find the secret phrase.

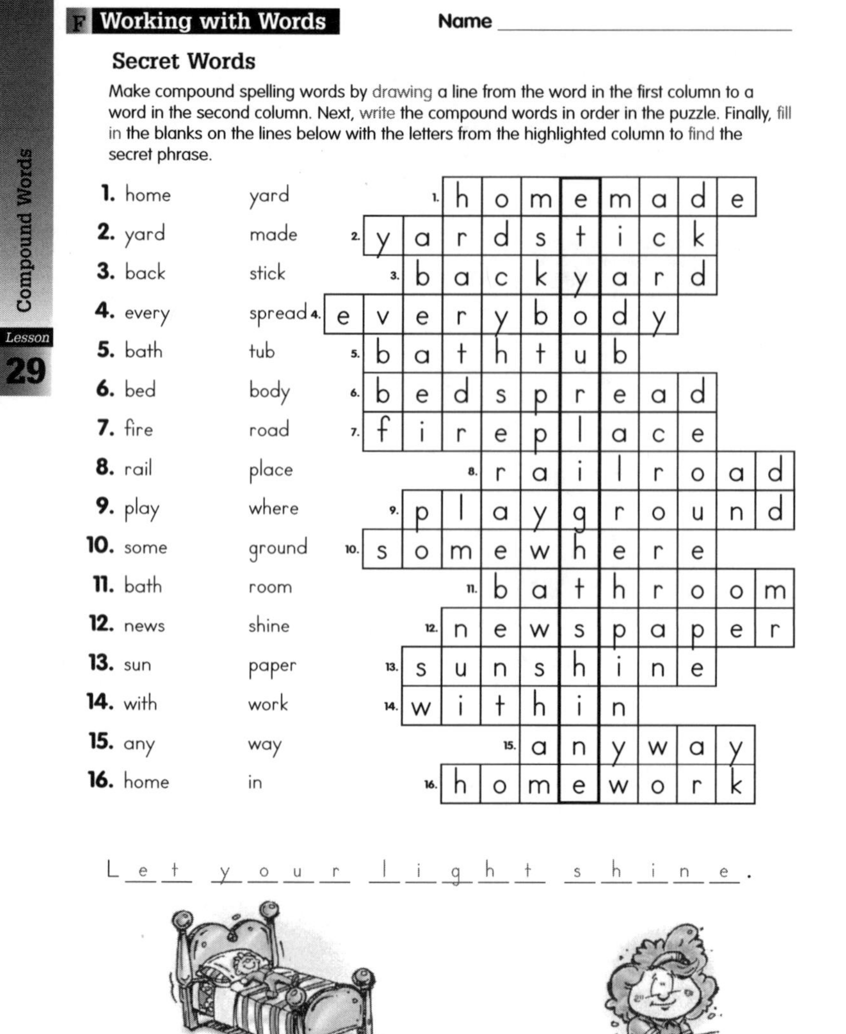

Compound Words | Lesson 29

F **Working with Words** Name ____________________

Secret Words

Make compound spelling words by drawing a line from the word in the first column to a word in the second column. Next, write the compound words in order in the puzzle. Finally, fill in the blanks on the lines below with the letters from the highlighted column to find the secret phrase.

1. home	yard	1.	homemade
2. yard	made	2.	yardstick
3. back	stick	3.	backyard
4. every	spread	4.	everybody
5. bath	tub	5.	bathtub
6. bed	body	6.	bedspread
7. fire	road	7.	fireplace
8. rail	place	8.	railroad
9. play	where	9.	playground
10. some	ground	10.	somewhere
11. bath	room	11.	bathroom
12. news	shine	12.	newspaper
13. sun	paper	13.	sunshine
14. with	work	14.	within
15. any	way	15.	anyway
16. home	in	16.	homework

L e t y o u r l i g h t s h i n e .

184

Take a minute to memorize...

Luke 11:33

G Dictation

Name ____________

Write each sentence as your teacher dictates. Use correct punctuation.

1. Wicker lay in the backyard in the sunshine.
2. She didn't like the show anyway, so she sat in the bathroom.
3. I lost my homework somewhere.

Compound Words

Lesson 29

H Proofreading

If a word is misspelled, fill in the oval by that word. If all the words are spelled correctly, fill in the oval by **no mistake**.

1. ● inyway ○ what's ○ she'll ○ no mistake
2. ○ couldn't ○ didn't ● bakyard ○ no mistake
3. ○ it'll ○ we've ○ bathroom ● no mistake
4. ○ there's ○ sunshine ○ bathtub ● no mistake
5. ○ I'd ○ they'd ● bedspred ○ no mistake
6. ○ he'd ○ yardstick ○ bedroom ● no mistake
7. ○ wouldn't ○ she's ● evrybody ○ no mistake
8. ● railrode ○ who's ○ newspaper ○ no mistake
9. ○ he'll ○ within ○ herself ● no mistake
10. ○ hadn't ○ weren't ● hommade ○ no mistake
11. ● playgrownd ○ here's ○ homework ○ no mistake
12. ○ somewhere ○ where's ○ fireplace ● no mistake

185

1 Dictation

Reinforce correct spelling by using current and previous words in context.

Listen as I read each sentence and then write it in your Worktext. Remember to use correct capitalization and punctuation. (Slowly read each sentence twice. Sentences are found in the Student Worktext to the left.)

2 Proofreading

Familiarize students with standardized test format and reinforce recognition of misspelled words.

Look at each set of words. If a word is misspelled, fill in the oval by that word. If all the words are spelled correctly, fill in the oval by **no mistake**.

3 Hide and Seek

Reinforce correct spelling of current spelling words. Repeat this activity from Day 2. (A reproducible master is provided in Appendix A as shown on the inset page to the right.)

4 Other Word Forms

Have your students complete this activity to strengthen spelling ability and expand vocabulary.

1 Posttest

Visit the **A Reason For** website to download free, printable Posttest pages.

I will say the word once, use it in a sentence, then say it again. Write your words on a separate sheet of paper.

Progress Chart

Students may record scores. (Appendix B)

Personal Dictionary

Students may add any words they have misspelled to their personal dictionaries. (Appendix B)

Hide and Seek

Play Hide and Seek with your words. Create a bar graph by filling in a box (left to right) for each word you spell correctly.

LOOK SAY HIDE WRITE SEEK CHECK

Other Word Forms

Spelling and Writing

Write sentences using words from the Word Bank. Check your spelling.

1. (Answers will vary)
2. (Answers will vary)
3. (Answers will vary)
4. (Answers will vary)
5. (Answers will vary)
6. (Answers will vary)
7. (Answers will vary)

Syllables

A syllable is a unit of sound in a word. A syllable contains a vowel and possibly one or more consonants. Count how many syllables each word has and write the number on the line.

1. 3 homemaking
2. 2 bedrooms
3. 2 backyards
4. 3 railroading
5. 2 playgrounds
6. 3 fireplaces

Word Bank

everybody's, herself, railroads, yardsticks, homemaker, newspapers, sunshiny

1.	playground	On the **playground**, Laney invited Rachel to her house.
2.	railroad	There is not a **railroad** near Rachel's house.
3.	yardstick	She used a **yardstick** to complete her math word problems.
4.	homework	Rachel finished her **homework** so she could go to Laney's house.
5.	bedroom	Rachel got to see Laney's big **bedroom**.
6.	bedspread	She thought Laney's **bedspread** was beautiful.
7.	homemade	Rachel enjoyed one of Mrs. Larkin's **homemade** cookies.
8.	fireplace	The **fireplace** in their family room had a huge mantel.
9.	newspaper	Rachel moved a **newspaper** out of the way and sat down.
10.	anyway	Despite the violent content, Laney watched the show **anyway**.
11.	within	**Within** a few minutes, Rachel knew she had to leave the room quickly.
12.	everybody	In Rachel's house **everybody** obeyed their family TV rules.
13.	bathroom	Rachel went into the **bathroom** to avoid seeing the program.
14.	bathtub	Sitting on the edge of the **bathtub**, she tried to forget what she'd seen.
15.	herself	Rachel talked to **herself** to get the picture out of her mind.
16.	backyard	The girls ran out into the **backyard** to see Wicker.
17.	sunshine	The dog's black coat glistened in the **sunshine**.
18.	somewhere	Is there **somewhere** you need to let your light shine brightly?

I Game Name ______________________

Play a game of tic-tac-toe by marking the grid each time you or your team spells a word correctly from this week's word list.

Compound Words

Lesson 29

Remember: Hold up the light Jesus put in your heart; share it with those around you.

J Journaling

What situation could someone your age be in where it would be hard to let their light shine? Make a list of at least 3 situations in your journal.

186

How to Play:

- Divide students into two teams (the X's and the O's).
- Have a student from team X choose a number from 1 to 9.
- Say the word that matches that number from the Game Word List (Game 1).
- Have the student write the word on the board.
- If correct, have each member of both teams put an X on that number.
- Alternate between teams X and O.
- The first team to score three marks in a row (up, down, across, or diagonally) is the winner.
- Word lists and tic-tac-toe grids are provided for two additional games.

Small Group Option: Students may play this game without teacher direction in groups of two.

2 Game

Reinforce spelling skills and provide motivation and interest.

Materials

- game page (from Student Worktext)
- pencils (1 per child)
- game word list

Game 1 Word List

1. **within**
2. **yardstick**
3. **anyway**
4. **bedspread**
5. **fireplace**
6. **railroad**
7. **herself**
8. **newspaper**
9. **homework**

Game 2 Word List

1. **somewhere**
2. **backyard**
3. **homemade**
4. **playground**
5. **bathtub**
6. **sunshine**
7. **bedroom**
8. **everybody**
9. **bathroom**

Game 3 Word List

1. **bedspread**
2. **newspaper**
3. **backyard**
4. **everybody**
5. **yardstick**
6. **railroad**
7. **homework**
8. **somewhere**
9. **anyway**

3 Journaling

Provide a meaningful reason for correct spelling through personal writing.

Review the story using discussion leads provided on the following page. Encourage students to apply the Scriptural value in their journaling.

Journaling (continued)

- When Rachel heard Wicker barking, what did she remember about the dog? (How he was attracted by light.)
- What did Benjamin want left on in his room at night? (His lamp.)
- What did Rachel see at Laney's house that made her feel uncomfortable? (A violent TV program.)
- What did Rachel say to Laney about the TV show? (She didn't say anything.)
- Raise your hand if you think Rachel should say how she feels about the TV show.
- What could Rachel say about the TV show? (Brainstorm with your class. You may wish to write student responses on the board.)
- Is letting your light shine always easy? (No.)

"Evade Dave!" is a palindrome.

Word Wow!

1 **Literature Connection**
Topic: Wise Counsel
Theme Text: Matthew 12:35

Wicker the Wonder Dog

Laney learns she can trust Rachel and depend on her word.

"I can't believe Wicker's my dog!" Laney swung the kennel gate open and watched the beautiful Gordon Setter romp across the fenced-in back yard. She took a tennis ball out of her pocket and called her pet's name. At the sound of her voice, Wicker whirled around and cocked his head to one side in anticipation. His attention zeroed in on the yellow ball in Laney's hand. He backed up slowly, his muscles tense—ready to spring into action!

Laney threw the ball high into the air. Wicker calculated where it was going and raced to catch it before it hit the ground. He caught it. He usually did. "Good boy," Laney called. The black and tan dog raced back across the yard and dropped the ball at her feet. She pretended not to notice. Wicker nudged the ball with his nose to get it closer to her foot. When she still didn't respond, Wicker cocked his head and looked at her pleadingly with his big brown eyes. When he did that Laney could seldom resist throwing it again.

Laney had told the kids at school about her wonderful new dog. Rachel was on her way over to see Wicker's latest accomplishments for herself. Laney could hardly wait to see the surprise on her friend's face when Wicker leaped to catch a tremendous throw.

Just one thing troubled Laney about her pet. *I wish I didn't have to leave him in his kennel,* she thought. *He thinks he should live in the house—so he howls when I lock him up in his kennel and go inside. But if I leave him loose in the back yard, he slobbers all over the sliding glass door, and Mom can't stand that. Dad says none of the Gordon Setters he's owned before salivated like that. The neighbors are probably tired of hearing him bark—I know I am. Poor baby! I think he should be allowed to come inside and sleep with me. Mom doesn't, and Dad won't give his opinion. I think he agrees with me but doesn't want to take sides against Mom.*

"Hi, Laney!" Rachel waved at her friend from the sidewalk.

"Come on back!" Laney called. "I need to hold Wicker while the gate's open. I sure don't want him to slip out and run around the neighborhood. We could probably catch him though. All I need is a flashlight if it's dark or a tennis ball if it's daytime. He's such a funny dog. Watch this." Laney threw the tennis ball high into the air. Wicker watched it intently for a split second then tore across the lawn to the place where he anticipated the ball would land. He deftly caught the ball, then ran back and dropped it at the girls' feet!

"Amazing! I want to try." Rachel picked up the ball. The two girls and the dog played hard. When they sat down for a breather, Rachel said, "I'm impressed with Wicker the Wonder Dog! You'd better not ever throw him a baseball or a rock—he might break his teeth."

Laney threw the ball again, and Wicker raced across the yard to fetch it. He loped back and dropped it at Rachel's feet. She was thrilled to be selected as his ball-playing partner. "If you ever decide you don't want Wicker, I'll take him," she told her friend.

After three more throws, Laney tossed the ball into the kennel. Wicker chased after it energetically. "That's all for now." Laney smiled. "We'll be back in a little while, boy." Wicker looked sadly through the wire. "I think he knows what I said," Laney said as she shut the gate.

Wicker howled. "I'm sure he does," Rachel agreed.

The big dog ran to his water dish. He stuck his whole head into the metal bowl and slurped loudly. Some of the water dribbled out of his mouth; more sloshed out onto the cement. "He may be messy, but he sure is happy!" Rachel giggled.

"I'm thirsty, too." Laney led the way into the house. Mrs. Larkin poured each girl a tall glass of juice that they carefully carried into the family room. Laney grabbed the TV remote before she flopped onto a huge cushion on the floor. She looked at her watch and announced, "Hey, it's time for my favorite afternoon show." She punched a bunch of buttons. "Let's watch this before we go back outside."

Rachel didn't say a word. She picked up the glasses and took them out to the kitchen. "Thanks for the juice, Mrs. Larkin."

Rachel returned to the family room. "Laney, I told your Mom I'd be outside. I'm going to go play with Wicker."

"Just a sec—I don't want to miss this part," Laney mumbled as her friend quietly disappeared. Soon she was absorbed in the fast-paced action. For the next few minutes she concentrated on the bad guys who were trying to defeat the good guys. There were so many chases and fights and angry conversations that Laney didn't even realize Rachel was no longer in the room.

When the credits scrolled down the screen Laney stood up slowly and hit the off button on the remote. She glanced around the room. *Where'd Rach go? I guess I'd better find her.* Laney yawned and stretched. *I wonder why she didn't watch the show with me?*

Laney found her friend sitting on the back steps, halfheartedly throwing the ball for Wicker. She didn't look like she was having as much fun as they'd had earlier in the afternoon.

"You okay?" Laney inquired.

Review 30 | Day 1

Story Continued

Rachel shook her head. She didn't answer immediately. Finally she began. "I've been scared to tell you this," There was a long pause. "But that show you were watching is bad. When I saw part of it here last week it really bothered me. I had nightmares and I can't get that poor woman's screams out of my mind. My folks have a rule...We aren't supposed to watch it—at our house or anywhere else."

Laney's eyes were wide as her friend continued. "The words the big man said today were so... so...vile, as my mom would say. I know you like that show, Laney, but I can't watch it."

The two girls were quiet for a while. Laney had never had one of her friends tell her she was making a bad choice. She wasn't sure what to say so she didn't say anything. Finally Rachel picked up the ball Wicker had dropped by her feet and threw it with all her might. Wicker ran across the yard, turned, jumped, and caught it near the fence. Both girls laughed at his mighty effort. The tension caused by the difficult conversation was broken.

The next morning Mrs. B's students were surprised. Their teacher's husband had come to school with her. He carried in two big boxes and put them at the front of the classroom.

When the bell rang, Mrs. Burton stepped to the board and wrote the Scripture verse: "A good man's speech reveals the rich treasures within him. An evil-hearted man is filled with venom, and his speech reveals it."

"Mr. Burton is going to share something about this verse," Mrs. B said before she turned the worship over to her husband and sat down behind her desk.

"Have you ever heard of a Herp Society?" Mr. Burton caught everyone's attention with that question. He gave them one clue, "'Herp' refers to a kind of animal." Laney chuckled and whispered to Tony, "I thought at first he said burp." Tony smiled. Still no one guessed what he was talking about.

"I guess I'll have to show you something," Mr. Burton said with a twinkle. He cautiously opened the first box—and took out a snake! Some students jumped. Heather screamed. "It's okay, kids." Mr. Burton talked calmly. "This is a corn snake. I've had her for about 10 years. She's a very good pet."

Laney leaned over and whispered to Rachel, "I think I'd rather have a dog."

Mr. Burton continued, "She lives in a cage at our house. I feed her dead mice I buy frozen from a pet store. She eats once every 10 days. She's tame and has never bitten me." He told the students that corn snakes are easy to take care of and breed easily in captivity. Before he put her away, he let anyone who was interested touch her to feel her scaly skin. Laney decided just to look.

Nobody was bored by Mr. Burton's talk. He opened the second box and pulled out...a rattlesnake! Laney recognized the rattles on the snake's tail, and she screamed—loudly.

"Don't be alarmed," Mr. Burton soothed. "Nobody's going to get hurt." He held the snake tightly right behind its head, and continued his talk. "There are four kinds of venomous snakes in North America—water moccasins, copperheads, rattlesnakes, and coral snakes. Copperheads are the most common in this part of the country, but we also have water moccasins and rattlesnakes, too."

Several of the students leaned forward in their seats to get a better look. Others wished he'd put the snake back in its box. "Rattlesnakes are pit vipers," Mr. Burton continued. "They kill their prey by biting and injecting it with venom."

Mr. Burton showed everyone the snake's fangs by placing them over the edge of a drinking glass. The class could see them clearly. "If you squeeze right behind the head, the venom will come out into the glass. It's called milking," he said.

Tony raised his hand and asked, "Have you ever been bitten by a snake?"

Mr. B smiled, "Yes—and it hurts! Most snakebites in the United States happen to people who keep venomous snakes as pets. But don't worry about this one," he added, "it has had a ductectomy, meaning it no longer has any venom."

Most of the kids looked relaxed and interested. "Can I touch the rattlesnake?" Tony asked.

"Better not. This guy isn't very tame." Mr. Burton returned the snake to its box and locked it. Laney's heartbeat returned to normal. She looked again at the text written on the board, "A good man's speech reveals the rich treasures within him. An evil-hearted man is filled with venom, and his speech reveals it." She shivered and thought about Mr. Burton's pet rattlesnake and compared it in her mind to her new pet. "I prefer dogs!" she said to herself.

She thought about Wicker and what Rachel had told her the day before after they had played with him. *It must have been hard for her to say what she did to me. I think she's a good person. In fact, she's a real treasure. I've never had a friend like her before. Those characters on my TV show are filled with venom—I can tell by the terrible way they talk. I think I'll spend more time with Rachel,* Laney vowed, *and less time watching TV!*

2 Discussion Time

Check understanding of the story and development of personal values.

- What does Wicker like to play?
- What does he do when he wants to come inside?
- How does Laney feel about Wicker?
- What does Mr. Burton bring to school?
- What comes out of rattlesnakes' fangs?
- How does Laney feel about Mr. Burton's rattlesnake?
- What does Rachel tell Laney about the TV show she starts to watch?
- How does Laney feel about what Rachel said?

A Test-Words Name ____________

Write each spelling word on the line as your teacher says it.

1.	curtain	8.	dare
2.	backyard	9.	kitchen
3.	robin	10.	pear
4.	appear	11.	button
5.	glare	12.	common
6.	share	13.	she's
7.	bare	14.	hadn't

Review Lesson 30

B Test-Sentences

Write the sentences on the lines below, correcting each misspelled word, as well as all capitalization and punctuation errors. There are two misspelled words in each sentence.

the giant went upstares to trim his beerd'

1. The giant went **upstairs** to trim his **beard.**

a frightened hair darted across the playgrownd.

2. A frightened **hare** darted across the **playground.**

the young lyon was weery from the hunt?

3. The young **lion** was **weary** from the hunt**.**

Sit in the bathtubb when you hear the tornado sirin:

4. Sit in the **bathtub** when you hear the tornado **siren.**

187

4 Test-Sentences

Reinforce recognizing misspelled words.

Read each sentence carefully. Write the sentences on the lines in your Worktext. There are two misspelled words in each sentence. Correct each misspelled word, as well as all capitalization and punctuation errors.

Take a minute to memorize...

Matthew 12:35

3 Test-Words

Test for knowledge of the correct spellings of these words.

I will say each word once, use the word in a sentence, then say the word again. Write the words on the lines in your Worktext.

1. curtain	Laney pulled back the **curtain** and saw Rachel coming up the sidewalk.
2. backyard	Wicker has a nice kennel in the **backyard.**
3. robin	The dog bounded toward a **robin** and made the girls laugh.
4. appear	It is not uncommon for Wicker to **appear** at the sliding glass doors.
5. glare	The **glare** from the sun often catches his attention.
6. share	He leaves his fair **share** of slobber all over the glass.
7. bare	Wicker could easily catch the tennis ball with his **bare** teeth.
8. dare	Laney would not **dare** take Wicker into her room.
9. kitchen	In the **kitchen,** Mrs. Larkin poured each girl a glass of juice.
10. pear	It was a combination of **pear,** apple, and kiwi juice.
11. button	Laney grabbed the remote control and pushed the "on" **button.**
12. common	It was **common** for Laney to watch violent programs on TV.
13. she's	"Oh, no, **she's** watching that bad show again," Rachel groaned to herself.
14. hadn't	Laney **hadn't** noticed that Rachel left the room.

Test-Dictation

Reinforce correct spelling by using current and previous words in context.

Listen as I read each sentence, then write it in your Worktext. Remember to use correct capitalization and punctuation. (Slowly read each sentence twice. Sentences are found in the Student Worktext at right. The words **dragon**, **champion**, **dairy**, and **wear** are found in this unit.)

Test-Proofreading

Familiarize students with standardized test format and reinforce recognizing misspelled words.

Look at each set of words. If a word is misspelled, fill in the oval by that word. If all the words are spelled correctly, fill in the oval by **no mistake**.

Review Lesson 30

C Test-Dictation

Name ____________________

Write each sentence as your teacher dictates. Use correct punctuation.

1. The angry dragon in the story was blue and red.
2. The champion horse wears a wreath around his neck.
3. That farmer to the north runs a dairy.
4. We are thankful for the clothes we have to wear.

D Test-Proofreading

If a word is misspelled, fill in the oval by that word. If all the words are spelled correctly, fill in the oval by **no mistake**.

1. ● theres	○ curtain	○ backyard	○ no mistake		
2. ○ robin	○ appear	● coton	○ no mistake		
3. ○ share	○ fair	○ glare	● no mistake		
4. ○ kitchen	○ pear	● reer	○ no mistake		
5. ● tair	○ button	○ common	○ no mistake		
6. ○ listen	○ didn't	○ bedroom	● no mistake		
7. ● chear	○ she's	○ hadn't	○ no mistake		
8. ○ dare	● geer	○ bare	○ no mistake		
9. ○ disappear	● ceereal	○ what's	○ no mistake		
10. ○ reason	○ scare	○ he'd	● no mistake		
11. ○ steer	○ ruin	● bedspred	○ no mistake		
12. ○ sincerely	○ weird	● fireplase	○ no mistake		

188

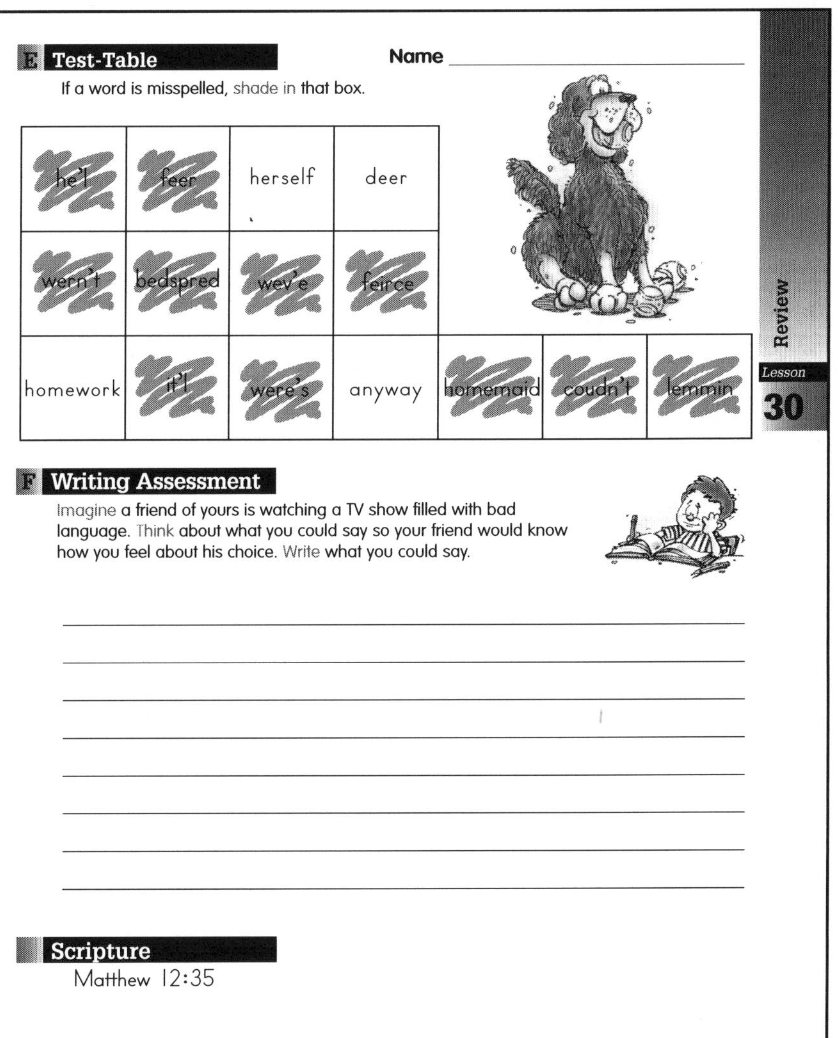

E Test-Table
Name
If a word is misspelled, shade in that box.
he'l
feer
herself
deer
wern't
bedspred
wev'e
feirce
homework
it'l
were's
anyway
homemaid
coudn't
lemmin
Review
Lesson
30
F Writing Assessment
Imagine a friend of yours is watching a TV show filled with bad language. Think about what you could say so your friend would know how you feel about his choice. Write what you could say.
Scripture
Matthew 12:35
189

Connecticut is the only state whose name is two words connected by a letter: "connect," "i," and "cut."

Test-Table

Test mastery of words in this unit.

If a word is misspelled, fill in the space on the grid.

Writing Assessment

Assess student's spelling, grammar, and composition skills through personal writing.

- Why does Rachel come over to Laney's house? (To see Wicker play catch.)
- How do you think Rachel feels when Laney turns on the TV again? (Upset.)
- Where did Rachel go when she felt uncomfortable about the TV show Laney was watching? (Outside on the back porch with Wicker.)
- What did Rachel say about the TV show? (She said the show was bad and gave her nightmares. The language was vile.)
- How would you feel if one of your friends told you, you were making a bad choice? (Brainstorm with your class. You may wish to write their responses on the board.)
- Raise your hand if you think Rachel is letting her light shine now.

Test-Sentences

Reinforce recognizing misspelled words.

Read each sentence carefully. Write the sentences on the lines in your Worktext, correcting each misspelled word, as well as all capitalization and punctuation errors.

Review Lesson 30

G Test-Sentences Name ______________

Write the sentences on the lines below, correcting each misspelled word, as well as all capitalization and punctuation errors. There are two misspelled words in each sentence.

The plumber will repare the fountin in the park

1. The plumber will repair the fountain in the park.

my Aunt told us not to get neer that chikin.

2. My aunt told us not to get near that chicken.

did you stair at the dog with the purple hare.

3. Did you stare at the dog with the purple hair?

Heres five dollars for your cab fair

4. Here's five dollars for your cab fare.

H Test-Words

Write each spelling word on the line as your teacher says it.

1. disappear
2. what's
3. reason
4. scare
5. listen
6. didn't
7. steer
8. ruin
9. sincerely
10. weird
11. compare
12. scarce
13. they'd
14. I'd

190

Test-Words

Test for knowledge of the correct spellings of these words.

I will say the word once, use the word in a sentence, then say the word again. Write the word on the lines in your Worktext.

1. disappear — "Why does Rachel **disappear** like that?" Laney wondered.
2. what's — "**What's** wrong?" she asked Rachel.
3. reason — Rachel explained her **reason** for leaving the family room.
4. scare — "I don't want to watch things on TV that **scare** me," said Rachel.
5. listen — "It's not good for me to **listen** to that bad language, either," she continued.
6. didn't — Rachel **didn't** want to hurt Laney's feelings, but she had to tell her.
7. steer — "I want to **steer** clear of programs like that," she explained.
8. ruin — Laney did not want to **ruin** her friendship with Rachel.
9. sincerely — Rachel **sincerely** wants to please God with what she watches.
10. weird — Laney did not think Rachel was **weird** for choosing not to watch the show.
11. compare — Laney has never had a friend that could **compare** with Rachel.
12. scarce — She realized that friends like Rachel were **scarce**.
13. they'd — Laney hoped **they'd** continue to be good friends.
14. I'd — "**I'd** like to spend more time with Rachel and less time watching TV," she said.

I Test-Editing

Name ____________________

If a word is spelled correctly, fill in the oval under **Correct**. If the word is misspelled, fill in the oval under **Incorrect**, and write the word correctly on the blank.

	Correct	Incorrect	
1. peeriod	○	●	period
2. anywhere	●	○	
3. newzpaper	○	●	newspaper
4. somewere	○	●	somewhere
5. within	●	○	
6. bathroom	●	○	
7. whos'	○	●	who's
8. speer	○	●	spear
9. she'l	○	●	she'll
10. ribbon	●	○	
11. sunshine	●	○	
12. ralerode	○	●	railroad
13. woudn't	○	●	wouldn't
14. everybody	●	○	
15. oven	●	○	

Review Lesson 30

191

3 Test-Editing

Reinforce recognizing and correcting misspelled words.

4 Action Game

Reinforce spelling skills and provide motivation and interest.

Materials

- Word Lists
- Several Balloons

BALLOON BOP

How to Play:

Divide students into two or more groups. Choose a "Caller" for each group and provide him/her with a list of spelling words to be reviewed. Have the groups sit in circles. The Caller for each group will say a spelling word and set the balloon in motion. The first player to hit the balloon says the first letter of the called word and hits it to another group member. The balloon is hit around the circle until the word is correctly spelled. A point is earned each time a word is spelled right. If the balloon hits the ground, the group looses a point. The team with the most points wins!

Game

Reinforce spelling skills and provide motivation and interest.

Materials

- game pages (from Student Worktext)
- stickers (13 per child)
- game word list

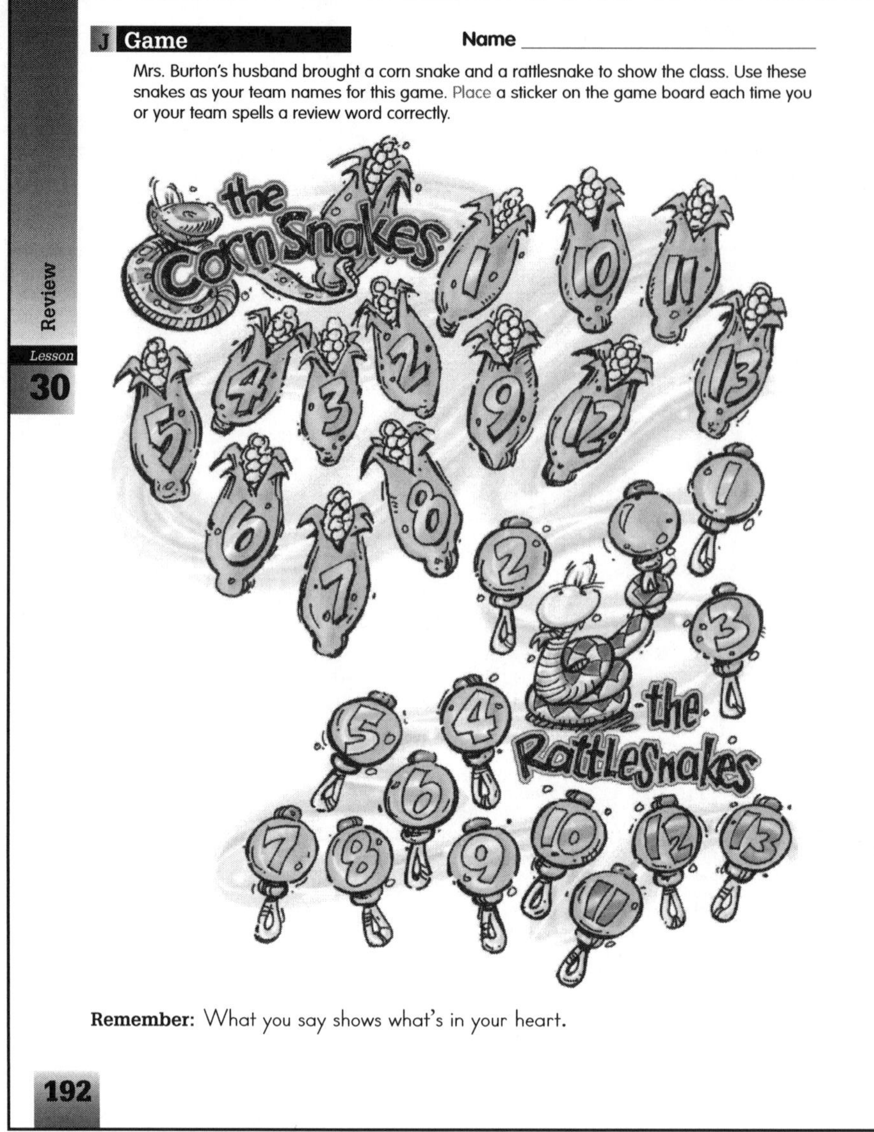

J **Game** Name ______________________

Mrs. Burton's husband brought a corn snake and a rattlesnake to show the class. Use these snakes as your team names for this game. Place a sticker on the game board each time you or your team spells a review word correctly.

Remember: What you say shows what's in your heart.

Review Lesson 30

192

Game Word List

Check off each word lightly in pencil as it is used.

The Corn Snakes	The Rattlesnakes
1. **there's**	1. **weren't**
2. **cotton**	2. **homework**
3. **fair**	3. **fear**
4. **gear**	4. **yardstick**
5. **rear**	5. **it'll**
6. **tear**	6. **herself**
7. **bedroom**	7. **we've**
8. **cheer**	8. **where's**
9. **cereal**	9. **fierce**
10. **he'd**	10. **anyway**
11. **bedspread**	11. **homemade**
12. **fireplace**	12. **couldn't**
13. **he'll**	13. **lemon**

How to Play:

- Divide students into two teams. Name one team The Corn Snakes, one The Rattlesnakes. (Optional: If you have an even number of students, you may wish to pair students from opposing teams and have them share a game page.)
- Read the instructions from the student game page aloud.
- Have a student from the first team choose a number from 1 to 13.
- Say the word that matches that number from the team's word list.
- Have the student write the word on the board.
- If correct, have each member of that team put a sticker on that number by his/her team name. If the word is misspelled, have him/her put an X through that number. That number may not be chosen again.
- Repeat this process with the second team.
- When the words from both lists have been used, the team with the most stickers is the winner.

Date ______________________

This certificate is awarded to

____

for completing activities using the following spelling words:

curtain	bare	appear	he'd	anyway
fountain	compare	beard	I'd	backyard
chicken	dare	disappear	they'd	bathroom
kitchen	fare	fear	he'll	bathtub
listen	glare	gear	it'll	bedroom
oven	hare	near	she'll	bedspread
siren	scare	rear	couldn't	everybody
robin	share	spear	didn't	fireplace
ruin	stare	tear	hadn't	herself
champion	scarce	weary	weren't	homemade
lion	pear	cheer	wouldn't	homework
button	wear	deer	here's	newspaper
common	anywhere	steer	she's	yardstick
cotton	dairy	fierce	there's	playground
dragon	fair	cereal	what's	railroad
lemon	hair	period	where's	somewhere
reason	repair	sincerely	who's	sunshine
ribbon	upstairs	weird	we've	within

2 Certificate

Provide an opportunity for parents or guardians to encourage and assess their child's progress.

Fill in today's date and your name on your certificate.

Take a minute to memorize...

Matthew 12:35

3 Letter

Provide the parent or guardian with the spelling word lists for the next unit.

Give your parents or guardian this letter that lists your spelling words for the next unit. Put it where you will remember to practice the words together.

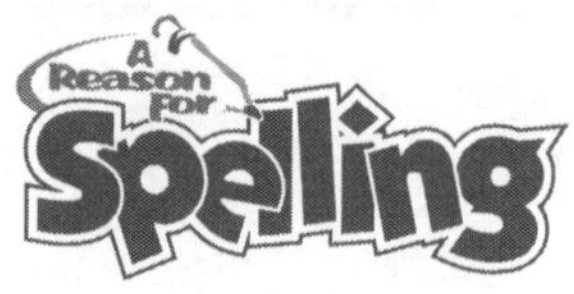

Dear Parent,

We are about to begin the last spelling unit of the year containing only one lesson. A set of eighteen words will be studied next week. All the words will be reviewed the following week. Values based on the Scripture listed below will be taught.

Lesson 31

April Fool's Day
Arbor Day
Christmas
Columbus Day
Easter
Independence Day
Groundhog Day
Halloween
Hanukkah
Labor Day
Martin Luther King Day
May Day
Memorial Day
New Year's Day
Passover
Presidents' Day
Thanksgiving
Valentine's Day

John 13:34, 35

1 **Literature Connection**
Topic: Love for others
Theme Text: John 13:34, 35

Under Construction

Thorny sees real love in action when he ruins his foster father's saw.

"What magnificent plumage!" Hubert Thornton Remington III—better known as Thorny—leaned toward the windows surrounding the breakfast table at the Simmons' home. He held his fork in midair as he stared at the little birds flitting around the bird feeder just outside the windows. "Such vivid color. I find it truly amazing that I never really noticed the avian species before coming to live with you." The hash browns on the fork plopped back onto his plate unnoticed.

"Those little goldfinches are flashy, all right." Thorny's foster father relaxed in his chair enjoying the slower pace of a weekend morning. "Especially now that they've got their summer feathers. Looks like I need to fill that thistle feeder again. They've cleaned it out pretty quickly."

"Look!" Thorny pointed with the fork. "What type of bird just flew into that tree?"

"What color was it, Thorny?" Mrs. Simmons stood up and moved to stand behind his chair. "Where did it land?"

"Right there. No, well, I don't see it now." Thorny finally laid his fork down. "It appeared to be primarily orange and black."

Mrs. Simmons squeezed Thorny's thin shoulders. "Probably an oriole, Son. They really like the oranges we put out." She picked up an empty dish and carried it over to the sink. "After you finish your breakfast, why don't you see what Pop's bird books say about them?"

When he'd polished off the last of Mrs. Simmons' yummy hash browns, Thorny went in search of the bird books. The floor-to-ceiling bookshelves in the family room held a wide variety of books, and Thorny soon spotted a group that were about birds.

"Hmmmm. Orioles. Let's see. 'Formerly considered two species... common in open woodlands, river groves, and suburban shade trees.'" Thorny checked out the goldfinches and other kinds of birds as well, but the bluebirds really caught his interest. "'Provision of specially designed nesting boxes by concerned bird-watchers has resulted in a promising comeback of this once declining species.'"

Thorny leafed through some of the other books. He stopped at a page that had pictures of several different birdhouses on it. *I could make this bluebird house!* Thorny jumped up from the big chair where he'd been reading. *Mr. and Mrs. Simmons enjoy the birds a great deal. I'm sure they'd be pleased to assist me in a project that would provide additional habitat for the bluebirds.*

Thorny continued the discussion with himself as he went looking for Mr. Simmons. *It cannot possibly be too difficult. After all, there are simply four sides, a roof, a floor and a hole for the door.*

As he entered the kitchen he called, "Mrs. Simmons?"

"Just a minute, Deborah." Mrs. Simmons spoke to the person on the other end of the phone connection and then turned to her foster son. "What is it, Thorny?"

Thorny felt bad about bothering her while she was on the phone but she didn't seem to mind. "Could you tell me where I might find Mr. Simmons?"

"He had to run over to the plant for a few minutes. Is there something I can help you with?" She held her hand over the phone.

"No, thank you." Thorny could hear her continuing her conversation as he wandered away from the kitchen.

Thorny sank back into the overstuffed chair in the family room and opened the book. *This birdhouse really doesn't appear to be difficult. The measurements are listed right here. I wonder how you cut the hole in front. It has to be 29 mm across. Oh! Perhaps that hand-held jigsaw Mr. Simmons showed me would be just the thing. He said it was used to cut rounded or curved lines!*

Thorny picked up the book and went to the garage. It was easy to find the jigsaw since Mr. Simmons kept all his tools neatly arranged in the work area at the back of the garage. Thorny fingered some wood scraps. *These smaller pieces of wood are almost the right size already. Perhaps I could build this birdhouse myself. How hard could it be?*

Thorny selected the pieces of wood he wanted and started measuring and marking. He decided it would be smart to cut the wood outside so he wouldn't have to clean up the sawdust. After carrying the wood out behind the garage, he plugged the small saw into an extension cord and carried it out, too. *Now, I just need to cut off the part I've marked on each board.* He picked up the saw and set it down again. *How am I going to cut that little strip off just holding the wood in my hand? I need something to set it on. That stack of cement blocks would work.* Thorny set the piece of wood on the top cement block and turned on the little jigsaw.

The next evening after supper Thorny and his foster parents gathered in the family room to watch a program about birds on television. The doorbell rang. Mr. Simmons went to the door and was gone for several minutes. When he came back into the room a man was with him.

"Sally, have you seen my jigsaw? I told Dan Holcomb that he could borrow it for some woodwork he's doing. It's not in the garage,

Story (continued)

and for the life of me I can't remember what I did with it."

"Um, Mr. Simmons?" Thorny's voice squeaked a little. "I, um, I believe I know precisely where your jigsaw is."

"Great!" Mr. Simmons grabbed Thorny's hand and pulled him up from the beanbag chair where he'd flopped. "Come and show us, Thorny." He wrapped an arm around the boy's shoulders as they walked through the house to the garage. "This boy's as smart as they come, Dan." He spoke over his shoulder to the man following them. "I can always count on him to keep track of things around here!"

Oh, no; oh, no; oh, no!

Thorny felt sick inside. *What will he do when he sees the jigsaw? He's sure to shout and call me names like Mr. Kincaid did, but I wonder if he'll shove me like Mr. Davis did? One thing's for sure, he won't have anything else good to say about me after this!*

But Mr. Simmons didn't do any of those things when Thorny led the men behind the garage. He just picked up the saw and turned it over in his hands a couple of times. "Well, Dan, it looks like you'll need to find another saw to borrow." His voice was as calm and quiet as ever. "I'm awfully sorry to have put you to the effort of driving over here for nothing. You might check with John Pace. He doesn't live far from here and does a bit of woodworking. Why don't we give him a call?"

Thorny retreated to his room, the rest of the TV program forgotten. If only he didn't have to face Mr. Simmons again. He buried his face in his hands. Mr. and Mrs. Simmons had been so kind to him, treating him as if he were their own son. They were so much nicer than any of the other foster parents he'd had—and how had he repaid them for their kindness? By ruining something and not telling them about it. He was sure to be in big trouble now! They might even ask Child Services to place him in a different foster home!

"Well, thanks anyway." Thorny could hear Mr. Holcomb talking to Mr. Simmons as he walked to the front door. "I appreciate your helping me locate another saw to borrow. I'm afraid it's just too much for me to buy one right now." There was a pause and Thorny could hear the familiar sounds of the door opening. "I was wondering...that is, would you mind if I asked you a personal question? Are you a Christian, a church-goer?" Mr. Holcomb's voice sounded a little nervous and he rushed on so fast Thorny could barely catch the words from his room down the hall. "I just wondered because of the way you treated that boy. I mean, most people would've been furious with him—and he's not even your own son, just a foster kid!"

"I don't mind your questions at all, Dan." Mr. Simmons sounded like he was smiling. Thorny crept over to the door to hear better. "Yes, Sally and I are Christians, and we do attend church. And Thorny isn't 'just a foster kid.' He's a very important part of our family and we love him."

"Well, now, doesn't that just beat all!" Dan Holcomb's voice faded as he stepped out the door. "Maybe there really is something to this church business!"

Maybe there really is something to this church business! Thorny repeated the statement in his mind. *Maybe believing in God really does make you different—better! It sure seems to make a difference in how Mr. and Mrs. Simmons treat me.*

Thorny found his foster parents in the family room. "I'm sorry. I didn't intend to break the saw. It was harder to maneuver than I realized and the blade broke when it hit the cement under the piece of wood. I didn't know how to tell you, so I left it outside and then it rained and..." Thorny dropped his head.

"It's all right, Thorny." Mr. Simmons looked up from the open book in his lap. "I forgive you. We'll get the saw fixed or replaced, and then I think we'd better get this birdhouse built." He tapped the page he'd been reading. It was the one that showed how to build bluebird houses. "After all, these birds need a home right away to raise their youngsters."

"Yes, sir." Thorny smiled in relief. Under his breath he added, "Everyone needs a home."

2 Discussion Time

Check understanding of the story and development of personal values.

- What did the Simmons enjoy watching in their backyard?
- What gave Thorny the idea of building a bluebird house?
- Why didn't Thorny get Mr. or Mrs. Simmons to help him?
- How did Mr. Simmons find out about the broken saw?
- What did Thorny expect Mr. Simmons to do when he realized Thorny had ruined the saw?
- How did Mr. Simmons react?
- What did Dan Holcomb ask after he saw how Mr. Simmons treated Thorny?

A Preview Name ______________

Write each word as your teacher says it.

1. Easter
2. Thanksgiving
3. Valentine's Day
4. Martin Luther King Day
5. Christmas
6. Columbus Day
7. Halloween
8. Independence Day
9. Groundhog Day
10. President's Day
11. Labor Day
12. Arbor Day
13. May Day
14. Memorial Day
15. April Fool's Day
16. Passover
17. Hanukkah
18. New Year's Day

Holidays

Lesson 31

Scripture

John 13:34, 35

195

3 Preview

Test for knowledge of the correct spellings of these words.

Customize Your List

On a separate sheet of paper, additional words of your choice may be tested.

I will say each word once, use the word in a sentence, then say the word again. Write the words on the lines in your Worktext.

Correct Immediately!

Let's correct our Preview. I will spell each word out loud. If you spelled a word incorrectly, rewrite it correctly.

Progress Chart

Students may record scores. (Reproducible master provided in Appendix B.)

Lesson 31 | Day 1

1.	Easter	We celebrate Christ's resurrection on **Easter** Sunday.
2.	Thanksgiving	Many American families have special foods on **Thanksgiving** Day.
3.	Valentine's Day	Cards are often exchanged on **Valentine's Day**.
4.	Martin Luther King Day	**Martin Luther King Day** honors the life of a civil rights leader.
5.	Christmas	During the **Christmas** season we celebrate the birth of Jesus.
6.	Columbus Day	**Columbus Day** is on October twelfth each year.
7.	Halloween	**Halloween** always falls on October thirty-first.
8.	Independence Day	On July fourth, Americans celebrate **Independence Day**.
9.	Groundhog Day	On **Groundhog Day** people watch for signs of an early spring.
10.	Presidents' Day	**Presidents' Day** celebrates Washington's and Lincoln's birthdays.
11.	Labor Day	Government offices, like the post office, are closed on **Labor Day**.
12.	Arbor Day	Communities often gather to plant trees on **Arbor Day**.
13.	May Day	People sometimes give each other fresh flowers on **May Day**.
14.	Memorial Day	**Memorial Day** honors men who died in the service of this country.
15.	April Fool's Day	Some people play jokes on others on **April Fool's Day**.
16.	Passover	The Jewish **Passover** is traditionally celebrated for eight days.
17.	Hanukkah	**Hanukkah**, or the Feast of Lights, is also celebrated for eight days.
18.	New Year's Day	At midnight on December thirty-first, **New Year's Day** begins.

Word Shapes

Help students form a correct image of whole words.

Look at each word and think about its shape. Now, write the word in the correct Word Shape Boxes. You may check off each word as you use it.

(The name of a holiday is a proper noun. Proper nouns begin with capital letters.)

In the Word Shape Boxes, fill in the boxes containing the capital letters in each word.

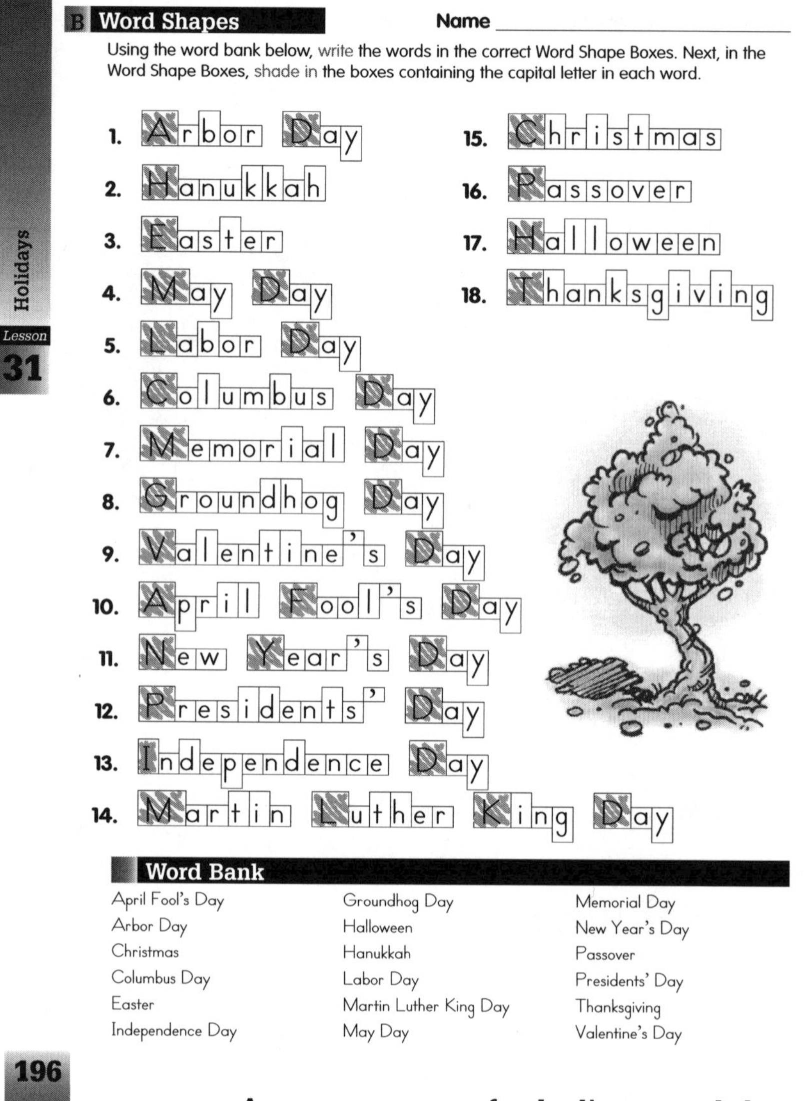

Holidays

Lesson 31

B **Word Shapes** Name ______________

Using the word bank below, write the words in the correct Word Shape Boxes. Next, in the Word Shape Boxes, shade in the boxes containing the capital letter in each word.

1. Arbor Day
2. Hanukkah
3. Easter
4. May Day
5. Labor Day
6. Columbus Day
7. Memorial Day
8. Groundhog Day
9. Valentine's Day
10. April Fool's Day
11. New Year's Day
12. Presidents' Day
13. Independence Day
14. Martin Luther King Day
15. Christmas
16. Passover
17. Halloween
18. Thanksgiving

Word Bank

April Fool's Day	Groundhog Day	Memorial Day
Arbor Day	Halloween	New Year's Day
Christmas	Hanukkah	Passover
Columbus Day	Labor Day	Presidents' Day
Easter	Martin Luther King Day	Thanksgiving
Independence Day	May Day	Valentine's Day

196

Answers may vary for duplicate word shapes.

Take a minute to memorize...

John 13:34, 35

Be Prepared For Fun

Check these supply lists for **Fun Ways to Spell** - presented **Day 2**. Purchase and/or gather these items ahead of time!

General

- Pencil
- Graph Paper (1 sheet per child)
- Spelling List

Auditory

- Voice Recorder
- Spelling List

Visual

- Water Color Paint Box (1 per child)
- Paint Brush (1 per child)
- Art Paper (3 or 4 sheets per child)
- Spelling List

Tactile

- Soccer Ball, Basketball, tennis ball, or 4-Square Ball
- Spelling List

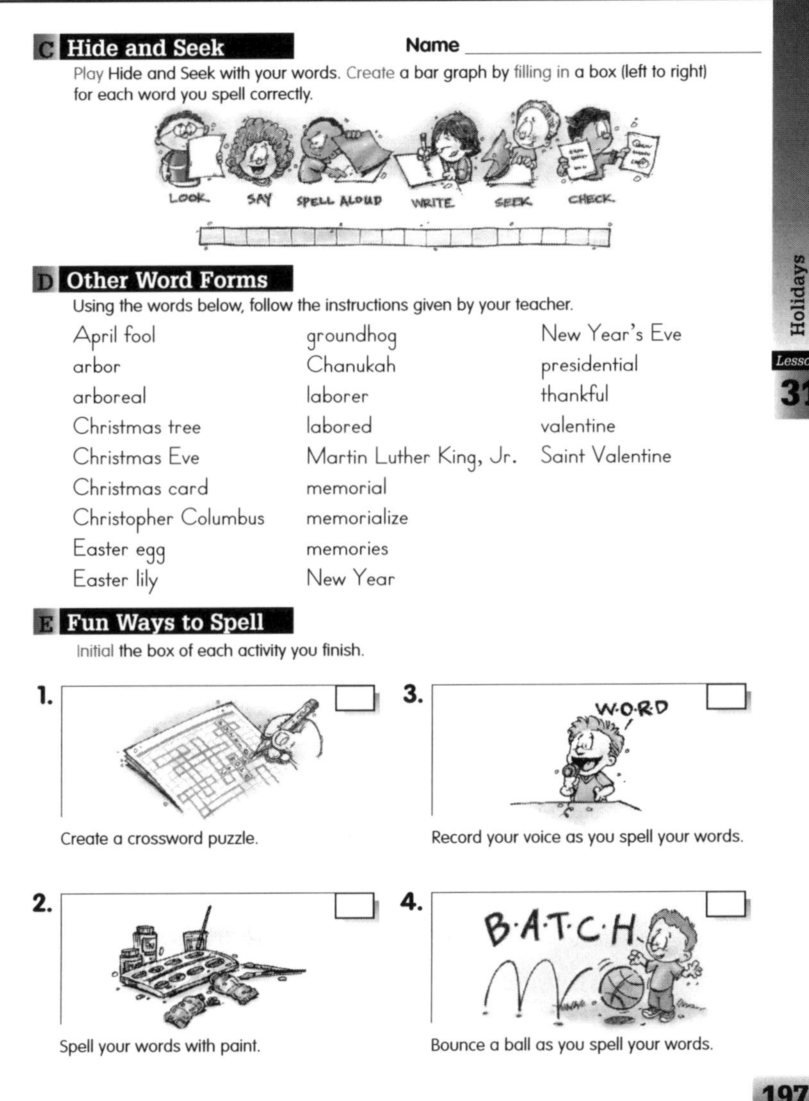
C Hide and Seek
Name
Play Hide and Seek with your words. Create a bar graph by filling in a box (left to right) for each word you spell correctly.
LOOK
SAY
SPELL ALOUD
WRITE
SEEK
CHECK
D Other Word Forms
Using the words below, follow the instructions given by your teacher.
April fool
arbor
arboreal
Christmas tree
Christmas Eve
Christmas card
Christopher Columbus
Easter egg
Easter lily
groundhog
Chanukah
laborer
labored
Martin Luther King, Jr.
memorial
memorialize
memories
New Year
New Year's Eve
presidential
thankful
valentine
Saint Valentine
E Fun Ways to Spell
Initial the box of each activity you finish.
1. Create a crossword puzzle.
3. WORD
Record your voice as you spell your words.
2. Spell your words with paint.
4. B·A·T·C·H
Bounce a ball as you spell your words.
Holidays
Lesson 31
197

1 Hide and Seek

Reinforce spelling by using multiple styles of learning.

On a white board, Teacher writes each word — one at a time. **Have students:**

- **Look** at the word.
- **Say** the word out loud.
- **Spell** the word out loud.
- **Hide** (teacher erases word.)
- **Write** the word on paper.
- **Seek** (teacher rewrites word.)
- **Check** spelling. If incorrect, rewrite word correctly.

2 Other Word Forms

This activity is optional. Have students write original sentences using these Other Word Forms:

arbor
presidential
memorial
thankful

3 Fun Ways to Spell

Four activities are provided. Use one, two, three, or all of the activities. Have students initial the box for each activity they complete.

Options:

- assign activities to students according to their learning styles
- set up the activities in learning centers for students to do throughout the day
- divide students into four groups and assign one activity per group
- do one activity per day

General

To create a crossword puzzle…
- Use a pencil to arrange your words on graph paper.
- Overlap words where letters are shared.
- Don't create any new words.
- Outline each word with a marker and number them.
- Write a clue for each word.
- Erase your words.
- Trade with a classmate and work each other's puzzles.

Auditory

To spell your words using a voice recorder…
- Record yourself as you say and spell each word on your spelling list.
- Listen to your recording and check your spelling.

Visual

To spell your words with paint…
- Paint each spelling word on your paper.
- Trade papers with a classmate and check each other's spelling.

Tactile

To bounce a ball as you spell your words…
- Look at the first word on your list.
- Bounce the ball as you say each letter of the word aloud.
- Do this with each word on your list.

Working with Words

Familiarize students with word meaning and usage.

Missing Letters

On the board, write **S__ __nt P__tr__ck's D__y**. Have students tell which letters are missing and write them in the blanks. Remind students that the names of holidays are proper nouns, so they will begin with capital letters.

Each of the holidays is missing its vowels. Fill in the missing letters to complete each word.

Spelling Clues

Write the correct spelling words on the lines. Be sure to use capital letters and apostrophes as needed.

Take a minute to memorize...

John 13:34, 35

Holidays | Lesson 31

F **Working with Words** Name ____________

Missing Letters

Each of the holidays is missing its vowels. Fill in the missing letters to complete each word. Remember to use capital letters where needed.

1. Chr_i_stm_a_s
2. C_o_l_u_mb_u_s D_a_y
3. Gr_o_u_ndh_o_g D_a_y
4. H_a_ll_o_w_e_e_n
5. H_a_n_u_kk_a_h
6. L_a_b_o_r D_a_y
7. M_a_y D_a_y
8. M_e_m_o_r_i_a_l D_a_y
9. _I_nd_e_p_e_nd_e_nc_e_ D_a_y
10. M_a_rt_i_n L_u_th_e_r K_i_ng D_a_y
11. Th_a_nksg_i_v_i_ng
12. N_e_w Y_e_a_r's D_a_y
13. _A_pr_i_l F_o_o_ls' D_a_y
14. Pr_e_s_i_d_e_nts' D_a_y
15. P_a_ss_o_v_e_r
16. _A_rb_o_r D_a_y
17. V_a_l_e_nt_i_n_e_'s D_a_y
18. _E_a_st_e_r

Spelling Clues

Write the correct spelling words on the lines. Be sure to use capital letters and punctuation as needed.

1. The short word **or** is in the holiday names Arbor Day, Labor Day, and Memorial Day.
2. The short word **as** is in the holiday names Christmas, Easter, and Passover.
3. The short word **in** is in the holiday names Independence Day, Thanksgiving, Martin Luther King Day, and Valentine's Day.

Word Bank

April Fools' Day	Groundhog Day	Memorial Day
Arbor Day	Halloween	New Year's Day
Christmas	Hanukkah	Passover
Columbus Day	Labor Day	Presidents' Day
Easter	Martin Luther King Day	Thanksgiving
Independence Day	May Day	Valentine's Day

198

G Dictation

Name ______________________

Write each sentence as your teacher dictates. Use correct punctuation.

1. We usually visit my grandfather and grandmother at Thanksgiving.
2. We had a party on Independence Day.
3. Our class will practice a play for Easter.

Holidays

Lesson 31

H Proofreading

If a word is misspelled, fill in the oval by that word. If all the words are spelled correctly, fill in the oval by **no mistake**.

1. ○ April Fool's Day
   ○ Christmas
   ● Arber Day
   ○ no mistake
2. ● Presidents Day
   ○ Easter
   ○ May Day
   ○ no mistake
3. ○ Thanksgiving
   ○ New Year's Day
   ○ Groundhog Day
   ● no mistake
4. ○ Passover
   ● Valentines Day
   ○ Memorial Day
   ○ no mistake
5. ○ Hanukkah
   ● Martin Luther King's Day
   ○ Columbus Day
   ○ no mistake
6. ○ Labor Day
   ● Haloween
   ○ Independence Day
   ○ no mistake
7. ● Eester
   ○ Arbor Day
   ○ Halloween
   ○ no mistake
8. ● Independance Day
   ○ Labor Day
   ○ Columbus Day
   ○ no mistake

199

Dictation

Reinforce correct spelling by using current and previous words in context.

Listen as I read each sentence and then write it in your Worktext. Remember to use correct capitalization and punctuation. (Slowly read each sentence twice. Sentences are found in the Student Worktext to the left.)

Proofreading

Familiarize students with standardized test format and reinforce recognition of misspelled words.

Look at each set of words. If a word is misspelled, fill in the oval by that word. If all the words are spelled correctly, fill in the oval by **no mistake**.

3 Hide and Seek

Reinforce correct spelling of current spelling words. Repeat this activity from Day 2. (A reproducible master is provided in Appendix A as shown on the inset page to the right.)

4 Other Word Forms

Have your students complete this activity to strengthen spelling ability and expand vocabulary.

1 Posttest

Visit the **A Reason For** website to download free, printable Posttest pages.

I will say the word once, use it in a sentence, then say it again. Write your words on a separate sheet of paper.

Progress Chart

Students may record scores. (Appendix B)

Personal Dictionary

Students may add any words they have misspelled to their personal dictionaries. (Appendix B)

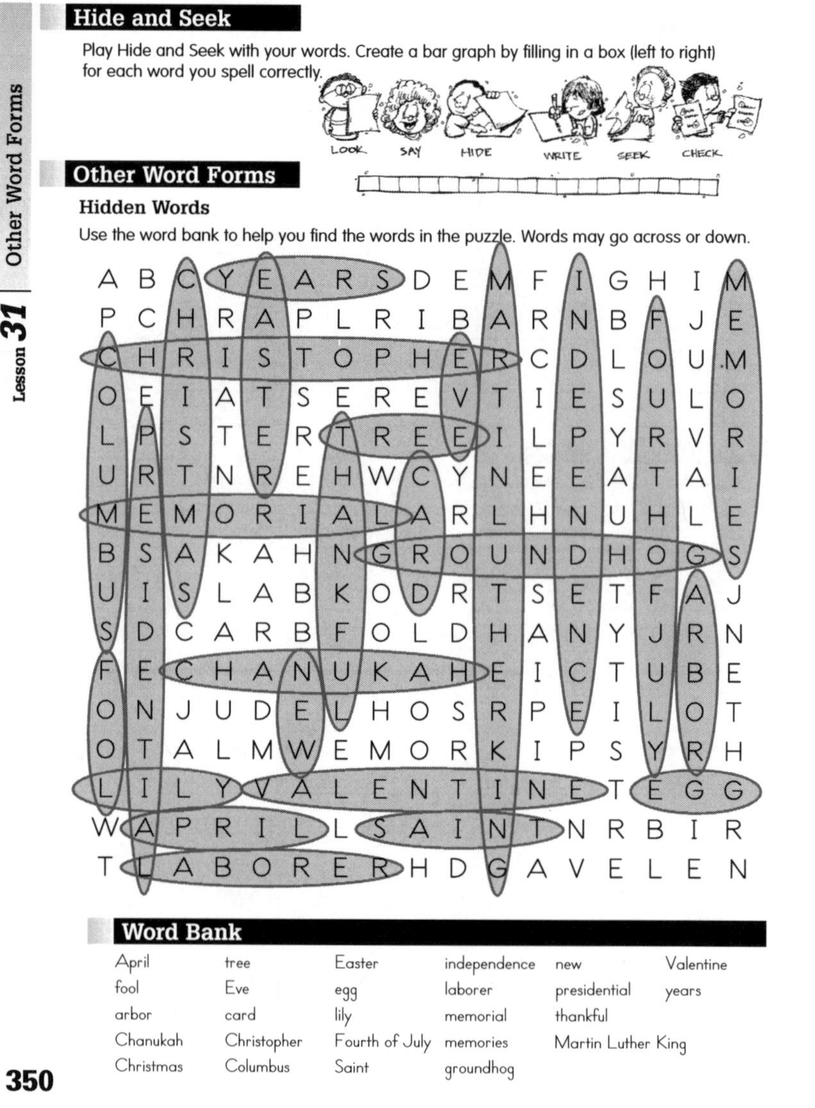

Lesson 31 | Other Word Forms

Hide and Seek

Play Hide and Seek with your words. Create a bar graph by filling in a box (left to right) for each word you spell correctly.

Other Word Forms

Hidden Words

Use the word bank to help you find the words in the puzzle. Words may go across or down.

A B C Y E A R S D E M F I G H I M
P C H R A P L R I B A R N B F J E
C H R I S T O P H E R C D L O U M
O E I A T S E R E V T I E S U L O
L P S T E R T R E E I L P Y R V R
U R T N R E H W C Y N E E A T A I
M E M O R I A L A R L H N U H L E
B S A K A H N G R O U N D H O G S
U I S L A B K O D R T S E T F A J
S D C A R B F O L D H A N Y J R N
F E C H A N U K A H E I C T U B E
O N J U D E L H O S R P E I L O T
O T A L M W E M O R K I P S Y R H
L I L Y V A L E N T I N E T E G G
W A P R I L L S A I N T N R B I R
T L A B O R E R H D G A V E L E N

Word Bank

April	tree	Easter	independence	new	Valentine
fool	Eve	egg	laborer	presidential	years
arbor	card	lily	memorial	thankful	
Chanukah	Christopher	Fourth of July	memories	Martin Luther King	
Christmas	Columbus	Saint	groundhog		

350

1. Christmas	**Christmas** is traditionally celebrated on December twenty-fifth.
2. May Day	**May Day** is designated for the celebration of the arrival of Spring.
3. Arbor Day	Many people plant a sapling on **Arbor Day.**
4. Labor Day	**Labor Day** is frequently celebrated with rest and relaxation.
5. Thanksgiving	**Thanksgiving** is always on the third Thursday in November.
6. Columbus Day	We remember Christopher Columbus on **Columbus Day.**
7. Independence Day	Americans celebrate this country's liberty on **Independence Day.**
8. New Year's Day	In America, **New Year's Day** is always January first.
9. Groundhog Day	**Groundhog Day** is always on February second.
10. Martin Luther King Day	**Martin Luther King Day** honors an important civil rights leader.
11. Presidents' Day	We celebrate Washington's and Lincoln's births on **Presidents' Day.**
12. Valentine's Day	Chocolates in a heart-shaped box are a traditional **Valentine's Day** gift.
13. Easter	Many people hide colored eggs on or around **Easter.**
14. Hanukkah	**Hanukkah** is also known as the Feast of Lights.
15. Passover	**Passover** commemorates the Israelites' exodus from Egypt.
16. Halloween	By **Halloween** the weather is often crisp and cool.
17. April Fool's Day	The first day of April is always called **April Fool's Day.**
18. Memorial Day	Wreaths are often placed on servicemen's graves on **Memorial Day.**

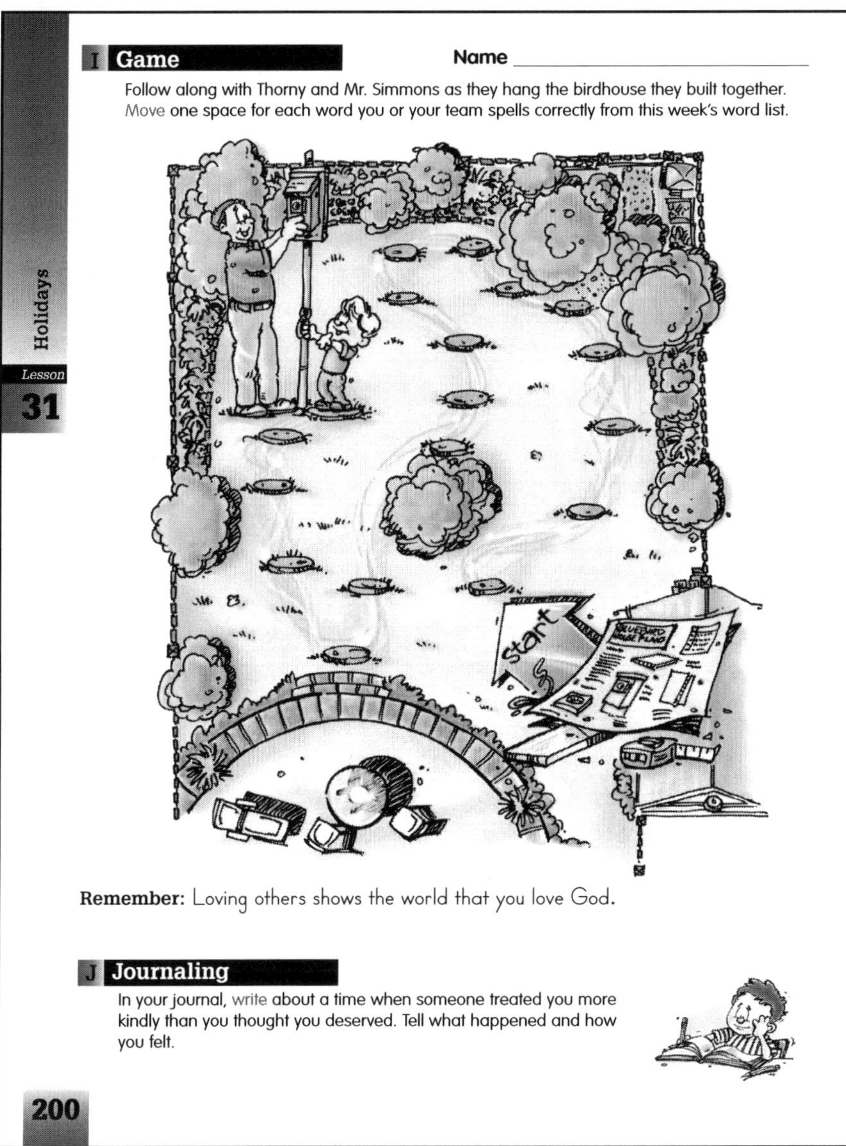

I Game Name ____________________

Follow along with Thorny and Mr. Simmons as they hang the birdhouse they built together. Move one space for each word you or your team spells correctly from this week's word list.

Remember: Loving others shows the world that you love God.

J Journaling

In your journal, write about a time when someone treated you more kindly than you thought you deserved. Tell what happened and how you felt.

How to Play:

- Divide students into two teams.
- Have each student place his/her game piece on Start.
- Have a student from team A go to the board.
- Say the spelling word.
- Have the student write the word on the board.
- If correct, instruct each member of team A to move his/her game piece forward one space.
- Alternate between teams A and B as you go down the word list.
- The team to reach Thorny and Mr. Simmons first is the winner.

Small Group Option: Students may play this game without teacher direction in small groups of two or more.

2 Game

Reinforce spelling skills and provide motivation and interest.

Materials

- game page (from Student Worktext)
- game pieces (1 per child)
- game word list

Game Word List

1. **April Fool's Day**
2. **Arbor Day**
3. **Christmas**
4. **Columbus Day**
5. **Easter**
6. **Independence Day**
7. **Groundhog Day**
8. **Halloween**
9. **Hanukkah**
10. **Labor Day**
11. **Martin Luther King Day**
12. **May Day**
13. **Memorial Day**
14. **New Year's Day**
15. **Passover**
16. **Presidents' Day**
17. **Thanksgiving**
18. **Valentine's Day**

3 Journaling

Provide a meaningful reason for correct spelling through personal writing.

Review the story using discussion leads provided on the following page. Encourage students to apply the Scriptural value in their journaling.

Journaling (continued)

- What kinds of birds did the Simmons see in their backyard? (Goldfinches and orioles.)
- What kind of bird did Thorny want to build a house for? Why? (Bluebirds. Because, for a while, bluebirds were disappearing. The houses help the number of bluebirds increase.)
- What happened to the jigsaw Thorny was using? (He broke the blade on the concrete block and then he left the saw out in the rain.)
- Why did Thorny think Mr. Simmons might yell at him or push him? (Because in the foster homes he'd been in before he was treated that way.)
- What made Mr. Holcomb think Mr. Simmons might be a "church goer?" (He saw the kind way he treated Thorny even though Thorny had made a big mistake.)

The longest word in any major English dictionary is "pneumonoultramicroscopicsilicovolcanoconiosis," which is a lung disease caused by inhaling volcanic silica particles. There are 45 letters in the word.

Word Wow!

1 **Literature Connection**
Topic: Unkind Words
Theme Text: Luke 6:45

What's Inside?

Rosa discovers things aren't always what they appear.

"Hey, look at these flowers!" Kristin stopped her bike at the side of the country road. "What are they, Rosa?"

"Wild roses." Rosa pedaled slowly back to join her friend. "Mmmmmm. I love how they smell." She held her bike up with one hand and with the other reached out to lift a bunch of blossoms to her face. "Especially these little white ones. They're so little but they smell a lot sweeter than the bigger pink ones."

"Are you guys coming?" Maria, Rosa's older sister, called from the top of the hill.

"Okay!" Rosa yelled, "Wait at the Andersons' for us!"

Kristin and Rosa were huffing and puffing by the time they reached the white farmhouse on the hilltop. "You two have really been getting the exercise!" Grandma Ruth Anderson backed out the door carrying a tray with glasses and a pitcher of ice-cold lemonade balanced on it.

"Yeah, you guys must not be in as good a shape as I am." Carlos flexed the muscles in his arm. "See, I'm not even breathing hard after that hill."

"That's just because you got here a few minutes before us and have had time to rest." Rosa flopped down in a lawn chair in the shady yard. "I bet you were panting just as hard as we are when you first got here!"

Maria settled herself in the swing and held her glass to her face. The moisture on the side of the glass cooled her skin. "Ahhh! There's nothing quite like ice-cold lemonade."

"It is a bit warm for this early in the spring." Grandma Ruth set the tray on the redwood picnic table and sat on its bench fanning herself. "We may be in for a long hot summer."

"I don't care!" The ice clinked in her glass when Rosa set it down. "I'm glad it's summer! We can just go swimming every day if it's too hot."

"Mrs. Anderson, what's this flower called?" Kristin was wandering along by one of Grandma Ruth's flower beds.

Grandma walked over to join her. "That's a bearded iris. And these are peonies."

"She sure likes flowers and plants and stuff, doesn't she?" Carlos closed his eyes and leaned his head against the back of his chair.

"Who—Kristin or Grandma Ruth?" Maria took another gulp of lemonade.

"Both." Carlos waved his hand to shoo a fly away. "But Kristin doesn't know anything about them. She didn't even know that was an iris!"

"So?" Rosa defended her friend. "She hasn't been around all kinds of flowers and plants like we have. Her mom always plants petunias in their yard because she likes them best and they're easy to take care of. After all, she doesn't have a lot of time to spend like Grandma Ruth does."

"C'mon, guys." Maria set her empty glass back on the tray. "Let's ride down to the meadow."

"Thanks for the lemonade, Grandma Ruth!" Rosa called. "Kristin, you ready to go?"

"Sure." Kristin picked up her helmet and fastened it. "Thank you for showing me your flowers, Mrs. Anderson."

"You're very welcome." Grandma Ruth picked up the tray and started back to the house. "You children have a good time, but be careful."

"We will!" Carlos popped a wheely with his bike. "Bye!"

The wind felt good in their faces as they flew down the hill to the meadow. Rosa let her bike coast as long as it would. When it finally slowed to a stop, she turned to look for Kristin.

As soon as Rosa saw what Kristin was doing, she raced back as fast as she could go. "Watch out!" she cried. "Stop, Kristin! DON'T TOUCH THAT!" Carlos and Maria turned to see what the commotion was about and came rushing back.

"Don't touch what?" Kristin stood knee deep in weeds and grass at the side of the road with a bewildered look on her face. "I just wanted to get a good look at this purple flower. I won't pick it! You already told me I'm not supposed to pick any wildflowers so their seeds will make more flowers next year."

"That's not it—you're standing in a whole patch of poison ivy!"

"Where?" Kristin looked around like the poison ivy was hiding behind her.

"Right there." Rosa pointed to the bright green plants surrounding Kristin. "All those plants with the points on the leaves. That's all poison ivy."

Kristin shot out of the weeds like a startled rabbit. "Oh, no! That's poison ivy? I had no idea! What'll I do?"

"Do you get it badly?" Maria wiped the sweat off her forehead.

Kristin nodded. "I think so. That's what the nurse said I had at camp last summer. It was awful." She shuddered. "I itched forever and had to have this pink stuff smeared on the bumps all the time."

"Well, we need to clean off your skin as soon as possible." Carlos turned his bike back down the road. "The Smiths' house is closer than the Andersons' from here, and it's not uphill. Let's see if they'll let you wash there."

The Vasquez children didn't know the Smiths well, but Carlos knocked on the front door. Nobody answered. "I guess they're not home. We'll have to head back to Grandma Ruth's or home."

"Maybe Kristin should rinse off with that hose over

Story Continued

there before we go." Maria bit her lip and pointed at the green garden hose lying in the grass. "Would that help?"

"I don't know." Carlos followed the hose to the faucet around the corner. "I think you have to use soap to get it all off, but it probably wouldn't hurt anything, and it might get some of it off. C'mon, Kristin."

Kristin rolled up her shorts and stuck her legs in the spray of water that Carlos directed her way. "Whadaya think yer doin' in my yard!" When the man shouted out the window Carlos jumped in surprise and the hose squirted water all over Kristin. "Buncha trouble-making delinquents! This is private property. MY property! You kids get outta here and don't come back! You hear me? Now, SCRAM!"

The four children were all panting when they pedaled into the Andersons' yard a few minutes later. When Grandma Ruth heard what had happened, she rushed Kristin into the tub with a special soap and dumped her clothes in the washing machine. After a thorough scrubbing, Kristin sat at the kitchen table wrapped in Grandma Anderson's robe and munched raisin cookies while her clothes tossed in the dryer.

"I don't know why Mr. Smith was so mean." Carlos took a bite of his cookie and talked around it. "He's always looked nice enough before."

"Well, now, I don't know about Mr. Smith, but I do know you can't always tell what someone's like by looking at him—or her." Grandma Ruth opened the oven door to check the next batch of cookies. "The Scriptures say that 'an evil man produces evil deeds from his hidden wickedness.'"

"Hey, I know that Scripture!" Rosa licked the cookie crumbs off her fingers. "We're learning it at school this week. There's more to it, isn't there, Kristin?"

"Yes, but I don't remember what." Kristin stared at the skin on her arms checking for poison ivy blisters.

"Run get my Bible, Rosa. It's on the rocking chair in the living room. I think you'll find the verse in Luke six or seven."

"Here it is." Rosa walked back into the kitchen slowly while she read the verse out loud. "'A good man produces good deeds from a good heart. And an evil man produces evil deeds from his hidden wickedness. Whatever is in the heart overflows into speech.' It's in Luke 6, verse 45."

"It's like that poison ivy Kristin got into." Grandma Ruth scooped the hot cookies off the baking sheet with a spatula before she continued, "She probably will still break out from it, although I hope it's not too bad. Some plants give us foods or even medicines that save lives, but not poison ivy! A poison ivy plant doesn't look much different. It's not ugly or scary. It's just a plant like any other. Nice green leaves. No thorns or stickers. But what's inside will eventually be known by what happens when we come into contact with it."

"That's the way it is with people. Most don't look ugly or scary. There's nothing on the outside to show what they're like. But what's inside will eventually be known by what they say, whether it be good, like these irises," she touched one of the velvety purple blooms in the vase on the table, "or bad like poison ivy. Remember, 'Whatever is in the heart overflows into speech.'"

2 Discussion Time

Check understanding of the story and development of personal values.

- To where did Kristin and the Vasquez kids ride?
- How can you tell Kristin didn't know much about plants and flowers?
- Why did the kids decide to head to the Smith's house when Kristin got in the poison ivy?
- What did Mr. Smith do when he saw the kids in his yard?
- What did Grandma Ruth do for Kristin?
- How are some people like poison ivy plants?

A Test-Editing Name ____________________

If a word is spelled correctly, fill in the oval under **Correct**. If the word is misspelled, fill in the oval under **Incorrect**, and spell the word correctly on the blank.

	Correct	Incorrect	
1. April fools day	○	●	April Fool's Day
2. Aber Day	○	●	Arbor Day
3. chrismas	○	●	Christmas
4. culumbus day	○	●	Columbus Day
5. eester	○	●	Easter
6. independance day	○	●	Independence Day
7. Groundhog Day	●	○	
8. haloween	○	●	Halloween
9. Hannuka	○	●	Hanukkah
10. Laber day	○	●	Labor Day
11. martin luth king day	○	●	Martin Luther King Day
12. may day	○	●	May Day
13. Memoriel Day	○	●	Memorial Day
14. new years day	○	●	New Year's Day
15. Passover	●	○	
16. President's Day	○	●	President's Day
17. Thanksgiving	●	○	
18. valintines day	○	●	Valentine's Day

Review Lesson 32

201

Take a minute to memorize...
Luke 6:45

Review 32 | Day 1

3 Test-Editing

Reinforce recognizing and correcting misspelled words.

1 Game

Reinforce spelling skills and provide motivation and interest.

Materials

- game page (from Student Worktext)
- space cards (move 1 space, move 2 spaces, and move 3 spaces--each written on a separate card)
- game pieces (1 per child)
- game word list

Game Word List

1. **April Fool's Day**
2. **Arbor Day**
3. **Christmas**
4. **Columbus Day**
5. **Easter**
6. **Independence Day**
7. **Groundhog Day**
8. **Halloween**
9. **Hanukkah**
10. **Labor Day**
11. **Martin Luther King Day**
12. **May Day**
13. **Memorial Day**
14. **New Year's Day**
15. **Passover**
16. **Presidents' Day**
17. **Thanksgiving**
18. **Valentine's Day**

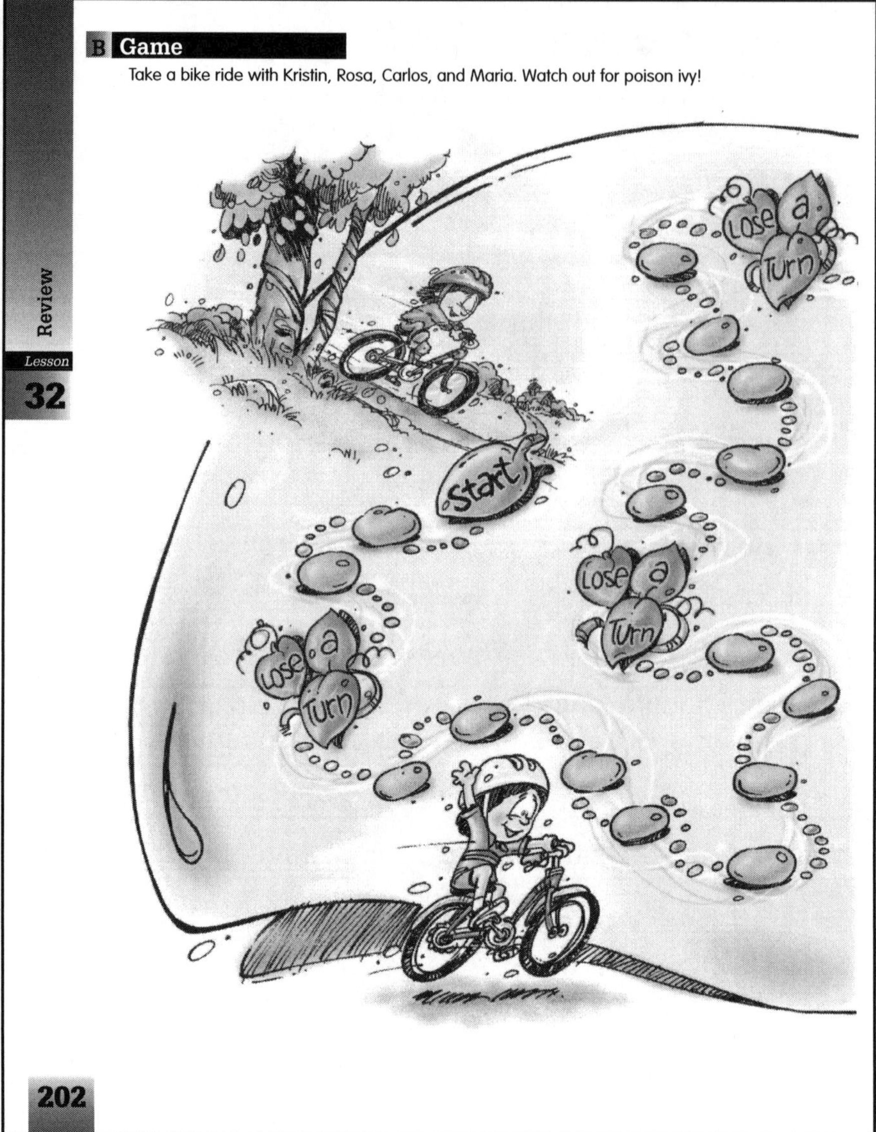

How to Play:

- Fold the cards (see **Materials**) in half, and put them in a container.
- Divide students into two teams.
- Have each student place their game piece on Start.
- Have a student from team A draw a card from the container, and go to the board.
- Say the spelling word.
- Have the student write the word on the board.
- If correct, instruct each member of team A to move his/her game piece forward one, two, or three spaces, as designated on the card drawn.
- Alternate between teams A and B as you go down the word list.
- The team to reach Grandma Ruth's yard first is the winner.

Name ________________________

Review

Lesson

32

Remember: Wickedness in your heart eventually slips out of your mouth.

Writing Assessment

Assess student's spelling, grammar, and composition skills through personal writing.

- How come Kristin and Rosa were tired when they got to the Anderson's house? (They had to pedal their bikes uphill to get there.)
- What was Kristin interested in at the Anderson's house? (Grandma Ruth's flowers.)
- Why did Kristin get into the poison ivy by the roadside? (She stepped off the road to get a good look at a purple flower.)
- What did the kids decide to do when it seemed no one was home at the Smith house? (To wash Kristin off with the hose in the yard before going back to the Anderson's house.)
- Why was Carlos surprised that Mr. Smith yelled at them and told them to leave? (Because Mr. Smith had always looked nice enough when they'd ridden past his house before.)
- What did Grandma Ruth say about people? (That you can't always tell what they're like by just looking at them, but that, sooner or later, what they're really like will show in their speech.)

Review | Lesson 32

C Writing Assessment Name ______________________

Write a story illustrating how a person's words show whether God's love is working to change them inside. In your journal, write about a time you showed your love for others by your actions, or a time when someone else showed their love for others by helping you.

____

____

____

____

____

____

____

____

____

____

____

____

____

Scripture

Luke 6:45

204

A rebus is a word or a phrase represented by pictures, letters, numbers, or other words or phrases. For example,

The weather report:

wether

Means: A bad spell of weather.

Word Wow!

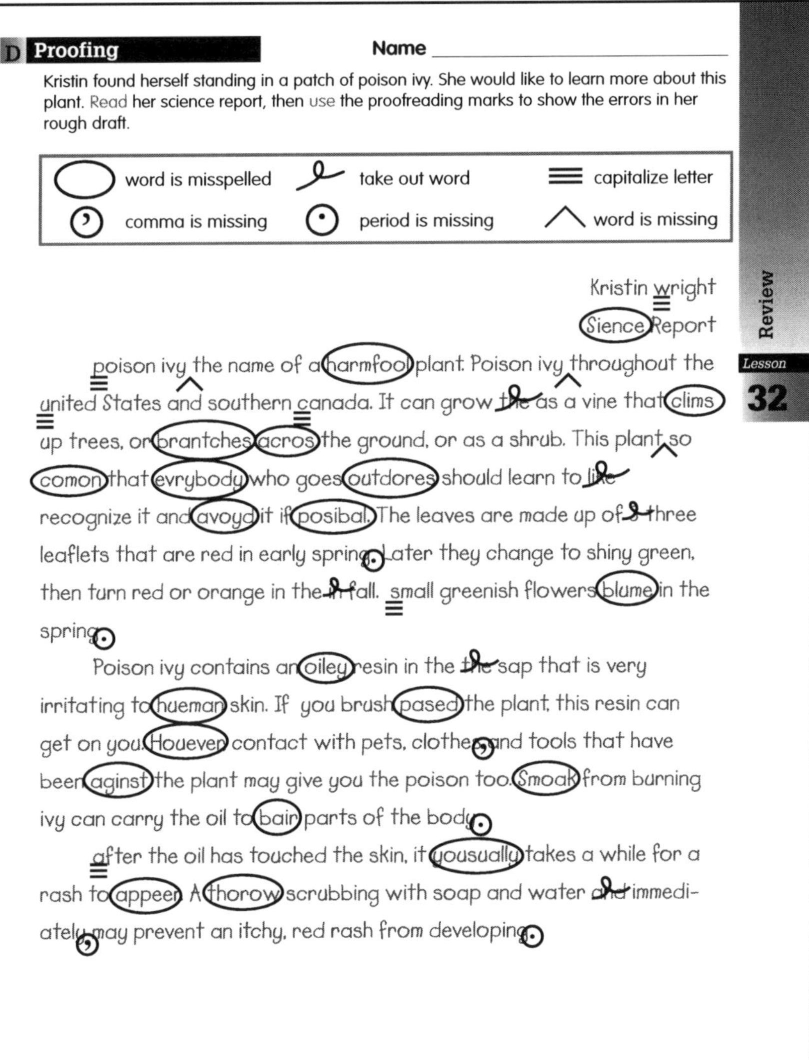
D Proofing Name ____________

Kristin found herself standing in a patch of poison ivy. She would like to learn more about this plant. Read her science report, then use the proofreading marks to show the errors in her rough draft.

word is misspelled	take out word	capitalize letter
comma is missing	period is missing	word is missing

Kristin wright
Sience Report

poison ivy the name of a harmfool plant. Poison ivy throughout the united States and southern canada. It can grow the as a vine that clims up trees, or brantches acros the ground, or as a shrub. This plant so comon that evrybody who goes outdores should learn to like recognize it and avoyd it if posibal The leaves are made up of 3 three leaflets that are red in early spring Later they change to shiny green, then turn red or orange in the in fall. small greenish flowers blume in the spring

Poison ivy contains an oiley resin in the the sap that is very irritating to hueman skin. If you brush pased the plant, this resin can get on you. Houever contact with pets, clothes and tools that have been aginst the plant may give you the poison too. Smoak from burning ivy can carry the oil to bair parts of the body

after the oil has touched the skin, it yousually takes a while for a rash to appeer A thorow scrubbing with soap and water and immediately may prevent an itchy, red rash from developing

Review Lesson 32

205

3 Proofing

Reinforce recognizing capitalization, punctuation, and spelling errors.

Write this sentence on the board: **kristin likes and the roases, iris, and poenies.** Have volunteers come to the board to insert the **proofing marks** needed for a misspelled word, letter to capitalize, missing comma, and unnecessary words.

You will be using these and other proofreading marks to show the errors in Kristin's science report. Read her report, then use the proofreading marks to show the errors in her rough draft.

2 Action Game

Reinforce spelling skills and provide motivation and interest.

Materials

- Two Bells

PROOF RINGING

How to Play:

Divide students into two teams. Each team sits around their game bell. Say a word aloud then slowly spell it. (Spell most words incorrectly.) When a word is spelled incorrectly, teams compete to ring their bell first. If the student who rings the bell first can correct the mistake, his/her team receives a point. If a student rings the bell when a mistake has not been made, his/her team loses a point. Repeat this process until all the words have been spelled. The team with the most points wins!

Word Find

Familiarize students with word meaning and usage.

Write the letters **lleps** on the board. Ask students to read the letters backwards to spell the word **spell**. Now, write the letters **sdrawkcab** on the board. Allow time for the students to decide that the letters spell the word **backwards**. Students will be challenged with some words that are hidden backwards in this puzzle.

Read each of the bold words in the sentences below and circle them in the puzzle. Words may go down, across, forwards, or backwards.

Review Lesson 32

E **Word Find** Name ____________________

Read each of the bold words in the sentences below and circle them in the puzzle. Words may go across, down, or backwards.

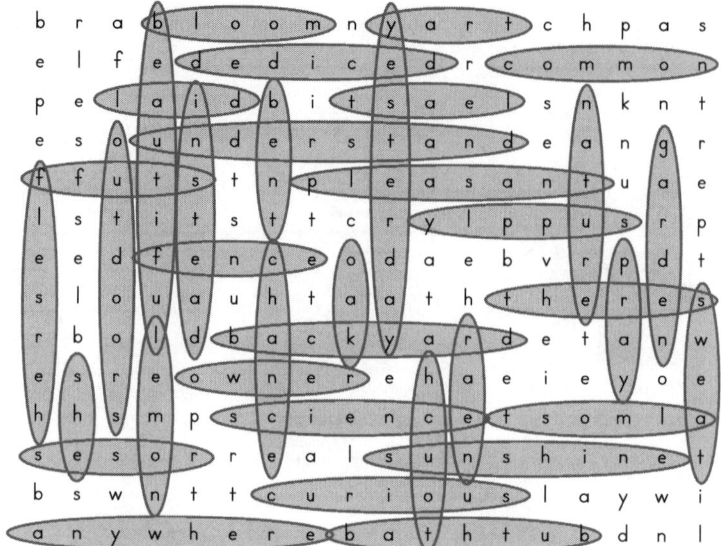

1. **Yesterday** we swam **instead** of riding bikes.
2. The hot **sunshine** made us **sweat**.
3. Her **backyard** is **beautiful** when the irises **bloom**.
4. Kristin **bent** over to smell the **roses** by the **fence**.
5. She **laid** a slice of **lemon** on the **tray**.
6. Do not go **near** or **touch** poison ivy or poison **oak**.
7. This plant is **common** and can grow **almost anywhere**.
8. Kristin got in the **bathtub** to wash **herself** off.
9. At **least there's** a **chance** you will not get it.
10. Mom has a **supply** of **stuff** to **spray** on the rash.
11. Kristin is **curious** about **nature** and the **outdoors**.
12. **She decided** to write a **science** report about poison ivy.
13. Let's ask the **owner** if we can use his **garden** hose.
14. We do not **understand** why he was not **pleasant**.

206

Date ____________________

This certificate is awarded to

____

for completing activities using the following spelling words:

April Fool's Day	Labor Day
Arbor Day	Martin Luther King Day
Christmas	May Day
Columbus Day	Memorial Day
Easter	New Year's Day
Independence Day	Passover
Groundhog Day	Presidents' Day
Halloween	Thanksgiving
Hanukkah	Valentine's Day

2 Certificate

Provide an opportunity for parents or guardians to encourage and assess their child's progress.

Fill in today's date and your name on your certificate.

Take a minute to memorize...

Luke 6:45

The End

PLEASE PHOTOCOPY!*

The following pages contain Black Line Masters for use with the ***A Reason For Spelling***® Student Worktext.

*Photocopy privileges extend only to the material in this section, and permission is granted only for those classrooms or homeschools using ***A Reason For Spelling***® Student Worktexts. Any other use of this material is expressly forbidden and all copyright laws apply.

Hide and Seek

Play Hide and Seek with your words. Create a bar graph by filling in a box (left to right) for each word you spell correctly.

LOOK SAY HIDE WRITE SEEK CHECK

Other Word Forms

Sentence Clues

Use the sentence clue to help you unscramble each word. Write the unscrambled word in the sentence.

abdelmoorst **1.** Exercise will improve the circulation of your ______________.

giiknns **2.** He dove to keep the keys from ______________ in the pond.

horrstttuwy **3.** If you are ______________, people will respect you.

cfklos **4.** Large ______________ of ducks flew over, heading south.

–choptuu **5.** Mom gave the scratched furniture a careful ______________.

abdnr **6.** Now there are scratches on my ______________ new car.

eepsw **7.** Please ______________ up the dirt you tracked into the house.

cdehotu **8.** She carefully ______________ the soft chinchilla.

bbeelps **9.** She stood and tossed ______________ into the creek.

degirs **10.** The ______________ on my boots kept me from sliding.

abcehnrs **11.** The large ______________ are perfect for building a tree house.

ffilstu **12.** The little boy grabbed a ______________ of candy.

dehosv **13.** Tommy ______________ another bite of pizza into his mouth.

cdkos **14.** We hurried to the ______________ to see which boat had won.

dginstu **15.** When I finish ______________, I will vacuum the carpet.

eeilprst **16.** We found two snakes for our collection of ______________.

Prefixes and Suffixes

Add the prefixes and suffixes to make new words. Write the words on the lines.

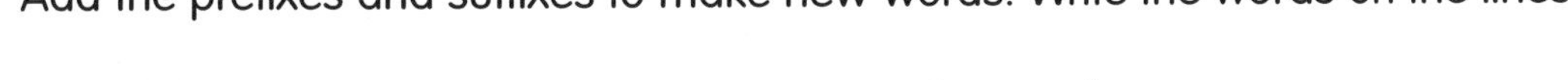

1. touch + y = ______________

2. self – f + v + es = ______________

3. en + trust = ______________

4. touchy – y + i + ness = ______________

5. reptile – e + ian = ______________

6. your + self = ______________

Hide and Seek

Play Hide and Seek with your words. Create a bar graph by filling in a box (left to right) for each word you spell correctly.

Other Word Forms

Hidden Words

Use the word bank to help you find the words in the puzzle. Words may go across or down.

o b j e c t s a r e p u b l i c f

c b a x d e n c e g p x i n o o l

b a r c g y d r q u a w e r b l o

a r r e s t e d c o c u y t j l r

n i o p h o p u m p k i n s e e d

d n w t z i e k l u a p o i c c e

a k s s e h n p o b g l t l t t c

g p f l i m d r s l i k h k i i o

e l e e x c e p t i n g i j v o l

d a m a g i n g t c g j n h e n l

a s d d x w c v u i h a g g m f e

c t c e y a e t r z g c n f n d c

n i b p r w o y e e f c e d b s t

a c c e p t a b l e d e s s v a i

p s i n m n b v c x z p s a c x n

l t a d a s r p r a c t i c i n g

a c i s d f g h j k l s p o i u y

Word Bank

acceptable	bandaged	dependence	nothingness	packaging	publicize
accepts	collecting	depends	objective	plastics	pumpkinseed
arrested	collection	excepting	objects	practicing	republic
arrows	damaging	excepts			

Hide and Seek

Play Hide and Seek with your words. Create a bar graph by filling in a box (left to right) for each word you spell correctly.

Other Word Forms

Sentence Fun

Circle the word that completes each sentence.

1. A repairman came to (troubleshoot, troublesome) the computer.
2. Daniel (coupled, couplet) his model engine to the coal car.
3. I hope we get rain so the tomato plants don't (deader, die).
4. If you are hungry, grab a (couple, coupler) of pieces of fruit.
5. Mama (comforter, comforted) Tony during the electrical storm.
6. My three (cousin, cousins) are coming over for dinner.
7. Our neighbor waved and smiled (pleasantry, pleasantly).
8. We will be (breakfasting, breakfasts) on the terrace this morning.
9. What are you (build, building) with your blocks?
10. Our puppy likes to chew on (leathers, leathery) objects.
11. The boys' team was (leading, leaden) until the end of the game.
12. The next unit in math is about (measures, measuring).
13. These new shoes are not very (comfortable, comforted).
14. We were (sweats, sweating) by the time we finished running.
15. What is the (meaning, means) of this word?
16. This old, rusty bicycle is very (troublesome, troubles).

Prefixes and Suffixes

Add the prefixes or suffixes to make new words. Write the words on the lines.

1. trouble – e + ing = ______________
2. measure + ment = ______________
3. wealthy – y + iest = ______________
4. couple – e + ing = ______________
5. wealth + y = ______________
6. dis + comfort = ______________

Hide and Seek

Play Hide and Seek with your words. Create a bar graph by filling in a box (left to right) for each word you spell correctly.

Other Word Forms

Prefixes and Suffixes

Circle the correct prefix or suffix to make a new word, write the word correctly on the line. Remember, when a base word ends with a long vowel sound spelled with **y**, change the **y** to **i** when adding the ending. When words have the consonant-vowel-consonant-silent **e** pattern (CVCe), drop the **e** when adding an ending that begins with a vowel.

1. secret + (s, es) = ____________

2. believe + (ed, ly) = ____________

3. (mis, dis) + agree = ____________

4. behave + (ior, ion) = ____________

5. freight + (er, ior) = ____________

6. jelly + (ing, ed) = ____________

7. lazy + (or, er) = ____________

8. agree + (able, ible) = ____________

9. freight + (ness, ing) = ____________

10. (dis, mis) + belief = ____________

11. fail + (ed, er) = ____________

12. lean + (iest, est) = ____________

13. lay + (ing, est) = ____________

14. cane + (ing, able) = ____________

15. (un, mis) + believe + (able, ible) = ____________

16. (dis, un) + become + (ing, ness) = ____________

17. (mis, dis) + agree + (able, tion) = ____________

18. agree + (ness, ment) = ____________

19. fail + (ure, es) = ____________

Hide and Seek

Play Hide and Seek with your words. Create a bar graph by filling in a box (left to right) for each word you spell correctly.

Other Word Forms

Synonyms

Use the synonyms to write the words. Remember, a synonym is a word that means the same or nearly the same as another word.

1. aloneness ________
2. Asian cats ________
3. black birds ________
4. elevated ________
5. frogman ________
6. providing ________
7. visible ________
8. made of wood ________
9. answered ________
10. been selected ________
11. directs athletics ________
12. emptiness ________
13. heaped ________
14. removing wrinkles ________
15. yearning ________
16. binding ________

Syllables

A syllable is a unit of sound in a word containing a vowel and possibly one or more consonants. Count how many syllables each word has and write the number on the line.

1. ______ chosen
2. ______ risen
3. ______ diver
4. ______ loneliness
5. ______ replying
6. ______ pining
7. ______ tigers
8. ______ coaches
9. ______ hollowness
10. ______ noticeable
11. ______ stoves
12. ______ replied
13. ______ supplying
14. ______ crowed
15. ______ ironing
16. ______ piled
17. ______ coached
18. ______ ties

Word Bank

chosen	diver	loneliness	piled	risen	tigers
coaches	hollowness	noticeable	pining	supplying	tying
crows	ironing	oaken	replied		

Hide and Seek

Play Hide and Seek with your words. Create a bar graph by filling in a box (left to right) for each word you spell correctly.

LOOK SAY HIDE WRITE SEEK CHECK

Other Word Forms

Sentence Fun

Circle the word that correctly completes each sentence.

1. A piano (tuning, tuner) has come to work on our piano.
2. Have you paid the (dews, dues) to join the stamp club?
3. I carefully (gluey, glued) all the pieces, but it fell apart!
4. I like this game with all the little (moves, movable) objects.
5. Our class is going to help clean up that (pollution, polluted) river.
6. It will be fun to help (beautify, beauty) our town.
7. My dad went to help with a (roofing, roofs) project.
8. My grandmother really likes this recording of a (flutist, fluting) playing.
9. Some of the (clueing, clues) for this treasure hunt are difficult.
10. The emergency team (rescues, rescued) several people last year.
11. I love June when the roses are (bloomed, blooming).
12. We (unusual, usually) have spaghetti on Friday nights.
13. What kind of (moving, movies) do you watch at home?
14. Dad is busy (tuning, tuned) his favorite guitar.
15. My hands are all (gluing, gluey) from making a toothpick tower.
16. His sprained ankle hurt whenever he (move, moved) it.
17. The vet did all that was (humanness, humanly) possible to save the bird.
18. This car is burning oil and needs a (tune-up, tuneful).
19. That is a very (usualness, unusual) kind of plant.
20. Her address is 32261 Maple (Av., Ave.).

Hide and Seek

Play Hide and Seek with your words. Create a bar graph by filling in a box (left to right) for each word you spell correctly.

Other Word Forms

Suffixes

Add each suffix to the word in each row to make a new word. Remember, normally when a one-syllable word ends in one vowel followed by one consonant, double the consonant before adding an ending that begins with a vowel.

	+ ed	+ ing	+ s
1. snap	__________	__________	__________
2. blanket	__________	__________	__________
3. cream	__________	__________	__________
4. flour	__________	__________	__________
5. dream	__________	__________	__________
6. drum	__________	__________	__________
7. bridge	__________	__________	__________
8. clear	__________	__________	__________
9. crack	__________	__________	__________
10. groan	__________	__________	__________
11. smoke	__________	__________	__________
12. plank	__________	__________	__________

When words have the consonant-vowel-consonant-**e** pattern, drop the **e** when adding an ending that begins with a vowel. Add the suffix to make a new word. Write it on the line.

1. smoky – y + i + er = __________
2. snappy – y + i + ly = __________
3. grave – e + en = __________
4. clear + ness = __________
5. bridge + able = __________
6. crack + er = __________

Hide and Seek

Play Hide and Seek with your words. Create a bar graph by filling in a box (left to right) for each word you spell correctly.

Other Word Forms

Code Words

Use the code to write each other word form.

0 = h 1 = l 2 = n 3 = p 4 = r 5 = s 6 = t

1. 6 0 4 i 1 1 5 ____________________
2. 5 6 e a d i e 4 ____________________
3. 5 6 4 e 6 c 0 y ____________________
4. 5 3 1 i 6 6 i 2 g ____________________
5. 6 0 4 o a 6 5 ____________________
6. 5 3 4 a y e d ____________________
7. 5 m a 5 0 e 5 ____________________
8. 5 6 4 o k i 2 g ____________________
9. 5 6 4 u c k ____________________
10. 5 1 i 3 3 e 4 i 2 e 5 5 ____________________
11. 5 1 i 3 5 ____________________
12. 5 6 4 a 3 5 ____________________
13. 6 0 4 e a d 5 ____________________
14. 6 4 u e 5 6 ____________________

Hide and Seek

Play Hide and Seek with your words. Create a bar graph by filling in a box (left to right) for each word you spell correctly.

Other Word Forms

Scrambled Words

Use the sentence clue to help you unscramble each word. Write the unscrambled word in the sentence.

adeeglnry	**1.** We read a book about a ______________ man.
deilmts	**2.** This is the ______________ weather we have had.
ddeeenprt	**3.** Matthew ______________ to correct his math problems.
fginorst	**4.** I like to lick the ______________ out of the bowl.
ceirssttu	**5.** I like the ______________ part of the bread best.
aeilmmnorty	**6.** I ______________ forgot to watch the ball.
bdeelt	**7.** Dad asked if everyone was ______________ in his seat belt.
ddeeimnr	**8.** Mom ______________ me to take my homework to school.
aabddelnnrstuy	**9.** He was ______________ tired after the 5k run.
dgginnoorw	**10.** Matthew was sorry for his ______________.
abdekln	**11.** His mind ______________ out when he took the math test.
agmnost	**12.** Mrs. Burton divided the candy ______________ the students.
emmnoostu	**13.** Choosing to follow Christ is a ______________ decision.
addeforrw	**14.** The post office ______________ the letter to his new address.

Prefixes and Suffixes

Add the prefixes or suffixes to make new words. Write the words on the lines.

1. guard + ian = ______________

2. frost + y = ______________

3. mild + ness = ______________

4. pretend + ing = ______________

5. frosty – y + i + er = ______________

6. understand + able = ______________

7. crusty – y + i + ly = ______________

8. mis + understand = ______________

Hide and Seek

Play Hide and Seek with your words. Create a bar graph by filling in a box (left to right) for each word you spell correctly.

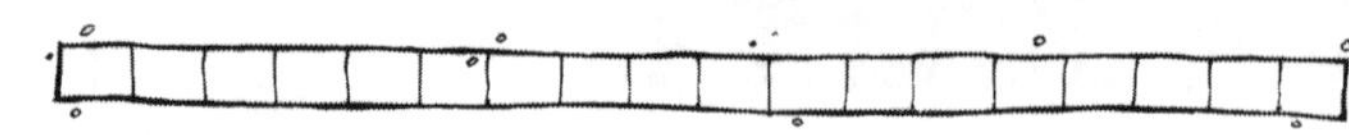

Other Word Forms

Hidden Words

Use the word bank to help you find the words in the puzzle. Words may go across or down.

k a w i r e i g w r e l i g r n y
c l i m b i n g d c l i w r e n s
l w e b b r o u e l k m r c i n d
i a t e i t g c l i m b e r g r b
m y h d g h t m i m j i a a n d m
b d o w h o l b g b t n t g s e n
t e r r t r o g h i h g h d l l h
h r o e a o u h t n o m e d p i l
o s u a d u m b f o u n d e d g o
u a g t c g t o u p g n o r o h u
g t h h o h e m l a h b k e i t y
h c l i m b s b o s t k n i v e s
f u y n b r r p b f h n i g u d t
u l l g e e a r o d g o w n y e r
l t h o d d b o m b e b e e t w e
l t h o r o h o b o m b e d r a d
t h o u g h t f u l l y d w e s s

Word Bank

bombed	combed	knives	reigns	thought	wreathed
bombproof	delighted	knobby	thoroughbred	thoughtfully	wreathing
climber	delightful	limbs	thoroughly	who	wrens
climbing	dumbfounded	reigned			

Hide and Seek

Play Hide and Seek with your words. Create a bar graph by filling in a box (left to right) for each word you spell correctly.

Other Word Forms

Sentence Fun

Circle the word that correctly completes each sentence.

1. Brutus (laughing, laughed) as he took Stephen's candy.
2. We began (crafting, craftily) a cabin with the sticks and pebbles.
3. Who is the (swiftest, swiftness) runner in our class?
4. We had to put our spelling words in (alphabetize, alphabetical) order.
5. Brutus is the (toughest, toughen) kid to pray for.
6. He choked on the candy and began (coughing, coughed).
7. In math, we are (graphed, graphing) the colors of M&M®s.
8. These baby raccoons have been (orphaned, orphanage).
9. The (photographer, photographic) is coming to take school pictures.
10. Stephen (stuffing, stuffed) the candy in his pocket.
11. The police (offices, officer) is directing traffic.
12. Mom made several (loaves, loafs) of bread for the neighbors.
13. Our tubes began (drifted, drifting) downstream with the current.
14. We tried (bluffing, bluffed) so Brutus wouldn't know we had candy.
15. This trail is (rougher, roughest) than the one we hiked last week.
16. It was hard to keep from (laughs, laughing) when he tripped.
17. This test seems (tougher, toughens) than the last one.
18. We opened the windows because the room felt hot and (stuffy, stuffily).
19. My brother is taking a (photographed, photography) class.
20. We watched a (craftsman, crafty) carving wood.

Hide and Seek

Play Hide and Seek with your words. Create a bar graph by filling in a box (left to right) for each word you spell correctly.

Other Word Forms

Prefixes and Suffixes

Circle the correct prefix or suffix to make a new word, then write the word correctly on the line. Remember, when words have the consonant-vowel-consonant-**e** pattern, drop the **e** when adding an ending that begins with a vowel.

1. decide + (s, ly) = ______________
2. peace + (ing, ably) = ______________
3. recess + (s, es) = ______________
4. chance + (ing, er) = ______________
5. police + (ing, ment) = ______________
6. fence + (ably, ing) = ______________
7. excite + (ment, ness) = ______________
8. (de, un) + excite + (ed, ly) = ______________
9. (im, ir) + press + (ied, ion) = ______________
10. glance + (ed, ness) = ______________
11. beast + (ly, ably) = ______________
12. citizen + (ment, ship) = ______________
13. scene + (ic, ish) = ______________
14. peace + (ing, ful) = ______________
15. press + (ure, ful) = ______________
16. (il, in) + famous = ______________

Hide and Seek

Play Hide and Seek with your words. Create a bar graph by filling in a box (left to right) for each word you spell correctly.

Other Word Forms

Synonyms

Use the synonyms to write the words. Remember, a synonym is a word that means the same or nearly the same as another word.

1. banging ____________
2. dusting ____________
3. exploring ____________
4. lofty ____________
5. kennels ____________
6. rural divisions ____________
7. snarling ____________
8. parts of speech ____________
9. fine grains ____________
10. stubbornly ____________
11. countrified ____________
12. evening dresses ____________
13. inhabitant ____________
14. noisily ____________
15. clothed ____________
16. scowling ____________
17. springiest ____________
18. plumpness ____________
19. skyscrapers ____________
20. young bird of prey ____________

Syllables

Count how many syllables each word has and write the number on the line.

1. _____ powdery
2. _____ bouncy
3. _____ loudly
4. _____ owlish
5. _____ impounded
6. _____ scoutmaster
7. _____ stoutness
8. _____ nouns
9. _____ towering
10. _____ powdering
11. _____ pounds
12. _____ growled
13. _____ frowned
14. _____ bouncier
15. _____ scouted

Word Bank

bounciest	gowns	nouns	pounds	stoutly
counties	growling	outdoorsy	powdering	stoutness
frowning	householder	owlet	powders	towering
gowned	loudly	pounding	scouting	towers

Hide and Seek

Play Hide and Seek with your words. Create a bar graph by filling in a box (left to right) for each word you spell correctly.

Other Word Forms

Sentence Fun

Circle the word that correctly completes each sentence.

1. Milli bought a book by an (authoring, authority) on model trains.
2. The vegetables simmered in a (saucepan, sauces).
3. The audience (applauding, applauded) after the recital.
4. Usually one (falsely, falsehood) leads to another.
5. Daniel could have (quarreled, quarrels) with Dalton.
6. The switch on the train set seems to be (faulted, faulty).
7. Daniel's train ran through a little (forests, forested) section.
8. Daniel (paused, pausing) in the doorway of the playroom.
9. Mom is (awfulness, awfully) tired after staying up late.
10. The mirror (fogging, fogged) up when I took a shower.
11. This money is my (offering, offers) for church.
12. The (cords, corded) on the computer are tangled.
13. She is feeling tired and (quarrelsome, quarreler).
14. A man stood by the road (hawker, hawking) his fruits and vegetables.
15. We began (hauled, hauling) bags of groceries in from the car.
16. It does not feel good to be (false, falsely) accused of something.
17. We drove carefully through the (fogging, foggy) streets.

Hide and Seek

Play Hide and Seek with your words. Create a bar graph by filling in a box (left to right) for each word you spell correctly.

Other Word Forms

Prefixes and Suffixes

Add each suffix to the word in each row to make a new word. Remember, when words have the consonant-vowel-consonant-**e** pattern, drop the **e** when adding an ending that begins with a vowel.

	+ ed	+ ing	+ s
1. spark	________	________	________
2. garden	________	________	________
3. carpet	________	________	________
4. starve	________	________	________
5. harm	________	________	________
6. barber	________	________	________
7. cart	________	________	________
8. farm	________	________	________
9. marble	________	________	________

Add the prefixes and suffixes to make new words. Write the words on the lines.

1. barber + shop = ________
2. harm + ful = ________
3. yarn + s = ________
4. harsh + ness = ________
5. farm + er = ________
6. harsh + er = ________
7. un + harm + ed = ________
8. garden + er = ________
9. harsh + ly = ________
10. harm + less = ________
11. scarf − f + ves = ________
12. hard + est = ________
13. un + carpet + ed = ________
14. harsh + est = ________

Lesson 17 | Other Word Forms

Hide and Seek

Play Hide and Seek with your words. Create a bar graph by filling in a box (left to right) for each word you spell correctly.

LOOK SAY HIDE WRITE SEEK CHECK

Other Word Forms

Scrambled Words

Use the sentence clue to help you unscramble each word. Write the unscrambled word in the sentence.

egmrs	**1.** Mrs. Wright used peroxide to kill the ______________.
limrfy	**2.** Christopher laced his skates ______________ on his feet.
deikrst	**3.** Daniel ______________ around the boy who had fallen.
cgilnru	**4.** I like ______________ up by the fire with a good book.
denrsu	**5.** Christopher felt better after Mom ______________ his hurt foot.
ceeflprty	**6.** Cory's castle stood up ______________ on the hearth.
abdhirty	**7.** I invited the whole class to my ______________ party.
deiorrw	**8.** Cory was ______________ because Christopher disobeyed Mom.
brsstu	**9.** When a blister ______________ it hurts more.
cginruv	**10.** The ______________ sidewalk is a fun place to ride bikes.
elopprsuy	**11.** He ______________ chose not to wear wool socks.
hortwy	**12.** We are not ______________, but God forgives our sins.
bginrstu	**13.** Kristin was ______________ with excitement about the field trip.
eorsw	**14.** He felt ______________ about disobeying than about his blister.
efhrsttu	**15.** Thorny rounded the ______________ corner of the ice rink.
ceilrstu	**16.** Kristin has the ______________ hair in her class.
abhikmrrt	**17.** There is a ______________ on my right ankle.
eedrssst	**18.** There were five yummy ______________ at my birthday party.

Hide and Seek

Play Hide and Seek with your words. Create a bar graph by filling in a box (left to right) for each word you spell correctly.

Other Word Forms

Code Words

Use the code to write each other word form.

0 = a   1 = e   2 = i   3 = o   4 = u   5 = r   6 = s   7 = t

1. c 4 5 2 3 6 2 7 y ____________________

2. b 4 7 c h 1 5 2 n g ____________________

3. 3 v 1 5 l 3 3 k 1 d ____________________

4. p l 4 5 0 l 2 6 7 ____________________

5. 6 4 5 1 6 7 ____________________

6. w 3 3 d 1 n l y ____________________

7. f 3 3 7 p 5 2 n 7 6 ____________________

8. c 4 5 2 n g ____________________

9. 7 3 4 5 2 n g ____________________

10. 6 4 5 1 n 1 6 6 ____________________

11. p 4 5 1 b 5 1 d ____________________

12. c 5 3 3 k 1 d l y ____________________

13. 7 3 4 5 2 6 m ____________________

14. b 4 l l 1 7 2 n 6 ____________________

Hide and Seek

Play Hide and Seek with your words. Create a bar graph by filling in a box (left to right) for each word you spell correctly.

Other Word Forms

Prefixes and Suffixes

Circle the correct prefix or suffix to make a new word, then write the word correctly on the line. Remember, sometimes base words change when adding a suffix.

1. choice + (est, ness) = ________________
2. joint + (ly, er) = ________________
3. moist + (ed, en) = ________________
4. point + (er, ment) = ________________
5. royal + (en, ist) = ________________
6. (dis, il) + loyal = ________________
7. enjoy + (er, able) = ________________
8. destroy + (ed, ty) = ________________
9. appoint + (ed, er) = ________________
10. (mis, dis) + jointed = ________________
11. disappoint + (ly, ment) = ________________
12. loyal + (ty, ed) = ________________
13. oily + (ness, mess) = ________________
14. rejoice + (ship, ing) = ________________
15. soybean + (ed, s) = ________________
16. voyage + (er, ly) = ________________
17. employ + (ment, ance) = ________________
18. avoid + (er, ance) = ________________
19. annoy + (able, ing) = ________________
20. (un, dis) + employment = ________________

Hide and Seek

Play Hide and Seek with your words. Create a bar graph by filling in a box (left to right) for each word you spell correctly.

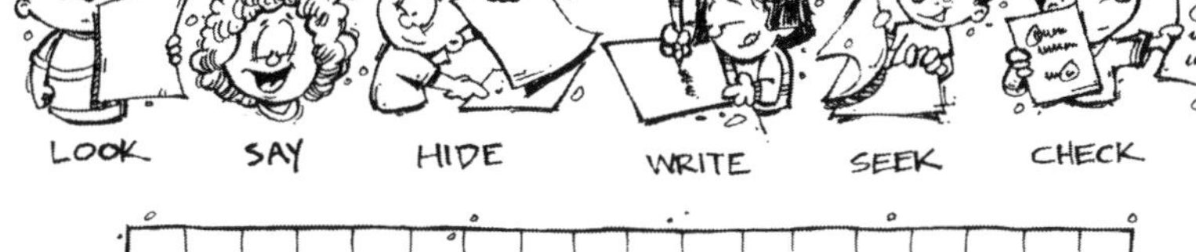

Other Word Forms

Sentence Fun

Circle the word that correctly completes each sentence.

1. Dalton got (fingering, fingerprints) on the glass aquarium.
2. Daniel thought (owning, owned) the aquarium was exciting.
3. The clown fish was his (favorite, favoring).
4. That book I'm reading is (humored, humorous).
5. The (motored, motorist) drove carefully on the slick streets.
6. Mr. and Mrs. DeVore are (donor, donors) to many charities.
7. Mrs. Fitzsimmons is (visiting, visited) again.
8. The long box (captured, capturing) Daniel's attention.
9. All set up, the aquarium looked very (nature, natural).
10. These (pictured, pictures) are from our vacation.
11. The bridge is (dangerous, endangered) when it snows.
12. Milli stood in the (entering, entrance) of the playroom.
13. The (feathery, feathering) snowflakes floated softly down.
14. Mrs. DeVore was (honors, honored) at a special dinner.
15. Our neighbor (pasturing, pastures) his horses at a nearby farm.
16. The aquarium looked (picturesque, picturing) when it was set up.
17. Many kinds of animals are on the (dangers, endangered) species list.

Hide and Seek

Play Hide and Seek with your words. Create a bar graph by filling in a box (left to right) for each word you spell correctly.

Other Word Forms

Hidden Words

Use the word bank to help you find the words in the puzzle. Words may go across or down.

f	e	g	e	n	t	l	e	m	a	n	z	e	e	d	m	p
e	g	e	n	t	l	e	s	t	e	l	i	s	b	m	i	l
s	f	e	s	t	i	v	e	l	y	i	l	e	a	o	s	i
g	s	i	m	p	l	e	s	t	r	c	a	s	t	l	e	s
l	j	u	n	u	g	l	e	n	a	b	a	t	t	l	e	d
e	n	p	o	d	l	e	g	f	l	z	t	v	l	d	n	c
v	e	h	n	d	o	d	r	e	w	e	i	e	e	e	a	i
e	g	o	d	l	e	t	l	s	v	d	t	r	f	l	m	g
l	s	s	t	e	a	r	a	t	u	r	o	a	i	e	o	e
h	a	p	o	s	s	i	b	i	l	i	t	i	e	s	w	n
e	c	i	h	l	j	s	e	v	e	r	a	l	l	y	e	e
a	t	t	o	l	u	n	l	i	b	h	l	l	d	d	l	r
d	a	a	s	o	n	d	e	t	e	o	i	y	l	i	t	a
e	b	l	p	e	g	a	d	y	i	s	t	l	e	n	n	l
d	f	i	n	a	l	i	z	e	d	p	y	a	b	g	e	l
b	d	z	e	g	e	n	t	l	s	m	s	i	m	p	l	y
m	o	e	d	a	s	o	m	o	d	e	l	i	n	g	g	t

Word Bank

battled
battlefield
castles
festively
festivity
finalized
generally
gentleman
gentlest
hospitalize
jungles
labeled
leveled
levelheaded
modeling
possibilities
puddles
severally
simplest
simply
totality

Hide and Seek

Play Hide and Seek with your words. Create a bar graph by filling in a box (left to right) for each word you spell correctly.

Other Word Forms

Synonyms

Use the synonyms to write the words. Remember, a synonym is a word that means the same or nearly the same as another word.

1. draperies ______________
2. sensible ______________
3. jets of water ______________
4. hearing ______________
5. African cat ______________
6. ordinarily ______________
7. like a citrus fruit ______________
8. thinking ______________
9. ordinary ______________
10. beyond repair ______________
11. was scared ______________
12. winners ______________
13. fastening ______________
14. poisonous snake ______________
15. cowardly ______________
16. kind of tree ______________
17. small place to cook ______________
18. covered with trimming ______________

Syllables

Remember, a syllable is a unit of sound in a word. A syllable contains a vowel and possibly one or more consonants. Count how many syllables each word has and write the number on the line.

1. ______ fountainhead
2. ______ championship
3. ______ buttonhole
4. ______ listening
5. ______ unreasonable
6. ______ reasonability
7. ______ chickenhearted
8. ______ lionhearted
9. ______ commonsense
10. ______ dragonfly
11. ______ ruinously
12. ______ kitchenware
13. ______ ruination
14. ______ curtained
15. ______ cottony

Word Bank

beribboned	chickenhearted	cottonwood	lemony	reasonable
buttoning	commonly	curtains	lioness	reasoning
champions	commonplace	fountains	listening	ruined
chickened	cottonmouth	kitchenette		

Hide and Seek

Play Hide and Seek with your words. Create a bar graph by filling in a box (left to right) for each word you spell correctly.

LOOK SAY HIDE WRITE SEEK CHECK

Other Word Forms

Sentence Fun

Circle the word that correctly completes each sentence.

1. They decided to ride the horses (barely, bareback).
2. The (repairing, repairman) is downstairs fixing the dishwasher.
3. I got a stain on my shirt the first time I (wore, worn) it.
4. We used to buy milk from a (dairys, dairyman) who lives nearby.
5. Sarah and Nellie (shared, sharing) a bedroom.
6. Daniel (scary, scarcely) heard what his mom was saying.
7. We bought a bushel of (pears, pares) to can.
8. The little boy felt (daring, dares) as he climbed up the slide.
9. We enjoy going (barely, barefoot) in the summertime.
10. Our Pekingese dog is very (hairier, hairy) and bouncy.
11. Each autumn we go to the (fairgrounds, fairest) for the county fair.
12. The sun (glaring, glaringly) through the window makes me hot.
13. Mom is busy (comparison, comparing) prices in the grocery store.
14. I couldn't sleep after watching a (scared, scary) movie.
15. We will be (wearing, wearer) uniforms at my school next year.
16. Dad took me to the barber to get a (haircut, hairless).
17. I don't think her bike computer is (repairing, repairable).
18. Grandma waved (fared, farewell) when we took her to the airport.
19. This car doesn't look good, (compared, comparing) to our new one.
20. Sarah checked to see how her mother was (faring, fared).

Hide and Seek

Play Hide and Seek with your words. Create a bar graph by filling in a box (left to right) for each word you spell correctly.

Other Word Forms

Prefixes and Suffixes

Add each suffix to the word in each row to make a new word.

	+ ed	+ ing	+ s
1. near	________	________	________
2. cheer	________	________	________
3. appear	________	________	________
4. fear	________	________	________
5. gear	________	________	________
6. spear	________	________	________
7. rear	________	________	________
8. tear	________	________	________
9. steer	________	________	________
10. beard	________	________	________
11. disappear	________	________	________

Add the prefixes and suffixes to make new words. Write the words on the lines. Remember, when a base word ends with a long vowel sound spelled with **y**, change the **y** to **i** when adding the ending. Also, when words have the consonant-vowel-consonant-**e** pattern, drop the **e** when adding an ending that begins with a vowel.

1. tear + ful + ly = ________

2. fear + less = ________

3. in + sincere = ________

4. near + by = ________

5. weird + est = ________

6. period + ic = ________

7. cheery – y + i + ness = ________

8. dis + appear + ance = ________

9. weary – y + i + some = ________

10. weary – y + i + ly = ________

11. sincere – e + ity = ________

12. fierce + ly = ________

Hide and Seek

Play Hide and Seek with your words. Create a bar graph by filling in a box (left to right) for each word you spell correctly.

Other Word Forms

Code Words

Using the word plus the code word, write the contracted form on the line.

0 = am   1 = will   2 = is   3 = would

4 = not   5 = have   6 = are   7 = did

1. he + 2 = ____________
2. I + 1 = ____________
3. does + 4 = ____________
4. who + 1 = ____________
5. they + 5 = ____________
6. she + 1 = ____________
7. there + 1 = ____________
8. we + 1 = ____________
9. we + 3 = ____________
10. they + 1 = ____________
11. what + 1 = ____________
12. here + 2 = ____________
13. we + 6 = ____________
14. she + 3 = ____________
15. they + 6 = ____________
16. there + 3 = ____________
17. I + 0 = ____________
18. it + 3 = ____________
19. has + 4 = ____________
20. where + 7 = ____________
21. I + 5 = ____________
22. it + 2 = ____________
23. was + 4 = ____________
24. who + 3 = ____________
25. where + 1 = ____________
26. had + 4 = ____________

Hide and Seek

Play Hide and Seek with your words. Create a bar graph by filling in a box (left to right) for each word you spell correctly.

LOOK SAY HIDE WRITE SEEK CHECK

Other Word Forms

Spelling and Writing

Write sentences using words from the Word Bank. Check your spelling.

1. ______________________________

____

2. ______________________________

____

3. ______________________________

____

4. ______________________________

____

5. ______________________________

____

6. ______________________________

____

7. ______________________________

____

Syllables

A syllable is a unit of sound in a word. A syllable contains a vowel and possibly one or more consonants. Count how many syllables each word has and write the number on the line.

1. ______ homemaking
2. ______ bedrooms
3. ______ backyards
4. ______ railroading
5. ______ playgrounds
6. ______ fireplaces

Word Bank

everybody's herself railroads yardsticks
homemaker newspapers sunshiny

Hide and Seek

Play Hide and Seek with your words. Create a bar graph by filling in a box (left to right) for each word you spell correctly.

Other Word Forms

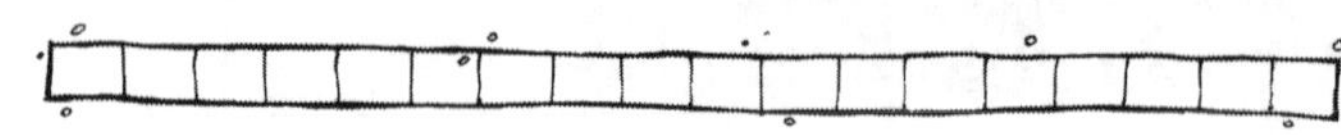

Hidden Words

Use the word bank to help you find the words in the puzzle. Words may go across or down.

```
A B C Y E A R S D E M F I G H I M
P C H R A P L R I B A R N B F J E
C H R I S T O P H E R C D L O U M
O E I A T S E R E V T I E S U L O
L P S T E R T R E E I L P Y R V R
U R T N R E H W C Y N E E A T A I
M E M O R I A L A R L H N U H L E
B S A K A H N G R O U N D H O G S
U I S L A B K O D R T S E T F A J
S D C A R B F O L D H A N Y J R N
F E C H A N U K A H E I C T U B E
O N J U D E L H O S R P E I L O T
O T A L M W E M O R K I P S Y R H
L I L Y V A L E N T I N E T E G G
W A P R I L L S A I N T N R B I R
T L A B O R E R H D G A V E L E N
```

Word Bank

April	tree	Easter	independence	new	Valentine
fool	Eve	egg	laborer	presidential	years
arbor	card	lily	memorial	thankful	
Chanukah	Christopher	Fourth of July	memories	Martin Luther King	
Christmas	Columbus	Saint	groundhog		

PLEASE PHOTOCOPY!*

The following pages contain Black Line Masters for use with the ***A Reason For Spelling®*** Student Worktext.

*Photocopy privileges extend only to the material in this section, and permission is granted only for those classrooms or homeschools using ***A Reason For Spelling®*** Student Worktexts. Any other use of this material is expressly forbidden and all copyright laws apply.

Spelling Progress Chart

Fill in the five lesson numbers for the unit in the first row of blocks. Use the first half of the column under each block to record the score for the Preview, and the second half of the column for the Posttest. To record the score, begin at the bottom of the column and color the blanks to show the number of words spelled correctly. Use one color for Preview and another for Postest.

Words Spelled Correctly	Lesson Numbers									
	Preview	Posttest	Preview	Posttest	Preview	Posttest	Preview	Posttest	Preview	Posttest
18.										
17.										
16.										
15.										
14.										
13.										
12.										
11.										
10.										
9.										
8.										
7.										
6.										
5.										
4.										
3.										
2.										
1.										

Rubric for Scoring

You may wish to use this rubric at the end of each unit to track student progress.

	Standard	Usually	Sometimes	Not Yet
1.	Writes all letters correctly and legibly (upper and lower case)			
2.	Uses correct spelling on words from current and previous lessons			
3.	Writes a paragraph in response to a prompt			
4.	Uses appropriate punctuation			
5.	Uses capital letters correctly			
6.	Writes complete, coherent, and organized sentences			
7.	Includes descriptive language			
8.	Forms plurals correctly			
9.	Subjects and verbs agree			
10.	Uses a logical sequence of events			

my dictionary
bulb:(n)
bulge:(a)
bulletin:(n)

my journal
March 16

The End